5th EDITION

Organizational Behavior

Steven L. McShane
University of Newcastle (Australia)

Mary Ann Von Glinow
Florida International University

Mc Graw Hill

M: ORGANIZATIONAL BEHAVIOR: FIFTH EDITION

Some ancillaries, including electronic and print components, may not be available to customers outside the United States.

This book is printed on acid-free paper.

1 2 3 4 5 6 7 8 9 0 LMN 26 25 24 23 22 21

ISBN 978-1-260-26156-1 (bound edition)
MHID 1-260-26156-5 (bound edition)
ISBN 978-1-260-47872-3 (loose-leaf edition)
MHID 1-260-47872-6 (loose-leaf edition)

Director: *Michael Ablassmeir*
Product Developer: *Anne Ehrenworth*
Product Coordinator: *Allison Marker*
Executive Marketing Manager: *Debbie Clare*
Content Project Managers: *Harvey Yep (Core)/Keri Johnson (Assessment)/George Theofanopoulos (Assessment)*
Buyer: *Susan K. Culbertson*
Designer: *Matt Diamond*
Content Licensing Specialist: *Sarah Flynn (Image and Text)*
Cover Image: *Thomas Barwick/Getty Images*
Compositor: *Aptara®, Inc.*

All credits appearing on page or at the end of the book are considered to be an extension of the copyright page.

Library of Congress Cataloging-in-Publication Data

Names: McShane, Steven Lattimore, author. | Von Glinow, Mary Ann Young, 1949- author.
Title: Oganizational behavior / Steven L. McShane, University of Victoria (Canada), Mary Ann Von Glinow, Florida International University.
Description: 5th edition. | New York, NY : McGraw Hill Education, [2022] | Includes index.
Identifiers: LCCN 2020047309 (print) | LCCN 2020047310 (ebook) | ISBN 9781260261561 (hardcover) | ISBN 9781260478723 (spiral bound) | ISBN 9781260478716 (ebook) | ISBN 9781260478761 (ebook other)
Subjects: LCSH: Organizational behavior.
Classification: LCC HD58.7 .M42 2021 (print) | LCC HD58.7 (ebook) | DDC 658–dc23
LC record available at https://lccn.loc.gov/2020047309
LC ebook record available at https://lccn.loc.gov/2020047310

The Internet addresses listed in the text were accurate at the time of publication. The inclusion of a website does not indicate an endorsement by the authors or McGraw-Hill Education, and McGraw-Hill Education does not guarantee the accuracy of the information presented at these sites.

www.mheducation.com

about the Authors

Steven L. McShane

Courtesy of Donna McClement

Steven L. McShane is Conjoint Professor at Newcastle Business School, University of Newcastle (Australia). He previously held the positions of Professor at Simon Fraser University's Faculty of Business Administration (Canada), Winthrop Professor of Management at the University of Western Australia Graduate School of Management and Business School, and Adjunct Professor at Gustavson School of Business, University of Victoria (Canada). He also taught organizational behavior in the IMBA program at the Antai College of Economics and Management at Shanghai Jiao Tong University in Shanghai, China. Steve has received awards for his teaching quality and innovation and receives high ratings from students in Perth, Shanghai, Singapore, Manila, and other cities where he has taught. He is also a popular visiting speaker, having given dozens of invited talks and seminars to faculty and students in the United States, China, Canada, Malaysia, India, and other countries.

Steve earned his PhD from Michigan State University, where he specialized in organizational behavior and labor relations. He also holds a Master's of Industrial Relations from the University of Toronto and an undergraduate degree from Queen's University in Canada. Steve is a past president of the Administrative Sciences Association of Canada (the Canadian equivalent of the Academy of Management) and served as Director of Graduate Programs in Simon Fraser University's business faculty. He has conducted executive programs with Nokia, TÜV-SÜD, Wesfarmers Group, Main Roads WA, McGraw-Hill, ALCOA World Alumina Australia, and many other organizations.

Along with coauthoring *M: Organizational Behavior*, Fifth Edition, Steve is lead coauthor of *Organizational Behavior*, Ninth Edition (2021); *Canadian Organizational Behaviour*, Eleventh Edition (2021); and *Organisational Behaviour: Asia Pacific*, Sixth Edition (2019). He is also coauthor of editions or translations of his organizational behavior books in China, India, Quebec, Taiwan, and Brazil. Steve has published several dozen articles and conference papers on workplace values, training transfer, organizational learning, exit-voice-loyalty, employee socialization, wrongful dismissal, media bias in business magazines, and other diverse topics.

Steve enjoys spending his leisure time hiking, swimming, body board surfing, canoeing, skiing, and traveling with his wife and two daughters.

Mary Ann Von Glinow

Mary Ann Von Glinow

Dr. Von Glinow is a Knight Ridder Eminent Scholar Chair in International Management at Florida International University and is senior editor for the *Journal of International Business Studies (JIBS)*. She served as 2010 to 2012 president of the Academy of International Business (AIB) and the 1994–1995 president of the Academy of Management (AOM). Previously on the Marshall School faculty of the University of Southern California, she has an MBA and a PhD in management science from Ohio State University, and is a Fellow of the Academy of Management, the Academy of International Business, and the Pan-Pacific Business Association. She sits on 13 editorial review boards and numerous international panels and teaches in executive programs in Latin America, Asia, and the United States.

Dr. Von Glinow has authored over 100 journal articles and 13 books, most of which have been translated into Chinese, Hindi, and Spanish. Her book on organizational learning capability won a Gold Book Award from the Ministry of Economic Affairs in Taiwan in 2002. She is the 2005 recipient of the Academy of Management's Distinguished Service Award, one of the highest honors bestowed by the Academy.

Mary Ann has consulted widely and is on the board of directors of several organizations, including the advisory board to Volvo-Geely in China. She is actively involved in several animal welfare organizations and received the 1996 Humanitarian Award of the Year from Miami's Adopt-a-Pet.

Dedication

Dedicated with love and devotion to Donna, and to our wonderful daughters, Bryton and Madison

–S.L.M.

Dedicated to Zack, Emma, Googun, Blue, Chloe, Jackson, and Boomer

–M.A.V.G.

Brief Contents

part one Introduction 2

part two Individual Behavior and Processes 30

part three Team Processes 158

part four Organizational Processes 276

Contents

part one Introduction 2

Jacob Ammentorp Lund/Ammentorp/123RF

Yuri Arcurs/E+/Getty Images

Dean Drobot/Shutterstock

Kaiskynet Studio/Shutterstock

Compassionate Eye Foundation/Mark Langridge/Getty Images

Drazen Zigic/Getty Images

11 Leadership in Organizational Settings 256

part four Organizational Processes 276

12 Designing Organizational Structures 276

13 Organizational Culture 296

Westend61/Getty Images

What's New
in the Fifth Edition

M: Organizational Behavior, Fifth Edition, has received more updating and revision than any previous edition of this book. Most chapters have new conceptual content and literature foundation; a few chapters have completely new sections and reorganization. All chapters have new examples and either new or revised factoids. The most substantial changes have occurred in Chapter 1 (Introduction to the Field of Organizational Behavior), Chapter 2 (Individual Differences: Personality and Values), Chapter 5 (Employee Motivation), Chapter 7 (Team Dynamics), Chapter 8 (Communicating in Teams and Organizations), and Chapter 10 (Conflict and Negotiation in the Workplace). This edition also relates the COVID-19 pandemic to several OB concepts and practices.

The authors personally researched, selected, and wrote all of this content, thereby providing superior integration of knowledge and ensuring that the examples are relevant and recent. Here are the key changes we've made to this Fifth edition, broken out by chapter.

Chapter 1: Introduction to the Field of Organizational Behavior

Almost every section of this chapter has been revised, updated, or replaced. This edition has a new section on the emerging workplace landscape, which includes new content on work–life integration, the inclusive workplace, and employment relationships. It also significantly updates the topic of remote work (the narrower topic of telecommuting was covered in previous editions). The section on the importance of organizational behavior now more fully explains why OB is important for students. It also succinctly introduces key organizational effectiveness concepts to explain why OB is vital for organizations. The section on OB anchors now includes a fifth anchor on OB's practical orientation. This chapter also has a stronger micro-OB focus by including the MARS model of individual behavior and the five types of individual behavior (previously in Chapter 2).

Chapter 2: Individual Differences: Personality, and Values

Along with its slightly revised title, this edition brings a number of noticeable updates and changes to the chapter. It now has a full discussion about the dark triad (Machiavellianism, narcissism, and psychopathy) and its relevance to organizational behavior. This edition also has a new separate discussion regarding four caveats when applying the five-factor model of personality in organizations. Also included in this edition is a fourth ethical principle: the ethic of care. We have also moved the topics of the MARS model and types of individual behavior from this chapter to Chapter 1.

Chapter 3: Perceiving Ourselves and Others in Organizations

This book pioneered the full model of self-concept and its relevance to organizational behavior. This edition further refines that discussion, particularly in explaining how people develop self-concept clarity and how self-concept characteristics affect behavior and performance. This chapter also updates writing on perceptual organization and interpretation, intentional discrimination, and improving self-awareness of perceptual biases.

Chapter 4: Workplace Emotions, Attitudes, and Stress

This was the first OB book to fully incorporate the concept of emotions in organizational behavior across various topics (perceptions, attitudes, motivation, decisions, etc.). This edition further develops this topic by revising the section on managing emotions and adding recent knowledge about the five strategies that people use to regulate their emotions. This edition also updates the topic of organizational commitment, incorporates normative commitment, and has minor rewriting on managing workplace stress.

Chapter 5: Employee Motivation

This edition significantly revises and updates the topics of procedural and interactional justice, including a new exhibit listing the specific rules of these two forms of organizational justice. The characteristics of effective feedback are discussed more fully, including the addition of an exhibit that defines and illustrates each characteristic. The section on drive-based motivation theories has been reorganized to give more emphasis on the recent four-drive theory. This edition also revises the chapter's opening topic on the meaning of motivation and employee engagement.

Chapter 6: Decision Making and Creativity

This chapter further updates and refines the discussion of information processing when choosing alternatives. Design thinking was fully introduced in the previous edition. In this edition, we have added an exhibit that outlines the four main rules or practices of design thinking. This edition also has minor revisions on the topic of escalation of commitment and ways to evaluate decisions more effectively.

Chapter 7: Team Dynamics

We have revised, clarified, updated, and generally improved several sections of this chapter. Most of the team processes section has been reorganized and rewritten. That section now has a more complete and updated discussion of team mental models, team development, team norms, and team roles. This edition also more completely discusses psychological safety as a factor in effective team decision making than previous editions. Other topics that benefited from minor rewriting and updating include team process losses and the prevalence of remote (virtual) teams.

Chapter 8: Communicating in Teams and Organizations

The previous edition apparently pioneered writing on the four key factors for choosing the best communication channel (synchronicity, social presence, social acceptance, and media richness). This edition further refines that content. We have also substantially updated the topic of digital communication, including a new exhibit on the rapidly changing popularity of various digital communication channels, along with associated discussion about why these changes are occurring. Social media communication is also more fully defined and discussed.

Chapter 9: Power and Influence in the Workplace

The topic of nonsubstitutability as a contingency of power has been rewritten, and the associated topic of personal brand is discussed more fully. We also discuss more fully the troubling issue of deference to power in organizations. The definition of organizational politics is explained in more detail, particularly with reference to recent writing about "positive politics."

Chapter 10: Conflict and Negotiation in the Workplace

This chapter has received several changes and updates. The topic of task and relationship conflict has been further refined for greater clarity. That section also significantly updates strategies to minimize relationship conflict during task conflict, including the role of psychological safety. The topic of conflict handling contingencies has been revised and updated. Along with other changes, it now includes the contingency of maintaining harmony. You will also find revision and updates on communication as a source of conflict, structural ways to manage conflict (particularly on reducing differentiation and on improving communication and mutual understanding), preparing for negotiation, and gathering information during negotiation.

Chapter 11: Leadership in Organizational Settings

This chapter has a few minor updates and revisions. The discussion about transformational leadership and charisma has an updated conceptualization of charisma. The section on strategic vision of transformational leadership has also been revised.

Chapter 12: Designing Organizational Structures

This edition revises the exhibit on mechanistic-organic structures for better clarity and style. The exhibit depicting various types of divisional structure has also been revised with new company examples, and the discussion about divisional structures has been updated. The section and exhibit on matrix organizational structures has similarly been revised with new writing and examples.

Chapter 13: Organizational Culture

Parts of the organizational socialization section have been revised, including the inherent conflicts in pre-employment socialization and the issue of whether socialization changes employee values or mostly communicates values-consistent behavior. This chapter has also revised and updated writing on the meaning and strategies for creating a strong organizational culture.

Chapter 14: Organizational Change

The discussion of appreciative inquiry principles has been revised and slightly expanded and now includes a new exhibit to summarize these principles. This edition has also minor rewriting on the section on creating an urgency for change as well as on the evaluation of appreciative inquiry.

McGraw Hill connect®

Instructors: Student Success Starts with You

Tools to enhance your unique voice

Want to build your own course? No problem. Prefer to use our turnkey, prebuilt course? Easy. Want to make changes throughout the semester? Sure. And you'll save time with Connect's auto-grading too.

65%
Less Time Grading

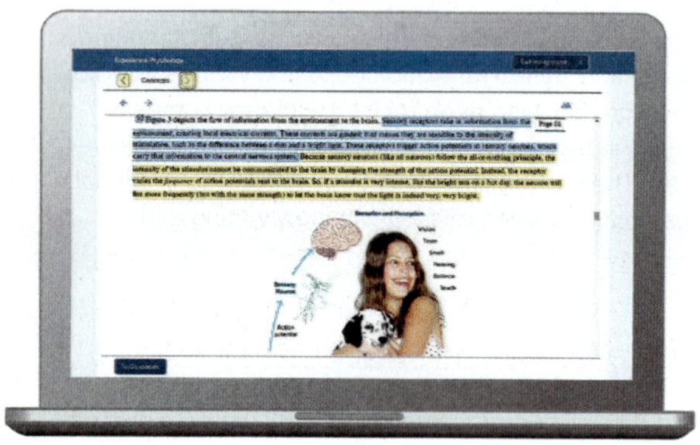

Laptop: McGraw Hill; Woman/dog: George Doyle/Getty Images

Study made personal

Incorporate adaptive study resources like SmartBook® 2.0 into your course and help your students be better prepared in less time. Learn more about the powerful personalized learning experience available in SmartBook 2.0 at **www.mheducation.com/highered/connect/smartbook**

Affordable solutions, added value

Make technology work for you with LMS integration for single sign-on access, mobile access to the digital textbook, and reports to quickly show you how each of your students is doing. And with our Inclusive Access program you can provide all these tools at a discount to your students. Ask your McGraw Hill representative for more information.

Padlock: Jobalou/Getty Images

Solutions for your challenges

A product isn't a solution. Real solutions are affordable, reliable, and come with training and ongoing support when you need it and how you want it. Visit **www.supportateverystep.com** for videos and resources both you and your students can use throughout the semester.

Checkmark: Jobalou/Getty Images

SUPPORT AT every step

Students: Get Learning that Fits You

Effective tools for efficient studying

Connect is designed to make you more productive with simple, flexible, intuitive tools that maximize your study time and meet your individual learning needs. Get learning that works for you with Connect.

Study anytime, anywhere

Download the free ReadAnywhere app and access your online eBook or SmartBook 2.0 assignments when it's convenient, even if you're offline. And since the app automatically syncs with your eBook and SmartBook 2.0 assignments in Connect, all of your work is available every time you open it. Find out more at **www.mheducation.com/readanywhere**

> ***"I really liked this app—it made it easy to study when you don't have your text-book in front of you."***
>
> - Jordan Cunningham, Eastern Washington University

Calendar: owattaphotos/Getty Images

Everything you need in one place

Your Connect course has everything you need—whether reading on your digital eBook or completing assignments for class, Connect makes it easy to get your work done.

Learning for everyone

McGraw Hill works directly with Accessibility Services Departments and faculty to meet the learning needs of all students. Please contact your Accessibility Services Office and ask them to email accessibility@mheducation.com, or visit **www.mheducation.com/about/accessibility** for more information.

Top: Jenner Images/Getty Images, Left: Hero Images/Getty Images, Right: Hero Images/Getty Images

PART 1

1 Introduction to the Field of Organizational Behavior

Jacob Ammentorp Lund/Ammentorp/123RF

Learning Objectives

After you read this chapter, you should be able to:

LO1-1 Define organizational behavior and organizations.

LO1-2 Explain why organizational behavior knowledge is important for you and for organizations.

LO1-3 Describe the anchors on which organizational behavior knowledge is based.

LO1-4 Summarize the workplace trends of diversity and the inclusive workplace, work–life integration, remote work, and emerging employment relationships.

LO1-5 Describe the four factors that directly influence individual behavior and performance.

LO1-6 Summarize the five types of individual behavior in organizations.

organizational behavior (OB) the study of what people think, feel, and do in and around organizations

organizations groups of people who work interdependently toward some purpose

Jerry Jones lives near Columbia, Missouri, where he was recently hired as a software engineer at Automattic. Jones and his team members work well together, even though they don't physically work together. In fact, his coworkers live in other countries and continents. Automattic, which makes the blogging platform WordPress and other popular website-building products, is a completely distributed organization. All of its 1,100 employees are remote workers located across 75 countries.

Automattic's entire hiring process, including interviews, is conducted through text-based interactions. The company reasons that its employees communicate mainly through chat and text messaging, so applicants need to demonstrate their ability to communicate well through these channels. "No one sees or hears you until after you're hired," says Jerry Jones. Employees are responsible for output, not for being at work at specific times. This creates accountability, but it also gives everyone considerable flexibility for work–life integration. The company even has a no-limits vacation policy.

Automattic team leaders regularly convene video-based meetings, partly to discuss complex issues but also so employees feel part of a team. To support team dynamics, organizational culture, and employee well-being, Automattic ensures that team members meet in person twice each year. One "meetup" is arranged for each team alone. For example, Jerry Jones and his team met for several days in Los Angeles two months after he was hired. The other event is the Grand Meetup, an annual week-long conference attended by all Automattic employees.[1]

WELCOME TO THE FIELD OF ORGANIZATIONAL BEHAVIOR!

Automattic is a somewhat unusual company, yet it has become a highly respected model of how organizations might operate in the future. Work is becoming something we do, not the place where we do it. The recent coronavirus (COVID-19) pandemic necessitated and accelerated this shift. Employers quickly set up or expanded remote work arrangements so employees could fulfill social distancing and self-isolation requirements from home. Along with remote working, this opening case study about Automattic highlights several other organizational behavior themes, such as teams, work–life integration, leadership, communication, and organizational culture.

Our purpose is to help you understand what goes on in organizations. We examine the factors that make companies effective, improve employee well-being, and drive successful collaboration among coworkers. We look at organizations from numerous and diverse perspectives, from the deepest foundations of employee thoughts and behavior (personality, self-concept, attitudes, etc.) to the complex interplay between the organization's structure and culture and its external environment. Along this journey, we emphasize why things happen and what you can do to predict and guide organizational events.

We begin this chapter by introducing you to the field of organizational behavior (OB) and its historical origins. This is followed by details about why OB is important for your career and why organizations depend on OB knowledge to survive and thrive. An integrative model of organizational behavior is presented, which illustrates the interconnectedness of OB topics and serves as a road map to guide you through this book. We then describe the philosophical anchors that guide the development of organizational behavior knowledge. This is followed by an overview of four emerging features of the workplace environment: diversity and the inclusive workplace, work–life integration, remote work, and emerging employment relationships. The latter part of this chapter introduces the MARS model, which outlines the four direct drivers of individual behavior and performance. The final section identifies the five main types of individual behavior.

LO1-1 Define organizational behavior and organizations.

What Is Organizational Behavior?

Organizational behavior (OB) is the study of what people think, feel, and do in and around organizations. It looks at employee behaviors, decisions, perceptions, and emotional responses. It examines how individuals and teams in organizations relate to one another and to their counterparts in other organizations. OB also encompasses the study of how organizations interact with their external environments, particularly in the context of employee behavior and decisions. OB researchers systematically study these topics at multiple levels of analysis, namely, the individual, team (including interpersonal), and organization.[2]

The definition of organizational behavior begs the question: What are organizations? **Organizations** are groups of people who work interdependently toward some purpose.[3] Notice that organizations are not buildings or government-registered entities. In fact, many organizations exist with neither physical walls nor government documentation to confer their legal status.[4]

One key feature of all organizations is that they are collective entities.[5] They consist of human beings—typically, but not necessarily, employees—who interact with one another in an *organized* way. This organized relationship requires communication, coordination, and collaboration to achieve organizational objectives. As such, all organizational members have degrees of interdependence; they accomplish goals by sharing materials, information, or expertise with coworkers.

One key feature of all organizations is that they consist of human beings who interact with each other in an *organized* way.
Image Source

A second key feature of organizations is that their members have a collective sense of purpose. This collective purpose isn't always well defined or agreed on. Companies typically have vision and mission statements, but they are sometimes out of date or don't describe what employees actually try to achieve. Still, some sense of collective purpose does exist, even if it is implicit or informally understood. Otherwise, an organization would be nothing more than an assemblage of people without direction or unifying force.

> A company is one of humanity's most amazing inventions . . . [It's] this abstract construct we've invented, and it's incredibly powerful.[6]
>
> —Steve Jobs, Apple and Pixar Animation Studios cofounder

Historical Foundations of Organizational Behavior

Organizational behavior emerged as a distinct field sometime around the early 1940s.[7] During that decade, a few researchers began describing their research as organizational (rather than sociological or psychological). And by the late 1940s, Harvard University had changed the name of its MBA human relations course to "Organizational Behavior."

Although the field of OB is recent, experts in other fields have been studying organizations for many centuries. The Greek philosopher Plato (400 bc) wrote about the essence of leadership, and the Chinese philosopher Confucius (500 bc) extolled the virtues of ethics and leadership. Economist Adam Smith (1770s) discussed the benefits of job specialization and division of labor. German sociologist Max Weber (early 1900s) wrote about rational organizations, the work ethic, and charismatic leadership. Industrial engineer Frederick Winslow Taylor proposed systematic ways to organize work processes and motivate employees through goal setting and rewards.[8]

Political scientist Mary Parker Follett (1920s) offered new ways of thinking about constructive conflict, team dynamics, power, and leadership. Harvard professor Elton Mayo and his colleagues (1930s and 1940s) established the "human relations" school of management, which pioneered research on employee attitudes, formal team dynamics, informal groups, and supervisor leadership style. American executive and Harvard associate Chester Barnard (1930s) wrote insightful views regarding organizational communication, coordination, leadership and authority, organizations as open systems, and team dynamics.[9] This brief historical tour indicates that OB has been in existence for a long time; it just wasn't organized into a unified discipline until around World War II.

LO1-2 Explain why organizational behavior knowledge is important for you and for organizations.

WHY ORGANIZATIONAL BEHAVIOR IS IMPORTANT

In all likelihood, you are reading this book as part of a required course in organizational behavior. Apart from degree or diploma requirements, why should you learn the ideas and practices discussed in this book? After all, who ever heard of a career path leading to a "vice president of OB" or a "chief OB officer"? Our answer to this question comes in two parts: why OB is important for you personally and why OB is important for organizations generally.

Why OB Is Important for You

Throughout our careers teaching undergraduate, graduate, and executive programs, we noticed that the more work experience students have, the more they tend to consider organizational behavior as one of their most valued courses. Why? Because they have learned over time that OB is important to them, whether as technical specialists or senior executives.[10] This observation is supported by numerous surveys that ask employers to identify the most important skills and knowledge they look for in new hires. Technical skills are important, of course, particularly for highly specialized jobs and professions. But the skills and knowledge that employers tend to rank above anything else are the topics found in this and other organizational behavior books.

Exhibit 1.1 lists the most important skills identified by employers in four recent major surveys. Every list identifies problem solving (including analytic thinking and strategic thinking), which you will learn about along with creativity and employee involvement in Chapter 6. The ability to work effectively in teams (also listed as collaboration, interpersonal skills, and people management) is another top-ranked skill that employers look for in job applicants. The team dynamics theme is fully discussed in Chapter 7, but it also relates to several others topics, such as understanding and managing emotions (Chapter 4), influencing others (Chapter 9), and managing conflict (Chapter 10).

Communication, which is featured in Chapter 8, is a third skill that employers in all four recent surveys identify as important for new hires. Leadership appears in three lists (in the Canadian survey, leadership is the second most important for mid-level hires, but not among the top five for entry-level hires). Leadership perspectives are discussed in Chapter 11, but this skill is also associated with other topics, such as motivating people (Chapter 5) and leading organizational change (Chapter 14). Overall, these and other surveys suggest that OB offers a core foundation of knowledge and skill development for your success in organizations.[11]

Better Personal Theories to Predict and Influence Along with providing the specific knowledge and skills identified in these surveys, this book serves a broader purpose: to help you develop better personal theories to understand, predict, and

Organizational behavior knowledge helps you to refine your personal theories, so you can understand, predict, and influence organizational events.
Chaay Tee/Shutterstock

Exhibit 1.1 Most Important Skills for New Hires

National Association of Colleges and Employers (United States)	Bloomberg Skills Report (United States)	Business Council of Canada (entry-level hires list)	Australian Institute of Management
• Problem solving • Ability to work in a team • Communication (written) • Leadership • Strong work ethic	• Communication skills • Analytical thinking • Work collaboratively • Strategic thinking • Leadership skills	• Collaboration, teamwork, interpersonal skills • Communication skills • Problem-solving skills • Analytical capabilities • Resiliency	• Communication • Leadership • Emotional intelligence • People management • Problem solving

Sources: "The Bloomberg Job Skills Report 2016: What Recruiters Want," *Bloomberg*, February 9, 2016; "Job Outlook 2018" (Bethlehem, PA: National Association of Colleges and Employers, November 2017); Morneau Shepell, "Navigating Change: 2018 Business Council Skills Survey" (Ottawa: Business Council of Canada, April 2018); "AIM Soft Skills Survey 2019" (Sydney: Australian Institute of Management, December 2018).

organizational effectiveness a broad concept represented by several perspectives, including the organization's fit with the external environment, internal subsystems' configuration for high performance, emphasis on organizational learning, and ability to satisfy the needs of key stakeholders

open systems a perspective that holds that organizations depend on the external environment for resources, affect that environment through their output, and consist of internal subsystems that transform inputs to outputs

human capital the knowledge, skills, abilities, creative thinking, and other valued resources that employees bring to the organization

influence organizational events. Every one of us has an inherent drive to understand our surroundings.[12] This need is particularly strong in organizational settings because they are highly complex and ambiguous contexts that have a profound effect on us. Throughout our lives, we develop personal theories to make sense of our environments. These personal theories are sometimes accurate, sometimes too simplified to fit specific situations, and occasionally wrong. Even some ideas that appear to be "common sense" may be inaccurate or oversimplified.[13]

The field of organizational behavior applies systematic research to develop evidence-based theories. This knowledge helps you to refine your personal theories, so you are better able to understand, predict, and influence organizational events.[14] Organizations are people who work together to accomplish things. Therefore, no matter what career path you choose, OB theories and practices are enormously valuable to help you perform your job and work more effectively within organizations.

Organizational Behavior Is for Everyone You may have noticed that we haven't mentioned "managers" in this discussion on why OB is important for you. Effective management (and leadership) does depend on OB concepts and practices, but this book pioneered the broader view that OB is valuable for everyone who works in and around organizations. Whether you are a software engineer, customer service representative, foreign exchange analyst, or chief executive officer, you need to understand and apply the many organizational behavior topics that are discussed in this book. In fact, OB knowledge is probably more valuable than ever before because employees increasingly need to be proactive, self-motivated, and able to work effectively with coworkers without management intervention. In the words of one forward-thinking OB writer almost a half century ago: Everyone is a manager.[15]

Why OB Is Important for Organizations

Along with benefiting you as an individual, the field of organizational behavior is vital to the organization's survival and success.[16] For instance, the best 100 companies to work for in America (i.e., companies with the highest levels of employee satisfaction) enjoy significantly higher financial performance than other businesses within the same industry. Companies with higher levels of employee engagement have higher sales and profitability. OB practices are also associated with various indicators of hospital performance, such as lower patient mortality rates and higher patient satisfaction. Other studies have consistently found a positive relationship between the quality of leadership and the company's financial performance. Financial analysts also rely on several organizational behavior variables—including leadership, performance-based rewards, employee development, and employee attitudes—as "positive screens" for selecting companies with the highest and most consistent long-term investment returns.[17]

Almost all organizational behavior theories have the implicit or explicit objective of making organizations more effective.[18] In fact, **organizational effectiveness** is considered the "ultimate dependent variable" in organizational behavior.[19] Organizational performance, success, goodness, health, competitiveness, and excellence are alternative labels for organizational effectiveness. Organizations are effective when they have a good fit with their external environment, effectively transform inputs to outputs through human capital, and satisfy the needs of key stakeholders.[20] Let's look at these elements to understand how OB knowledge improves organizational effectiveness.

Organizations as Open Systems One of the fundamental views in organizational behavior is that organizations are **open systems**.[21] They are complex organisms that "live" within an external environment, as Exhibit 1.2 illustrates. The word *open* describes this permeable relationship, whereas *closed systems* operate without dependence on or interaction with an external environment. Organizations depend on the external environment for resources, including raw materials, job applicants, financial funding, information, and equipment. The environment also consists of laws, cultural norms, and other expectations that place demands on how organizations should operate.

The open systems view recognizes that organizations have numerous subsystems (departments, teams, technological processes, etc.) that transform the incoming resources into outputs. Organizations also have outputs to the external environment. Some outputs, such as products and services, may be valued by the external environment; other outputs, such as employee layoffs and pollution, are undesirable by-products. Throughout this process, organizations receive feedback regarding the value of their outputs, the availability of future inputs, and the appropriateness of the transformation process.

As open systems, organizations are effective when they maintain a good "fit" with their external environment.[22] A good fit exists when the organization's inputs, processes, and outputs are aligned with the resources available in the external environment and with the needs and expectations of that environment. Organizational behavior knowledge is highly relevant to the open systems view by identifying organizational characteristics that "fit" some external environments better than others. For example, the external environment is a key factor in choosing the best organizational structure (Chapter 12) and organizational culture

Exhibit 1.2 Organizations as Open Systems

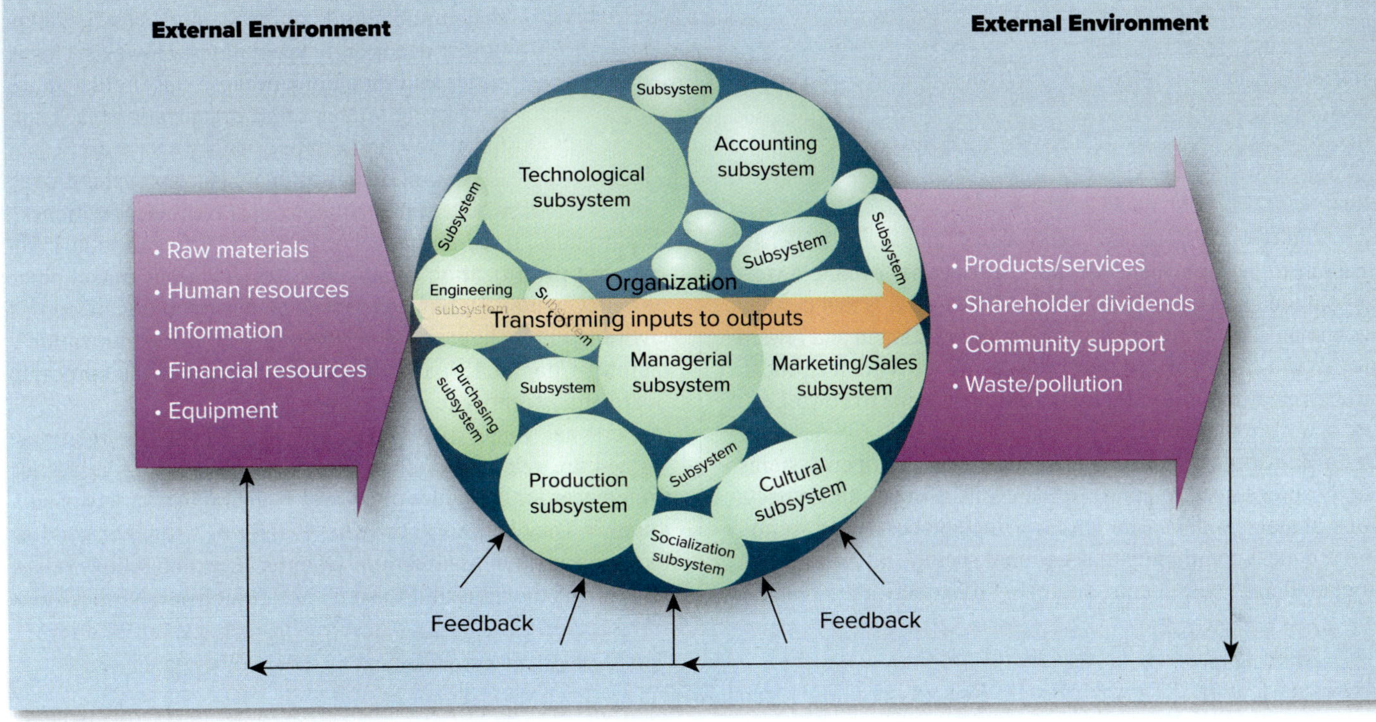

(Chapter 13). This topic also relates to leadership (Chapter 11), organizational change (Chapter 14), and job characteristics (Chapter 5).

OB theories also offer guidance regarding the transformation of inputs to outputs, including how internal subsystems coordinate with one another.[23] For instance, we discuss how to create and support effective teams (Chapter 7), how organizations rely on a variety of coordinating mechanisms (Chapter 12), how employees use various methods every day to successfully influence each other (Chapter 9), and how successful companies improve coordination through a strong organizational culture (Chapter 13).

As open systems, organizations are effective when they maintain a good "fit" with their external environment.
Palto/iStock/Getty Images

Human Capital as the Organization's Competitive Advantage The most important ingredient in the organization's process of transforming inputs to outputs is human capital. **Human capital** refers to the knowledge, skills, abilities, creativity, and other valued resources that employees bring to the organization. It is a competitive advantage because employees are essential for the organization's survival and success. Furthermore, their talents are difficult to find, copy, and replace with technology.[24] Consequently, effective organizations introduce workplace practices that enhance human capital.[25] These practices are identified and discussed throughout this book. For example, some OB themes identify ways to strengthen employee motivation through enriched jobs, rewards, feedback, and fair work practices (Chapter 5). Other topics discuss the value of employee involvement (Chapter 6) and the features of effective self-directed work teams (Chapter 7).

Organizations potentially boost their effectiveness through human capital development in three ways.[26] First, human capital development partly occurs by improving employee skills and knowledge. When employees improve their ability, they tend to improve their performance, which, in turn, improves the organization's success. Second, companies with superior human capital are better at adapting to rapidly changing environments. This

stakeholders individuals, groups, and other entities that affect, or are affected by, the organization's objectives and actions

values relatively stable, evaluative beliefs that guide a person's preferences for outcomes or courses of action in a variety of situations

corporate social responsibility (CSR) organizational activities intended to benefit society and the environment beyond the firm's immediate financial interests or legal obligations

adaptability occurs because highly skilled employees who have freedom to perform their work are better at performing diverse tasks in unfamiliar situations. A third explanation is that developing human capital means the company is investing in and rewarding its workforce, which motivates employees to reciprocate through greater effort in their jobs and assistance to coworkers.

Organizations and Their Stakeholders As open systems, organizations need to adjust to the evolving needs and expectations of stakeholders. **Stakeholders** include customers, suppliers, the local community and national society, interest groups, stockholders, governments, and many other entities that affect, or are affected by, the company's objectives and actions.[28] Organizations are more effective when they understand, manage, and satisfy stakeholder needs and expectations. However, this is easier said than done because stakeholders have conflicting interests and organizations lack sufficient resources to fully satisfy everyone.

Several organizational behavior topics give us a better understanding of stakeholder relations.[29] In particular, research has identified several factors that influence the prioritization of stakeholders, including stakeholder power (Chapter 9), how executives perceive the organization's environment (Chapter 3 and Chapter 12), the organization's culture (Chapter 13), and the personal values of the corporate board and executive team (Chapter 2).

Personal values play a key role in stakeholder relations. **Values** are relatively stable, evaluative beliefs that guide our preferences for outcomes or courses of action in a variety of situations.[30] They help us know what is right or wrong, or good or bad, in a particular situation. Chapter 2 explains how values anchor our thoughts and to some extent motivate our decisions

Human Capital Practices in Selected OECD and Partner Countries[27]

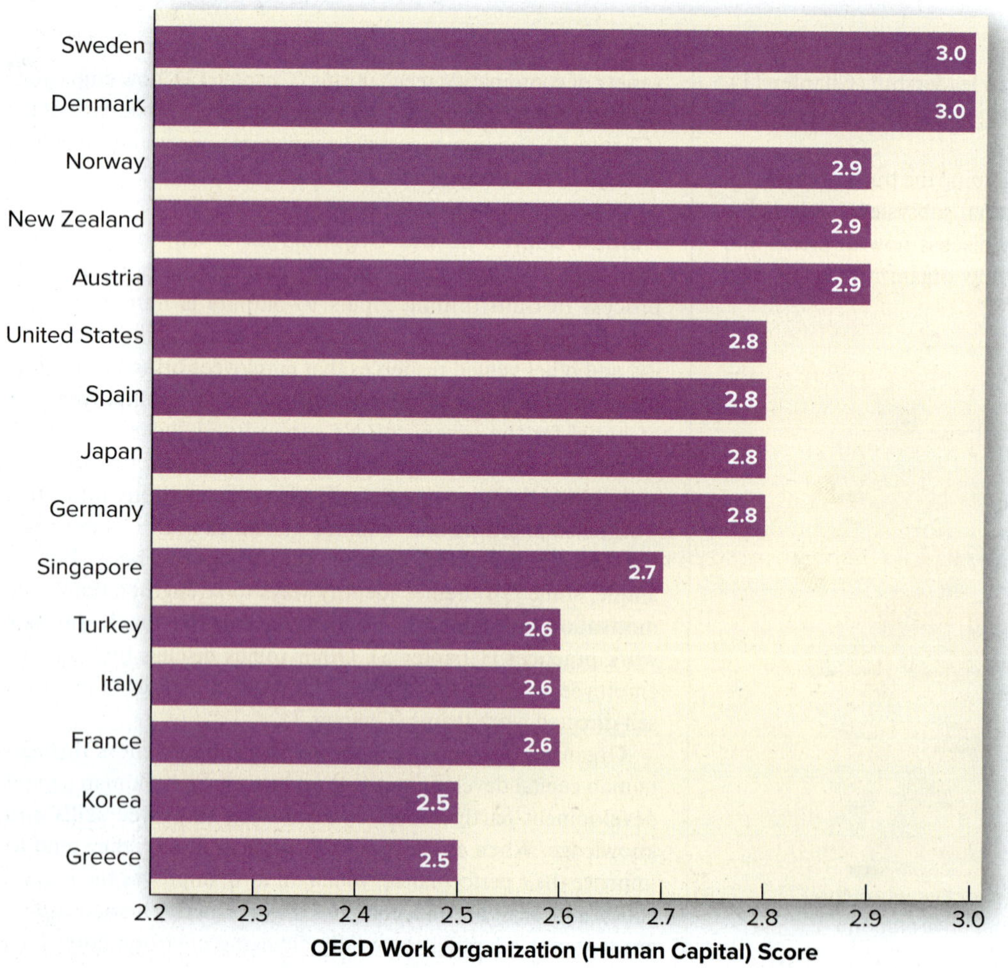

Average composite score on work organization (human capital) practices reported by employees in selected countries. Higher scores indicate a higher incidence of human capital practices in that country. This scale represents "work organization" practices, which exclude rewards but include work flexibility/autonomy, planning one's own work, cooperating and sharing information with coworkers, and training others. Data were collected from more than 215,000 adults in OECD and partner countries with a minimum 4,000 respondents per country. This chart shows a subset of the 34 countries measured in the study.

and behavior. With regard to stakeholders, the company's executive team and board of directors rely on their personal values to decide how the company should prioritize its investments for future growth and how its current earnings should be distributed (e.g., to stockholders, employees, community, etc.).

One topic that is closely aligned with personal values and stakeholders is corporate social responsibility. **Corporate social responsibility (CSR)** consists of organizational activities intended to benefit society and the environment beyond the firm's immediate financial interests or legal obligations.[31] It is the view that companies have a contract with society, in which they must serve stakeholders beyond stockholders and customers. This is known as the triple-bottom-line philosophy. Firms that adopt the triple bottom line aim to survive and be profitable in the marketplace (economic), but they also intend to maintain or improve conditions for society (social) as well as the physical environment. The emerging evidence is that companies with a positive CSR reputation tend to have better financial performance, more loyal employees, and better relations with customers, job applicants, and other stakeholders.[32]

> Corporate social responsibility applies the triple bottom line; organizations strive to be financially successful as well as to improve society and the environment.

Connecting the Dots: An Integrative Model of Organizational Behavior

So far, we have explained how organizational behavior benefits you as well as the organization. This discussion also reveals that OB is a diverse and interconnected field of knowledge. Exhibit 1.3 is an integrative road map to help you navigate the various organizational behavior topics throughout this book. It is a metamodel—a model that connects more specific OB models and concepts. As such, Exhibit 1.3 gives you a bird's-eye view of the book and its various topics, so you can more easily see how they fit together.

As Exhibit 1.3 illustrates, individual inputs and processes influence individual outcomes, which have a direct effect on the organization's effectiveness. For example, how well organizations transform inputs to outputs and satisfy key stakeholders is dependent on how well employees perform their jobs and make logical and creative decisions. Individual inputs, processes, and outcomes are identified in the two left-side boxes of our integrative OB model and are the center of attention in Part 2 of this book. We will learn about personality and values—two of the most important individual characteristics—and later examine self-concept, perceptions, emotions, attitudes, and motivation.

Part 3 of this book directs our attention to team and interpersonal inputs, processes, and outcomes. These topics are found

Exhibit 1.3 An Integrative Model of Organizational Behavior

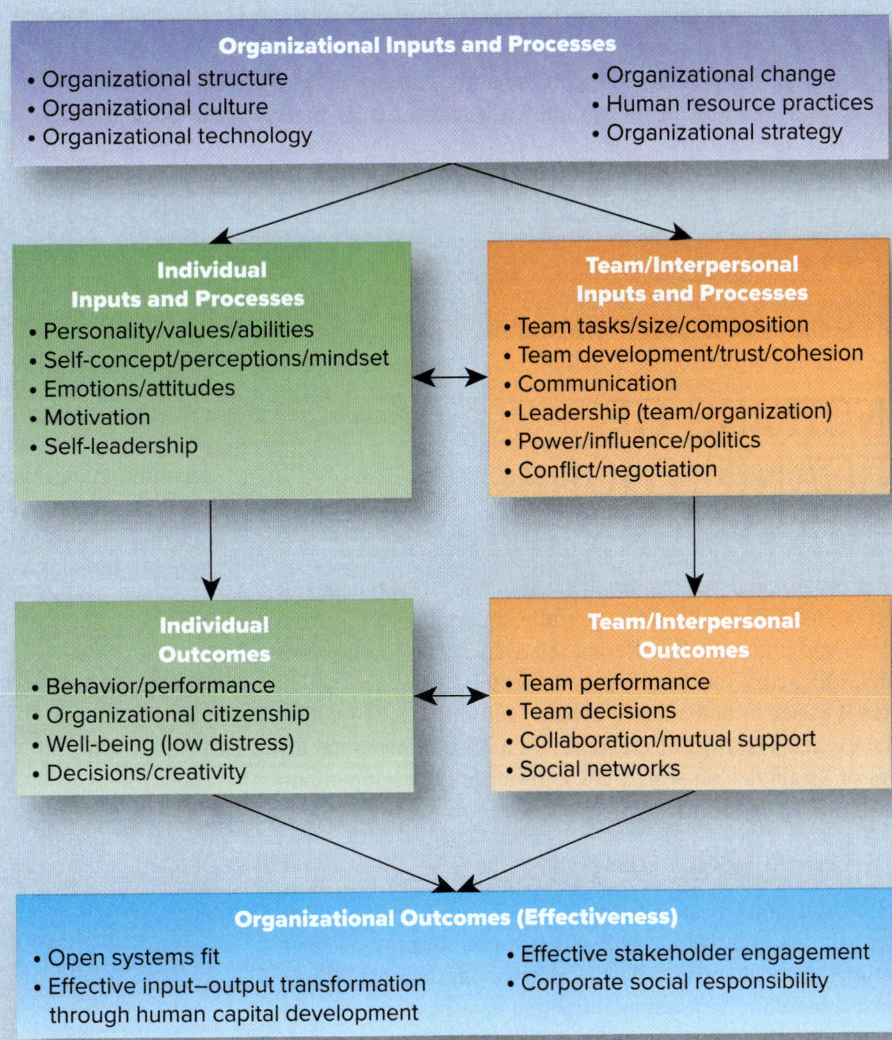

evidence-based management the practice of making decisions and taking actions based on research evidence

in the two boxes on the right side of Exhibit 1.3. The chapter on team dynamics (Chapter 7) explains how team inputs (e.g., team composition, size, and other team characteristics) influence team processes (team development, cohesion, and others), which then affect team performance and other outcomes. Later chapters in Part 3 examine specific interpersonal and team processes listed in Exhibit 1.3, including communication, power and influence, conflict, and leadership.

Exhibit 1.3 illustrates that team processes and outcomes affect individual processes and outcomes. As an example, an individual's personal well-being is partly affected by the mutual support received from team members and other coworkers. The opposite is also true; individual processes affect team and interpersonal dynamics in organizations. For instance, self-concept among individual team members influences the team's cohesion.

The top area of Exhibit 1.3 highlights the macro-level influence of organizational inputs and processes on both teams and individuals. These organizational-level variables are mainly discussed in Part 4, including organizational structure, organizational culture, and organizational change. However, we will also refer to human resource practices, information systems, and additional organizational-level variables throughout this book where they have a known effect on individual, interpersonal, and team dynamics.

LO1-3 Describe the anchors on which organizational behavior knowledge is based.

ANCHORS OF ORGANIZATIONAL BEHAVIOR KNOWLEDGE

Earlier, we pointed out that the field of organizational behavior benefits you because it offers carefully constructed and tested theories and practices. By offering relatively accurate models of reality, OB helps you to refine your personal theories, which makes it easier to understand, predict, and influence organizational events. The field of OB relies on a set of conceptual anchors or principles on which OB knowledge is developed and refined (see Exhibit 1.4).[33]

The Systematic Research Anchor

A key feature of OB knowledge is that it should be based on systematic research, which typically involves forming research questions, systematically collecting data, and testing hypotheses against those data.[34] Systematic research investigation is the basis for **evidence-based management**—making decisions and taking actions guided by research evidence. It makes perfect sense that management practice should be founded on the best available systematic knowledge. Yet corporate leaders and other staff often embrace fads, untested consulting models, and their own pet beliefs without bothering to find out if they actually work![35]

There are several reasons why corporate decision makers overlook evidence-based knowledge:

1. People are bombarded with ideas from consultant reports, newspaper articles, and other public sources, many of which provide only vague evidence to validate their claims. This volume and opacity of popular advice makes it difficult for executives to quickly determine which ideas have sufficient evidence-based foundation.
2. Busy executives tend to rely on a few favorite publications, rather than evaluate the accuracy of specific ideas published in those sources and continuously seek out other sources. Meanwhile, OB research often receives limited attention in many popular sources.[36]
3. Executives sometimes ignore or dismiss evidence-based knowledge that contradicts their preconceived beliefs. This problem is caused by various perceptual errors and decision-making biases (see Chapter 3 and Chapter 6).
4. The developers of many popular management fads are rewarded for marketing their ideas, not for testing to see if they actually work. Consequently, some management fads gain the most public attention because of their excellent packaging and promotion, not because they have the strongest evidence-based foundation.
5. Good OB research is necessarily generic rather than relevant to a specific situation or industry. Managers therefore have the difficult task of figuring out which theories are relevant to their unique situation.

OB experts have proposed a few simple suggestions to create a more evidence-based organization.[37] First, be skeptical of hype, which is apparent when so-called experts say the idea is "new," "revolutionary," and "proven." In reality, most management ideas are adaptations, evolutionary, and never proven (science can only disprove, but never prove; it can only find evidence to support a practice). Second, the company should embrace collective expertise rather than rely on charismatic stars and management gurus. Third, stories provide useful illustrations and possibly preliminary evidence of a useful practice, but they should never become the main foundation to support management action. Instead, rely on more systematic investigation with a larger sample. Finally, take a neutral stance toward

OB THEORY TO PRACTICE

Creating an Evidence-Based Management Organization

1. Be skeptical of hyped management practices ("new," "revolutionary," "proven").
2. Embrace collective expertise, not charismatic stars or management gurus.
3. Use stories as examples and ideas, not conclusive evidence.
4. Take a neutral stance to popular trends and ideologies.

Exhibit 1.4 Anchors of Organizational Behavior Knowledge

Systematic research anchor	Study organizations using systematic research methods
Practical orientation anchor	Ensure that OB theories are useful in organizations
Multidisciplinary anchor	Import knowledge from other disciplines, not just create its own knowledge
Contingency anchor	Recognize that the effectiveness of an action may depend on the situation
Multiple levels of analysis anchor	Understand OB events from three levels of analysis: individual, team, organization

popular trends and ideologies. Executives tend to get caught up in what their counterparts at other companies are doing without determining the validity or relevance of those trendy practices to their own organizations.

The Practical Orientation Anchor

Most OB theories are interesting, but they also need to be useful in practice, whether for executive teams or for the rest of us in everyday work activities.[38] This is consistent with our statement earlier in this chapter that almost all organizational behavior theories have the implicit or explicit objective of making organizations more effective. The true "impact" of an OB theory is how well it finds its way into organizational life and becomes a valuable asset for improving the organization's effectiveness. OB theories offer specific advice on how to energize employees, improve customer service through employee attitudes, create more effective teams, determine the best communication channel for a specific situation, build a strong corporate culture, determine when to involve others in your decisions, handle conflict effectively, and so forth. After reading this book, you will have a toolkit of theories that are not only interesting, but are practical to use in organizations.

The Multidisciplinary Anchor

Another organizational behavior anchor is that the field should welcome theories and knowledge from other disciplines, not just from its own isolated research base. For instance, psychological research has aided our understanding of individual and interpersonal behavior. Sociologists have contributed to our knowledge of team dynamics, organizational socialization, organizational power, and other aspects of the social system. OB knowledge has also benefited from knowledge in emerging fields such as communications, marketing, and information systems.

This practice of borrowing theory from other disciplines is inevitable. Organizations have central roles in society, so they are studied in many social sciences.[39] Furthermore, organizations consist of people who interact with one another, so there is an inherent intersection between OB and most disciplines that study human beings. However, by relying too much on theories developed in other fields, OB faces the risk of lagging rather than leading in knowledge production. In contrast, OB-bred theories allow researchers to concentrate on the quality and usefulness of the theory and be the first to understand and apply that knowledge.[40]

The Contingency Anchor

OB research embraces the contingency anchor—namely, that the effect of one variable on another variable often depends on the characteristics of the situation or people involved. People and their work environments are complex, so a particular action may have different consequences under different conditions. The same outcome or solution rarely applies in every circumstance.[41]

For example, later in this chapter we discuss how the success of remote work depends on specific characteristics of the employee, job, and organization. Contingencies are identified in many OB theories, such as the best leadership style, the best conflict-handling style, and the best organizational structure. Of course, it would be so much simpler if we could rely on "one best way" theories, in which a particular concept or practice has the same results in every situation. OB experts do try to keep theories as simple as possible, but the contingency anchor is always on their mind.[42]

People and their work environments are complex, so a particular action may have different consequences under different conditions (the contingency anchor).
Elnur/Shutterstock

The Multiple Levels of Analysis Anchor

Organizational behavior recognizes that what goes on in organizations can be placed into three levels of analysis: individual, team (including interpersonal), and organization. In fact, advanced empirical research carefully identifies the appropriate level of analysis for each variable in the study and then measures at that level of analysis. For example, team norms and cohesion are measured as team variables, not as characteristics of individuals within each team.

Although OB research and writing pegs each variable within one of these levels of analysis, most variables are understood best by thinking of them from all three levels of analysis.[43] Communication is located in this book as a team (interpersonal) process, for instance, but it also includes individual and organizational processes. Therefore, you should try to think about each OB topic at the individual, team, and organizational levels, not just at one of these levels.

LO1-4 Summarize the workplace trends of diversity and the inclusive workplace, work–life integration, remote work, and emerging employment relationships.

THE EMERGING WORKPLACE LANDSCAPE

Organizations are experiencing unprecedented change. Global competition, rapid and disruptive technological change, and many other factors have substantially altered business strategy and everyday workplace activities. The field of organizational behavior plays a vital role in guiding organizations through this continuous turbulence. In this section, we look at four emerging workplace developments: diversity/inclusive workplace, work-life integration, remote work, and employment relationships.

Diversity and the Inclusive Workplace

An important objective of successful organizations is to create an **inclusive workplace**. Inclusive workplaces value diversity and allow people of all identities to be fully themselves while contributing to the organization.[44] At the individual level, an inclusive workplace enables people of all backgrounds to feel psychologically safe, engaged, valued, authentic, listened to, and respected. At a collective level, an inclusive workplace gives diverse groups voice through formal structures, such as diversity councils, and everyday processes, such as representation in teams and casual gatherings. It also continually assesses recruitment, rewards, social and information networks, and other organizational systems to ensure that they do not unfairly favor some groups over others.

Most people initially think about diversity in terms of **surface-level diversity**, that is, the observable demographic and other overt differences among members of a group, such as their race, ethnicity, gender, age, and physical capabilities.[45] Surface-level diversity in the United States and many other countries has increased substantially over the past few decades. Another form of diversity—called **deep-level diversity**—refers to differences in the psychological characteristics of employees, including personalities, beliefs, values, and attitudes.[46] We can't directly see deep-level diversity, but it is evident in a person's words, decisions, and actions. Some deep-level diversity is associated with surface-level attributes. For example, studies report significant differences between men and women regarding their preference of conflict-handling styles, ethical principles, and approaches to communicating with other people in various situations.[47]

The combination of surface-level and deep-level diversity is also evident in the multigenerational workforce, which is usually organized into cohorts: *Silents* (born earlier than 1946), *Baby Boomers* (born from 1946 to 1964), *Generation Xers* (born from 1965 to 1980), *Millennials* (born from 1981 to 1996), and *Generation Zs* (born after 1996).[48] Research suggests that differences in needs, expectations, and attitudes do exist across age groups, although not necessarily as much as some popular books and articles claim. Also, much of this deep-level diversity is due more to the person's stage in life and less to whether they were born into a specific cohort. For instance, one analysis of German data over 25 years found that generational groups held similar attitudes (importance of job success, importance of self-actualization, confidence in the future, worry about job security, etc.) when they were a particular age. In other words, Baby Boomers had similar beliefs and attitudes as Millennials do when they were that age.[49]

Consequences of Diversity Inclusive workplaces produce better decisions, employee attitudes, team performance, and a host of other favorable outcomes for employees and the organization.[50] Teams with high informational diversity (members have different knowledge and skills) tend to be more creative and make better decisions in complex situations compared to teams with less informational diversity. A workforce with surface-level and deep-level diversity is also more representative of most communities, so companies are better able to recognize and address community needs. However, the many benefits of

> **The many benefits of an inclusive workplace depend on leadership, team structure, psychological safety perceptions, and employees' personal values.**

inclusive workplace a workplace that values people of all identities and allows them to be fully themselves while contributing to the organization

surface-level diversity the observable demographic or physiological differences in people, such as their race, ethnicity, gender, age, and physical disabilities

deep-level diversity differences in the psychological characteristics of employees, including personalities, beliefs, values, and attitudes

work–life integration the degree that people are effectively engaged in their various work and nonwork roles and have a low degree of role conflict across those life domains

Inclusive workplaces value diversity and allow people of all identities to be fully themselves while contributing to the organization.
Ariel Skelley/Blend Images

an inclusive workplace are contingent on a variety of factors, such as leadership, team structure, psychological safety perceptions, and employees' personal values.[51]

Diversity also poses challenges in the workplace.[52] One problem is that employees with diverse backgrounds usually take longer to perform effectively together because they experience numerous communication problems and create "faultlines" in informal group dynamics (see Chapter 7). One recent study found that research teams in the Formula 1 race car industry performed better as their diversity (range of experience) increased to a point, but performance was lower in highly diverse teams because they couldn't communicate or coordinate as well as less diverse teams. Some forms of diversity also increase the risk of dysfunctional conflict, which reduces information sharing and satisfaction with coworkers (see Chapter 10). These problems can offset the advantages of diversity in some situations.

But even with these challenges, companies need to make diversity a priority because surface-level diversity, as well as some forms of deep-level diversity, are moral and legal imperatives. Companies that offer an inclusive workplace are, in essence, fulfilling the ethical standard of fairness in their decisions regarding employment and the allocation of rewards. Inclusive workplace practices improve the quality of hiring and promotion, and increase employee satisfaction and loyalty. Companies that create an inclusive workplace also nurture a culture of respect that, in turn, improves cooperation and coordination among employees.

Work–Life Integration

Before the digital age, most employees would finish work after eight or nine hours at the office or factory and could separate their personal time from their employment. Few people had complete separation of these roles, of course. Employees either brought paperwork home or thought about workplace issues long after their official work day had ended. Even so, the past is a stark contrast to the situation today in which information technology tethers a large percentage of employees to work on a 24/7 schedule. Globalization has contributed to this blending of work and nonwork because employees need to be "on-call" with coworkers, suppliers, and clients who now live in different time zones around the planet.

Little wonder that one feature employees value in a job is the ability to integrate work with nonwork activities.[53] **Work–life integration** refers to the degree that people are effectively engaged in their various work and nonwork roles and have a low degree of role conflict across those life domains.[54] This phrase has replaced *work-life balance*, which incorrectly implies that work and nonwork roles are completely separate and opposing partitions (like a balance of a scale). "There is no such thing as work–life balance," says Lisa Sterling, executive vice president and chief people & culture officer at human resource software company Ceridian in Minneapolis. "You've got to get to a point at which work and life integrate, and you figure out organizationally and individually how to make those two things work together."[55]

Work–life integration occurs by satisfying the demands and experiencing the positive emotions of our multiple roles, which are inherently integrated because the resources generated and consumed by one role enhance or starve other roles.
chaponta/Shutterstock

To understand work-life integration, consider that each of us has multiple roles and associated self-concepts, such as accountant, parent, friend, manager, and sports fan (see Chapter 3). Work-life integration occurs by satisfying the demands and experiencing the positive emotions of our various segments of life. These roles are inherently integrated because the resources generated and consumed by one role enhance or starve other roles.[56] People with a fulfilling home life, for example, develop social support, positive moods, relaxation, and other resources that can enrich their work and other roles. Similarly, the resources gained at work—such as new skills, financial rewards, and feelings of success—contribute to home and other nonwork roles.

Unfortunately, many people don't experience resource enrichment across roles. Instead, the heavy demands of one role deplete personal resources, which starve other roles. Employees who spend most waking hours performing or thinking about their job—whether at the workplace, at home, or on vacation—have insufficient time and energy remaining for other aspects of their lives. They experience what is widely known as work-life conflict. In summary, a person's work roles and nonwork roles are inherently integrated because the physical, cognitive, and emotional resources produced or consumed by one role potentially enrich or undermine the success and enjoyment of other roles.

Practicing Work–Life Integration How do individuals and organizations maximize work-life integration?[57] One strategy is to literally integrate two or more roles. An increasingly popular trend is to conduct meetings during an exercise walk. Some companies encourage staff to bring their dogs to work, which is both comforting and requires an occasional break to walk the four-legged friend. Onsite child care is a form of integration because it allows employees to switch from work to parent roles throughout the day. These integration efforts are not always effective, but they illustrate that blending work and nonwork roles is more viable than we previously understood.

A second work-life integration strategy occurs through flexible work scheduling.[58] For instance, you might remotely attend a meeting from home in the evening with coworkers who live in other time zones, then arrive at work late the next morning after doing a few household chores. Organizations also have parental and other personal leave benefits to support higher demands at home in the short term. A third work-life integration strategy is to ensure that your various work and nonwork roles are sufficiently compatible with each other and with your personal characteristics. In other words, your job, family life, sports activities, and so forth should roughly be consistent with your personality and values. This relates to self-concept consistency, which we discuss in Chapter 3.

Although work is integrated with other life roles, a fourth strategy is to engage in some degree of "boundary management"

OB THEORY TO PRACTICE

Strategies to Improve Work–Life Integration

Work–Life Integration Strategy	Description	Example
Integrate multiple roles	Find ways to perform work and nonwork activities simultaneously or proximally.	Have a meeting with a coworker while doing exercise that allows conversation (e.g., walking).
Flexible work scheduling	Establish work (and nonwork) roles that allow work time to have variable time frames.	Seek jobs and companies that allow you to vary your start and finish times as well as work remotely on some days.
Align roles with personal attributes	Choose work and nonwork roles that are sufficiently compatible with each other and with your personality and values.	Assess your personality and values, then choose work and life activities that are compatible with those personal attributes.
Boundary management	Establish methods that prevent your work roles from encroaching on time and attention devoted to your nonwork roles.	Establish personal or organizational rules that prohibit communication with coworkers at times that are formally outside company work hours.

across those roles.[59] Employees are more likely to set aside work-free times in their private lives when they observe this behavior in managers. Several organizations adopt more structured boundary management through rules that prohibit work-related communication (except in extreme emergencies) after the regular work day. The French government has taken this one step further: It recently passed legislation giving employees the "right to disconnect"—that is, they have a legal right to ignore company messages after hours.

Remote Work

Blending work with other life roles is particularly apparent as more people sometimes perform their job remotely rather than at the organization's physical work site.[60] *Remote work* (formerly known as telecommuting or teleworking) occurs when employees work from home or other nonwork site (such as a café). It also occurs when employees are temporarily or indefinitely assigned to a client's workplace—an arrangement that we describe in the next section on employment relationships. Remote work is increasingly common because employees can connect relatively easily with coworkers, clients, and company data through various forms of information technology.

> I never wrote anything in the office—too many distractions.[61]
>
> —David Ogilvy, founder of Ogilvy, known as the "Father of Advertising"

A small percentage of the American workforce over the past two decades has worked remotely at least a few days each month. However, remote working skyrocketed when the COVID-19 pandemic forced businesses in the United States and elsewhere to apply social distancing and self-isolation practices. One very large panel survey reported that 61 percent of full-time American employees were working from home due to COVID-19 a few weeks after it became a serious health concern (but before the peak of its first wave). In comparison, 33 percent of these employees were working at home two weeks earlier, just as the social distancing requirements were being introduced. Some companies, such as Optus (a large Australian telecommunications firm), intend to transition its call center employees permanently to remote work arrangements, even after the pandemic is over.[62]

Some companies employed a completely remote workforce long before the COVID-19 pandemic motivated many employers to apply this work arrangement. As we described at the beginning of this chapter, all of Automattic's 1,200 employees work from home and cafés across dozens of countries, every day. Buffer, Emsisoft, and Sonatype are a few other organizations in which all employees are remote workers. These *distributed organizations* have learned how to recruit, train, support, retain, and lead employees who rarely (if ever) meet in person. "When I started doing all-remote, it was a special thing," says Christian Mairoll, who launched anti-malware software company Emsisoft 15 years ago in Austria. Mairoll now has three dozen staff located around the world and runs the business from his sheep farm in New Zealand. "As we celebrate our 15th anniversary, I'm proud to say that Emsisoft is living proof that all-remote is a viable, effective, and sustainable business model."[63]

Remote Work Benefits and Risks Remote work is a controversial topic because it has both benefits and risks for organizations as well as remote workers (see Exhibit 1.5).[64] Several contingencies also enhance and undermine its effectiveness. One benefit is that remote workers usually experience better work-life integration because they have more time and somewhat more control to juggle work with family obligations. Work-life integration is more difficult, however, when employees lack sufficient workspace and privacy at home and have increased family responsibilities on days when they work from home.

Job applicants—particularly Millennials and Gen Zers—identify remote work as an attractive job feature, and turnover is usually lower among employees who are able to work from home. Research also indicates that remote workers have higher productivity than other employees, likely because they experience less stress and tend to convert some of the former commuting time into work time. Working remotely also improves productivity by enabling employees to perform their jobs at times when natural disasters (such as the COVID-19 pandemic) prohibit access to the office.

Due to less commuting, remote work offers considerable financial benefits for employees, including less vehicle use, fuel costs, unpaid time traveling, and other commuting expenses.[65] Remote work benefits society in the form of lower greenhouse gas emissions and less need for taxpayer-funded transportation infrastructure. Companies also benefit from lower real estate costs.

Remote work also has several disadvantages or risks.[66] People who regularly or mostly work from home report higher

Exhibit 1.5 Potential Benefits and Risks of Remote Working

Potential Benefits	Potential Risks
• Better employee work–life integration • Attractive benefit for job applicants • Low employee turnover • Higher employee productivity • Reduced greenhouse gas emissions • Reduced corporate real estate and office costs	• More social isolation • Lower team cohesion • Weaker organizational culture • Higher stress due to home space and roles

Remote work tends to be more successful when employers help remote workers maintain sufficient cohesion with their team and psychological connectedness with the organization.
fizkes/Shutterstock

levels of social isolation, including weaker relationships with coworkers. They also receive less word-of-mouth information, which may have implications for promotional opportunities and workplace relations. Teams potentially suffer from lower cohesion. Organizations risk having a weaker culture when most employees work from home for a significant part of their work week.

The success of remote working depends on several characteristics of the employee, job, and organization.[67] Employees who work effectively from home typically have high self-motivation, self-organization, need for autonomy, and information technology skills. They also fulfill their social needs more from sources outside the workplace. Jobs are better suited to remote work when the tasks require few resources at the workplace, the work is performed independently from coworkers, and task performance is measurable.

Remote work tends to be more successful when organizations reward and promote employees based on their performance rather than their presence in the office (face time). These firms also help remote workers maintain sufficient cohesion with their team and psychological connectedness with the organization. This occurs through regular supportive communication with the supervisor and teammates. In some instances, companies may need to limit the number of days that employees work from home, such as by having special meetings or events where all employees assemble at the workplace. Visual communication channels, such a video conferences with cameras turned on, also improve personal relatedness.

Employment Relationships

Another rapidly evolving workplace arrangement is the individual's formal employment relationship with the organization.[68] Historically, most workers have been in full-time, permanent jobs (called direct employment). This relationship assumes continuous employment (lifetime employment, in rare cases), usually with expectations of career advancement and the organization's investment in the employee's skills. An increasing percentage of the workforce has a more fragile form of direct employment relationship, such as part-time, on-call, casual, and seasonal employment.

Although direct employment still dominates, indirect employment and self-employed contract work are the fastest growing work relationships. Indirect employment occurs when people hold positions in an agency and are temporarily assigned (temps) or indefinitely "leased" to client firms. One annual survey estimates that agency-based placements alone represent almost 10 percent of the U.S. workforce.[69] The rapid growth of indirect employment has occurred as companies outsource noncore work activities, such as information technology and customer contact centers, to firms that specialize in these services.

Self-employed contract work, the third type of employment relationship, has recently dominated the public's attention because of the increasing number of freelancers in the "gig economy." Traditionally, a self-employed contractor represents an independent organization that provides services to a client organization. The emergence of Uber, Airbnb, Uber Eats, and other branded platforms has created a less independent form of this relationship. Some experts suggest that platform-based workers are more like on-call direct employment staff than contractors because they are dependent on the platform, abide by its work standards, and in some instances provide transportation, food delivery, or accommodation services when required by the platform.[70]

Consequences of Emerging Employment Relationships

People in indirect and self-employment relationships have higher job performance under some circumstances, but those with direct employment relationships tend to produce higher work quality, innovation, and agility. This is because permanent employees tend to have lower turnover, higher commitment, and more involvement in the company. They also tend to receive more organizational investment in their training, rewards, and other high-performance work practices.[71]

Teams that include both direct employment and agency workers tend to have weaker social networks, which results in less information sharing (see Chapter 9).

McGraw Hill connect

SELF-ASSESSMENT 1.1: Are You a Good Remote Worker?

Contract workers generally have similar levels of job satisfaction as direct employment workers, whereas agency workers tend to have lower job satisfaction. In fact, the presence of agency (outsourced) workers can adversely affect the satisfaction and commitment of permanent employees in the client organization. Direct employment anchors an individual's self-concept (see Chapter 3), whereas people working in outsourced/agency and contract relationships need to discover how to replicate this stability in their self-view and role. Finally, managers in client firms seem to experience more ambiguity in their roles and less discretion in their daily attempts to guide the work of indirect employment and contract people who are technically not their own employees.[72]

> People in indirect and self-employment relationships have higher job performance under some circumstances, but those with direct employment relationships tend to produce higher work quality, innovation, and agility.

LO1-5 Describe the four factors that directly influence individual behavior and performance.

MARS MODEL OF INDIVIDUAL BEHAVIOR AND PERFORMANCE

For most of the past century, experts have investigated the direct predictors of individual behavior and performance.[73] One of the earliest formulas was *performance = person × situation*, where *person* includes individual characteristics and *situation* represents external influences on the individual's behavior. Another frequently mentioned formula is *performance = ability × motivation*.[74] Sometimes known as the "skill-and-will" model, this formula elaborates two specific characteristics within the person that influence individual performance. Some organizational studies use the *ability-motivation-opportunity (AMO)* model, which refers to the three variables but with a limited interpretation of the situation. Along with ability, motivation, and situation, researchers have more recently identified a fourth key direct predictor of individual behavior and performance: role perceptions (the individual's expected role obligations).[75]

These four variables—motivation, ability, role perceptions, and situational factors—are represented in the **MARS model** of individual behavior and performance (see Exhibit 1.6). MARS is the acronym for these four concepts.[76] All four factors are essential influences on an individual's voluntary behavior and performance; if any one of them is low in a given situation, the employee is less likely to engage in the behavior or will perform it poorly. For example, motivated salespeople with clear role perceptions and sufficient resources (situational factors) will not perform their jobs as well if they lack sales skills and related knowledge (ability).

MARS model a model depicting the four variables—motivation, ability, role perceptions, and situational factors—that directly influence an individual's voluntary behavior and performance

motivation the forces within a person that affect his or her direction, intensity, and persistence of voluntary behavior

Motivation, ability, and role perceptions are clustered together in the model because they are located within the person. Situational factors are external to the individual but still affect his or her behavior and performance.[77] The four MARS variables are the direct predictors of employee performance, customer service, coworker collegiality, ethical behavior, and all other forms of voluntary behavior in the workplace. Let's look at each of the four factors in the MARS model.

Employee Motivation

Motivation represents the forces within a person that affect his or her direction, intensity, and persistence of effort for voluntary behavior.[78] *Direction* refers to the path along which people steer their effort. In other words, motivation is goal-directed, not random. People have choices about what they are trying to achieve and at what level of quality, quantity, and so forth. They are motivated to arrive at work on time, finish a project a few hours early, or aim for many other targets.

The second element of motivation, called *intensity*, is the amount of effort allocated to the goal. Intensity refers to how much people push themselves to complete a task. Two employees might be motivated to finish their project within the next few hours (direction), but only one of them puts forth enough effort (intensity) to achieve this goal. The third element of motivation is *persistence*, which refers to the length of time that the individual continues to exert effort toward an objective. Employees sustain their effort until they reach their goal or give up beforehand.

Exhibit 1.6 MARS Model of Individual Behavior and Results

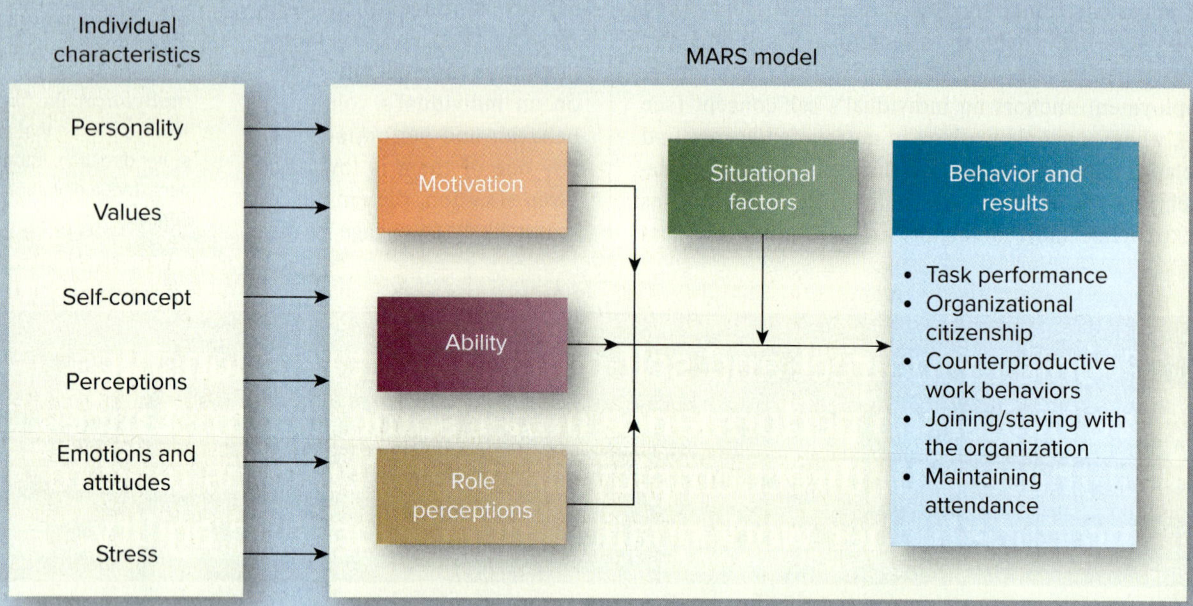

To help remember these three elements of motivation, consider the metaphor of driving a car in which the thrust of the engine is your effort. Direction refers to where you steer the car, intensity is how much you put your foot down on the gas pedal, and persistence is for how long you keep your foot on that accelerator and drive toward your destination. Remember that motivation is a force that exists within individuals; it is not their actual behavior. Thus, direction, intensity, and persistence are cognitive (thoughts) and emotional conditions that directly cause us to move.

Ability

Employee abilities have a well-known influence on behavior and task performance. **Ability** includes both the learned capabilities and natural aptitudes required to successfully complete a task. *Learned capabilities* include the skills and knowledge that people acquire through training, practice, and other forms of learning. Learned capabilities tend to wane over time if they are not regularly put to use. *Aptitudes* are the natural talents that help employees learn specific tasks more quickly and perform them better. For example, finger dexterity is an aptitude by which individuals learn more quickly and potentially achieve higher performance at picking up and handling small objects with their fingers. Employees with high finger dexterity are not necessarily better than others at first; rather, they usually learn the skill faster and potentially reach a higher level of performance.[79]

How well an individual's abilities affect his or her performance and well-being depends on how well those abilities are compatible with the job's requirements. One matching strategy is to select applicants with the required abilities. For example, companies ask applicants to perform work samples, provide references for checking their past performance, and complete various selection tests. A second strategy is to train employees who lack specific knowledge or skills needed for the job.[80] The third person–job matching strategy is to redesign the job so that employees are given tasks only within their current abilities. For example, a complex task might be simplified–some aspects of the work are transferred to others–so a new employee is only assigned tasks that he or she is currently able to perform. As the employee becomes more competent at these tasks, other tasks are added back into the job.

Role Perceptions

Along with motivation and ability, employees require accurate **role perceptions** to perform their jobs well. Role perceptions refer to how clearly people understand what is expected of them in their organizational roles. These perceptions range from role clarity to role ambiguity. Role clarity exists when the individual:

1. Understands the specific duties or consequences for which the employee is accountable.
2. Understands the priority of assigned tasks and performance expectations (e.g. performance quality versus quantity).
3. Understands the preferred behaviors or procedures for accomplishing tasks.

The first of these may seem obvious, but employees are occasionally evaluated on job duties they were never told were within their zone of responsibility. The priority dimension of

ability the learned capabilities and natural aptitudes required to successfully complete a task

role perceptions the degree to which a person understands the job duties assigned to or expected of him or her

Mind the MARS Gap on Ability, Role Perceptions, and Situational Factors[81]

40% of 20,000 employees surveyed worldwide strongly agree that their managers have clearly defined their roles and responsibilities.

67% of 615,395 U.S. federal government employees say they are given a real opportunity to improve their skills in the organization.

60% of 2.2 million employees surveyed worldwide strongly agree that they know what is expected of them.

83% of 181,754 Canadian federal government employees strongly or somewhat agree that they have the materials and equipment they need to do their job.

75% of 1,500 American employees surveyed question whether their workplace has given them the sufficient training necessary to do their current job.

(Photo): Maren Wischnewski/Alamy Stock Photo

role clarity is illustrated in the classic dilemma of quantity versus quality, such as how many customers to serve in an hour (quantity) versus how well each customer should be served (quality). The "preferred behaviors or procedures" dimension of role clarity exists when an employee knows two or three ways to perform a task and knows which of these the company prefers.

Role perceptions are important because they represent how well employees know where to direct their effort.[82] Employees with role clarity perform work more accurately and efficiently, whereas those with role ambiguity waste considerable time and energy performing the wrong tasks or in the wrong way. Furthermore, role clarity is essential for coordination with coworkers and other stakeholders. This not only improves team performance, but it also ensures that everyone performs their work safely. Finally, role clarity motivates employees because they have a higher belief that their effort will produce the expected outcomes. In other words, people are more confident when they know what is expected of them.

OB THEORY TO PRACTICE

Walmart Employees Improve Role Perceptions through Virtual Reality Training[83]

Through virtual reality training, Walmart employees are improving their role clarity for everyday situations. An employee slips on VR goggles and acts out the role while classmates view a projection of the same scene. The Black Friday scenario, for example, shows long lines, confused shoppers, a toddler standing on a shopping cart seat, and a manager searching for lost keys.

The instructor coaches employee role perceptions by asking the class to prioritize what should be done and to describe the preferred behaviors for each incident. For example, Walmart has a preferred way to correct the child's risky behavior in the shopping cart (*hint:* don't tell the child directly). "Black Friday is a busy, hectic day for everyone," says Sandi Hughes, a Walmart employee in St. Petersburg, Florida. "With the VR, an associate can feel how it can play out."

Julio Cortez/AP Images

Situational Factors

Individual behavior and performance also depend on the situation, which is any context beyond the employee's immediate control.[84] The situation has two main influences on individual behavior and performance.[85] One influence is that the work context constrains or facilitates behavior and performance. Employees who are motivated and skilled and know their role obligations will nevertheless perform poorly if they lack time, budget, physical work facilities, and other resources. The second influence is that the work environment provides cues to guide and motivate people. For example, companies install barriers and warning signs in dangerous areas. These workplace features are situational factors that cue employees to avoid the nearby hazards.

LO1-6 Summarize the five types of individual behavior in organizations.

TYPES OF INDIVIDUAL BEHAVIOR

The four elements of the MARS model—motivation, ability, role perceptions, and situational factors—affect all voluntary workplace behaviors and performance. There are many varieties of individual behavior, but most can be organized into the five categories described in this section: task performance, organizational citizenship, counterproductive work behaviors, joining and staying with the organization, and maintaining work attendance (Exhibit 1.7).

Task Performance

Task performance refers to the individual's voluntary goal-directed behaviors that contribute to organizational objectives.[86] Most jobs require incumbents to complete several tasks. For example, foreign exchange traders at Morgan Stanley must be able to identify and execute profitable trades, work cooperatively with clients and coworkers, assist in training new staff, and work on special telecommunications equipment without error. All tasks involve working with people, data, things, and ideas.[87] Foreign exchange traders, for instance, mainly work with data (e.g., performing technical analysis of trends), but also with people (e.g., sharing information with coworkers and clients), and ideas (interpreting charts and company reports).

There are three types of task performance: proficient, adaptive, and proactive.[88]

- *Proficient task performance* refers to performing the work efficiently and accurately. It involves accomplishing the assigned work at or above the expected standards of quality, quantity, and other indicators of effectiveness.
- *Adaptive task performance* refers to how well employees modify their thoughts and behavior to align with and support a new or changing work process or work setting. Essentially, adaptive task performance is about how well employees respond to change in the workplace and in their job duties.
- *Proactive task performance* refers to how well employees take the initiative to anticipate and introduce new work patterns that benefit the organization. Proactive behaviors bring about change in oneself, coworkers, and the workplace to achieve what is perceived to be a better future for the organization.

Employees in almost every job are expected to perform their work proficiently. However, adaptive and proactive task performance are also important, particularly when the work is ambiguous or dynamic. These conditions exist when the client's expectations are unclear, resources to perform the work have uncertain availability, and the methods used to perform the work are rapidly evolving due to emerging technology.

Organizational Citizenship

Task performance refers to behaviors engaged in *work content*, whereas **organizational citizenship behaviors (OCBs)** refer to behaviors associated with the *work context*. Specifically, OCBs are various forms of cooperation and helpfulness to others that support the organization's social and psychological context.[89] Some OCBs are directed toward individuals, such as assisting coworkers with their work problems, adjusting your work

Exhibit 1.7 Five Types of Individual Behavior in the Workplace

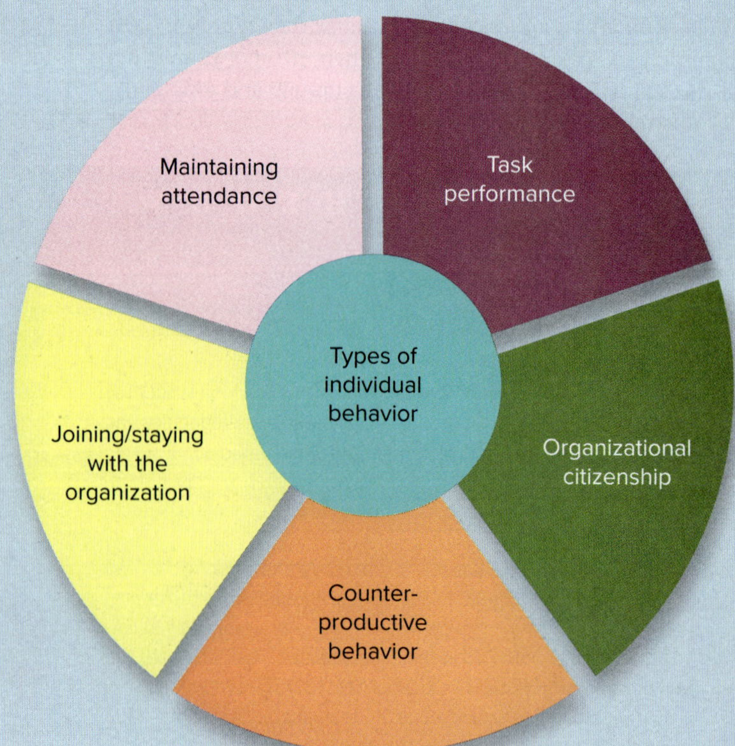

schedules to accommodate coworkers, showing genuine courtesy toward coworkers, and sharing your work resources (supplies, technology, staff) with coworkers. Other OCBs represent cooperation and helpfulness toward the organization, such as supporting the company's public image, offering ideas beyond those required for your own job, attending events that support the organization, and keeping up with new developments in the organization. Some organizational citizenship behaviors are discretionary (employees don't have to perform them), whereas other OCBs are job requirements even if they aren't explicitly stated in job descriptions. In fact, research suggests that managers often evaluate performance by the employee's organizational citizenship behaviors as much as by their task performance.[90]

OCBs can have a significant effect on individual, team, and organizational effectiveness.[91] High-OCB employees receive more support from coworkers, which, in turn, supports their own task performance. OCBs also increase team performance because members depend on one another. However, engaging in OCBs can have negative consequences.[92] OCBs take time and energy away from performing work content, so employees who give more attention to OCBs risk lower career success in companies that reward task performance. Also, employees who frequently perform OCBs tend to have higher work–life conflict because of the amount of time required for these activities.

Counterproductive Work Behaviors

Organizational behavior is interested in all workplace behaviors, including dysfunctional activities collectively known as **counterproductive work behaviors (CWBs)**. CWBs are voluntary behaviors that have the potential to directly or indirectly harm the organization or its stakeholders.[93] This concept includes a wide array of intentional and unintentional behaviors, such as harassing coworkers, creating unnecessary conflict, deviating from preferred work methods (e.g., shortcuts that undermine work quality), being untruthful, stealing, sabotaging work, and wasting resources. CWBs are not minor concerns; research suggests that they can substantially undermine the organization's effectiveness.

Joining and Staying with the Organization

Companies suffer and potentially fail if they can't hire and retain enough people with the right skills and knowledge to perform the work.[94] This isn't a hypothetical statement. During times of economic growth, companies have been unable to keep up with demand because they can't hire enough qualified people. The impact of staff shortages on organizational effectiveness is particularly dramatic during crises, such as the coronavirus (COVID-19) pandemic. Governors in states hardest hit by the virus used social media to urgently invite medical staff elsewhere in the United States to help them treat the burgeoning number of patients. Veterans Affairs hospitals were so understaffed that some nurses were handling five intensive care patients rather than usual two patients. VA staff who would normally enter two-week self-isolation when a coworker tested positive for the virus were apparently told to report for work.[95]

Even when companies are able to hire enough qualified staff, they need these employees to stay with the company.[96] Earlier in this chapter, we explained that human capital is the organization's main source of competitive advantage. The importance of human capital is particularly apparent when employees quit. Those who leave remove valuable knowledge, skills, and relationships with coworkers and external stakeholders, all of which take time for new staff to acquire. Other problems with employee turnover are discussed in later chapters, such as its adverse effect on customer service, team development, and corporate culture strength. Employee turnover does offer some benefits, such as opening up positions so new employees with fresh ideas can be hired and removing people with a tendency for counterproductive work behaviors. But overall, turnover usually has a negative effect on organizational effectiveness.

task performance the individual's voluntary goal-directed behaviors that contribute to organizational objectives

organizational citizenship behaviors (OCBs) various forms of cooperation and helpfulness to others that support the organization's social and psychological context

counterproductive work behaviors (CWBs) voluntary behaviors that have the potential to directly or indirectly harm the organization

Maintaining Work Attendance

Along with attracting and retaining employees, organizations need everyone to show up for work at scheduled times. Unscheduled absenteeism can lead to increased workloads or overtime among coworkers, lower performance by temporary staff filling the vacant positions, poorer coordination in the work process, poorer customer service, and potentially more workplace accidents.[97]

What are the main causes of absenteeism and lateness?[98] Much absenteeism is due to situational factors, such as personal

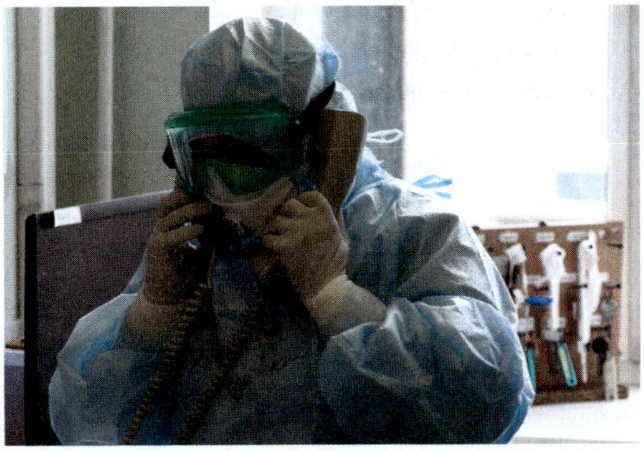

The impact of staff shortages on organizational effectiveness is particularly dramatic during crises, such as the recent coronavirus (COVID-19) pandemic.
Yegor Aleyev/TASS/Getty Images

illness, family demands (e.g., sick children) and bad weather. Other absenteeism occurs because employees need to get away from workplace bullying, difficult customers, boring work, and other stressful conditions. Absenteeism is also higher in organizations with generous sick leave payments. Absenteeism also varies from one employee to the next due to personal values and personality. Finally, studies report that absenteeism is higher in teams with strong absence norms, meaning that team members tolerate and even expect coworkers to take time off.

Although most companies focus on minimizing absenteeism, a more serious behavior may be *presenteeism*—showing up for work when unwell, injured, preoccupied by personal problems, or faced with dangerous conditions getting to work.[99] Employees who show up for work when they should be absent tend to be less productive and may reduce the productivity of coworkers. They may also worsen their own health and spread disease to coworkers. This latter risk of presenteeism had particularly serious consequences during the COVID-19 pandemic. Entire offices and production facilities shut down after just one employee went to work while ill, which quickly spread the virus to dozens or hundreds of other people.

Presenteeism is more common among employees with low job security (such as new and temporary staff), employees who lack sick leave pay or similar financial buffers, and those whose absence would immediately affect many people. Personality characteristics also motivate some people to show up for work when others would gladly recover at home.[100]

THE JOURNEY BEGINS

This chapter introduced you to the field of organizational behavior, described the emerging landscape of organizations, and explained why OB is important for you and for organizations. It also introduced the foundations of individual behavior and performance as well as the main types of individual behavior. But this is only the beginning of our journey. Throughout this volume, we will challenge you to learn new ways of thinking about how people work in and around organizations. We begin this process in Chapter 2 through Chapter 6 by looking at personality, values, and other individual differences that indirectly predict individual behavior through the MARS model.

Study Checklist

Connect® is available for *M Organizational Behavior.* Additional resources include:

✓ Exercises:

- **Case Analysis:** Apply concepts within the context of a real-world situation.
- **Click and Drag:** Helps make the connection between theory and application through matching, ranking, or grouping activities.
- **Video Case:** See management in action through interactive videos.
- **Self-Assessment:** Designed to promote student self-awareness and reflection, these research-based surveys contain detailed feedback for students.
- **Application-Based Activities:** These highly interactive, application- and analysis-based exercises allow students to take on specific roles to complete management-related tasks within a real-world context.

✓ **SmartBook 2.0™**—Smartbook 2.0 is an adaptive learning solution that provides personalized learning to individual student needs, continually adapts to pinpoint knowledge gaps and focuses learning on concepts requiring additional study. It fosters more productive learning, takes the guesswork out of what to study, and helps students better prepare for class.

Notes

1. G. Leibowitz, "This CEO Runs a Billion-Dollar Company With No Offices or Email," *Inc*, March 16, 2016; M.K. Saltzman, "Best Practices for Distributed Teams: Automattic Shares All," *True Ventures* (blog), March 13, 2020, https://trueventures.com/blog/automattic-distributed-team; J. Jones, "Getting Hired at Automattic," *Jerry Jones Blog* (blog), April 16, 2020, https://jerryjones.dev/2020/04/16/getting-hired-at-automattic/. Information about Automattic's workforce is available on its website. See: https://automattic.com/about/

2. M. Warner, "Organizational Behavior Revisited," *Human Relations* 47 (1994): 1151–66; R. Westwood and S. Clegg, "The Discourse of Organization Studies: Dissensus, Politics, and Paradigms," in *Debating Organization: Point-Counterpoint in Organization Studies*, ed. R. Westwood and S. Clegg (Malden, MA: Wiley-Blackwell, 2003), 1–42.

3. R.N. Stern and S.R. Barley, "Organizations as Social Systems: Organization Theory's Neglected Mandate," *Administrative Science Quarterly* 41 (1996): 146–62; D. Katz and R.L. Kahn, *The Social Psychology of Organizations* (New York: Wiley, 1966), Chap. 2.

4. L.E. Greiner, "A Recent History of Organizational Behavior," in *Organizational Behavior*, ed. S. Kerr (Columbus, OH: Grid, 1979), 3–14; J. Micklethwait and A. Wooldridge, *The Company: A Short History of a Revolutionary Idea* (New York: Random House, 2003).

5. T. Lawson, "The Nature of the Firm and Peculiarities of the Corporation," *Cambridge Journal of Economics* 39, no. 1 (2015): 1–32.

6. B. Schlender, "The Three Faces of Steve," *Fortune*, November 9, 1998, 96–101.

7. "A Field Is Born," *Harvard Business Review* 86, no. 7/8 (2008): 164; P.R. Lawrence, "The Key Job Design Problem Is Still Taylorism," *Journal of Organizational Behavior* 31, no. 2/3 (2010): 412–21; L.W. Porter and B. Schneider, "What Was, What Is, and What May Be in OP/OB," *Annual Review of Organizational Psychology and Organizational Behavior* 1, no. 1 (2014): 1–21.

8. T. Takala, "Plato on Leadership," *Journal of Business Ethics* 17(1998): 785–98; J.A. Fernandez, "The Gentleman's Code of Confucius: Leadership by Values," *Organizational Dynamics* 33, no. 1 (2004): 21–31; A.M. Blake and J.L. Moseley, "Frederick Winslow Taylor: One Hundred Years of Managerial Insight," *International Journal of Management* 28, no. 4 (2011): 346–53; J.W. Stutje, ed., *Charismatic Leadership and Social Movements: The Revolutionary Power of Ordinary Men and Women, International Studies in Social History* (New York: Berghahn Books, 2012).

9. C.D. Wrege, "Solving Mayo's Mystery: The First Complete Account of the Origin of the Hawthorne Studies–the Forgotten Contributions of C. E. Snow and H. Hibarger" (paper presented at the Academy of Management Proceedings, August 1976), 12–16; P. Graham, ed., *Mary Parker Follett: Prophet of Management* (Boston: Harvard Business School Press, 1995); J.H. Smith, "The Enduring Legacy of Elton Mayo," *Human Relations* 51, no. 3 (1998): 221–49; R. Busse and M. Warner, "The Legacy of the Hawthorne Experiments: A Critical Analysis of the Human Relations School of Thought," *History of Economic Ideas* 25, no. 2 (2017): 91–114, https://doi.org/10.19272/201706102004; G.M. Nelson, "Mary Parker Follett–Creativity and Democracy," *Human Service Organizations: Management, Leadership & Governance* 41, no. 2 (2017): 178–85, https://doi.org/10.1080/23303131.2016.1263073.

10. The extent to which OB influences career success depends on course pedagogy as well as the practical value of the OB concepts covered in the course. In fact, OB scholars have an ongoing debate about the practical relevance of OB research. See, for example: J.P. Walsh et al., "On the Relationship between Research and Practice: Debate and Reflections," *Journal of Management Inquiry* 16, no. 2 (2007): 128–54; R. Gulati, "Tent Poles, Tribalism, and Boundary Spanning: The Rigor-Relevance Debate in Management Research," *Academy of Management Journal* 50, no. 4 (2007): 775–82; J. Pearce and L. Huang, "The Decreasing Value of Our Research to Management Education," *Academy of Management Learning & Education* 11, no. 2 (2012): 247–62; J.M. Bartunek and S.L. Rynes, "Academics and Practitioners Are Alike and Unlike: The Paradoxes of Academic–Practitioner Relationships," *Journal of Management* 40, no. 5 (2014): 1181–201; N. Butler, H. Delaney, and S. Spoelstra, "Problematizing 'Relevance' in the Business School: The Case of Leadership Studies," *British Journal of Management* 26, no. 4 (2015): 731–44.

11. The skills identified in these recent surveys are almost identical to those reported in a recent review of more than two dozen surveys on employability skills of higher education graduates. See M. Osmani et al., "Graduates Employability Skills: A Review of Literature against Market Demand," *Journal of Education for Business* 94, no. 7 (2019): 423–32.

12. G. Loewenstein, "The Psychology of Curiosity: A Review and Reinterpretation," *Psychological Bulletin* 116, no. 1 (1994): 75–98; C. Kidd and B.Y. Hayden, "The Psychology and Neuroscience of Curiosity," *Neuron* 88, no. 3 (November 2015): 449–60, https://doi.org/10.1016/j.neuron.2015.09.010; M. Livio, *Why?: What Makes Us Curious* (New York: Simon and Schuster, 2017).

13. R.L. Priem and J. Rosenstein, "Is Organization Theory Obvious to Practitioners? A Test of One Established Theory," *Organization Science* 11, no. 5 (2000): 509–24.

14. R.S. Rubin and E.C. Dierdorff, "How Relevant Is the MBA? Assessing the Alignment of Required Curricula and Required Managerial Competencies," *Academy of Management Learning & Education* 8, no. 2 (2009): 208–24; Y. Baruch and O. Lavi-Steiner, "The Career Impact of Management Education from an Average-Ranked University: Human Capital Perspective," *Career Development International* 20, no. 3 (2015): 218–37.

15. M.S. Myers, *Every Employee a Manager* (New York: McGraw-Hill, 1970).

16. For example, see: M.A. West et al., "Reducing Patient Mortality in Hospitals: The Role of Human Resource Management," *Journal of Organizational Behavior* 27, no. 7 (2006): 983–1002; I.S. Fulmer and R.E. Ployhart, "'Our Most Important Asset': A Multidisciplinary/Multilevel Review of Human Capital Valuation for Research and Practice," *Journal of Management* 40, no. 1 (2014): 161–92; M.C. Díaz-Fernández, M.R. González-Rodríguez, and B. Simonetti, "Top Management Team's Intellectual Capital and Firm Performance," *European Management Journal* 33, no. 5 (2015): 322–31, https://doi.org/10.1016/j.emj.2015.03.004; N. Taylor et al., "High Performing Hospitals: A Qualitative Systematic Review of Associated Factors and Practical Strategies for Improvement," *BMC Health Services Research* 15, no. 1 (2015): 244, https://doi.org/10.1186/s12913-015-0879-z; S. Hauff, D. Alewell, and N.K. Hansen, "Further Exploring the Links between High-Performance Work Practices and Firm Performance: A Multiple-Mediation Model in the German Context," *German Journal of Human Resource Management* 32, no. 1 (2018): 5–26, https://doi.org/10.1177/2397002217728251.

17. J.T. Comeault and D. Wheeler, "Human Capital-Based Investment Criteria for Total Shareholder Returns," in *Pensions at Work: Socially Responsible Investment of Union-Based Pension Funds*, ed. J. Quarter, I. Carmichael, and S. Ryan (Toronto: University of Toronto Press, 2008); S. Abhayawansa, M. Aleksanyan, and J. Bahtsevanoglou, "The Use of Intellectual Capital Information by Sell-Side Analysts in Company Valuation," *Accounting and Business Research* 45, no. 3 (2015): 279–306; S. Abhayawansa and J. Guthrie, "Drivers and Semantic Properties of Intellectual Capital Information in Sell-Side Analysts' Reports," *Journal of Accounting & Organizational Change* 12, no. 4 (2016): 434–71, https://doi.org/10.1108/JAOC-05-2014-0027.

18. S.A. Mohrman, C.B. Gibson, and A.M. Mohrman Jr., "Doing Research That Is Useful to Practice: A Model and Empirical Exploration," *Academy of Management Journal* 44 (2001): 357–75; J.P. Walsh et al., "On the Relationship between Research and Practice," *Journal of Management Inquiry* 16, no. 2 (June 2007): 128–54. Similarly, in 1961, Harvard business professor Fritz Roethlisberger proposed that the field of OB is concerned with human behavior "from the points of view of both (a) its determination . . . and (b) its improvement." See P.B. Vaill, "F. J. Roethlisberger and the Elusive Phenomena of Organizational Behavior," *Journal of Management Education* 31, no. 3 (2007): 321–38.

19. R.H. Hall, "Effectiveness Theory and Organizational Effectiveness," *Journal of Applied Behavioral Science* 16, no. 4 (1980): 536–45; K. Cameron, "Organizational Effectiveness: Its Demise and Re-Emergence through Positive Organizational Scholarship," in *Great Minds in Management*, ed. K.G. Smith and M.A. Hitt (New York: Oxford University Press, 2005), 304–30.

20. A.A. Amirkhanyan, H.J. Kim, and K.T. Lambright, "The Performance Puzzle: Understanding the Factors Influencing Alternative Dimensions and Views of Performance," *Journal of Public Administration Research and Theory* 24, no. 1 (2014): 1–34.

21. Chester Barnard gives one of the earliest descriptions of organizations as systems interacting with external environments and that are composed of subsystems. See C. Barnard, *The Functions of the Executive* (Cambridge, MA: Harvard University Press, 1938), esp. Chap. 6. Also see F.E. Kast and J.E. Rosenzweig, "General Systems Theory: Applications for Organization and Management," *Academy of Management Journal* 15, no. 4 (1972): 447–65; P.M. Senge, *The Fifth Discipline: The Art and Practice of the Learning Organization* (New York: Doubleday Currency, 1990); G. Morgan, *Images of Organization*, 2nd ed. (Newbury Park: Sage, 1996); A. de Geus, *The Living Company* (Boston: Harvard Business School Press, 1997).

22. D. Katz and R.L. Kahn, *The Social Psychology of Organizations* (New York: Wiley, 1966), Chap. 2; J. McCann, "Organizational Effectiveness: Changing Concepts for Changing Environments," *Human Resource Planning* 27, no. 1 (2004): 42–50; A.H. Van de Ven, M. Ganco, and C.R. Hinings, "Returning to the Frontier of Contingency Theory of Organizational and Institutional Designs," *Academy of Management Annals* 7, no. 1 (2013): 391–438.

23. K.E. Weick, *The Social Psychology of Organizing* (Reading, MA: Addison-Wesley, 1979); J.L. Claggett and E. Karahanna, "Unpacking the Structure of Coordination Mechanisms and the Role of Relational Coordination in an Era of Digitally Mediated Work Processes," *Academy of Management Review* 43, no. 4 (2018): 704–22, https://doi.org/10.5465/amr.2016.0325; R.M. Burton and B. Obel, "The Science of Organizational Design: Fit between Structure and Coordination," *Journal of Organization Design* 7, no. 5 (2018), https://doi.org/10.1186/s41469-018-0029-2.

24. J. Barney, "Firm Resources and Sustained Competitive Advantage," *Journal of Management* 17, no. 1 (1991): 99–120. The scholarly literature has separated human capital from social capital (social networks) and psychological capital (personal cognitive and emotional resources such as hope and optimism). On closer inspection, however, social and psychological capital may be embedded in, or consequences of, human capital. Consequently, the three concepts may be integrated in some ways.

25. J. Combs et al., "How Much Do High-Performance Work Practices Matter? A Meta-Analysis of Their Effects on Organizational Performance," *Personnel Psychology* 59, no. 3 (2006): 501–28; P. Tharenou, A.M. Saks, and C. Moore, "A Review and Critique of Research on Training and Organizational-Level Outcomes," *Human Resource Management Review* 17, no. 3 (2007): 251–73; D.Y. Jeong and M. Choi, "The Impact of High-Performance Work Systems on Firm Performance: The Moderating Effects of the Human Resource Function's Influence," *Journal of Management & Organization* 22, no. 3 (2016): 328–48.

26. J. Camps and R. Luna-Arocas, "A Matter of Learning: How Human Resources Affect Organizational Performance," *British Journal of Management* 23, no. 1 (2012): 1–21; R.R. Kehoe and P.M. Wright, "The Impact of High-Performance Human Resource Practices on Employees' Attitudes and Behaviors," *Journal of Management* 39, no. 2 (2013): 366–91; B. Fabi, R. Lacoursière, and L. Raymond, "Impact of High-Performance Work Systems on Job Satisfaction, Organizational Commitment, and Intention to Quit in Canadian Organizations," *International Journal of Manpower* 36, no. 5 (2015): 772–90.

27. OECD, *Skills Matter: Further Results from the Survey of Adult Skills*, OECD Skills Studies (Paris: OECD Publishing, June 2016). Also from Annex A, spreadsheet data file associated with tables in the OECD publication.

28. R.E. Freeman, J.S. Harrison, and A.C. Wicks, *Managing for Stakeholders: Survival, Reputation, and Success* (New Haven, CT: Yale University Press, 2007); B.L. Parmar et al., "Stakeholder Theory: The State of the Art," *Academy of Management Annals* 4, no. 1 (2010): 403–45; S. Sachs and E. Rühli, *Stakeholders Matter: A New Paradigm for Strategy in Society* (Cambridge, UK: Cambridge University Press, 2011).

29. R.B. Adams, A.N. Licht, and L. Sagiv, "Shareholders and Stakeholders: How Do Directors Decide?" *Strategic Management Journal* 32, no. 12 (2011): 1331–55; A. Santana, "Three Elements of Stakeholder Legitimacy," *Journal of Business Ethics* 105, no. 2 (2012): 257–65; D. Crilly and P. Sloan, "Autonomy or Control? Organizational Architecture and Corporate Attention to Stakeholders," *Organization Science* 25, no. 2 (2014): 339–55; M. Hall, Y. Millo, and E. Barman, "Who and What Really Counts? Stakeholder Prioritization and Accounting for Social Value," *Journal of Management Studies* 52, no. 7 (2015): 907–34; D. Weitzner and Y. Deutsch, "Understanding Motivation and Social Influence in Stakeholder Prioritization," *Organization Studies* 36, no. 10 (2015): 1337–60.

30. B.M. Meglino and E.C. Ravlin, "Individual Values in Organizations: Concepts, Controversies, and Research," *Journal of Management* 24, no. 3 (1998): 351–89; S. Hitlin and J.A. Pilavin, "Values: Reviving a Dormant Concept," *Annual Review of Sociology* 30 (2004): 359–93; L. Sagiv et al., "Personal Values in Human Life," *Nature Human Behaviour* 1, no. 9 (September 2017): 630-39, https://doi.org/10.1038/s41562-017-0185-3.

31. M. van Marrewijk, "Concepts and Definitions of CSR and Corporate Sustainability: Between Agency and Communion," *Journal of Business Ethics* 44 (2003): 95–105; H. Aguinis and A. Glavas, "What We Know and Don't Know about Corporate Social Responsibility: A Review and Research Agenda," *Journal of Management* 38, no. 4 (2012): 932–68; T. Meynhardt and P. Gomez, "Building Blocks for Alternative Four-Dimensional Pyramids of Corporate Social Responsibilities," *Business & Society* 58, no. 2 (2019): 404–38, https://doi.org/10.1177/0007650316650444.

32. A.B. Carroll and K.M. Shabana, "The Business Case for Corporate Social Responsibility: A Review of Concepts, Research and Practice," *International Journal of Management Reviews* 12, no. 1 (2010): 85–105; J. Kim and J. Kim, "Corporate Sustainability Management and Its Market Benefits," *Sustainability* 10, no. 5 (May 2018): 1455, https://doi.org/10.3390/su10051455; M. Ong et al., "When Corporate Social Responsibility Motivates Employee Citizenship Behavior: The Sensitizing Role of Task Significance," *Organizational Behavior and Human Decision Processes* 144 (2018): 44–59, https://doi.org/10.1016/j.obhdp.2017.09.006; B. Lis, "Corporate Social Responsibility's Influence on Organizational Attractiveness: An Investigation in the Context of Employer Choice," *Journal of General Management* 43, no. 3 (2018): 106–14, https://doi.org/10.1177/0306307017749627.

33. Most of these anchors are mentioned in J.D. Thompson, "On Building an Administrative Science," *Administrative Science Quarterly* 1, no. 1 (1956): 102–11.

34. This anchor has a colorful history dating back to critiques of business schools in the 1950s. Soon after, systematic research became a mantra for many respected scholars. See, for example, J.D. Thompson, "On Building an Administrative Science," *Administrative Science Quarterly* 1, no. 1 (1956): 102–11.

35. J. Pfeffer and R.I. Sutton, *Hard Facts, Dangerous Half-Truths, and Total Nonsense* (Boston: Harvard Business School Press, 2006); D.M. Rousseau and S. McCarthy, "Educating Managers from an Evidence-Based Perspective," *Academy of Management Learning & Education* 6, no. 1 (2007): 84–101; R.B. Briner and D.M. Rousseau, "Evidence-Based I-O Psychology: Not There Yet," *Industrial and Organizational Psychology* 4, no. 1 (2011): 3–22.

36. J. Hamet and F. Maurer, "Is Management Research Visible Outside the Academic Community?" *M@n@gement* 20, no. 5 (2017): 492–516.

37. J. Pfeffer and R.I. Sutton, *Hard Facts, Dangerous Half-Truths, and Total Nonsense* (Boston: Harvard Business School Press, 2006).

38. E. Abrahamson, H. Berkowitz, and H. Dumez, "A More Relevant Approach to Relevance in Management Studies: An Essay on Performativity," *Academy of Management Review* 41, no. 2 (2016): 367–81, https://doi.org/10.5465/amr.2015.0205; J.M. Bartunek and J. McKenzie, eds., *Academic-Practitioner Relationships: Developments, Complexities and Opportunities* (New York: Routledge, 2017); G. Carton and P. Mouricou, "Is Management Research Relevant? A Systematic Analysis of the Rigor-Relevance Debate in Top-Tier Journals (1994–2013)," *M@n@gement* 20, no. 2 (2017): 166–203; J. Hamet and S. Michel, "Rigor, Relevance, and the Knowledge 'Market,'" *European Business Review* 30, no. 2 (2018): 183–201, https://doi.org/10.1108/EBR-01-2017-0025.

39. P.H. Kim, R.E. Ployhart, and C.B. Gibson, "Editors' Comments: Is Organizational Behavior Overtheorized?" *Academy of Management Review* 43, no. 4 (October 2018): 541–45, https://doi.org/10.5465/amr.2018.0233.

40. M.N. Zald, "More Fragmentation? Unfinished Business in Linking the Social Sciences and the Humanities," *Administrative Science Quarterly* 41 (1996): 251–61; C. Oswick, P. Fleming, and G. Hanlon, "From Borrowing to Blending: Rethinking the Processes of Organizational Theory Building," *Academy of Management Review* 36, no. 2 (2011): 318–37; B.M. Staw, "Stumbling Toward a Social Psychology of Organizations: An Autobiographical Look at the Direction of Organizational Research," *Annual Review of Organizational Psychology and Organizational Behavior* 3, no. 1 (2016): 1–19, https://doi.org/10.1146/annurev-orgpsych-041015-062524.

41. C.M. Christensen and M.E. Raynor, "Why Hard-Nosed Executives Should Care about Management Theory," *Harvard Business Review* (2003): 66–74; C.E.J. Härtel and J.M. O'Connor, "Contextualizing Research: Putting Context Back into Organizational Behavior Research," *Journal of Management & Organization* 20, no. 4 (2014): 417–22. For excellent critique of the "one best way" approach in early management scholarship, see P.F. Drucker, "Management's New Paradigms," *Forbes* (1998): 152–77.

42. H.L. Tosi and J.W. Slocum Jr., "Contingency Theory: Some Suggested Directions," *Journal of Management* 10 (1984): 9–26.

43. D.M. Rousseau and R.J. House, "Meso Organizational Behavior: Avoiding Three Fundamental Biases," in *Trends in Organizational Behavior*, ed. C.L. Cooper and D.M. Rousseau (Chichester, UK: Wiley, 1994), 13–30.

44. B.M. Ferdman, "Paradoxes of Inclusion: Understanding and Managing the Tensions of Diversity and Multiculturalism," *Journal of Applied Behavioral Science* 53, no. 2 (2017): 235–63, https://doi.org/10.1177/0021886317702608; A.E. Randel et al., "Inclusive Leadership: Realizing Positive Outcomes through Belongingness and Being Valued for Uniqueness," *Human Resource Management Review* 28, no. 2 (2018): 190–203, https://doi.org/10.1016/j.hrmr.2017.07.002; L.M. Shore, J.N. Cleveland, and D. Sanchez, "Inclusive Workplaces: A Review and Model," *Human Resource Management Review* 28, no. 2 (2018): 176–89, https://doi.org/10.1016/j.hrmr.2017.07.003.

45. D.A. Harrison et al., "Time, Teams, and Task Performance: Changing Effects of Surface- and Deep-Level Diversity on Group Functioning," *Academy of Management Journal* 45, no. 5 (2002): 1029–46; W.J. Casper, J.H. Wayne, and J.G. Manegold, "Who Will We Recruit? Targeting Deep- and Surface-Level Diversity with Human Resource Policy Advertising," *Human Resource Management* 52, no. 3 (2013): 311–32; J.E. Mathieu et al., "A Review and Integration of Team Composition Models: Moving toward a Dynamic and Temporal Framework," *Journal of Management* 40, no. 1 (2014): 130–60.

46. J. Qin, N. Muenjohn, and P. Chhetri, "A Review of Diversity Conceptualizations: Variety, Trends, and a Framework," *Human Resource Development Review* 13, no. 2 (2014): 133–57.

47. M.H. Davis, S. Capobianco, and L.A. Kraus, "Gender Differences in Responding to Conflict in the Workplace: Evidence from a Large Sample of Working Adults," *Sex Roles* 63, no. 7 (2010): 500–14; J.L. Locke, *Duels and Duets: Why Men and Women Talk So Differently* (New York: Cambridge University Press, 2011); R. Friesdorf, P. Conway, and B. Gawronski, "Gender Differences in Responses to Moral Dilemmas: A Process Dissociation Analysis," *Personality and Social Psychology Bulletin* 41, no. 5 (2015): 696–713.

48. E. Bolland and C. Lopes, *Generations and Work* (New York: Palgrave Macmillan, 2014); P. Taylor, *The Next America: Boomers, Millennials, and the Looming Generational Showdown* (New York: Public Affairs, 2014); J. Bristow, *Baby Boomers and Generational Conflict* (London: Palgrave Macmillan, 2015).

49. S. Lyons and L. Kuron, "Generational Differences in the Workplace: A Review of the Evidence and Directions for Future Research," *Journal of Organizational Behavior* 35, no. S1 (2014): S139–57, https://doi.org/10.1002/job.1913; K.L. Zabel et al., "Generational Differences in Work Ethic: Fact or Fiction?" *Journal of Business and Psychology* 32, no. 3 (2017): 301–15, https://doi.org/10.1007/s10869-016-9466-5; J.M. Cucina et al., "Generational Differences in Workplace Attitudes and Job Satisfaction: Lack of Sizable Differences across Cohorts," *Journal of Managerial Psychology* 33, no. 3 (2018): 246–64, https://doi.org/10.1108/JMP-03-2017-0115; M. Schröder, "Der Generationenmythos (The Generation Myth)," *Kölner Zeitschrift für Soziologie und Sozialpsychologie* 70, no. 3 (2018): 469–94, https://doi.org/10.1007/s11577-018-0570-6.

50. M.-E. Roberge and R. van Dick, "Recognizing the Benefits of Diversity: When and How Does Diversity Increase Group Performance?" *Human Resource Management Review* 20, no. 4 (2010): 295–308; M. Singal, "The Business Case for Diversity Management in the Hospitality Industry," *International Journal of Hospitality Management* 40 (2014): 10–19; C.-M. Lu et al., "Effect of Diversity on Human Resource Management and Organizational Performance," *Journal of Business Research* 68, no. 4 (2015): 857–61; Y. Zhang and M.-Y. Huai, "Diverse Work Groups and Employee Performance: The Role of Communication Ties," *Small Group Research* 47, no. 1 (2016): 28–57.

51. Q. Roberson, O. Holmes, and J.L. Perry, "Transforming Research on Diversity and Firm Performance: A Dynamic Capabilities Perspective," *Academy of Management Annals* 11 (2017): 189–216; Y.R.F. Guillaume et al., "Harnessing Demographic Differences in Organizations: What Moderates the Effects of Workplace Diversity?" *Journal of Organizational Behavior* 38, no. 2 (2017): 276–303, https://doi.org/10.1002/job.2040; N. Luanglath, M. Ali, and K. Mohannak, "Top Management Team Gender Diversity and Productivity: The Role of Board Gender Diversity," *Equality, Diversity and Inclusion: An International Journal* 38, no. 1 (2019): 71–86, https://doi.org/10.1108/EDI-04-2018-0067.

52. T. Kochan et al., "The Effects of Diversity on Business Performance: Report of the Diversity Research Network," *Human Resource Management* 42 (2003): 3–21; S.T. Bell et al., "Getting Specific about Demographic Diversity Variable and Team Performance Relationships: A Meta-Analysis," *Journal of Management* 37, no. 3 (2011): 709–43; S.M.B. Thatcher and P.C. Patel, "Group Faultlines: A Review, Integration, and Guide to Future Research," *Journal of Management* 38, no. 4 (2012): 969–1009; C. Ozgen et al., "Does Cultural Diversity of Migrant Employees Affect Innovation?" *International Migration Review* 48 (2014): S377–S416; K. Hoisl, M. Gruber, and A. Conti, "R&D Team Diversity and Performance in Hypercompetitive Environments," *Strategic Management Journal* 38, no. 7 (2017): 1455–77, https://doi.org/10.1002/smj.2577.

53. "The 2016 Deloitte Millennial Survey: Winning over the Next Generation of Leaders" (New York: Deloitte Touche Tohmatsu, January 2016); B.W. Reynolds, "2017 Annual Survey Finds Workers Are More Productive at Home, And More," *FlexJobs* (blog), August 21, 2017, https://www.flexjobs.com/blog/post/productive-working-remotely-top-companies-hiring/.

54. J.H. Greenhaus and L.L. ten Brummelhuis, "Models and Frameworks Underlying Work–Life Research: Challenges and Opportunities," in *Handbook of Work-Life Integration Among Professionals: Challenges and Opportunities*, ed. D.A. Major and R.J. Burke (Cheltenham, UK: Edward Elgar Publishing, 2013), 14–34; M.J. Sirgy and D.-J. Lee, "Work-Life Balance: An Integrative Review," *Applied Research in Quality of Life* 13, no. 1 (2018): 229–54, https://doi.org/10.1007/s11482-017-9509-8.

55. Katie Clarey, "Work-Life Balance? There's No Such Thing," *HR Dive*, December 18, 2018.

56. L.L. ten Brummelhuis and A.B. Bakker, "A Resource Perspective on the Work–Home Interface: The Work–Home Resources Model.," *American Psychologist* 67, no. 7 (2012): 545–56, https://doi.org/10.1037/a0027974; L.L. ten Brummelhuis and J.H. Greenhaus, "How Role Jugglers Maintain Relationships at Home and at Work: A Gender Comparison," *Journal of Applied Psychology* 103, no. 12 (2018): 1265–82, https://doi.org/10.1037/apl0000340; A. Li, A. Butler, and J. Bagger, "Depletion or Expansion? Understanding the Effects of Support Policy Use on Employee Work and Family Outcomes," *Human Resource Management Journal* 28, no. 2 (2018): 216–34, https://doi.org/10.1111/1748-8583.12174.

57. S.D. Friedman, *Leading the Life You Want: Skills for Integrating Work and Life* (Boston: Harvard Business Press, 2014); A.M. Foreman et al., "Dogs in the Workplace: A Review of the Benefits and Potential Challenges," *International Journal of Environmental Research and Public Health* 14, no. 5 (2017), https://doi.org/10.3390/ijerph14050498; K. Goldin, "Why Meetings on the Move Should Be the New Normal (And How to Ensure They're Productive)," *Forbes*, April 20, 2018; Kris Fannin, "Why Work-Life Integration Is the New Work-Life Balance and How To..." *Intelivate* (blog), January 29, 2018, https://www.intelivate.com/team-strategy/work-life-integration-work-life-balance; K. Lockwood. "Achieving Work-Life Integration in This New World of Work," *Forbes*, April 18, 2018. Although almost all firms have practices that support work-life integration, many employers implicitly limit the career progress of those who use some of these practices. See S. Bourdeau, A. Ollier-Malaterre, and N. Houlfort, "Not All Work-Life Policies Are Created Equal: Career Consequences of Using Enabling versus Enclosing Work-Life Policies," *Academy of Management Review* 44, no. 1 (2019): 172–93, https://doi.org/10.5465/amr.2016.0429.

58. E.E. Kossek and R.J. Thompson, "Workplace Flexibility: Integrating Employer and Employee Perspectives to Close the Research–Practice Implementation Gap," in *The Oxford Handbook of Work and Family*, ed. T.D. Allen and L.T. Eby (New York: Oxford University Press, 2016), 255–70, https://doi.org/10.1093/oxfordhb/9780199337538.013.19; M. Beatson, "Megatrends: Flexible Working" (London: Chartered Institute of Personnel and Development, January 15, 2019).

59. L.A. Perlow, *Sleeping with Your Smartphone: How to Break the 24/7 Habit and Change the Way You Work* (Boston: Harvard Business Press, 2012); T.D. Allen, E. Cho, and L.L. Meier, "Work–Family Boundary Dynamics," *Annual Review of Organizational Psychology and Organizational Behavior* 1, no. 1 (2014): 99–121, https://doi.org/10.1146/annurev-orgpsych-031413-091330; A.R. Koch and C. Binnewies, "Setting a Good Example: Supervisors as Work-Life-Friendly Role Models within the Context of Boundary Management," *Journal of Occupational Health Psychology* 20, no. 1 (2015): 82–92, https://doi.org/10.1037/a0037890; N.P. Rothbard and A. Ollier-Malaterre, "Boundary Management," in *The Oxford Handbook of Work and Family*, ed. T.D. Allen and L.T. Eby (New York: Oxford University Press, 2016), 109–24, https://doi.org/10.1093/oxfordhb/9780199337538.013.19; R. Hackwill, "French First to Protect 'the Right to Disconnect,'" *EuroNews*, January 2, 2017.

60. T.L. Johns, "The Third Wave of Virtual Work," *Harvard Business Review* 91, no. 1 (2013): 66–73.

61. R. Sutherland, H. Matthews, and S. Tatam, "Ogilvy on Managed Remote Working: Building a Sustainable Way of Working" (London: Ogilvy UK, March 20, 2020).

62. A. Mann and A. Adkins, "America's Coming Workplace: Home Alone," *Gallup Business Journal*, March 15, 2017.

63. J. Trigwell, "What I've Learned about Running an All-Remote Company during 15-Years as the CEO of the World's First All-Remote AV Company," *Emsisoft Security Blog* (blog), November 20, 2018, https://blog.emsisoft.com/en/32308/what-ive-learned-about-running-an-all-remote-company-during-15-years-as-the-ceo-of-the-worlds-first-all-remote-av-company/; R. Chan, "How a Tech CEO Runs His 40-Employee Company from a Farm in New Zealand," *stuff.co.nz*, January 21, 2019.

64. E.J. Hill et al., "Workplace Flexibility, Work Hours, and Work–Life Conflict: Finding an Extra Day or Two," *Journal of Family Psychology* 24, no. 3 (2010): 349–58; M.C. Noonan and J.L. Glass, "The Hard Truth about Telecommuting," *Monthly Labor Review* 135, no. 6 (2012): 38–45; B.H. Martin and R. MacDonnell, "Is Telework Effective for Organizations?" *Management Research Review* 35, no. 7 (2012): 602–16; T.D. Allen, T.D. Golden, and K.M. Shockley, "How Effective Is Telecommuting? Assessing the Status of Our Scientific Findings," *Psychological Science in the Public Interest* 16, no. 2 (2015): 40–68; N. Bloom et al., "Does Working from Home Work? Evidence from a Chinese Experiment," *Quarterly Journal of Economics* 130, no. 1 (2015): 165–218; R.S. Gajendran, D.A. Harrison, and K. Delaney-Klinger, "Are Telecommuters Remotely Good Citizens? Unpacking Telecommuting's Effects on Performance Via I-Deals and Job Resources," *Personnel Psychology* 68, no. 2 (2015): 353–93. The WestJet quotation is from: R. Marowits, "More Employees Working from Home in Shift to 'Telecommuting,'" *Toronto Star*, 23 May 2016.

65. D. Meinert, "Make Telecommuting Pay Off," *HR Magazine*, June 2011, 33; M. McQuigge, "A Panacea for Some, Working from Home Still a Tough Sell for Some Employers," *Canadian Press* (Toronto), June 26, 2013; Aetna, "Teleworking on the Rise, Saving Costs and the Environment," May 2015, https://news.aetna.com/2015/05/teleworking-rise-saving-costs-environment/ (accessed March 4, 2016).

66. C.A. Bartel, A. Wrzesniewski, and B.M. Wiesenfeld, "Knowing Where You Stand: Physical Isolation, Perceived Respect, and Organizational Identification among Virtual Employees," *Organization Science* 23, no. 3 (2011): 743–57; E.E. Kossek, R.J. Thompson, and B.A. Lautsch, "Balanced Workplace Flexibility: Avoiding the Traps," *California Management Review* 57, no. 4 (2015): 5–25.

67. T.A. O'Neill, L.A. Hambley, and G.S. Chatellier, "Cyberslacking, Engagement, and Personality in Distributed Work Environments," *Computers in Human Behavior* 40 (2014): 152–60; N.W. Van Yperen, E.F. Rietzschel, and K.M.M. De Jonge, "Blended Working: For Whom It May (Not) Work," *PLoS ONE* 9, no. 7 (2014): e102921; D. Karis, D. Wildman, and A. Mané, "Improving Remote Collaboration with Video Conferencing and Video Portals," *Human-Computer Interaction* 31, no. 1 (2016): 1–58.

68. P. Cappelli and J. Keller, "Classifying Work in the New Economy," *Academy of Management Review* 38, no. 4 (2013): 575–96, https://doi.org/10.5465/amr.2011.0302; T.S.-C. Poon, "Independent Workers: Growth Trends, Categories, and Employee Relations Implications in the Emerging Gig Economy," *Employee Responsibilities and Rights Journal* 31, no. 1 (2019): 63–69, https://doi.org/10.1007/s10672-018-9318-8.

69. L.F. Katz and A.B. Krueger, "The Rise and Nature of Alternative Work Arrangements in the United States, 1995–2015," *ILR Review* 72, no. 2 (2019): 382–416, https://doi.org/10.1177/0019793918820008; World Employment Federation, "Economic Report, 2018" (Brussels, Belgium: World Employment Federation, July 2018).

70. M.A. Cherry and A. Aloisi, "'Dependent Contractors' in the Gig Economy: A Comparative Approach," *American University Law Review* 66 (2017): 635–89, https://doi.org/10.2139/ssrn.2847869; K.M. Kuhn and A. Maleki, "Micro-Entrepreneurs, Dependent Contractors, and Instaserfs: Understanding Online Labor Platform Workforces," *Academy of Management Perspectives* 31, no. 3 (2017): 183–200, https://doi.org/10.5465/amp.2015.0111; UpWork, "New 5th Annual 'Freelancing in America' Study Finds That the U.S. Freelance Workforce, Now 56.7 Million People, Grew 3.7 Million Since 2014," news release (New York: Upwork and Freelancers Union, October 31, 2018).

71. M. Banerjee, P.S. Tolbert, and T. DiCiccio, "Friend or Foe? The Effects of Contingent Employees on Standard Employees' Work Attitudes," *International Journal of Human Resource Management* 23, no. 11 (2012): 2180–2204, https://doi.org/10.1080/09585192.2011.637061; S.L. Fisher and C.E. Connelly, "Lower Cost or Just Lower Value? Modeling the Organizational Costs and Benefits of Contingent Work," *Academy of Management Discoveries* 3, no. 2 (2016): 165–86, https://doi.org/10.5465/amd.2015.0119; G.M. Spreitzer, L. Cameron, and L. Garrett, "Alternative Work Arrangements: Two Images of the New World of Work," *Annual Review of Organizational Psychology and Organizational Behavior* 4, no. 1 (March 21, 2017): 473–99, https://doi.org/10.1146/annurev-orgpsych-032516-113332; C.L. Wilkin, J.P. de Jong, and C. Rubino, "Teaming up with Temps: The Impact of Temporary Workers on Team Social Networks and Effectiveness," *European Journal of Work and Organizational Psychology* 27, no. 2 (2018): 204–18, https://doi.org/10.1080/1359432X.2017.1418329; T.A. Kochan et al., "The Changing Nature of Employee and Labor-Management Relationships," *Annual Review of Organizational Psychology and Organizational Behavior* 6, no. 1 (2019): 195–219, https://doi.org/10.1146/annurev-orgpsych-012218-015335.

72. E. Selenko et al., "On the Dynamics of Work Identity in Atypical Employment: Setting out a Research Agenda," *European Journal of Work and Organizational Psychology* 27, no. 3 (2018): 324–34, https://doi.org/10.1080/1359432X.2018.1444605; T.A. Kochan et al., "The Changing Nature of Employee and Labor-Management Relationships," *Annual Review of Organizational Psychology and Organizational Behavior* 6, no. 1 (2019): 195–219, https://doi.org/10.1146/annurev-orgpsych-012218-015335; G. Petriglieri, S.J. Ashford, and A. Wrzesniewski, "Agony and Ecstasy in the Gig Economy: Cultivating Holding Environments for Precarious and Personalized Work Identities," *Administrative Science Quarterly* 64, no. 1 (2019): 124–70, https://doi.org/10.1177/0001839218759646.

73. L.L. Thurstone, "Ability, Motivation, and Speed," *Psychometrika* 2, no. 4 (1937): 249–54; N.R.F. Maier, *Psychology in Industry*, 2nd ed. (Boston: Houghton Mifflin, 1955); V.H. Vroom, *Work and Motivation* (New York: Wiley, 1964); J.P. Campbell et al., *Managerial Behavior, Performance, and Effectiveness* (New York: McGraw-Hill, 1970).

74. R.S. Dalal, D.P. Bhave, and J. Fiset, "Within-Person Variability in Job Performance: A Theoretical Review and Research Agenda," *Journal of Management* 40, no. 5 (2014): 1396–436; S. Aryee et al., "Developing and Leveraging Human Capital Resource to Promote Service Quality: Testing a Theory of Performance," *Journal of Management* 42, no. 2 (2016): 480–99.

75. E.E. Lawler III and L.W. Porter, "Antecedent Attitudes of Effective Managerial Performance," *Organizational Behavior and Human Performance* 2 (1967): 122–42; O.-P. Kauppila, "So, What Am I Supposed to Do? A Multilevel Examination of Role Clarity," *Journal of Management Studies* 51, no. 5 (2014): 737–63.

76. Only a few sources have included all four factors. These include J.P. Campbell and R.D. Pritchard, "Motivation Theory in Industrial and Organizational Psychology," in *Handbook of Industrial and Organizational Psychology*, ed. M.D. Dunnette (Chicago: Rand McNally, 1976), 62–130; T.R. Mitchell, "Motivation: New Directions for Theory, Research, and Practice," *Academy of Management Review* 7, no. 1 (1982): 80–88; G.A.J. Churchill et al., "The Determinants of Salesperson Performance: A Meta-Analysis," *Journal of Marketing Research* 22, no. 2 (1985): 103–18; R.E. Plank and D.A. Reid, "The Mediating Role of Sales Behaviors: An Alternative Perspective of Sales Performance and Effectiveness," *Journal of Personal Selling & Sales Management* 14, no. 3 (1994): 43–56. The "MARS" acronym was coined by senior officers in the Singapore Armed Forces during a senior officer program taught by Steve McShane.

77. Technically, the model proposes that situation factors moderate the effects of the three within-person factors. For instance, the effect of employee motivation on behavior and performance depends on (is moderated by) the situation.

78. G.P. Latham and C.C. Pinder, "Work Motivation Theory and Research at the Dawn of the Twenty-First Century," *Annual Review of Psychology* 56 (2005): 485–516; G.P. Latham, *Work Motivation: History, Theory, Research, and Practice*, revised ed. (Thousand Oaks, CA: Sage, 2012), 7.

79. L.M. Spencer and S.M. Spencer, *Competence at Work: Models for Superior Performance* (New York: Wiley, 1993); D. Bartram, "The Great Eight Competencies: A Criterion-Centric Approach to Validation," *Journal of Applied Psychology* 90, no. 6 (2005): 1185–203; R.A. Roe, "Using Competences in Employee Development," in *Wiley Blackwell Handbook of the Psychology of Training, Development, and Performance Improvement*, ed. K. Kraiger et al. (Chichester: Wiley, 2014), 303–35.

80. P. Tharenou, A.M. Saks, and C. Moore, "A Review and Critique of Research on Training and Organizational-Level Outcomes," *Human Resource Management Review* 17, no. 3 (2007): 251–73; Y. Kim and R.E. Ployhart, "The Effects of Staffing and Training on Firm Productivity and Profit Growth before, during, and after the Great Recession," *Journal of Applied Psychology* 99, no. 3 (2014): 361–89; M. Choi and H.J. Yoon, "Training Investment and Organizational Outcomes: A Moderated Mediation Model of Employee Outcomes and Strategic Orientation of the HR Function," *International Journal of Human Resource Management* 26, no. 20 (2015): 2632–51.

81. *The Interserve Society Report* (Reading, UK: Interserve, January 30, 2015); J. Harter, "Obsolete Annual Review: Gallup's Advice" (Washington, DC: Gallup, Inc., September 28, 2015); Randstad, "Prospects for Older Workers Shrink While the Skills Gap Widens," *Randstad Workmonitor* (Amsterdam, The Netherlands: Randstad Holding nv, June 2016); TINYpulse, *The Tinypulse 2015 Employee Engagement & Organizational Culture Report: The Era of Personal and Peer Accountability* (Seattle: TINYpulse, February 2016); Gallup Inc., *State of the American Workplace* (Washington, DC: Gallup, February 23, 2017).

82. E.C. Dierdorff, R.S. Rubin, and D.G. Bachrach, "Role Expectations as Antecedents of Citizenship and the Moderating Effects of Work Context," *Journal of Management* 38, no. 2 (2012): 573–98; A. Newman, B. Allen, and Q. Miao, "I Can See Clearly Now: The Moderating Effects of Role Clarity on Subordinate Responses to Ethical Leadership," *Personnel Review* 44, no. 4 (2015): 611–28.

83. L. Mirabella, "Walmart Employees Get Real Look at Retail World; Virtual Reality Technology Prepares Supervisors for Situations That Might Arise," *Baltimore Sun*, December 3, 2017; H. Shively, "Area Stores Training Employees Using Virtual Reality," *TCA Regional News*, November 12, 2018; S. DiNatale, "What's It Like to Train for Walmart's Black Friday? Local Stores Use Virtual Reality Goggles," *Tampa Bay Times*, November 13, 2018.

84. W.H. Cooper and M.J. Withey, "The Strong Situation Hypothesis," *Personality and Social Psychology Review* 13, no. 1 (2009): 62–72; N.A. Bowling et al., "Situational Strength as a Moderator of the Relationship between Job Satisfaction and Job Performance: A Meta-Analytic Examination," *Journal of Business and Psychology* 30, no. 1 (2015): 89–104; T.A. Judge and C.P. Zapata, "The Person–Situation Debate Revisited: Effect of Situation Strength and Trait Activation on the Validity of the Big Five Personality Traits in Predicting Job Performance," *Academy of Management Journal* 58, no. 4 (2015): 1149–79; J.F. Rauthmann and R.A. Sherman, "Situation Change: Stability and Change of Situation Variables between and within Persons," *Frontiers in Psychology* 6 (2016).

85. L.H. Peters and E.J. O'Connor, "Situational Constraints and Work Outcomes: The Influences of a Frequently Overlooked Construct," *Academy of Management Review* 5, no. 3 (1980): 391–97; G. Johns, "Commentary: In Praise of Context," *Journal of Organizational Behavior* 22 (2001): 31–42; C.E.J. Härtel and J.M. O'Connor, "Contextualizing Research: Putting Context Back into Organizational Behavior Research," *Journal of Management & Organization* 20, no. 4 (2014): 417–22.

86. R.D. Hackett, "Understanding and Predicting Work Performance in the Canadian Military," *Canadian Journal of Behavioural Science* 34, no. 2 (2002): 131–40; J.P. Campbell and B.M. Wiernik, "The Modeling and Assessment of Work Performance," *Annual Review of Organizational Psychology and Organizational Behavior* 2, no. 1 (2015): 47–74.

87. L. Tay, R. Su, and J. Rounds, "People-Things and Data-Ideas: Bipolar Dimensions?" *Journal of Counseling Psychology* 58, no. 3 (2011): 424–40.

88. E.D. Pulakos et al., "Predicting Adaptive Performance: Further Tests of a Model of Adaptability," *Human Performance* 15, no. 4 (2002): 299–323; M.A. Griffin, A. Neal, and S.K. Parker, "A New Model of Work Role Performance: Positive Behavior in Uncertain and Interdependent Contexts," *Academy of Management Journal* 50, no. 2 (2007): 327–47; S.K. Baard, T.A. Rench, and S.W.J. Kozlowski, "Performance Adaptation: A Theoretical Integration and Review," *Journal of Management* 40, no. 1 (2014): 48–99; D.K. Jundt, M.K. Shoss, and J.L. Huang, "Individual Adaptive Performance in Organizations: A Review," *Journal of Organizational Behavior* 36, no. S1 (2015): S53–S71; J.A. Carpini, S.K. Parker, and M.A. Griffin, "A Look Back and a Leap Forward: A Review and Synthesis of the Individual Work Performance Literature," *Academy of Management Annals* 11, no. 2 (2017): 825–85, https://doi.org/10.5465/annals.2015.0151.

89. D.W. Organ, "Organizational Citizenship Behavior: It's Construct Clean-up Time," *Human Performance* 10 (1997): 85–97; J.A. LePine, A. Erez, and D.E. Johnson, "The Nature and Dimensionality of Organizational Citizenship Behavior: A Critical Review and Meta-Analysis," *Journal of Applied Psychology* 87 (2002): 52–65; N.P. Podsakoff et al., "Consequences of Unit-Level Organizational Citizenship Behaviors: A Review and Recommendations for Future Research," *Journal of Organizational Behavior* 35, no. S1 (2014): S87–S119.

90. E.W. Morrison, "Role Definitions and Organizational Citizenship Behavior: The Importance of the Employee's Perspective," *Academy of Management Journal* 37, no. 6 (1994): 1543–67; N. Podsakoff et al., "Individual- and Organizational-Level Consequences of Organizational Citizenship Behaviors: A Meta-Analysis," *Journal of Applied Psychology* 94, no. 1 (2009): 122–41; E.C. Dierdorff, R.S. Rubin, and D.G. Bachrach, "Role Expectations as Antecedents of Citizenship and the Moderating Effects of Work Context," *Journal of Management* 38, no. 2 (2012): 573–598.

91. M. Ozer, "A Moderated Mediation Model of the Relationship between Organizational Citizenship Behaviors and Job Performance," *Journal of Applied Psychology* 96, no. 6 (2011): 1328–36; S.B. Mackenzie, N.P. Podsakoff, and P.M. Podsakoff, "Individual- and Organizational-Level Consequences of Organizational Citizenship Behaviors," in *The Oxford Handbook of Organizational Citizenship Behavior*, ed. P.M. Podsakoff, S.B. MacKenzie, and N.P. Podsakoff (New York: Oxford University Press, 2018).

92. M.C. Bolino, A.C. Klotz, and W.H. Turnley, "The Unintended Consequences of Organizational Citizenship Behaviors for Employees, Teams, and Organizations," in *The Oxford Handbook of Organizational Citizenship Behavior*, ed. P.M. Podsakoff, S.B. Mackenzie, and N.P. Podsakoff (New York: Oxford University Press, 2018), 185–202.

93. M. Rotundo and P. Sackett, "The Relative Importance of Task, Citizenship, and Counterproductive Performance to Global Ratings of Job Performance: A Policy-Capturing Approach," *Journal of Applied Psychology* 87 (2002): 66–80; N.A. Bowling and M.L. Gruys, "Overlooked Issues in the Conceptualization and Measurement of Counterproductive Work Behavior," *Human Resource Management Review* 20, no. 1 (2010): 54–61; B. Marcus et al., "The Structure of Counterproductive Work Behavior: A Review, a Structural Meta-Analysis, and a Primary Study," *Journal of Management* 42, no. 1 (2016): 203–33; R.S. Dalal and N.C. Carpenter, "The Other Side of the Coin?: Similarities and Differences between Organizational Citizenship Behavior and Counterproductive Work Behavior," in *The Oxford Handbook of Organizational Citizenship Behavior*, ed. P.M. Podsakoff, S.B. MacKenzie, and N.P. Podsakoff (New York: Oxford University Press, 2018), 69–90.

94. The relationship between employee turnover and firm performance is actually very low, but this is due to moderators and is stronger for some forms of firm performance. See: J.I. Hancock et al., "Meta-Analytic Review of Employee Turnover as a Predictor of Firm Performance," *Journal of Management* 39, no. 3 (2013): 573–603.

95. K. Burns, "Governors Plead with Other States for More Health Care Workers to Fight Coronavirus," *Vox*, March 31, 2020; M. Casey and H. Yen, "VA Medical Facilities Struggle to Cope with the Coronavirus," *Associated Press*, April 23, 2020.

96. T.-Y. Park and J. Shaw, "Turnover Rates and Organizational Performance: A Meta-Analysis," *Journal of Applied Psychology* 98, no. 2 (2013): 268–309; J.I. Hancock et al., "Meta-Analytic Review of Employee Turnover as a Predictor of Firm Performance," *Journal of Management* 39, no. 3 (2013): 573–603; J.G. Messersmith et al., "Turnover at the Top: Executive Team Departures and Firm Performance," *Organization Science* 25, no. 3 (2014): 776–93; B.C. Holtom and T.C. Burch, "A Model of Turnover-Based Disruption in Customer Services," *Human Resource Management Review* 26, no. 1 (2016): 25–36.

97. P.S. Goodman and R.S. Atkin, "Effects of Absenteeism on Individuals and Organizations," in *Absenteeism: New Approaches to Understanding, Measuring and Managing Employee Attendance*, ed. P.S. Goodman and R.S. Atkin (San Francisco: Jossey-Bass, 1984), 276–321; D.A. Harrison and J.J. Martocchio, "Time for Absenteeism: A 20-Year Review of Origins, Offshoots, and Outcomes," *Journal of Management* 24, no. 3 (1998): 305–50.

98. W. Beemsterboer et al., "A Literature Review on Sick Leave Determinants (1984–2004)," *International Journal of Occupational Medicine and Environmental Health* 22, no. 2 (2009): 169–79; C.M. Berry, A.M. Lelchook, and M.A. Clark, "A Meta-Analysis of the Interrelationships between Employee Lateness, Absenteeism, and Turnover: Implications for Models of Withdrawal Behavior," *Journal of Organizational Behavior* 33, no. 5 (2012): 678–99; C. Magee et al., "Workplace Bullying and Absenteeism: The Mediating Roles of Poor Health and Work Engagement," *Human Resource Management Journal* 27, no. 3 (2017): 319–34.

99. G. Johns, "Presenteeism in the Workplace: A Review and Research Agenda," *Journal of Organizational Behavior* 31, no. 4 (2010): 519–42; R.K. Skagen and A.M. Collins, "The Consequences of Sickness Presenteeism on Health and Wellbeing over Time: A Systematic Review," *Social Science & Medicine* 161 (2016): 169–77.

100. G. Johns, "Attendance Dynamics at Work: The Antecedents and Correlates of Presenteeism, Absenteeism, and Productivity Loss," *Journal of Occupational Health Psychology* 16, no. 4 (2011): 483–500; D. Baker-McClearn et al., "Absence Management and Presenteeism: The Pressures on Employees to Attend Work and the Impact of Attendance on Performance," *Human Resource Management Journal* 20, no. 3 (2010): 311–28; R. Pohling et al., "Work-Related Factors of Presenteeism: The Mediating Role of Mental and Physical Health," *Journal of Occupational Health Psychology* 21, no. 2 (2016): 220–34.

PART 2

2 Individual Differences: Personality and Values

Yuri Arcurs/E+/Getty Images

Learning Objectives

After you read this chapter, you should be able to:

LO2-1 Define personality and discuss how the Big Five personality factors relate to workplace behavior and performance.

LO2-2 Describe the dark triad of personality and the MBTI types and discuss their implications for organizational behavior.

LO2-3 Summarize Schwartz's model of individual values and discuss the conditions where values influence behavior.

LO2-4 Describe four ethical principles and discuss three factors that influence ethical behavior.

LO2-5 Describe five values commonly studied across cultures.

personality the relatively enduring pattern of thoughts, emotions, and behaviors that characterize a person, along with the psychological processes behind those characteristics

Julie Averill's decision to join Lululemon was partly motivated by the opportunity to guide the athletic apparel firm's digital transformation. But the veteran information technology executive also considered the fit between her personal values and Lululemon's culture. "I choose to work with companies that have values that align with my own, and who care about important things in the world," says Averill, who is located in Seattle with Lululemon's technology team. "I get inspired every day by people who live their lives to their values and find their passion along the way."[1]

Julie Averill's psychological attachment to Lululemon illustrates that personal values have a powerful influence on individual attitudes, decisions, and behavior. This chapter takes a close look at personal values as well as personality, which are the two most stable foundations of individual behavior. We begin by describing the meaning of personality and how it is affected by nature and nurture. The five-factor personality model is introduced, followed by an explanation of how each dimension of this highly regarded model relates to job performance and related behaviors. Two other personality models are then discussed: the dark triad (Machiavellianism, narcissism, and psychopathy) and the Jungian personality theory applied by the Myers-Briggs Type Indicator (MBTI). Next, our attention turns to personal values. We describe Schwartz's values circumplex model, explain how personal values influence workplace decisions and behavior, and introduce the concept of values congruence. Later, we examine ethical values and the mechanisms through which they influence a person's decisions and behavior. The final section of this chapter describes the best known cross-cultural values and explains their relevance to organizational behavior.

> One regrets the loss even of one's worst habits. . . . They are such an essential part of one's personality.[3]
>
> —Oscar Wilde, author (from *The Picture of Dorian Gray*)

LO2-1 Define personality and discuss how the Big Five personality factors relate to workplace behavior and performance.

PERSONALITY AND THE FIVE-FACTOR MODEL IN ORGANIZATIONS

On any given day in almost every workplace, employees will invariably mention either their own or someone else's personality. **Personality** refers to the relatively enduring pattern of thoughts, emotions, and behaviors that characterize a person, along with the psychological processes behind those characteristics.[2] In essence, it is the bundle of characteristics that make us similar to or different from other people. We estimate an individual's personality by what he or she says and does, and we infer the person's internal states—including thoughts and emotions—from these observable behaviors.

People engage in a wide range of behaviors in their daily lives, yet close inspection of those actions reveals discernible patterns called *personality traits*.[4] Traits are broad concepts that allow us to label and understand individual differences. For example, some of your friends are probably quite talkative whereas others tend to be quieter. Some people like to take risks whereas others are risk-averse. Each trait implies that there is something within the person, rather than environmental influences alone, that predicts this behavioral tendency. In fact, studies report that an individual's personality traits measured in childhood predict many behaviors and outcomes in adulthood, including educational attainment, employment success, marital relationships, illegal activities, and health-risk behaviors.[5]

Although people have behavioral tendencies, they do not act the same way in all situations. Such consistency would be considered abnormal because it indicates a person's insensitivity to social norms, reward systems, and other external conditions.[6] People vary their behavior to suit the situation, even if the behavior is at odds with their personality. For example, talkative people remain relatively quiet in a library where "no talking" rules are explicit and strictly enforced. But even there, personality differences are apparent because talkative people tend to do more chatting in libraries relative to how much other people talk in that setting.

What Causes Personality: Nature versus Nurture

Personality is shaped by both nature and nurture, although the relative importance of each continues to be debated and studied.[7] *Nature* refers to our genetic or hereditary origins—the genes

five-factor (Big Five) model (FFM) the five broad dimensions representing most personality traits: conscientiousness, emotional stability, openness to experience, agreeableness, and extraversion

conscientiousness a personality dimension describing people who are organized, dependable, goal-focused, thorough, disciplined, methodical, and industrious

agreeableness a personality dimension describing people who are trusting, helpful, good-natured, considerate, tolerant, selfless, generous, and flexible

neuroticism a personality dimension describing people who tend to be anxious, insecure, self-conscious, depressed, and temperamental

openness to experience a personality dimension describing people who are imaginative, creative, unconventional, curious, nonconforming, autonomous, and aesthetically perceptive

extraversion a personality dimension describing people who are outgoing, talkative, sociable, and assertive

that we inherit from our parents. Studies of identical twins reveal that heredity has a very large effect on personality; up to 50 percent of variation in behavior and 30 percent of temperament preferences can be attributed to a person's genetic characteristics. In other words, genetic code not only determines our eye color, skin tone, and physical shape; it also significantly affects our attitudes, decisions, and behavior.

Personality is also shaped by *nurture*—our socialization, life experiences, and other forms of interaction with the environment. Personality develops and changes mainly from childhood to young adulthood, typically stabilizing by around age 30. However, some personality changes continue to occur later in life. For instance, a few traits (openness to experience, social vitality) increase through to young adulthood, then decline in later years, whereas other traits (agreeableness, conscientiousness) tend to increase through to late life. Our personality can also change somewhat due to the job we work in over a long time period. Even migrating to another culture can change our personality to some extent.[8]

The main explanation for why personality becomes more stable by adulthood is that we form a clearer and more rigid self-concept. This increasing clarity of "who we are" anchors our behavior with the help of our *executive function.* This is the part of the brain that monitors and regulates goal-directed behavior to keep it consistent with our self-concept. Our self-view becomes clearer and more stable with age, which increases the stability and consistency of our personality and behavior.[9] We discuss the elements and influences of self-concept in Chapter 3. The main point here is that personality is not completely determined by heredity; life experiences, particularly early in life, also shape each individual's personality traits.

Studies of identical twins reveal that heredity has a very large effect on personality.
Elnur/Shutterstock

Five-Factor Model of Personality

Sociable, anxious, curious, dependable, suspicious, talkative, adventurous, and hundreds of other personality traits have been described over the years, so experts have tried to organize them into smaller clusters. The most researched and respected clustering of personality traits is the **five-factor model**, also known as the *Big Five.*[10] Several decades ago, personality experts identified more than 17,000 words that describe an individual's personality. These words were distilled down to five broad personality factors, each with a cluster of specific traits. Similar results were found in studies of different languages, suggesting that the five-factor model is fairly robust across cultures. These Big Five factors, represented by the handy acronym *CANOE,* are outlined in Exhibit 2.1 and described below.

- **Conscientiousness.** Characterizes people who are organized, dependable, goal-focused, thorough, disciplined, methodical, and industrious. People with low conscientiousness tend to be careless, disorganized, and less thorough.
- **Agreeableness.** Describes people who are trusting, helpful, good-natured, considerate, tolerant, selfless, generous, and flexible. People with low agreeableness tend to be uncooperative and intolerant of others' needs as well as more suspicious and self-focused.
- **Neuroticism.** Refers to people who tend to be anxious, insecure, self-conscious, depressed, and temperamental. In contrast, people with low neuroticism (high emotional stability) are poised, secure, and calm.
- **Openness to experience.** Characterizes people who are imaginative, creative, unconventional, curious, nonconforming, autonomous, and aesthetically perceptive. Those with low scores on this factor tend to be more resistant to change, less open to new ideas, and more conventional and fixed in their ways.
- **Extraversion.** Describes people who are outgoing, talkative, energetic, sociable, and assertive. The opposite is *introversion*, which applies to those who are quiet, cautious, and less interactive with others. Extraverts get their energy from the outer world (people and things around them), whereas introverts get their energy from the internal world, such as personal reflection on concepts and ideas. Introverts do not necessarily lack social skills. Instead, they are more inclined to direct their interests to ideas than to social events. Introverts feel more comfortable being alone than do extraverts.

Exhibit 2.1 Five-Factor Model of Personality

Personality factor	People with higher scores on this factor tend to be more:
Conscientiousness	Organized, dependable, goal-focused, thorough, disciplined, methodical, industrious
Agreeableness	Trusting, helpful, good-natured, considerate, tolerant, selfless, generous, flexible
Neuroticism	Anxious, insecure, self-conscious, depressed, temperamental
Openness to experience	Imaginative, creative, unconventional, curious, nonconforming, autonomous, perceptive
Extraversion	Outgoing, talkative, energetic, sociable, assertive

connect

SELF-ASSESSMENT 2.1: What is Your Big Five Personality?

connect

SELF-ASSESSMENT 2.2: Are You Introverted or Extraverted?

Five-Factor Model and Work Performance Personality mainly affects behavior and performance through motivation, specifically by influencing the individual's choice of goals (direction) as well as intensity and persistence of effort toward those goals. Consequently, all of the Big Five factors predict one or more types of employee behavior and performance to some extent.

Exhibit 2.2 highlights which Big Five personality factors best predict the three types of task performance as well as organizational citizenship and counterproductive work behaviors (see Chapter 1).[11] Conscientiousness stands out as the best overall personality predictor of proficient task performance for most jobs. The specific conscientiousness traits of industriousness (achievement, self-discipline, purposefulness) and dutifulness are the best predictors of proficient task performance. Conscientious employees set higher personal goals for themselves and are more persistent. They also engage in more organizational citizenship and in less counterproductive work behavior. Conscientiousness is a weak predictor of adaptive (responding to change) and proactive performance (taking initiative toward new work patterns). In fact, two specific conscientiousness traits—orderliness and dependability—tend to suppress adaptivity.

Extraversion is the second best overall personality predictor of proficient task performance but is a much weaker predictor than is conscientiousness. Among the specific traits within the extraversion factor, assertiveness and positive emotionality are the strongest predictors of proficient task performance. Assertiveness is also a strong predictor of adaptive and proactive performance. Assertive employees tend to have a "take charge" approach to situations, which is consistent with adapting to change and proactively initiating change. Extraversion is associated with influencing others and being comfortable in social settings, which (along with being assertive) explains why effective leaders and salespeople tend to be somewhat more extraverted than the general population.

Agreeableness is positively associated with organizational citizenship and negatively associated with counterproductive work behaviors.[12] The reason is that employees with high agreeableness are motivated to be cooperative, sensitive, flexible, and supportive. Agreeableness does not predict proficient or proactive task performance very well, mainly because it is associated with lower motivation to set goals and achieve results. However, employees with higher (but not too high) agreeableness tend to improve team performance through better knowledge sharing and motivation to help the team. Agreeableness also has a positive effect on friendliness behavior in customer service jobs.[13]

Openness to experience is a weak predictor of proficient task performance, but it is one of the best personality predictors of adaptive and proactive performance. The main reason is that employees with higher openness scores have more curiosity, imagination, and tolerance of change.[14] These traits also explain why openness to change is associated with successful performance in creative work.

Emotional stability (low neuroticism) is one of the best personality predictors of adaptive performance.[15] The main explanation is that employees with higher emotional stability cope better with the ambiguity and uncertainty of change. In contrast, those with higher neuroticism view change as a threat, so they tend to avoid change and experience more stress when faced with workplace adjustments. These characteristics would

Exhibit 2.2 Big Five Personality and Work Performance

Type of Performance	Proficient task performance	Adaptive task performance	Proactive task performance

Relevant Personality Factors	• Conscientiousness • Extraversion	• Emotional stability • Extraversion (assertiveness) • Openness to experience	• Extraversion (assertiveness) • Openness to experience

Type of Performance	Organizational citizenship	Counterproductive work behaviors

Relevant Personality Factors	• Conscientiousness • Agreeableness	• Conscientiousness* • Agreeableness*

*Negative relationship.

(Top-left): Ildar Galeev/Shutterstock; *(Top-center):* Fred Ho Yeow Hui/Shutterstock; *(Top-right):* malika.1028/Shutterstock; *(Bottom-left):* Aha-Soft/Shutterstock; *(Bottom-right):* Sign N Symbol Production/Shutterstock

connect

SELF-ASSESSMENT 2.3: Can You Identify Personality Traits from Blogging Words?

suggest that emotional stability also predicts proactive performance, but the limited research has reported mixed results.

Caveats When Applying the Five-Factor Model The five-factor model of personality is well established, but there is a tendency for people to make false assumptions about it. First, the "perfect employee" isn't the individual with the highest scores on all of the Big Five personality factors. This false assumption likely exists because the labels and structure of the Big Five factors have a strong linear bias (high is good, low is bad). But research indicates that the relationship between some Big Five factors and performance is nonlinear. For instance, employees with moderate extraversion perform better in sales jobs than those with high or low extraversion.[16]

Second, some behaviors are predicted better by a specific personality trait than by the overall Big Five factor for that trait. For example, the specific extraversion traits of assertiveness and positive emotionality predict proficient task performance better than the overall extraversion factor.

Third, personality isn't completely static. As we explained earlier, an individual's personality does stabilize around age 30, but some Big Five factors tend to increase or decrease as we age. Some personality factors also change over a long time when our environment significantly changes.

Fourth, although the five-factor model captures a large portion of the domain we call *personality*, it doesn't

> Some behaviors are predicted better by a specific personality trait than by the overall Big Five factor for that trait.

dark triad a cluster of three socially undesirable (dark) personality traits: Machiavellianism, narcissism, and psychopathy

Machiavellianism a personality trait of people who demonstrate a strong motivation to achieve their own goals at the expense of others, who believe that deceit is a natural and acceptable way to achieve their goals, who take pleasure in outwitting and misleading others using crude influence tactics, and who have a cynical disregard for morality

narcissism a personality trait of people with a grandiose, obsessive belief in their superiority and entitlement, a propensity to aggressively engage in attention-seeking behaviors, an intense envy of others, and tendency to exhibit arrogance, callousness, and exploitation of others for personal aggrandizement

psychopathy a personality trait of people who ruthlessly dominate and manipulate others without empathy or any feelings of remorse or anxiety, use superficial charm, yet are social predators who engage in antisocial, impulsive, and often fraudulent thrill-seeking behavior

represent all of it.[17] There are several perspectives or approaches to personality, each of which has a somewhat different view or emphasis. For example, the next section of this chapter looks at two other models of personality that only partially overlap with the Big Five factors.

LO2-2 Describe the dark triad of personality and the MBTI types and discuss their implications for organizational behavior.

OTHER PERSONALITY CONCEPTS: THE DARK TRIAD AND MBTI TYPES

The Dark Triad

When personality experts developed the five-factor model, they deliberately excluded words with noticeably positive or negative valence, such as *humble* (positive) or *sinister* (negative). More recently, researchers re-examined the emotionally charged words that were previously excluded. Out of these studies has emerged a cluster of three socially undesirable personality traits–Machiavellianism, narcissism, and psychopathy–called the **dark triad**.[18] Although these traits are distinct, they have a common "dark core" consisting of either low humility/honesty or a tendency to malevolently undermine others to maximize one's own gains.[19]

- **Machiavellianism.** People with high Machiavellianism (*high-Machs*) demonstrate a strong motivation to get what they want at the expense of others. They believe that deceit is a natural and acceptable way to achieve their goals; indeed, they take pleasure in misleading, outwitting, and otherwise controlling others. High-Machs routinely use lies, manipulation, exploitation, and other undesirable influence tactics (see Chapter 9). They have a cynical disregard for moral principles, believe that getting more than one deserves is acceptable, and seldom empathize with or trust coworkers.[20]
- **Narcissism.** Often called grandiose narcissism, this personality trait is evident in people who have an obsessive belief in their superiority and entitlement. Due to their excessive need for attention, narcissists aggressively engage in self-promotion, exhibitionism, and other attention-seeking behaviors. They can be initially charming, but are intensely envious of others. This envy is eventually manifest in the form of arrogance, schadenfreude (deriving pleasure from another person's misfortune), callous disregard for others' feelings (i.e., low empathy), and exploitation of others for personal aggrandizement.[21]
- **Psychopathy.** Considered the most sinister personality trait in the dark triad, psychopathy refers to social predators who ruthlessly dominate and manipulate others, yet without empathy or any feelings of remorse or anxiety. They are selfish self-promoters who use superficial charm (called the "mask" of psychopathy), yet engage in antisocial, impulsive, and often fraudulent thrill-seeking behavior. These people callously do as they please and take what they want.[22]

The Dark Triad in the Workplace Machiavellianism, narcissism, and psychopathy may seem like they belong in textbooks on criminology or medieval politics, not organizational behavior. Yet these traits are gaining attention because they are prevalent throughout the workplace. As one personality researcher warned in his keynote address to a national police association: "Not all psychopaths are in prison. Some are in the board room."[23]

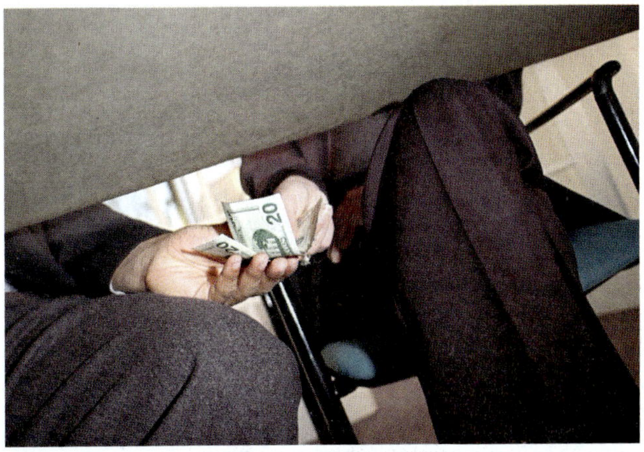

People with dark triad personality traits are more likely to engage in white-collar crime, workplace bullying, and riskier decisions with poorer investment returns.
Thinkstock Images/Comstock Images/Getty Images

counterproductive work behaviors (CWBs) voluntary behaviors that have the potential to directly or indirectly harm the organization

organizational politics the use of influence tactics for personal gain at the perceived expense of others and the organization

Myers–Briggs Type Indicator (MBTI) an instrument designed to measure the elements of Jungian personality theory, particularly preferences regarding perceiving and judging information

McGraw Hill connect

SELF-ASSESSMENT 2.4: How Machiavellian are You?

The dark triad traits are strongly associated with serious white-collar crime behavior. For instance, one study reported that a dark triad measure from video analysis was highly effective at identifying chief executive officers who were implicated in unethical misconduct and fraud.[24] People with dark triad personality traits are more likely to engage in bullying and other forms of workplace aggression.[25] They also tend to make decisions that produce poorer absolute and risk-adjusted investment returns. In particular, those with high psychopathy take excessive risks, due to their overconfidence and disregard for consequences.[26] The dark triad predicts **counterproductive work behaviors**, but not as well as do the specific Big Five factors of low agreeableness and conscientiousness.

Dishonesty is a core characteristic of the dark triad, so people with these traits are more likely to lie and deceive others at work. Similarly, they malevolently undermine others to maximize their own gains. This is the essence of **organizational politics** (see Chapter 9), which is about using influence tactics for personal gain at the expense of others and the interests of the entire organization. Political tactics produce a host of dysfunctional outcomes, ranging from employee stress and dissatisfaction to unproductive use of organizational resources. People with dark triad personality traits are dysfunctional team members in the long term because, by definition, they don't trust coworkers and focus on their own goals at the expense of team goals.[27] At the same time, they are known to help others in the short run when it serves their self-interest.

People who possess dark triad personality traits aren't always worse off. They have a manipulative political skill, which some supervisors rate favorably in employee performance. Being manipulative also occasionally helps employees move into more powerful positions in informal employee networks. Narcissistic CEOs tend to have higher direct pay as well as a larger gap in pay from other members of the executive team.[28]

Jungian Personality Theory and the Myers–Briggs Type Indicator

The five-factor model of personality has the most research support, but it is not the most popular personality test in practice. That distinction goes to Jungian personality theory, which is measured through the **Myers–Briggs Type Indicator (MBTI)** (see Exhibit 2.3).

Nearly a century ago, Swiss psychiatrist Carl Jung suggested that personality is mainly represented by the individual's preferences regarding perceiving and judging information.[29] Jung explained that the perceiving function—how people prefer to gather information—occurs through two competing orientations: *sensing (S)* and *intuition (N)*. Sensing involves perceiving

Exhibit 2.3 Jungian and Myers–Briggs Type Indicator Types

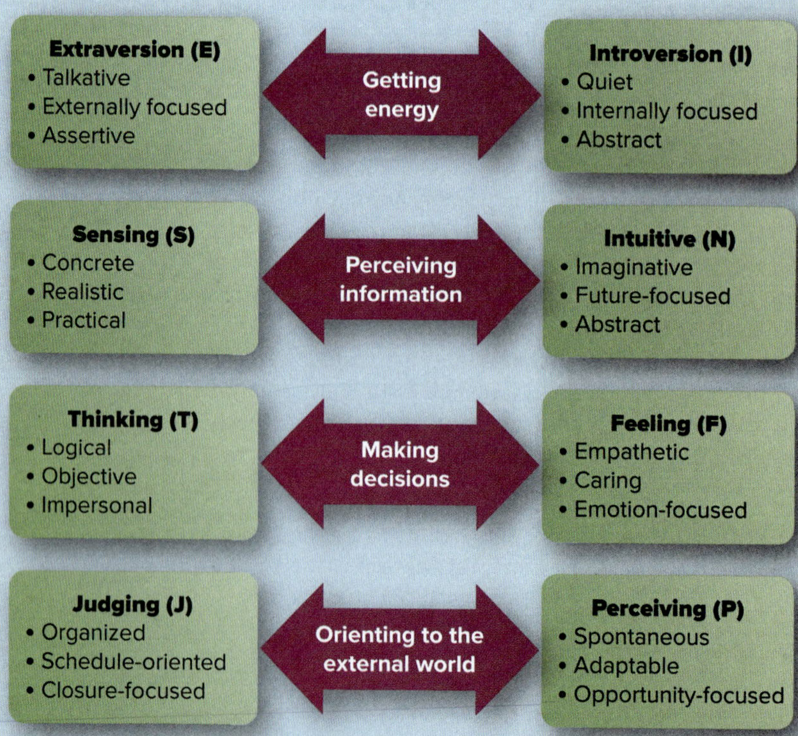

Sources: Adapted from an exhibit found at http://www.16-personality-types.com. Based on data from CPP, Inc., Sunnyvale, CA 94086 from *Introduction to Type and Careers* by Allen L. Hammer.

The MBTI should not be used for employment selection and promotion decisions, but it may be helpful in career counseling and executive coaching.
Trinette Reed/Blend Images LLC

information directly through the five senses; it relies on an organized structure to acquire factual and preferably quantitative details. In contrast, intuition relies more on insight and subjective experience to see relationships among variables. Sensing types focus on the here and now, whereas intuitive types focus more on future possibilities.

Jung also proposed that the judging function—how people prefer making decisions based on what they have perceived—consists of two competing processes: *thinking (T)* and *feeling (F)*. People with a thinking orientation rely on rational cause-effect logic and systematic data collection to make decisions. Those with a strong feeling orientation, on the other hand, give more weight to their emotional responses to the options presented, as well as to how those choices affect others. Jung noted that in addition to the four core processes of sensing, intuition, thinking, and feeling, people differ in their level of extraversion-introversion, which was introduced earlier as one of the Big Five personality traits.

The MBTI extends Jung's list of personality traits described above by also measuring Jung's broader categories of *perceiving* and *judging*, which represent a person's attitude toward the external world. People with a perceiving orientation are open, curious, and flexible. They like to keep their options open and to adapt spontaneously to events as they unfold. Judging types prefer order and structure and want to resolve problems quickly.

values relatively stable, evaluative beliefs that guide a person's preferences for outcomes or courses of action in a variety of situations

MBTI has a number of benefits, but it is usually a poor predictor of job performance and should be avoided for employment selection and promotion decisions.[30] There are also issues with its measurement. MBTI can potentially identify employees who prefer face-to-face versus virtual teamwork, but it does not seem to predict how well a team develops. It also has questionable value in predicting leadership effectiveness.

In spite of these limitations, the MBTI is the most widely studied measure of cognitive style in management research and may be helpful in career counseling and executive coaching (where it is the most popular personality assessment).[31] It is even being used by artificial intelligence engineers to adapt the behavior of robots to user preferences. MBTI takes a neutral or balanced approach by recognizing both the strengths and limitations of each personality type in different situations. In contrast, the five-factor model views people with higher scores as better than those with lower scores on each dimension. As such, the Big Five model may have adopted a restrictive view of personality that is more difficult to apply in coaching and development settings.[32]

Mc Graw Hill connect

SELF-ASSESSMENT 2.5: Are You a Sensing or Intuitive Type?

LO2-3 Summarize Schwartz's model of individual values and discuss the conditions where values influence behavior.

VALUES IN THE WORKPLACE

Liam (not his real name) felt uncomfortable working in his previous project team at a consumer goods company. His coworkers were friendly and knowledgeable, but their views about customers and getting ahead in the company were irritating. Most of the other team members discussed new products as money makers without much thought to whether they actually satisfied customer needs. Conversations about getting ahead in the company focused on networking rather than achieving objectives. At one point, Liam felt so uncomfortable with the views of other team members that he began looking for a job at another company. Fortunately, he was transferred to a new project where most colleagues held values that were similar to his own.

Most of us have experienced situations similar to what Liam went through, where the values expressed by others clash with our own personal values. **Values**, a concept that we introduced in Chapter 1,

Personal values serve as a moral compass; they influence our motivation and potentially our decisions and actions in various situations.
Colin Anderson/Blend Images LLC

are stable, evaluative beliefs that guide our preferences for outcomes or courses of action in a variety of situations.[33] They are perceptions about what is good or bad, right or wrong. They tell us to what we "ought" to do. Personal values serve as a moral compass; they influence our motivation and potentially our decisions and actions in various situations. They also provide justification for past decisions and behavior.

People arrange values into a hierarchy of preferences, called a *value system* (or, more correctly, a *values system*). Some individuals value new challenges more than they value conformity. Others value generosity more than frugality. Each person's unique value system is developed and reinforced through socialization from parents, religious institutions, friends, personal experiences, and the society in which he or she lives. As such, a person's hierarchy of values is stable and long-lasting. For example, one study found that a sample of adolescents had values systems that were remarkably similar 20 years later as adults.[34]

Values exist only within individuals—we call them *personal values*. However, groups of people might hold the same or similar values, so we tend to ascribe these *shared values* to the team, department, organization, profession, or entire society. The values shared by people throughout an organization (*organizational values*) receive fuller discussion in Chapter 13 because they are a central component of organizational culture. The values shared across a society (*cultural values*) receive attention in the last section of this chapter.

Values and personality traits are related to each other, but the two concepts differ in a few ways.[35] The most noticeable distinction is that values are evaluative (they tell us what we *ought* to do) whereas personality traits describe what we naturally *tend* to do. A second distinction is that personality traits have minimal conflict with each other—you can have high agreeableness and high introversion, for example—whereas some values are opposed to other values. This opposing effect means that someone who values excitement and challenge would have difficulty also valuing stability and moderation. Third, although personality and values are both partly determined by heredity, values are influenced more by socialization whereas heredity has a stronger influence on an individual's personality traits.

Types of Values

Values come in many forms, and experts on this topic have conducted considerable research on organizing them into clusters. By far, the most widely accepted model of personal values is Schwartz's values circumplex, developed and tested by social psychologist Shalom Schwartz and his colleagues.[36] This model clusters 57 values into 10 broad categories that are organized into the circular model (circumplex) shown in Exhibit 2.4. The

Exhibit 2.4 Schwartz's Values Circumplex

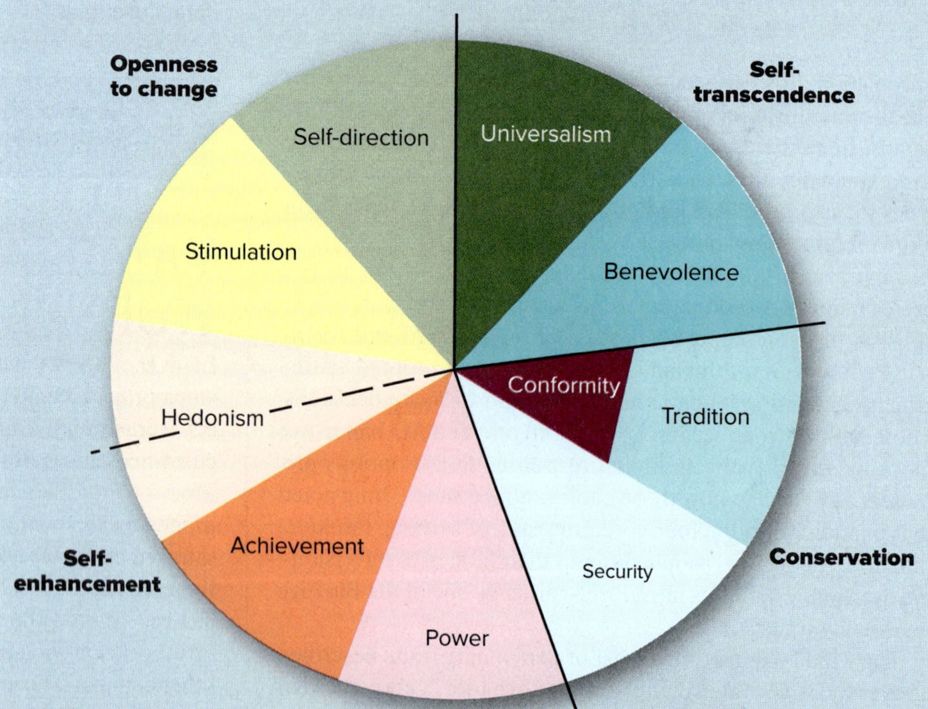

Sources: S.H. Schwartz, "Universals in the Content and Structure of Values: Theoretical Advances and Empirical Tests in 20 Countries," *Advances in Experimental Social Psychology* 25 (1992): 1–65; S.H. Schwartz and K. Boehnke, "Evaluating the Structure of Human Values with Confirmatory Factor Analysis," *Journal of Research in Personality* 38, no. 3 (2004): 230–55; Academic Rss. Inc.

10 categories include universalism, benevolence, tradition, conformity, security, power, achievement, hedonism, stimulation, and self-direction. Each category is a cluster of several specific values (not shown in the exhibit). For example, conformity includes the values of politeness, honoring parents, self-discipline, and obedience.

The 10 broad values categories are further clustered into four quadrants. One quadrant, called *openness to change*, refers to the extent to which a person is motivated to pursue innovative ways. It includes the values categories of self-direction (creativity, independent thought), stimulation (excitement and challenge), and hedonism (pursuit of pleasure, enjoyment, gratification of desires). The opposing quadrant is *conservation*, which is the extent to which a person is motivated to preserve the status quo. The conservation quadrant includes the value categories of conformity (adherence to social norms and expectations), security (safety and stability), and tradition (moderation and preservation of the status quo).

> The more choices you have, the more your values matter.[38]
>
> —Michael Schrage, **MIT Research Fellow and author**

The third quadrant in Schwartz's circumplex model, called *self-enhancement*, refers to how much a person is motivated by self-interest. This quadrant includes the values categories of achievement (pursuit of personal success), power (dominance over others), and hedonism (a values category shared with openness to change). The opposite of self-enhancement is *self-transcendence*, which refers to motivation to promote the welfare of others and nature. Self-transcendence includes the values categories of benevolence (concern for others in one's life) and universalism (concern for the welfare of all people and nature).

Mc Graw Hill **connect**

SELF-ASSESSMENT 2.6: What Are Your Dominant Values?

Values and Individual Behavior

Personal values influence decisions and behavior in at least three ways.[37]

- *Values influence the attractiveness of choices.* Our decisions are guided by personal values because those values generate positive or negative feelings (valences) toward the available choices. We experience more positive feelings toward choices that are aligned with our values and negative feelings toward alternatives that are contrary to our values. If stimulation is at the top of your values hierarchy, for instance, then jobs that offer new experiences will appeal to you more than jobs that have predictable and stable tasks.
- *Values frame our perceptions of reality.* We are constantly bombarded with stimuli from our surroundings. Personal values influence whether we notice something as well as how we interpret it (see Chapter 3). Our decisions and actions are affected by how we perceive those situations.
- *Values help regulate the consistency of behavior.* People are motivated to act consistently with their personal values and other aspects of their self-concept. If achievement is a key feature of your self-view and public image, then you are motivated to act in ways that are consistent with that value. The more clearly a behavior is aligned with a specific value that identifies us, the more motivated we are to engage in that behavior.

Personal values motivate behavior to some extent, but this connection isn't as strong as we might like to believe.[39] One reason for this "disconnect" between personal values and individual behavior is the situation. Personal values motivate us to engage in specific behavior, but the MARS model points out that the situation can prevent us from engaging in values-consistent behavior. For example, individuals with strong self-transcendent values are motivated to engage in recycling and other environmentally friendly behaviors, but lack of recycling facilities prevents or severely limits this behavior. A second reason an individual's behavior deviates from personal values is the presence of strong counter-motivational forces. Employees caught in illegal business dealings sometimes attribute their unethical activities to pressure from management to achieve their performance target at any cost.

A third reason why our personal values are sometimes inconsistent with our decisions and behavior is that we don't actively think about our values much of the time.[40] Values are abstract concepts, so their relevance is not obvious in many situations. Furthermore, many daily decisions and actions occur routinely, so we don't actively evaluate their consistency with our values. We do consciously consider our values in some situations, of course, such as realizing how much we value security when deciding whether to perform a risky task. However, many daily events do not trigger values awareness, so we act without their guidance. We literally need to be reminded of our values so they can guide our decisions and actions.

The effect of values awareness on behavior was apparent in a study in which students were given a math test and received a payment for each correct answer.[41] One group couldn't lie about their results because they submitted their results to the experimenter for scoring. A second group could lie because they scored the test themselves and told the experimenter their test score. A third group was similar to the second (they scored their own test), but that test included the following statement, and students were required to sign their name below that statement: "I understand that this short survey falls under (the university's) honor system." The researchers estimated that some students cheated when they scored their own test without the "honor system" statement, whereas no one given the "honor system" form lied about the results. The university didn't actually have an honor system, but the message made students pay attention to their honesty. In short, people are more likely to apply their values (honesty, in this case) when they are explicitly reminded of those values and see their relevance to the situation.

The Value of Personal Values at Work[42]

55% of 7,700 Millennials in 29 countries say their personal values/morals have a high degree of influence on their decision making at work.

73% of 5,113 working adults in the United States, France, Germany, and the UK say they would not apply to a company unless its values align with their own personal values.

68% of 181,009 Canadian federal government employees somewhat or strongly agree that their department or agency does a good job of promoting values and ethics in the workplace.

70% of 7,700 Millennials in 29 countries believe their personal values are shared by the organizations they work for.

18% of 600 corporate board directors in Australia identify "values" (leaders and employees aligned with company values) as the most important measure of the company's long-term value (2nd most important factor, following customer satisfaction/loyalty).

(Photo): mattjeacock/Getty Images

Values Congruence

Values tell us what is right or wrong and what we ought to do. This evaluative characteristic affects how comfortable we are with specific organizations and individuals. The key concept here is *values congruence*, which refers to how similar a person's values hierarchy is to the values hierarchy of another entity, such as the employee's team or organization. When personal values are congruent with the organization's values, employees tend to have higher job satisfaction, loyalty, and organizational citizenship. They also have less stress and turnover. Furthermore, employees are more likely to make decisions that are compatible with organizational expectations when their personal values are congruent with the organization's shared values.[43]

Are organizations the most successful when every employee's personal values align with the company's values? Not at all! While a large degree of values congruence is necessary for the reasons just noted, organizations also benefit from some level of incongruence. Employees with diverse values offer different perspectives, which potentially lead to better decision making. Also, too much congruence can create a "corporate cult" that potentially undermines creativity, organizational flexibility, and business ethics (see Chapter 13).

OB THEORY TO PRACTICE

"Your Values Are More Important Than Your CV" at IKEA[44]

IKEA describes itself as a values-driven company, so job applicants need to reflect on whether their personal values are congruent with the global retailer's organizational values. "We recruit by values," explains Anna Carin Månsson, Country HR Manager, IKEA India. "We like to understand personal values of a candidate and how these come out in typical behavior in everyday life."

Månsson's team pays attention to whether job applicants have really considered values congruence. "When recruiting for IKEA, it is attractive to recognize that the applicant has read up about the company and managed to describe the connection—i.e., what are the values they have as a person which makes them the perfect fit for working with the organization."

D'neale Prosser echoes Månsson's views. "Your values are more important than your CV," says the national talent manager at IKEA Australia. Prosser adds that the importance of values congruence extends beyond getting hired at IKEA. It is central to a person's success and happiness in life. "Find an organization that connects with your personal values and allows you to be yourself at work," advises Prosser. "This will add value and meaning to your everyday life."

LO2-4 Describe four ethical principles and discuss three factors that influence ethical behavior.

ETHICAL VALUES AND BEHAVIOR

When 195 business leaders across 15 countries were asked to identify the most important leader attributes, "high ethics and moral standards" was the top-rated item from the list of 74 items. Similarly, when 1,000 CEOs and other top-level executives around the world were asked to list the most important characteristics of effective leaders, the most frequently mentioned characteristic was *integrity*—the leader's ethical standards.[45] These surveys reveal the importance of ethics in the workplace. *Ethics* refers to the study of moral principles or values that determine whether actions are right or wrong and outcomes are good or bad (see Chapter 1). People rely on their ethical values to determine "the right thing to do."

Four Ethical Principles

Most ethical issues are associated with four ethical principles: utilitarianism, individual rights, distributive justice, and the ethic of care.[46] Your personal values might sway you more toward one principle than the others, but all four should be actively considered to put important ethical issues to the test.

- *Utilitarianism.* This principle says the only moral obligation is to seek the greatest good for the greatest number of people. It advocates choosing the option that produces the highest satisfaction to those affected. One problem is that utilitarianism requires a cost–benefit analysis, yet many outcomes aren't measurable. Another problem is that utilitarianism focuses only on outcomes, whereas the means of achieving those outcomes may be considered unethical by other principles.
- *Individual rights.* This principle says that everyone has the same set of natural rights, such as freedom of speech, freedom of movement, right to physical security, and right to fair trial. The individual rights principle includes human rights that are considered a moral norm of society. One problem with this principle is that some individual rights may conflict with others. The right of stockholders to be informed about corporate activities may ultimately conflict with an executive's right to privacy, for example.
- *Distributive justice.* This principle says that the benefits and burdens of similar individuals should be the same; otherwise they should be proportional. For example, employees who contribute equally in their work should receive similar rewards, whereas those who make a lesser contribution should receive less. A variation of this principle says that inequalities are acceptable when they benefit the least well off in society. The main problem with the distributive justice principle is that it is difficult to agree on who is "similar" and what factors are "relevant." We discuss distributive justice further in Chapter 5.
- *Ethic of care.* This principle states that everyone has a moral obligation to help others within their relational sphere to grow and self-actualize.[47] Thus, caring for others is a fundamental characteristic of humanity and an ethical virtue. Ethic of care includes being attentive to others' needs, using one's abilities to give care to others, and being responsive to (having empathy for) the person receiving care. This principle is found in writing about how organizations should serve stakeholders and how leaders should serve employees (see servant leadership in Chapter 11).[48]

moral intensity the degree to which an issue demands the application of ethical principles

moral sensitivity a person's ability to recognize the presence of an ethical issue and determine its relative importance

Moral Intensity, Moral Sensitivity, and Situational Influences

Along with ethical principles and their underlying values, three other factors influence ethical conduct in the workplace: the moral intensity of the issue, the individual's moral sensitivity, and situational influences.[49]

Moral Intensity

Moral intensity is the degree to which an issue demands the application of ethical principles. The higher the moral intensity of an issue, the more the decision maker needs to carefully apply ethical principles to make the best choice. The moral intensity of an issue is essentially about (1) how seriously (good or bad) people will be affected by the decision, (2) the probability that those good or bad outcomes will occur, and (3) how many people will be affected.[50] This is a variation of the classic expectancy-valence decision model that is applied in many organizational behavior concepts, including attitudes (Chapter 4), employee motivation (Chapter 5), and rational choice decision making (Chapter 6).

> It takes many good deeds to build a good reputation and only one bad one to lose it.
>
> —Attributed to Benjamin Franklin

Ethic of care includes being attentive to others' needs, giving care to others, and being responsive to (having empathy for) the person receiving care.
Rawpixel.com/Shutterstock

Moral Sensitivity

Moral sensitivity (also called *ethical sensitivity*) is a person's ability to detect a moral dilemma and estimate its relative importance.[51] People with high moral sensitivity can more quickly and accurately estimate the moral intensity of the issue. This awareness does not necessarily translate into more ethical behavior; it just means that people with higher moral sensitivity are more likely to know when unethical behavior occurs.

mindfulness a person's receptive and impartial attention to and awareness of the present situation as well as to one's own thoughts and emotions in that moment

> People with high moral sensitivity can more quickly and accurately estimate the moral intensity of the issue.

Several factors are associated with a person's moral sensitivity.[52]

- *Expertise or knowledge of prescriptive norms and rules.* Some people are more aware of illegal or otherwise unethical conduct due to their professional training. For example, accountants are more morally sensitive regarding specific accounting procedures than are people who lack experience in this profession.
- *Previous experience with specific moral dilemmas.* Past incidents likely generate internal cues that trigger awareness of future ethical dilemmas with similar characteristics.
- *Ability to empathize with those affected by the decision.* People with higher empathy for those affected by the decision would have greater moral sensitivity regarding the moral intensity of the issue. On average, women have higher moral sensitivity compared to men, partly because women tend to have higher empathy.
- *A strong self-view of being a morally sensitive person.*[53] Employees who strongly define themselves by their moral character (called their *moral identity*) tend to have higher moral sensitivity because they put more energy into maintaining ethical conduct.
- *A high degree of situational mindfulness.*[54] **Mindfulness** refers to a person's receptive and impartial attention to and awareness of the present situation as well as to one's own thoughts and emotions in that moment. Mindfulness increases moral sensitivity because it involves actively monitoring the environment as well as being sensitive to our responses to that environment. This vigilance requires effort as well as skill to receptively evaluate our thoughts and emotions. Unfortunately, we have a natural tendency to minimize effort, which leads to less mindfulness. For instance, employees don't pay attention to possible illegal activity by highly-regarded professionals and executives because these people are assumed to be ethical by virtue of their expertise and reputation.

Situational Factors Along with moral intensity and moral sensitivity, ethical conduct is influenced by the situation in which the conduct occurs.[55] Some employees say they regularly experience pressure from top management that motivates them to lie to customers, breach regulations, or otherwise act unethically. Situational factors do not justify unethical conduct. Rather, we need to be aware of these factors so organizations can reduce their influence.

Supporting Ethical Behavior

Most large and medium-sized organizations in the United States and other developed countries apply one or more strategies to improve ethical conduct. The most common ethics initiative is a code of ethical conduct—a statement about desired practices, rules of conduct, and philosophy about the organization's relationship to its stakeholders and the environment.[57] These codes, which are found in most large organizations, are supposed to motivate and guide employee behavior, signal the importance of ethical conduct, and build the firm's trustworthiness to stakeholders. However, critics suggest that they do little to reduce unethical conduct.

Another strategy to improve ethical conduct is to train and regularly evaluate employees on their knowledge of proper ethical conduct. Many large firms have annual quizzes to test employee awareness of company rules and practices concerning important ethical issues such as giving gifts and receiving sensitive information about competitors or governments. In some firms, employees participate in elaborate games that present increasingly challenging and complex moral dilemmas.

A growing ethics practice is a confidential telephone hotline and website, typically operated by an independent organization, whereby employees can anonymously report suspicious behavior. A few very

Ethical Challenges in the Workplace[56]

60% of Americans in a large Gallup survey believe there is widespread corruption within American businesses.

57% of 2,000 UK adults believe that British businesses behave very or fairly ethically.

24% of 759 Singaporean employees say they have felt pressured to compromise ethical standards.

46% of 9,000 American employees who received ethics training from their organization agree that they are able to apply that training in their day-to-day work.

19% of more than 18,000 employees surveyed worldwide say they observed corruption in their organization within the previous 12 months (ranging from 14% in Europe to 27% in Africa/Middle East).

(Photo): pathdoc/Shutterstock

large businesses also employ ombudspersons who receive information confidentially from employees and proactively investigate possible wrongdoing.[58] Likely the most powerful way to improve ethical conduct is to instill a set of shared values that reinforces ethical conduct. As we describe in Chapter 13 (organizational culture), an ethical culture is supported by the conduct and vigilance of corporate leaders. By acting with the highest moral standards, leaders not only gain support and trust from followers; they role-model the ethical standards that employees are more likely to follow.[59]

individualism a cross-cultural value describing the degree to which people in a culture emphasize independence and personal uniqueness

OB THEORY TO PRACTICE

The Texas Instruments Ethics Quick Test[60]

Texas Instruments takes ethical conduct seriously. Employees at the Dallas-based technology company receive a code of ethical conduct, are trained to understand and respond to ethical dilemmas, and have a confidential hotline to report ethical misconduct. Texas Instruments also distributes a business-card-sized mini-pamphlet, which asks employees to consider these questions when making ethical decisions.

1. Is the action legal?
2. Does it comply with our values?
3. If you do it, will you feel bad?
4. How will it look in a news story?
5. If you know it's wrong, don't do it! If you're not sure, ask. Keep asking until you get an answer.

LO2-5 Describe five values commonly studied across cultures.

VALUES ACROSS CULTURES

Values differ not only among individuals and across organizations. They also vary across societies. In this final section of the chapter, we introduce five values that have been studied across cultures: individualism, collectivism, power distance, uncertainty avoidance, and achievement-nurturing orientation. Exhibit 2.5 summarizes these values and lists a sample of countries that have high, medium, or low emphasis on these values.

Individualism and Collectivism

Two seemingly inseparable cross-cultural values are individualism and collectivism. **Individualism** is the extent to which we value independence and personal uniqueness. Highly individualist people value personal freedom, self-sufficiency, control over their own

Exhibit 2.5 Five Cross-Cultural Values

Value	Sample Countries	Representative Beliefs/Behaviors in "High" Cultures
Individualism	High: United States, Chile, Canada, South Africa Medium: Japan, Denmark Low: Taiwan, Venezuela	Defines self more by one's uniqueness; personal goals have priority; decisions have low consideration of effect on others; relationships are viewed as more instrumental and fluid.
Collectivism	High: Israel, Taiwan Medium: India, Denmark Low: United States, Germany, Japan	Defines self more by one's in-group membership; goals of self-sacrifice and harmony have priority; behavior regulated by in-group norms; in-group memberships are viewed as stable with a strong differentiation with out-groups.
Power distance	High: India, Malaysia Medium: United States, Japan Low: Denmark, Israel	Reluctant to disagree with or contradict the boss; managers are expected and preferred decision makers; perception of dependence on (versus interdependence with) the boss.
Uncertainty avoidance	High: Belgium, Greece Medium: United States, Norway Low: Denmark, Singapore	Prefer predictable situations; value stable employment, strict laws, and low conflict; dislike deviations from normal behavior.
Achievement-nurturing orientation	High: Austria, Japan Medium: United States, Brazil Low: Sweden, Netherlands	Focus on outcomes (versus relationships); decisions based on contribution (equity versus equality); low empathy or showing emotions (versus strong empathy and caring).

Sources: Individualism and collectivism descriptions and results are from the meta-analysis reported in D. Oyserman, H.M. Coon, and M. Kemmelmeier, "Rethinking Individualism and Collectivism: Evaluation of Theoretical Assumptions and Meta-Analyses," *Psychological Bulletin*, 128 (2002): 3–72. The other information is from G. Hofstede, *Culture's Consequences*, 2nd ed. (Thousand Oaks, CA: Sage, 2001).

collectivism a cross-cultural value describing the degree to which people in a culture emphasize duty to groups to which they belong and to group harmony

power distance a cross-cultural value describing the degree to which people in a culture accept unequal distribution of power in a society

uncertainty avoidance a cross-cultural value describing the degree to which people in a culture tolerate ambiguity (low uncertainty avoidance) or feel threatened by ambiguity and uncertainty (high uncertainty avoidance)

achievement-nurturing orientation cross-cultural value describing the degree to which people in a culture emphasize competitive versus cooperative relations with other people

lives, and appreciation of the unique qualities that distinguish them from others. Americans, Chileans, Canadians, and South Africans generally exhibit high individualism, whereas Taiwan and Venezuela are countries with low individualism.[61] **Collectivism** is the extent to which we value our duty to groups to which we belong and to group harmony. Highly collectivist people define themselves by their group memberships, emphasize their personal connection to others in their in-groups, and value the goals and well-being of people within those groups.[62] Low collectivism countries include the United States, Japan, and Germany, whereas Israel and Taiwan have relatively high collectivism.

Contrary to popular belief, individualism is not the opposite of collectivism. In fact, the two concepts are typically uncorrelated.[63] For example, cultures that highly value duty to one's group do not necessarily give a low priority to personal freedom and uniqueness. Generally, people across all cultures define themselves by both their uniqueness and their relationship to others. It is an inherent characteristic of everyone's self-concept, which we discuss in the next chapter. Some cultures clearly emphasize either personal uniqueness or group obligations, but both have a place in a person's values and self-concept.

Power Distance

People with high **power distance** value unequal power.[64] Those in higher positions expect obedience to authority; those in lower positions are comfortable receiving commands from their superiors without consultation or debate. People with high power distance also prefer to resolve differences through formal procedures rather than direct informal discussion. In contrast, people with low power distance expect relatively equal power sharing. They view the relationship with their boss as one of interdependence, not dependence; that is, they believe their boss is also dependent on them, so they expect power sharing and consultation before decisions affecting them are made. People in India and Malaysia tend to have high power distance, whereas people in Denmark and Israel generally have low power distance. Americans collectively have medium-low power distance.

Uncertainty Avoidance

Uncertainty avoidance is the degree to which people tolerate ambiguity (low uncertainty avoidance) or feel threatened by ambiguity and uncertainty (high uncertainty avoidance). Employees with high uncertainty avoidance value structured situations in which rules of conduct and decision making are clearly documented. They usually prefer direct rather than indirect or ambiguous communications. Uncertainty avoidance tends to be high in Belgium and Greece and very high in Japan. It is generally low in Denmark and Singapore. Americans collectively have medium-low uncertainty avoidance.

Achievement-Nurturing Orientation

Achievement-nurturing orientation reflects a competitive versus cooperative view of relations with other people.[65] People with a high achievement orientation value assertiveness, competitiveness, and materialism. They appreciate people who are tough, and they favor the acquisition of money and material goods. In contrast, people in nurturing-oriented cultures emphasize relationships and the well-being of others. They focus on human interaction and caring rather than competition and personal success. People in Sweden, Norway, and the Netherlands have a very low achievement orientation (i.e., they have a high nurturing orientation). In contrast, very high achievement orientation scores have been reported in Japan and Austria. The United States is located a little above the middle of the range on achievement-nurturing orientation.

Caveats about Cross-Cultural Knowledge

Cross-cultural organizational research has gained considerable attention over the past two decades, likely due to increased globalization and cultural diversity within organizations. Our knowledge of cross-cultural dynamics has blossomed, and many of these findings will be discussed in other chapters, such as leadership, conflict, and influence. However, we also need to raise a few warning flags about cross-cultural knowledge. One problem is that too many studies have relied on small, convenient samples (such as students attending one university) to represent an entire culture.[66] The result is that many cross-cultural studies draw conclusions that might not generalize to the cultures they intended to represent.

Mc Graw Hill connect

SELF-ASSESSMENT 2.7: How Much Do You Value Individualism and Collectivism?

Mc Graw Hill connect

SELF-ASSESSMENT 2.8: What is Your Level of Power Distance?

Cultural diversity exists within many countries; for example, personal values and personalities vary somewhat across regions within the United States.
Ollyy/Shutterstock

A second caveat is that cross-cultural research and writing continues to rely on a major study conducted almost four decades ago of 116,000 IBM employees across dozens of countries. That study helped ignite subsequent cross-cultural research, but its findings are becoming out-of-date as values in some cultures have shifted over the years.[67]

A third concern is that cross-cultural studies often assume that each country has one culture.[68] In reality, the United States and many other countries have become culturally diverse. For example, African Americans have significantly higher individualism than European and Hispanic Americans, whereas Asian Americans have the lowest individualism among these demographic groups.[69] Several studies also report cultural variations across geographic regions within the United States.[70] Collectivism is highest across the southern states, California, and Hawaii and lowest in the Mountain, Northwest, and Great Plains states, for instance. The personality profiles of Americans also vary from one region to the next. The New England, Middle Atlantic, and Pacific regions have high openness to experience, whereas people living in the Great Plains and midwestern and southeastern states have the lowest scores.[71] One study found that Americans have fairly accurate stereotypes of these regional differences. In summary, cultural diversity exists within many countries, such as within the United States.

Study Checklist

Connect® is available for *M Organizational Behavior.* Additional resources include:

✓ Exercises:

- **Case Analysis:** Apply concepts within the context of a real-world situation.
- **Click and Drag:** Helps make the connection between theory and application through matching, ranking, or grouping activities.
- **Video Case:** See management in action through interactive videos.
- **Self-Assessment:** Designed to promote student self-awareness and reflection, these research-based surveys contain detailed feedback for students.
- **Application-Based Activities:** These highly interactive, application- and analysis-based exercises allow students to take on specific roles to complete management-related tasks within a real-world context.

✓ **SmartBook 2.0™**—Smartbook 2.0 is an adaptive learning solution that provides personalized learning to individual student needs, continually adapts to pinpoint knowledge gaps and focuses learning on concepts requiring additional study. It fosters more productive learning, takes the guesswork out of what to study, and helps students better prepare for class.

©Natthawat Jamnapa/123RF

Notes

1. "Reign FC Legend: Julie Averill," Medium, May 12, 2017; S.A. Schwartz, "Lululemon CTO Aligns Personal Values with the Company's Mission through Tech," CIO Dive, December 5, 2018; R. Torres, "CTO of the Year: Julie Averill, Lululemon," CIO Dive, December 12, 2019.
2. The definition presented here is based on: D.C. Funder, *The Personality Puzzle* (New York: W.W. Norton & Company, 2016); C.S. Carver and M.F. Scheier, *Perspectives on Personality*, 8th ed. (Hoboken, NJ: Pearson Education, 2017). Both of these books recognize the varied perspectives of and approaches to personality. Several recent articles also recognize and attempt to address this conceptual diversity, such as: D. Cervone and B.R. Little, "Personality Architecture and Dynamics: The New Agenda and What's New about It," *Personality and Individual Differences* 136 (2019): 12–23, https://doi.org/10.1016/j.paid.2017.07.001; E. Jayawickreme, C.E. Zachry, and W. Fleeson, "Whole Trait Theory: An Integrative Approach to Examining Personality Structure and Process," *Personality and Individual Differences* 136 (2019): 2–11, https://doi.org/10.1016/j.paid.2018.06.045.
3. O. Wilde, *The Picture of Dorian Gray* (New York: Barnes & Noble, 2003), 340.
4. J. Anglim and P. O'Connor, "Measurement and Research Using the Big Five, HEXACO, and Narrow Traits: A Primer for Researchers and Practitioners," *Australian Journal of Psychology* 71, no. 1 (2019): 16–25, https://doi.org/10.1111/ajpy.12202.
5. B.W. Roberts and A. Caspi, "Personality Development and the Person-Situation Debate: It's Déjà Vu All over Again," *Psychological Inquiry* 12, no. 2 (2001): 104–9; N.A. Turiano et al., "Personality and Substance Use in Midlife: Conscientiousness as a Moderator and the Effects of Trait Change," *Journal of Research in Personality* 46, no. 3 (2012): 295–305; C.R. Gale et al., "Neuroticism and Extraversion in Youth Predict Mental Wellbeing and Life Satisfaction 40 Years Later," *Journal of Research in Personality* 47, no. 6 (2013): 687–97; M. Pluess and M. Bartley, "Childhood Conscientiousness Predicts the Social Gradient of Smoking in Adulthood: A Life Course Analysis," *Journal of Epidemiology and Community Health* 69, no. 4 (2015): 330–38; M. Blatný et al., "Personality Predictors of Successful Development: Toddler Temperament and Adolescent Personality Traits Predict Well-Being and Career Stability in Middle Adulthood," *PLoS ONE* 10, no. 4 (2015): e0126032.
6. W. Mischel, "Toward an Integrative Science of the Person," *Annual Review of Psychology* 55 (2004): 1–22; W.H. Cooper and M.J. Withey, "The Strong Situation Hypothesis," *Personality and Social Psychology Review* 13, no. 1 (2009): 62–72; T.A. Judge and C.P. Zapata, "The Person–Situation Debate Revisited," *Academy of Management Journal* 58, no. 4 (2015): 1149–79.
7. T. Vukasović and D. Bratko, "Heritability of Personality: A Meta-Analysis of Behavior Genetic Studies.," *Psychological Bulletin* 141, no. 4 (2015): 769–85, https://doi.org/10.1037/bul0000017; W. Bleidorn, "What Accounts for Personality Maturation in Early Adulthood?" *Current Directions in Psychological Science* 24, no. 3 (2015): 245–52; T.J.C. Polderman et al., "Meta-Analysis of the Heritability of Human Traits Based on Fifty Years of Twin Studies," *Nature Genetics* 47, no. 7 (2015): 702–9; L. Penke and M. Jokela, "The Evolutionary Genetics of Personality Revisited," *Current Opinion in Psychology* 7 (2016): 104–9; M.-T. Lo et al., "Genome-Wide Analyses for Personality Traits Identify Six Genomic Loci and Show Correlations with Psychiatric Disorders," *Nature Genetics* 49, no. 1 (2017): 152–56, https://doi.org/10.1038/ng.3736.
8. R. Mıttus et al., "Within-Trait Heterogeneity in Age Group Differences in Personality Domains and Facets: Implications for the Development and Coherence of Personality Traits," *PLoS ONE* 10, no. 3 (2015): e0119667; M. Liu and J.L. Huang, "Cross-Cultural Adjustment to the United States: The Role of Contextualized Extraversion Change," *Frontiers in Psychology* 6 (2015), https://doi.org/10.3389/fpsyg.2015.01650; S. Tasselli, M. Kilduff, and B. Landis, "Personality Change: Implications for Organizational Behavior," *Academy of Management Annals* 12, no. 2 (2018): 467–93, https://doi.org/10.5465/annals.2016.0008; W. Bleidorn, C.J. Hopwood, and R.E. Lucas, "Life Events and Personality Trait Change," *Journal of Personality* 86, no. 1 (2018): 83–96, https://doi.org/10.1111/jopy.12286; P.T. Costa, R.R. McCrae, and C.E. Löckenhoff, "Personality Across the Life Span," *Annual Review of Psychology* 70, no. 1 (2019): 423–48, https://doi.org/10.1146/annurev-psych-010418-103244.
9. R.F. Baumeister, B.J. Schmeichel, and K.D. Vohs, "Self-Regulation and the Executive Function: The Self as Controlling Agent," in *Social Psychology: Handbook of Basic Principles*, ed. A.W. Kruglanski and E.T. Higgins (New York: Guilford, 2007), 516–39; K. Murdock, K. Oddi, and D. Bridgett, "Cognitive Correlates of Personality: Links between Executive Functioning and the Big Five Personality Traits," *Journal of Individual Differences* 34, no. 2 (2013): 97–104; P. Baggetta and P.A. Alexander, "Conceptualization and Operationalization of Executive Function," *Mind, Brain, and Education* 10, no. 1 (2016): 10–33.
10. J.M. Digman, "Personality Structure: Emergence of the Five-Factor Model," *Annual Review of Psychology* 41 (1990): 417–40; O.P. John and S. Srivastava, "The Big Five Trait Taxonomy: History, Measurement, and Theoretical Perspectives," in *Handbook of Personality: Theory and Research*, ed. L.A. Pervin and O.P. John (New York: Guilford Press, 1999), 102–38; R.R. McCrae, J.F. Gaines, and M.A. Wellington, "The Five-Factor Model in Fact and Fiction," in *Handbook of Psychology*, ed. I.B. Weiner (2012), 65–91.
11. M.R. Barrick and M.K. Mount, "Yes, Personality Matters: Moving on to More Important Matters," *Human Performance* 18, no. 4 (2005): 359–72; P.R. Sackett and P.T. Walmsley, "Which Personality Attributes Are Most Important in the Workplace?" *Perspectives on Psychological Science* 9, no. 5 (2014): 538–51; L.M. Penney, E. David, and L.A. Witt, "A Review of Personality and Performance: Identifying Boundaries, Contingencies, and Future Research Directions," *Human Resource Management Review* 21, no. 4 (2011): 297–310; T. Judge et al., "Hierarchical Representations of the Five-Factor Model of Personality in Predicting Job Performance: Integrating Three Organizing Frameworks with Two Theoretical Perspectives," *Journal of Applied Psychology* 98, no. 6 (2013): 875–925; J. Huang et al., "Personality and Adaptive Performance at Work: A Meta-Analytic Investigation," *Journal of Applied Psychology* 99, no. 1 (2014): 162–79.
12. R.D.S. Chiaburu et al., "The Five-Factor Model of Personality Traits and Organizational Citizenship Behaviors: A Meta-Analysis," *Journal of Applied Psychology* 96, no. 6 (2011): 1140–66; D.S. Chiaburu, I.-S. Oh, and S.V. Marinova, "Five-Factor Model of Personality Traits and Organizational Citizenship Behavior: Current Research and Future Directions," in *The Oxford Handbook of Organizational Citizenship Behavior*, ed. P.M. Podsakoff, S.B. Mackenzie, and N.P. Podsakoff (New York: Oxford University Press, 2018), 203–20.
13. R.F. Hurley, "Customer Service Behavior in Retail Settings: A Study of the Effect of Service Provider Personality," *Journal of the Academy of Marketing Science* 26, no. 2 (1998): 115–27, https://doi.org/10.1177/0092070398262003; M.A.G. Peeters et al., "Personality and Team Performance: A Meta-Analysis," *European Journal of Personality* 20, no. 5 (2006): 377–96, https://doi.org/10.1002/per.588; J.L. Huang and A.M. Ryan, "Beyond Personality Traits: A Study of Personality States and Situational Contingencies in Customer Service Jobs," *Personnel Psychology* 64, no. 2 (2011): 451–88, https://doi.org/10.1111/j.1744-6570.2011.01216.x;

B.H. Bradley et al., "Team Players and Collective Performance: How Agreeableness Affects Team Performance over Time," *Small Group Research* 44, no. 6 (2013): 680–711, https://doi.org/10.1177/1046496413507609.

14. A. Neal et al., "Predicting the Form and Direction of Work Role Performance from the Big 5 Model of Personality Traits," *Journal of Organizational Behavior* 33, no. 2 (2012): 175–92.
15. J. L. Huang et al., "Personality and Adaptive Performance at Work," *Journal of Applied Psychology* 99, no. 1 (2014): 162–79.
16. H. Le et al., "Too Much of a Good Thing: Curvilinear Relationships between Personality Traits and Job Performance," *Journal of Applied Psychology* 96, no. 1 (2011): 113–33; A.M. Grant, "Rethinking the Extraverted Sales Ideal: The Ambivert Advantage," *Psychological Science* 24, no. 6 (2013): 1024–30; G. Blickle et al., "Extraversion and Job Performance: How Context Relevance and Bandwidth Specificity Create a Non-Linear, Positive, and Asymptotic Relationship," *Journal of Vocational Behavior* 87 (2015): 80–88; P.L. Curşeu et al., "Personality Characteristics That Are Valued in Teams: Not Always 'More Is Better'?" *International Journal of Psychology*, 2019, https://doi.org/10.1002/ijop.12511.
17. J. Anglim and P. O'Connor, "Measurement and Research Using the Big Five, HEXACO, and Narrow Traits: A Primer for Researchers and Practitioners," *Australian Journal of Psychology* 71, no. 1 (2019): 16–25, https://doi.org/10.1111/ajpy.12202.
18. D.L. Paulhus and K.M. Williams, "The Dark Triad of Personality: Narcissism, Machiavellianism, and Psychopathy," *Journal of Research in Personality* 36, no. 6 (2002): 556–63, https://doi.org/10.1016/S0092-6566(02)00505-6; J.M. LeBreton, L.K. Shiverdecker, and E.M. Grimaldi, "The Dark Triad and Workplace Behavior," *Annual Review of Organizational Psychology and Organizational Behavior* 5, no. 1 (2018): 387–414, https://doi.org/10.1146/annurev-orgpsych-032117-104451; R. Rogoza and J. Cieciuch, "Dark Triad Traits and Their Structure: An Empirical Approach," *Current Psychology*, March 19, 2018, https://doi.org/10.1007/s12144-018-9834-6; S.M. Spain, "The Dark Side of Personality," in *Leadership, Work, and the Dark Side of Personality*, ed. S.M. Spain (Academic Press, 2019), 41–93, https://doi.org/10.1016/B978-0-12-812821-3.00003-7. A fourth trait–sadism–has recently been suggested, but it is early days to add this as a dark tetrad to our discussion.
19. D.N. Jones and D.L. Paulhus, "Differentiating the Dark Triad within the Interpersonal Circumplex," in *Handbook of Interpersonal Psychology*, ed. L.M. Horowitz and S. Strack (Hoboken, NJ, USA: John Wiley & Sons, Inc., 2012), 249–67, https://doi.org/10.1002/9781118001868.ch15; A. Book et al., "Unpacking More 'Evil': What Is at the Core of the Dark Tetrad?" *Personality and Individual Differences* 90 (2016): 269–72, https://doi.org/10.1016/j.paid.2015.11.009; M. Moshagen, B.E. Hilbig, and I. Zettler, "The Dark Core of Personality," *Psychological Review* 125, no. 5 (2018): 656–88, https://doi.org/10.1037/rev0000111; G. Hodson et al., "Is the Dark Triad Common Factor Distinct from Low Honesty-Humility?" *Journal of Research in Personality* 73 (2018): 123–29, https://doi.org/10.1016/j.jrp.2017.11.012.
20. R. Christie and F. Geis, *Studies in Machiavellianism* (New York: Academic Press, 1970); S. R. Kessler et al., "Re-Examining Machiavelli: A Three-Dimensional Model of Machiavellianism in the Workplace," *Journal of Applied Social Psychology* 40, no. 8 (2010): 1868–96; E. O'Boyle et al., "A Meta-Analysis of the Dark Triad and Work Behavior: A Social Exchange Perspective," *Journal of Applied Psychology* 97, no. 3 (2012): 557–79.
21. Z. Krizan and O. Johar, "Envy Divides the Two Faces of Narcissism," *Journal of Personality* 80, no. 5 (2012): 1415–51, https://doi.org/10.1111/j.1467-6494.2012.00767.x.
22. C.J. Patrick, "Psychopathy as Masked Pathology," in *Handbook of Psychopathy*, 2nd ed. (New York: The Guilford Press, 2018), 3–21.
23. S.F. Smith and S.O. Lilienfeld, "Psychopathy in the Workplace: The Knowns and Unknowns," *Aggression and Violent Behavior* 18, no. 2 (2013): 204–18, https://doi.org/10.1016/j.avb.2012.11.007; A. Cohen, "Are They among Us? A Conceptual Framework of the Relationship between the Dark Triad Personality and Counterproductive Work Behaviors (CWBs)," *Human Resource Management Review* 26, no. 1 (2016): 69–85, https://doi.org/10.1016/j.hrmr.2015.07.003; A. Harrison, J. Summers, and B. Mennecke, "The Effects of the Dark Triad on Unethical Behavior," *Journal of Business Ethics* 153, no. 1 (2018): 53–77, https://doi.org/10.1007/s10551-016-3368-3.
24. H.L. DeShong, D.M. Grant, and S.N. Mullins-Sweatt, "Comparing Models of Counterproductive Workplace Behaviors: The Five-Factor Model and the Dark Triad," *Personality and Individual Differences* 74 (2015): 55–60, https://doi.org/10.1016/j.paid.2014.10.001; J.R. Van Scotter and K.D.D. Roglio, "CEO Bright and Dark Personality: Effects on Ethical Misconduct," *Journal of Business Ethics*, 2019, https://doi.org/10.1007/s10551-018-4061-5.
25. C.R. Boddy, "Corporate Psychopaths, Bullying and Unfair Supervision in the Workplace," *Journal of Business Ethics* 100, no. 3 (2011): 367–79, https://doi.org/10.1007/s10551-010-0689-5; S.F. Smith and S.O. Lilienfeld, "Psychopathy in the Workplace: The Knowns and Unknowns," *Aggression and Violent Behavior* 18, no. 2 (2013): 204–18, https://doi.org/10.1016/j.avb.2012.11.007.
26. D.N. Jones, "Risk in the Face of Retribution: Psychopathic Individuals Persist in Financial Misbehavior among the Dark Triad," *Personality and Individual Differences*, The Dark Triad of Personality, 67 (2014): 109–13, https://doi.org/10.1016/j.paid.2014.01.030; L. ten Brinke, A. Kish, and D. Keltner, "Hedge Fund Managers with Psychopathic Tendencies Make for Worse Investors," *Personality and Social Psychology Bulletin* 44, no. 2 (2018): 214–23, https://doi.org/10.1177/0146167217733080.
27. M.A. Baysinger, K.T. Scherer, and J.M. LeBreton, "Exploring the Disruptive Effects of Psychopathy and Aggression on Group Processes and Group Effectiveness.," *Journal of Applied Psychology* 99, no. 1 (2014): 48–65, https://doi.org/10.1037/a0034317; A.G. Nassif, "Heterogeneity and Centrality of 'Dark Personality' within Teams, Shared Leadership, and Team Performance: A Conceptual Moderated-Mediation Model," *Human Resource Management Review*, December 2018, https://doi.org/10.1016/j.hrmr.2018.11.003.
28. C.A. O'Reilly et al., "Narcissistic CEOs and Executive Compensation," *The Leadership Quarterly* 25, no. 2 (2014): 218–31, https://doi.org/10.1016/j.leaqua.2013.08.002; K.J. Templer, "Dark Personality, Job Performance Ratings, and the Role of Political Skill: An Indication of Why Toxic People May Get Ahead at Work," *Personality and Individual Differences* 124 (2018): 209–14, https://doi.org/10.1016/j.paid.2017.11.030; W. Hart, K. Richardson, and G.K. Tortoriello, "Meet Your Public Relations Team: People with Dark Traits May Help You Manage Your Image," *Personality and Individual Differences* 134 (2018): 164–73, https://doi.org/10.1016/j.paid.2018.06.019; D.K. Marcus, J. Preszler, and V. Zeigler-Hill, "A Network of Dark Personality Traits: What Lies at the Heart of Darkness?," *Journal of Research in Personality* 73 (2018): 56–62, https://doi.org/10.1016/j.jrp.2017.11.003.
29. C.G. Jung, *Psychological Types*, trans. H.G. Baynes (Princeton, NJ: Princeton University Press, 1971); I.B. Myers, *The Myers-Briggs Type Indicator* (Palo Alto, CA: Consulting Psychologists Press, 1987).

30. J. Michael, "Using the Myers-Briggs Type Indicator as a Tool for Leadership Development? Apply with Caution," *Journal of Leadership & Organizational Studies* 10 (2003): 68–81; R.M. Capraro and M.M. Capraro, "Myers-Briggs Type Indicator Score Reliability across Studies: A Meta-Analytic Reliability Generalization Study," *Educational and Psychological Measurement* 62 (2002): 590–602; B.S. Kuipers et al., "The Influence of Myers-Briggs Type Indicator Profiles on Team Development Processes," *Small Group Research* 40, no. 4 (2009): 436–64; F.W. Brown and M.D. Reilly, "The Myers-Briggs Type Indicator and Transformational Leadership," *Journal of Management Development* 28, no. 10 (2009): 916–32; A. Luse et al., "Personality and Cognitive Style as Predictors of Preference for Working in Virtual Teams," *Computers in Human Behavior* 29, no. 4 (2013): 1825–32.

31. R.B. Kennedy and D.A. Kennedy, "Using the Myers-Briggs Type Indicator in Career Counseling," *Journal of Employment Counseling* 41, no. 1 (2004): 38–44; K.-H. Lee, Y. Choi, and D.J. Stonier, "Evolutionary Algorithm for a Genetic Robot's Personality Based on the Myers-Briggs Type Indicator," *Robotics and Autonomous Systems* 60, no. 7 (2012): 941–61; S.J. Armstrong, E. Cools, and E. Sadler-Smith, "Role of Cognitive Styles in Business and Management: Reviewing 40 Years of Research," *International Journal of Management Reviews* 14, no. 3 (2012): 238–62.

32. J.B. Lloyd, "Unsubstantiated Beliefs and Values Flaw the Five-Factor Model of Personality," *Journal of Beliefs & Values* 36, no. 2 (2015): 156–64.

33. B.M. Meglino and E.C. Ravlin, "Individual Values in Organizations: Concepts, Controversies, and Research," *Journal of Management* 24, no. 3 (1998): 351–89; B.R. Agle and C.B. Caldwell, "Understanding Research on Values in Business," *Business and Society* 38, no. 3 (1999): 326–87; S. Hitlin and J.A. Pilavin, "Values: Reviving a Dormant Concept," *Annual Review of Sociology* 30 (2004): 359–93; L. Sagiv et al., "Personal Values in Human Life," *Nature Human Behaviour* 1, no. 9 (September 2017): 630–39, https://doi.org/10.1038/s41562-017-0185-3.

34. D. Lubinski, D.B. Schmidt, and C.P. Benbow, "A 20-Year Stability Analysis of the Study of Values for Intellectually Gifted Individuals from Adolescence to Adulthood," *Journal of Applied Psychology* 81 (1996): 443–51. A more recent example of values stability is reported in R. Sundberg, "Value Stability and Change in an ISAF Contingent," *Journal of Personality* 84, no. 1 (2016): 91–101, https://doi.org/10.1111/jopy.12142.

35. L. Parks and R.P. Guay, "Personality, Values, and Motivation," *Personality and Individual Differences* 47, no. 7 (2009): 675–84; L. Parks-Leduc, G. Feldman, and A. Bardi, "Personality Traits and Personal Values: A Meta-Analysis," *Personality and Social Psychology Review* 19, no. 1 (2015): 3–29.

36. S.H. Schwartz, "Universals in the Content and Structure of Values: Theoretical Advances and Empirical Tests in 20 Countries," *Advances in Experimental Social Psychology* 25 (1992): 1–65; S.H. Schwartz and K. Boehnke, "Evaluating the Structure of Human Values with Confirmatory Factor Analysis," *Journal of Research in Personality* 38, no. 3 (2004): 230–55; I. Borg, A. Bardi, and S.H. Schwartz, "Does the Value Circle Exist within Persons or Only across Persons?" *Journal of Personality* 85, no. 2 (2017): 151–62, https://doi.org/10.1111/jopy.12228. Schwartz's model is currently being revised, but the new model is similar in overall design and still requires refinement. One recent study found that Schwartz's new model is the strongest predictor among various values models. See S.H. Schwartz et al., "Refining the Theory of Basic Individual Values," *Journal of Personality and Social Psychology* 103, no. 4 (2012): 663–88; P.H.P. Hanel, L.F. Litzellachner, and G.R. Maio, "An Empirical Comparison of Human Value Models," *Frontiers in Psychology* 9 (September 25, 2018), https://doi.org/10.3389/fpsyg.2018.01643.

37. N.T. Feather, "Values, Valences, and Choice: The Influence of Values on the Perceived Attractiveness and Choice of Alternatives," *Journal of Personality and Social Psychology* 68, no. 6 (1995): 1135–51; L. Sagiv, N. Sverdlik, and N. Schwarz, "To Compete or to Cooperate? Values' Impact on Perception and Action in Social Dilemma Games," *European Journal of Social Psychology* 41, no. 1 (2011): 64–77; S.H. Schwartz and T. Butenko, "Values and Behavior: Validating the Refined Value Theory in Russia," *European Journal of Social Psychology* 44, no. 7 (2014): 799–813.

38. M. Schrage, *Serious Play: How the World's Best Companies Simulate to Innovate* (Cambridge, MA: Harvard Business School Press, 1999), 98.

39. G.R. Maio et al., "Addressing Discrepancies between Values and Behavior: The Motivating Effect of Reasons," *Journal of Experimental Social Psychology* 37, no. 2 (2001): 104–17; A. Bardi and S.H. Schwartz, "Values and Behavior: Strength and Structure of Relations," *Personality and Social Psychology Bulletin* 29, no. 10 (2003): 1207–20; L. Sagiv, N. Sverdlik, and N. Schwarz, "To Compete or to Cooperate? Values' Impact on Perception and Action in Social Dilemma Games," *European Journal of Social Psychology* 41, no. 1 (2011): 64–77; K.M. Sheldon and L.S. Krieger, "Walking the Talk: Value Importance, Value Enactment, and Well-Being," *Motivation and Emotion* 38 (2014): 609–19.

40. E. Dreezens et al., "The Missing Link: On Strengthening the Relationship between Values and Attitudes," *Basic and Applied Social Psychology* 30, no. 2 (2008): 142–52; S. Arieli, A.M. Grant, and L. Sagiv, "Convincing Yourself to Care About Others: An Intervention for Enhancing Benevolence Values," *Journal of Personality* 82, no. 1 (2014): 15–24.

41. N. Mazar, O. Amir, and D. Ariely, "The Dishonesty of Honest People: A Theory of Self-Concept Maintenance," *Journal of Marketing Research* 45 (2008): 633–44.

42. "The 2016 Deloitte Millennial Survey: Winning over the Next Generation of Leaders" (New York: Deloitte Touche Tohmatsu, January 2016); "Creating Value and Balancing Stakeholder Needs: The Board's Role," AICD-KPMG Survey: Australian Governance Summit 2019 (Sydney: Australian Institute of Company Directors, March 1, 2019); "Mission & Culture Survey 2019" (Mill Valley, CA: Glassdoor, July 9, 2019); "2019 Public Service Employee Survey Results for the Public Service" (Ottawa: Government of Canada, Treasury Board of Canada Secretariat, January 15, 2020).

43. M.L. Verquer, T.A. Beehr, and S.H. Wagner, "A Meta-Analysis of Relations between Person–Organization Fit and Work Attitudes," *Journal of Vocational Behavior* 63 (2003): 473–89; J.W. Westerman and L.A. Cyr, "An Integrative Analysis of Person–Organization Fit Theories," *International Journal of Selection and Assessment* 12, no. 3 (2004): 252–61; J.R. Edwards and D.M. Cable, "The Value of Value Congruence," *Journal of Applied Psychology* 94, no. 3 (2009): 654–77. We use the phrase "values congruence" (plural, NOT the singular "value congruence") because values operate as a set, not individually. Also, "value" is easily confused with the economic concept of worth of something relative to price.

44. "'We Believe That Your Values Are More Important than Your CV,'" *Human Resources Director Australia*, April 11, 2018; V. Sawhney, "What I Look for in Candidates: An Interview with Anna-Carin Månsson," *HBR Ascend* (blog), August 2018, https://hbrascend.org/topics/look-candidate-interview-anna-carin-mansson/; N. Yazxhi, "BM Expert: How to Future Proof Your Career," *Bellamumma* (blog), October 17, 2018, http://bellamumma.com/2018/10/17/bm-expert-how-to-future-proof-your-career/; C. Lamba, "Understanding the HR Policies of IKEA," *India Retailing*, December 17, 2018.

45. The Conference Board, *CEO Challenge 2014* (New York: The Conference Board, January 2014); S. Giles, "The Most Important Leadership Competencies, According to Leaders around the World," *Harvard Business Review Digital Articles*(March 2016): 2–6.

46. P.L. Schumann, "A Moral Principles Framework for Human Resource Management Ethics," *Human Resource Management Review* 11(2001): 93–111; J.A. Boss, *Analyzing Moral Issues*, 6th ed. (New York: McGraw-Hill, 2013), Chap. 1; A. Gustafson, "In Defense of a Utilitarian Business Ethic," *Business and Society Review* 118, no. 3 (2013): 325-60.

47. J.C. Tronto, *Moral Boundaries: A Political Argument for an Ethic of Care* (New York: Routledge, 1993), Chap. 5; T.F. Hawk, "An Ethic of Care: A Relational Ethic for the Relational Characteristics of Organizations," in *Applying Care Ethics to Business*, ed. M. Hamington and M. Sander-Staudt (Dordrecht: Springer Netherlands, 2011), 3–34.

48. D. Engster, "Care Ethics and Stakeholder Theory," in *Applying Care Ethics to Business*, ed. M. Hamington and M. Sander-Staudt (Dordrecht: Springer Netherlands, 2011), 93–110, https://doi.org/10.1007/978-90-481-9307-3_5; J. Nicholson and E. Kurucz, "Relational Leadership for Sustainability: Building an Ethical Framework from the Moral Theory of 'Ethics of Care,'" *Journal of Business Ethics*, 2017, https://doi.org/10.1007/s10551-017-3593-4; G.J. Lemoine, C.A. Hartnell, and H. Leroy, "Taking Stock of Moral Approaches to Leadership: An Integrative Review of Ethical, Authentic, and Servant Leadership," *Academy of Management Annals* 13, no. 1 (2018): 148–87, https://doi.org/10.5465/annals.2016.0121.

49. For analysis of these predictors of ethical conduct, see J.J. Kish-Gephart, D.A. Harrison, and L.K. Treviño, "Bad Apples, Bad Cases, and Bad Barrels: Meta-Analytic Evidence about Sources of Unethical Decisions at Work," *Journal of Applied Psychology* 95, no. 1 (2010): 1–32.

50. T.M. Jones, "Ethical Decision Making by Individuals in Organizations: An Issue-Contingent Model," *Academy of Management Review* 16 (1991): 366–95; T. Barnett, "Dimensions of Moral Intensity and Ethical Decision Making: An Empirical Study," *Journal of Applied Social Psychology* 31, no. 5 (2001): 1038–57; S. Valentine and D. Hollingworth, "Moral Intensity, Issue Importance, and Ethical Reasoning in Operations Situations," *Journal of Business Ethics* 108, no. 4 (2012): 509–23; T.T. Moores, H.J. Smith, and M. Limayem, "Putting the Pieces Back Together: Moral Intensity and Its Impact on the Four-Component Model of Morality," *Business and Society Review* 123, no. 2 (2018): 243–68, https://doi.org/10.1111/basr.12141.

51. K. Weaver, J. Morse, and C. Mitcham, "Ethical Sensitivity in Professional Practice: Concept Analysis," *Journal of Advanced Nursing* 62, no. 5 (2008): 607–18; L.J.T. Pedersen, "See No Evil: Moral Sensitivity in the Formulation of Business Problems," *Business Ethics: A European Review* 18, no. 4 (2009): 335–48. According to one recent neuroscience study, the emotional aspect of moral sensitivity declines and the cognitive aspect increases between early childhood and young adulthood. See J. Decety, K.J. Michalska, and K.D. Kinzler, "The Contribution of Emotion and Cognition to Moral Sensitivity: A Neurodevelopmental Study," *Cerebral Cortex* 22, no. 1 (2012): 209–20.

52. D. You, Y. Maeda, and M.J. Bebeau, "Gender Differences in Moral Sensitivity: A Meta-Analysis," *Ethics & Behavior* 21, no. 4 (2011): 263–82; A.H. Chan and H. Cheung, "Cultural Dimensions, Ethical Sensitivity, and Corporate Governance," *Journal of Business Ethics* 110, no. 1 (2012): 45–59; J.R. Sparks, "A Social Cognitive Explanation of Situational and Individual Effects on Moral Sensitivity," *Journal of Applied Social Psychology* 45, no. 1 (2015): 45–54; S.J. Reynolds and J.A. Miller, "The Recognition of Moral Issues: Moral Awareness, Moral Sensitivity and Moral Attentiveness," *Current Opinion in Psychology* 6 (2015): 114–17.

53. J. Boegershausen, K. Aquino, and A. Reed II, "Moral Identity," *Current Opinion in Psychology* 6 (2015): 162–66.

54. N. Ruedy and M. Schweitzer, "In the Moment: The Effect of Mindfulness on Ethical Decision Making," *Journal of Business Ethics* 95, no. 1 (2010): 73–87.

55. M.H. Bazerman and F. Gino, "Behavioral Ethics: Toward a Deeper Understanding of Moral Judgment and Dishonesty," *Annual Review of Law and Social Science* 8, no. 1 (2012): 85–104; M. Knoll et al., "Examining the Moral Grey Zone: The Role of Moral Disengagement, Authenticity, and Situational Strength in Predicting Unethical Managerial Behavior," *Journal of Applied Social Psychology* 46, no. 1 (2016): 65–78. The survey results are reported in A. Tenbrunsel and J. Thomas, *The Street, the Bull and the Crisis: A Survey of the US & UK Financial Services Industry*, University of Notre Dame and Labaton Sucharow (Indiana and New York: May 2015); D. Johnson, *Ethics at Work 2015 Survey of Employees: Main Findings and Themes* (London: Institute of Business Ethics, November 2015).

56. G. Khoury and S. Crabtree, "Are Businesses Worldwide Suffering From a Trust Crisis?" *Gallup Workplace*, February 6, 2019; "A Quarter of Singaporean Employees Felt Pressured to Compromise Ethical Standards, Reveals Institute of Business Ethics' Survey," news release (London: Institute of Business Ethics, September 23, 2019); "2019 Global Business Ethics Survey—Workplace Misconduct and Reporting: A Global Look" (Vienna, VA: Ethics & Compliance Initiative, November 27, 2019); "Attitudes of the British Public to Business Ethics: 2019" (London: Institute of Business Ethics, January 2020).

57. H. Donker, D. Poff, and S. Zahir, "Corporate Values, Codes of Ethics, and Firm Performance: A Look at the Canadian Context," *Journal of Business Ethics* 82, no. 3 (2008): 527–37; G. Svensson et al., "Ethical Structures and Processes of Corporations Operating in Australia, Canada, and Sweden: A Longitudinal and Cross-Cultural Study," *Journal of Business Ethics* 86, no. 4 (2009): 485–506; L. Preuss, "Codes of Conduct in Organisational Context: From Cascade to Lattice-Work of Codes," *Journal of Business Ethics* 94, no. 4 (2010): 471–87.

58. G. Svensson et al., "Ethical Structures and Processes of Corporations Operating in Australia, Canada, and Sweden: A Longitudinal and Cross-Cultural Study," *Journal of Business Ethics* 86, no. 4 (2009): 485–506.

59. S.L. Grover, T. Nadisic, and D.L. Patient, "Bringing Together Different Perspectives on Ethical Leadership," *Journal of Change Management* 12, no. 4 (2012): 377–81; J. Jordan et al., "Someone to Look Up To: Executive–Follower Ethical Reasoning and Perceptions of Ethical Leadership," *Journal of Management* 39, no. 3 (2013): 660–83; J. Jaeger, "Compliance Culture Depends on Middle Management," *Compliance Week*, February 2014, 47–61.

60. "Code of Conduct: Our Values and Ethics" (Dallas: Texas Instruments, May 21, 2019).

61. Individualism and collectivism information is from the meta-analysis by Oyserman et al., not the earlier findings by Hofstede. See D. Oyserman, H.M. Coon, and M. Kemmelmeier, "Rethinking Individualism and Collectivism: Evaluation of Theoretical Assumptions and Meta-Analyses," *Psychological Bulletin* 128 (2002): 3–72. Consistent with Oyserman et al., a recent study found high rather than low individualism among Chileans. See A. Kolstad and S. Horpestad, "Self-Construal in Chile and Norway," *Journal of Cross-Cultural Psychology* 40, no. 2 (2009): 275–81.

62. F.S. Niles, "Individualism–Collectivism Revisited," *Cross-Cultural Research* 32 (1998): 315–41; C.P. Earley and C.B. Gibson, "Taking Stock in Our Progress on Individualism–Collectivism: 100 Years of Solidarity and Community," *Journal of Management* 24 (1998): 265–304; C.L. Jackson et al., "Psychological Collectivism: A Measurement Validation and Linkage to Group Member Performance," *Journal of Applied Psychology* 91, no. 4 (2006): 884–99.

63. D. Oyserman, H.M. Coon, and M. Kemmelmeier, "Rethinking Individualism and Collectivism: Evaluation of Theoretical Assumptions and Meta-Analyses," *Psychological Bulletin* 128 (2002): 3–72; H. Vargas and M. Kemmelmeier, "Ethnicity and Contemporary American Culture: A Meta-Analytic Investigation of Horizontal–Vertical Individualism–Collectivism," *Journal of Cross-Cultural Psychology* 44, no. 2 (2013): 195–222; Y. Kashima, P.G. Bain, and A. Perfors, "The Psychology of Cultural Dynamics: What Is It, What Do We Know, and What Is Yet to Be Known?" *Annual Review of Psychology* 70, no. 1 (2019): 499–529, https://doi.org/10.1146/annurev-psych-010418-103112.

64. G. Hofstede, *Culture's Consequences: Comparing Values, Behaviors, Institutions, and Organizations across Nations*, 2nd ed. (Thousand Oaks, CA: Sage, 2001).

65. G. Hofstede, *Culture's Consequences: Comparing Values, Behaviors, Institutions, and Organizations across Nations,* 2nd ed. (Thousand Oaks, CA: Sage, 2001). Hofstede used the terms *masculinity* and *femininity* for *achievement* and *nurturing orientation*, respectively. We (along with other writers) have adopted the latter two terms to minimize the sexist perspective of these concepts. Also, readers need to be aware that achievement orientation is assumed to be opposite of nurturing orientation, but this opposing relationship might be questioned.

66. V. Taras, J. Rowney, and P. Steel, "Half a Century of Measuring Culture: Review of Approaches, Challenges, and Limitations Based on the Analysis of 121 Instruments for Quantifying Culture," *Journal of International Management* 15, no. 4 (2009): 357–73.

67. N. Jacob, "Cross-Cultural Investigations: Emerging Concepts," *Journal of Organizational Change Management* 18, no. 5 (2005): 514–28; V. Taras, B.L. Kirkman, and P. Steel, "Examining the Impact of Culture's Consequences: A Three-Decade, Multilevel, Meta-Analytic Review of Hofstede's Cultural Value Dimensions," *Journal of Applied Psychology* 95, no. 3 (2010): 405–39.

68. R.L. Tung and A. Verbeke, "Beyond Hofstede and GLOBE: Improving the Quality of Cross-Cultural Research," *Journal of International Business Studies* 41, no. 8 (2010): 1259–74.

69. D. Oyserman, H.M. Coon, and M. Kemmelmeier, "Rethinking Individualism and Collectivism: Evaluation of Theoretical Assumptions and Meta-Analyses," *Psychological Bulletin* 128 (2002): 3–72. However, a recent meta-analysis found only minor differences across ethnic groups. See J.H. Vargas and M. Kemmelmeier, "Ethnicity and Contemporary American Culture: A Meta-Analytic Investigation of Horizontal–Vertical Individualism–Collectivism," *Journal of Cross-Cultural Psychology* 44, no. 2 (2013): 195–222.

70. J.A. Vandello and D. Cohen, "Patterns of Individualism and Collectivism across the United States," *Journal of Personality and Social Psychology* 77, no. 2 (1999): 279–92; B. MacNab, R. Worthley, and S. Jenner, "Regional Cultural Differences and Ethical Perspectives within the United States: Avoiding Pseudo-Emic Ethics Research," *Business and Society Review* 115, no. 1 (2010): 27–55; J. Lun, B. Mesquita, and B. Smith, "Self- and Other-Presentational Styles in the Southern and Northern United States: An Analysis of Personal Ads," *European Journal of Social Psychology* 41, no. 4 (2011): 435–45; P.J. Rentfrow et al., "Divided We Stand: Three Psychological Regions of the United States and Their Political, Economic, Social, and Health Correlates," *Journal of Personality and Social Psychology* 105, no. 6 (2013): 996–1012.

71. V.C. Plaut, H. Rose Markus, and M.E. Lachman, "Place Matters: Consensual Features and Regional Variation in American Well-Being and Self," *Journal of Personality and Social Psychology* 83, no. 1 (2002): 160–84; P.J. Rentfrow, "Statewide Differences in Personality: Toward a Psychological Geography of the United States," *American Psychologist* 65, no. 6 (2010): 548–58; K.H. Rogers and D. Wood, "Accuracy of United States Regional Personality Stereotypes," *Journal of Research in Personality* 44, no. 6 (2010): 704–13; J. Lieske, "The Changing Regional Subcultures of the American States and the Utility of a New Cultural Measure," *Political Research Quarterly* 63, no. 3 (2010): 538–52.

3 Perceiving Ourselves and Others in Organizations

Learning Objectives

After you read this chapter, you should be able to:

LO3-1 Describe the elements of self-concept and explain how each affects an individual's behavior and well-being.

LO3-2 Outline the perceptual process and discuss the effects of categorical thinking and mental models in that process.

LO3-3 Discuss how stereotyping; attribution; self-fulfilling prophecy; and the halo, false-consensus, recency, and primacy effects influence the perceptual process.

LO3-4 Discuss three ways to improve perceptions, with specific application to organizational situations.

self-concept an individual's self-beliefs and self-evaluations

South African restaurant chain Nando's recently launched a witty advertisement that pokes fun at our tendency to stereotype people who are different from us. The "You People" video has several brief scenes in which viewers easily misperceive the actors' role in the scene (upscale customer versus employee) or the meaning of their actions (running for exercise versus running away from police). It also shows that those who stereotype "you people" fail to recognize similar behavior in themselves.

"'You people' is a phrase often used by South Africans when describing people who are different to them," says Doug Place, Nando's chief marketing officer in Johannesburg. "It's a phrase that goes hand in hand with an unconscious bias." Place explains that Nando's created the ad to encourage discussion about stereotyping and to promote greater harmony in society. "If you're watching our ad and say 'I've done that' (hopefully with a guilty smile), then we've been successful at starting a crucial conversation—hopefully one that starts with 'us people.'"[1]

The Nando's advertisement pokes fun at the human propensity to stereotype others. Yet our inability to accurately perceive things and people often creates serious difficulties and injustices in the workplace. This chapter looks at how we perceive ourselves and others in organizational settings. First, we look at the details of self-concept—how we perceive ourselves—and how that self-perception affects our decisions and behavior. We then turn our attention to perceptions of others in organizational settings, beginning with how we select, organize, and interpret information. Next, we examine several specific perceptual processes, such as stereotyping, attribution, and self-fulfilling prophecy. The final section of this chapter discusses potentially effective ways to improve perceptions in the workplace.

LO3-1 Describe the elements of self-concept and explain how each affects an individual's behavior and well-being.

SELF-CONCEPT: HOW WE PERCEIVE OURSELVES

Self-concept refers to an individual's self-beliefs and self-evaluations.[2] It is the "Who am I?" and "How do I feel about myself?" that people ask themselves and that guide their decisions and actions. Whether contemplating a career as a health care executive or in any other occupation, we compare our perceptions of that job with our current (perceived self) and desired (ideal self) images of ourselves. We also evaluate our current and desired abilities to determine whether there is a good fit with that type of work. Our self-concept is defined at three levels: individual, relational, and collective. Specifically, we view ourselves in terms of our personal traits (individual self); connections to friends and coworkers (relational self); and membership in teams, organizations, social groups, and other entities (collective self).[3]

Self-Concept Complexity, Consistency, and Clarity

An individual's self-concept can be described by three characteristics: complexity, consistency, and clarity (see Exhibit 3.1). *Complexity* refers to the number of distinct and important roles or identities that people perceive about themselves.[5] Everyone has multiple self-views because each person sees himself or herself in different roles at various times (student, friend, daughter, sports fan, etc.). People are generally motivated to increase their complexity (called *self-expansion*) as they seek out new opportunities and social connections. A person's self-concept becomes more complex, for example, as he or she moves from being an accountant to a manager because the person has acquired additional roles.

> **Whenever two people meet there are really six people present. There are the two people as they see themselves, the two people as they see each other, and the two people as they really are.[4]**
>
> —Restated from Oliver Wendell Holmes Sr., medical scholar and author (in *The Autocrat of the Breakfast-Table*, 1858)

Exhibit 3.1 Self-Concept Characteristics and Processes

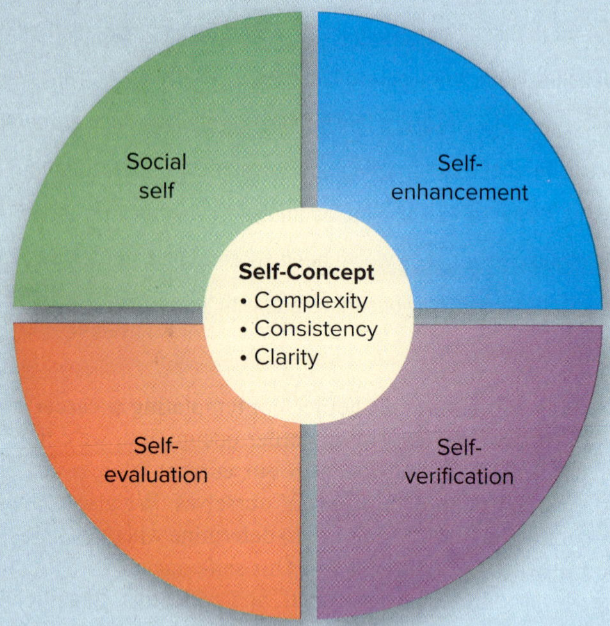

> **Self-concept clarity refers to the degree to which a person's self-concept is clear, confidently defined, and stable.**

Self-concept complexity is defined by more than just the number of identities that a person has; it is also defined by the separation of those identities. An individual with several identities might still have low self-concept complexity when those identities are highly interconnected, such as when they are all work related (manager, engineer, family income earner). Complexity is higher when the multiple identities have a low correlation with each other, such as when you have a successful career but also carve out sufficient time and focus to be a dedicated parent, a helpful neighbor, and a talented mountain biker.

Although people have multiple selves, only some of those identities dominate their attention at one time.[6] A particular self-view (parent, manager, etc.) is usually domain specific; it is more likely to be activated in some settings than in others. People shift their self-concept more easily when the activated self-view is important and compatible with the situation. For instance, as employees travel from home to work, they can usually shift their self-view from being a parent to being an executive because each role is important and fits into the home and work contexts, respectively. In contrast, some individuals struggle to focus on their occupational self-concept when working from home (remote work).

Consistency, the second self-concept characteristic, is the degree to which a person's identities require similar personal attributes and are compatible with the person's actual attributes. Low consistency occurs when some self-views require personal attributes that conflict with attributes required for other self-views, such as when a safety-conscious engineer also defines himself or herself as a risk-oriented snowboarder. Low consistency also occurs when an individual's dominant self-views are incompatible with his or her actual personal attributes. As an example, low consistency would occur when someone has a self-concept as a highly creative individual yet has moderately low openness-to-experience personality and values.

Clarity, the third characteristic of self-concept, refers to the degree to which a person's self-concept is clear, confidently defined, and stable.[7] People with high self-concept clarity are confident about "who I am," can describe their identities to others, and provide the same description of themselves across time. Self-concept clarity increases with age because personality and values become relatively stable by adulthood and people develop better self-awareness through life experiences. Self-concept is also clearer when a person's multiple selves have higher consistency. This makes sense because low consistency produces ambiguity about a person's underlying characteristics. For example, someone whose self-view includes both cautious engineer and risk-oriented snowboarder would have difficulty defining himself or herself clearly or with much confidence.[8]

Effects of Self-Concept Characteristics on Well-Being and Behavior

Psychological well-being tends to be higher among people with fairly distinct multiple selves (complexity) that are well established (clarity) and require similar personal attributes that are compatible with the individual's character (consistency).[9] Self-concept complexity protects our self-esteem when some roles are threatened or damaged. A complex self is rather like a ship with several compartments that can be sealed off from one another. If one

McGraw Hill connect

SELF-ASSESSMENT 3.1: How Much Does Work Define Your Self-Concept?

People tend to have better psychological well-being when their multiple selves are in harmony with one another other and with their personality and values (high consistency).
alphaspirit/Shutterstock

compartment is damaged, the other compartments remain intact so the ship remains afloat. A complex self offers the same benefits: If one identity is damaged by events—job loss, for example—the person's mental health stays afloat because the other selves remain intact. In contrast, people with low complexity, including those whose multiple selves are highly interconnected, suffer severe loss when they experience failure because these events affect a large part of themselves.

People also tend to have better well-being when their multiple selves are in harmony with one another other and with their personality and values (high consistency).[10] Self-concept complexity helps people adapt, but too much variation causes internal tension and conflict. Well-being also tends to increase with self-concept clarity. People who are unsure of their self-views are more easily influenced by others, experience more stress when making decisions, and feel more threatened by social forces that undermine their self-confidence and self-esteem.[11]

Self-concept complexity, consistency, and clarity have both positive and negative influences on individual behavior and performance.[12] Employees with complex identities tend to have more adaptive decision making and performance. This likely occurs because multiple selves generate more diverse experiences and role patterns, so these employees can more easily alter their thinking and behavior to suit new tasks and work environments. A second benefit is that self-concept complexity often produces more diverse social networks, which gives employees access to more resources and social support to perform their jobs.

People are inherently motivated to perceive themselves, and to be perceived by others, as above average in important ways.
Spark Studio/Getty Images

Against these benefits is the problem that highly complex self-concepts require more effort to maintain and juggle, which can be stressful and less efficient. Low complexity self-concepts, on the other hand, require less effort and resources to develop. For example, people who define themselves mainly by their work (low complexity) tend to have better job performance due to their longer work hours, more investment in skill development, and more concentration on work. They also have lower absenteeism and turnover.

self-enhancement a person's inherent motivation to have a positive self-concept (and to have others perceive him or her favorably), such as being competent, attractive, lucky, ethical, and important

Self-concept clarity tends to improve performance and is considered vital for leadership roles.[13] Clarity also provides a more discernible career path, which enables people to direct their effort more efficiently toward career success. Another benefit is that people with high self-concept clarity feel less threatened by interpersonal conflict, which increases their ability to resolve conflicts through constructive problem-solving behaviors. However, those with very high clarity may have role inflexibility, with the result that they cannot adapt to changing job duties or environmental conditions.

Along with the three self-concept characteristics, Exhibit 3.1 illustrates four processes that shape self-concept and motivate a person's decisions and behavior. Let's look at each of these four "selves": self-enhancement, self-verification, self-evaluation, and social self (social identity).

Self-Enhancement

People are inherently motivated to perceive themselves, and to be perceived by others, as above average in important ways, such as being competent, attractive, lucky, ethical, and valuable.[14] This phenomenon, called **self-enhancement**, occurs when individuals rate themselves above average, believe that they have a better-than-average probability of success, and attribute their successes to personal motivation or ability while blaming the situation for their mistakes. People don't believe they are above average in all circumstances, only for things that are important to them, and are relatively common rather than rare.[15]

Self-enhancement has both positive and negative consequences in organizational settings.[16] On the positive side, individuals tend to experience better mental and physical health when they amplify their self-concept. Overconfidence also generates a "can-do" attitude (which we discuss later) that motivates persistence in difficult or risky tasks. On the negative side, self-enhancement causes people to overestimate future returns in investment decisions and to engage in unsafe behavior, such as dangerous driving. It also accounts for executives repeating poor decisions (because they ignore negative feedback), launching misguided corporate diversification strategies, and acquiring excessive corporate debt.

> The deepest urge in human nature is the desire to be important.[17]
>
> — John Dewey, educational philosopher

Self-Verification

Individuals try to confirm and maintain their existing self-concept.[18] This process, called **self-verification**, stabilizes an individual's self-view, which in turn provides an important anchor that guides his or her thoughts and actions. Employees actively communicate their self-concept so coworkers understand it and provide verifying feedback when observed. For example, you might let coworkers know that you are a very organized person; later, they compliment you on occasions where you have indeed been very organized. Unlike self-enhancement, self-verification includes seeking feedback that is not necessarily flattering (e.g., "I'm a numbers person, not a people person"). Experts continue to debate whether and under what conditions people prefer information that supports self-enhancement or self-verification.[19] Do we prefer compliments rather than accurate critique about weaknesses that we readily acknowledge? The answer is likely complex; we enjoy compliments, but less so if they are significantly contrary to our self-view.

Self-verification is associated with several OB topics.[20] First, it affects the perceptual process that we describe later in this chapter. Specifically, employees are more likely to remember information that is consistent with their self-concept and nonconsciously screen out information (particularly negative information) that seems inconsistent with it. Second, people with high self-concept clarity will consciously dismiss feedback that contradicts their self-concept. Third, employees prefer interacting with others who affirm their self-views, which affects how well they get along with their boss and team members.

Self-Evaluation

Almost everyone strives to have a positive self-concept, but some people have a more positive evaluation of themselves than do others. This *self-evaluation* is mostly defined by three elements: self-esteem, self-efficacy, and locus of control.[21]

Self-Esteem

Self-esteem—the extent to which people like, respect, and are satisfied with themselves—represents a comprehensive self-evaluation. People have degrees of self-esteem for each of their various roles, such as being a good student, a good driver, and a good parent. From these multiple self-appraisals, people form an overall evaluation of themselves, known as their global self-esteem. Those with high self-esteem are less influenced by others, tend to persist in spite of failure, and have a higher propensity to think logically.[23]

Self-Efficacy

Self-efficacy refers to a person's belief about successfully completing a task.[24] Those with high self-efficacy have a "can-do" attitude. They believe they possess the energy (motivation), ability, clear expectations (role perceptions), and resources (situational factors) to perform the task. In other words, self-efficacy is an individual's perception regarding the MARS model in a specific situation. Self-efficacy is often task specific, but it also can be more generalized. People have a general self-efficacy when they believe they can be successful across a variety of situations.[25] Those with higher general self-efficacy have a more positive overall self-evaluation.

Self-Efficacy of Managers and Employees[26]

93% of 1,000 executives surveyed say they felt a material dip in their self-confidence and self-esteem within the past six months due to something that happened at work.

51% of 666 employees surveyed say that workplace training gives them more self-confidence.

45% of managers in a large survey say they don't feel confident in their ability to develop the skills employees need today.

79% of women (compared to 62% of men) among 2,499 UK employees surveyed say they regularly lack confidence when it comes to their careers and speaking up at work.

33% of more than 25,000 employees globally say their employer makes them feel undervalued (26% feel highly valued).

(Photo): Ljupco Smokovski/Shutterstock

self-verification a person's inherent motivation to confirm and maintain his or her existing self-concept

self-efficacy a person's belief that he or she has the ability, motivation, correct role perceptions, and favorable situation to complete a task successfully

locus of control a person's general belief about the amount of control he or she has over personal life events

social identity theory a theory stating that people define themselves by the groups to which they belong or have an emotional attachment

> **OB THEORY TO PRACTICE**
>
> **Girls Gain Confidence in Software Coding Workshops**
>
> One reason women represent only 17 percent of information technology graduates is that girls have unfounded low self-efficacy regarding their performance in this field. One study found that 14-year-old girls significantly underestimated their performance on science and technology tests, whereas boys slightly overrated themselves, even though average scores are about the same for both genders. Several programs have been launched to help young women develop a more positive self-evaluation about their performance in information technology careers. For example, Google launched "Made with Code," a series of workshops in which girls gain confidence in coding software apps and learn how software can be a positive force in society. "Ours is a perception campaign," says Made with Code's program manager.[22]

> McGraw Hill connect
>
> **SELF-ASSESSMENT 3.2: How Much General Self-Efficacy Do You Have?**

Locus of Control

Locus of control is defined as a person's general beliefs about the amount of control he or she has over personal life events.[27] Individuals with an internal locus of control believe that life events are caused mainly by their personal characteristics (i.e., motivation and abilities). Those with an external locus of control believe events are due mainly to fate, luck, or conditions in the external environment. Locus of control is a generalized belief, but this belief varies to some extent with the situation. People with an external locus of control generally believe that life's outcomes are beyond their control, but they also believe they have control over the results of tasks they perform often. An individual's general locus of control tendency is most apparent in new situations, where his or her ability to control events is uncertain.

People with an internal locus of control have a more positive self-evaluation. They also tend to perform better in most employment situations, are more successful in their careers, earn more money, and are better suited for leadership positions. Internals also are more satisfied with their jobs, cope better in stressful situations, and are more motivated by performance-based reward systems.[28]

> McGraw Hill connect
>
> **SELF-ASSESSMENT 3.3: What Is Your Locus of Control?**

The Social Self

We began this topic by stating that an individual's self-concept exists at three levels: individual, relational, and collective. These three levels recognize two opposing human motives that influence how people view themselves.[29] One motivation is to be distinctive and different from other people. The individual self, called *personal identity* or *internal self-concept*, fulfills the need for distinctiveness because it involves defining ourselves by our personality, values, abilities, qualifications, achievements and other personal attributes. Everyone has a unique combination of personal characteristics, and we embrace this uniqueness to some degree. For instance, an unusual skill or accomplishment that distinguishes you from coworkers is part of your personal identity.

The opposing motivation—for inclusion and assimilation with other people—is fulfilled through our relational and collective self-concepts.[30] Human beings are social animals; they have an inherent drive to be associated with others and to be recognized as part of social communities. Thus, everyone defines himself or herself to some degree by his or her interpersonal and collective relationships.[31] *Social identity* (also called *external self-concept*) is the foundation of **social identity theory**, which says that people define themselves by the groups to which they belong or have an emotional attachment. For instance, someone might have a social identity as an American citizen, a University of Oregon alumnus, and an employee at Boston Consulting Group (see Exhibit 3.2).

Social identity is a complex combination of many memberships arranged in a hierarchy of importance. One factor that determines importance is how easily you are identified as a member of the reference group, such as by your gender, age, and ethnicity. A second factor is your minority status in a group. It is difficult to ignore your gender in a class where most other students are another gender, for example. In that context, gender tends to become a stronger defining feature of your social identity than it is in social settings where there are many people of your gender.

The group's status is another important social identity factor because association with the group makes us feel better about ourselves (i.e., self-enhancement).

Exhibit 3.2 Social Identity Theory Example

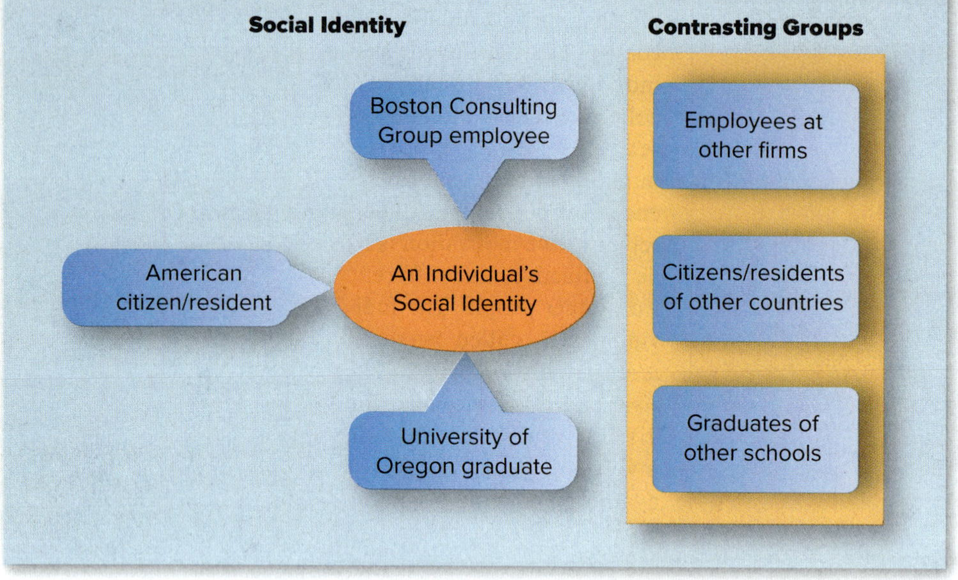

Medical doctors usually define themselves by their profession because of its high status. Some people describe themselves by where they work ("I work at Microsoft") because their employer has a good reputation. Others never mention where they work because their employer is noted for poor relations with employees or has a poor reputation in the community.[32]

Everyone tries to balance personal and social identities to some degree, but the priority for uniqueness (personal identities) versus relatedness (social identities) differs from one person to the next. People whose self-concepts are heavily defined by social rather than personal identities are more motivated to abide by team norms and more easily influenced by peer pressure. Those who place more emphasis on personal identities, on the other hand, speak out more frequently against the majority and are less motivated to follow the team's wishes. Furthermore, expressing disagreement with others is a sign of distinctiveness and can help employees form a clearer self-concept, particularly when that disagreement is based on differences in personal values.[33]

People whose self-concepts are heavily defined by social rather than personal identities are more motivated to abide by team norms and more easily influenced by peer pressure.
andresr/Getty Images

Self-Concept and Organizational Behavior

Self-concept has become a hot topic in the social sciences and is starting to bloom in organizational behavior research.[34] This section briefly noted that self-concept influences human perceptions, decision making, motivation, stress, team dynamics, leadership development, and several other OB topics. Consequently, we will refer to self-concept later in this chapter and in many other topics throughout this book.

LO3-2 Outline the perceptual process and discuss the effects of categorical thinking and mental models in that process.

PERCEIVING THE WORLD AROUND US

We spend considerable time perceiving ourselves, but most of our perceptual energy is directed toward the outer world. Whether as a forensic accountant, mechanical engineer, or senior executive, we need to make sense of our surroundings and to manage the conditions that challenge the accuracy of those perceptions. **Perception** is the process of receiving information about and making sense of the world around us. It includes determining which information to notice, as well as how to categorize and interpret it within the framework of our existing knowledge.

The perceptual process generally follows the steps shown in Exhibit 3.3. Perception begins when environmental stimuli are received through our senses. We are continually bombarded by external stimuli. Most are screened out; the rest are organized and interpreted. The process of attending to some information received by our senses and ignoring other information is called **selective attention**. Selective attention is influenced by characteristics of the person or object being perceived, particularly size, intensity, motion, repetition, and novelty. For example, a small, flashing red light on a nurses' workstation console is immediately noticed because it is bright (intensity), flashing (motion), and a rare event (novelty) and has symbolic meaning that a patient's vital signs are failing. Notice that selective attention also is influenced by the context in which the target is perceived. For instance, selective attention is triggered by things or people who might be out of context, such as someone with a foreign accent in a setting where most people have a local accent.

Characteristics of the perceiver also influence selective attention, usually without the perceiver's awareness.[35] When information is received through the senses, our brain quickly and nonconsciously assesses whether it is relevant or irrelevant to us and then attaches emotional markers (worry, happiness, boredom) to the retained information.[36] Emotional markers help us to store information in memory; those emotions are later reproduced when recalling the perceived information. The selective attention process is far from perfect, however. The Greek philosopher Plato acknowledged this imperfection long ago when he wrote that we see reality only as shadows reflecting against the rough wall of a cave.[37]

perception the process of receiving information about and making sense of the world around us

selective attention the process of attending to some information received by our senses and ignoring other information

confirmation bias the process of screening out information that is contrary to our values and assumptions, and to more readily accept confirming information

One selective attention bias is the effect of our assumptions and expectations about future events. You are more likely to notice a particular coworker's email among the daily avalanche of messages when you are expecting to receive that email (even more so if it is important). Unfortunately, expectations and assumptions also cause us to screen out potentially important information. In one study, students were asked to watch a 30-second video clip in which several people passed around two basketballs. Students in one group were instructed simply to watch the video clip. Most of them readily noticed a person dressed in a gorilla suit walking among the players for nine seconds and stopping to thump his or her chest. Students in a second group were asked to count the number of times one of the two basketballs was passed around. Only half of the people in this latter group noticed the intruding gorilla.[38]

Another selective attention problem, called **confirmation bias**, is the nonconscious tendency for people to screen out information that is contrary to their decisions, beliefs, values, and assumptions, while more readily accepting information that confirms those elements.[39] When we make important decisions, such as investing in a costly project, we tend to pay attention to information that supports that decision, ignore information that questions the wisdom of the decision, and more easily recall the supportive than the opposing information. Confirmation bias is a well-known perceptual problem in which law enforcement professionals form a theory too early in an investigation.[40]

Exhibit 3.3 Model of the Perceptual Process

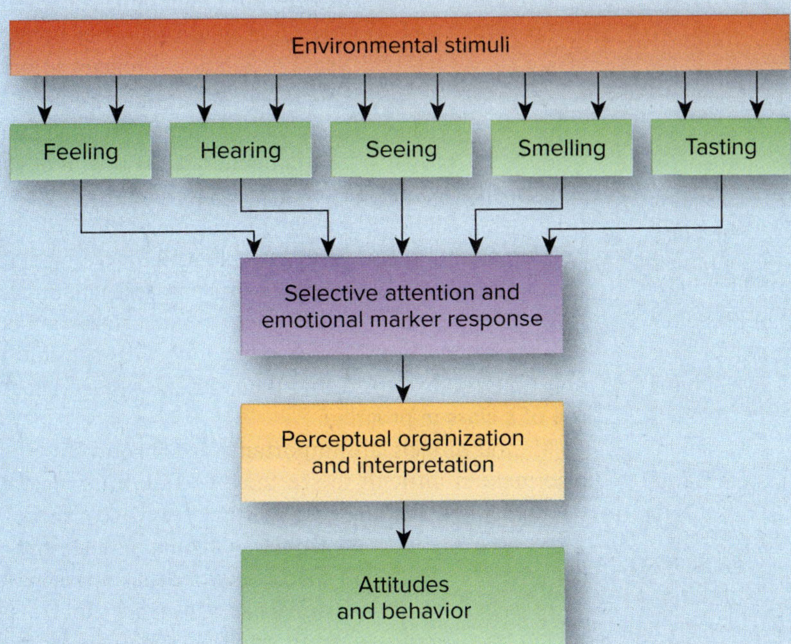

Perceptual Organization and Interpretation

We pay attention to a tiny fraction of the stimuli received by the senses. Even so, the human brain further reduces the huge volume and complexity

categorical thinking organizing people and objects into preconceived categories that are stored in our long-term memory

mental models knowledge structures that we develop to describe, explain, and predict the world around us

of selected information through various perceptual grouping strategies. Perceptual grouping occurs mostly without our awareness, yet it is the foundation for making sense of things and fulfilling our need for cognitive closure.

The most common and far-reaching perceptual grouping process is **categorical thinking**—the mostly nonconscious process of organizing people and objects into preconceived categories that are stored in our long-term memory.[42] We tend to group people together based on their observable similarity, such as gender, age, race, or clothing style. This categorization process also groups people together by their proximity to one another. If you notice a group of employees working in the same area and know that some of them are marketing staff, you will likely assume that the others in that group are also marketing staff.

One form of perceptual grouping involves filling in missing information about people or places.
Romolo Tavani/Shutterstock

Another form of perceptual grouping involves filling in missing information about people or places. Everyone wants to make sense of what goes on around them, so they rely on past images and experiences to make sense of similar situations. For instance, people assume what happened at a meeting that they didn't attend (e.g., who was there, where it was held). A related process is one in which people tend to see patterns that, in fact, are random events. For example, people incorrectly believe that a sports player or gambler with a string of wins is more likely to win next time as well.[43]

> **Theory like mist on eyeglasses. Obscure facts.**[41]
>
> —Robert Ellis and Helen Logan (screenwriters of the film *Charlie Chan in Egypt*, 1935)

The process of "making sense" of the world around us involves interpreting incoming information, not just organizing it. This happens as quickly as selecting and organizing because the previously mentioned emotional markers are tagged to incoming stimuli, which are essentially quick judgments about whether that information is good or bad for us. How much time does it take to make these quick judgments? Recent studies estimate that we make reliable (but not necessarily accurate) judgments about another individual's trustworthiness after viewing a facial image for as little as 50 milliseconds (1/20th of a second). In fact, our opinion regarding whether we like or trust a stranger is about the same whether we see the person's face for a minute or a fraction of a second.[44] Collectively, these studies reveal that selective attention, perceptual organization, and interpretation operate very quickly and to a large extent without our awareness.

Mental Models To achieve our goals with some degree of predictability and sanity, we need road maps of the environments in which we live. These road maps, called **mental models**, are knowledge structures that we develop to describe, explain, and predict the world around us.[45] They consist of visual or relational images in our mind, such as what the classroom looks like or what happens when we submit an assignment late. Mental models partly rely on the process of perceptual grouping to make sense of things; they fill in the missing pieces, including the causal connection among events. For example, you have a mental model about attending a class lecture or seminar, including assumptions or expectations about where the instructor and students arrange themselves in the room, how they ask and answer questions, and so forth. In other words, we have a mental image of a class in progress.

Mental models are important for sense making, yet they also make it difficult to see the world in different ways. For example, accounting professionals tend to see corporate problems from an accounting perspective, whereas marketing professionals see the same problems from a marketing perspective. Mental models also block our recognition of new opportunities.

McGraw Hill connect

SELF-ASSESSMENT 3.4: How Much Perceptual Structure Do You Need?

How do we change mental models? That's a tough challenge. After all, we developed these knowledge structures from several years of experience and reinforcement. The most important strategy is to be aware of and frequently question our mental models. We also need to be more aware of our assumptions, which are often based on mental models. Working with people from diverse backgrounds is another way to break out of existing mental models. Colleagues from different cultures and areas of expertise tend to have different mental models, so working with them makes our own assumptions more obvious.

LO3-3 Discuss how stereotyping; attribution; self-fulfilling prophecy; and the halo, false-consensus, recency, and primacy effects influence the perceptual process.

SPECIFIC PERCEPTUAL PROCESSES AND PROBLEMS

Within the general perceptual process are specific subprocesses and associated perceptual errors. In this section of the chapter, we examine several of these perceptual processes and biases as well as their implications for organizational behavior, beginning with the most widely known one: stereotyping.

Stereotyping in Organizations

Stereotyping is the perceptual process in which we assign characteristics to an identifiable group and then automatically transfer those features to anyone we believe is a member of that group.[46] The assigned characteristics tend to be difficult to observe, such as personality traits and abilities, but they also can include physical characteristics and a host of other qualities. If we learn that someone is a professor, for example, we implicitly assume the person is probably also intelligent, absent-minded, and socially challenged.

Stereotypes are formed to some extent from personal experience, but they are mainly provided to us through media images (e.g., movie characters) and other cultural prototypes. Consequently, stereotypes are shared beliefs across an entire society and sometimes across several cultures, rather than beliefs that differ from one person to the next. Most stereotypes have a few kernels of truth; they are more likely to characterize people within the group than the rest of us.[47] Still, stereotypes embellish or distort the kernels of truth and include other features that are false.

stereotyping the process of assigning traits to people based on their membership in a social category

Why People Stereotype People engage in stereotyping because, as a form of categorical thinking, it is usually a nonconscious "energy-saving" process that simplifies our understanding of the world. It is easier to remember features of a stereotype than the constellation of characteristics unique to each person we meet. A second reason is that we have an innate need to understand and anticipate how others will behave. We don't have much information when first meeting someone, so we rely on stereotypes to fill in the missing pieces. The higher the perceiver's need for cognitive closure, the higher their reliance on stereotypes.[48]

A third explanation for stereotyping is that it is motivated by the observer's need for social identity and self-enhancement. Earlier in this chapter we explained that people define themselves by the groups to which they belong or have an emotional attachment. They also are motivated to maintain a positive self-concept. This combination of social identity and self-enhancement leads to the stereotyping process of categorization, homogenization, and differentiation:[49]

- *Categorization.* Social identity is a comparative process, and the comparison begins by categorizing people into distinct groups. By viewing someone (including yourself) as a Texan, for example, you remove that person's individuality and, instead, see him or her as a prototypical representative of the group called Texans. This categorization then allows you to distinguish Texans from people who live in, say, California or Maine.
- *Homogenization.* To simplify the comparison process, we tend to think that people within each group are very similar to each other. For instance, we surmise that Texans collectively have similar attitudes and characteristics, whereas Californians collectively have their own set of characteristics. Of course, every individual is unique, but we often lose sight of this fact when thinking about our social identity and how we compare to people in other social groups.
- *Differentiation.* Along with categorizing and homogenizing people, we tend to assign more favorable characteristics to people in our groups than to people in other groups.[50] This differentiation is motivated by self-enhancement because being in a "better" group produces higher self-esteem. Differentiation is often subtle, but when out-group members threaten our self-concept, we are particularly motivated (often without our awareness) to assign negative stereotypes to them.

"Social identity and self-enhancement motivate us to engage in the stereotyping process of categorization, homogenization, and differentiation."

Problems with Stereotyping Everyone engages in stereotyping, yet it is highly inaccurate. Most features of a stereotype are distorted and embellished to such an extent that they describe very few people in the group. Even though a stereotype often has kernels of truth, that information doesn't describe everyone—often less than the majority—of members in the category. As a result, stereotyping leads to perceptual biases. For instance, the traditional accountant stereotype (boring, cautious, calculating) perhaps describes a few accountants, but it is certainly not characteristic of all, or even most, people in this profession. Nevertheless, when someone is categorized as an accountant, the nonobservable stereotypical features of accountants are transferred to that individual, even though we have no evidence that he or she actually has those characteristics.

Most features of a stereotype are distorted and embellished to such an extent that they describe very few people in the group.
wavebreakmedia/Shutterstock

A second problem with stereotypes is that they generate **stereotype threat**. This is a condition whereby members of a group are so concerned about the negative stereotype assigned to their group that they end up displaying the stereotype trait they are trying to avoid.[51] Stereotype threat occurs because people anxiously try to avoid confirming the undesirable stereotype traits of their group and try to push the negative image from their mind. These two cognitive activities divert energy and attention, which makes it more difficult to perform the task well. The negative stereotype also can weaken self-efficacy; it is difficult to be confident in your ability when your group's stereotype suggests otherwise.

For example, women perform worse on math and science tests when sensitized to the generally false but widely held belief that women perform worse than men in these subjects. They also tend to have lower scores when there are few women in the group being tested. Women achieve much higher scores when the gender stereotype or their minority status is not apparent, such as when taking the test with many women in the class. Almost anyone can be affected by stereotype threat, but studies have particularly observed it for women, some minority groups, and older people.

A third problem with stereotyping is that it lays the foundation for unfair discrimination. Most of this perceptual bias occurs as *unintentional (systemic) discrimination*, whereby decision makers rely on stereotypes to establish notions of the "ideal" person in specific roles. Those who don't fit the ideal tend to receive a less favorable evaluation than someone who is compatible with the occupational stereotype.

Unintentional systemic discrimination is particularly evident in employment and salary decisions. Consider the following example: Science faculty from several research intensive universities were given the fictitious application materials of either a male or female undergraduate student who was applying for a science laboratory manager job. The applications were identical other than the name and gender of the applicant, yet the male applicant received significantly higher ratings than the female applicant on competence and hireability. The male applicant also received a 15 percent higher recommended salary than did the female applicant. Female faculty exhibited as much gender bias as the male faculty.[52]

Worse than systemic discrimination is *intentional discrimination* or *prejudice*, in which people hold unfounded negative attitudes toward people belonging to a particular stereotyped group.[53] Systemic discrimination is implicit, automatic, and unintentional, whereas intentional discrimination deliberately puts the target person at an unfair disadvantage.

If stereotyping is such a problem, shouldn't we try to avoid this process altogether? Unfortunately, it's not that simple. Most experts agree that categorical thinking (including stereotyping) is an automatic and nonconscious process. Specialized training programs can minimize stereotype activation to some extent, but for the most part the process is hardwired in our brain cells.[54] Also remember that stereotyping helps us in several valuable (although fallible) ways described earlier: minimizing mental effort, filling in missing information, and supporting our social identity.

Stereotype *activation* is automatic and nonconscious, but the good news is that we can minimize stereotype *application* – the extent to which we rely on that information. In other words, we

> **Stereotype *activation* is automatic and nonconscious, but we can minimize stereotype *application*—the extent to which we rely on that information.**

automatically categorize people and assign stereotypic traits to them, but we can consciously minimize our reliance on that stereotypic information.[55] Later in this chapter, we identify ways to minimize stereotype application and other perceptual biases.

Attribution Theory

Another widely discussed perceptual phenomenon in organizational settings is the **attribution process**.[56] Attribution involves forming beliefs about the causes of behavior or events. Generally, we perceive whether an observed behavior or event is caused mainly by characteristics of the person (internal factors) or by the environment (external factors). Internal factors include the person's ability or motivation, whereas external factors include resources, coworker support, or luck. If someone doesn't show up for an important meeting, for instance, we infer either internal attributions (the coworker is forgetful, lacks motivation, etc.) or external attributions (traffic, a family emergency, etc.) to make sense of the person's absence.

People rely on the three attribution rules—consistency, distinctiveness, and consensus—to decide whether someone's behavior and performance are mainly caused by their personal characteristics or environmental influences (see Exhibit 3.4).[57] To illustrate how these three attribution rules operate, imagine a situation in which an employee is making poor-quality products on a particular machine. We would probably conclude that the employee lacks skill or motivation (an internal attribution) if the employee consistently makes poor-quality products on this machine (high consistency), the employee makes poor-quality products on other machines (low distinctiveness), and other employees make good-quality products on this machine (low consensus). In contrast, we would believe something is wrong with the machine (an external attribution) if the employee consistently makes poor-quality products on this machine (high consistency), the employee makes good-quality products on other machines (high distinctiveness), and other employees make poor-quality products on this machine (high consensus).

stereotype threat an individual's concern about confirming a negative stereotype about his or her group

attribution process the perceptual process of deciding whether an observed behavior or event is caused largely by internal or external factors

Exhibit 3.4 Attribution Theory Rules

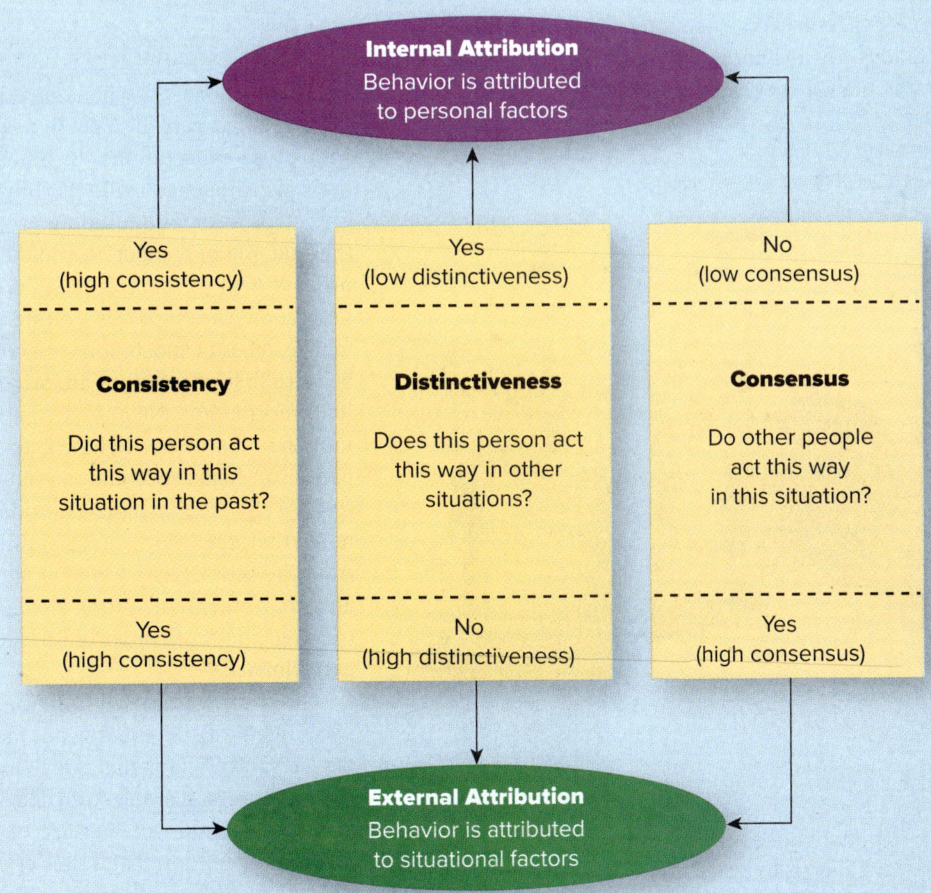

self-serving bias the tendency to attribute our favorable outcomes to internal factors and our failures to external factors

fundamental attribution error the tendency to see the person rather than the situation as the main cause of that person's behavior

self-fulfilling prophecy the perceptual process in which our expectations about another person cause that person to act more consistently with those expectations

Notice that "consistency" is high for both internal and external attributions. This occurs because low consistency (the person's output quality on this machine is sometimes good and sometimes poor) weakens our confidence about whether the source of the problem is the person or the machine. In other words, distinctiveness and consensus determine whether the attribution should be internal or external, whereas consistency determines how confident we should be in that attribution.

The attribution process is important because understanding cause–effect relationships enables us to work more effectively with others and to assign praise or blame to them.[58] Suppose a coworker didn't complete his or her task on a team project. You would approach this situation differently if you believed the coworker was lazy or lacked sufficient skill (an internal attribution) than if you believed the poor performance was due to lack of time or resources available to the coworker (an external attribution). We also react differently to attributions of our own behavior and performance. Students who make internal attributions about their poor grades, for instance, are more likely to drop out of their programs than if they make external attributions about those grades.[59]

Attribution Errors The attribution process is susceptible to errors. One such error is **self-serving bias**—the tendency to attribute our failures to external causes more than internal causes, while successes are due more to internal than external factors.[60] Simply put, we take credit for our successes and blame others or the situation for our mistakes. In annual reports, for example, executives mainly refer to their personal qualities as reasons for the company's successes and to external factors (competitors, economic problems, skill shortages, etc.) as reasons for the company's failures.[61] Self-serving bias occurs mainly because of the self-enhancement process described earlier in this chapter. By pointing to external causes of their own failures, and internal causes of their successes, people generate a more positive self-concept.

Another widely studied attribution error, **fundamental attribution error** (also called *correspondence bias*), is the tendency to overemphasize internal causes of another person's behavior and to discount or ignore external causes of his or her behavior.[62] We are more likely to attribute a coworker's late arrival for work to lack of motivation rather than to situational constraints (such as traffic congestion). This occurs because observers can't easily see the external factors that constrain another person's behavior. Also, people like to think that human beings (not the situation) are the prime sources of their behavior. Although fundamental attribution error does occur, recent reviews suggest it may be less common than previously thought.[63]

Self-Fulfilling Prophecy

Self-fulfilling prophecy occurs when our expectations about another person cause that person to act in a way that is consistent with those expectations. In other words, our perceptions can influence reality. Exhibit 3.5 illustrates the four steps in the self-fulfilling prophecy process using the example of a supervisor and a subordinate.[64] The process begins when the supervisor forms expectations about the employee's future behavior and performance. These expectations are sometimes inaccurate because first impressions are usually formed from limited information. Next, the supervisor's expectations influence his or her behavior toward employees. In particular, high-expectancy employees (those expected to do well) receive more emotional support through nonverbal cues (e.g., more smiling and eye contact from the boss), more frequent and valuable feedback and reinforcement, more challenging goals, better training, and more opportunities to demonstrate good performance.[65]

The third step in self-fulfilling prophecy includes two effects of the supervisor's behavior on the employee. One effect is that a high-expectancy employee learns more skills and knowledge than does a low-expectancy employee because of better training and more practice opportunities. The other effect is that the high-expectancy employee becomes more self-confident, which results in stronger motivation and willingness to set challenging

The attribution process is important because understanding cause–effect relationships enables us to work more effectively with others and to assign praise or blame to them.
Wavebreakmedia Ltd UC4/Alamy Stock Photo

halo effect a perceptual error whereby our general impression of a person, usually based on one prominent characteristic, colors our perception of other characteristics of that person

false-consensus effect a perceptual error in which we overestimate the extent to which others have beliefs and characteristics similar to our own

Exhibit 3.5 The Self-Fulfilling Prophecy Cycle

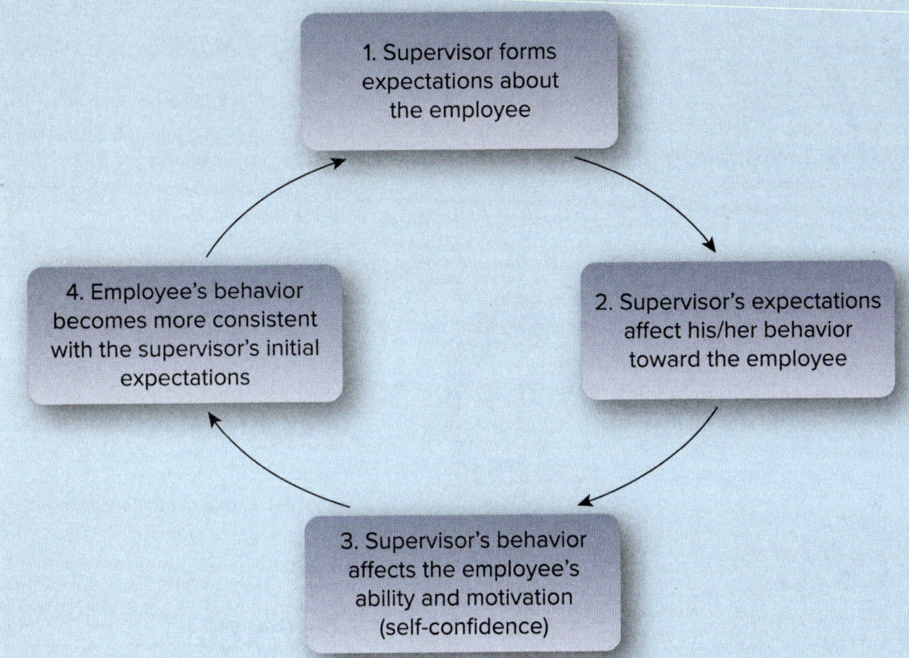

goals.[66] In the final step, high-expectancy employees are more motivated and skilled, resulting in better performance, while the opposite is true of low-expectancy employees.

Self-fulfilling prophecy has been observed in many contexts. In one study, four Israeli Defense Force combat command course instructors were told that one-third of the incoming trainees had high command potential, one-third had normal potential, and the rest had unknown potential. The trainees had been randomly placed into these categories by the researchers, but the instructors were led to believe that the information they received was accurate. Consistent with self-fulfilling prophecy, high-expectancy soldiers performed significantly better by the end of the course than did trainees in the other groups. They also had more favorable attitudes toward the course and the instructor's leadership effectiveness. An analysis of dozens of leader intervention studies over the years found that self-fulfilling prophecy is one of the most powerful leadership effects on follower behavior and performance.[67]

Contingencies of Self-Fulfilling Prophecy Self-fulfilling prophecy has a stronger effect at the beginning of a relationship, such as when employees are first hired. It is also stronger when several people (rather than just one person) hold the same expectations of the individual. In other words, we might be able to ignore one person's doubts about our potential but not the collective doubts of several people. The self-fulfilling prophecy effect is also stronger among people with a history of low achievement. These people tend to have lower self-esteem, so they are more easily influenced by others' opinions of them.[68]

The main lesson from the self-fulfilling prophecy literature is that leaders need to develop and maintain positive, yet realistic, expectations toward all employees. Communicating realistic hope and optimism is so important that it has been identified as one of the critical success factors for physicians and surgeons. Training programs that make leaders aware of the power of positive expectations seem to have minimal effect, however. Instead, generating positive expectations and hope depends on a corporate culture of support and learning. Hiring supervisors who are inherently optimistic toward their staff is another way of increasing the incidence of positive self-fulfilling prophecies.[69]

Other Perceptual Effects

Self-fulfilling prophecy, attribution, and stereotyping are among the most common perceptual processes and biases in organizational settings, but there are many others. Four additional biases that have received attention in organizational settings are briefly described below.

Halo Effect The **halo effect** occurs when our general impression of a person, usually based on one prominent characteristic, distorts our perception of other characteristics of that person.[70] If a supervisor who values punctuality notices that an employee is sometimes late for work, the supervisor might form a negative overall opinion of the employee and evaluate that person's other performance dimensions unfavorably as well. The halo effect is most likely to occur when important information about the other person is unavailable or we are not sufficiently motivated to search for it. Instead, we use our general impression of the person to fill in the missing information.

False-Consensus Effect The **false-consensus effect** (also called *similar-to-me effect*) occurs when people overestimate the extent to which others have similar beliefs or behaviors to their own.[71] Employees who are thinking of quitting their jobs overestimate the percentage of coworkers who also are thinking about

recency effect a perceptual error in which the most recent information dominates our perception of others

primacy effect a perceptual error in which we quickly form an opinion of people based on the first information we receive about them

Johari window a model of mutual understanding that encourages disclosure and feedback to increase our own open area and reduce the blind, hidden, and unknown areas

First Impressions Count in Job Applications[74]

77% of 1,138 employers say they instantly reject résumés with typos or bad grammar.

67% of 1,014 employers say they would not hire an applicant who sends text messages or uses their phone during the job interview.

48% of 1,014 employers say they would not hire an applicant who talks negatively during the job interview about current or previous employers.

Some Résumé Gaffes

"Dear Sir or **Madman**."

"Assisted company executives with travel **arraignments**."

"I would like to work for a company that is **very lax** when it comes to **tardiness**."

"Instrumental for **ruining** entire operation for a Midwest chain store."

"My last employer **fried** me for no reason."

"Earned a diploma from a very **repudiated** college."

"Hope to hear from you, **shorty**."

32% of 2,076 employers say they automatically dismiss a job applicant whose résumé includes a large amount of wording from the job posting.

23% of 1,138 employers say they spend less than 30 seconds looking at a résumé.

(Photo): pathdoc/Shutterstock

quitting, for example. The false-consensus effect occurs partly because we are comforted by the belief that others are similar to us, particularly regarding less acceptable or divisive behavior. A second explanation is that we interact more with people who have similar views and frequent interaction with like-minded people causes us to overestimate how common those views are throughout the company or society.

A third explanation for the false-consensus effect is confirmation bias. We are more likely to notice and remember people whose views are similar to our own and ignore or forget about incidents in which individuals express views that oppose our own. A fourth explanation is that our social identity process homogenizes people within groups, so we tend to think that everyone in that group has similar opinions and behavior, including the false-consensus attitude or behavior.

Recency Effect The **recency effect** occurs when the most recent information dominates our perceptions.[72] This perceptual bias is most common when people (especially those with limited experience) make a decision involving complex information. For instance, auditors need to digest large volumes of information for their assessments about financial documents. They are susceptible to recency effect because the most recent information received prior to rendering their judgment may receive more weight than information received at the beginning of the audit. Similarly, when supervisors evaluate the performance of employees over the previous year, the most recent performance information dominates the evaluation because it is the most easily recalled.

Primacy Effect The **primacy effect** is our tendency to rely on the first information we receive about people to quickly form an opinion of them.[73] This perceptual bias is captured in the well-known statement: First impressions are lasting impressions. We rapidly organize and interpret new information to fulfill our inherent need to make sense of the situation and, in particular, to trust others. The problem is that first impressions—particularly negative first impressions—are difficult to change. After categorizing someone, we tend to select subsequent information that supports our first impression and screen out information that opposes that impression.

LO3-4 Discuss three ways to improve perceptions, with specific application to organizational situations.

IMPROVING PERCEPTIONS

We can't bypass the perceptual process, but we should try to minimize perceptual biases and distortions. Three potentially effective ways to improve perceptions include awareness of perceptual biases, self-awareness, and meaningful interaction.

Awareness of Perceptual Biases

One of the most obvious and widely practiced ways to reduce perceptual biases is by knowing that they exist. For example, diversity awareness training tries to minimize discrimination by making people aware of systemic discrimination as well as prejudices that occur through stereotyping. This training also attempts to dispel myths about people from various cultural and demographic groups. Awareness of perceptual biases can reduce these biases to some extent by making people more mindful of their thoughts and actions. However, awareness training has only a limited effect.[75] One problem is that teaching people to reject incorrect stereotypes has the unintended effect of reinforcing rather than reducing reliance on those stereotypes. Another problem is that diversity training is ineffective for people with deeply held prejudices against those groups.

Improving Self-Awareness

A more successful way to minimize perceptual biases is by increasing self-awareness.[76] By discovering our own perceptual biases, we begin to reduce those biases through increased open-mindedness toward others. Self-awareness is also the first step in a person's ability to become an authentic leader (see Chapter 11). Essentially, leaders need to understand their own values, strengths, and biases as a foundation for creating a vision and leading others toward that vision.[77]

But how do we become more self-aware? One approach is to complete formal tests that indicate any implicit biases we might have toward others. One such instrument is the Implicit Association Test (IAT), which attempts to detect subtle racial, age, gender, disability, and other forms of bias by associating positive and negative words with specific groups of people.[78] Although the reliability and accuracy of the IAT is still being debated by scholars, the test does seem to provide some evidence of specific biases. Many people are much more cautious about their stereotypes and prejudices after discovering that their test results show a personal bias against older people or individuals from different ethnic backgrounds.[79]

Another way to reduce perceptual biases through increased self-awareness is by applying the **Johari window**.[81] Developed by Joseph Luft and Harry Ingram (hence the name "Johari"), this model of self-awareness and mutual understanding divides information about you into four "windows"—open, blind, hidden, and unknown—based on whether your own values, beliefs, and experiences are known to you and to others (see Exhibit 3.6). The *open area* includes information about you that is known both to you and to others. The *blind area* refers to information that is known to others but not to you. For example, your colleagues might notice that you are self-conscious and awkward when meeting the company's chief executive officer, but you are unaware of this fact. Information known to you but unknown to others is found in the *hidden area*. Finally, the *unknown area* includes your values, beliefs, and experiences that are buried so deeply that neither you nor others are aware of them.

The main objective of the Johari window is to increase the size of the open area so that both you and your colleagues are aware of your perceptual limitations. This objective is

OB THEORY TO PRACTICE

Nonconscous Bias Training at Manulife

Manulife Financial (which owns John Hancock Financial) strives to be an inclusive workplace in which everyone can bring their authentic and whole self to work. To achieve this, the company's entire global senior executive group and more than 26,000 of its managers and employees have completed a nonconscious bias training program. The program gives each participant confidential feedback on his or her personal biases (through the IAT or similar test) and provides guidance on how to manage those perceptions and attitudes. "There needs to be a focus on inclusion, and unconscious bias training is one way that we're working to shift our culture," explains Sandeep Tatla, Manulife's Global Head of Diversity & Inclusion.[80]

GaudiLab/Shutterstock

Exhibit 3.6 Johari Window Model of Self-Awareness and Mutual Understanding

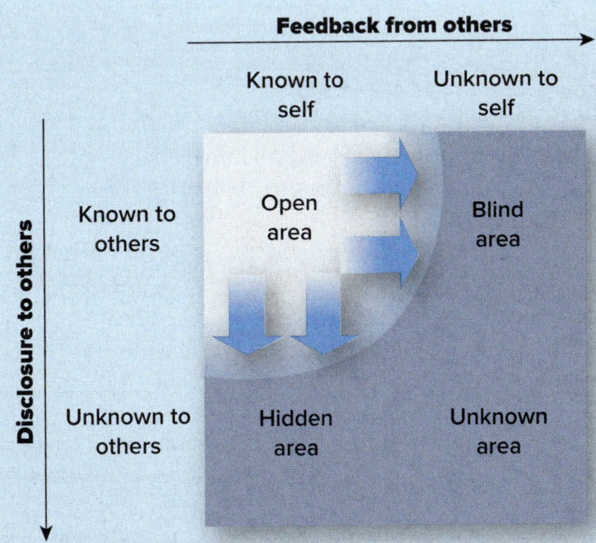

Source: Based on J. Luft, *Of Human Interaction* (Palo Alto, CA: National Press Books, 1969).

contact hypothesis a theory stating that the more we interact with someone, the less prejudiced or perceptually biased we will be against that person

empathy a person's understanding of and sensitivity to the feelings, thoughts, and situations of others

partly accomplished by reducing the hidden area through *disclosure*—informing others of your beliefs, feelings, and experiences that may influence the work relationship. The open area also increases through *feedback* from others about your behavior. Feedback reduces your blind area because, according to recent studies, people near you are good sources of information about many (but not all) of your traits and behaviors.[82] Finally, the combination of disclosure and feedback occasionally produces revelations about you in the unknown area.

The Johari window and Implicit Association Test improve self-awareness, which potentially minimizes biases by being more open-minded and nonjudgmental. However, two problems may limit these benefits. First, implicit biases are similar to stereotypes—they are automatically activated and, consequently, difficult to prevent. However, as with stereotypes, even though implicit biases are still activated, we can potentially minimize the application of those biases in our decisions and behavior. The second problem is that perceptual bias self-awareness can cause people to become more sensitized and self-conscious when interacting with people who are the target of that bias.[83]

Meaningful Interaction

Meaningful interaction is any activity in which people engage in valued (meaningful, not trivial) activities.[84] This process is founded on the **contact hypothesis**, which states that, under specific conditions, people who interact with each other will be less perceptually biased because they have a more personal understanding of the other person and their group.[85] Meaningful interaction occurs when executives work beside front line staff or when any employee performs tasks with co-workers from other parts of the organization. It is strongest when people work closely and frequently with each other on a shared goal that requires mutual cooperation and reliance. Furthermore, everyone should have equal status in that context, should be engaged in a meaningful task, and should have positive experiences with each other in those interactions.

Meaningful interaction reduces dependence on stereotypes because it diminishes psychological distance, improves our knowledge about individuals, and helps us to observe their unique attributes in action.[86] Meaningful interaction also potentially improves empathy toward others. **Empathy** refers to understanding and being sensitive to the feelings, thoughts, and situations of others.[87] People empathize when they visualize themselves in the other person's place as if they are the other person. This perceptual experience is cognitive, emotional, and experiential. In other words, empathy occurs when we understand the other person's situation, feel his or her emotions in that context, and to some degree react to those thoughts and feelings as the other person does. Empathizing reduces attribution errors by improving our sensitivity to the external causes of another person's performance and behavior. However, trying to empathize with others without spending time with them might actually increase rather than reduce stereotyping and other perceptual biases.[88]

McGraw Hill connect

SELF-ASSESSMENT 3.5: How Strong Is Your Perspective Taking (Cognitive Empathy)?

McGraw Hill connect

SELF-ASSESSMENT 3.6: How Strong Is Your Emotional Empathy?

Study Checklist

Connect® is available for *M Organizational Behavior*. Additional resources include:

✓ Exercises:

- **Case Analysis:** Apply concepts within the context of a real-world situation.
- **Click and Drag:** Helps make the connection between theory and application through matching, ranking, or grouping activities.
- **Video Case:** See management in action through interactive videos.
- **Self-Assessment:** Designed to promote student self-awareness and reflection, these research-based surveys contain detailed feedback for students.
- **Application-Based Activities:** These highly interactive, application- and analysis-based exercises allow students to take on specific roles to complete management-related tasks within a real-world context.

✓ **SmartBook 2.0™**—Smartbook 2.0 is an adaptive learning solution that provides personalized learning to individual student needs, continually adapts to pinpoint knowledge gaps and focuses learning on concepts requiring additional study. It fosters more productive learning, takes the guesswork out of what to study, and helps students better prepare for class.

Notes

1. J. Richardson, "Nando's Takes on Stereotypes with Their Hilarious New Ad: #YouPeople [Video]," *The South African*, November 26, 2018; J. Tennant, "#New-Campaign: All You People, This Ad's for You," *Advertising News*, November 26, 2018; *Nando's–#YOUPEOPLE*, YouTube (South Africa: M&C Saatchi Abel, 2018), https://www.youtube.com/watch?v=Rl8wYtCgZAk (accessed April 8, 2020).
2. J. Schaubroeck, Y.J. Kim, and A.C. Peng, "The Self-Concept in Organizational Psychology: Clarifying and Differentiating the Constructs," in *International Review of Industrial and Organizational Psychology* (New York: Wiley, 2012), 1–38; J.J. Skowronski and C. Sedikides, "Evolution of Self," in *Encyclopedia of Evolutionary Psychological Science*, ed. T.K. Shackelford and V.A. Weekes-Shackelford (Cham: Springer International Publishing, 2018), 1–10.
3. V.L. Vignoles, S.J. Schwartz, and K. Luyckx, "Introduction: Toward an Integrative View of Identity," in *Handbook of Identity Theory and Research*, ed. J.S. Schwartz, K. Luyckx, and L.V. Vignoles (New York: Springer New York, 2011), 1–27; L. Gaertner et al., "A Motivational Hierarchy within: Primacy of the Individual Self, Relational Self, or Collective Self?" *Journal of Experimental Social Psychology* 48, no. 5 (2012).
4. O.W. Holmes, *The Autocrat of the Breakfast-Table* (Boston: Phillips, Sampson, 1858), 58–59. This quotation, which Steve McShane slightly rewrote to remove sexist language, has a long and convoluted history. Pioneering psychology professor William James is almost always cited as the source, yet there is no evidence that he wrote this statement or anything similar. The first attribution of this quotation to William James may have been a 1958 *RAND Memoranda* publication (p. 925), and later in *Reader's Digest* (1962). Even if James did publish something similar, it is a highly condensed version of the humorous discussion of "six persons" that Oliver Wendell Holmes Sr. published decades before James began his career. Most likely, a RAND Corporation editor crafted this quotation from vague memory of Holmes's story and misattributed William James as the author because one of Holmes's characters in the story was "James." We cite Holmes as the source because he wrote the story from which this quotation is derived.
5. E.J. Koch and J.A. Shepperd, "Is Self-Complexity Linked to Better Coping? A Review of the Literature," *Journal of Personality* 72, no. 4 (2004): 727–60; A.R. McConnell, "The Multiple Self-Aspects Framework: Self-Concept Representation and Its Implications," *Personality and Social Psychology Review* 15, no. 1 (2011): 3–27; L.F. Emery, C. Walsh, and E.B. Slotter, "Knowing Who You Are and Adding to It: Reduced Self-Concept Clarity Predicts Reduced Self-Expansion," *Social Psychological and Personality Science* 6, no. 3 (2015): 259–66.
6. C.M. Brown et al., "Between Two Selves: Comparing Global and Local Predictors of Speed of Switching between Self-Aspects," *Self and Identity* 15, no. 1 (2016): 72–89.
7. J.D. Campbell et al., "Self-Concept Clarity: Measurement, Personality Correlates, and Cultural Boundaries," *Journal of Personality and Social Psychology* 70, no. 1 (1996): 141–56.
8. J. Lodi-Smith and B.W. Roberts, "Getting to Know Me: Social Role Experiences and Age Differences in Self-Concept Clarity during Adulthood," *Journal of Personality* 78, no. 5 (2010): 1383–410.
9. E.J. Koch and J.A. Shepperd, "Is Self-Complexity Linked to Better Coping? A Review of the Literature," *Journal of Personality* 72, no. 4 (2004): 727–60; A.T. Church et al., "Relating Self-Concept Consistency to Hedonic and Eudaimonic Well-Being in Eight Cultures," *Journal of Cross-Cultural Psychology* 45, no. 5 (2014): 695–712, https://doi.org/10.1177/0022022114527347; A.W. Hanley and E.L. Garland, "Clarity of Mind: Structural Equation Modeling of Associations between Dispositional Mindfulness, Self-Concept Clarity and Psychological Well-Being," *Personality and Individual Differences* 106 (2017): 334–39, https://doi.org/10.1016/j.paid.2016.10.028; M. Parise et al., "Self-Concept Clarity and Psychological Adjustment in Adolescence: The Mediating Role of Emotion Regulation," *Personality and Individual Differences* 138 (2019): 363–65, https://doi.org/10.1016/j.paid.2018.10.023.
10. A.T. Brook, J. Garcia, and M.A. Fleming, "The Effects of Multiple Identities on Psychological Well-Being," *Personality and Social Psychology Bulletin* 34, no. 12 (2008): 1588–600; A.T. Church et al., "Relating Self-Concept Consistency to Hedonic and Eudaimonic Well-Being in Eight Cultures," *Journal of Cross-Cultural Psychology* 45, no. 5 (2014): 695–712.
11. J.D. Campbell, "Self-Esteem and Clarity of the Self-Concept," *Journal of Personality and Social Psychology* 59, no. 3 (1990).
12. S. Hannah et al., "The Psychological and Neurological Bases of Leader Self-Complexity and Effects on Adaptive Decision-Making," *Journal of Applied Psychology* 98, no. 3 (2013): 393–411; S.J. Creary, B.B. Caza, and L M. Roberts, "Out of the Box? How Managing a Subordinate's Multiple Identities Affects the Quality of a Manager-Subordinate Relationship," *Academy of Management Review* 40, no. 4 (2015): 538–62.
13. C. Peus et al., "Authentic Leadership: An Empirical Test of Its Antecedents, Consequences, and Mediating Mechanisms," *Journal of Business Ethics* 107, no. 3 (2012): 331–48; F.O. Walumbwa, M.A. Maidique, and C. Atamanik, "Decision-Making in a Crisis: What Every Leader Needs to Know," *Organizational Dynamics* 43, no. 4 (2014): 284–93; B. Mittal, "Self-Concept Clarity: Exploring Its Role in Consumer Behavior," *Journal of Economic Psychology* 46 (2015): 98–110.
14. C.L. Guenther and M.D. Alicke, "Deconstructing the Better-Than-Average Effect," *Journal of Personality and Social Psychology* 99, no. 5 (2010): 755–70; S. Loughnan et al., "Universal Biases in Self-Perception: Better and More Human Than Average," *British Journal of Social Psychology* 49 (2010): 627–36; D.L. Ferris and C. Sedikides, "Self-Enhancement in Organizations," in *The Self at Work: Fundamental Theory and Research*, ed. D.L. Ferris, R.E. Johnson, and C. Sedikides (New York: Routledge, 2018), 91–118.
15. D. Dunning, C. Heath, and J.M. Suls, "Flawed Self-Assessment: Implications for Health, Education, and the Workplace," *Psychological Science in the Public Interest* 5, no. 3 (2004): 69–106; D.A. Moore, "Not So above Average after All: When People Believe They Are Worse Than Average and Its Implications for Theories of Bias in Social Comparison," *Organizational Behavior and Human Decision Processes* 102, no. 1 (2007): 42–58.
16. D. Gosselin et al., "Comparative Optimism among Drivers: An Intergenerational Portrait," *Accident Analysis & Prevention* 42, no. 2 (2010): 734–40; P.M. Picone, G. Battista Dagnino, and A. Minà, "The Origin of Failure: A Multidisciplinary Appraisal of the Hubris Hypothesis and Proposed Research Agenda," *Academy of Management Perspectives* 28, no. 4 (2014): 447–68; G. Chen, C. Crossland, and S. Luo, "Making the Same Mistake All over Again: CEO Overconfidence and Corporate Resistance to Corrective Feedback," *Strategic Management Journal* 36, no. 10 (2015): 1513–35; M. Dufner et al., "Self-Enhancement and Psychological Adjustment: A Meta-Analytic Review," *Personality and Social Psychology Review* 23, no. 1 (2019): 48–72, https://doi.org/10.1177/1088868318756467.

17. This quotation has been cited since the 1930s, yet we were unable to find it in any of Dewey's writing. The earliest known reference to this quotation is Dale Carnegie's famous self-help book, where the statement is attributed to Dewey. See D. Carnegie, *How to Win Friends and Influence People*, 1st ed. (New York: Simon & Schuster, 1936), 43–44 (p. 19 in later editions).

18. W.B. Swann Jr., P.J. Rentfrow, and J.S. Guinn, "Self-Verification: The Search for Coherence," in *Handbook of Self and Identity*, ed. M.R. Leary and J. Tagney (New York: Guilford, 2002), 367–83; D.M. Cable and V.S. Kay, "Striving for Self-Verification during Organizational Entry," *Academy of Management Journal* 55, no. 2 (2012): 360–80.

19. T. Kwang and W.B. Swann, "Do People Embrace Praise Even When They Feel Unworthy? A Review of Critical Tests of Self-Enhancement versus Self-Verification," *Personality and Social Psychology Review* 14 (2010): 263–80; G.S. Preuss and M.D. Alicke, "My Worst Faults and Misdeeds: Self-Criticism and Self-Enhancement Can Co-Exist," *Self and Identity* 16 (2017): 645–63.

20. M.R. Leary, "Motivational and Emotional Aspects of the Self," *Annual Review of Psychology* 58, no. 1 (2007): 317–44; A. Meister, K.A. Jehn, and S.M.B. Thatcher, "Feeling Misidentified: The Consequences of Internal Identity Asymmetries for Individuals at Work," *Academy of Management Review* 39, no. 4 (2014): 488–512.

21. We have described three components of core self-evaluation. The remaining component is the personality trait emotional stability, which was described in Chapter 2. However, personality is a behavior tendency, whereas core self-evaluation includes only "evaluation-focused" variables. Some also question whether locus of control is part of self-evaluation. See R.E. Johnson, C.C. Rosen, and P.E. Levy, "Getting to the Core of Core Self-Evaluation: A Review and Recommendations," *Journal of Organizational Behavior* 29 (2008): 391–413; C.-H. Chang et al., "Core Self-Evaluations: A Review and Evaluation of the Literature," *Journal of Management* 38 (2012): 81–128; R.E. Johnson et al., "Getting to the Core of Locus of Control: Is It an Evaluation of the Self or the Environment?" *Journal of Applied Psychology* 100 (2015): 1568–78.

22. E. Dockterman, "Google Invests $50 Million to Close the Tech Gender Gap," *Time*, June 21, 2014, 16; M. della Cava, "Google, Pixar Team Up to Teach Kids Joy of Coding," *USA Today*, December 7, 2015, B4; C. Preece, "Is a Lack of Self-Belief Pushing Girls Away from STEM?" *IT Pro*, February 9, 2016; A.T. Kearney and Your Life, *Tough Choices: The Real Reasons A-Level Students Are Steering Clear of Science and Maths* (London: A.T. Kearney, February 2016).

23. W.B. Swann Jr., C. Chang-Schneider, and K.L. McClarty, "Do People's Self-Views Matter?: Self-Concept and Self-Esteem in Everyday Life," *American Psychologist* 62, no. 2 (2007): 84–94; J.L. Pierce, D.G. Gardner, and C. Crowley, "Organization-Based Self-Esteem and Well-Being: Empirical Examination of a Spillover Effect," *European Journal of Work and Organizational Psychology* 25, no. 2 (2016): 181–99.

24. A. Bandura, *Self-Efficacy: The Exercise of Control* (New York: W. H. Freeman, 1997); J.B. Vancouver and J.D. Purl, "A Computational Model of Self-Efficacy's Various Effects on Performance: Moving the Debate Forward.," *Journal of Applied Psychology* 102 (2017): 599–616.

25. G. Chen, S.M. Gully, and D. Eden, "Validation of a New General Self-Efficacy Scale," *Organizational Research Methods* 4, no. 1 (2001): 62–83.

26. S. Mautz, "A New Deloitte Study of 10,455 Millennials Shows They Need Help Improving These 4 Skills," *Inc.*, May 21, 2018; J. Gitlin, "Why Employees Crave More Training and How Employers Aren't Delivering It," SurveyMonkey, *Curiosity at Work* (blog), August 30, 2018, https://www.surveymonkey.com/curiosity/why-employees-crave-more-training-and-how-employers-arent-delivering-it/; "Getting to Equal," news release (Glasgow: My Confidence Matters, 2019), https://www.myconfidencematters.com/research-2019; "The TINYpulse 2019 Employee Engagement Report: The End of Employee Loyalty" (Seattle: TINYpulse, February 2019); "Gartner Says 45% of Managers Lack Confidence To Help Employees Develop the Skills They Need Today," news release (London: Gartner, September 18, 2019).

27. J.B. Rotter, "Generalized Expectancies for Internal versus External Control of Reinforcement," *Psychological Monographs* 80 (1966): 1–28; D.A. Cobb-Clark, "Locus of Control and the Labor Market," *IZA Journal of Labor Economics* 4 (2015): 1–19; B.M. Galvin et al., "Changing the Focus of Locus (of Control): A Targeted Review of the Locus of Control Literature and Agenda for Future Research," *Journal of Organizational Behavior* 39 (2018): 820–33.

28. T.W.H. Ng, K.L. Sorensen, and L.T. Eby, "Locus of Control at Work: A Meta-Analysis," *Journal of Organizational Behavior* 27 (2006): 1057–87; Q. Wang, N.A. Bowling, and K.J. Eschleman, "A Meta-Analytic Examination of Work and General Locus of Control," *Journal of Applied Psychology* 95, no. 4 (2010): 761–68.

29. G.J. Leonardelli, C.L. Pickett, and M.B. Brewer, "Optimal Distinctiveness Theory: A Framework for Social Identity, Social Cognition, and Intergroup Relations," in *Advances in Experimental Social Psychology*, ed. M.P. Zanna and J.M. Olson (San Diego, CA: Academic Press, 2010), 63–113; M. Ormiston, "Explaining the Link between Objective and Perceived Differences in Groups: The Role of the Belonging and Distinctiveness Motives," *Journal of Applied Psychology* 101, no. 2 (2016): 222–36.

30. We describe relational self-concept as a form of social identity because such connections are inherently social and the dyads are typically members of a collective entity. For example, an employee has a relationship identity with his/her boss, but this is connected to a social identity with the team or department. However, recent discussion suggests that relational self-concept also may be part of personal identity or a separate form of self-concept. See B.E. Ashforth, B.S. Schinoff, and K.M. Rogers, "'I Identify with Her,' 'I Identify with Him': Unpacking the Dynamics of Personal Identification in Organizations," *Academy of Management Review* 41, no. 1 (2016): 28–60.

31. C. Sedikides and A.P. Gregg, "Portraits of the Self," in *The Sage Handbook of Social Psychology*, ed. M.A. Hogg and J. Cooper (London: Sage, 2003), 110–38; S.A. Haslam and N. Ellemers, "Identity Processes in Organizations," in *Handbook of Identity Theory and Research*, ed. J.S. Schwartz, K. Luyckx, and L.V. Vignoles (New York: Springer New York, 2011), 715–44; M.A. Hogg and M.J. Rinella, "Social Identities and Shared Realities," *Current Opinion in Psychology*, 23 (October 2018): 6–10.

32. M.R. Edwards, "Organizational Identification: A Conceptual and Operational Review," *International Journal of Management Reviews* 7, no. 4 (2005): 207–30; E.S. Lee, T.Y. Park, and B. Koo, "Identifying Organizational Identification as a Basis for Attitudes and Behaviors: A Meta-Analytic Review," *Psychological Bulletin* 141, no. 5 (2015): 1049–80.

33. M.B. Brewer, "The Social Self: On Being the Same and Different at the Same Time," *Personality and Social Psychology Bulletin* 17, no. 5 (1991): 475–82; R. Imhoff and H.-P. Erb, "What Motivates Nonconformity? Uniqueness Seeking Blocks Majority Influence," *Personality and Social Psychology Bulletin* 35, no. 3 (2009):

309–20; K.R. Morrison and S.C. Wheeler, "Nonconformity Defines the Self: The Role of Minority Opinion Status in Self-Concept Clarity," *Personality and Social Psychology Bulletin* 36, no. 3 (2010): 297–308; M.G. Mayhew, J. Gardner, and N.M. Ashkanasy, "Measuring Individuals' Need for Identification: Scale Development and Validation," *Personality and Individual Differences* 49, no. 5 (2010): 356–61.

34. See, for example: L. Ramarajan, "Past, Present and Future Research on Multiple Identities: Toward an Intrapersonal Network Approach," *The Academy of Management Annals* 8 (2014): 589–659; D.L. Ferris, R.E. Johnson, and C. Sedikides, eds., *The Self at Work: Fundamental Theory and Research* (New York: Routledge/ Taylor & Francis Group, 2018).
35. E.I. Knudsen, "Fundamental Components of Attention," *Annual Review of Neuroscience* 30, no. 1 (2007): 57–78. For an evolutionary psychology perspective of selective attention and organization, see L. Cosmides and J. Tooby, "Evolutionary Psychology: New Perspectives on Cognition and Motivation," *Annual Review of Psychology* 64, no. 1 (2013): 201–29.
36. A. Bechara and A.R. Damasio, "The Somatic Marker Hypothesis: A Neural Theory of Economic Decision," *Games and Economic Behavior* 52 (2005): 336–72; T.S. Saunders and M.J. Buehner, "The Gut Chooses Faster Than the Mind: A Latency Advantage of Affective over Cognitive Decisions," *Quarterly Journal of Experimental Psychology* 66 (2012): 381–88; R. Smith and R. D. Lane, "The Neural Basis of One's Own Conscious and Unconscious Emotional States," *Neuroscience & Biobehavioral Reviews* 57 (2015): 1–29.
37. Plato, *The Republic*, trans. D. Lee (Harmondsworth, UK: Penguin, 1955). For the importance of emotions on memory, see: I. Xenakis, A. Arnellos, and J. Darzentas, "The Functional Role of Emotions in Aesthetic Judgment," *New Ideas in Psychology* 30 (2012): 212–26; S. Sheldon and J. Donahue, "More than a Feeling: Emotional Cues Impact the Access and Experience of Autobiographical Memories," *Memory & Cognition* 45 (2017): 731–44; H.J. Bowen, S.M. Kark, and E.A. Kensinger, "NEVER Forget: Negative Emotional Valence Enhances Recapitulation," *Psychonomic Bulletin & Review* 25 (2018): 870–91.
38. D.J. Simons and C.F. Chabris, "Gorillas in Our Midst: Sustained Inattentional Blindness for Dynamic Events," *Perception* 28 (1999): 1059–74.
39. R. S. Nickerson, "Confirmation Bias: A Ubiquitous Phenomenon in Many Guises," *Review of General Psychology* 2, no. 2 (1998): 175–220; A. Gilbey and S. Hill, "Confirmation Bias in General Aviation Lost Procedures," *Applied Cognitive Psychology* 26, no. 5 (2012): 785–95; A. M. Scherer, P. D. Windschitl, and A. R. Smith, "Hope to Be Right: Biased Information Seeking Following Arbitrary and Informed Predictions," *Journal of Experimental Social Psychology* 49, no. 1 (2013): 106–12.
40. C. Wastell et al., "Identifying Hypothesis Confirmation Behaviors in a Simulated Murder Investigation: Implications for Practice," *Journal of Investigative Psychology and Offender Profiling* 9, no. 2 (2012): 184–98; D.K. Rossmo, "Case Rethinking: A Protocol for Reviewing Criminal Investigations," *Police Practice and Research* 17, no. 3 (2016): 212–28.
41. Earl Derr Biggars, the author of the Charlie Chan novels, is sometimes cited as the source of this quotation. However, this statement is found only in the 1935 film *Charlie Chan in Egypt*, which is based on Biggars' character. It does not appear in any Charlie Chan novels.
42. C.N. Macrae and G.V. Bodenhausen, "Social Cognition: Thinking Categorically about Others," *Annual Review of Psychology* 51 (2000): 93–120; K.A. Quinn and H.E.S. Rosenthal, "Categorizing Others and the Self: How Social Memory Structures Guide Social Perception and Behavior," *Learning and Motivation* 43, no. 4 (2012): 247–58; L.T. Phillips, M. Weisbuch, and N. Ambady, "People Perception: Social Vision of Groups and Consequences for Organizing and Interacting," *Research in Organizational Behavior* 34 (2014): 101–27.
43. S. Avugos et al., "The 'Hot Hand' Reconsidered: A Meta-Analytic Approach," *Psychology of Sport and Exercise* 14, no. 1 (2013): 21–27. For a discussion of cognitive closure and perception, see A. Roets et al., "The Motivated Gatekeeper of Our Minds: New Directions in Need for Closure Theory and Research," in *Advances in Experimental Social Psychology*, ed. M.O. James and P.Z. Mark (San Diego, CA: Academic Press, 2015), 221–83.
44. J. Willis and A. Todorov, "First Impressions: Making Up Your Mind after a 100-Ms Exposure to a Face," *Psychological Science* 17 (2006): 592–98; D. Kahneman, *Thinking Fast and Slow* (New York: Farrar, Strauss and Giroux, 2011); A. Todorov, *Face Value: The Irresistible Influence of First Impressions* (Princeton, NJ: Princeton University Press, 2017).
45. P.M. Senge, *The Fifth Discipline: The Art and Practice of the Learning Organization* (New York: Doubleday Currency, 1990), chap. 10; T.J. Chermack, "Mental Models in Decision Making and Implications for Human Resource Development," *Advances in Developing Human Resources* 5, no. 4 (2003): 408–22; P.N. Johnson-Laird, "Mental Models and Deductive Reasoning," in *Reasoning: Studies of Human Inference and Its Foundations*, ed. J.E. Adler and L. . Rips (Cambridge: Cambridge University Press, 2008); S. Ross and N. Allen, "Examining the Convergent Validity of Shared Mental Model Measures," *Behavior Research Methods* 44, no. 4 (2012): 1052–62.
46. G.W. Allport, *The Nature of Prejudice* (Reading, MA: Addison-Wesley, 1954); J.C. Brigham, "Ethnic Stereotypes," *Psychological Bulletin* 76, no. 1 (1971): 15–38; D.J. Schneider, *The Psychology of Stereotyping* (New York: Guilford, 2004); S. Kanahara, "A Review of the Definitions of Stereotype and a Proposal for a Progressional Model," *Individual Differences Research* 4, no. 5 (2006): 306–21.
47. L. Jussim, J.T. Crawford, and R.S. Rubinstein, "Stereotype (in)Accuracy in Perceptions of Groups and Individuals," *Current Directions in Psychological Science* 24, no. 6 (2015): 490–97.
48. C.N. Macrae, A.B. Milne, and G.V. Bodenhausen, "Stereotypes as Energy-Saving Devices: A Peek inside the Cognitive Toolbox," *Journal of Personality and Social Psychology* 66 (1994): 37–47; J.W. Sherman et al., "Stereotype Efficiency Reconsidered: Encoding Flexibility under Cognitive Load," *Journal of Personality and Social Psychology* 75 (1998): 589–606; C.K. Soderberg et al., "The Effects of Psychological Distance on Abstraction: Two Meta-Analyses," *Psychological Bulletin* 141 (2015): 525–48.
49. J.C. Turner and S.A. Haslam, "Social Identity, Organizations, and Leadership," in *Groups at Work: Theory and Research*, ed. M.E. Turner (Mahwah, NJ: Erlbaum, 2001), 25–65; J. Jetten, R. Spears, and T. Postmes, "Intergroup Distinctiveness and Differentiation: A Meta-Analytic Integration," *Journal of Personality and Social Psychology* 86, no. 6 (2004): 862–79; M.A. Hogg et al., "The Social Identity Perspective: Intergroup Relations, Self-Conception, and Small Groups," *Small Group Research* 35, no. 3 (2004): 246–76; K. Hugenberg and D.F. Sacco, "Social Categorization and Stereotyping: How Social Categorization Biases Person Perception and Face Memory," *Social and Personality Psychology Compass* 2, no. 2 (2008): 1052–72.

50. N. Halevy, G. Bornstein, and L. Sagiv, "'In-Group Love' and 'Out-Group Hate' as Motives for Individual Participation in Intergroup Conflict: A New Game Paradigm," *Psychological Science* 19, no. 4 (2008): 405–11; T. Yamagishi and N. Mifune, "Social Exchange and Solidarity: In-Group Love or Out-Group Hate?," *Evolution and Human Behavior* 30, no. 4 (2009): 229–37; N. Halevy, O. Weisel, and G. Bornstein, "'In-Group Love' and 'Out-Group Hate' in Repeated Interaction between Groups," *Journal of Behavioral Decision Making* 25, no. 2 (2012): 188–95; M. Parker and R. Janoff-Bulman, "Lessons from Morality-Based Social Identity: The Power of Outgroup 'Hate,' Not Just Ingroup 'Love,'" *Social Justice Research* 26, no. 1 (2013): 81–96.

51. T. Schmader and W.M. Hall, "Stereotype Threat in School and at Work: Putting Science into Practice," *Policy Insights from the Behavioral and Brain Sciences* 1, no. 1 (2014): 30–37; C.R. Pennington et al., "Twenty Years of Stereotype Threat Research: A Review of Psychological Mediators," *PLoS ONE* 11, no. 1 (2016): e0146487.

52. C.A. Moss-Racusin et al., "Science Faculty's Subtle Gender Biases Favor Male Students," *Proceedings of the National Academy of Sciences* 109, no. 41 (2012): 16474–79.

53. S.T. Fiske, "Stereotyping, Prejudice, and Discrimination," in *Handbook of Social Psychology*, ed. D.T. Gilbert, S.T. Fiske, and G. Lindzey (New York: McGraw-Hill, 1998): 357–411; M. Hewstone, M. Rubin, and H. Willis, "Intergroup Bias," *Annual Review of Psychology* 53 (2002): 575–604; C. Stangor, "The Study of Stereotyping, Prejudice, and Discrimination within Social Psychology: A Quick History of Theory and Research," in *Handbook of Prejudice, Stereotyping, and Discrimination*, ed. T.D. Nelson (New York: Psychology Press, 2016), 1–22.

54. J.A. Bargh and T.L. Chartrand, "The Unbearable Automaticity of Being," *American Psychologist* 54 (1999): 462–79; B. Gawronski et al., "When 'Just Say No' Is Not Enough: Affirmation versus Negation Training and the Reduction of Automatic Stereotype Activation," *Journal of Experimental Social Psychology* 44 (2008): 370–77; M.D. Burns, M.J. Monteith, and L.R. Parker, "Training away Bias: The Differential Effects of Counterstereotype Training and Self-Regulation on Stereotype Activation and Application," *Journal of Experimental Social Psychology* 73 (2017): 97–110; I.R. Johnson, B.M. Kopp, and R.E. Petty, "Just Say No! (And Mean It): Meaningful Negation as a Tool to Modify Automatic Racial Attitudes," *Group Processes & Intergroup Relations* 21 (2018): 88–110; G.B. Humiston and E.J. Wamsley, "Unlearning Implicit Social Biases during Sleep: A Failure to Replicate," *PLOS ONE* 14, no. 1 (January 25, 2019): e0211416, https://doi.org/10.1371/journal.pone.0211416.

55. A.M. Rivers et al., "On the Roles of Stereotype Activation and Application in Diminishing Implicit Bias," *Personality and Social Psychology Bulletin* 46 (2020): 349–64.

56. H.H. Kelley, *Attribution in Social Interaction* (Morristown, NJ: General Learning Press, 1971); B.F. Malle, "Attribution Theories: How People Make Sense of Behavior," in *Theories of Social Psychology*, ed. D. Chadee (Chichester, UK: Blackwell, 2011), 72–95. This "internal-external" or "person-situation" perspective of the attribution process differs somewhat from the original "intentional-unintentional" perspective, which says that we try to understand the deliberate or accidental/involuntary reasons why people engage in behaviors, as well as the reasons for behavior. Some writers suggest the original perspective is more useful. See B.F. Malle, "Time to Give Up the Dogmas of Attribution: An Alternative Theory of Behavior Explanation," in *Advances in Experimental Social Psychology*, vol. 44, ed. K.M. Olson and M.P. Zanna (San Diego: Elsevier Academic, 2011), 297–352.

57. H.H. Kelley, "The Processes of Causal Attribution," *American Psychologist* 28 (1973): 107–28.

58. D. Lange and N.T. Washburn, "Understanding Attributions of Corporate Social Irresponsibility," *Academy of Management Review* 37, no. 2 (2012): 300–26. Recent reviews explain that attribution is an incomplete theory for understanding how people determine causation and assign blame. See S.A. Sloman and D. Lagnado, "Causality in Thought," *Annual Review of Psychology* 66, no. 1 (2015): 223–47; M.D. Alicke et al., "Causal Conceptions in Social Explanation and Moral Evaluation: A Historical Tour," *Perspectives on Psychological Science* 10, no. 6 (2015): 790–812.

59. J.M. Crant and T.S. Bateman, "Assignment of Credit and Blame for Performance Outcomes," *Academy of Management Journal* 36 (1993): 7–27; B. Weiner, "Intrapersonal and Interpersonal Theories of Motivation from an Attributional Perspective," *Educational Psychology Review* 12 (2000): 1–14; N. Bacon and P. Blyton, "Worker Responses to Teamworking: Exploring Employee Attributions of Managerial Motives," *International Journal of Human Resource Management* 16, no. 2 (2005): 238–55.

60. D.T. Miller and M. Ross, "Self-Serving Biases in the Attribution of Causality: Fact or Fiction?" *Psychological Bulletin* 82, no. 2 (1975): 213–25; J. Shepperd, W. Malone, and K. Sweeny, "Exploring Causes of the Self-Serving Bias," *Social and Personality Psychology Compass* 2, no. 2 (2008): 895–908.

61. E.W.K. Tsang, "Self-Serving Attributions in Corporate Annual Reports: A Replicated Study," *Journal of Management Studies* 39, no. 1 (2002): 51–65; N.J. Roese and J.M. Olson, "Better, Stronger, Faster: Self-Serving Judgment, Affect Regulation, and the Optimal Vigilance Hypothesis," *Perspectives on Psychological Science* 2, no. 2 (2007): 124–41; R. Hooghiemstra, "East-West Differences in Attributions for Company Performance: A Content Analysis of Japanese and U.S. Corporate Annual Reports," *Journal of Cross-Cultural Psychology* 39, no. 5 (2008): 618–29.

62. D.T. Gilbert and P.S. Malone, "The Correspondence Bias," *Psychological Bulletin* 117, no. 1 (1995): 21–38.

63. B.F. Malle, "The Actor-Observer Asymmetry in Attribution: A (Surprising) Meta-Analysis," *Psychological Bulletin* 132 (2006): 895–919; C.W. Bauman and L.J. Skitka, "Making Attributions for Behaviors: The Prevalence of Correspondence Bias in the General Population," *Basic and Applied Social Psychology* 32 (2010): 269–77; S.G. Goto et al., "Cultural Differences in Sensitivity to Social Context: Detecting Affective Incongruity Using the N400," *Social Neuroscience* 8 (2012): 63–74; I. Scopelliti et al., "Individual Differences in Correspondence Bias: Measurement, Consequences, and Correction of Biased Interpersonal Attributions," *Management Science* 64 (2017): 1879–1910.

64. Similar models are presented in D. Eden, "Self-Fulfilling Prophecy as a Management Tool: Harnessing Pygmalion," *Academy of Management Review* 9 (1984): 64–73; R. H. G. Field and D. A. Van Seters, "Management by Expectations (MBE): The Power of Positive Prophecy," *Journal of General Management* 14 (1988): 19–33; D. O. Trouilloud et al., "The Influence of Teacher Expectations on Student Achievement in Physical Education Classes: Pygmalion Revisited," *European Journal of Social Psychology* 32 (2002): 591–607.

65. P. Whiteley, T. Sy, and S.K. Johnson, "Leaders' Conceptions of Followers: Implications for Naturally Occurring Pygmalion Effects," *Leadership Quarterly* 23, no. 5 (2012): 822–34; J. Weaver, J.F. Moses, and M. Snyder, "Self-Fulfilling Prophecies in Ability Settings," *Journal of Social Psychology* 156, no. 2 (2016): 179–89.

66. D. Eden, "Interpersonal Expectations in Organizations," in *Interpersonal Expectations: Theory, Research, and Applications*, ed. P.D. Blanck (Cambridge: Cambridge University Press, 1993), 154–78.

67. D. Eden, "Pygmalion Goes to Boot Camp: Expectancy, Leadership, and Trainee Performance," *Journal of Applied Psychology* 67 (1982): 194–99; B.J. Avolio et al., "A Meta-Analytic Review of Leadership Impact Research: Experimental and Quasi-Experimental Studies," *The Leadership Quarterly* 20, no. 5 (2009): 764–84; P. Whiteley, T. Sy, and S.K. Johnson, "Leaders' Conceptions of Followers: Implications for Naturally Occurring Pygmalion Effects," *Leadership Quarterly* 23, no. 5 (2012): 822–34.

68. S. Madon, L. Jussim, and J. Eccles, "In Search of the Powerful Self-Fulfilling Prophecy," *Journal of Personality and Social Psychology* 72 (1997): 791–809; A. E. Smith, L. Jussim, and J. Eccles, "Do Self-Fulfilling Prophecies Accumulate, Dissipate, or Remain Stable over Time?," *Journal of Personality and Social Psychology* 77 (1999): 548–65; S. Madon et al., "Self-Fulfilling Prophecies: The Synergistic Accumulative Effect of Parents' Beliefs on Children's Drinking Behavior," *Psychological Science* 15 (2005): 837–45.

69. J. Hoffman, "Doctors' Delicate Balance in Keeping Hope Alive," *New York Times*, December 24, 2005, A1, A14; K. Blakely et al., "Optimistic Honesty: Understanding Surgeon and Patient Perspectives on Hopeful Communication in Pancreatic Cancer Care," *HPB* 19 (2017): 611–19; D.S. Dunn, ed. *Positive Psychology: Established and Emerging Issues* (New York: Routledge, 2018).

70. W.H. Cooper, "Ubiquitous Halo," *Psychological Bulletin* 90 (1981): 218–44; P. Rosenzweig, *The Halo Effect . . . and the Eight Other Business Delusions That Deceive Managers* (New York: Free Press, 2007); J.W. Keeley et al., "Investigating Halo and Ceiling Effects in Student Evaluations of Instruction," *Educational and Psychological Measurement* 73, no. 3 (2013): 440–57.

71. B. Mullen et al., "The False Consensus Effect: A Meta-Analysis of 115 Hypothesis Tests," *Journal of Experimental Social Psychology* 21, no. 3 (1985): 262–83; F.J. Flynn and S.S. Wiltermuth, "Who's with Me? False Consensus, Brokerage, and Ethical Decision Making in Organizations," *Academy of Management Journal* 53, no. 5 (2010): 1074–89; B. Roth and A. Voskort, "Stereotypes and False Consensus: How Financial Professionals Predict Risk Preferences," *Journal of Economic Behavior & Organization* 107, Part B (2014): 553–65.

72. D. D. Steiner and J. S. Rain, "Immediate and Delayed Primacy and Recency Effects in Performance Evaluation," *Journal of Applied Psychology* 74 (1989): 136–42; K. T. Trotman, "Order Effects and Recency: Where Do We Go from Here?," *Accounting & Finance* 40 (2000): 169–82; W. Green, "Impact of the Timing of an Inherited Explanation on Auditors' Analytical Procedures Judgements," *Accounting and Finance* 44 (2004): 369–92.

73. E.A. Lind, L. Kray, and L. Thompson, "Primacy Effects in Justice Judgments: Testing Predictions from Fairness Heuristic Theory," *Organizational Behavior and Human Decision Processes* 85 (2001): 189–210; T. Mann and M. Ferguson, "Can We Undo Our First Impressions? The Role of Reinterpretation in Reversing Implicit Evaluations," *Journal of Personality & Social Psychology* 108, no. 6 (2015): 823–49; B.C. Holtz, "From First Impression to Fairness Perception: Investigating the Impact of Initial Trustworthiness Beliefs," *Personnel Psychology* 68, no. 3 (2015): 499–546.

74. Careerbuilder, "Careerbuilder Releases Study of Common and Not-So-Common Resume Mistakes That Can Cost You the Job," news release (Chicago: Careerbuilder, September 11, 2013); Accountemps, "Survey: Job Interview Trips up More Candidates Than Any Other Step in Hiring Process," news release (Menlo Park, CA: Accountemps, April 2, 2014); Careerbuilder, "Careerbuilder's Annual Survey Reveals the Most Outrageous Resume Mistakes Employers Have Found," news release (Chicago: Careerbuilder, September 22, 2016); "Top 25 Worst Resume Objective Statements," *Robert Half Blog*, May 17, 2017, https://www.roberthalf.com/blog/top-25-worst-resume-objective-statements.

75. B. Gawronski et al., "When 'Just Say No' Is Not Enough: Affirmation versus Negation Training and the Reduction of Automatic Stereotype Activation," *Journal of Experimental Social Psychology* 44 (2008): 370–77; M.M. Duguid and M.C. Thomas-Hunt, "Condoning Stereotyping? How Awareness of Stereotyping Prevalence Impacts Expression of Stereotypes," *Journal of Applied Psychology* 100 (2015): 343–59; F. Dobbin and A. Kalev, "Why Diversity Programs Fail," *Harvard Business Review* 94, no. 7/8 (2016): 52–60; L.M. Leslie, "Diversity Initiative Effectiveness: A Typological Theory of Unintended Consequences," *Academy of Management Review* 44 (2019): 538–63.

76. T.W. Costello and S.S. Zalkind, *Psychology in Administration: A Research Orientation* (Englewood Cliffs, NJ: Prentice Hall, 1963), 45–46; J.M. Kouzes and B.Z. Posner, *The Leadership Challenge*, 4th ed. (San Francisco: Jossey-Bass, 2007), Chap. 3.

77. W. L. Gardner et al., "'Can You See the Real Me?' A Self-Based Model of Authentic Leader and Follower Development," *Leadership Quarterly* 16 (2005): 343–72; C. Peus et al., "Authentic Leadership: An Empirical Test of Its Antecedents, Consequences, and Mediating Mechanisms," *Journal of Business Ethics* 107, no. 3 (2012): 331–48.

78. A.G. Greenwald et al., "Understanding and Using the Implicit Association Test: III. Meta-Analysis of Predictive Validity," *Journal of Personality and Social Psychology* 97, no. 1 (2009): 17–41; M.C. Wilson and K. Scior, "Attitudes Towards Individuals with Disabilities as Measured by the Implicit Association Test: A Literature Review," *Research in Developmental Disabilities* 35, no. 2 (2014): 294–321; B.A. Nosek et al., "Understanding and Using the Brief Implicit Association Test: Recommended Scoring Procedures," *PLoS ONE* 9, no. 12 (2014): e110938; B. Schiller et al., "Clocking the Social Mind by Identifying Mental Processes in the IAT with Electrical Neuroimaging," *Proceedings of the National Academy of Sciences* 113, no. 10 (2016): 2786–91.

79. J.T. Jost et al., "The Existence of Implicit Bias Is Beyond Reasonable Doubt: A Refutation of Ideological and Methodological Objections and Executive Summary of Ten Studies That No Manager Should Ignore," *Research in Organizational Behavior* 29 (2009): 39–69. The science-as-male implicit stereotype is discussed in F.L. Smyth and B.A. Nosek, "On the Gender-Science Stereotypes Held by Scientists: Explicit Accord with Gender-Ratios, Implicit Accord with Scientific Identity," *Frontiers in Psychology* 6 (2015).

80. S. Tatla, "A Great Start to 2019 - Manulife Named to Bloomberg's 2019 Gender-Equality Index," LinkedIn, *Pulse* (blog), January 16, 2019, https://www.linkedin.com/pulse/great-start-2019-manulife-named-bloombergs-index-sandeep-tatla; "2018 Sustainability Report" (Toronto: Manulife Financial Corporation, June 4, 2019).

81. J. Luft, *Of Human Interaction* (Palo Alto, CA: National Press, 1969). For a variation of this model, see J. Hall, "Communication Revisited," *California Management Review* 15 (1973): 56–67. For recent discussion of the Johari blind spot, see A.-M.B. Gallrein et al., "You Spy with Your Little Eye: People Are 'Blind' to Some of the Ways in Which They Are Consensually Seen by Others," *Journal of Research in Personality* 47, no. 5 (2013): 464–71; A.-M.B. Gallrein et al., "I Still Cannot See It—A Replication of Blind Spots in Self-Perception," *Journal of Research in Personality* 60 (2016): 1–7.

82. S. Vazire and M.R. Mehl, "Knowing Me, Knowing You: The Accuracy and Unique Predictive Validity of Self-Ratings and Other-Ratings of Daily Behavior," *Journal of Personality and Social Psychology* 95, no. 5 (2008): 1202–16; D. Leising, A.-M.B. Gallrein, and M. Dufner, "Judging the Behavior of People We Know: Objective Assessment, Confirmation of Preexisting Views, or Both?" *Personality and Social Psychology Bulletin* 40 (2014): 153–63. However, too much self-disclosure may have unintended negative consequences for individuals in team settings. See K.R. Gibson, D. Harari, and J.C. Marr, "When Sharing Hurts: How and Why Self-Disclosing Weakness Undermines the Task-Oriented Relationships of Higher Status Disclosers," *Organizational Behavior and Human Decision Processes* 144 (2018): 25–43.

83. J.D. Vorauer, "Completing the Implicit Association Test Reduces Positive Intergroup Interaction Behavior," *Psychological Science* 23 (2012): 1168–75.

84. T.F. Pettigrew and L.R. Tropp, "A Meta-Analytic Test of Intergroup Contact Theory," *Journal of Personality and Social Psychology* 90 (2006): 751–83; S.C. Wright, A. Mazziotta, and L.R. Tropp, "Contact and Intergroup Conflict: New Ideas for the Road Ahead," *Journal of Peace Psychology* 23 (2017): 317–27; J.F. Dovidio et al., "Reducing Intergroup Bias through Intergroup Contact: Twenty Years of Progress and Future Directions," *Group Processes & Intergroup Relations* 20 (2017): 606–20.

85. The contact hypothesis was first introduced in G.W. Allport, *The Nature of Prejudice* (Reading, MA: Addison-Wesley, 1954), Chap. 16.

86. C.K. Soderberg et al., "The Effects of Psychological Distance on Abstraction: Two Meta-Analyses," *Psychological Bulletin* 141 (2015): 525–48.

87. R. Elliott et al., "Empathy," *Psychotherapy* 48, no. 1 (2011): 43–49; J. Zaki, "Empathy: A Motivated Account," *Psychological Bulletin* 140, no. 6 (2014): 1608–47; E. Teding van Berkhout and J. Malouff, "The Efficacy of Empathy Training: A Meta-Analysis of Randomized Controlled Trials," *Journal of Counseling Psychology* 63, no. 1 (2016): 32–41.

88. M. Tarrant, R. Calitri, and D. Weston, "Social Identification Structures the Effects of Perspective Taking," *Psychological Science* 23, no. 9 (2012): 973–78; J.L. Skorinko and S.A. Sinclair, "Perspective Taking Can Increase Stereotyping: The Role of Apparent Stereotype Confirmation," *Journal of Experimental Social Psychology* 49, no. 1 (2013): 10–18.

4 Workplace Emotions, Attitudes, and Stress

Paul Bradbury/Caiaimage/Getty Images

Learning Objectives

After you read this chapter, you should be able to:

LO4-1 Explain how emotions and cognition (conscious reasoning) influence attitudes and behavior.

LO4-2 Discuss the dynamics of emotional labor and the role of emotional intelligence in the workplace.

LO4-3 Summarize the consequences of job dissatisfaction, as well as strategies to increase organizational (affective) commitment.

LO4-4 Describe the stress experience and review four major stressors.

LO4-5 Identify five ways to manage workplace stress.

Circles.Life doesn't wait a year or even six months to measure employee attitudes. "At Circles.Life, we launched an initiative called monthly pulse check (quick rating of 1 to 5) that helps us evaluate how our employees feel," says cofounder Rameez Ansar. The Singapore-based digital telco, which operates across five countries, provides quarterly feedback to employees about the pulse survey results and the company's actions to address employee concerns.

Circles.Life and many other companies are replacing or supplementing their annual attitude survey with more timely pulse checks, in which employees respond to a handful of easily answered questions online several times each year. "Offering a fast and secure way for employees to voice their opinion can give businesses a clear understanding of the engagement of their people and insight into their views on particular issues," explains an executive in Boulder, Colorado.

Companies also create special pulse surveys to quickly gauge employee feelings about specific, timely issues such as the devastating COVID-19 pandemic. "In normal times, we conduct a quarterly pulse survey to keep on top of employee satisfaction," explains an executive at a Chicago-based e-commerce platform. "This week, we conducted a quick COVID-related version to check in on employees and understand their feelings regarding a variety of topics." The pulse check discovered that employees' top concerns were about working from home, health risks of the virus, and how the virus might affect the company's financial situation.[1]

Corporate leaders increasingly recognize that emotions and attitudes influence employee behavior and well-being, and ultimately affect the organization's performance and customer service. This chapter begins by describing emotions and explaining how they influence attitudes and behavior. Next, we consider the dynamics of emotional labor, followed by the popular topic of emotional intelligence. The specific work attitudes of job satisfaction and organizational commitment are then discussed, including their association with various employee behaviors and work performance. The final section looks at work-related stress, including the stress experience, four prominent stressors, individual differences in stress, and ways to combat excessive stress.

LO4-1 Explain how emotions and cognition (conscious reasoning) influence attitudes and behavior.

EMOTIONS IN THE WORKPLACE

Emotions influence almost everything we do in the workplace. This is a strong statement, and one that would have rarely been expressed by organizational behavior experts two decades ago. Most OB theories still assume that a person's thoughts and actions are governed primarily or exclusively by logical thinking (called *cognitions*).[2] Yet groundbreaking neuroscience discoveries have revealed that our perceptions, attitudes, decisions, and behavior are influenced by emotions as well as cognitions.[3] In fact, emotions may have a greater influence because they often occur before cognitive processes and, consequently, influence the latter. By ignoring emotionality, many theories have overlooked a large piece of the puzzle about human behavior in the workplace.

Emotions are physiological, behavioral, and psychological episodes experienced toward an object, person, or event that create a state of readiness.[4] These "episodes" are very brief events, some

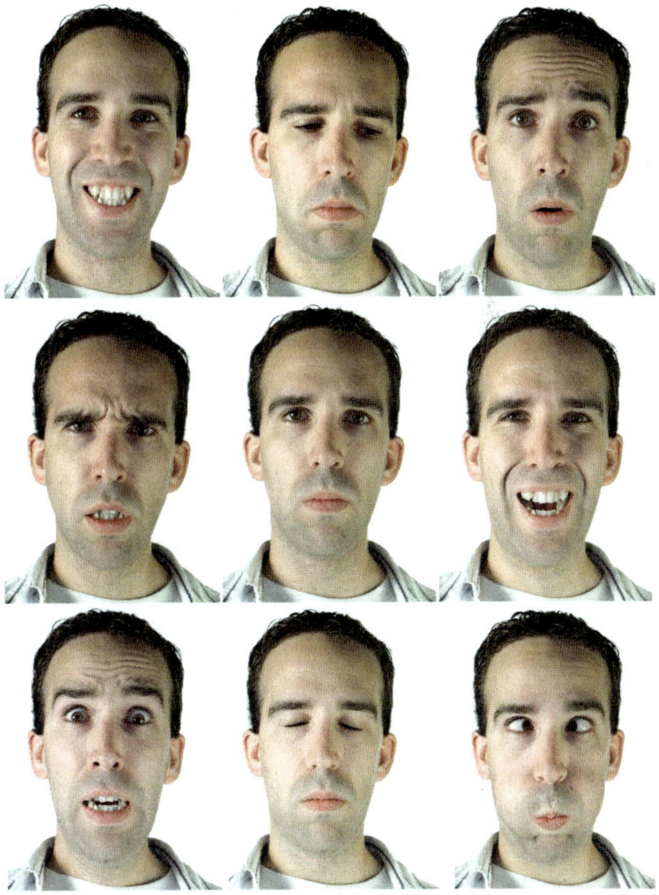

Emotions are physiological, behavioral, and psychological episodes experienced toward an object, person, or event that create a state of readiness.
Richard Nelson/Cutcaster

emotions physiological, behavioral, and psychological episodes experienced toward an object, person, or event that create a state of readiness

lasting less than a second. However, we usually experience emotions over several minutes or longer because they occur in waves as we continue to think about the source of the emotion. Emotions are directed toward someone or something. For example, we experience joy, fear, anger, and other emotional episodes toward tasks, customers, or a mobile phone app we are using. This differs from *moods,* which are not directed toward anything in particular and tend to be longer-term background emotional states.

Emotions are experiences. They represent changes in our physiological state (e.g., blood pressure, heart rate), psychological state (e.g., thought process), and behavior (e.g., facial expression).[5] Most of these emotional reactions are subtle; they occur without our awareness. This is an important point because the topic of emotions often conjures up images of people "getting emotional." In reality, most emotions are fleeting, usually nonconscious events that influence our conscious thinking and behavior.[6] Finally, emotions put us in a state of readiness. When we get worried, for example, our heart rate and blood pressure increase to make our body better prepared to engage in fight or flight. Strong emotions trigger our conscious awareness of a threat or opportunity in the external environment. The "state of readiness" generated by emotions is the engine of our motivation, which we discuss more fully in Chapter 5.[7]

Types of Emotions

People experience many emotions and various combinations of emotions, but all of them have two common features, illustrated in Exhibit 4.1.[9] One feature is that emotions vary in their level of

> **Don't let us forget that the small emotions are the great captains of our lives, and that we obey them without knowing it.[8]**
>
> —Vincent Van Gogh (late 1800s Dutch painter)

Exhibit 4.1 Circumplex Model of Emotions

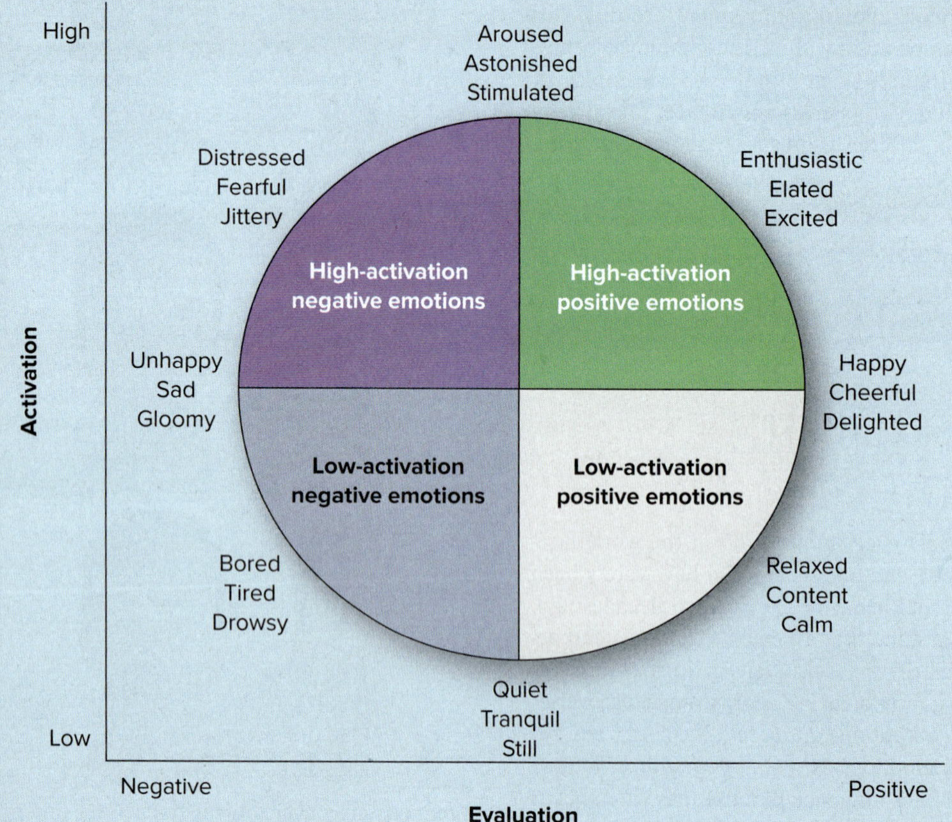

Sources: Adapted from J.A. Russell, "Core Affect and the Psychological Construction of Emotion," *Psychological Review* 110, no. 1 (2003): 145–72; M. Yik, J.A. Russell, and J.H. Steiger, "A 12-Point Circumplex Structure of Core Affect," *Emotion* 11, no. 4 (2011): 705–31.

attitudes the cluster of beliefs, assessed feelings, and behavioral intentions toward a person, object, or event (called an attitude object)

activation. By definition, emotions put us in a state of readiness and, as we discuss in the next chapter, are the primary source of a person's motivation. Some emotional experiences, such as when we are suddenly surprised, are strong enough to consciously motivate us to act without careful thought. Most emotional experiences are more subtle, but even they activate enough to make us more aware of our environment.

A second feature is that all emotions evaluate the situation as positive or negative, good or bad, helpful or harmful, and so forth. In other words, all emotions have an associated valence (called *core affect*) signaling that the perceived object or event should be approached or avoided. Negative emotions tend to generate stronger levels of activation than do positive emotions.[10] Fear and anger, for instance, are more intense experiences than are joy and delight, so they have a stronger effect on our actions. This valence asymmetry likely occurs because negative emotions protect us from harm and are therefore more critical for our survival.

Emotions, Attitudes, and Behavior

To understand how emotions influence our thoughts and behavior in the workplace, we first need to know about attitudes. **Attitudes** represent the cluster of beliefs, assessed feelings, and behavioral intentions toward a person, object, or event (called an *attitude object*).[11] Attitudes are *judgments*, whereas emotions are *experiences*. In other words, attitudes involve evaluations of an attitude object, whereas emotions operate as events that we experience, usually without our awareness. Attitudes sometimes operate nonconsciously, but most of the time we are aware of and consciously think about our attitudes. Another distinction is that we experience most emotions very briefly, whereas our attitude toward someone or something is more stable over time.[12]

Until recently, experts believed that attitudes could be understood just by the three cognitive components illustrated on the left side of Exhibit 4.2: beliefs, feelings, and behavioral intentions. Now evidence suggests that a parallel emotional process is also at work, shown on the right side of the exhibit.[13] Using attitude toward mergers as an example, let's look more closely at this model, beginning with the traditional cognitive perspective of attitudes.

- *Beliefs.* These are your established perceptions about the attitude object—what you believe to be true.[14] For example, you might believe that mergers reduce job security for employees in the merged firms or that mergers increase the company's competitiveness in this era of globalization. These beliefs are perceived facts that you acquire from experience and other forms of learning. Each of these beliefs also has a valence; that is, you have a positive or negative feeling about each belief (e.g., less job security is bad).
- *Feelings.* This element represents your conscious positive or negative evaluations of the attitude object. Some people think mergers are good; others think they are bad. Your positive or negative opinion of mergers represents your assessed feelings. According to the traditional cognitive perspective of attitudes (left side of the model), feelings are calculated from your beliefs about mergers and the associated feelings about those beliefs. Consider the example of your attitude toward mergers. If you believe that mergers typically have negative consequences such as layoffs and organizational politics, then you will form negative feelings toward mergers in general or about a specific planned merger in your organization.
- *Behavioral intentions.* This third element represents your motivation to engage in a particular behavior regarding the attitude object.[15] Upon hearing that the company will merge with another organization, you might become motivated to look for a job elsewhere or possibly to complain to management about the merger decision. Your feelings toward mergers motivate your behavioral intentions, and which actions you choose depends on your past experience, personality, and social norms of appropriate behavior.

Exhibit 4.2 Model of Emotions, Attitudes, and Behavior

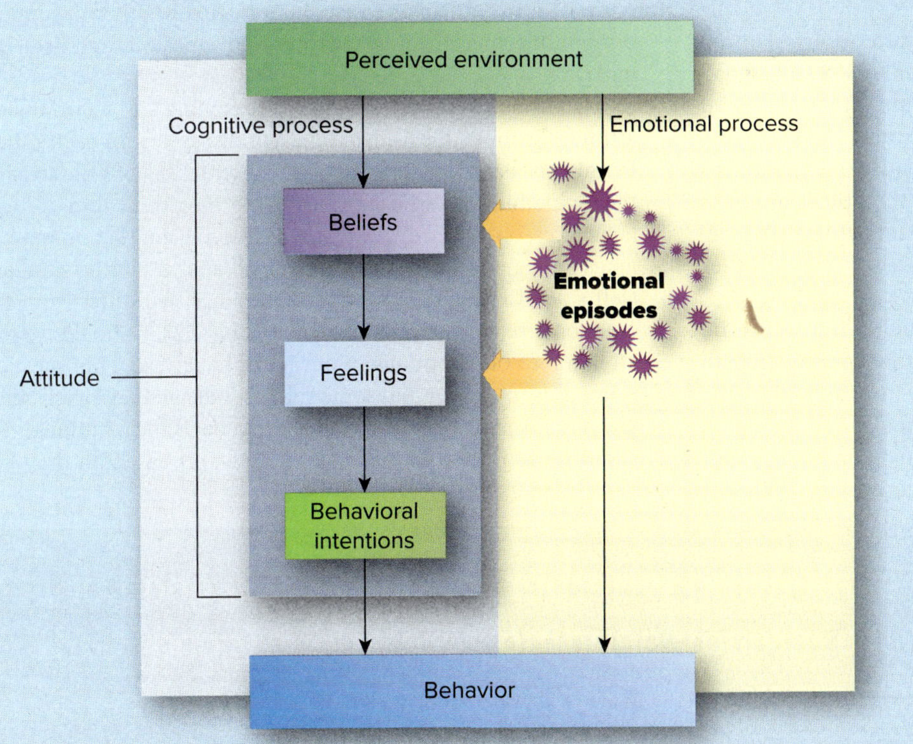

Attitude–Behavior Contingencies

The cognitive model of attitudes (beliefs-feelings-intentions) gives the impression that we can predict behavior from each element of the

Several contingencies at each stage in the cognitive model of attitudes weaken the ability to predict behavior from beliefs, feelings, and behavioral intentions.
ImageFlow/Shutterstock

individual's attitude. This is potentially true, but several contingencies at each stage in the model usually weaken that predictability. Let's begin with the beliefs–feelings link. People with the same beliefs might form quite different feelings toward the attitude object because they have different valences for those beliefs. Two employees who report to the same boss have the same belief that their boss makes them work hard. Yet one employee dislikes the boss because of a negative valence toward hard work whereas the other employee likes the boss because of a positive valence toward hard work.

The effect of feelings on behavioral intentions also depends on contingencies, particularly an individual's personality, values, self-concept, experiences, and other personal characteristics. For instance, two employees might equally dislike their boss, but one employee intends to complain to the union or upper management whereas the other employee intends to find a job elsewhere. Later in this chapter we describe the four main responses to dissatisfaction and other negative attitudes.

Finally, the model indicates that behavioral intentions are the best predictors of a person's behavior. However, the strength of this link also depends on situational factors as well as the person's ability and role perceptions (see the MARS model in Chapter 1). For example, two people might intend to quit because they dislike their boss, but only one does so because the other employee can't find another job.

How Emotions Influence Attitudes and Behavior

The cognitive model describes to some extent how employees form and change their attitudes, but emotions also have a central role in this process.[16] The right side of Exhibit 4.2 illustrates this process, which (like the cognitive process) also begins with perceptions of the world around us. Our brain tags incoming sensory information with emotional markers based on a quick and imprecise evaluation of whether that information supports or threatens our innate drives. These markers are not calculated feelings; they are automatic and nonconscious emotional responses based on very thin slices of sensory information.[17] The experienced emotions then influence our feelings about the attitude object.

Consider once again your attitude toward mergers. You might experience worry, nervousness, or relief upon learning that your company intends to merge with a competitor. The fuzzy dots on the right side of Exhibit 4.2 depict the numerous emotional episodes you experience upon hearing the merger announcement, subsequently thinking about the merger, discussing the merger with coworkers, and so forth. These emotions are transmitted to your brain's cognitive centers, where they are logically analyzed along with other information about the attitude object.[18] So, while you are consciously evaluating whether the merger is good or bad, your emotions are already sending core affect (good–bad) signals, which sway your conscious evaluation. In fact, we often deliberately "listen in" on our emotions to help us consciously decide whether to support or oppose something (see Chapter 6 on emotions and decision making).[19]

The influence of both cognitive reasoning and emotions on attitudes is most apparent when they disagree with each other. People occasionally experience this mental tug-of-war, sensing that something isn't right even though they can't think of any logical reason to be concerned. This internal conflict or ambivalence indicates that the person's logical analysis of the situation (left side of Exhibit 4.2) generates feelings that differ from the emotional response (right side of Exhibit 4.2).[20] Should we pay attention to our emotions or our logical analysis? This question is not easy to answer, but some studies indicate that logical analysis should play a central role in most decisions. Although executives are known to make quick decisions based on their gut

> **While consciously evaluating whether something is good or bad, your emotions are already sending core affect (good–bad) signals, which sway your conscious evaluation.**

feelings (emotional response), their best decisions tend to occur after logically working through the alternatives.[21] Therefore, we should pay attention to both the cognitive and emotional sides of the attitude model and hope they agree with each other most of the time!

Generating Positive Emotions at Work Many organizational leaders seem to be well aware of the dual cognitive-emotional attitude process because they try to craft a workplace that will generate more positive emotional experiences. Google is famous for its superb perks, including in-house coffee bars, gourmet cafeterias, conversation areas that look like vintage subway cars, personal development courses, game rooms, free haircuts, and slides to descend to the floor below. Zoom Video Communications has an entire team—called the happiness crew—at each location dedicated to maintaining a positive and engaging workplace. "If you get an offer to work at Zoom, take it," advises a Zoom employee in Atlanta, Georgia. "Zoom takes employee happiness seriously and people genuinely love the company."[22]

Some critics argue that the organization's main focus should be to create positive emotions through the job itself as well as natural everyday occurrences such as polite customers and supportive coworkers. These are, indeed, important sources of positive emotions. Still, most people perform work that produces some negative emotions, and research has found that humor and fun at work—whether natural or contrived—can potentially counteract the negative experiences.[23] Overall, we need to keep in mind that emotions shape employee attitudes and, as we will discuss later, attitudes influence various forms of work-related behavior.

One last comment about Exhibit 4.2: Notice the arrow from the emotional episodes to behavior. It indicates that emotions directly influence a person's behavior without conscious thought. This occurs when we jump suddenly if someone sneaks up on us. It also occurs in everyday situations because even low-intensity emotions automatically change our facial expressions. These actions are not carefully thought out. They are automatic emotional responses that are learned or hardwired by heredity for particular situations.[25]

Cognitive Dissonance

Imagine that you have just signed a contract for new digital whiteboards to be installed throughout the company's meeting rooms. The deal was expensive but, after consulting several staff, you felt that the technology would be valuable in this electronic age. Yet, you felt a twinge of regret soon after signing the contract. This emotional experience is

---

OB THEORY TO PRACTICE

Short List of Fun Events for the Workplace[24]

Interesting work, supportive coworkers, a healthy work environment, and good pay are some of the well-established ways to make employees happier at work. But companies also try to introduce specific events to inject more positive emotions. Here are some of the more interesting (and apparently effective) fun strategies:

- Office races—individual and team races down hallways with tricycles, wheeled chairs, or scooters. At some fun-oriented businesses, employees start these races without formal planning.
- Orienteering challenge—employee teams use maps, compasses, and topographical awareness to navigate their way to several control points The event can be staged within the cityscape, at a large city park, at a national forest, or on a lake (where the teams travel by canoe). Some orienteering events include physical or cognitive challenges at each control point.
- Peer learning classes on nonwork skills—from music lessons to printmaking, employees enjoy learning something different during lunch, after hours, or on special learning days.
- Attending sports games—baseball, hockey, and many other sporting events are great to watch and share the enthusiasm with coworkers.
- Board games—from Monopoly to Settlers of Catan, board games have surprised many (initially skeptical) employees about how much fun they are as office events. Some companies schedule board game events over an extended lunch break (with company-provided food, of course) or on special games days.
- Nature hikes—a noncompetitive half-day hike in the woods with coworkers through terrain that most can handle is a healthy break from office stress and builds positive relations with coworkers.
- Go-kart and bumper car races—these competitive activities rev up excitement for most employees without being dangerous (the vehicles are designed for anyone over 12 years old). For those with a more aggressive bent, there are also paintball and smurf battles.

g-stockstudio/Shutterstock

cognitive dissonance an emotional experience caused by a perception that our beliefs, feelings, and behavior are incongruent with one another

emotional labor the effort, planning, and control needed to express organizationally desired emotions during interpersonal transactions

cognitive dissonance, which occurs when people perceive that their beliefs, feelings, and behavior are incongruent with each other.[26] The inconsistency among these three attitude components generates emotions (such as feeling hypocritical) that motivate the person to create more consistency by changing one or more of them.

Cognitive dissonance occurs because your attitude (it's good to be cost conscious) is inconsistent with your behavior (buying expensive digital whiteboards). Most people like to think of themselves–and be viewed by others–as rational and logical. Cognitive dissonance occurs when our behavior and beliefs conflict, which is not so rational. How do we reduce cognitive dissonance?[27] Most behaviors can't be undone or are too expensive to reverse. Also, reversing the behavior rarely reduces dissonance because the event is publicly known—you and your coworkers already know that you bought the digital whiteboards and did so willingly.

People reduce cognitive dissonance by changing their beliefs and feelings. One dissonance-reducing strategy is to amplify or discover additional positive features of their selected alternative (e.g., the digital whiteboards can change handwriting into typed text). A second strategy is to do amplify or discover additional problems or weaknesses with the alternatives they didn't choose (e.g., traditional boards are ineffective as projection screens). A third strategy is more indirect; rather than try to ignore the high price of the digital whiteboards, you reduce dissonance by emphasizing how your other decisions have been frugal. This framing compensates for your expensive digital whiteboard fling and thereby maintains your self-concept as a thrifty decision maker. Each of these mental acrobatics maintains some degree of consistency between the person's behavior (buying expensive digital whiteboards) and attitudes (being thrifty).

Emotions and Personality

Throughout this section, we have implied that emotional experiences are triggered by workplace experiences. This is mostly true, but emotions are also partly determined by an individual's personality.[28] Individuals with higher emotional stability and extraverted personalities (see Chapter 2) tend to experience more positive emotions. Those with higher neuroticism (lower emotional stability) and introverted personalities tend to experience more negative emotions. Although positive and negative emotional traits have some effect, studies have found that the actual situation in which people work has a noticeably stronger influence on their attitudes and behavior.[29]

LO4-2 Discuss the dynamics of emotional labor and the role of emotional intelligence in the workplace.

MANAGING EMOTIONS AT WORK

Employees are expected to manage their emotions in the workplace. They must conceal their frustration when serving an irritating customer, display compassion to an ill patient, and hide their boredom in a long meeting with other executives. These are all forms of **emotional labor**–the effort, planning, and control needed to express organizationally desired emotions during interpersonal transactions.[30]

Almost everyone is expected to abide by *display rules*. These norms or explicit rules require employees to display behaviors representing specific emotions and to hide observable evidence of other emotions. Emotional labor demands are higher in jobs requiring a variety of emotions (e.g., anger as well as joy) and more intense emotions (e.g., showing delight rather than smiling weakly), as well as in jobs where interaction with clients is frequent and longer. Emotional labor also increases when employees must precisely rather than casually abide by the display rules.[31] This work requirement is most common in service industries, where employees have frequent face-to-face interaction with clients.

Employees sometimes need to show emotions that are quite different from–sometimes opposite to–the emotions they actually experience at that moment. For instance, they must display patience and positive feelings toward a customer who they actually dislike. This incongruence requires considerable mental effort and can be very stressful. Emotional labor may also require employees to act contrary to their self-concept, which can lead to psychological separation from self as well as job dissatisfaction.[32]

McGraw Hill connect

SELF-ASSESSMENT 4.1: What Is Your Emotional Personality?

> Emotional labor requires considerable mental effort and can be stressful when employees must display emotions that differ significantly from the emotions they actually experience at that moment.

Emotional Display Norms across Cultures

Norms about displaying or hiding your true emotions vary considerably across cultures.[33] One large global study reports that several countries in Asia and Africa strongly discourage emotional expression. Instead, people are expected to be subdued, have relatively monotonic voice intonation, and avoid physical movement and touching that display emotions. In contrast, several Latin and Middle Eastern cultures allow or encourage more vivid display of emotions and expect people to act more consistently with their true emotions. In these cultures, people are expected to reveal their thoughts and feelings, be dramatic in their conversational tones, and be animated in their use of nonverbal behaviors. For example, 81 percent of Ethiopians and 74 percent of Japanese agreed that it is considered unprofessional to express emotions overtly in their culture, whereas 43 percent of Americans, 33 percent of Italians, and only 19 percent of Spaniards, Cubans, and Egyptians agreed with this statement.[34] When required to suppress their true emotions at work, employees from cultures that tolerate or encourage emotional expression experience more stress and lower life satisfaction compared to coworkers from cultures that discourage emotional expression.

Strategies for Displaying Expected Emotions

Emotional labor is ultimately about displaying expected emotions through facial expressions and other forms of behavior. Two general approaches to emotional labor are (1) pretending to have the expected emotions by consciously trying to display behaviors depicting those emotions and (2) actively changing our perceptions and situation so they naturally produce the expected emotions and associated behaviors.

The first approach—consciously pretending to display the expected emotions—is known as *surface acting*. For example, we try to show interest in a client's lengthy explanation even though we are actually weary from hearing it. We act out the verbal and nonverbal behaviors that symbolize the expected emotions, even though our actual emotions are quite different.[35]

Surface acting is usually a poor strategy for emotional labor. It requires considerable mental effort that is often stressful and alienating.[36] A genuine emotion automatically activates a complex set of facial muscles and body positions, all of which are difficult to replicate when pretending to have this emotion. Meanwhile, our true emotions tend to reveal themselves as subtle gestures, usually without our awareness. More often than not, observers recognize fake emotions, which undermines the social exchange.[37]

A genuine emotion automatically activates a complex set of facial muscles and body positions, all of which are difficult to replicate when pretending to have this emotion (surface acting).
RapidEye/Getty Images

Regulating Emotions The second approach to displaying the expected emotions is to actually experience those emotions (rather than faking them). In other words, we consciously alter our perceptions or situation to naturally generate the desired emotions and the behaviors that display those emotions. Employees who actually produce the emotions that are expected in a particular situation are engaging in *deep acting*, whereas surface acting pretends to have the desired emotion by acting out the behavior associated with that emotion.[38]

There are five main strategies for regulating our emotions.[39] One approach is to change the situation, such as moving out of or into work settings that produce or avoid specific emotions. For instance, when feeling lethargic performing a task, you might have a short walking break outside to regain vigor. A second tactic is to modify the existing situation, such changing tasks or altering physical arrangements in the work area. A third way to regulate emotions is by consciously trying to suppress or amplify them.[40] Medical staff might try to avoid becoming too emotionally attached to patients with serious health conditions. A fourth strategy is to changing the focus of attention. If you had a terrible client presentation in the morning, you might actively seek out a work activity in the afternoon that makes you feel happier and more confident in your abilities. A fifth approach to emotion regulation is to reframe the situation. This involves cognitively re-evaluating a particular event so it generates more desirable emotions. Flight attendants apply reframing when they define an incident with an unruly passenger as a test of their customer service skill. These interactions are challenging accomplishments rather than dreaded chores.[41]

All five emotion regulation strategies generate deep acting, but reframing the situation and shifting attention are likely the most common. Changing and modifying the situation can be applied when employees work alone, but seldom when attending a client meeting, interacting with an upset passenger, or in most other work-related social interactions. Suppressing or amplifying emotions produces deep acting, but these cognitive activities may actually involve reframing the situation and shifting attention. But no matter which strategy is applied to manage emotions, emotion regulation requires emotional intelligence, which we discuss next.

OB THEORY TO PRACTICE

Strategies for Regulating Emotions (Deep Acting)

Strategy	Description	Example
Change the situation	Move out of or into work settings that produce or avoid specific emotions.	• Temporarily leave a work area that makes us feel lethargic. • Keep away from a particular client who is deeply irritating.
Modify the situation	Modify the current setting to create or avoid specific emotions.	• Switch from a task that is aggravating to one that is more enjoyable. • Shift a conversation away from an awkward or sensitive topic (e.g., politics) to a less emotionally laden topic.
Suppress or amplify emotions	Consciously block out thoughts that produce dysfunctional emotions or more actively think about things that produce expected emotions.	• Maintain an impersonal relationship with patients (avoid becoming emotionally attached to their plight).
Shift attention	Change the focus of one's attention.	• Switch to an engaging and enjoyable work activity that takes your mind off something that caused negative emotions earlier that day.
Reframe the situation	Cognitively reevaluate a particular event so it generates desired emotions.	• Rather than viewing a client presentation as a failure, reframe the event as a learning moment that had a low probability of success.

EMOTIONAL INTELLIGENCE

Emotional intelligence (EI) is a set of *abilities* that enable us to recognize and regulate our own emotions as well as the emotions of other people. This definition refers to the four main dimensions shown in Exhibit 4.3.[42]

- *Awareness of our own emotions.* This is the ability to perceive and understand the meaning of our own emotions. People with higher EI have better awareness of their emotions and are better able to make sense of them. They can eavesdrop on their emotional responses to specific situations and use this awareness as conscious information.[43]
- *Management of our own emotions.* Everyone manages their own emotions to some extent. We suppress disruptive impulses and try not to feel angry or frustrated when events go against us. We try to feel joy and happiness toward others on such occasions. We re-energize ourselves to break out of mid-day lethargy. More generally, management of our own emotions involves deep acting and the associated emotion regulation practices described earlier.
- *Awareness of others' emotions.* This is the ability to perceive and understand the emotions of other people.[44] It relates to *empathy*—having an understanding of and sensitivity to the feelings, thoughts, and situations of others (see Chapter 3). This ability includes comprehending the other person's situation, experiencing his or her emotions, and knowing his or her needs, even when unstated. Awareness of others' emotions also includes being organizationally aware, such as sensing office politics and the presence of informal social networks.
- *Management of others' emotions.* This dimension of EI includes consoling people who feel sad, emotionally inspiring team members to complete a class project on time, getting strangers to feel comfortable working with you, and dissipating coworker stress and other dysfunctional emotions that they experience.

The four dimensions of emotional intelligence form a foundational hierarchy.[45] Awareness of your own emotions is the base of that foundation

Exhibit 4.3 Dimensions of Emotional Intelligence

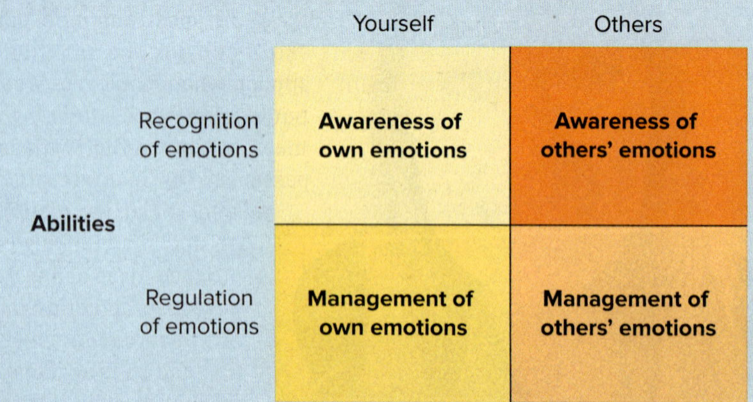

Sources: D. Goleman, "An EI-Based Theory of Performance," in *The Emotionally Intelligent Workplace*, ed. C. Cherniss and D. Goleman (San Francisco: Jossey-Bass, 2001), 28; P.J. Jordan and S.A. Lawrence, "Emotional Intelligence in Teams: Development and Initial Validation of the Short Version of the Workgroup Emotional Intelligence Profile (WEIP-S)," *Journal of Management & Organization* 15 (2009): 452–69.

emotional intelligence (EI) a set of abilities to perceive and express emotion, assimilate emotion in thought, understand and reason with emotion, and regulate emotion in oneself and others

Mc Graw Hill connect

SELF-ASSESSMENT 4.2: How Well Do You Recognize and Regulate Emotions?

Importance of Emotional Intelligence in the Workplace[48]

92% of 800 American and Canadian employees surveyed believe they have strong emotional intelligence.

22% of 860 UK and Australian managers surveyed say too little emphasis is put on emotional intelligence by employers during the hiring process.

74% of 750 executives from Europe, United States, India, and China believe that emotional intelligence will become a "must-have" skill for all employees.

61% of 800 American and Canadian employees surveyed admit they've let emotions get the better of them at work.

17% of 750 executives from Europe, United States, India, and China say their organization conducts emotional intelligence training for nonsupervisory employees.

(Photo): Jack Hollingsworth/Blend Images LLC

because you need that awareness to engage in the higher levels of EI. You can't manage your own emotions if you don't know what they are (i.e., low self-awareness). Managing other people's emotions is the highest level of EI because this ability requires awareness of your own and others' emotions. To diffuse an angry conflict between two employees, for example, you need to understand the emotions they are experiencing and manage your emotions (and display of emotions). To manage your own emotions, you also need to be aware of your current emotions.

Emotional Intelligence Outcomes and Development

Most jobs involve social interaction with coworkers or external stakeholders, so employees need emotional intelligence to work effectively.[46] Studies suggest that people with high EI are more effective team members, perform better in jobs requiring emotional labor, make better decisions involving other people, and maintain a more positive mindset for creative work. EI also is associated with effective leadership because leaders engage in emotional labor (e.g., showing patience to employees even when they might feel frustrated) and actively regulate the emotions of others (e.g., helping staff members feel optimism for the future even though they just lost an important contract). However, emotional intelligence does not improve some forms of performance, such as tasks that require minimal social interaction.[47]

Given the potential value of emotional intelligence, it's not surprising that some organizations try to measure this ability in job applicants. Several organizations also have training programs to improve employees' emotional intelligence.[49] These programs usually teach participants about the concept, test their EI when the program begins, and provide ongoing feedback about how well they understand and manage others' emotions. For instance, the San Diego Police Department conducts a course in which officers develop emotional intelligence and effective communication skills, including de-escalation role-playing scenarios. "If you describe how a good officer anywhere does their job, you're describing what we've come to recognize as emotional intelligence," explains San Diego police psychologist Dan Blumberg. "It's someone who understands himself or herself and can understand emotions evoked during the job and manage their emotions effectively. They understand the emotions of others and are able to use emotions to create positive encounters."[50] Emotional intelligence also increases with age; it is part of the process called maturity.

So far, this chapter has introduced the model of emotions and attitudes, as well as emotional intelligence, as the means by which we manage emotions in the workplace. The next two sections look at two specific attitudes: job satisfaction and organizational commitment. These two attitudes are so important in our understanding of workplace behavior that some experts suggest the two combined should be called "overall job attitude."[51]

OB THEORY TO PRACTICE

Training Emotional Intelligence at Indian Railways

Indian Railways is experiencing rapid change, which requires managers with high emotional intelligence to effectively lead that change. Thousands of managers at India's largest employer are attending workshops to help them understand emotional intelligence and its relevance to their daily leadership roles. Managers complete a well-known emotional intelligence test, which is followed by feedback and coaching by specialist trainers to help them improve weaker aspects of their emotional intelligence.

"Emotional intelligence is just one component of a larger canvas of better training for railway officers," explains Indian Railways Board chairman Ashwani Lohani, who initiated the massive program. "My emphasis across the organization is 'satyanishtha'—a mission for inculcating ethics and integrity among our employees. EI is an input in that direction."

LO 4-3 Summarize the consequences of job dissatisfaction, as well as strategies to increase organizational (affective) commitment.

JOB SATISFACTION

When people mention work attitudes, they are typically referring to **job satisfaction**, a person's evaluation of his or her job and work context.[52] It is an *appraisal* of the perceived job characteristics, work environment, and emotional experiences at work. Satisfied employees have a favorable evaluation of their jobs, based on their observations and emotional experiences. Job satisfaction is best viewed as a collection of attitudes about different aspects of the job and work context. You might like your coworkers but be less satisfied with your workload, for instance.

How satisfied are employees at work? The answer depends on the person, the workplace, and the country. Global surveys, such as the one shown in Exhibit 4.4, indicate that job satisfaction is currently highest in India, Mexico, Turkey, and the United States. The lowest levels of overall job satisfaction have recently been recorded in Japan, Hong Kong, and Singapore.

Can we conclude from these surveys that most employees in India, Mexico, Turkey, and the United States are happy at work? Possibly, but their overall job satisfaction probably isn't as high as these statistics suggest. One problem is that surveys often use a single direct question, such as "How satisfied are you with your job?" Many dissatisfied employees are reluctant to reveal their feelings in a direct question because this is tantamount to admitting that they made a poor job choice and are not enjoying a large part of their life. The inflated results are evident in the fact that employees tend to report less satisfaction when asked about specific aspects of their work. Furthermore, studies report that many employees plan to look for work within the next year or would leave their current employer if the right opportunity came along.[54]

A second problem is that cultural values make it difficult to compare job satisfaction across countries. People in Japan tend to subdue their emotions in public, and there is evidence that they also avoid extreme survey ratings such as "very satisfied." A third problem is that job satisfaction changes with economic conditions. Employees with the highest job satisfaction in current surveys tend to be in countries where the economies are chugging along quite well.[55]

Job Satisfaction and Work Behavior

Job satisfaction influences task performance, organizational citizenship, employee turnover, and other individual behaviors described in Chapter 1.[56] However, the relationship is somewhat more complex because two dissatisfied employees might engage in different behaviors, depending on their personal attributes

Exhibit 4.4 Job Satisfaction in Selected Countries[53]

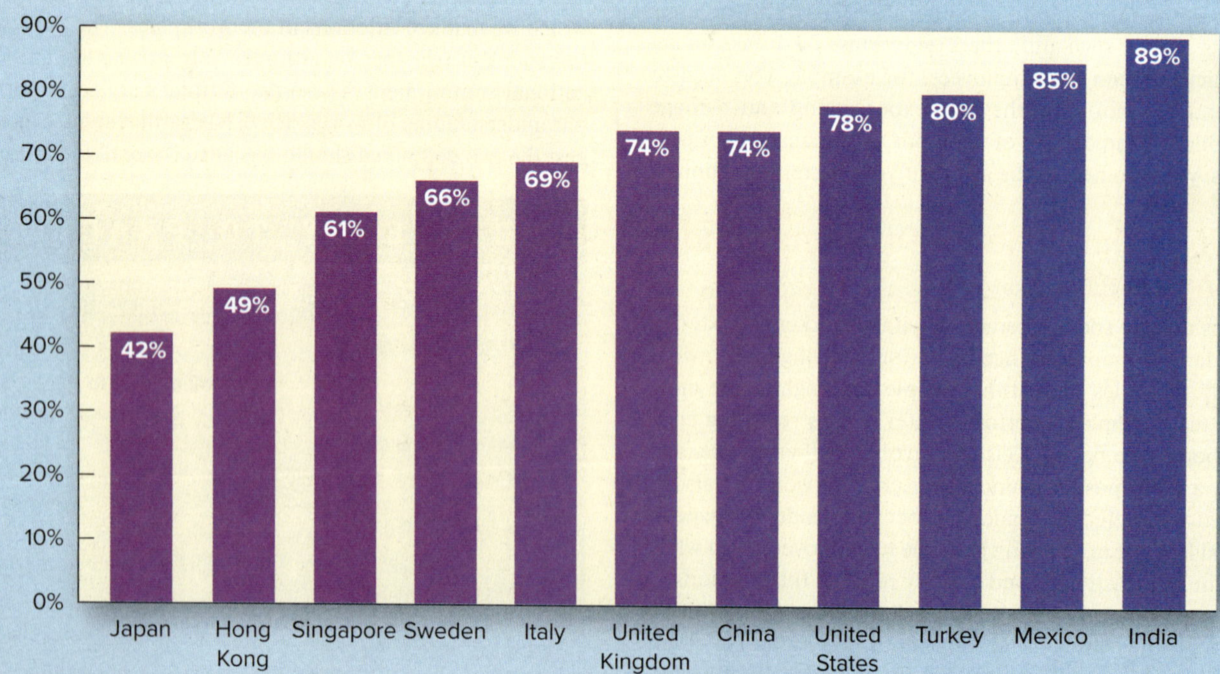

Percentage of employees in each country who said they are, in general, satisfied or very satisfied working for their current employer. Survey data were collected in 2019 for Randstad Holdings nv, with a minimum of 400 employees in each country. This exhibit shows results from selected countries across the full range of 34 countries studied.

job satisfaction a person's evaluation of his or her job and work context

exit–voice–loyalty–neglect (EVLN) model the four ways, as indicated in the name, that employees respond to job dissatisfaction

and the situation. A useful template for organizing and understanding the consequences of job dissatisfaction is the **exit–voice–loyalty–neglect (EVLN) model**. As the name suggests, the EVLN model identifies four ways that employees respond to dissatisfaction:[57]

- *Exit.* Exit includes leaving the organization, transferring to another work unit, or at least trying to get away from the dissatisfying situation. The traditional theory is that job dissatisfaction builds over time and eventually becomes strong enough that the employee is motivated to search for better work opportunities elsewhere. This is likely true to some extent, but it is more likely that specific "shock events" quickly energize employees to think about and engage in exit behavior. For example, the emotional reaction you experience to an unfair management decision or a conflict episode with a coworker motivates you to look at job ads and speak to friends about job opportunities where they work. This begins the process of visualizing yourself working at another company and psychologically withdrawing from your current employer.[58]
- *Voice.* Voice is any attempt to change, rather than escape from, the dissatisfying situation. Voice can be a constructive response, such as recommending ways for management to improve the situation, or it can be more confrontational, such as filing formal grievances or forming a coalition to oppose a decision.[59] In the extreme, some employees might engage in counterproductive behaviors to get attention and force changes in the organization.
- *Loyalty.* In the original version of this model, loyalty was only briefly mentioned as an outcome of dissatisfaction. Instead, the original model stated that loyalty predicted whether people chose exit or voice (i.e., high loyalty resulted in voice; low loyalty produced exit).[60] More recent writers describe loyalty as an outcome, but in various and somewhat unclear ways. Generally, they suggest that "loyalists" are employees who respond to dissatisfaction by patiently waiting—some say they "suffer in silence"—for the problem to work itself out or be resolved by others.[61]
- *Neglect.* Neglect includes reducing work effort, paying less attention to quality, and increasing absenteeism and lateness. It is generally considered a passive activity that has negative consequences for the organization.

Which of the four EVLN alternatives do employees use? It depends on the person and the situation.[62] Voice is preferred by employees with higher extraversion and conscientiousness, likely because these personality factors relate to a person's assertiveness, dutifulness, and outgoing nature. Past experience also influences which EVLN action is applied. Dissatisfied employees are more likely to apply exit or neglect if they were unsuccessful with voice in the past. Loyalty, as it was intended in the original exit–voice–loyalty model, is another important factor. Specifically, employees are more likely to quit when they have low loyalty to the company, and they are more likely to engage in voice when they have high loyalty. An employee's response to dissatisfaction also depends on the situation. Employees are less likely to use the exit option when there are few alternative job prospects, for example. Dissatisfied employees are more likely to use voice than the other options when they are aware that other employees are dependent on them and when organizational leaders encourage employees to discuss their concerns.[63]

Voice is any attempt to change, rather than escape from, the dissatisfying situation, such as providing recommendations, complaining about the problem, mounting opposition through a coalition, or filing a formal grievance.
fizkes/Getty Images

Job Satisfaction and Performance

Does job satisfaction predict job performance? In other words, is a happy worker a productive worker? This is one of the oldest debates in workplace attitudes, and one that has flip-flopped over the years.[64] In recent years, studies have fairly consistently concluded that the "happy worker" hypothesis is true, but only to some extent. In other words, there is a moderately positive relationship between job satisfaction and performance.[65]

Why does job satisfaction affect employee performance only "to some extent"? One reason is that general attitudes (such as job satisfaction) don't predict specific behaviors very well. As the EVLN model explained, reduced performance (a form of neglect) is only one of four possible responses to dissatisfaction. A second reason is that some employees have little control over their performance because their work effort is paced by technology or interdependence with coworkers in the production process. An assembly-line worker, for instance, installs a fixed number of windshields each hour with about the same quality of installation whether he or she has high or low job satisfaction.

A third consideration is that job performance might cause job satisfaction, rather than vice versa.[66] Higher performers tend to have higher satisfaction because they receive more rewards and recognition than do low-performing employees. The connection between job satisfaction and performance isn't stronger because many organizations do not reward good performance very well.

Job Satisfaction and Customer Satisfaction

Wegmans Food Markets in Rochester, New York, has an unusual motto: *Employees first, customers second.* The supermarket chain definitely values its customers, but it does so by caring as much for its employees. "What's most important to us is that our employees feel that Wegmans is a great place to work," explains chairman and former CEO Danny Wegman. "When our people feel cared about and respected, they turn around and make our customers feel that way too."

Research supports Wegmans' philosophy. In fact, evidence suggests that job satisfaction has a stronger effect on customer service than on overall performance. The effect of job satisfaction on customer service and company profits is detailed in the **service profit chain model**, diagrammed in Exhibit 4.5. This model shows that job satisfaction has a positive effect on customer service, which eventually benefits shareholder financial returns.

The service profit chain model process begins with workplace practices that increase or decrease job satisfaction. Job satisfaction then influences whether employees stay (employee retention) as well as their motivation and behavior on the job. Retention, motivation, and behavior affect service quality, which influences the customer's satisfaction, perceived value of the service, and tendency to recommend the service to others (referrals). These customer activities influence the company's profitability and growth. The service profit chain model has strong research support. However, the benefits of job satisfaction take considerable time to flow through to the organization's bottom line.[68]

Within the service profit chain model are two key explanations for why satisfied employees tend to produce happier and more loyal customers.[69] One explanation is that job satisfaction tends to put employees in a more positive mood, and people in a good mood more naturally and frequently display friendliness and positive emotions. When employees have good feelings, their display of positive emotions "rubs off" on most customers, so customers feel happier and consequently form a positive evaluation of the service experience (i.e., higher service quality). The effect is also mutual—happy customers make employees happier—which can lead to a virtuous cycle of positive emotions in the service experience.

> It just seems common sense to me that if you start with a happy, well-motivated workforce, you're much more likely to have happy customers.[67]
>
> —Sir Richard Branson, founder of Virgin Group

Exhibit 4.5 Service Profit Chain Model

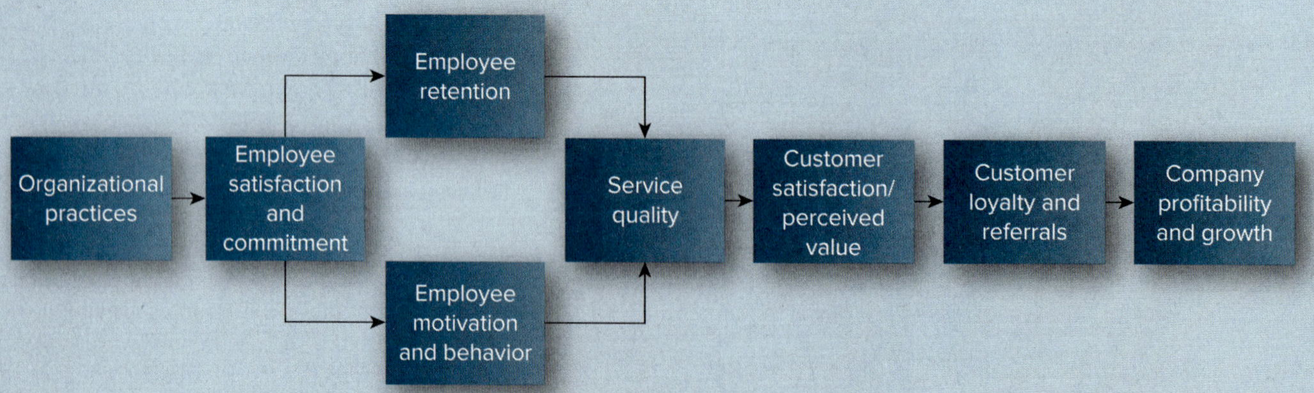

Sources: This model is based on J.I. Heskett, W.E. Sasser, and L.A. Schlesinger, *The Service Profit Chain* (New York: Free Press, 1997); A.J. Rucci, S.P. Kirn, and R.T. Quinn, "The Employee-Customer-Profit Chain at Sears," *Harvard Business Review* 76 (1998): 83–97; S.P. Brown and S.K. Lam, "A Meta-Analysis of Relationships Linking Employee Satisfaction to Customer Responses," *Journal of Retailing* 84 (2008): 243–55.

The second explanation is that satisfied employees are less likely to quit their jobs, so they have more work experience (i.e., better knowledge and skills) to serve clients. Lower turnover also enables customers to have the same employees serve them on different occasions, thereby providing more consistent service. Some evidence indicates that customers build their loyalty to specific employees, not to the organization, so keeping employee turnover low tends to build customer loyalty.

Job Satisfaction and Business Ethics

Along with its significant effect on employee behavior, job satisfaction is an ethical issue that influences the organization's reputation in the community. People spend a large portion of their time working in organizations, and many societies now expect companies to provide work environments that are safe and enjoyable. Indeed, employees in several countries closely monitor ratings of the best companies to work for, an indication that employee satisfaction is a virtue worth considerable goodwill to employers. The importance of this reputation is apparent when an organization has low job satisfaction. The company typically tries to hide this fact, and when morale problems become public, corporate leaders are usually quick to take steps to improve the situation.

ORGANIZATIONAL COMMITMENT

Organizational commitment—specifically **affective organizational commitment**—represents the other half (with job satisfaction) of what some experts call "overall job attitude." Affective commitment is the employee's emotional attachment to, involvement in, and identification with an organization. It is a psychological bond whereby one chooses to be dedicated to and responsible for the organization. Furthermore, affective commitment is intrinsically motivated because it originates from the employee's self-concept and values alignment rather than from external forces.[70]

Affective commitment differs from **continuance commitment**, which is a calculative attachment to the organization. Employees develop continuance commitment when leaving the organization would incur significant financial or social costs (e.g., "I hate this place but can't afford to quit!").[71] This happens when quitting forfeits a large deferred financial bonus or risks weakening social bonds with friends at work. Continuance commitment also occurs when employees have limited employment opportunities elsewhere (e.g., "I dislike working here but there are no other jobs available"). In each situation, continuance commitment is motivation to remain with and participate in the organization due to external forces, whereas the motivation of affective commitment originates internally from the person's identity, bond, and psychological attachment to the organization.

Affective and continuance commitment have a third sibling, called *normative commitment,* which refers to a felt obligation or moral duty to the organization.[72] Felt obligation applies the **norm of reciprocity**—a natural human motivation to support, contribute, and otherwise "pay back" the organization because it has invested in and supported the employee (see Chapter 9). The sense of moral duty is the motivation to remain with and contribute to the organization because it is the right thing to do as a member of the organization. Normative commitment receives less attention because it overlaps somewhat with affective commitment and its meaning is somewhat ambiguous.

service profit chain model a theory explaining how employees' job satisfaction influences company profitability indirectly through service quality, customer loyalty, and related factors

affective organizational commitment an individual's emotional attachment to, involvement in, and identification with an organization

continuance commitment an individual's calculative attachment to an organization

norm of reciprocity a felt obligation and social expectation of helping or otherwise giving something of value to someone who has already helped or given something of value to you

Consequences of Affective and Continuance Commitment

Affective commitment can be a significant competitive advantage.[73] Employees with a strong psychological bond to the organization are less likely to quit their jobs and be absent from work. They also have higher work motivation and organizational citizenship, as well as somewhat higher job performance. Affective commitment also improves customer satisfaction because long-tenure employees have better

Mc Graw Hill connect

SELF-ASSESSMENT 4.3: How Committed Are You to Your School?

> Employees develop continuance commitment when leaving the company would incur significant financial or social costs or when they have limited employment opportunities elsewhere.

knowledge of work practices and because clients like to do business with the same employees. One concern is that employees with very high affective commitment tend to have high conformity, which results in lower creativity. Another problem is that employees with very high commitment are more motivated to engage in illegal activity in defense of the organization. However, most companies suffer from too little rather than too much affective commitment.

In contrast to the benefits of affective commitment, employees with high levels of continuance commitment tend to have *lower* performance and are *less* likely to engage in organizational citizenship behaviors. Furthermore, unionized employees with high continuance commitment are more likely to use formal grievances, whereas employees with high affective commitment engage in more cooperative problem solving when employee–employer relations sour.[74] In general, employers should not rely on continuance commitment to retain staff. Instead, they should focus on winning employees' hearts through affective commitment.

Organizational comprehension is a necessary prerequisite to affective commitment because it is difficult to identify with or feel loyal to something that you don't know very well.
pathdoc/Shutterstock

Building Organizational Commitment

There are almost as many ways to build and maintain affective commitment as there are topics in this textbook, but here are the most frequently mentioned strategies in the literature:

- *Justice and support.* Affective commitment is higher in organizations that support organizational justice, which we discuss in the next chapter. Similarly, organizations that support employee well-being tend to cultivate higher levels of loyalty in return.[75]
- *Shared values.* The definition of affective commitment refers to a person's identification with the organization, and that identification is highest when employees believe their values are congruent with the organization's dominant values. Employees also experience more positive emotions when their personal values are aligned with corporate values and actions, and these positive emotions increase their motivation to stay with the organization.[76]
- *Trust.* **Trust** refers to positive expectations one person has toward another person in situations involving risk.[77] Trust means putting faith in others. It is also a reciprocal activity: To receive trust, you must demonstrate trust. Employees identify with and feel obliged to work for an organization only when they trust its leaders. This explains why layoffs are one of the greatest blows to affective commitment. By reducing job security, companies reduce the trust employees have in their employer and the employment relationship.[78]
- *Organizational comprehension.* Organizational comprehension refers to how well employees understand the organization, including its strategic direction, social dynamics, and physical layout.[79] This awareness is a necessary prerequisite to affective commitment because it is difficult to identify with or feel loyal to something that you don't know very well. Furthermore, lack of information produces uncertainty, and the resulting stress can distance employees from that source of uncertainty (i.e., the organization). The practical implication here is to ensure that employees develop a reasonably clear and complete mental model of the organization. This occurs by giving staff information and opportunities to keep up to date about organizational events, to interact with coworkers, to discover what goes on in different parts of the organization, and to learn about the organization's history and future plans.[80]
- *Employee involvement.* Employee involvement increases affective commitment by strengthening the employee's psychological ownership and social identity with the organization.[81] Employees feel that they are an integral part of the organization when they participate in decisions that guide the organization's future (see Chapter 6). Participation also builds loyalty because it demonstrates the company's trust in its employees.

Organizational commitment and job satisfaction represent two of the most often studied and discussed attitudes in the workplace. Each is linked to emotional episodes and cognitive judgments about the workplace and relationship with the company. Emotions also play an important role in another concept that is on everyone's mind these days: stress. The final section of this chapter provides an overview of work-related stress and how it can be managed.

LO 4-4 Describe the stress experience and review four major stressors.

WORK-RELATED STRESS AND ITS MANAGEMENT

When asked if they often feel stressed by their work, most employees these days will answer with an emphatic Yes! Not only do most people understand the concept; they claim to have plenty of personal experience with it. **Stress** is most often described as an adaptive response to a situation that is perceived as challenging or threatening to the person's well-being.[82] It is a physiological and psychological condition that prepares us to adapt to hostile or noxious environmental conditions. One school of thought suggests that stress is a negative evaluation of the external environment. However, critics of this *cognitive appraisal* perspective point out that stress is more accurately described as an emotional experience, which may occur before or after a conscious evaluation of the situation.[83]

Whether stress is a complex emotion or a cognitive evaluation of the environment, it has become a pervasive experience in

trust positive expectations one person has toward another person in situations involving risk

stress an adaptive response to a situation that is perceived as challenging or threatening to the person's well-being

general adaptation syndrome a model of the stress experience, consisting of three stages: alarm reaction, resistance, and exhaustion

Stressed Out, Burnt Out[85]

65% of 1,951 American professionals surveyed say that their level of stress at work today is higher than it was 5 years ago.

40% of National Health Service employees in the UK report feeling unwell as a result of work-related stress over the previous year.

24% of more than 100,000 Canadian adults (18–64 years) surveyed say that most days in their life are quite a bit or extremely stressful.

35% of 151,000 adults interviewed across 142 countries say they had experienced significant stress the previous day.

12% of 13,200 adults representative of the population in 22 countries say their work-related stress is unmanageable.

(Photo): donskarpo/Getty Images

connect

SELF-ASSESSMENT 4.4: How Stressed Are You?

the daily lives of most people. Stress is typically described as a negative experience. This is known as *distress*—the degree of physiological, psychological, and behavioral deviation from healthy functioning. However, some level and form of stress—called *eustress*—is a necessary part of life because it activates and motivates people to achieve goals, change their environments, and succeed in life's challenges.[84] Our focus is on the causes and management of distress because it has become a chronic problem in many societies.

General Adaptation Syndrome

In the 1930s, Hans Selye (often described as the "father" of stress research) first documented the stress experience, called the **general adaptation syndrome**. Selye determined that people have a fairly consistent and automatic physiological response to stressful situations, which helps them cope with environmental demands.[86]

The general adaptation syndrome consists of the three stages shown in Exhibit 4.6. The *alarm reaction* stage occurs when a threat or challenge activates the physiological stress responses that we described a few paragraphs ago. The individual's energy level and coping effectiveness decrease in response to the initial shock. The second stage, *resistance*, activates various biochemical, psychological, and behavioral mechanisms that give the individual more energy and engage coping mechanisms to overcome or remove the source of stress. People have a limited resistance capacity, and if the source of stress persists, the individual will eventually move into the third stage, *exhaustion*. Most of us are able to remove the source of stress or remove ourselves from that source before becoming too exhausted. However, people who frequently reach exhaustion have an increased risk of long-term physiological and psychological damage.[87]

Exhibit 4.6 General Adaptation Syndrome

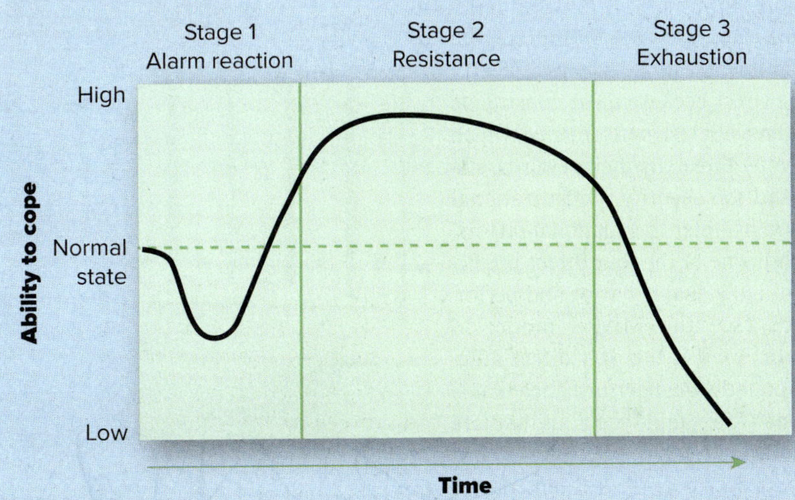

Source: Adapted from H. Selye, *The Stress of Life* (New York: McGraw-Hill, 1956).

Consequences of Distress

Stress takes its toll on the human body.[88] Many people experience tension headaches, muscle pain, and related problems mainly due to muscle contractions from the stress response. High stress levels also contribute to cardiovascular disease, including heart attacks and strokes, and may be associated with

> Technology and globalization contribute to work overload because they tether employees to their job for more hours of the day.

some forms of cancer. One major review estimated that more than 100,000 deaths annually and as much as 8 percent of health care costs in the United States are due to the consequences of work-related stress. Stress also produces various psychological consequences such as job dissatisfaction, moodiness, depression, and lower organizational commitment. Furthermore, various behavioral outcomes have been linked to high or persistent stress, including lower job performance, poor decision making, and increased workplace accidents and aggressive behavior. Most people react to stress through "fight or flight," so, as a form of flight, increased absenteeism is another outcome of stress.[89]

Stressors: The Causes of Stress

Before identifying ways to manage work-related stress, we must first understand its causes, known as stressors. **Stressors** include any environmental conditions that place a physical or emotional demand on a person.[90] There are numerous stressors in the workplace and in life in general. Four of the most common work-related stressors are organizational constraints, interpersonal conflict, work overload, and low task control.[91]

Organizational Constraints Stress research has identified organizational constraints as one of the most pervasive causes of workplace stress.[92] This stressor includes lack of equipment, supplies, budget funding, coworker support, information, and other resources necessary to complete the required work. Most employees experience stress because these constraints interfere with task performance, which indirectly threatens their rewards, status, and job security. Organizational constraints refer to situational factors, which is one of the four direct predictors of individual behavior and performance (see the MARS model in Chapter 1). It is the only direct influence on individual performance that is beyond the employee's immediate control. This lack of control is a powerful stressor because it threatens the individual's fundamental drive to influence his or her external environment.

Interpersonal Conflict As we will learn in Chapter 10, dysfunctional conflict can easily flair up and, left unchecked, escalate to a level that produces considerable stress and counterproductive work behaviors. In organizational settings, most interpersonal conflict is caused by structural sources such as ambiguous rules, lack of resources, and conflicting goals between employees or departments. However, conflict is more stressful when the parties attack each other's personal attributes (intelligence, experience, etc.) rather than focus on the logic and factual foundation of the arguments presented. Also, one form of interpersonal conflict that has become an increasing concern is workplace harassment, including workplace bullying, sexual harassment, and other forms of incivility and mistreatment by coworkers, managers, or customers.[93]

Work Overload Work overload is a common workplace stressor. Employees are under pressure to complete more work with more effort than they can provide within the allotted time.[94] Work overload is evident when employees consume more of their personal time to get the job done. Technology and globalization also contribute to work overload because they tether employees to their job for more hours of the day. People

Work overload is a common workplace stressor because employees are under pressure to complete more work with more effort than they can provide within the allotted time.
Antonio Guillem/Shutterstock

increasingly work with coworkers in distant time zones, and their communication habits of being constantly "on" make it difficult to separate work from personal life. Some employees amplify their work overload by adopting an "ideal worker norm" in which they expect themselves and others to work longer hours.[95]

Low Task Control Workplace stress is higher when employees lack control over how and when they perform their tasks as well as lack control over the pace of work activity. Work is potentially more stressful when it is paced by a machine, it involves monitoring equipment, or the work schedule is controlled by someone else. Low task control is a stressor because employees face high workloads without the ability to adjust the pace of the load to their own energy, attention span, and other resources. Furthermore, the degree to which low task control is a stressor increases with the burden of responsibility the employee must carry.[96] Assembly-line workers have low task control, but they experience fairly low stress if their level of responsibility is also low. In contrast, sports coaches are under immense pressure to win games (high responsibility), yet they have little control over what happens on the playing field (low task control).

Individual Differences in Stress

Two employees exposed to the same stressor often experience different levels of stress. One reason is the employee's physical health. Regular exercise and a healthy lifestyle produce a larger store of energy to cope with stress. A second reason is that people use different strategies to cope with the stressor.[97] Some try to remove the stressor or to minimize its presence. Others seek out support from coworkers and friends or try to reframe the stressor in a more positive light. Some coping strategies work better for specific stressors and some are better across all stressors.[98] Those who prefer a less effective coping mechanism in a particular situation would experience more stress in response to that situation.

Personality is the third reason people experience different levels of stress when faced with the same stressor.[99] Individuals with low neuroticism (high emotional stability) usually experience lower stress levels because, by definition, they are less prone to anxiety, depression, and other negative emotions. Extraverts also tend to experience lower stress than do introverts, likely because extraversion includes a degree of positive thinking and extraverts interact with others, which helps buffer the effect of stressors. Those with a positive self-concept—high self-esteem, self-efficacy, and internal locus of control (see Chapter 3)—feel more confident and in control when faced with a stressor. In other words, they tend to have a stronger sense of optimism.[100]

Stress also tends to be higher among those who suffer from *workaholism*. Workaholics have an uncontrollable work motivation, constantly think about work, and have low work enjoyment.[101]

stressors any environmental conditions that place a physical or emotional demand on the person

work–life integration the degree that people are effectively engaged in their various work and nonwork roles and have a low degree of role conflict across those life domains

SELF-ASSESSMENT 4.5: Are You a Workaholic?

LO 4-5 Identify five ways to manage workplace stress.

Managing Work-Related Stress

Many people deny the existence of their stress until it has more serious outcomes. This avoidance strategy amplifies the stress, because the failure to cope with stress becomes another stressor on top of the one that created the stress in the first place. To prevent this vicious cycle, employers and employees need to apply one or more of the stress management strategies described next: remove the stressor, withdraw from the stressor, change stress perceptions, control stress consequences, and receive social support.[102]

Remove the Stressor There are many ways to remove the stressor, but some of the more common actions involve assigning employees to jobs that match their skills and preferences, reducing excessive workplace noise, having a complaint system that takes corrective action against harassment, and giving employees more control over the work process. Another important way that companies can remove stressors is through **work–life integration** initiatives (see Chapter 1). For example, personal leave benefits, such as maternity and paternity leave, temporarily offer employees paid nonwork time to manage special circumstances. Remote work potentially improves work-life integration by reducing or eliminating commuting time and increasing flexibility to perform nonwork obligations (such as picking up the kids from school). Some companies and at least one government (France) have introduced policies that prohibit managers and employees from communicating work-related issues during nonwork hours.[103]

Withdraw from the Stressor Removing the stressor may be the ideal solution, but it isn't feasible in every situation. Another strategy is to permanently or temporarily remove employees from the stressor. Permanent withdrawal occurs when employees are transferred to jobs that are more compatible with their abilities and values. Temporarily withdrawing from stressors is the most frequent way that employees manage stress. Vacations and holidays are important opportunities for employees to recover from stress and reenergize for future challenges.[104] Many firms also provide innovative ways for employees to withdraw from stressful work throughout the day such as game rooms, ice-cream cart breaks, nap rooms, and cafeterias that include live piano recitals.

Change Stress Perceptions How much stress employees experience depends on how they perceive the stressor.[105] Consequently, another way to manage stress is by coaching employees to improve their self-concept, personal goal setting, and self-reinforcement practices. Job challenges are perceived as less threatening when employees develop these self-views and self-management activities. In addition, research suggests that some (but not all) forms of humor can improve optimism and create positive emotions by taking some psychological weight off a stressful situation.[106]

Control Stress Consequences Keeping physically fit, maintaining a healthy lifestyle, and getting plenty of sleep, are effective stress management strategies because they control stress consequences. Good physical fitness reduces the adverse physiological consequences of stress by helping employees moderate their breathing and heart rate, muscle tension, and stomach acidity. The key variable here is physical fitness, not exercise. Exercise leads to physical fitness, but research suggests that exercise does not reduce stress symptoms among people who are not yet physically fit.[107] Various forms of meditation reduce anxiety and other symptoms of stress, but their effect on blood pressure and other physiological symptoms is minimal.[108] Wellness programs also can assist in controlling the consequences of stress. These programs inform employees about better nutrition and fitness, regular sleep, and other good health habits. Many large companies offer *employee assistance programs (EAPs)*—counseling services that help employees resolve marital, financial, or work-related troubles.

Receive Social Support Social support occurs when coworkers, supervisors, family members, friends, and others provide emotional and/or informational support to buffer an individual's stress experience. Social support potentially improves the person's optimism and self-confidence because support makes people feel valued and worthy. Social support also provides information to help the person interpret, comprehend, and possibly remove the stressor. For instance, to reduce a new employee's stress, coworkers could describe ways to handle difficult customers. Seeking social support is called a "tend and befriend" response to stress, and research suggests that women often take this route rather than the "fight-or-flight" response mentioned earlier.[110]

OB THEORY TO PRACTICE

Reducing Stress by Rewarding Longer Sleeps

SOURCENEXT/Alamy Stock Photo

Japanese employees are chronically overworked and sleep deprived. On average, Japanese men and women sleep only 6 hours and 35 minutes each day, which is the lowest among 28 countries studied. One upscale wedding organizer in Japan hopes to reduce the Japanese penchant for overwork by motivating its employees to sleep longer. The Tokyo-based company awards points to staff members who sleep at least six hours every night for at least five days each week. Employee sleep patterns are tracked by an app. The points, which are exchanged for food in the company cafeteria, can add up to more than $500 per year.[109]

Mc Graw Hill connect

SELF-ASSESSMENT 4.6: How Do You Cope with Stressful Situations?

Study Checklist

Connect® is available for *M Organizational Behavior.* Additional resources include:

✓ Exercises:

- **Case Analysis:** Apply concepts within the context of a real-world situation.
- **Click and Drag:** Helps make the connection between theory and application through matching, ranking, or grouping activities.
- **Video Case:** See management in action through interactive videos.
- **Self-Assessment:** Designed to promote student self-awareness and reflection, these research-based surveys contain detailed feedback for students.
- **Application-Based Activities:** These highly interactive, application- and analysis-based exercises allow students to take on specific roles to complete management-related tasks within a real-world context.

✓ **SmartBook 2.0™**—Smartbook 2.0 is an adaptive learning solution that provides personalized learning to individual student needs, continually adapts to pinpoint knowledge gaps and focuses learning on concepts requiring additional study. It fosters more productive learning, takes the guesswork out of what to study, and helps students better prepare for class.

©Natthawat Jamnapa/123RF

Notes

1. N. Fearn, "Employee Activism: How Staff Revolts Are Shaking up the IT Recruitment Landscape," *Computer Weekly*, June 27, 2019; R. Ansar, "Creating a Culture beyond Ping Pong Tables and Sleeping Pods," *E27*, November 16, 2019; M. Hines, "Here's How HR Leaders Are Keeping a Pulse on Remote Teams," *Built In Chicago*, April 7, 2020.
2. Emotions are also cognitive processes. However, we use the narrow definition of *cognition* as a well-used label referring only to reasoning processes. Also, this and other chapters emphasize that emotional and cognitive processes are intertwined. For recent discussion of this in neuroscience, see L. Pessoa, "Understanding Emotion with Brain Networks," *Current Opinion in Behavioral Sciences*, 19 (2018): 19-25.
3. For discussion of emotions in marketing, economics, and sociology, see W. Kalkhoff, S.R. Thye, and J. Pollock, "Developments in Neurosociology," *Sociology Compass* 10 (2016): 242-58; H. Lin and O. Vartanian, "A Neuroeconomic Framework for Creative Cognition," *Perspectives on Psychological Science* 13 (2018): 655-77; W.M. Lim, "Demystifying Neuromarketing," *Journal of Business Research* 91 (2018): 205-20; A. Konovalov and I. Krajbich, "Over a Decade of Neuroeconomics: What Have We Learned?" *Organizational Research Methods* 22 (2019): 148-73.
4. Although definitions of *emotion* vary, the definition stated here seems to be the most widely accepted. See, for example, N.H. Frijda, "Varieties of Affect: Emotions and Episodes, Moods, and Sentiments," in *The Nature of Emotion: Fundamental Questions*, ed. P. Ekman and R.J. Davidson (New York: Oxford University Press, 1994), 59-67; G. Van Kleef, H. van den Berg, and M. Heerdink, "The Persuasive Power of Emotions: Effects of Emotional Expressions on Attitude Formation and Change," *Journal of Applied Psychology* 100 (2015): 1124-42; A. Scarantino, "The Philosophy of Emotions and Its Impact on Affective Science," in *Handbook of Emotions*, ed. L.F. Barrett, M. Lewis, and J.M. Haviland-Jones, 4th ed. (New York: Guilford Press, 2016), 3-47; R. Smith and R.D. Lane, "Unconscious Emotion: A Cognitive Neuroscientific Perspective," *Neuroscience & Biobehavioral Reviews* 69 (2016): 216-38; M. Résibois et al., "The Relation between Rumination and Temporal Features of Emotion Intensity," *Cognition and Emotion* 32 (2018): 259-74; L.F. Barrett and A.B. Satpute, "Historical Pitfalls and New Directions in the Neuroscience of Emotion," *Neuroscience Letters*, 693 (2019): 9-18.
5. R. Reisenzein, M. Studtmann, and G. Horstmann, "Coherence between Emotion and Facial Expression: Evidence from Laboratory Experiments," *Emotion Review* 5, no. 1 (2013): 16-23; M.D. Lieberman, "Boo! The Consciousness Problem in Emotion," *Cognition and Emotion* 33, no. 1 (2019): 24-30.
6. R.B. Zajonc, "Emotions," in *Handbook of Social Psychology*, ed. D.T. Gilbert, S.T. Fiske, and L. Gardner (New York: Oxford University Press, 1998), 591-634; P. Winkielman, "Bob Zajonc and the Unconscious Emotion," *Emotion Review* 2, no. 4 (2010): 353-62.
7. A.R. Damasio, *The Feeling of What Happens: Body and Emotion in the Making of Consciousness* (New York: Harcourt Brace, 1999), 286; B.Q. Ford and J.J. Gross, "Emotion Regulation: Why Beliefs Matter," *Canadian Psychology* 59 (2018): 1-14; K.C. Berridge, "Evolving Concepts of Emotion and Motivation," *Frontiers in Psychology* 9 (2018), https://doi.org/10.3389/fpsyg.2018.01647.
8. V. van Gogh, T. van Gogh, and I. Stone, *Dear Theo: The Autobiography* (New York: Doubleday, 1937; repr., 1995), 441. This quotation originally appeared in a letter sent by Vincent van Gogh to his brother Théo in 1889.
9. R.J. Larson, E. Diener, and R.E. Lucas, "Emotion: Models, Measures, and Differences," in *Emotions in the Workplace*, ed. R.G. Lord, R.J. Klimoski, and R. Kanfer (San Francisco: Jossey-Bass, 2002), 64-113; L.F. Barrett et al., "The Experience of Emotion," *Annual Review of Psychology* 58, no. 1 (2007): 373-403; M. Yik, J.A. Russell, and J.H. Steiger, "A 12-Point Circumplex Structure of Core Affect," *Emotion* 11, no. 4 (2011): 705-31.
10. R.F. Baumeister, E. Bratslavsky, and C. Finkenauer, "Bad Is Stronger Than Good," *Review of General Psychology* 5, no. 4 (2001): 323-70; A. Vaish, T. Grossmann, and A. Woodward, "Not All Emotions Are Created Equal: The Negativity Bias in Social-Emotional Development," *Psychological Bulletin* 134, no. 3 (2008): 383-403; R.H. Fazio et al., "Positive versus Negative Valence: Asymmetries in Attitude Formation and Generalization as Fundamental Individual Differences," in *Advances in Experimental Social Psychology*, vol. 51, ed. J.M. Olson and M.P. Zanna (Waltham, MA: Academic Press, 2015), 97-146; K. Bebbington et al., "The Sky Is Falling: Evidence of a Negativity Bias in the Social Transmission of Information," *Evolution and Human Behavior* 38, no. 1 (2017): 92-101.
11. A.P. Brief, *Attitudes in and around Organizations* (Thousand Oaks, CA: Sage, 1998); A.H. Eagly and S. Chaiken, "The Advantages of an Inclusive Definition of Attitude," *Social Cognition* 25, no. 5 (2007): 582-602; G. Bohner and N. Dickel, "Attitudes and Attitude Change," *Annual Review of Psychology* 62, no. 1 (2011): 391-417; R.S. Dalal, "Job Attitudes: Cognition and Affect," in *Industrial and Organizational Psychology*, ed. I.B. Weiner, N.W. Schmitt, and S. Highhouse, *Handbook of Psychology*, 2nd ed., ed. I. B. Weiner, vol. 12 (New York: Wiley, 2012), 341-66.
12. Neuroscience has a slightly more complicated distinction between conscious "feeling a feeling" and nonconscious "feeling." See A.R. Damasio, *The Feeling of What Happens: Body and Emotion in the Making of Consciousness* (New York: Harcourt Brace, 1999); F. Hansen, "Distinguishing between Feelings and Emotions in Understanding Communication Effects," *Journal of Business Research* 58, no. 10 (2005): 1426-36; T. Bosse, C.M. Jonker, and J. Treur, "Formalisation of Damasio's Theory of Emotion, Feeling and Core Consciousness," *Consciousness and Cognition* 17, no. 1 (2008): 94-113.
13. W.A. Cunningham and P.D. Zelazo, "Attitudes and Evaluations: A Social Cognitive Neuroscience Perspective," *TRENDS in Cognitive Sciences* 11, no. 3 (2007): 97-104; M.D. Lieberman, "Social Cognitive Neuroscience: A Review of Core Processes," *Annual Review of Psychology* 58, no. 1 (2007): 259-89; M. Fenton-O'Creevy et al., "Thinking, Feeling and Deciding: The Influence of Emotions on the Decision Making and Performance of Traders," *Journal of Organizational Behavior* 32 (2011): 1044-61. The dual emotion-cognition processes are likely the same as the implicit-explicit attitude processes reported by several scholars, as well as tacit knowledge structures. See W.J. Becker and R. Cropanzano, "Organizational Neuroscience: The Promise and Prospects of an Emerging Discipline," *Journal of Organizational Behavior* 31, no. 7 (2010): 1055-59; D. Kahneman, *Thinking Fast and Slow* (New York: Farrar, Straus and Giroux, 2011).
14. D. Albarracín, M.S. Chan, and D. Jiang, "Attitudes and Attitude Change: Social and Personality Considerations About Specific and General Patterns of Behavior," in *The Oxford Handbook of Personality and Social Psychology*, ed. K. Deaux and M. Snyder, 2nd ed. (New York: Oxford University Press, 2018), 439-64.
15. S. Orbell, "Intention-Behavior Relations: A Self-Regulation Perspective," in *Contemporary Perspectives on the Psychology of Attitudes*, ed. G. Haddock and G.R. Maio (East Sussex, UK: Psychology Press, 2004), 145-68.
16. H.M. Weiss and R. Cropanzano, "Affective Events Theory: A Theoretical Discussion of the Structure, Causes and Consequences of Affective Experiences at Work," *Research in Organizational Behavior* 18 (1996): 1-74; A. Bechara et al., "Deciding Advantageously before Knowing the Advantageous Strategy," *Science*

275, no. 5304 (1997): 1293–95; B. Russell and J. Eisenberg, "The Role of Cognition and Attitude in Driving Behavior: Elaborating on Affective Events Theory," in *Experiencing and Managing Emotions in the Workplace*, ed. N.M. Ashkanasy, C.E.J. Hartel, and W.J. Zerbe (Bingley, UK: Emerald Group, 2012), 203–24.

17. J.A. Bargh and M.J. Ferguson, "Beyond Behaviorism: On the Automaticity of Higher Mental Processes," *Psychological Bulletin* 126, no. 6 (2000): 925–45; P. Winkielman and K.C. Berridge, "Unconscious Emotion," *Current Directions in Psychological Science* 13, no. 3 (2004): 120–23; A. Moors, "Automaticity: Componential, Causal, and Mechanistic Explanations," *Annual Review of Psychology* 67, no. 1 (2016): 263–87.

18. A.R. Damasio, *Descartes' Error: Emotion, Reason, and the Human Brain* (New York: Putnam Sons, 1994); P. Ekman, "Basic Emotions," in *Handbook of Cognition and Emotion*, ed. T. Dalgleish and M. Power (San Francisco: Jossey-Bass, 1999), 45–60; A.R. Damasio, *The Feeling of What Happens: Body and Emotion in the Making of Consciousness* (New York: Harcourt Brace and Company, 1999); J.E. LeDoux, "Emotion Circuits in the Brain," *Annual Review of Neuroscience* 23 (2000): 155–84; R. Smith and R.D. Lane, "The Neural Basis of One's Own Conscious and Unconscious Emotional States," *Neuroscience & Biobehavioral Reviews* 57 (2015): 1–29.

19. M.T. Pham, "The Logic of Feeling," *Journal of Consumer Psychology* 14, no. 4 (2004): 360–69; N. Schwarz, "Feelings-as-Information Theory," in *Handbook of Theories of Social Psychology*, ed. P. Van Lange, A. Kruglanski, and E.T. Higgins (London: Sage, 2012), 289–308.

20. We have described likely the most common form of emotion–attitude conflict and ambivalence, but other forms exist. See: A.I. Snyder and Z.L. Tormala, "Valence Asymmetries in Attitude Ambivalence," *Journal of Personality and Social Psychology* 112 (2017): 555–76; I.K. Schneider and N. Schwarz, "Mixed Feelings: The Case of Ambivalence," *Current Opinion in Behavioral Sciences, Mixed Emotions*, 15 (2017): 39–45; N.B. Rothman and S. Melwani, "Feeling Mixed, Ambivalent, and in Flux: The Social Functions of Emotional Complexity for Leaders," *Academy of Management Review* 42 (2017): 259–82.

21. P.C. Nutt, *Why Decisions Fail* (San Francisco, CA: Berrett-Koehler, 2002); S. Finkelstein, *Why Smart Executives Fail* (New York: Viking, 2003); P.C. Nutt, "Search During Decision Making," *European Journal of Operational Research* 160 (2005): 851–76.

22. B. Nordlo, "Why Zoom Video Communications Built a Team Dedicated to Happiness," *Built In Colorado* (blog), July 27, 2018, https://www.builtincolorado.com/2018/07/27/spotlight-working-at-zoom-video-communications-culture; Globe Newswire, "Zoom Is a Glassdoor Employees' Choice Award Winner, Honored as a Top Workplace Again," news release (San Jose, CA: Zoom Video Communications, December 4, 2018). The quotation was retrieved from an employee comment submitted to Glassdoor on June 24, 2019.

23. J. Mesmer-Magnus, D.J. Glew, and C. Viswesvaran, "A Meta-Analysis of Positive Humor in the Workplace," *Journal of Managerial Psychology* 27 (2012): 155–90; C. Robert and M.V.S.P. da, "Conversational Humor and Job Satisfaction at Work: Exploring the Role of Humor Production, Appreciation, and Positive Affect," *HUMOR* 30 (2017): 417–438; C. Robert, ed., *The Psychology of Humor at Work: A Psychological Perspective* (London: Routledge, 2017).

24. M. Kohrman, "10 Ways to Make Your Office More Fun," *Fast Company*, July 23, 2013; J. Ball, "80 Unique & Quirky Corporate Event Ideas," *Friday Funnies* (Sutton Coldfield, UK: Coburg Banks, May 19, 2016), https://www.coburgbanks.co.uk/blog/friday-funnies/corporate-event-ideas/ (accessed June 23, 2017); "39 Insanely Fun Team Building Activities for Work ('Trust Falls' Not Included)," *SnackNation Blog* (Los Angeles: SnackNation, August 29, 2016), http://www.snacknation.com/blog/team-building-activities-for-work/ (accessed June 23, 2017).

25. H.M. Weiss and R. Cropanzano, "Affective Events Theory: A Theoretical Discussion of the Structure, Causes and Consequences of Affective Experiences at Work," *Research in Organizational Behavior* 18 (1996): 1–74.

26. L. Festinger, *A Theory of Cognitive Dissonance* (Evanston, IL: Row, Peterson, 1957); J. Cooper, *Cognitive Dissonance: Fifty Years of a Classic Theory* (London: Sage, 2007); J. Hagège et al., "Suggestion of Self-(in)Coherence Modulates Cognitive Dissonance," *PLOS ONE* 13, no. 8 (August 30, 2018): e0202204, https://doi.org/10.1371/journal.pone.0202204.

27. G.R. Salancik, "Commitment and the Control of Organizational Behavior and Belief," in *New Directions in Organizational Behavior*, ed. B.M. Staw and G.R. Salancik (Chicago: St. Clair, 1977), 1–54; A. McGrath, "Dealing with Dissonance: A Review of Cognitive Dissonance Reduction," *Social and Personality Psychology Compass* 11, no. 12 (2017): e12362, https://doi.org/10.1111/spc3.12362.

28. T.A. Judge, E.A. Locke, and C.C. Durham, "The Dispositional Causes of Job Satisfaction: A Core Evaluations Approach," *Research in Organizational Behavior* 19 (1997): 151–88; T.W.H. Ng and K.L. Sorensen, "Dispositional Affectivity and Work-Related Outcomes: A Meta-Analysis," *Journal of Applied Social Psychology* 39, no. 6 (2009): 1255–87.

29. J. Schaubroeck, D.C. Ganster, and B. Kemmerer, "Does Trait Affect Promote Job Attitude Stability?" *Journal of Organizational Behavior* 17 (1996): 191–96; C. Dormann and D. Zapf, "Job Satisfaction: A Meta-Analysis of Stabilities," *Journal of Organizational Behavior* 22 (2001): 483–504; A.C. Keller and N.K. Semmer, "Changes in Situational and Dispositional Factors as Predictors of Job Satisfaction," *Journal of Vocational Behavior* 83, no. 1 (2013): 88–98.

30. A.S. Wharton, "The Sociology of Emotional Labor," *Annual Review of Sociology* 35 (2009): 147–65; H. Wang, N.C. Hall, and J.L. Taxer, "Antecedents and Consequences of Teachers' Emotional Labor: A Systematic Review and Meta-Analytic Investigation," *Educational Psychology Review*, 2019; A.A. Grandey and G.M. Sayre, "Emotional Labor: Regulating Emotions for a Wage," *Current Directions in Psychological Science* 28 (2019): 131–37.

31. J.A. Morris and D.C. Feldman, "The Dimensions, Antecedents, and Consequences of Emotional Labor," *Academy of Management Review* 21 (1996): 986–1010; J. Li, B.F. Canziani, and C. Barbieri, "Emotional Labor in Hospitality: Positive Affective Displays in Service Encounters," *Tourism and Hospitality Research* 18, no. 2 (2018): 242–53.

32. A.A. Grandey and R.C. Melloy, "The State of the Heart: Emotional Labor as Emotion Regulation Reviewed and Revised," *Journal of Occupational Health Psychology* 22 (2017): 407–22; H. Wang, N.C. Hall, and J.L. Taxer, "Antecedents and Consequences of Teachers' Emotional Labor: A Systematic Review and Meta-Analytic Investigation," *Educational Psychology Review* 31 (2019): 663–98.

33. D. Matsumoto, S.H. Yoo, and J. Fontaine, "Mapping Expressive Differences around the World," *Journal of Cross-Cultural Psychology* 39 (2008): 55–74; B.Q. Ford and I.B. Mauss, "Culture and Emotion Regulation," *Current Opinion in Psychology* 3 (2015): 1–5; N. Gullekson and A. Dumaisnil, "Expanding Horizons on Expatriate Adjustment: A Look at the Role of Emotional Display and Status," *Human Resource Management Review* 26 (2016): 260–69.

34. F. Trompenaars and C. Hampden-Turner, *Riding the Waves of Culture*, 2nd ed. (New York: McGraw-Hill, 1998), Chap. 6. This major survey is two decades old, but recent studies report similar emotional display rules in the cultures reported by Trompenaars and Hampden-Turner. For example, see: Ю. Менджерицкая, М. Ханзен, and Х. Хорц, "Правила выражения эмоций преподавателями российских и немецких университетов (The Rules of Emotional Display in Lecturers of Russian and German Universities)," *Российский психологический журнал* 12 (2015): 54-77; H.C. Hwang et al., "Self-Reported Expression and Experience of Triumph across Four Countries," *Motivation and Emotion* 40 (2016): 731-39.

35. D.P. Bhave and T.M. Glomb, "The Role of Occupational Emotional Labor Requirements on the Surface Acting–Job Satisfaction Relationship," *Journal of Management* 42 (2016): 722-41; T. Huyghebaert et al., "Investigating the Longitudinal Effects of Surface Acting on Managers' Functioning through Psychological Needs," *Journal of Occupational Health Psychology* 23 (April 2018): 207-22.

36. A.A. Grandey and R.C. Melloy, "The State of the Heart: Emotional Labor as Emotion Regulation Reviewed and Revised," *Journal of Occupational Health Psychology* 22 (2017): 407-22. However, recent evidence suggests that deep acting can also be stressful because it requires cognitive effort. Also, faking negative emotions may be less stressful than faking positive emotions. Another recent study concluded that both surface and deep acting are effortful activities, so both produce emotional exhaustion. See F. Cheung, V.M.C. Lun, and M.W.-L. Cheung, "Emotional Labor and Occupational Well-Being: Latent Profile Transition Analysis Approach," *Frontiers in Psychology* 9 (2018); A.C. Lennard, B.A. Scott, and R.E. Johnson, "Turning Frowns (and Smiles) Upside down: A Multilevel Examination of Surface Acting Positive and Negative Emotions on Well-Being.," *Journal of Applied Psychology* 104 (2019): 1164-80.

37. S. Côté, I. Hideg, and G.A. van Kleef, "The Consequences of Faking Anger in Negotiations," *Journal of Experimental Social Psychology* 49 (2013): 453-63; Y. Zhan, M. Wang, and J. Shi, "Interpersonal Process of Emotional Labor: The Role of Negative and Positive Customer Treatment," *Personnel Psychology* 69 (2016): 525-57; K. Picard, M. Cossette, and D. Morin, "Service with a Smile: A Source of Emotional Exhaustion or Performance Incentive in Call-Centre Employees," *Canadian Journal of Administrative Sciences* 35 (2018): 214-27.

38. J.D. Kammeyer-Mueller et al., "A Meta-Analytic Structural Model of Dispositonal Affectivity and Emotional Labor," *Personnel Psychology* 66 (2013): 47-90; R.H. Humphrey, B.E. Ashforth, and J.M. Diefendorff, "The Bright Side of Emotional Labor," *Journal of Organizational Behavior* 36 (2015): 749-69. Deep acting is considered an adaptation of method acting used by professional actors.

39. J.J. Gross, "Emotion Regulation: Current Status and Future Prospects," *Psychological Inquiry* 26 (2015): 1-26; J.M. Diefendorff et al., "Emotion Regulation in the Context of Customer Mistreatment and Felt Affect: An Event-Based Profile Approach.," *Journal of Applied Psychology* 104 (2019): 965-83; J. Yih et al., "Better Together: A Unified Perspective on Appraisal and Emotion Regulation," *Cognition and Emotion* 33 (2019): 41-47.

40. Y. Kivity and J.D. Huppert, "Emotion Regulation in Social Anxiety: A Systematic Investigation and Meta-Analysis Using Self-Report, Subjective, and Event-Related Potentials Measures," *Cognition and Emotion* 33 (2019): 213-30.

41. R. Brockman et al., "Emotion Regulation Strategies in Daily Life: Mindfulness, Cognitive Reappraisal and Emotion Suppression," *Cognitive Behaviour Therapy* 46, no. 2 (2017): 91-113.

42. This model is an ability-based adaptation of the original mixed model by Goleman et al. Most recent models and measures of emotional intelligence have also adopted a similar four-quadrant model. These studies have adopted a "trait" approach to EI measurement, which might be more accurately described as a self-perceived EI ability approach. See D. Goleman, R. Boyatzis, and A. McKee, *Primal Leadership* (Boston: Harvard Business School Press, 2002), Chap. 3; R.P. Tett and K.E. Fox, "Confirmatory Factor Structure of Trait Emotional Intelligence in Student and Worker Samples," *Personality and Individual Differences* 41 (2006): 1155-68; D.L. Joseph and D.A. Newman, "Emotional Intelligence: An Integrative Meta-Analysis and Cascading Model," *Journal of Applied Psychology* 95 (2010): 54-78; X. Wei, Y. Liu, and N. Allen, "Measuring Team Emotional Intelligence: A Multimethod Comparison," *Group Dynamics: Theory, Research, & Practice* 20 (2016): 34-50; K.A. Pekaar et al., "Self- and Other-Focused Emotional Intelligence: Development and Validation of the Rotterdam Emotional Intelligence Scale (REIS)," *Personality and Individual Differences* 120 (2018): 222-33.

43. H.A. Elfenbein and N. Ambady, "Predicting Workplace Outcomes from the Ability to Eavesdrop on Feelings," *Journal of Applied Psychology* 87 (2002): 963-71; T. Quarto et al., "Association between Ability Emotional Intelligence and Left Insula during Social Judgment of Facial Emotions," *PLoS ONE* 11, no. 2 (2016): e0148621.

44. For neurological evidence that people with higher EI have higher sensitivity to others' emotions, see W.D.S. Killgore et al., "Emotional Intelligence Correlates with Functional Responses to Dynamic Changes in Facial Trustworthiness," *Social Neuroscience* 8, (2013): 334-46.

45. The hierarchical nature of the four EI dimensions is discussed by Goleman, but it is more explicit in the Salovey and Mayer model. See D.R. Caruso and P. Salovey, *The Emotionally Intelligent Manager* (San Francisco: Jossey-Bass, 2004). Aspects of this hierarchy are also incorporated in recent studies. For example, see K.A. Pekaar et al., "Managing Own and Others' Emotions: A Weekly Diary Study on the Enactment of Emotional Intelligence," *Journal of Vocational Behavior* 109 (2018): 137-51.

46. S. Côté, "Emotional Intelligence in Organizations," *Annual Review of Organizational Psychology and Organizational Behavior* 1 (2014): 459-88; M. Parke, M.-G. Seo, and E. Sherf, "Regulating and Facilitating: The Role of Emotional Intelligence in Maintaining and Using Positive Affect for Creativity," *Journal of Applied Psychology* 100 (2015): 917-34; D. Delpechitre and L. Beeler, "Faking It: Salesperson Emotional Intelligence's Influence on Emotional Labor Strategies and Customer Outcomes," *Journal of Business & Industrial Marketing* 33 (2017): 53-71; C. Miao, R.H. Humphrey, and S. Qian, "Emotional Intelligence and Authentic Leadership: A Meta-Analysis," *Leadership & Organization Development Journal* 39 (2018): 679-90.

47. D. Joseph et al., "Why Does Self-Reported Emotional Intelligence Predict Job Performance? A Meta-Analytic Investigation of Mixed EI," *Journal of Applied Psychology* 100 (2015): 298-342; P. Checa and P. Fernández-Berrocal, "Cognitive Control and Emotional Intelligence: Effect of the Emotional Content of the Task. Brief Reports," *Frontiers in Psychology* 10 (2019) 195, https://doi.org/10.3389/fpsyg.2019.00195.

48. "Why You Need Emotional Intelligence at Work," News Release (Toronto: OfficeTeam, February 22, 2017); "Emotional Intelligence Undervalued by One in Four Firms," news release (London: Robert Half, August 16, 2018); "Survey Shows Lack of Emphasis Put on EQ during Hiring Process for One in Five Australian Companies," news release (Sydney: Robert Half, March 12, 2019); C. Crummeneri et al., "Emotional Intelligence–the Essential Skillset for the Age of AI" (Paris: Capgemini Research Institute, November 2019).

49. J. Shaw, S. Porter, and L. ten Brinke, "Catching Liars: Training Mental Health and Legal Professionals to Detect High-Stakes Lies," *Journal of Forensic Psychiatry & Psychology* 24 (2013): 145–59; P. Risan, P.-E. Binder, and R.J. Milne, "Emotional Intelligence in Police Interviews–Approach, Training and the Usefulness of the Concept," *Journal of Forensic Psychology Practice* 16, no. 5 (October 19, 2016): 410–24; S. Hodzic et al., "How Efficient Are Emotional Intelligence Trainings: A Meta-Analysis," *Emotion Review* 10 (2018): 138–48; "Building and Sustaining an Officer Wellness Program: Lessons from the San Diego Police Department" (Washington, D.C.: U.S. Department of Justice, Office of Community Oriented Policing Services, and Police Executive Research Forum, October 2018).

50. L. Winkley, "Teaching Cops Empathy to Deter Use of Force," *San Diego Union-Tribune*, February 12, 2016.

51. D.A. Harrison, D.A. Newman, and P.L. Roth, "How Important Are Job Attitudes? Meta-Analytic Comparisons of Integrative Behavioral Outcomes and Time Sequences," *Academy of Management Journal* 49, no. 2 (2006): 305–25. Another recent study concluded that job satisfaction and organizational commitment are so highly correlated that they represent the same construct. See H. Le et al., "The Problem of Empirical Redundancy of Constructs in Organizational Research: An Empirical Investigation," *Organizational Behavior and Human Decision Processes* 112, no. 2 (2010): 112–25. They also are considered the two central work-related variables in the broader concept of happiness at work. See C.D. Fisher, "Happiness at Work," *International Journal of Management Reviews* 12, no. 4 (2010): 384–412.

52. E.A. Locke, "The Nature and Causes of Job Satisfaction," in *Handbook of Industrial and Organizational Psychology*, ed. M. Dunnette (Chicago: Rand McNally, 1976), 1297–350; H.M. Weiss, "Deconstructing Job Satisfaction: Separating Evaluations, Beliefs and Affective Experiences," *Human Resource Management Review*, no. 12 (2002): 173–94. Some definitions still include emotion as an element of job satisfaction, whereas the definition presented in this book views emotion as a cause of job satisfaction. Also, this definition views job satisfaction as a "collection of attitudes," not several "facets" of job satisfaction.

53. "Randstad Workmonitor Q4 2019" (Amsterdam: Randstad Holding nv, December 2019). Survey data were collected from 34 countries with a minimum of 400 interviews per country of adults working 24 hours or more per week as employees. Respondents were asked, "How satisfied are you in general about working with your current employer?" This exhibit shows results from selected countries across the full range of results.

54. For example, see Randstad's work mobility index across countries. "Randstad Workmonitor Q4 2019" (Amsterdam: Randstad Holding nv, December 2019).

55. The problems with measuring attitudes and values across cultures are discussed in L. Saari and T.A. Judge, "Employee Attitudes and Job Satisfaction," *Human Resource Management* 43, no. 4 (2004): 395–407; A.K. Uskul et al., "How Successful You Have Been in Life Depends on the Response Scale Used: The Role of Cultural Mindsets in Pragmatic Inferences Drawn from Question Format," *Social Cognition* 31, no. 2 (2013): 222–36.

56. For a review of the various job satisfaction outcome theories, see R.S. Dalal, "Job Attitudes: Cognition and Affect," in *Handbook of Psychology, Second Edition*, ed. I.B. Weiner (New York: John Wiley & Sons, 2013), 341–66.

57. D. Farrell, "Exit, Voice, Loyalty, and Neglect as Responses to Job Dissatisfaction: A Multidimensional Scaling Study," *Academy of Management Journal* 26, no. 4 (1983): 596–607; M.J. Withey and W.H. Cooper, "Predicting Exit, Voice, Loyalty, and Neglect," *Administrative Science Quarterly*, no. 34 (1989): 521–39; A.B. Whitford and S.-Y. Lee, "Exit, Voice, and Loyalty with Multiple Exit Options: Evidence from the US Federal Workforce," *Journal of Public Administration Research and Theory* 25, no. 2 (2015): 373–98. For a critique and explanation of historical errors in the EVLN model, see S.L. McShane, "Reconstructing the Meaning and Dimensionality of Voice in the Exit-Voice-Loyalty-Neglect Model," paper presented at the Voice and Loyalty Symposium, Annual Conference of the Administrative Sciences Association of Canada, Organizational Behaviour Division, Halifax, 2008.

58. K. Morrell, J. Loan-Clarke, and A. Wilkinson, "The Role of Shocks in Employee Turnover," *British Journal of Management* 15 (2004): 335–49; M. Zhang, D.D. Fried, and R.W. Griffeth, "A Review of Job Embeddedness: Conceptual, Measurement Issues, and Directions for Future Research," *Human Resource Management Review* 22 (2012): 220–31; P.W. Hom et al., "One Hundred Years of Employee Turnover Theory and Research," *Journal of Applied Psychology* 102 (2017): 530–45; A.L. Rubenstein et al., "Surveying the Forest: A Meta-Analysis, Moderator Investigation, and Future-Oriented Discussion of the Antecedents of Voluntary Employee Turnover," *Personnel Psychology* 71 (2018): 23–65.

59. E.W. Morrison, "Employee Voice and Silence," *Annual Review of Organizational Psychology and Organizational Behavior* 1, no. 1 (2014): 173–97; M.R. Bashshur and B. Oc, "When Voice Matters: A Multilevel Review of the Impact of Voice in Organizations," *Journal of Management* 41, no. 5 (2015): 1530–54; P.K. Mowbray, A. Wilkinson, and H.H.M. Tse, "An Integrative Review of Employee Voice: Identifying a Common Conceptualization and Research Agenda," *International Journal of Management Reviews* 17, no. 3 (2015): 382–400.

60. A.O. Hirschman, *Exit, Voice, and Loyalty: Responses to Decline in Firms, Organizations, and States* (Cambridge, MA: Harvard University Press, 1970); P. John, "Finding Exits and Voices: Albert Hirschman's Contribution to the Study of Public Services," *International Public Management Journal* 20 (2017): 512–29.

61. J.D. Hibbard, N. Kumar, and L.W. Stern, "Examining the Impact of Destructive Acts in Marketing Channel Relationships," *Journal of Marketing Research* 38 (2001): 45–61; J. Zhou and J. M. George, "When Job Dissatisfaction Leads to Creativity: Encouraging the Expression of Voice," *Academy of Management Journal* 44 (2001): 682–96.

62. M.J. Withey and I.R. Gellatly, "Situational and Dispositional Determinants of Exit, Voice, Loyalty and Neglect," *Proceedings of the Administrative Sciences Association of Canada, Organizational Behaviour Division*, 1998; R.D. Zimmerman et al., "Who Withdraws? Psychological Individual Differences and Employee Withdrawal Behaviors," *Journal of Applied Psychology* 101 (2016): 498–519; É. Lapointe and C. Vandenberghe, "Examination of the Relationships between Servant Leadership, Organizational Commitment, and Voice and Antisocial Behaviors," *Journal of Business Ethics* 148, (2018): 99–115; M. Zare and C. Flinchbaugh, "Voice, Creativity, and Big Five Personality Traits: A Meta-Analysis," *Human Performance* 32 (2019): 30–51.

63. V.V. Venkataramani and S. Tangirala, "When and Why Do Central Employees Speak Up? An Examination of Mediating and Moderating Variables," *Journal of Applied Psychology* 95 (2010): 582–91; M. Weiss et al., "We Can Do It! Inclusive Leader Language Promotes Voice Behavior in Multi-Professional Teams," *The Leadership Quarterly* 29 (2018): 389–402; I. Hussain et al., "The Voice Bystander Effect: How Information Redundancy Inhibits Employee Voice," *Academy of Management Journal* 62 (2019): 828–49.

64. D.P. Schwab and L.L. Cummings, "Theories of Performance and Satisfaction: A Review," *Industrial Relations* 9 (1970): 408–30.

65. D.J. Schleicher, J.D. Watt, and G.J. Greguras, "Reexamining the Job Satisfaction-Performance Relationship: The Complexity of Attitudes," *Journal of Applied Psychology* 89 (2004): 165–77; D.A. Harrison, D.A. Newman, and P.L. Roth, "How Important Are Job Attitudes? Meta-Analytic Comparisons of Integrative Behavioral Outcomes

and Time Sequences," *Academy of Management Journal* 49 (2006): 305–25; N.A. Bowling et al., "Situational Strength as a Moderator of the Relationship Between Job Satisfaction and Job Performance: A Meta-Analytic Examination," *Journal of Business and Psychology* 30 (2015): 89–104; T.A. Judge et al., "Job Attitudes, Job Satisfaction, and Job Affect: A Century of Continuity and of Change," *Journal of Applied Psychology* 102 (2017): 356–74; P. Warr and and K. Nielsen, "Wellbeing and Work Performance," In E. Diener, S. Oishi, and L. Tay (eds.), *Handbook of Well-Being* (Salt Lake City, UT: DEF Publishers, 2018); J. Peiró et al., "The Happy-Productive Worker Model and Beyond: Patterns of Wellbeing and Performance at Work," *International Journal of Environmental Research and Public Health* 16 (2019): 479.

66. However, panel studies suggest that satisfaction has a stronger effect on performance than the other way around. For a summary, see C.D. Fisher, "Happiness at Work," *International Journal of Management Reviews* 12, no. 4 (2010): 384–412.

67. "The Greatest Briton in Management and Leadership," *Personnel Today* (2003): 20.

68. J.I. Heskett, W.E. Sasser, and L.A. Schlesinger, *The Service Profit Chain* (New York: Free Press, 1997); S.P. Brown and S.K. Lam, "A Meta-Analysis of Relationships Linking Employee Satisfaction to Customer Responses," *Journal of Retailing* 84, no. 3 (2008): 243–55; T.J. Gerpott and M. Paukert, "The Relationship between Employee Satisfaction and Customer Satisfaction: A Meta-Analysis (*Der Zusammenhang Zwischen Mitarbeiter-Und Kundenzufriedenheit: Eine Metaanalyse*)," *Zeitschrift für Personalforschung* 25, no. 1 (2011): 28–54; H. Evanschitzky, F.V. Wangenheim, and N.V. Wünderlich, "Perils of Managing the Service Profit Chain: The Role of Time Lags and Feedback Loops," *Journal of Retailing* 88, no. 3 (2012): 356–66; Y. Hong et al., "Missing Link in the Service Profit Chain: A Meta-Analytic Review of the Antecedents, Consequences, and Moderators of Service Climate," *Journal of Applied Psychology* 98, no. 2 (2013): 237–67.

69. W.-C. Tsai and Y.-M. Huang, "Mechanisms Linking Employee Affective Delivery and Customer Behavioral Intentions," *Journal of Applied Psychology* 87, no. 5 (2002): 1001–08; P. Guenzi and O. Pelloni, "The Impact of Interpersonal Relationships on Customer Satisfaction and Loyalty to the Service Provider," *International Journal of Service Industry Management* 15, no. 3/4 (2004): 365–84; S.J. Bell, S. Auh, and K. Smalley, "Customer Relationship Dynamics: Service Quality and Customer Loyalty in the Context of Varying Levels of Customer Expertise and Switching Costs," *Journal of the Academy of Marketing Science* 33, no. 2 (2005): 169–83; P.B. Barger and A.A. Grandey, "Service with a Smile and Encounter Satisfaction: Emotional Contagion and Appraisal Mechanisms," *Academy of Management Journal* 49, no. 6 (2006): 1229–38. On the reciprocal effect, see E. Kim and D.J. Yoon, "Why Does Service with a Smile Make Employees Happy? A Social Interaction Model," *Journal of Applied Psychology* 97, no. 5 (2012): 1059–67.

70. R.T. Mowday, L.W. Porter, and R.M. Steers, *Employee Organization Linkages: The Psychology of Commitment, Absenteeism, and Turnover* (New York: Academic Press, 1982); J.P. Meyer, "Organizational Commitment," *International Review of Industrial and Organizational Psychology* 12 (1997): 175–228. The definition and dimensions of organizational commitment continue to be debated. Some writers even propose that *affective commitment* refers only to one's psychological attachment to and involvement in the organization, whereas *identification* with the organization is a distinct concept further along a continuum of bonds. See O.N. Solinger, W. van Olffen, and R.A. Roe, "Beyond the Three-Component Model of Organizational Commitment," *Journal of Applied Psychology* 93, no. 1 (2008): 70–83; H.J. Klein, J.C. Molloy, and C.T. Brinsfield, "Reconceptualizing Workplace Commitment to Redress a Stretched Construct: Revisiting Assumptions and Removing Confounds," *Academy of Management Review* 37, no. 1 (2012): 130–51.

71. M. Taing et al., "The Multidimensional Nature of Continuance Commitment: Commitment Owing to Economic Exchanges versus Lack of Employment Alternatives," *Journal of Business and Psychology* 26 (2011): 269–84; C. Vandenberghe and A. Panaccio, "Perceived Sacrifice and Few Alternatives Commitments: The Motivational Underpinnings of Continuance Commitment's Subdimensions," *Journal of Vocational Behavior* 81 (2012): 59–72; S. Jaros and R.A. Culpepper, "An Analysis of Meyer and Allen's Continuance Commitment Construct," *Journal of Management & Organization* 20 (2014): 79–99.

72. J.P. Meyer and N.M. Parfyonova, "Normative Commitment in the Workplace: A Theoretical Analysis and Re-Conceptualization," *Human Resource Management Review* 20 (2010): 283–94; S. Jaros, "A Critique of Normative Commitment in Management Research," *Management Research Review* 40 (2017): 517–37.

73. J.P. Meyer et al., "Affective, Continuance, and Normative Commitment to the Organization: A Meta-Analysis of Antecedents, Correlates, and Consequences," *Journal of Vocational Behavior* 61 (2002): 20–52; A.S.D. Semedo, A.F.M. Coelho, and N.M.P. Ribeiro, "Effects of Authentic Leadership, Affective Commitment and Job Resourcefulness on Employees' Creativity and Individual Performance," *Leadership & Organization Development Journal* 37 (2016): 1038–55; J.C. Wombacher and J. Felfe, "Dual Commitment in the Organization: Effects of the Interplay of Team and Organizational Commitment on Employee Citizenship Behavior, Efficacy Beliefs, and Turnover Intentions," *Journal of Vocational Behavior* 102 (2017): 1–14; S.L. Blader, S. Patil, and D.J. Packer, "Organizational Identification and Workplace Behavior: More than Meets the Eye," *Research in Organizational Behavior* 37 (2017): 19–34; D. Charbonneau and V.M. Wood, "Antecedents and Outcomes of Unit Cohesion and Affective Commitment to the Army," *Military Psychology* 30 (2018): 43–53.

74. J.P. Meycr et al., "Organizational Commitment and Job Performance: It's the Nature of the Commitment That Counts," *Journal of Applied Psychology* 74 (1989): 152–56; H. Gill et al., "Affective and Continuance Commitment and Their Relations with Deviant Workplace Behaviors in Korea," *Asia Pacific Journal of Management* 28 (2011): 595–607. The negative effect on performance might depend on the type of continuance commitment. See M. Taing et al., "The Multidimensional Nature of Continuance Commitment: Commitment Owing to Economic Exchanges versus Lack of Employment Alternatives," *Journal of Business and Psychology* 26 (2011): 269–84.

75. K.Y. Kim, R. Eisenberger, and K. Baik, "Perceived Organizational Support and Affective Organizational Commitment: Moderating Influence of Perceived Organizational Competence," *Journal of Organizational Behavior* 37 (2016): 558–83; J.N. Kurtessis et al., "Perceived Organizational Support: A Meta-Analytic Evaluation of Organizational Support Theory," *Journal of Management* 43 (2017): 1854–84; D. Charbonneau and V.M. Wood, "Antecedents and Outcomes of Unit Cohesion and Affective Commitment to the Army," *Military Psychology* 30, no. 1 (2018): 43–53.

76. A.L. Kristof-Brown, R.D. Zimmerman, and E.C. Johnson, "Consequences of Individuals' Fit at Work: A Meta-Analysis of Person-Job, Person-Organization, Person-Group, and Person-Supervisor Fit," *Personnel Psychology* 58 (2005): 281–342; M.E. Bergman et al., "An Event-Based Perspective on the Development of Commitment," *Human Resource Management Review* 23 (2013): 148–60; O.A.U. Byza et al., "When Leaders and Followers Match: The Impact of Objective Value Congruence, Value Extremity, and Empowerment on Employee Commitment and Job Satisfaction," *Journal of Business Ethics* 158 (2019): 1097–1112.

77. D.M. Rousseau et al., "Not So Different after All: A Cross-Discipline View of Trust," *Academy of Management Review* 23 (1998): 393–404.

78. D.K. Datta et al., "Causes and Effects of Employee Downsizing: A Review and Synthesis," *Journal of Management* 36, no. 1 (2010): 281–348; R. van Dick, F. Drzensky, and M. Heinz, "Goodbye or Identify: Detrimental Effects of Downsizing on Identification and Survivor Performance," *Frontiers in Psychology* 7 (2016), https://doi.org/10.3389/fpsyg.2016.00771.

79. C. Leighton and S.L. McShane, "Being 'in the Know': Introducing Organisational Comprehension and Its Nomological Net" (paper presented at the ANZAM Annual Conference, Brisbane, Australia, August 8, 2016). For similar concepts on information acquisition, see P. Bordia et al., "Uncertainty during Organizational Change: Types, Consequences, and Management Strategies," *Journal of Business and Psychology* 18, no. 4 (2004): 507–32; H.D. Cooper-Thomas and N. Anderson, "Organizational Socialization: A Field Study into Socialization Success and Rate," *International Journal of Selection and Assessment* 13, no. 2 (2005): 116–28; T.N. Bauer, "Newcomer Adjustment During Organizational Socialization: A Meta-Analytic Review of Antecedents, Outcomes, and Methods," *Journal of Applied Psychology* 92, no. 3 (2007): 707–21.

80. T.S. Heffner and J.R. Rentsch, "Organizational Commitment and Social Interaction: A Multiple Constituencies Approach," *Journal of Vocational Behavior* 59 (2001): 471–90.

81. M. Mayhew et al., "A Study of the Antecedents and Consequences of Psychological Ownership in Organizational Settings," *Journal of Social Psychology* 147 (2007): 477–500; T.-S. Han, H.-H. Chiang, and A. Chang, "Employee Participation in Decision Making, Psychological Ownership and Knowledge Sharing: Mediating Role of Organizational Commitment in Taiwanese High-Tech Organizations," *International Journal of Human Resource Management* 21 (2010): 2218–33; D. Gallie et al., "The Implications of Direct Participation for Organisational Commitment, Job Satisfaction and Affective Psychological Well-Being: A Longitudinal Analysis," *Industrial Relations Journal* 48 (2017): 174–91.

82. J.C. Quick et al., *Preventive Stress Management in Organizations* (Washington, DC: American Psychological Association, 1997), pp. 3–4; A.L. Dougall and A. Baum, "Stress, Coping, and Immune Function," in *Handbook of Psychology*, ed. M. Gallagher and R.J. Nelson (Hoboken, NJ: John Wiley & Sons, Inc., 2003), 441–55. For the various definitions and perspectives of stress, see T.A. Day, "Defining Stress as a Prelude to Mapping Its Neurocircuitry: No Help from Allostasis," *Progress in Neuro-Psychopharmacology and Biological Psychiatry* 29 (2005): 1195–200; D.C. Ganster and C.C. Rosen, "Work Stress and Employee Health: A Multidisciplinary Review," *Journal of Management* 39 (2013): 1085–122.

83. The cognitive appraisal view is described in R.S. Lazarus, *Stress and Emotion: A New Synthesis* (New York: Springer Publishing, 2006). In contrast, recent neuroscience studies and reviews indicate a dissociation between a person's subjective feeling of stress and their autonomic physiological responses (i.e., release of stress hormones into the blood stream). In other words, people respond physiologically to stressful situations even when they do not consciously feel stressed. See J. Campbell and U. Ehlert, "Acute Psychosocial Stress: Does the Emotional Stress Response Correspond with Physiological Responses?" *Psychoneuroendocrinology* 37 (2012): 1111–34; N. Ali et al., "Suppressing the Endocrine and Autonomic Stress Systems Does Not Impact the Emotional Stress Experience after Psychosocial Stress," *Psychoneuroendocrinology* 78 (2017): 125–30.

84. M.G. González-Morales and P. Neves, "When Stressors Make You Work: Mechanisms Linking Challenge Stressors to Performance," *Work & Stress* 29, no. 3 (2015): 213–29; M.B. Hargrove, W.S. Becker, and D.F. Hargrove, "The HRD Eustress Model: Generating Positive Stress with Challenging Work," *Human Resource Development Review* 14, no. 3 (2015): 279–98.

85. Statistics Canada, "Perceived Life Stress, by Age Group," Health Characteristics, Annual Estimates (Ottawa: Statistics Canada, June 26, 2018), https://doi.org/10.25318/1310009601-eng; "Worried Workers: Korn Ferry Survey Finds Professionals Are More Stressed Out at Work Today Than 5 Years Ago," News Release (Los Angeles: Korn Ferry, November 8, 2018); "2019 CIGNA 360 Well-Being Survey: Well and Beyond" (Bloomfield, CT: CIGNA, March 26, 2019); "2019 Global Emotions Report" (Washington, DC: Gallup, April 18, 2019); "NHS Staff Survey 2019: National Results Briefing" (London: National Health Service, February 2020).

86. H. Selye, *Stress without Distress* (Philadelphia: J.B. Lippincott, 1974); S.L. Buckner et al., "The General Adaptation Syndrome: Potential Misapplications to Resistance Exercise," *Journal of Science and Medicine in Sport* 20 (2017): 1015–17; A.J. Cunanan et al., "The General Adaptation Syndrome: A Foundation for the Concept of Periodization," *Sports Medicine* 48 (2018): 787–97.

87. K. Hasselberg et al., "Self-Reported Stressors among Patients with Exhaustion Disorder: An Exploratory Study of Patient Records," *BMC Psychiatry* 14 (2014): 1–10; I.H. Jonsdottir et al., "Working Memory and Attention Are Still Impaired after Three Years in Patients with Stress-Related Exhaustion," *Scandinavian Journal of Psychology* 58 (2017): 504–9; I. Savic, A. Perski, and W. Osika, "MRI Shows That Exhaustion Syndrome Due to Chronic Occupational Stress Is Associated with Partially Reversible Cerebral Changes," *Cerebral Cortex* 28 (2018): 894–906.

88. D.C. Ganster and C.C. Rosen, "Work Stress and Employee Health: A Multidisciplinary Review," *Journal of Management* 39 (2013): 1085–122; J. Goh, J. Pfeffer, and S.A. Zenios, "The Relationship between Workplace Stressors and Mortality and Health Costs in the United States," *Management Science* 62 (2016): 608–28; C. Johansen et al., "Stress and Cancer," in *The Handbook of Stress and Health*, ed. C.L. Cooper and J.C. Quick (John Wiley & Sons, Ltd, 2017), 125–34.

89. M. Lauzier, S. Melancon, and K. Cote, "The Effect of Stress Seen on Absenteeism and Presenteeism Behavior: The Mediating Role of Health," *Canadian Journal of Behavioural Science* 49 (2017): 221–30; B. Schmidt et al., "A Comparison of Job Stress Models: Associations with Employee Well-Being, Absenteeism, Presenteeism, and Resulting Costs," *Journal of Occupational and Environmental Medicine* 61 (2019): 535–44.

90. C.L. Cooper and J. Marshall, "Occupational Sources of Stress: A Review of the Literature Relating to Coronary Heart Disease and Mental Ill Health," in *From Stress to Wellbeing Volume 1: The Theory and Research on Occupational Stress and Wellbeing*, ed. C.L. Cooper (London: Palgrave Macmillan UK, 2013), 3–23.

91. C.C. Rosen et al., "Occupational Stressors and Job Performance: An Updated Review and Recommendations," in *New Developments in Theoretical and Conceptual Approaches to Job Stress*, ed. P.L. Perrewé and D.C. Ganster, Research in Occupational Stress and Well-Being, ed. P. Perrewé, J. Halbesleben, and C. Rose, vol. 8 (Bingley, UK: Emerald Group Publishing Limited, 2010), 1–60; A.E. Nixon et al., "Can Work Make You Sick? A Meta-Analysis of the Relationships between Job Stressors and Physical Symptoms," *Work & Stress* 25, no. 1 (2011): 1–22.

92. A.E. Nixon et al., "Can Work Make You Sick? A Meta-Analysis of the Relationships between Job Stressors and Physical Symptoms," *Work & Stress* 25, no. 1 (2011): 1–22; S. Pindek and P.E. Spector, "Organizational Constraints: A Meta-Analysis of a Major Stressor," *Work & Stress* 30, no. 1 (2016): 7–25.

93. P. McDonald, "Workplace Sexual Harassment 30 Years On: A Review of the Literature," *International Journal of Management Reviews* 14 (2012): 1–17; B. Verkuil, S. Atasayi, and M.L. Molendijk, "Workplace Bullying and Mental Health: A Meta-Analysis on Cross-Sectional and Longitudinal Data," *PLOS ONE* 10, no. 8 (2015): e0135225, https://doi.org/10.1371/journal.pone.0135225; J.D. Mackey et al., "Abusive Supervision: A Meta-Analysis and Empirical Review," *Journal of Management* 43 (2017): 1940–65.

94. N.A. Bowling et al., "A Meta-Analytic Examination of the Potential Correlates and Consequences of Workload," *Work & Stress* 29, no. 2 (2015): 95–113.

95. R. Drago, D. Black, and M. Wooden, *The Persistence of Long Work Hours*, Melbourne Institute Working Paper Series, Melbourne Institute of Applied Economic and Social Research, University of Melbourne, August 2005; L. Golden, "A Brief History of Long Work Time and the Contemporary Sources of Overwork," *Journal of Business Ethics* 84, no. S2 (2009): 217–27; M. Tarafdar, E. B. Pullins, and T.S. Ragu-Nathan, "Technostress: Negative Effect on Performance and Possible Mitigations," *Information Systems Journal* 25, no. 2 (2015): 103–32; E. Reid, "Embracing, Passing, Revealing, and the Ideal Worker Image: How People Navigate Expected and Experienced Professional Identities," *Organization Science* 26, no. 4 (2015): 997–1017; Project: Time Off, *The Work Martyr's Cautionary Tale: How the Millennial Experience Will Define America's Vacation Culture* (Washington, DC: Project: Time Off, August 17, 2016).

96. R. Karasek and T. Theorell, *Healthy Work: Stress, Productivity, and the Reconstruction of Working Life* (New York: Basic Books, 1990); M. Lavigne-Robichaud et al., "Job Strain and the Prevalence of Uncontrolled Hypertension among White-Collar Workers," *Hypertension Research* 42 (2019): 1616–23.

97. M.K. Holton, A.E. Barry, and J.D. Chaney, "Employee Stress Management: An Examination of Adaptive and Maladaptive Coping Strategies on Employee Health," *Work* 53 (2016): 299–305.

98. M. Zuckerman and M. Gagne, "The COPE Revised: Proposing a 5-Factor Model of Coping Strategies," *Journal of Research in Personality* 37 (2003): 169–204; S. Folkman and J.T. Moskowitz, "Coping: Pitfalls and Promise," *Annual Review of Psychology* 55 (2004): 745–74; C.A. Thompson et al., "On the Importance of Coping: A Model and New Directions for Research on Work and Family," *Research in Occupational Stress and Well-Being* 6 (2007): 73–113.

99. S.E. Taylor et al., "Psychological Resources, Positive Illusions, and Health," *American Psychologist* 55, no. 1 (2000): 99–109; F. Luthans and C.M. Youssef, "Emerging Positive Organizational Behavior," *Journal of Management* 33, no. 3 (2007): 321–49; P. Steel, J. Schmidt, and J. Shultz, "Refining the Relationship between Personality and Subjective Well-Being," *Psychological Bulletin* 134, no. 1 (2008): 138–61; G. Alarcon, K.J. Eschleman, and N.A. Bowling, "Relationships between Personality Variables and Burnout: A Meta-Analysis," *Work & Stress* 23, no. 3 (2009): 244–63; R. Kotov et al., "Linking 'Big' Personality Traits to Anxiety, Depressive, and Substance Use Disorders: A Meta-Analysis," *Psychological Bulletin* 136, no. 5 (2010): 768–821.

100. G.A. Bonanno, "Loss, Trauma, and Human Resilience: Have We Underestimated the Human Capacity to Thrive after Extremely Aversive Events?," *American Psychologist* 59, no. 1 (2004): 20–28; F. Luthans, C.M. Youssef, and B.J. Avolio, *Psychological Capital: Developing the Human Competitive Edge* (New York: Oxford University Press, 2007).

101. M.A. Clark et al., "All Work and No Play? A Meta-Analytic Examination of the Correlates and Outcomes of Workaholism," *Journal of Management* 42, no. 7 (2016): 1836–73; C.S. Andreassen et al., "The Relationships between Workaholism and Symptoms of Psychiatric Disorders: A Large-Scale Cross-Sectional Study," *PLoS ONE* 11, no. 5 (2016): e0152978.

102. This list is based on various reviews, but stress management interventions have been organized in several ways. See, for example, J.H. Ruotsalainen et al., "Preventing Occupational Stress in Healthcare Workers," *Cochrane Database of Systematic Reviews*, no. 4 (2015); L.E. Tetrick and C.J. Winslow, "Workplace Stress Management Interventions and Health Promotion," *Annual Review of Organizational Psychology and Organizational Behavior* 2 (2015): 583–603; M. Savic et al., "How Do Nurses Cope with Shift Work? A Qualitative Analysis of Open-Ended Responses from a Survey of Nurses," *International Journal of Environmental Research and Public Health* 16, no. 20 (October 10, 2019), https://doi.org/10.3390/ijerph16203821.

103. S.D. Friedman, *Leading the Life You Want: Skills for Integrating Work and Life* (Boston: Harvard Business Press, 2014); T.D. Allen, E. Cho, and L.L. Meier, "Work-Family Boundary Dynamics," *Annual Review of Organizational Psychology and Organizational Behavior* 1 (2014): 99–121; T.D. Allen, T.D. Golden, and K.M. Shockley, "How Effective Is Telecommuting? Assessing the Status of Our Scientific Findings," *Psychological Science in the Public Interest* 16 (2015): 40–68; E.E. Kossek and R.J. Thompson, "Workplace Flexibility: Integrating Employer and Employee Perspectives to Close the Research-Practice Implementation Gap," in *The Oxford Handbook of Work and Family*, ed. T.D. Allen and L.T. Eby (New York: Oxford University Press, 2016), 255–70; M.J. Sirgy and D.-J. Lee, "Work-Life Balance: An Integrative Review," *Applied Research in Quality of Life* 13 (2018): 229–54; M. Beatson, "Megatrends: Flexible Working" (London: Chartered Institute of Personnel and Development, January 15, 2019).

104. C. Fritz et al., "Happy, Healthy, and Productive: The Role of Detachment from Work during Nonwork Time," *Journal of Applied Psychology* 95, no. 5 (2010): 977–83.

105. M. Tuckey et al., "Hindrances Are Not Threats: Advancing the Multidimensionality of Work Stress," *Journal of Occupational Health Psychology* 20, no. 2 (2015): 131–47.

106. M.H. Abel, "Humor, Stress, and Coping Strategies," *Humor: International Journal of Humor Research* 15 (2002): 365–81; K. Ebner et al., "Coaching as Stress-Management Intervention: The Mediating Role of Self-Efficacy in a Framework of Self-Management and Coping.," *International Journal of Stress Management* 25 (2018): 209–33.

107. O. Kettunen et al., "Greater Levels of Cardiorespiratory and Muscular Fitness Are Associated with Low Stress and High Mental Resources in Normal but Not Overweight Men," *BMC Public Health* 16, no. 1 (2016): 788; M. Gerber et al., "Fitness Moderates the Relationship between Stress and Cardiovascular Risk Factors," *Medicine & Science in Sports & Exercise* 48, no. 11 (2016): 2075–81.

108. H.O. Dickinson et al., "Relaxation Therapies for the Management of Primary Hypertension in Adults," *Cochrane Database of Systematic Reviews* (January, 2008); O.L. Siu, "Stress Management Techniques in the Workplace," in *Routledge Companion to Wellbeing at Work*, ed. C.L. Cooper and M.P. Leiter (Routledge: 2017), 284–97.

109. M. Katanuma, "The Company That Pays Its Employees to Get a Full Night's Sleep," *Bloomberg*, October 21, 2018; L. Lewis, "Japan Wakes up to Sleep Shortage Problems," *Financial Times*, November 20, 2018; J. McCurry, "Snoozing on the Job: Japanese Firms Tackle Epidemic of Sleeplessness," *The Guardian*, January 8, 2019.

110. C. Viswesvaran, J.I. Sanchez, and J. Fisher, "The Role of Social Support in the Process of Work Stress: A Meta-Analysis," *Journal of Vocational Behavior* 54, no. 2 (1999): 314–34; S.E. Taylor et al., "Biobehavioral Responses to Stress in Females: Tend-and-Befriend, Not Fight-or-Flight," *Psychological Review* 107, no. 3 (2000): 411–29; T.A. Beehr, N.A. Bowling, and M.M. Bennett, "Occupational Stress and Failures of Social Support: When Helping Hurts," *Journal of Occupational Health Psychology* 15, no. 1 (2010): 45–59; B.A. Scott et al., "A Daily Investigation of the Role of Manager Empathy on Employee Well-Being," *Organizational Behavior and Human Decision Processes* 113, no. 2 (2010): 127–40; S.Y. Shin and S.G. Lee, "Effects of Hospital Workers? Friendship Networks on Job Stress," *PLoS ONE* 11, no. 2 (2016): e0149428.

5 Employee Motivation

Dean Drobot/Shutterstock

Learning Objectives

After you read this chapter, you should be able to:

LO5-1 Define employee motivation and engagement.

LO5-2 Explain how drives and emotions influence employee motivation.

LO5-3 Discuss the employee motivation implications of four-drive theory, Maslow's needs hierarchy, intrinsic and extrinsic motivation, and learned needs theory.

LO5-4 Discuss the expectancy theory model, including its practical implications.

LO5-5 Outline organizational behavior modification (OB Mod) and social cognitive theory and explain their relevance to employee motivation.

LO5-6 Describe the characteristics of effective goal setting and feedback.

LO5-7 Explain how equity theory, procedural justice, and interactional justice influence employee motivation.

LO5-8 List the advantages and disadvantages of job specialization and explain how to improve employee motivation through job design.

Accenture has launched a radically different way to motivate employees. The consulting firm ditched its traditional performance appraisal system in which managers annually evaluated employees, ranked their performance against peers on a forced distribution scale, and held a formal meeting to discuss the results for that time period. Accenture now takes a coaching approach to employee motivation and performance. Managers have regular informal, constructive, forward-looking discussions that focus on employee achievements and career development. Employee performance is no longer numerically scored or ranked.

"We realized that investing significant time in backward-looking performance appraisals—and figuring out the Holy Grail of forced rankings—simply does not yield the best outcomes for our company or our people," observes an Accenture executive. "Millennials and Gen Z-ers don't want hierarchy, formal feedback processes, and appraisals. They demand real-time, in-person feedback, forward-looking conversations and support to grow their careers."[1]

motivation the forces within a person that affect his or her direction, intensity, and persistence of voluntary behavior

employee engagement individual emotional and cognitive motivation, particularly a focused, intense, persistent, and purposive effort toward work-related goals

Corporate leaders around the world are discovering that their traditional performance appraisal systems don't motivate employees. Some traditional performance reviews even have the opposite effect; they disengage employees and motivate behavior that undermines the organization's success. This isn't news to organizational behavior scholars, who have warned over the past few decades about the adverse effects of rating, ranking, and other traditional performance management practices. The challenge now is to introduce practices that actually motivate and develop employees to their potential.

The theme of this chapter is employee motivation. We begin by introducing the definition of motivation and the often-stated associated phrase, employee engagement. Next, we explain how drives and emotions are the prime movers of employee motivation. The prominent drive-based theories of motivation are then described. Next, expectancy theory is described, including the practical implications of this popular cognitive decision model of employee motivation. Organizational behavior modification and social cognitive theory are then introduced and linked to expectancy theory. Next, we consider theory and practices related to the important motivation topics of goal setting and feedback, and organizational justice. The final section of this chapter examines the effect of job design on employee motivation and performance.

LO5-1 Define employee motivation and engagement.

EMPLOYEE MOTIVATION, DRIVES, AND NEEDS

Employee motivation should be on anyone's short list of the most important topics in organizational behavior. Why? Because motivation is one of the four elements of the MARS model, meaning that it is critical to understanding human behavior and performance (see Chapter 1). Even when people are able to perform the work (A), understand their role responsibilities (R), and work in a setting that supports their work objectives (S), they won't get the job done without sufficient motivation (M) to achieve those tasks.

Motivation is defined as the forces within a person that affect the direction, intensity, and persistence of his or her effort for voluntary behavior.[2] *Direction* refers to what people are focused on achieving; in other words, the goal or outcome toward which they steer their effort. *Intensity* is the amount of physical, cognitive, and emotional energy expended at a given moment to achieve a task or other objective. *Persistence,* the third element of motivation, refers to how long people sustain their effort as they move toward their goal. In short, motivated employees exert varying levels of effort (intensity), for varying lengths of time (persistence), toward various goals (direction).

When executives discuss employee motivation these days, they are just as likely to use the phrase **employee engagement**. Employee engagement is an individual's emotional and cognitive (logical) motivation, particularly a focused, intense, persistent, and purposive effort toward work-related goals.[3] It is associated with self-efficacy—the belief that you have the ability, role clarity, and resources to get the job done (see Chapter 3). Employee engagement also includes a high level of absorption in the work—the experience of focusing intensely on the task with limited awareness of events beyond that work.

Employee engagement predicts employee and work unit performance.[4] Unfortunately, surveys consistently report that few employees are fully engaged at work. The numbers vary across studies, but recent results from a widely recognized survey estimate that only 34 percent of employees in the United States are engaged, 53 percent are not engaged, and 13 percent are actively disengaged. Actively disengaged employees tend to be disruptive at work, not just disconnected from work.[5]

Motivated employees exert varying levels of effort (intensity), for varying lengths of time (persistence), toward various goals (direction).
K-PHOTOS/Alamy Stock Photo

LO5-2 Explain how drives and emotions influence employee motivation.

Employee Drives and Needs

To build a more engaged and motivated workforce, we first need to understand where motivation begins, that is, the motivational "forces" or prime movers of employee behavior.[6] Our starting point is **drives** (also called *primary needs*), which we define as hardwired characteristics of the brain that attempt to keep us in balance by correcting deficiencies. Neuroscience (brain) research has highlighted the central role of emotions in this process. Specifically, drives produce emotions that energize us to act on our environment.[7] There is no agreed-upon list of human drives, but research has consistently identified several, such as the drive to have social interaction, to develop our competence, to comprehend our surroundings, and to defend ourselves against physiological and psychological harm.[8]

Drives are universal and innate, which means that everyone has them and they exist from birth. Drives are the starting point of motivation because they generate emotions that, as we learned in Chapter 4, put people in a state of readiness to act on their environment. Cognition (logical thinking) also plays an important role in motivation, but emotions are the real sources of energy in human behavior.[9] In fact, both words (*emotion* and *motivation*) originate from the same Latin word, *movere*, which means "to move."

Exhibit 5.1 illustrates how drives and emotions translate into felt needs and behavior. Drives, and the emotions generated by these drives, form human needs. We define **needs** as goal-directed forces that people experience. They are the motivational forces of emotions channeled toward particular goals to correct deficiencies or imbalances. In other words, needs are the emotions we eventually become consciously aware of. For example, you sense a need to interact with people after being alone for a while, or to do something challenging after performing tedious activities.

Consider the following example: You arrive at work to discover a stranger sitting at your desk. Seeing this situation produces emotions (worry, curiosity) that motivate you to act. These emotions are generated from drives, such as the drive to defend and drive to comprehend. When strong enough, these emotions motivate you to do something about this situation, such as finding out who that person is and possibly seeking reassurance from coworkers that your job is still safe. In this case, you have a need to make sense of what is going on (comprehend), to feel secure, and possibly to correct a sense of personal violation (defend). Notice that your emotional reactions to seeing the stranger sitting at your desk represent the forces that move you, and that your logical thinking plays an active role in channeling those emotions toward specific goals.

> It is the paradox of Intelligence that it directs forces or energies without being itself a force or energy.[10]
>
> —William McDougall, early 20th century motivation scholar

Exhibit 5.1 Drives, Needs, and Behavior

drives hardwired characteristics of the brain that correct deficiencies or maintain an internal equilibrium by producing emotions to energize individuals

needs goal-directed forces that people experience

four-drive theory a motivation theory based on the innate drives to acquire, bond, learn, and defend that incorporates both emotions and rationality

Individual Differences in Needs

Everyone has the same drives; they are hardwired in us through evolution. However, people develop different intensities of needs in a particular situation. Exhibit 5.1 explains why this difference occurs. The left side of the model shows that the individual's self-concept (as well as personality and values), social norms, and past experience amplify or suppress emotions, thereby resulting in stronger or weaker needs.[11] For example, people who define themselves as very sociable typically experience a stronger need for social interaction if alone for a while, whereas less sociable types experience a less intense need to be with others over that time. These individual differences can be "learned" to some extent through socialization and reinforcement. We will discuss learned needs later in the chapter.

Along with amplifying or suppressing emotions, individual differences (self-concept, social norms, past experience) influence what goals and behaviors are motivated by the felt emotions, as the right side of Exhibit 5.1 illustrates. Visualize once again the stranger sitting at your desk. You probably wouldn't walk up to that person and demand that he or she leave; such blunt behavior is contrary to social norms in most cultures. Employees who view themselves as forthright might approach the stranger directly, whereas those who have a different personality and self-view are more likely to first gather information from coworkers before approaching the individual. In summary, your drives (to comprehend, to defend, to socialize with others, etc.) and resulting emotions energize you to act, and your personal characteristics (self-concept, social norms, and past experience) direct that energy toward goal-directed behavior.

Exhibit 5.1 provides a useful template for understanding how drives and emotions are the prime sources of employee motivation and how individual characteristics (self-concept, experience, social norms) influence goal-directed behavior. We will refer to elements of this drive theory of motivation when we discuss four-drive theory, expectancy theory, equity theory, and other concepts in this chapter. The next section describes theories that explain the dynamics of drives and needs.

LO5-3 Discuss the employee motivation implications of four-drive theory, Maslow's needs hierarchy, intrinsic and extrinsic motivation, and learned needs theory.

DRIVE-BASED MOTIVATION THEORIES

Four-Drive Theory

The process through which drives, emotions, and needs influence motivation is most effectively explained by **four-drive theory**. This theory states that emotions are the source of human motivation and that these emotions are generated through four drives:[12]

- *Drive to acquire.* This is the drive to seek out, take, control, and retain objects and personal experiences. It produces several needs, including achievement, competence, status, and self-esteem.[13] The drive to acquire also motivates competition.
- *Drive to bond.* This drive produces the need for belonging and affiliation.[14] It explains why our self-concept is partly defined by associations with social groups (see Chapter 3). The drive to bond motivates people to cooperate and, consequently, is essential for organizations and societies.
- *Drive to comprehend.* We are inherently curious and need to make sense of our environment and ourselves.[15] We are motivated to discover answers to unknown as well as conflicting ideas.
- *Drive to defend.* This is the drive to protect ourselves physically, psychologically, and socially. Probably the first drive to develop in human beings, it creates a fight-or-flight response when we are confronted with threats to our physical safety, our possessions, our self-concept, our values, and the well-being of people around us.[16]

All drives are hardwired in our brains and exist in all human beings. They are also independent of one another; there is no hierarchy of drives. Four-drive theory also claims that no fundamental drives are excluded from the model. Another key feature is that three of the four drives are proactive—we regularly try to fulfill them. Therefore, need "fulfillment" is brief and ongoing. Only the drive to defend is reactive—it is triggered by threat.

Four-drive theory states that emotions are the source of human motivation and that these emotions are generated through the drive to acquire, bond, comprehend, and defend.
LWA/Larry Williams/Blend Images

How Drives Influence Motivation and Behavior Recall from Chapter 3 that the stimuli received through our senses are quickly and nonconsciously tagged with emotional markers.[17] Four-drive theory proposes that the four drives determine which emotions are tagged to incoming stimuli. Most of the time, we aren't aware of our emotional experiences because they are subtle and fleeting. However, emotions do become conscious experiences when they are sufficiently strong or when they significantly conflict with one another.

Four-drive theory also recognizes that our social norms, personal values, and past experience—which the theory calls our "mental skill set"—guide our motivational energy and reduce the felt need (see Exhibit 5.2). In other words, our mental skill set chooses courses of action that are acceptable to society, consistent with our own moral compass, and have a high probability of achieving the goal of fulfilling our felt needs.[18]

Practical Implications of Four-Drive Theory Four-drive theory recommends that jobs and workplaces should provide a balanced opportunity for employees to fulfill the four drives.[19] There are really two recommendations here. The first is that the best workplaces help employees fulfill all four drives. Employees continually seek fulfillment of their innate drives, so successful companies provide sufficient rewards, learning opportunities, social interaction, and so forth for all employees.

The second recommendation is that fulfillment of the four drives must be kept in balance; that is, organizations shouldn't give employees too much or too little opportunity to fulfill each drive. The reason for this advice is that the four drives counterbalance each other. The drive to bond, which motivates mutual

Exhibit 5.2 Four-Drive Theory of Motivation

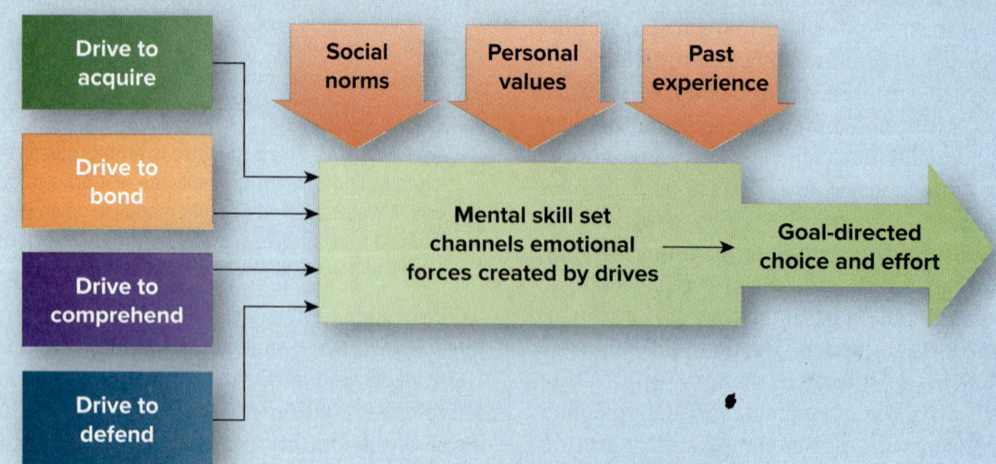

Source: Based on information in P.R. Lawrence and N. Nohria, *Driven: How Human Nature Shapes Our Choices* (San Francisco: Jossey-Bass, 2002).

Exhibit 5.3 Maslow's Needs Hierarchy

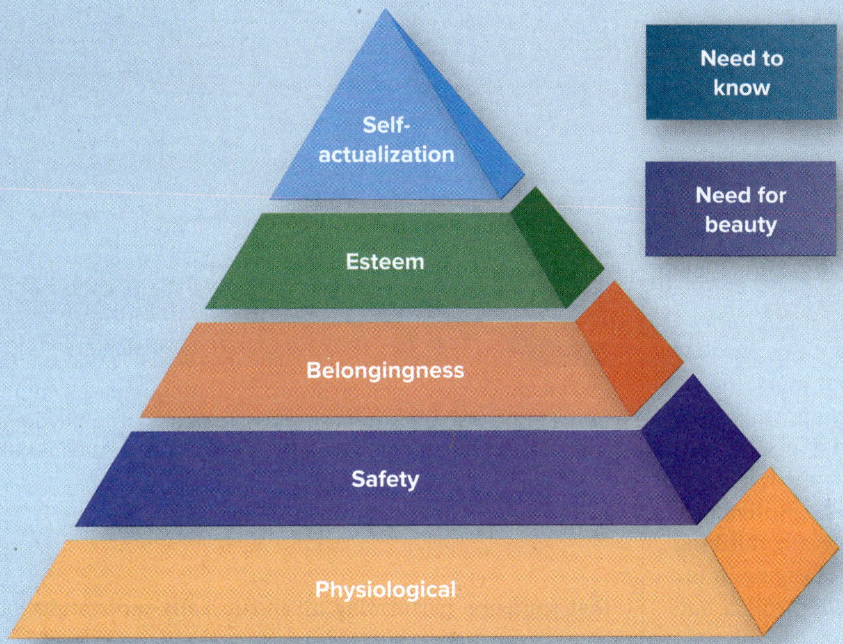

Source: Based on information in A.H. Maslow, "A Theory of Human Motivation," *Psychological Review* 50 (1943): 370–96.

Maslow's needs hierarchy theory a motivation theory of needs arranged in a hierarchy, whereby people are motivated to fulfill a higher need as a lower one becomes gratified

support and cohesion, counterbalances the drive to acquire, which motivates competitiveness. An organization that fuels the drive to acquire without encouraging the drive to bond may eventually suffer from organizational politics, dysfunctional conflict, and insufficient collaboration.[20] The drive to comprehend, which motivates investigation of the unknown, counterbalances the drive to defend, which motivates avoidance of the unknown. Change and novelty in the workplace will feed the drive to comprehend, but too much of it will trigger the drive to defend to such an extent that employees become territorial and resistant to change.

Maslow's Needs Hierarchy Theory

Mention needs and drives to most people and they will probably refer to **Maslow's needs hierarchy theory**, which was developed by psychologist Abraham Maslow in the 1940s.[21] Maslow condensed and organized the dozens of previously studied drives (which he called *primary needs*) into five basic categories, organized in a hierarchy from lowest to highest (see Exhibit 5.3):[22] *physiological* (need for food, air, water, shelter, etc.), *safety* (need for security and stability), *belongingness/love* (need for interaction with and affection from others), *esteem* (need for self-esteem and social esteem/status), and *self-actualization* (need for self-fulfillment, realization of one's potential). Along with these five categories, Maslow identified the need to know and the need for aesthetic beauty as two innate drives that do not fit within the hierarchy.

Maslow proposed we are motivated simultaneously by several needs, but the strongest motivation comes from the lowest unsatisfied need. When satisfied, the next higher need in the hierarchy becomes the strongest motivator and remains so even if never satisfied. The exception to this need fulfillment process is self-actualization, which is an ongoing need that is never fulfilled. Thus, while the bottom four groups are *deficiency needs* because they become activated when unfulfilled, self-actualization is known as a *growth need* because it continues to develop even when temporarily satiated.

In spite of its popularity, Maslow's needs hierarchy theory was dismissed decades ago by motivation experts.[23] The main flaw is that not everyone has the same needs hierarchy. Some people place social status at the top of their personal hierarchy whereas others view personal development and growth above social relations or status. This variation occurs because employee needs are strongly influenced by self-concept, personal values, and personality.[24] People have different hierarchies of values, so they also have parallel differences in their needs hierarchies. Furthermore, a person's values hierarchy can change over time, so his or her needs hierarchy also changes over time.[25]

Why have we introduced Maslow's needs hierarchy model? One reason is that the theory is widely known and incorrectly assumed to be accurate; therefore, organizational behavior students need to be aware of its true status. The other reason is that through this theory, Maslow transformed how we now think about human motivation.[26] Specifically, he emphasized that needs should be studied together

connect

SELF-ASSESSMENT 5.1: How Strong Are Your Growth Needs?

intrinsic motivation
motivation that occurs when people are fulfilling their needs for competence and autonomy by engaging in the activity itself, rather than from an externally controlled outcome of that activity

(holistically), not separately from one another; he recognized that motivation can be shaped by human thoughts (humanistic), not just from instincts; and his focus on self-actualization and growth needs introduced a more positive view of motivation, whereas previous motivation theories focused on need deficiencies such as hunger.

Intrinsic and Extrinsic Motivation

By extolling the importance of self-actualization, Maslow launched an entirely new way of thinking about human motivation. People experience self-actualization by applying their skills and knowledge, observing how their talents achieve meaningful results, and experiencing personal growth through learning. These are the conditions for **intrinsic motivation**, which is motivation that occurs when people are fulfilling their needs for competence and autonomy by engaging in the activity itself, rather than from an externally controlled outcome of that activity.[27] Intrinsically motivated employees apply their talents toward a meaningful task and experience progress or success in that task.[28] They feel competent when applying their skills and observing positive, meaningful outcomes from that effort. They feel autonomous when their motivation is self-initiated rather than controlled from an external source.

Intrinsic motivation contrasts with **extrinsic motivation**, which occurs when people are motivated to engage in an activity for instrumental reasons, that is, to receive something that is beyond their personal control. This involves directing one's effort toward a reward controlled by others that indirectly fulfills a need. Extrinsic motivators exist throughout organizations, such as pay incentives, recognition awards, and frequent reminders from the boss about work deadlines. Extrinsic motivation also occurs indirectly, such as when we are motivated to complete our part of a team project partly due to our concerns about how team members will react if we submit it late or with inferior quality.

Does Extrinsic Motivation Undermine Intrinsic Motivation?

There are two contrasting hypotheses about how extrinsic and intrinsic motivation work together.[29] The additive hypothesis is that someone performing an intrinsically motivating job becomes even more motivated by also receiving an extrinsic source of motivation for that work. The extrinsic motivator energizes the employee more than the intrinsic motivator alone. The contrasting hypothesis is that introducing extrinsic sources of motivation will reduce intrinsic motivation. For example, employees who were energized by the work itself will experience less of that intrinsic motivation when they receive extrinsic rewards, such as a performance bonus. The contrasting hypothesis suggests that introducing extrinsic motivators diminishes the employee's feeling of autonomy, which is a key source of intrinsic motivation.

Which hypothesis is correct? So far, the research evidence is mixed. Extrinsic motivators may reduce existing intrinsic motivation to some extent and under some conditions, but the effect is often minimal. Extrinsic rewards do not undermine intrinsic motivation when they are unexpected (such as receiving a surprise bonus), when they have low value relative to the intrinsic motivator, and when they are not contingent on specific behavior (such as receiving a fixed salary). Even so, when employees are engaged in intrinsically motivating work, employers should be careful about the potential unintended effect of undermining that motivation with performance bonuses and other sources of extrinsic motivation.[30]

Pay incentives, recognition awards, and frequent reminders from the boss about work deadlines are extrinsic motivators because the outcomes are controlled by others and are not need fulfillment in themselves.
Peshkova/Shutterstock

> Intrinsic motivation occurs when people are fulfilling their needs for competence and autonomy by engaging in the activity itself.

extrinsic motivation motivation that occurs when people want to engage in an activity for instrumental reasons, that is, to receive something that is beyond their personal control

need for achievement (nAch) a learned need in which people want to accomplish reasonably challenging goals and desire unambiguous feedback and recognition for their success

need for affiliation (nAff) a learned need in which people seek approval from others, conform to their wishes and expectations, and avoid conflict and confrontation

need for power (nPow) a learned need in which people want to control their environment, including people and material resources, to benefit either themselves (personalized power) or others (socialized power)

expectancy theory a motivation theory based on the idea that work effort is directed toward behaviors that people believe will lead to desired outcomes

Learned Needs Theory

In the previous section of this chapter, we explained that needs are shaped, amplified, or suppressed through self-concept, social norms, and past experience. Maslow noted this when he observed that individual differences influence the strength of higher-order needs, such as the need to belong. Psychologist David McClelland further investigated the idea that needs can be strengthened or weakened through reinforcement, learning, and social conditions. He examined three "learned" needs: achievement, affiliation, and power.[31]

- People with a high **need for achievement (nAch)** choose moderately challenging tasks, desire unambiguous feedback and recognition for their success, and prefer working alone rather than in teams. Except as a source of feedback, money is a weak motivator for people with high nAch, whereas it can be a strong motivator for those with low nAch.[32] Successful entrepreneurs tend to have high nAch, possibly because they establish challenging goals for themselves and thrive on competition.[33]
- People with a high **need for affiliation (nAff)** seek approval from others, want to conform to others' wishes and expectations, and avoid conflict and confrontation. High nAff employees generally work well in jobs where the main task is cultivating long-term relations. However, with a strong need for approval, high nAff employees tend to be less effective at allocating scarce resources and making other decisions that potentially generate conflict. This suggests that leaders should have low nAff, but a few studies have found that leaders should have at least moderate levels of nAff to be supportive of employee needs.[34]
- People with a high **need for power (nPow)** want to exercise control over others, are highly involved in team decisions, rely on persuasion, and are concerned about maintaining their leadership position. There are two types of nPow.[35] The need for *personalized power* occurs when individuals enjoy their power for its own sake, use it to advance personal interests, and wear their power as a status symbol. The need for *socialized power* exists when individuals desire power as a means to help others. Effective leaders have a high need for socialized rather than personalized power. They demonstrate altruism and social responsibility and are concerned about the consequences of their own actions on others.

McClelland developed training programs to test the idea that needs can be learned (amplified or suppressed) through reinforcement, learning, and social conditions. One program increased achievement motivation by having participants write achievement-oriented stories, practice achievement-oriented behaviors in business games, and meet frequently with a reference group with other trainees to maintain their newfound achievement motivation.[36] Essentially, McClelland's programs changed how people viewed themselves (their self-concept), which amplified their need for achievement, affiliation, or power.

Connect

SELF-ASSESSMENT 5.2: How Strong Are Your Learned Needs?

LO5-4 Discuss the expectancy theory model, including its practical implications.

EXPECTANCY THEORY OF MOTIVATION

The theories described so far mainly explain *what motivates us*—the prime movers of employee motivation—but they don't tell us *what we are motivated to do*. Four-drive theory recognizes that social norms, personal values, and past experience direct our effort, but it doesn't offer any detail about what goals we choose or where our effort is directed under various circumstances.

Expectancy theory offers more detail by predicting the goal-directed behavior where employees are most likely to direct their effort toward specific behavior. Essentially, the theory states that work effort is directed toward behaviors that people believe will produce the most favorable outcomes. It assumes that people are rational decision makers who choose a target that will best fulfill their needs. This choice is based on the probability that specific events will occur and the positive or negative valences (expected satisfaction) resulting from those events.[37] As Exhibit 5.4 illustrates, an individual's effort level depends on three factors: effort-to-performance (E-to-P) expectancy, performance-to-outcome (P-to-O) expectancy, and outcome valences. Employee motivation is influenced by all three components of the expectancy theory model.[38] If any component weakens, motivation weakens.

Exhibit 5.4 Expectancy Theory of Motivation

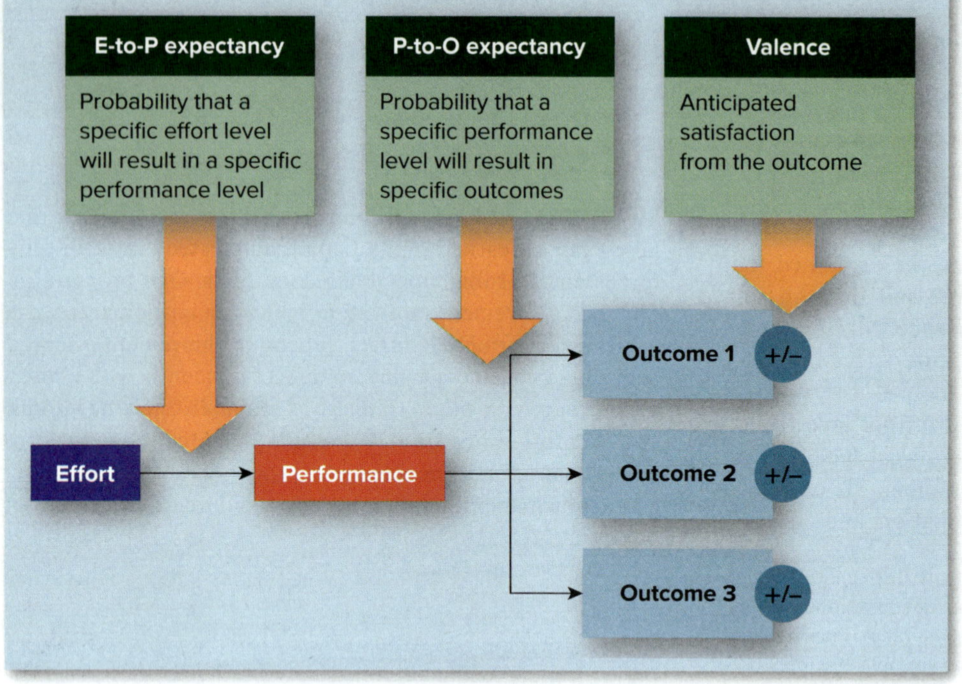

- *E-to-P expectancy.* This is the individual's perception that his or her effort will result in a particular level of performance. In some situations, employees may believe that they can unquestionably accomplish the task (a probability of 1.0). In other situations, they expect that even their highest level of effort will not result in the desired performance level (a probability of 0.0). In most cases, the E-to-P expectancy falls somewhere between these two extremes.
- *P-to-O expectancy.* This is the perceived probability that a specific behavior or performance level will lead to a particular outcome. In extreme cases, employees may believe that accomplishing a particular task (performance) will definitely result in a particular outcome (a probability of 1.0), or they may believe that successful performance will have no effect on this outcome (a probability of 0.0). More often, the P-to-O expectancy falls somewhere between these two extremes.
- *Outcome valences.* A *valence* is the anticipated satisfaction or dissatisfaction that an individual feels toward an outcome.[39] It ranges from negative to positive. (The actual range doesn't matter; it may be from −1 to +1 or from −100 to +100.) Outcomes have a positive valence when they are consistent with our values and satisfy our needs; they have a negative valence when they oppose our values and inhibit need fulfillment.

Expectancy Theory in Practice

One of the appealing characteristics of expectancy theory is that it provides clear guidelines for increasing employee motivation, at least extrinsic motivation.[40] Several practical applications of expectancy theory are described below.

Increasing E-to-P Expectancies E-to-P expectancies are influenced by the individual's belief that he or she can successfully complete the task. Some companies increase this can-do attitude by assuring employees that they have the required abilities and resources as well as clear role perceptions to reach the desired

Performance-to-Outcome Expectancy: A Weak Link in Employee Motivation[41]

56% of 8,254 employees surveyed in the United States, Canada, and five European countries say that they have a good understanding of how people are compensated at all levels of their company (36% say they don't have a good understanding).

37% of American employees surveyed see NO link at all between their performance and their pay.

39% of 615,395 U.S. federal government employees believe that differences in performance are recognized in a meaningful way in their work unit.

44% of 31,000 employees surveyed in 29 countries say they see a clear link between performance and pay in their organization.

44% of more than 4,000 employees in the United States and Canada say their manager differentiates between high and low performers.

alxpin/iStock/Getty Images

OB THEORY TO PRACTICE

Putting Expectancy Theory into Practice

Increasing E → P expectancies

- Select people with the required skills and knowledge.
- Provide required training and clarify job requirements.
- Provide sufficient time and resources.
- Assign simpler or fewer tasks until employees can master them.
- Provide examples of similar employees who have successfully performed the task.
- Provide coaching to employees who lack self-confidence.

Increasing P → O expectancies

- Measure job performance accurately.
- Clearly explain the outcomes that will result from successful performance.
- Describe how the employee's rewards were based on past performance.
- Provide examples of other employees whose good performance has resulted in higher rewards.

Increasing outcome valences

- Distribute rewards that employees value.
- Individualize rewards.
- Minimize the presence of countervalent outcomes.

levels of performance. An important part of this process involves matching employee abilities to job requirements and clearly communicating the tasks required for the job. Similarly, E-to-P expectancies are learned, so behavior modeling and supportive feedback typically strengthen the individual's belief that he or she is able to perform the task.

Increasing P-to-O Expectancies The most obvious ways to improve P-to-O expectancies are to measure employee performance accurately and distribute more valued rewards to those with higher job performance. P-to-O expectancies are perceptions, so employees also need to believe that higher performance will result in higher rewards. Furthermore, they need to know how that connection occurs, so leaders should use examples, anecdotes, and public ceremonies to illustrate when behavior has been rewarded.

Increasing Outcome Valences One size does not fit all when motivating and rewarding people. The valence of a reward varies from one person to the next because each person has different need priorities. One solution is to individualize rewards by allowing employees to choose the rewards of greatest value to them. When this isn't possible, companies should find a reward that everyone values to some degree. Finally, we need to watch out for countervalent outcomes. If a company offers individual performance bonuses, for example, it should beware of team norms that discourage employees from working above a minimum standard. These norms and associated peer pressure are countervalent outcomes to the bonus.

Overall, expectancy theory is a useful model that explains how people rationally figure out the best direction, intensity, and persistence of effort. It has been tested in a variety of situations and predicts employee motivation in different cultures.[42] One limitation, however, is that expectancy theory assumes people are perfectly rational decision makers; in reality, human decisions are not perfectly rational (see Chapter 6). A second concern is that the theory mainly explains extrinsic motivation, whereas applying the model's features to intrinsic motivation is more difficult (although not impossible). Third, expectancy theory ignores emotions as a source of motivation. The valence element of expectancy theory captures some of this emotional process, but only peripherally.[43] Fourth, E-to-P and P-to-O expectancies are critical components of expectancy theory, yet the theory doesn't explain how employees develop these expectancies. Two theories that provide this explanation are organizational behavior modification and social cognitive theory, which we describe next.

LO5-5 Outline organizational behavior modification (OB Mod) and social cognitive theory and explain their relevance to employee motivation.

ORGANIZATIONAL BEHAVIOR MODIFICATION AND SOCIAL COGNITIVE THEORY

Expectancy theory states that motivation is determined by employee beliefs about expected performance and outcomes. But how do employees learn these expectancy beliefs? For example, how do they form the impression that one level of task performance is more likely than another performance level to produce a pay increase, promotion, or other outcomes? Two theories—organizational behavior modification (OB Mod) and social cognitive theory—complement expectancy theory by explaining how people *learn* what to expect from their actions, which is how people develop the expectancies that affect motivation.

organizational behavior modification (OB Mod) a theory that explains employee behavior in terms of the antecedent conditions and consequences of that behavior

Organizational Behavior Modification

> **In most situations, positive reinforcement should follow desired behaviors and extinction (do nothing) should follow undesirable behaviors.**

For most of the first half of the 1900s, the dominant paradigm about managing individual behavior was *behaviorism*, which argues that a good theory should rely exclusively on behavior and the environment and ignore nonobservable cognitions and emotions.[44] Although behaviorists don't deny the existence of human thoughts and attitudes, they view them as unobservable and, therefore, irrelevant to scientific study. A variation of this paradigm, called **organizational behavior modification (OB Mod)**, eventually entered organizational studies of motivation and learning.[45]

A-B-Cs of OB Mod The core elements of OB Mod are depicted in the A-B-C model shown in Exhibit 5.5. Essentially, OB Mod attempts to change behavior (B) by managing its antecedents (A) and consequences (C).[46] *Consequences* are events following a particular behavior that influence its future occurrence. Consequences include receiving words of thanks from coworkers after assisting them, receiving preferred work schedules after being with the company longer than the average employee, and finding useful information on your smartphone after checking for new messages. Consequences also include no outcome at all, such as when no one says anything to you about how well you have been serving customers.

Antecedents are events preceding the behavior, informing employees that a particular action will produce specific consequences. An antecedent could be a sound from your smartphone signaling that a text message has arrived. Or it could be your supervisor's request to complete a specific task by tomorrow. Notice that antecedents do not cause behavior. The sound from your smartphone doesn't cause you to open the text message. Rather, the sound (antecedent) is a cue signaling that if you look at your phone messages (behavior), you will find a new message with potentially useful information (consequence).

Contingencies and Schedules of Reinforcement OB Mod identifies four types of consequences, called the *contingencies of reinforcement*.[47] *Positive reinforcement* occurs when the introduction of a consequence increases or maintains the frequency or future probability of a specific behavior. Receiving praise from coworkers is an example of positive reinforcement because the praise usually maintains or increases your likelihood of helping them in future. *Punishment* occurs when a consequence decreases the frequency or future probability of a specific behavior occurring. Most of us would consider being demoted or criticized by our coworkers as forms of punishment. A third type of consequence is *extinction*. The extinction consequence occurs when the target behavior decreases because no consequence follows it. For instance, research suggests that performance tends to decline when managers stop congratulating employees for their good work.[48]

The fourth consequence in OB Mod, called *negative reinforcement*, is often confused with punishment. It's actually the opposite—the removal of punishment. Negative reinforcement occurs when the removal or avoidance of a consequence increases or maintains the frequency or future probability of a specific behavior. For example, managers apply negative reinforcement when they *stop* criticizing employees whose substandard performance has improved.

Exhibit 5.5 A-B-Cs of Organizational Behavior Modification

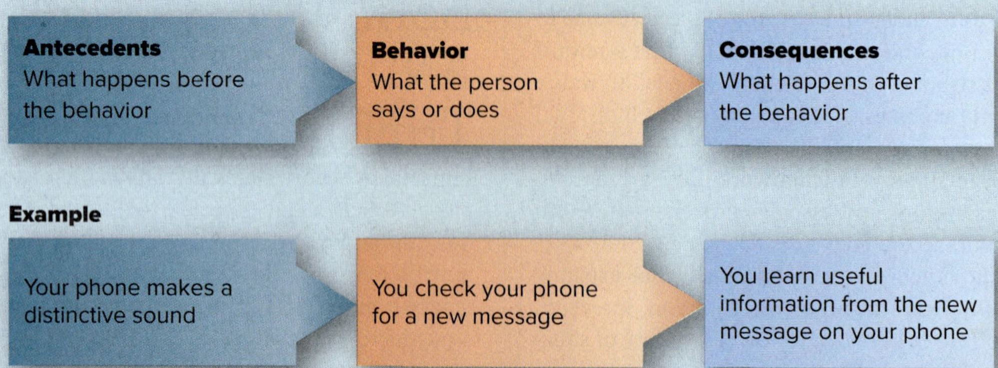

Source: Adapted from T.K. Connellan, *How to Improve Human Performance* (New York: Harper & Row, 1978), 50; F. Luthans and R. Kreitner, *Organizational Behavior Modification and Beyond* (Glenview, IL: Scott, Foresman, 1985), 85–88.

Which of these four consequences works best? In most situations, positive reinforcement should follow desired behaviors and extinction (do nothing) should follow undesirable behaviors. Positive reinforcement is preferred because focusing on the positive rather than negative aspects of life tends to improve organizational success and individual well-being.[49] In contrast, punishment and negative reinforcement generate negative emotions and attitudes toward the punisher (e.g., supervisor) and organization who initiated and later removed the punishment. However, punishment (dismissal, suspension, demotion, etc.) may be necessary for extreme behaviors, such as deliberately hurting a coworker or stealing inventory. Indeed, research suggests that, under some conditions, punishment maintains a sense of fairness among those affected by or aware of the employee's indiscretion.[50]

Along with the four consequences, OB Mod considers the frequency and timing of these reinforcers (called the *schedules of reinforcement*).[51] The most effective reinforcement schedule for learning new tasks is *continuous reinforcement*—providing positive reinforcement after every occurrence of the desired behavior. The most effective reinforcement schedule for skilled employees is the *variable ratio schedule* – providing positive reinforcement after a varying number of times. Salespeople experience variable ratio reinforcement because they make a successful sale (positive reinforcement) after a varying number of client calls. The variable ratio schedule makes behavior highly resistant to extinction because the reinforcer is never expected at a particular time or after a fixed number of behaviors.

Social Cognitive Theory

Social cognitive theory states that much learning occurs by observing and modeling others as well as by anticipating the consequences of our behavior.[52] There are several pieces to social cognitive theory, but the three most relevant to employee motivation are learning behavior consequences, behavior modeling, and self-regulation.

People learn the consequences of behavior by observing or hearing about what happened to others, not just by directly experiencing the consequences.
BulentBARIS/Getty Images

social cognitive theory a theory that explains how learning and motivation occur by observing and modeling others as well as by anticipating the consequences of our behavior

Learning Behavior Consequences People learn the consequences of behavior by observing or hearing about what happened to others, not just by directly experiencing the consequences.[53] Hearing that a coworker was fired for being rude to a client increases your belief that rude behavior will result in being fired. In the language of expectancy theory, learning behavior consequences changes a person's perceived P-to-O expectancy. Furthermore, people logically anticipate consequences in related situations. For instance, the story about the fired employee might also strengthen your P-to-O expectancy that being rude toward coworkers and suppliers (not just clients) will get you fired.

Behavior Modeling Along with observing others, people learn by imitating and practicing their behaviors.[54] Modeling the behavior of others gives learners direct sensory experience, which helps them to acquire knowledge and skills, such as the subtle person–machine interaction while driving a vehicle. Behavior modeling also increases E-to-P expectancy because people develop a stronger self-efficacy (see Chapter 3) after observing others and performing the task successfully themselves. Self-efficacy particularly improves when observers are similar to the model in age, experience, gender, and related characteristics.

Self-Regulation An important feature of social cognitive theory is that human beings set goals and engage in other forms of

Social cognitive theory states that people self-regulate through self-reinforcement; they reward and punish themselves for exceeding or falling short of their self-set goals.
Tim Teebken/Getty Images

self-reinforcement reinforcement that occurs when an employee has control over a reinforcer but doesn't "take" it until completing a self-set goal

goal a cognitive representation of a desired end state that a person is committed to attain

intentional, purposive action.[55] They establish their own short- and long-term objectives, choose their own standards of achievement, work out a plan of action, consider backup alternatives, and have the forethought to anticipate the consequences of their goal-directed behavior. Furthermore, people self-regulate by engaging in **self-reinforcement**; they reward and punish themselves for exceeding or falling short of their self-set goals. For example, you might have a goal of completing the rest of this chapter, after which you reward yourself by having a snack. Raiding the refrigerator is a form of self-induced positive reinforcement for completing this reading assignment.

OB Mod and social cognitive theory explain how people learn probabilities of successful performance (E-to-P expectancies) as well as probabilities of various outcomes from that performance (P-to-O expectancies). As such, these theories explain motivation through their relationship with expectancy theory of motivation, described earlier. Elements of these theories also help us to understand other motivation processes. For instance, self-regulation is the cornerstone of motivation through goal setting and feedback, which we discuss next.

LO5-6 Describe the characteristics of effective goal setting and feedback.

GOAL SETTING AND FEEDBACK

Key performance indicators, task objectives, stretch targets, job duties. No matter what they are called, goals figure prominently in everyone's job. A **goal** is a cognitive representation of a desired end state that a person is committed to attain.[56] Goals motivate people by clarifying role perceptions and, consequently, the direction of effort. Goals also amplify the intensity and persistence of effort because they make it easier to judge how much energy is required to reach them. However, the motivational potential of goals depends on how well they are stated.[57] Rather than just trying to "do your best," effective goals have several characteristics identified in the popular acronym SMARTER.[58] Specifically, goals are more effective when they are specific, measurable, achievable, relevant, time-framed, exciting, and reviewed.

OB THEORY TO PRACTICE

The SMARTER Approach to Goal Setting

Specific. Goals lead to better performance when they are specific. Specific goals state what needs to be accomplished; how it should be accomplished; and where, when, and with whom it should be accomplished. Specific goals clarify performance expectations, so employees can direct their effort more efficiently and reliably.

Measurable. Goals need to be measurable because motivation occurs when people have some indication of their progress and achievement of those goals. This measurement ideally includes how much (quantity), how well (quality), and at what cost the goal was achieved. However, some types of employee performance are difficult to measure, and those non-measurable tasks might be neglected in companies preoccupied with quantifiable outcomes.[59]

Achievable. One of the trickiest aspects of goal setting is developing goals that are sufficiently but not overly challenging.[60] Easier goals motivate employees to perform well below their potential. Yet, goals that are too challenging also may lead to substandard effort if employees believe there is a low probability of accomplishing them (i.e., low E-to-P expectancy). Recent studies also have found that very difficult goals increase the probability that employees will engage in unethical behavior to achieve them.[61]

Relevant. Goals need to be relevant to the job and within the individual's control. For example, a goal to reduce waste materials won't motivate employees who have negligible control over waste in the production process.

Time-framed. Goals need a due date. They should specify when the objective should be completed or when it will be assessed for comparison against a standard.

Exciting. Goals tend to be more effective when employees are committed to them, not just compliant. Challenging goals tend to be more exciting for most (but not all) employees because growth need fulfillment is stronger when difficult goals are achieved. Goal commitment also increases when employees are involved in goal setting.[62]

Reviewed. The motivational value of goal setting depends on employees receiving feedback about reaching those goals.[63] Effective feedback requires measurement, which we discussed earlier in this list, but it also includes reflecting or discussing with others your goal progress and accomplishment. Reviewing goal progress and accomplishment helps employees redirect their effort. It is also a potential source of recognition that fulfills growth needs.

McGraw Hill connect

SELF-ASSESSMENT 5.3: What Is Your Goal Orientation?

Characteristics of Effective Feedback

Feedback—information that lets us know whether we have achieved the goal or are properly directing our effort toward it—is an essential partner with goal setting. Feedback contributes to motivation and performance by clarifying role perceptions, improving employee skills and knowledge, and strengthening self-efficacy.[64]

strengths-based coaching an approach to coaching and feedback that focuses on building and leveraging the employee's strengths rather than trying to correct his or her weaknesses

Effective feedback has many of the same characteristics as effective goal setting (see Exhibit 5.6).[65] It should be *specific* and *relevant*—that is, the information should refer to specific metrics (e.g., sales increased by 5 percent last month) and to the individual's behavior or outcomes within his or her control. Feedback also should be *timely*—available soon after the behavior or results occur. Feedback also should be *credible*; that is, the person providing the feedback should have complete and accurate information about the employee's performance, is reliable at recalling that information, is unbiased in communicating and applying the feedback to decisions (such as performance ratings), and describes the feedback in a supportive and empathetic manner.

Finally, effective feedback is *sufficiently frequent*. "Sufficiently" means that the feedback is provided more often for employees learning new tasks and less often for employees who already know how to perform those tasks. It also means that feedback is provided in a time frame proportional to how long it takes to complete the task (i.e., the job cycle). Less frequent feedback usually occurs in jobs with a long cycle time (e.g., executives and scientists) because indicators of goal progress and accomplishment in these jobs are less frequent than in jobs with a short cycle time (e.g., grocery store cashiers).

Feedback through Strengths-Based Coaching **Strengths-based coaching** (also known as *appreciative coaching*) is a positive approach to feedback that maximizes employees' potential by focusing on their strengths rather than weaknesses.[66] In strengths-based coaching, employees describe areas of work where they excel or demonstrate potential. The coach guides this discussion by asking exploratory questions that help employees discover ways to build on these strengths. Situational barriers, as well as strategies to overcome those barriers, are identified to further support the employee's potential.

> **Success is achieved by developing our strengths, not by eliminating our weaknesses.**[67]
>
> —Marilyn vos Savant, author and magazine columnist

Exhibit 5.6 Characteristics of Effective Feedback

Feedback Characteristic	Description	Example
Specific	Information refers to identifiable behaviors and (when possible) measurable outcomes	"Inventory shrinkage (theft, damage) fell to 1% of inventory over the previous three months."
Relevant	Information should relate to behaviors and outcomes within the individual's or team's control	"You have submitted the monthly budget reports without error and on time every month over the past year, one of the few district managers to do so" (where district managers have few situational barriers to submitting the reports accurately or on schedule).
Timely	Information should be available soon after the behavior or results occur	"Two of our customers noted this week that you were unable to answer their questions about how the new widget model differs from the previous model."
Credible	Information source should: • Have complete and accurate information • Recall information reliably • Be unbiased in communicating and applying the feedback • Describe the feedback in a supportive and empathetic manner	Supervisor has good knowledge of the employee's job duties, regularly observes him/her performing the work, and offers constructive feedback with optimism and sensitivity on how the employee can perform specific tasks better.
Sufficiently frequent	Information is provided: • More often for those learning new tasks • According to the job cycle's frequency	Supervisor meets twice monthly with every experienced production employee and at least twice weekly with every new employee to discuss their individual safety behavior and output (where task cycle times are usually less than one hour).

> **Not everything that can be counted counts, and not everything that counts can be counted.**[75]
>
> —William Bruce Cameron, sociologist

Strengths-based coaching might not be best in all situations, but it is associated with higher employee motivation, satisfaction, self-efficacy, and relations with management.[68] One reason is that people are more receptive to information about their strengths than they are to information about their flaws. In fact, for more than three decades scholars have warned that traditional problem-focused feedback leads to employee defensiveness and potentially lower self-efficacy, which can result in reduced (rather than increased) employee performance.[69] Strengths-based coaching also makes sense because personality becomes quite stable in the early stages of a person's career, which limits his or her flexibility regarding interests, preferences, and abilities.[70] Consequently, employees become less motivated and less able to improve themselves in areas where they previously lacked interest or skill.

Sources of Feedback

Feedback can originate from nonsocial or social sources. Nonsocial sources provide feedback without someone communicating that information. Corporate intranets allow many executives to receive feedback instantaneously on their computer or other digital device, usually in the form of graphic output on an executive dashboard.

Some companies set up *multisource (360-degree) feedback*, which, as the name implies, is information about an employee's performance collected from a full circle of people, including subordinates, peers, supervisors, and customers. Multisource feedback tends to provide more complete and accurate information than feedback from a supervisor alone. It is particularly useful when the supervisor is unable to observe the employee's behavior or performance in every situation. Lower-level employees also feel a greater sense of fairness when they are able to provide upward feedback about their boss's performance.[71] However, multisource feedback can be expensive and time-consuming. It may also be biased by coworkers avoiding interpersonal conflict. Multisource feedback also tends to be ambiguous because several observers have different perspectives of the employee's behavior.

Feedback from nonsocial sources is better than from social sources when employees need to learn about goal progress and accomplishment.
Dan Bannister/Blend Images LLC

The preferred feedback source depends on the purpose of the information. Feedback from nonsocial sources, such as digital images or feedback directly from the job, is better when employees need to learn about goal progress and accomplishment. This is because information from nonsocial sources is considered more accurate than information from social sources. Negative feedback from nonsocial sources is also less damaging to self-esteem. In contrast, social sources tend to delay or exclude negative information, as well as distort the bad news in a positive way.[72] Employees should receive some positive feedback from social sources. It feels better to have coworkers say that you are performing the job well than to discover this from data on an impersonal digital dashboard.

Evaluating Goal Setting and Feedback

Goal setting (in partnership with feedback) is generally a highly effective practice for employee motivation and performance.[73] Putting goal setting into practice can be challenging, however.[74] It tends to focus employees on a narrow subset of measurable performance indicators while ignoring aspects of job performance that are difficult to measure. Another concern is that very difficult goals may motivate some people to engage in unethical behavior to achieve those targets. Difficult goals are also stressful, which can undermine overall job performance.

Yet another problem is that goal setting tends to interfere with the learning process in new, complex jobs. Therefore, setting performance goals may be effective for employees who are already experienced in a job but should be avoided where they are in the middle of an intense learning process. A final issue is that when goal achievement is tied to financial rewards, many employees are motivated to set easy goals (while making the boss think they are difficult) so that they have a higher probability of receiving the bonus or pay increase. As a former Ford Motor Company CEO once quipped: "At Ford, we hire very smart people. They quickly learn how to make relatively easy goals look difficult!"[76]

LO5-7 Explain how equity theory, procedural justice, and interactional justice influence employee motivation.

ORGANIZATIONAL JUSTICE

Treating employees fairly is both morally correct and good for employee motivation, loyalty, and well-being. Yet feelings of injustice are regular occurrences in the workplace. To minimize these incidents, we need to first understand the three most common types of justice (there are others): distributive, procedural, and interactional justice. All three refer to the perception that appropriate formal or informal rules have been applied to the situation. People have a sense of fairness when they believe those rules are being followed.[77]

- **Distributive justice** refers to the perception that appropriate decision criteria (rules) have been applied to calculate how various benefits and burdens are distributed. These criteria—such as effort, need, or membership—determine how much each person should receive, such as higher pay, more tedious tasks, better workspace, and so on.
- **Procedural justice** is the perception that appropriate procedural rules have been applied throughout the decision process. Procedural justice tends to be higher, for example, when the decision maker demonstrates neutrality (no favoritism), allows everyone involved to have their say, and allows an appeal of the decision.
- **Interactional justice** is the perception that appropriate rules have been applied in the way employees are treated throughout the decision process. For example, we believe there is interactional justice when the decision maker is polite toward the potential beneficiaries and is honest and candid in providing information about the decision.

Distributive Justice and Equity Theory

At its most basic level, employment in any organization is an exchange relationship; we provide our time, skills, and behavior in exchange for pay, fulfilling work, skill development opportunities, and so forth. What is considered "fair" in this exchange relationship depends on what criteria we use to determine distributive justice in various situations.[78] An *equality principle* operates when we believe that everyone in the group should receive the same outcomes, such as when everyone gets subsidized meals in the company cafeteria. The *need principle* is applied when we believe that those with the greatest need should receive more outcomes than others with less need. This occurs, for instance, when employees get paid time off to recover from illness. The *equity principle* infers that people should be paid in proportion to their contribution. The equity principle relates to the most common set of distributive justice rules in organizational settings, so let's look at equity-based distributive justice in more detail.

Equity-based fairness is explained by **equity theory**, which says that employees determine whether a decision is equitable by

distributive justice the perception that appropriate decision criteria (rules) have been applied to calculate how various benefits and burdens are distributed

procedural justice the perception that appropriate procedural rules have been applied throughout the decision process

interactional justice the perception that appropriate rules have been applied in the way the people involved are treated throughout the decision process

equity theory a theory explaining how people develop perceptions of fairness in the distribution and exchange of resources

Not Paid What (They Believe) They're Worth[79]

53% of 31,000 employees surveyed globally say they are being paid fairly compared with others who fill similar positions in other companies.

44% of 7,700 executives and managers surveyed in several countries (5,136 in the United States) say that employees at their companies are paid fairly.

20% of 71,000 employees surveyed (most in the United States) say that they are paid fairly.

36% of 1,000 Australian advertising professionals surveyed say their bosses are NOT overpaid (26% say they ARE overpaid).

26% of 14,000 New Zealand public servants surveyed agree that their pay is fair compared to similar jobs in the wider labor market (53% disagree; 21% neither agree nor disagree).

Don Farrall/Getty Images

Exhibit 5.7 Equity Theory Model

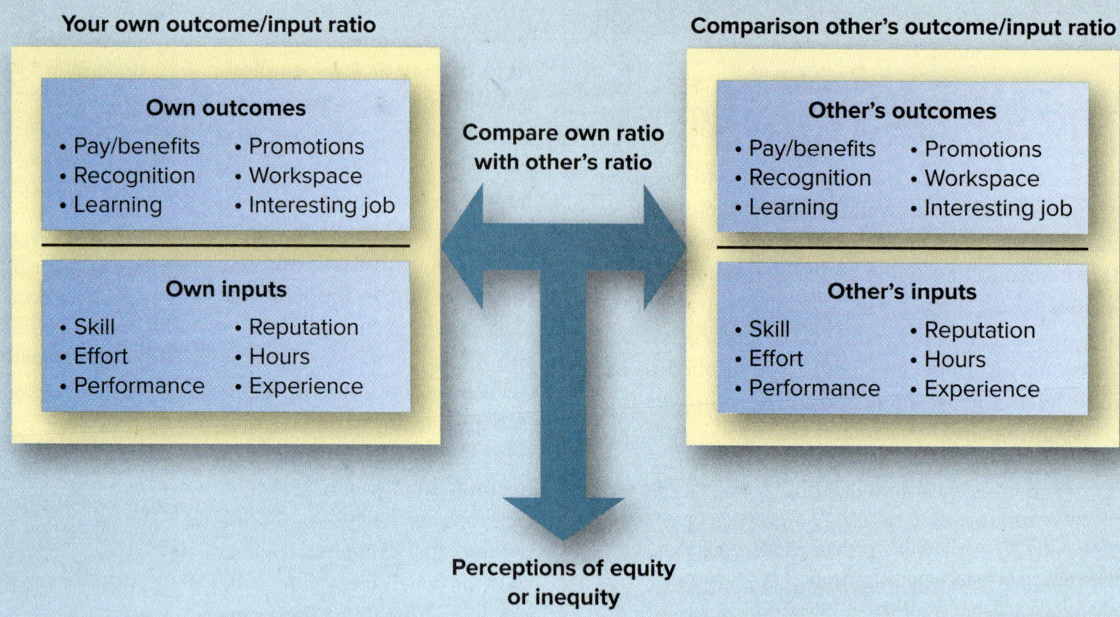

comparing their own outcome/input ratio to the outcome/input ratio of another person or group.[80] As Exhibit 5.7 illustrates, the *outcome/input ratio* is the value of the outcomes you receive divided by the value of the inputs you provide in the exchange relationship. Inputs include such things as skill, effort, reputation, performance, experience, and hours worked. Outcomes are what employees receive from the organization, such as pay, promotions, recognition, interesting jobs, and opportunities to improve one's skills and knowledge.

A central feature of equity theory is that individuals determine fairness in terms of a *comparison other*.[81] The comparison other might be another person or group of people in other jobs (e.g., comparing your pay with your boss's pay) or another organization. Some research suggests that employees frequently collect information on several referents to form a "generalized" comparison other.[82] For the most part, however, the comparison other varies from one person and situation to the next and is not easily identifiable.

The comparison of our own outcome/input ratio with the ratio of someone else results in perceptions of equity, underreward inequity, or overreward inequity. In the equity condition, people believe that their outcome/input ratio is similar to the ratio of the comparison other. In the underreward inequity situation, people believe their outcome/input ratio is lower than the comparison other's ratio. In the overreward inequity condition, people believe their outcome/input ratio is higher than the comparison other's ratio.

Inequity and Employee Motivation How do perceptions of equity or inequity affect employee motivation? The answer is illustrated in Exhibit 5.8. When people believe they are under- or

Exhibit 5.8 Motivational Effects of Inequity Perceptions

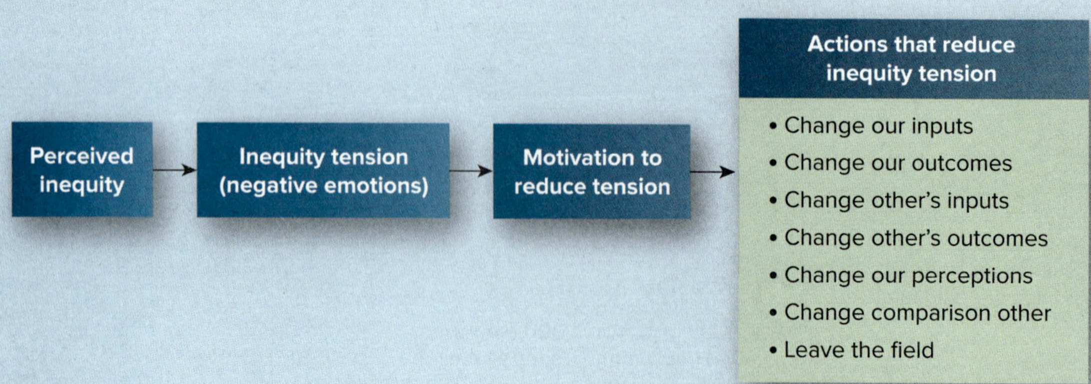

overrewarded, they experience negative emotions (called *inequity tension*).[83] As we have pointed out throughout this chapter, emotions are the engines of motivation. In the case of inequity, people are motivated to reduce the emotional tension. Most people have a strong emotional response when they believe a situation is unfair, and this emotion nags at them until they take steps to correct the perceived inequity.

> I was underpaid for the first half of my life. I don't mind being overpaid for the second half.[85]
>
> — Pierre Burton, journalist and popular history author

There are several ways to try to reduce the inequity tension.[84] Let's consider each of these in the context of underreward inequity. One action is to reduce our inputs so the outcome/input ratio is similar to that of the higher-paid coworker. Some employees do this by working more slowly, offering fewer suggestions, and engaging in less organizational citizenship behavior. A second action is to increase our outcomes. Some people who think they are underpaid ask for a pay raise. Others make unauthorized use of company resources. A third behavioral response is to increase the comparison other's inputs. We might subtly ask the better-paid coworker to do a larger share of the work, for instance. A fourth action is to reduce the comparison other's outcomes. This might occur by ensuring that the coworker gets less desirable jobs or working conditions. Another action, although uncommon, is to ask the company to reduce the coworker's pay so it is the same as yours.

A fifth action involves changing our beliefs about the situation rather than changing our behavior. For example, we might believe that the coworker really is providing more inputs (e.g., working longer hours) for that higher pay. Alternatively, we might change our perceived valence of some outcomes. Rather than viewing a coworker's work-related travel as a desirable perk, we instead perceive most of that travel as an undesirable nuisance. A sixth action to reduce the inequity tension is to change the comparison other. Instead of comparing ourselves with the higher-paid coworker, we might increasingly compare ourselves with a friend or neighbor who works in a similar job. Finally, if the inequity tension is strong enough and can't be reduced through other actions, we might leave the field. This occurs by moving to another department, joining another company, or keeping away from the work site where the overpaid coworker is located.

People who feel overreward inequity would reverse these actions. Some overrewarded employees reduce their feelings of inequity by working harder; others encourage the underrewarded coworker to work at a more leisurely pace. A common reaction, however, is that the overrewarded employee changes his or her perceptions to justify the more favorable outcomes, such as believing the assigned work is more difficult or his or her skills are more valuable than the lower-paid coworker's skills.

Evaluating Equity Theory Equity theory is quite successful at understanding (usually in hindsight) why people feel unfairly rewarded.[86] However, it is more difficult to use as a practical tool for preventing inequity in the future. The main problem is that people vary in their choice of comparison other and which inputs or outcomes are most valuable. The best solution here is for leaders to know their employees well enough to minimize the risk of inequity feelings. Open communication is also key, enabling employees to let decision makers know when they believe decisions are unfair. A second problem is that equity theory accounts for only some of our feelings of fairness in the workplace. Procedural and interactional justice can be just as important as distributive justice.

Procedural and Interactional Justice

Procedural justice is the perception that appropriate rules are applied in the procedures used throughout the course of deciding how to distribute workplace benefits and burdens. *Interactional justice* is the perception that appropriate rules are applied in the way the people involved are treated throughout that decision process.[87] Exhibit 5.9 lists the main rules that people consider when determining procedural and interactional justice.

There are several ways to maintain procedural justice.[88] Decision makers must be perceived as unbiased, without self-interest in the results, and not blinded by narrow doctrines. Their allocation decisions need to be based on as much relevant and accurate information as possible. Those decisions also need to take into account the positions and circumstances of the diverse groups affected by the outcomes. Another factor to consider in procedural justice is whether the decision criteria and decision procedures are compatible with ethical principles. For example, gathering accurate information might not be fair if it involves closely monitoring employees or violating their individual privacy. The decision criteria used to allocate benefits as well as the procedural justice rules need to be applied consistently to everyone (equality) and over time (stability).

Another important condition for procedural justice is that employees are given "voice" in the process—they have the opportunity to present their evidence and opinions to decision makers. Voice

Connect

SELF-ASSESSMENT 5.4: How Sensitive Are You to Inequities?

Exhibit 5.9 Procedural and interactional Justice Rules

Procedural Justice Rules	Interactional Justice Rules
• Decision makers are not biased by self-interest or restrictive doctrines. • Allocation decisions are based on a full complement of accurate information. • Decision makers consider the interests of all groups affected by the outcomes. • Decisions and procedures are compatible with ethical principles. • Decision criteria and procedures are applied consistently across persons and over time. • Employees have the opportunity to present their evidence and opinions to decision makers (voice). • Questionable decisions and procedures can be appealed and overturned.	• Employees are treated in a polite manner. • Employees are treated with respect. • Employees receive thorough and well-justified explanations about the decision. • Employees receive honest, candid, and timely information about the decision.

Sources: Based on information in: G.S. Leventhal, "What Should Be Done with Equity Theory? New Approaches to the Study of Fairness in Social Relationships," in *Social Exchange*, ed. K.J. Gergen, M.S. Greenberg, and R.H. Willis (Boston: Springer US, 1980), 27–55; J.A. Colquitt and J.B. Rodell, "Measuring Justice and Fairness," in *The Oxford Handbook of Justice in the Workplace*, ed. R.S. Cropanzano and M.L. Ambrose (New York: Oxford University Press, 2015), 187–202.

improves the quality of information applied to the decision. It also provides a value-expressive function; employees tend to feel better after having an opportunity to speak their mind. Lastly, employees should have a right to appeal the decision (so it is reviewed and possibly overturned) if they believe there were errors in how resources were distributed or flaws in the procedures leading to that decision.

Interactional justice also depends on a set of rules that people believe are being applied to the situation.[89] Two of these rules—treating people with politeness and with respect—support the feeling of fairness in the interpersonal relationship. Abusive supervision is a clear example of violation of these interactional justice rules because employees are treated rudely and their self-worth is attacked.[90] To generate a sense of fairness regarding the information provided, employees should receive thorough and well justified explanations about the decision, as well as honest, candid, and timely information about the decision. For instance, people are more likely to feel that a decision is unfair if decision makers refuse to explain how the decision was made, or if they seem evasive in their explanation.

An important condition for procedural justice is that employees are given "voice" in the process—they have the opportunity to present their evidence and opinions.
fizkes/Shutterstock

Consequences of Procedural and Interactional Injustice

Employees who believe procedural or interactional justice rules have been violated experience negative emotions, such as anger, frustration, insult, resentment, and shame.[91] Generally, procedural or interactional injustice often results in less work effort (and performance), fewer organizational citizenship behaviors, less cooperation with coworkers, increased involvement in union activities, and increased turnover. Victims of procedural and interactional injustice sometimes retaliate to restore their self-esteem, reinstate their status and power in the relationship, and to educate the perpetrator of the injustice.[92] A related outcome is increased aggression toward the decision maker (e.g., supervisor) and sometimes toward coworkers who are seemingly treated more favorably. Procedural or interactional justice can also lead to more extreme dysfunctional behaviors, such as theft, sabotage, and violence.

LO5-8 List the advantages and disadvantages of job specialization and explain how to improve employee motivation through job design.

JOB DESIGN

How do you build a better job? That question has challenged organizational behavior experts, psychologists, engineers, and economists for a few centuries. Some jobs have very few tasks and usually require very little skill. Other jobs are immensely complex and require years of experience and learning to master them. From one extreme to the other, jobs have different effects on work efficiency and employee motivation. The ideal, at least from the organization's perspective, is to find the right combination so that work is performed efficiently but employees are engaged and satisfied.[93] Job design—the process of assigning tasks

Supermarket cashier jobs have high job specialization; the cycle time is about 4 seconds to scan each grocery item before they repeat the activity with the next item.
Antenna/Getty Images

to a job, including the interdependency of those tasks with other jobs—tries to balance these potentially competing effects of efficiency and motivation. To understand this issue more fully, we'll begin by describing early job design efforts aimed at increasing work efficiency through job specialization.

Job Design and Work Efficiency

By any measure, supermarket cashiers have highly repetitive work. One consulting firm estimated that cashiers should be able to scan each item in an average of 4.6 seconds. Cashiers at five British supermarket chains took between 1.75 and 3.25 seconds to scan each item from a standardized list of 20 products. Along with scanning, cashiers process the payment, move the divider stick, and (in some stores) bag the checked groceries.[94]

Supermarket cashiers perform jobs with a high degree of **job specialization**. Job specialization occurs when the work required to serve a customer—or provide any other product or service—is subdivided into separate jobs assigned to different people. For instance, supermarkets have separate jobs for checking out customers, stocking shelves, preparing fresh foods, and so forth. Except in the smallest family grocery stores, one person would not perform all of these tasks as part of one job. Each resulting job includes a narrow subset of tasks, usually completed in a short cycle time. *Cycle time* is the time required to complete the task before starting over with another item or client. Supermarket cashiers have a cycle time of less than 5 seconds to scan each item before they repeat the activity with the next item. They also have a cycle time for serving each customer, which works out to somewhere between 20 and 40 times per hour in busy stores.

job specialization the result of a division of labor, in which work is subdivided into separate jobs assigned to different people

scientific management the practice of systematically partitioning work into its smallest elements and standardizing tasks to achieve maximum efficiency

Why would companies divide work into such tiny bits? The simple answer is that job specialization potentially improves work efficiency. It does so in four ways:

- *Fewer skills and less knowledge to learn*. Employees can master specialized jobs more quickly because there are fewer physical and mental skills and knowledge to learn and therefore less time required to become proficient in the job.
- *More frequent practice*. More specialized jobs typically have shorter cycle times. Shorter task cycles give employees more frequent practice with the task, so jobs are mastered more quickly.
- *Less attention residue from changing tasks*. Employees experience "attention residue" after they change from one type of task to another. Specifically, their mental attention lingers on the previous type of work, which slows down performance on the new task. Specialized jobs have fewer and less varied tasks, so there is less changeover and, consequently, less attention residue and productivity loss.[95]
- *Better person-job matching*. Job specialization tends to increase work efficiency by enabling employers to more precisely match employees with specific aptitudes, skills, knowledge, interests, and other characteristics to the jobs for which these talents are best suited.[96]

The benefits of job specialization were noted more than 2,300 years ago by the Chinese philosopher Mencius and the Greek philosopher Plato. Scottish economist Adam Smith wrote 250 years ago about the advantages of job specialization. Smith described a small factory where 10 pin makers collectively produced as many as 48,000 pins per day because they performed specialized tasks. One person straightened the metal, another cut it, another sharpened one end of the cut piece, yet another added a white tip to the other end, and so forth. By comparison, Smith suggested that if each of these 10 people was individually expected to produce complete pins, the group would collectively manufacture no more than 20 pins per day.[97]

Scientific Management

One of the strongest advocates of job specialization was Frederick Winslow Taylor, an American industrial engineer who introduced the principles of **scientific management** in the

job characteristics model a job design model that relates the motivational properties of jobs to specific personal and organizational consequences of those properties

skill variety the extent to which employees must use different skills and talents to perform tasks within their jobs

task identity the degree to which a job requires completion of a whole or an identifiable piece of work

task significance the degree to which a job has a substantial impact on the organization and/or larger society

early 1900s.[98] Scientific management consists of a toolkit of activities. Some of these interventions—employee selection, training, goal setting, and work incentives—are common today but were rare until Taylor popularized them. However, scientific management is mainly associated with high levels of job specialization and standardization of tasks to achieve maximum efficiency.

Taylor recommended that the most effective companies should have detailed procedures and work practices developed by engineers, enforced by supervisors, and executed by employees. Even supervisory tasks should be divided among different people (operations, inspection, discipline). Although the accuracy of Taylor's evidence is suspect, scientific management practices do improve work efficiency in many situations. These productivity gains are partly due to training, goal setting, and work incentives, but job specialization quickly became popular in its own right.

Problems with Job Specialization

Frederick Winslow Taylor and his contemporaries focused on how job specialization reduces labor "waste" by improving the mechanical efficiency of work (i.e., skills matching, faster learning, less switchover time). Yet they didn't seem to notice how this extreme job specialization adversely affects employee attitudes and motivation. Some jobs—such as scanning grocery items—are so specialized and repetitive that they become tedious, socially isolating, and cognitively dysfunctional. Specialized jobs with very short cycle times often produce higher employee turnover and absenteeism. Companies sometimes have to pay higher wages to attract job applicants to this dissatisfying, narrowly defined work.[99]

Job specialization affects output quality, but in two opposing ways. On the positive side, employees in specialized jobs tend to produce higher quality output because, as we mentioned earlier, they master their work faster compared to people in jobs with a wide variety of tasks. This higher proficiency explains why specialist lawyers tend to provide better quality service than do generalist lawyers.[100]

However, job specialization also has two negative effects on work quality. First, many specialized jobs (such as supermarket cashiers) are so tedious that they reduce work attentiveness and motivation, both of which undermine the quality of output. Second, by performing a tiny piece of the overall product or service, employees in specialized jobs have difficulty striving for better quality or even noticing flaws with the work unit's overall output.

Job Design and Work Motivation

Frederick Winslow Taylor may have overlooked the motivational effect of job characteristics, but it is now the central focus of many job design initiatives. The motivational potential of the job itself is the focus of the **job characteristics model**, shown in Exhibit 5.10. The model identifies five core job dimensions that produce three psychological states. Employees who experience these psychological states tend to have higher levels of intrinsic motivation, job satisfaction with the work itself, and work performance (quality and efficiency).[101]

Core Job Characteristics The job characteristics model identifies five core job characteristics. Under the right conditions, employees are more motivated and satisfied when jobs have higher levels of these characteristics:

- *Skill variety.* **Skill variety** refers to the use of different skills and talents to perform tasks within a job. For example, sales clerks who normally only serve customers might be assigned the additional duties of stocking inventory and changing storefront displays.

OB THEORY TO PRACTICE

Motivated by Enriched Jobs at Softcom Nigeria

Sam Diephuis/Blend Images LLC

Softcom Ltd. is a shining star in Nigeria's emerging technology industry. The company's 165 employees say they are motivated by the felt meaningfulness and responsibility of their jobs. "The sheer scale, size and audacity of what we're doing here is one of the motivating factors for me to come to work," enthuses the leader of one of Softcom's engineering development teams. "At Softcom, there is always a sense of purpose," observes another Softcom employee. "We are all committed to the goal of solving some of Africa's biggest challenges, and that in itself is what connects everything and everyone."

Softcom employees say they are also motivated by autonomy. "I've realized that maybe just the freedom is what comforts people. Nobody is ringing the bell for opening time and closing time," says Abiola Fajimi. "There's just that expectation for you to take ownership of your time and ideas. That level of expectation will drive you to find the most productive ways to work."[104]

Exhibit 5.10 The Job Characteristics Model

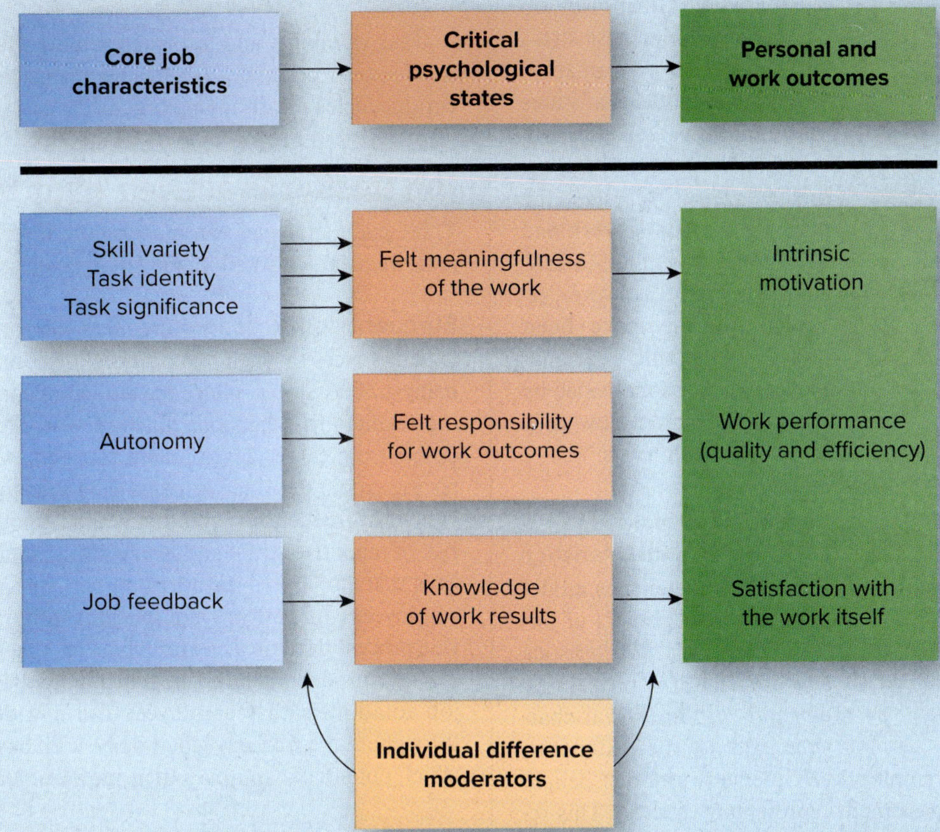

Sources: J.R. Hackman and E.E. Lawler, "Employee Reactions to Job Characteristics," *Journal of Applied Psychology* 55, no. 3 (1971): 259–86; J.R. Hackman and G.R. Oldham, "The Job Diagnostic Survey: An Instrument for the Diagnosis of Jobs and the Evaluation of Job Redesign Projects" (New Haven, CT: Department of Administrative Sciences, Yale University, May 1974); J.R. Hackman and G.R. Oldham, "Motivation through the Design of Work: Test of a Theory," *Organizational Behavior and Human Performance* 16, no. 2 (1976): 250–79; J.R. Hackman and G. Oldham, *Work Redesign* (Reading, MA: Addison-Wesley, 1980).

- *Task identity.* **Task identity** is the degree to which a job requires completion of a whole or identifiable piece of work, such as assembling an entire broadband modem rather than just soldering in the circuitry.

- *Task significance.* **Task significance** is the degree to which the job affects the organization and/or larger society. This job characteristic is most strongly felt when employees regularly and directly see how their work affects customers or others in society. As an example, when chefs in one study were able to directly observe the customers who ordered food (and vice versa), they felt more appreciated and, consequently, exerted more effort and felt more satisfied with their job. "When [the customers] can see us [make their food], they appreciate it, and I appreciate that. It makes me want to improve," says a cook who participated in the study.[102]

- *Autonomy.* As we discussed earlier in this chapter, autonomy is a key contributor to intrinsic motivation. In jobs with high levels of autonomy, employees make their own decisions rather than rely on detailed instructions from supervisors or procedure manuals. These jobs provide freedom, independence, and discretion in scheduling the work and determining the procedures to be used to complete the work.[103]

- *Job feedback.* Job feedback is the degree to which employees can tell how well they are doing from direct sensory information from the job itself. Airline pilots can tell how well they land their aircraft, and road crews can see how well they have prepared the roadbed and laid the asphalt.

Critical Psychological States The five core job characteristics affect employee motivation and satisfaction through three critical psychological states, shown in Exhibit 5.10. Skill variety, task identity, and task significance directly contribute to the job's *felt meaningfulness of the work*—the belief that one's work is worthwhile or important. Autonomy directly contributes to *felt responsibility for work outcomes*—a sense of being personally accountable for the work outcomes. The third critical psychological state is *knowledge of work results*—an awareness of the work outcomes based on information from the job itself.

Individual Differences Job design doesn't increase work motivation for everyone in every situation. Employees must have

task variability the degree to which job duties are nonroutine and unpredictable; employees perform diverse tasks from one day to the next because they are faced with unfamiliar and unexpected issues

task analyzability the degree to which job duties allow the application of established procedures and rules to guide decisions and behavior (high analyzability); employee creativity and judgment are necessary to perform jobs with low task analyzability

job enlargement the practice of adding more tasks to an existing job

job enrichment the practice of giving employees more responsibility for scheduling, coordinating, and planning their own work

the required skills and knowledge to master the more challenging work. Otherwise, job design tends to increase stress and reduce job performance. The original model also states that employees will be motivated only when they have a high *growth need strength* (the need for personal growth and development—similar to self-actualization).[105] However, research findings have been mixed, suggesting that employees might be motivated by the job no matter how they score on growth needs.[106]

Social and Information Processing Job Characteristics

The job characteristics model overlooks two clusters of job features: social characteristics and information processing demands.[107] One social characteristic is the extent to which the job requires employees to interact with other people (coworkers, clients, government representatives, etc.). This required social interaction is associated with emotional labor and regulation, discussed in Chapter 4. Social interaction also increases the complexity of the work due to the person's interdependence with these other people (see *task interdependence* in Chapter 7). A second social characteristic of the job is feedback from others. Jobs that include feedback from people may be just as motivating as jobs that provide feedback from the task itself. Feedback from others may be communicated explicitly through conversation or more implicitly through subtle nonverbal cues.

Job characteristics related to the information processing demands of the job include task variability and task analyzability:[108]

- **Task variability.** This information processing demand refers to how predictable the job duties are from one day to the next. Task variability increases employee motivation because employees in these jobs have nonroutine work patterns; they perform different types of tasks from one day to the next, and don't know which tasks are required until that time. Jobs with low task variability, on the other hand, are less motivating because the work is repetitive; employees perform similar tasks using similar skills in the same way every day.
- **Task analyzability.** This information processing demand refers to how much the job can be performed using known procedures and rules. Jobs with high task analyzability have low information processing demand because job incumbents rely on established guidelines for most decisions and actions. Consequently, employees are less motivated when performing jobs with high task analyzability. Jobs with low task analyzability, on the other hand, have higher motivational potential because employees need to rely on their creativity and judgment to determine the best courses of action for most tasks. The novel or complex work activities in low task analyzability jobs make it difficult to create fixed procedures and rules.

Task variability and task analyzability will be discussed again in Chapter 7 on task structures for teams and in Chapter 12 on contingencies for designing organizational structures.

Job Design Practices That Motivate

Three main strategies can increase the motivational potential of jobs: frequent job rotation, job enlargement, and job enrichment.

Frequent Job Rotation Frequent job rotation involves moving employees through two or more jobs each day. For example, many grocery stores reduce the tedium of checkout work by moving cashiers to other jobs during the work shift. This rotation differs from career development transfers, which involves transferring employees once or twice each year to different jobs. One benefit of frequent job rotation is that it potentially reduces the risk of repetitive strain and heavy lifting injuries. A second benefit is that employees learn how to perform multiple jobs. Third, employees who perform multiple jobs within a production or service process develop a clearer picture of that process and ways to improve product quality. The fourth potential benefit of frequent job rotation is that employees use a wider variety of skills throughout the workday—their daily work has more skill variety—which potentially improves their motivation and satisfaction.[109]

Job Enlargement **Job enlargement** is the practice of increasing the number and variety of related tasks assigned to a job held by an employee. This might involve combining two or more complete jobs into one or just adding one or two more tasks to an existing job. Either way, job enlargement offers the same benefits as job rotation because adding more and varied tasks gives employees more skill variety and reduces the risk of repetitive strain injuries.

Job Enrichment **Job enrichment** occurs when employees are given more responsibility for scheduling, coordinating, and planning their own work.[110] For example, employees have more enriched jobs when they are responsible for a variety of tasks and have enough autonomy to plan their work and choose when to perform each task. Job enrichment potentially increases job satisfaction and work motivation, and reduces absenteeism and turnover. Productivity is also higher when task identity and job feedback are improved. Product and service quality tend to improve because job enrichment increases the jobholder's felt responsibility and sense of ownership over the product or service.[111]

One way to increase job enrichment is by combining highly interdependent tasks into one job. This *natural grouping* approach occurs in the video journalist job because it naturally groups tasks together to complete an entire product (i.e., a news story). By forming natural work units, jobholders have stronger feelings of responsibility for an identifiable body of work. They

> **Putting employees in direct contact with clients increases task significance because employees more easily see how their work affects those clients.**

feel a sense of ownership and, therefore, tend to deliver higher quality work output. Forming natural work units increases task identity and task significance because employees perform a complete product or service and can more readily see how their work affects others.

A second job enrichment strategy, called *establishing client relationships*, involves putting employees in direct contact with their clients rather than using another job group or the supervisor as the liaison between the employee and the customer. Establishing client relationships increases task significance because employees more easily see how their work affects those clients. By being directly responsible for specific clients, employees also have more information and can make better decisions affecting those clients.[112]

Study Checklist

Connect® is available for *M Organizational Behavior.* Additional resources include:

✓ Exercises:

- **Case Analysis:** Apply concepts within the context of a real-world situation.
- **Click and Drag:** Helps make the connection between theory and application through matching, ranking, or grouping activities.
- **Video Case:** See management in action through interactive videos.
- **Self-Assessment:** Designed to promote student self-awareness and reflection, these research-based surveys contain detailed feedback for students.
- **Application-Based Activities:** These highly interactive, application- and analysis-based exercises allow students to take on specific roles to complete management-related tasks within a real-world context.

✓ **SmartBook 2.0™**—Smartbook 2.0 is an adaptive learning solution that provides personalized learning to individual student needs, continually adapts to pinpoint knowledge gaps and focuses learning on concepts requiring additional study. It fosters more productive learning, takes the guesswork out of what to study, and helps students better prepare for class.

Notes

1. D. Morris, "2017: The Year Performance Reviews Get the Axe," *Adobe Conversations-Perspectives* (blog), January 11, 2017, https://theblog.adobe.com/2017-the-year-performance-reviews-get-the-axe; J. Mendonca, "TCS Abandons Bell Curve Based Performance Appraisal; Shifting to System of Continuous Feedback," *The Economic Times (India)*, April 20, 2017; N. Singh, "Coca-Cola India Moves to Monthly Appraisals," *The Economic Times (India)*, October 8, 2017; V. Shiao, "Why We Fail at Grading Our Workers," *Business Times (Singapore)*, November 3, 2018.
2. C.C. Pinder, *Work Motivation in Organizational Behavior* (Upper Saddle River, NJ: Prentice Hall, 1998); A.M. Schmidt, J.W. Beck, and J.Z. Gillespie, "Motivation: Industrial and Organizational Psychology," in *Handbook of Psychology,* 2nd ed., ed. Schmidt, Neil and Highouse, S., vol. 12 (John Wiley & Sons, Inc., 2012), 311–40.
3. W.H. Macey and B. Schneider, "The Meaning of Employee Engagement," *Industrial and Organizational Psychology* 1 (2008): 3–30; A.M. Saks and J.A. Gruman, "What Do We Really Know about Employee Engagement?" *Human Resource Development Quarterly* 25, no. 2 (2014): 155–82; J.L. Whittington et al., *Enhancing Employee Engagement: An Evidence-Based Approach* (New York: Palgrave Macmillan, 2017), Chap. 1.
4. P.M. Bal and A.H. De Lange, "From Flexibility Human Resource Management to Employee Engagement and Perceived Job Performance across the Lifespan: A Multisample Study," *Journal of Occupational and Organizational Psychology* 88 (2015): 126–54; C. Bailey et al., *Evaluating the Evidence on Employee Engagement and Its Potential Benefits to NHS Staff: A Narrative Synthesis of the Literature*, Health Services and Delivery Research, Vol. 3, Issue 26 (London: NHS National Institute for Health Research, 2015). The outcomes of employee engagement are confounded by the various ways the concept has been studied, but most perspectives of engagement tend to predict meaningful outcomes. See A.M. Saks, "Translating Employee Engagement Research into Practice," *Organizational Dynamics* 46, no. 2 (2017): 76–86.
5. "2018 Trends in Global Employee Engagement" (Chicago: Aon Hewitt, March 2018); J. Hartell, "Employee Engagement on the Rise in the U.S." (Washington, DC: Gallup, Inc., August 26, 2018).

6. The confusing array of definitions about drives and needs has been the subject of criticism for a half century. See, for example, R.S. Peters, "Motives and Motivation," *Philosophy* 31 (1956): 117–30; H. Cantril, "Sentio, Ergo Sum: 'Motivation' Reconsidered," *Journal of Psychology* 65 (1967): 91–107; G.R. Salancik and J. Pfeffer, "An Examination of Need-Satisfaction Models of Job Attitudes," *Administrative Science Quarterly* 22 (1977): 427–456. For a recent effort to condense 162 human "motives" into a small set, see J.R. Talevich et al., "Toward a Comprehensive Taxonomy of Human Motives," *PLOS ONE* 12, no. 2 (2017): e0172279.

7. D.W. Pfaff, *Drive: Neurobiological and Molecular Mechanisms of Sexual Motivation* (Cambridge, MA: MIT Press, 1999); A. Blasi, "Emotions and Moral Motivation," *Journal for the Theory of Social Behaviour* 29 (1999): 1–19; K.C. Berridge, "Motivation Concepts in Behavioral Neuroscience," *Physiology & Behavior* 81 (2004): 179–209; D. Scheffer and H. Heckhausen, "Trait Theories of Motivation," in *Motivation and Action*, ed. J. Heckhausen and H. Heckhausen (Cham: Springer International Publishing, 2018), 67–112. We distinguish drives from emotions, but future research may find that the two concepts are not so different as is stated here. Woodworth is credited with either coining or popularizing the term *drives* in the context of human motivation. His classic book is certainly the first source to discuss the concept in detail. See R.S. Woodworth, *Dynamic Psychology* (New York: Columbia University Press, 1918).

8. P.R. Lawrence and N. Nohria, *Driven: How Human Nature Shapes Our Choices* (San Francisco: Jossey-Bass, 2002); N. Nohria, B. Groysberg, and L.-E. Lee, "Employee Motivation: A Powerful New Model," *Harvard Business Review* (2008): 78–84; P. Lawrence and M. Pirson, "Economistic and Humanistic Narratives of Leadership in the Age of Globality: Toward a Renewed Darwinian Theory of Leadership," *Journal of Business Ethics* 128, no. 2 (2015): 383–394. https://doi/10.1007/s10551-014-2090-2.

9. S.G. Barsade and D.E. Gibson, "Why Does Affect Matter in Organizations?" *Academy of Management Perspectives* 21 (2007): 36–59; K.C. Berridge, "Evolving Concepts of Emotion and Motivation," *Frontiers in Psychology* 9 (2018), https://doi.org/10.3389/fpsyg.2018.01647; E. Harmon-Jones, "On Motivational Influences, Moving beyond Valence, and Integrating Dimensional and Discrete Views of Emotion," *Cognition and Emotion* 33 (2019): 101–8.

10. W. McDougall, *Outline of Psychology* (New York: Charles Scribner's Sons, 1923), 440 fn#1.

11. B. Monin, D.A. Pizarro, and J.S. Beer, "Deciding Versus Reacting: Conceptions of Moral Judgment and the Reason-Affect Debate," *Review of General Psychology* 11 (2007): 99–111; S.H. Schwartz et al., "Refining the Theory of Basic Individual Values," *Journal of Personality and Social Psychology* 103 (2012): 663–88; M. Driver, "Motivation and Identity: A Psychoanalytic Perspective on the Turn to Identity in Motivation Research," *Human Relations* 70 (2017): 617–37.

12. P.R. Lawrence and N. Nohria, *Driven: How Human Nature Shapes Our Choices* (San Francisco: Jossey-Bass, 2002); N. Nohria, B. Groysberg, and L.-E. Lee, "Employee Motivation: A Powerful New Model," *Harvard Business Review* (2008): 78–84; P. Lawrence and M. Pirson, "Economistic and Humanistic Narratives of Leadership in the Age of Globality: Toward a Renewed Darwinian Theory of Leadership," *Journal of Business Ethics* 128 (2015): 383–94.

13. The drive to acquire is likely associated with research on getting ahead, desire for competence, the selfish gene, and desire for social distinction. See R.H. Frank, *Choosing the Right Pond: Human Behavior and the Quest for Status* (New York: Oxford University Press, 1985); L. Gaertner et al., "The 'I,' the 'We,' and the 'When': A Meta-Analysis of Motivational Primacy in Self-Definition," *Journal of Personality and Social Psychology* 83, no. 3 (2002): 574–91; J. Hogan and B. Holland, "Using Theory to Evaluate Personality and Job-Performance Relations: A Socioanalytic Perspective," *Journal of Applied Psychology* 88, no. 1 (2003): 100–12; R. Dawkins, *The Selfish Gene*, 30th Anniversary Ed. (Oxford, UK: Oxford University Press, 2006); M.R. Leary, "Motivational and Emotional Aspects of the Self," *Annual Review of Psychology* 58, no. 1 (2007): 317–44; F. Martela and T.J.J. Riekki, "Autonomy, Competence, Relatedness, and Beneficence: A Multicultural Comparison of the Four Pathways to Meaningful Work," *Frontiers in Psychology* 9 (2018), https://doi.org/10.3389/fpsyg.2018.01157.

14. R.E. Baumeister and M.R. Leary, "The Need to Belong: Desire for Interpersonal Attachments as a Fundamental Human Motivation," *Psychological Bulletin* 117 (1995): 497–529.

15. G. Loewenstein, "The Psychology of Curiosity: A Review and Reinterpretation," *Psychological Bulletin* 116 (1994): 75–98; J. Litman, "Curiosity and the Pleasures of Learning: Wanting and Liking New Information," *Cognition and Emotion* 19 (2005): 793–814; C. Kidd and B.Y. Hayden, "The Psychology and Neuroscience of Curiosity," *Neuron* 88 (2015): 449–60.

16. N. Nohria, B. Groysberg, and L.-E. Lee, "Employee Motivation: A Powerful New Model," *Harvard Business Review*, August 2008, 78–84; F. Beyer et al., "Hit or Run: Exploring Aggressive and Avoidant Reactions to Interpersonal Provocation Using a Novel Fight-or-Escape Paradigm (FOE)," *Frontiers in Behavioral Neuroscience* 11 (2017), https://doi.org/10.3389/fnbeh.2017.00190.

17. A.R. Damasio, *Descartes' Error: Emotion, Reason, and the Human Brain* (New York: Putnam's Sons, 1994); J.E. LeDoux, "Emotion Circuits in the Brain," *Annual Review of Neuroscience* 23 (2000): 155–184; M. Reimann and A. Bechara, "The Somatic Marker Framework as a Neurological Theory of Decision-Making: Review, Conceptual Comparisons, and Future Neuroeconomics Research," *Journal of Economic Psychology* 31, no. 5 (2010): 767–776; P. Winkielman, K. Berridge, and S. Sher, "Emotion, Consciousness, and Social Behavior," in *The Oxford Handbook of Social Neuroscience*, ed. J. Decety and J.T. Cacioppo (Oxford University Press, 2011), 195–211; T. Poppa and A. Bechara, "The Somatic Marker Hypothesis: Revisiting the Role of the 'Body-Loop' in Decision-Making," *Current Opinion in Behavioral Sciences* 19 (2018): 61–66.

18. P.R. Lawrence and N. Nohria, *Driven: How Human Nature Shapes Our Choices* (San Francisco: Jossey-Bass, 2002), 145–47; R.F. Baumeister, E.J. Masicampo, and K.D. Vohs, "Do Conscious Thoughts Cause Behavior?" *Annual Review of Psychology* 62, no. 1 (2011): 331–61.

19. P.R. Lawrence and N. Nohria, *Driven: How Human Nature Shapes Our Choices* (San Francisco: Jossey-Bass, 2002), Chap. 11.

20. For recent discussion on the benefits and risks of work practices that encourage employee competition, see: A. Sapegina and A. Weibel, "The Good, the Not So Bad, and the Ugly of Competitive Human Resource Practices: A Multidisciplinary Conceptual Framework," *Group & Organization Management* 42 (2017): 707–47.

21. A.H. Maslow, "A Theory of Human Motivation," *Psychological Review* 50 (1943): 370–96; A.H. Maslow, *Motivation and Personality* (New York: Harper & Row, 1954).

22. Maslow did not diagram his theory as a pyramid. He does not even mention pyramids in his writing on human motivation. Instead, Maslow mostly repeats the term *hierarchy* in describing how human needs (drives) are organized relative to each other. The earliest description of human needs as a pyramid is likely from Chapter 2 ("The Pyramid of Man's Needs") of a 1960 book on conflict by F. Alexander Magoun, a professor of human relations at MIT. Magoun's chapter discusses Maslow's needs hierarchy theory. A recent review also points to a step model of Maslow's model in Keith Davis's human relations book and of a pyramid model in a 1960 article by Charles McDermid. See F.A. Magoun, *Cooperation and Conflict in Industry* (New York: Harper, 1960), 20–31; T. Bridgman, S. Cummings, and J. Ballard, "Who Built Maslow's Pyramid? A History of the Creation of Management Studies' Most Famous Symbol and Its Implications for Management Education," *Academy of Management Learning & Education* 18 (2019): 81–98.

23. D.T. Hall and K.E. Nougaim, "An Examination of Maslow's Need Hierarchy in an Organizational Setting," *Organizational Behavior and Human Performance* 3, no. 1 (1968): 12; M.A. Wahba and L.G. Bridwell, "Maslow Reconsidered: A Review of Research on the Need Hierarchy Theory," *Organizational Behavior and Human Performance* 15 (1976): 212–40; E.L. Betz, "Two Tests of Maslow's Theory of Need Fulfillment," *Journal of Vocational Behavior* 24, no. 2 (1984): 204–20; P.A. Corning, "Biological Adaptation in Human Societies: A 'Basic Needs' Approach," *Journal of Bioeconomics* 2, no. 1 (2000): 41–86. For a recent proposed revision of the model, see D.T. Kenrick et al., "Renovating the Pyramid of Needs: Contemporary Extensions Built upon Ancient Foundations," *Perspectives on Psychological Science* 5, no. 3 (2010): 292–314.

24. L. Parks and R.P. Guay, "Personality, Values, and Motivation," *Personality and Individual Differences* 47, no. 7 (2009): 675–84; R. Fischer and D. Boer, "Motivational Basis of Personality Traits: A Meta-Analysis of Value-Personality Correlations," *Journal of Personality* 83, no. 5 (2015): 491–510, https://doi/10.1111/jopy.12125; L. Parks-Leduc, G. Feldman, and A. Bardi, "Personality Traits and Personal Values: A Meta-Analysis," *Personality and Social Psychology Review* 19, no. 1 (2015): 3–29, https://doi/10.1177/1088868314538548. Maslow did acknowledge that the needs hierarchy has a different ordering for some people, but he described these as relatively rare exceptions. See A.H. Maslow, "A Theory of Human Motivation," *Psychological Review* 50 (1943): 386–88.

25. B. Verplanken and R.W. Holland, "Motivated Decision Making: Effects of Activation and Self-Centrality of Values on Choices and Behavior," *Journal of Personality and Social Psychology* 82, no. 3 (2002): 434–47; J. Jin and J. Rounds, "Stability and Change in Work Values: A Meta-Analysis of Longitudinal Studies," *Journal of Vocational Behavior* 80, no. 2 (2012): 326–39. https://doi.org/10.1016/j.jvb.2011.10.007; C.M. Lechner et al., "The Development of Work Values during the Transition to Adulthood: A Two-Country Study," *Journal of Vocational Behavior* 99(2017): 52–65. https://doi.org/10.1016/j.jvb.2016.12.004.

26. K. Dye, A.J. Mills, and T.G. Weatherbee, "Maslow: Man Interrupted–Reading Management Theory in Context," *Management Decision* 43, no. 10 (2005): 1375–95.

27. M. Gagné and E.L. Deci, "Self-Determination Theory and Work Motivation," *Journal of Organizational Behavior* 26, no. 4 (2005): 331–62; C.P. Cerasoli, J.M. Nicklin, and M.T. Ford, "Intrinsic Motivation and Extrinsic Incentives Jointly Predict Performance: A 40-Year Meta-Analysis," *Psychological Bulletin* 140, no. 4 (2014): 980–1008.

28. M. Gagné and D. Bhave, "Autonomy in the Workplace: An Essential Ingredient to Employee Engagement and Well-Being in Every Culture," in *Human Autonomy in Cross-Cultural Context*, ed. V.I. Chirkov, R.M. Ryan and K.M. Sheldon, *Cross-Cultural Advancements in Positive Psychology* (Dordrecht, Netherlands: Springer Netherlands, 2011), 163–87; E.L. Deci and M.R. Ryan, "The Importance of Universal Psychological Needs for Understanding Motivation in the Workplace," in *The Oxford Handbook of Work Engagement, Motivation, and Self-Determination Theory*, ed. M. Gagne (New York: Oxford University Press, 2014), 13–32. For neuroscience research on intrinsic motivation (particularly need for competence), see W. Lee and J. Reeve, "Identifying the Neural Substrates of Intrinsic Motivation during Task Performance," *Cognitive, Affective, & Behavioral Neuroscience* 17, no. 5 (2017): 939–53; S.I. Di Domenico and R.M. Ryan, "The Emerging Neuroscience of Intrinsic Motivation: A New Frontier in Self-Determination Research," *Frontiers in Human Neuroscience* 11 (2017), https://doi.org/10.3389/fnhum.2017.00145.

29. C.P. Cerasoli, J.M. Nicklin, and M.T. Ford, "Intrinsic Motivation and Extrinsic Incentives Jointly Predict Performance: A 40-Year Meta-Analysis," *Psychological Bulletin* 140, no. 4 (2014): 980–1008; Y. Garbers and U. Konradt, "The Effect of Financial Incentives on Performance: A Quantitative Review of Individual and Team-Based Financial Incentives," *Journal of Occupational and Organizational Psychology* 87, no. 1 (2014): 102–37.

30. J. Schroeder and A. Fishbach, "How to Motivate Yourself and Others? Intended and Unintended Consequences," *Research in Organizational Behavior* 35 (2015): 123–41.

31. D.C. McClelland, *The Achieving Society* (New York: Van Nostrand Reinhold, 1961); D. McClelland and D. Burnham, "Power Is Great Motivator," *Harvard Business Review* 54, no. 2 (1976): 100–110; M.G. Köllner and O.C. Schultheiss, "Meta-Analytic Evidence of Low Convergence between Implicit and Explicit Measures of the Needs for Achievement, Affiliation, and Power," *Frontiers in Psychology* 5 (2014), https://doi.org/10.3389/fpsyg.2014.00826.

32. D.C. McClelland, *The Achieving Society* (New York: Van Nostrand Reinhold, 1961).

33. M. Frese and M.M. Gielnik, "The Psychology of Entrepreneurship," *Annual Review of Organizational Psychology and Organizational Behavior* 1, no. 1 (2014): 413–38.

34. S. Leroy et al., "Synchrony Preference: Why Some People Go with the Flow and Some Don't," *Personnel Psychology* 68, no. 4 (2015): 759–809; M.H. Do and A. Minbashian, "A Meta-Analytic Examination of the Effects of the Agentic and Affiliative Aspects of Extraversion on Leadership Outcomes," *Leadership Quarterly* 25, no. 5 (2014): 1040–53, https://doi.org/10.1016/j.leaqua.2014.04.004; B. Steinmann et al., "Implicit Motives and Leadership Performance Revisited: What Constitutes the Leadership Motive Pattern?" *Motivation and Emotion* 39, no. 2 (2015): 167–74, https://doi.org/10.1007/s11031-014-9458-6; B. Steinmann, S.K. Ötting, and G.W. Maier, "Need for Affiliation as a Motivational Add-On for Leadership Behaviors and Managerial Success," *Frontiers in Psychology* 7 (2016), https://doi.org/10.3389/fpsyg.2016.01972.

35. J.C. Magee and C.A. Langner, "How Personalized and Socialized Power Motivation Facilitate Antisocial and Prosocial Decision-Making," *Journal of Research in Personality* 42, no. 6 (2008): 1547–59; D. Rus, D. van Knippenberg, and B. Wisse, "Leader Self-Definition and Leader Self-Serving Behavior," *Leadership Quarterly* 21, no. 3 (2010): 509–29; C. Case and J. Maner, "Divide and Conquer: When and Why Leaders Undermine the Cohesive Fabric of Their Group," *Journal of Personality and Social Psychology* 107, no. 6 (2014): 1033–50.

36. D. Miron and D.C. McClelland, "The Impact of Achievement Motivation Training on Small Business," *California Management Review* 21 (1979): 13–28.

37. Expectancies and valences have a long history in motivation and decision making, dating back to the earliest writing on the economics of utilitarianism. See, for example, W.S. Jevons, *The Theory of Political Economy* (London: MacMillan, 1871), Chaps. 2 and 3. For recent discussion in organizational behavior, see S. Sun, J.B. Vancouver, and J.M. Weinhardt, "Goal Choices and Planning: Distinct Expectancy and Value Effects in Two Goal Processes," *Organizational Behavior and Human Decision Processes* 125 (2014): 220–33.

38. Expectancy theory of motivation in work settings originated in V.H. Vroom, *Work and Motivation* (New York: Wiley, 1964). The version of expectancy theory presented here was developed by Edward Lawler. Lawler's model provides a clearer presentation of the model's three components. P-to-O expectancy is similar to "instrumentality" in Vroom's original expectancy theory model. The difference is that instrumentality is a correlation whereas P-to-O expectancy is a probability. See J.P. Campbell et al., *Managerial Behavior, Performance, and Effectiveness* (New York: McGraw-Hill, 1970); E.E. Lawler III, *Motivation in Work Organizations* (Monterey, CA: Brooks-Cole, 1973); D.A. Nadler and E.E. Lawler, "Motivation: A Diagnostic Approach," in *Perspectives on Behavior in Organizations*, ed. J.R. Hackman, E.E. Lawler III, and L.W. Porter (New York: McGraw-Hill, 1983), 67–78.

39. The earliest economic theorists argued that valence is the positive or negative emotion that the decision maker anticipates from an outcome. See Steven L. McShane, "Organisational Decision-Making," in *Contemporary Issues in Management and Organisational Behaviour*, ed. P. Murray, D. Poole, and G. Jones (Sydney: Cengage Learning Australia, 2006), 136–65. The connection between valence and emotion is supported by recent neuroscience studies. See A. Bechara and A.R. Damasio, "The Somatic Marker Hypothesis: A Neural Theory of Economic Decision," *Games and Economic Behavior* 52, no. 2 (2005): 336–72; J. Bartol and S. Linquist, "How Do Somatic Markers Feature in Decision Making?" *Emotion Review* 7 (2014): 81–89, https://doi.org/10.1177/1754073914553000; J.S. Lerner et al., "Emotion and Decision Making," *Annual Review of Psychology* 66, no. 1 (2015): 799–823, https://doi.org/10.1146/annurev-psych-010213-115043.

40. D.A. Nadler and E.E. Lawler, "Motivation: A Diagnostic Approach," in *Perspectives on Behavior in Organizations,* ed. J.R. Hackman, E.E. Lawler III, and L.W. Porter (New York: McGraw-Hill, 1983), 70–73.

41. A. Fisher, "Expecting a Fat Year-End Bonus? Don't Get Your Hopes Up," *Fortune*, December 5, 2012; Willis Towers Watson, *Under Pressure to Remain Relevant, Employers Look to Modernize the Employee Value Proposition* (London: Willis Towers Watson, September 9, 2016); Willis Towers Watson, "U.S. Employees Give Performance Management Programs Mediocre Grades," news release (Arlington, VA: Willis Towers Watson, December 6, 2016); Glassdoor, *Global Salary Transparency Survey: Employee Perceptions of Talking Pay* (Mill Valley, CA: Glassdoor, April 2016); U.S. Office of Personnel Management, *Federal Employee Viewpoint Survey* (Washington, DC: Office of Personnel Management, October 2018).

42. For recent applications of expectancy in diverse settings, see R.L. Purvis, T.J. Zagenczyk, and G.E. McCray, "What's in It for Me? Using Expectancy Theory and Climate to Explain Stakeholder Participation, Its Direction and Intensity," *International Journal of Project Management* 33, no. 1 (2015): 3–14; E. Shweiki et al., "Applying Expectancy Theory to Residency Training: Proposing Opportunities to Understand Resident Motivation and Enhance Residency Training," *Advances in Medical Education and Practice* 6 (2015): 339–46; K.N. Bauer et al., "Re-Examination of Motivation in Learning Contexts: Meta-Analytically Investigating the Role Type of Motivation Plays in the Prediction of Key Training Outcomes," *Journal of Business and Psychology* 31, no. 1 (2016): 33–50; R. Meymandpour and P. Pawar, "Study of Expectancy Motivation in IT Developers," *Telecom Business Review* 11, no. 1 (2018): 6–11.

43. This limitation was acknowledged by Victor Vroom, who had introduced expectancy theory in his 1964 book. See G.P. Latham, *Work Motivation: History, Theory, Research, and Practice* (Thousand Oaks, CA: Sage, 2007), 47–48.

44. J.B. Watson, *Behavior: An Introduction to Comparative Psychology* (New York: Henry Holt, 1914).

45. B.F. Skinner, *About Behaviorism* (New York: Knopf, 1974); J. Komaki, T. Coombs, and S. Schepman, "Motivational Implications of Reinforcement Theory," in *Motivation and Leadership at Work*, ed. R.M. Steers, L.W. Porter, and G.A. Bigley (New York: McGraw-Hill, 1996), 34–52; R.G. Miltenberger, *Behavior Modification: Principles and Procedures* (Pacific Grove, CA: Brooks/Cole, 1997).

46. T.K. Connellan, *How to Improve Human Performance* (New York: Harper & Row, 1978), 48–57; F. Luthans and R. Kreitner, *Organizational Behavior Modification and Beyond* (Glenview, IL: Scott, Foresman, 1985), 85–88.

47. B.F. Skinner, *Science and Human Behavior* (New York: Free Press, 1965); R.G. Miltenberger, *Behavior Modification: Principles and Procedures* (Pacific Grove, CA: Brooks/Cole, 1997), Chap. 4–6.

48. T.R. Hinkin and C.A. Schriesheim, "'If You Don't Hear from Me You Know You Are Doing Fine,'" *Cornell Hotel & Restaurant Administration Quarterly* 45, no. 4 (2004): 362–72; T.R. Hinkin and C.A. Schriesheim, "An Examination of 'Nonleadership': From Laissez-Faire Leadership to Leader Reward Omission and Punishment Omission," *Journal of Applied Psychology* 93, no. 6 (2008): 1234–48, https://doi.org/10.1037/a0012875.

49. K. Cameron et al., "Effects of Positive Practices on Organizational Effectiveness," *Journal of Applied Behavioral Science* 47 (2011): 266–308; F. Luthans and C.M. Youssef-Morgan, "Psychological Capital: An Evidence-Based Positive Approach," *Annual Review of Organizational Psychology and Organizational Behavior* 4 (2017): 339–66; A.B. Bakker and M. van Woerkom, "Strengths Use in Organizations: A Positive Approach of Occupational Health," *Canadian Psychology* 59 (2018): 38–46.

50. L.K. Trevino, "The Social Effects of Punishment in Organizations: A Justice Perspective," *Academy of Management Review* 17 (1992): 647–76; L. Wang and J.K. Murnighan, "The Dynamics of Punishment and Trust," *Journal of Applied Psychology* 102, no. 10 (October 2017): 1385–1402, https://doi.org/10.1037/apl0000178; L. Wang et al., "Does Anger Expression Help or Harm Leader Effectiveness? The Role of Competence-Based versus Integrity-Based Violations and Abusive Supervision," *Academy of Management Journal* 61, no. 3 (June 2018): 1050–72, https://doi.org/10.5465/amj.2015.0460.

51. G.P. Latham and V.L. Huber, "Schedules of Reinforcement: Lessons from the Past and Issues for the Future," *Journal of Organizational Behavior Management* 13 (1992): 125–49; B.A. Williams, "Challenges to Timing-Based Theories of Operant Behavior," *Behavioural Processes* 62 (2003): 115–23.

52. A. Bandura, *Social Foundations of Thought and Action: A Social Cognitive Theory* (Englewood Cliffs, NJ: Prentice Hall, 1986); A. Bandura, "Social Cognitive Theory of Self-Regulation," *Organizational Behavior and Human Decision Processes* 50, no. 2 (1991): 248–87; A. Bandura, "Social Cognitive Theory: An Agentic Perspective," *Annual Review of Psychology* 52, no. 1 (2001): 1–26.

53. M.E. Schnake, "Vicarious Punishment in a Work Setting," *Journal of Applied Psychology* 71 (1986): 343–45; L.K. Trevino, "The Social Effects of Punishment in Organizations: A Justice Perspective," *Academy of Management Review* 17 (1992): 647–76; J. Malouff et al., "Effects of Vicarious Punishment: A Meta-Analysis," *Journal of General Psychology* 136, no. 3 (2009): 271–86.

54. A. Pescuric and W.C. Byham, "The New Look of Behavior Modeling," *Training & Development* 50 (1996): 24–30; P.J. Taylor, D.F. Russ-Eft, and D.W.L. Chan, "A Meta-Analytic Review of Behavior Modeling Training," *Journal of Applied Psychology* 90, no. 4 (2005): 692–709, https://doi.org/10.1037/0021-9010.90.4.692; C.G. Myers and D.S. DeRue, "Agency in Vicarious Learning at Work," in *Autonomous Learning in the Workplace*, ed. J.E. Ellingson and R.A. Noe (New York: Routledge, 2017), 15–37.

55. A. Bandura, "Self-Reinforcement: Theoretical and Methodological Considerations," *Behaviorism* 4 (1976): 135–55; J.B. Vancouver and D.V. Day, "Industrial and Organisation Research on Self-Regulation: From Constructs to Applications," *Applied Psychology: An International Journal* 54, no. 2 (2005): 155–85; A. Neal, T. Ballard, and J.B. Vancouver, "Dynamic Self-Regulation and Multiple-Goal Pursuit," *Annual Review of Organizational Psychology and Organizational Behavior* 4, no. 1 (2017): 401–23, https://doi.org/10.1146/annurev-orgpsych-032516-113156.

56. M. Milyavskaya and K.M. Werner, "Goal Pursuit: Current State of Affairs and Directions for Future Research," *Canadian Psychology* 59 (May 2018): 163–75.

57. E.A. Locke and G.P. Latham, *A Theory of Goal Setting and Task Performance* (Englewood Cliffs, NJ: Prentice Hall, 1990); G. Latham, G. Seijts, and J. Slocum, "The Goal Setting and Goal Orientation Labyrinth: Effective Ways for Increasing Employee Performance," *Organizational Dynamics* 45, no. 4 (2016): 271–77, https://doi.org/10.1016/j.orgdyn.2016.10.001.

58. The SMARTER goal-setting model is an extension of the earlier SMART model. SMARTER apparently originated from British sports psychology writing around the mid-1990s, such as: P. Butler, *Performance Profiling* (Leeds, UK: The National Coaching Foundation, 1996), 36. There are several variations of the SMARTER goal-setting model; "achievable" is sometimes "acceptable," "reviewed" is sometimes "recorded," and "exciting" is sometimes "ethical." For a summary of variations of meanings within the SMARTER acronym, see: G. Brown, C. Leonard, and M. Arthur-Kelly, "Writing SMARTER Goals for Professional Learning and Improving Classroom Practices," *Reflective Practice* 17, no. 5 (2016): 621–35, https://doi.org/10.1080/14623943.2016.1187120.

59. The value and limitations of measurement are discussed in J.M. Henshaw, *Does Measurement Measure Up? How Numbers Reveal and Conceal the Truth* (Baltimore, MD: Johns Hopkins Press, 2006).

60. A.C. Crossley, C. Cooper, and T. Wernsing, "Making Things Happen through Challenging Goals: Leader Proactivity, Trust, and Business-Unit Performance," *Journal of Applied Psychology* 98, no. 3 (2013): 540–49; A. Kruglanski et al., "The Rocky Road from Attitudes to Behaviors: Charting the Goal Systemic Course of Actions," *Psychological Review* 122, no. 4 (2015): 598–620; K.M. Roose and W.L. Williams, "An Evaluation of the Effects of Very Difficult Goals," *Journal of Organizational Behavior Management* 38, no. 1 (2018): 18–48. https://doi/10.1080/01608061.2017.1325820

61. Z. Zhang and M. Jia, "How Can Companies Decrease the Disruptive Effects of Stretch Goals? The Moderating Role of Interpersonal–and Informational–Justice Climates," *Human Relations* 66, no. 7 (2013): 993–1020; L.D. Ordóñez and D.T. Welsh, "Immoral Goals: How Goal Setting May Lead to Unethical Behavior," *Current Opinion in Psychology* 6 (2015): 93–96.

62. E.A. Locke and G.P. Latham, *A Theory of Goal Setting and Task Performance* (Englewood Cliffs, NJ: Prentice Hall, 1990), Chaps. 6 and 7; H. Klein, J.T. Cooper and C.A. Monahan, "Goal Commitment," in *New Developments in Goal Setting and Task Performance*, ed. E.A. Locke and G.P. Latham (London: Taylor and Francis, 2012), 65–89.

63. G.P. Latham and C.C. Pinder, "Work Motivation Theory and Research at the Dawn of the Twenty-First Century," *Annual Review of Psychology* 56 (2005): 485–516; S.J. Ashford and K.E.M. Stobbelier, "Feedback, Goal Setting, and Task Performance Revisited," in *New Developments in Goal Setting and Task Performance*, ed. E.A. Locke and G.P. Latham (New York: Routledge, 2013), 51–64.

64. G.P. Latham, *Work Motivation: History, Theory, Research, and Practice* (Thousand Oaks, CA: Sage, 2007), 198–203; A. Baker et al., "Feedback and Organizations: Feedback Is Good, Feedback-Friendly Culture Is Better," *Canadian Psychology* 54, no. 4 (2013): 260–68.

65. F. Anseel et al., "How Are We Doing after 30 Years? A Meta-Analytic Review of the Antecedents and Outcomes of Feedback-Seeking Behavior," *Journal of Management* 41 (2015): 318–48; M. London, *The Power of Feedback: Giving, Seeking, and Using Feedback for Performance Improvement* (New York: Routledge, 2015); B. Kuvaas, R. Buch and A. Dysvik, "Constructive Supervisor Feedback Is Not Sufficient: Immediacy and Frequency Is Essential," *Human Resource Management* 56 (2017): 519–31.

66. M. Buckingham, *Go Put Your Strengths to Work* (New York: Free Press, 2007); A.L. Clancy and J. Binkert, "Appreciative Coaching: Pathway to Flourishing," in *Excellence in Coaching: The Industry Guide*, ed. J. Passmore (London: Kogan Page, 2010), 147–56; H. Aguinis, R.K. Gottfredson, and H. Joo, "Delivering Effective Performance Feedback: The Strengths-Based Approach," *Business Horizons* 55, no. 2 (2012): 105–11; A.B. Bakker and M. van Woerkom, "Strengths Use in Organizations: A Positive Approach of Occupational Health," *Canadian Psychology* 59, no. 1 (February 2018): 38–46, https://doi.org/10.1037/cap0000120. While still encouraging a positive approach to coaching and feedback, some writers believe that negative feedback is also necessary. See, for example, A. Castiello D'Antonio, "Coaching Psychology and Positive Psychology in Work and Organizational Psychology," *Psychologist-Manager Journal* 21, no. 2 (May 2018): 130–50, https://doi.org/10.1037/mgr0000070.

67. Cited in H. Aguinis, R. K. Gottfredson, and H. Joo, "Delivering Effective Performance Feedback: The Strengths-Based Approach," *Business Horizons* 55, no. 2 (2012): 105–11.

68. A.N. Kluger and D. Nir, "The Feedforward Interview," *Human Resource Management Review* 20, no. 3 (2010): 235–46; H. Aguinis, R.K. Gottfredson, and H. Joo, "Delivering Effective Performance Feedback: The Strengths-Based Approach," *Business Horizons* 55, no. 2 (2012): 105–11; B. Kuvaas, R. Buch, and A. Dysvik, "Constructive Supervisor Feedback Is Not Sufficient: Immediacy and Frequency Is Essential," *Human Resource Management* 56, no. 3 (2017): 519–31, https://doi.org/10.1002/hrm.21785; J.V. Wingerden and J.V. der Stoep, "The Motivational Potential of Meaningful Work: Relationships with Strengths Use, Work Engagement, and Performance," *PLOS ONE* 13, no. 6 (June 13, 2018): e0197599, https://doi.org/10.1371/journal.pone.0197599.

69. H.H. Meyer, "A Solution to the Performance Appraisal Feedback Enigma," *Academy of Management Executive* 5, no. 1 (1991): 68–76.

70. A. Terracciano, P.T. Costa and R.R. McCrae, "Personality Plasticity after Age 30," *Personality and Social Psychology Bulletin* 32 (2006): 999–1009; R. Mõttus et al., "Within-Trait Heterogeneity in Age Group Differences in Personality Domains and Facets: Implications for the Development and Coherence of Personality Traits," *PLoS ONE* 10, no. 3 (2015): e0119667; L.H. Schultz et al., "Vocational Interests across 20 Years of Adulthood: Stability, Change, and the Role of Work Experiences," *Journal of Research in Personality* 71 (2017): 46–56.

71. J.W. Smither, M. London, and R.R. Reilly, "Does Performance Improve Following Multisource Feedback? A Theoretical Model, Meta-Analysis, and Review of Empirical Findings," *Personnel Psychology* 58, no. 1 (2005): 33–66; L.E. Atwater, J.F. Brett, and A.C. Charles, "Multisource Feedback: Lessons Learned and Implications for Practice," *Human Resource Management* 46, no. 2 (2007): 285–307; M.C. Campion, E.D. Campion, and M.A. Campion, "Improvements in Performance Management through the Use of 360 Feedback," *Industrial and Organizational Psychology* 8, no. 1 (2015): 85–93.

72. S.J. Ashford and G.B. Northcraft, "Conveying More (or Less) Than We Realize: The Role of Impression Management in Feedback Seeking," *Organizational Behavior and Human Decision Processes* 53 (1992): 310–34; J.R. Williams et al., "Increasing Feedback Seeking in Public Contexts: It Takes Two (or More) to Tango," *Journal of Applied Psychology* 84 (1999): 969–76.

73. J.B. Miner, "The Rated Importance, Scientific Validity, and Practical Usefulness of Organizational Behavior Theories: A Quantitative Review," *Academy of Management Learning and Education* 2, no. 3 (2003): 250–68; S. Asmus et al., "The Impact of Goal-Setting on Worker Performance - Empirical Evidence from a Real-Effort Production Experiment," *Procedia CIRP*, 12th Global Conference on Sustainable Manufacturing – Emerging Potentials, 26 (January 2015): 127–32, https://doi.org/10.1016/j.procir.2015.02.086.

74. P.M. Wright, "Goal Setting and Monetary Incentives: Motivational Tools That Can Work Too Well," *Compensation and Benefits Review* 26 (1994): 41–49; S. Kerr and D. LePelley, "Stretch Goals: Risks, Possibilities, and Best Practices," in *New Developments in Goal Setting and Task Performance*, ed. E.A. Locke and G.P. Latham (London: Taylor and Francis, 2012), 21–32; L.D. Ordóñez and D.T. Welsh, "Immoral Goals: How Goal Setting May Lead to Unethical Behavior," *Current Opinion in Psychology* 6 (2015): 93–96.

75. W.B. Cameron, *Informal Sociology: A Casual Introduction to Sociological Thinking* (Random House, 1963), 13; "Not Everything That Counts Can Be Counted–Quote Investigator," May 26, 2010, https://quoteinvestigator.com/2010/05/26/everything-counts-einstein/.

76. G.P. Latham, *Work Motivation: History, Theory, Research, and Practice* (Thousand Oaks, CA: Sage, 2007), 188.

77. The most widely studied types in organizational behavior are distributive, procedural, and interactional justice, the latter of which includes two subsets (informational and interpersonal). However, other writers have identified completely different typologies, such as legalistic, retributive, and restorative justice. See, for example, G.D. Paul and L.L. Putnam, "Emergent Paradigms of Organizational Justice," in *Transforming Conflict through Communication in Personal, Family, and Working Relationships*, ed. P.M. Kellett and T. Matyók, Peace and Conflict Studies (Lanham: Lexington Books, 2016), 271–92. For a detailed discussion and critique of the development of the justice domain, see D.E. Rupp et al., "A Critical Analysis of the Conceptualization and Measurement of Organizational Justice: Is It Time for Reassessment?" *Academy of Management Annals* 11, no. 2 (2017): 919–59, https://doi.org/10.5465/annals.2014.0051.

78. M. Deutsch, "Equity, Equality, and Need: What Determines Which Value Will Be Used as the Basis of Distributive Justice?," *Journal of Social Issues* 31, no. 3 (1975): 137–49; D.A. Morand and K.K. Merriman, "Equality Theory as a Counterbalance to Equity Theory in Human Resource Management," *Journal of Business Ethics* 111, no. 1 (2012): 133–44; T. Reeskens and W. van Oorschot, "Equity, Equality, or Need? A Study of Popular Preferences for Welfare Redistribution Principles across 24 European Countries," *Journal of European Public Policy* 20, no. 8 (2013): 1174–95.

79. "B&T Salary Survey," *B&T Magazine* 64, no. 2812 (2015): 56–63; G. Plimmer and C. Cantal, *Workplace Dynamics in New Zealand Public Services*, Centre for Labour, Employment and Work (Wellington, NZ: Victoria University of Wellington, November 2016); Willis Towers Watson, "Only Half of U.S. Employees Think They Are Paid Fairly Compared to Counterparts," news release (Arlington, VA: Willis Towers Watson, November 10, 2016); *Comp Is Culture: 2017 Compensation Best Practices Report* (Seattle: PayScale, February 14, 2017).

80. J.S. Adams, "Toward an Understanding of Inequity," *Journal of Abnormal and Social Psychology* 67 (1963): 422–36; P.H. Siegel, M. Schraeder, and R. Morrison, "A Taxonomy of Equity Factors," *Journal of Applied Social Psychology* 38, no. 1 (2008): 61–75; R. Cropanzana, D.E. Bowen, and S.W. Gilliland, "The Management of Organizational Justice," *Academy of Management Perspectives* 21, no. 4 (2007): 34–48; D.E. Rupp et al., "A Critical Analysis of the Conceptualization and Measurement of Organizational Justice: Is It Time for Reassessment?," *Academy of Management Annals* 11, no. 2 (2017): 919–59, https://doi.org/10.5465/annals.2014.0051.

81. C.T. Kulik and M.L. Ambrose, "Personal and Situational Determinants of Referent Choice," *Academy of Management Review* 17 (1992): 212–37; J. Shin and Y.W. Sohn, "Effects of Employees' Social Comparison Behaviors on Distributive Justice Perception and Job Satisfaction," *Social Behavior and Personality* 43, no. 7 (2015): 1071–83; C.M. Sterling and G. Labianca, "Costly Comparisons: Managing Envy in the Workplace," *Organizational Dynamics* 44, no. 4 (2015): 296–305.

82. T.P. Summers and A.S. DeNisi, "In Search of Adams' Other: Reexamination of Referents Used in the Evaluation of Pay," *Human Relations* 43 (1990): 497–511.

83. The emotive dynamics of feelings of inequity are studied in A.W. Cappelen et al., "Equity Theory and Fair Inequality: A Neuroeconomic Study," *Proceedings of the National Academy of Sciences* 111, no. 43 (2014): 15368–72.

84. Y. Cohen-Charash and P.E. Spector, "The Role of Justice in Organizations: A Meta-Analysis," *Organizational Behavior and Human Decision Processes* 86 (2001): 278–321; B. Walker and R.T. Hamilton, "Employee–Employer Grievances: A Review," *International Journal of Management Reviews* 13, no. 1 (2011): 40–58; R. Cropanzana and C. Moliner, "Hazards of Justice: Egocentric Bias, Moral Judgments, and Revenge-Seeking," in *Deviant and Criminal Behavior in the Workplace*, ed. S.M. Elias (New York: New York University Press, 2013), 155–77; B.C. Holtz and C.M. Harold, "Interpersonal Justice and Deviance: The Moderating Effects of Interpersonal Justice Values and Justice Orientation," *Journal of Management* 39, no. 2 (2013): 339–65; C.L. Wilkin and C.E. Connelly, "Green with Envy and Nerves of Steel: Moderated Mediation between Distributive Justice and Theft," *Personality and Individual Differences* 72 (2015): 160–64.

85. Canadian Press, "Pierre Berton, Canadian Cultural Icon, Enjoyed Long and Colourful Career," *Times Colonist* (Victoria, BC), November 30, 2004.

86. J. Fizel, A.C. Krautman, and L. Hadley, "Equity and Arbitration in Major League Baseball," *Managerial and Decision Economics* 23, no. 7 (2002): 427–35; M. Ezzamel and R. Watson, "Pay Comparability across and within UK Boards: An Empirical Analysis of the Cash Pay Awards to CEOs and Other Board Members," *Journal of Management Studies* 39, no. 2 (2002): 207–32.

87. D.R. Bobocel and L. Gosse, "Procedural Justice: A Historical Review and Critical Analysis," in *Oxford Handbook of Justice in the Workplace*, ed. R.S. Cropanzano and M.L. Ambrose (New York: Oxford University Press, 2015), 51–88; Robert J. Bies, "Interactional Justice: Looking Backward, Looking Forward," in *The Oxford Handbook of Justice in the Workplace*, ed. R. Cropanzano and M.L. Ambrose, Oxford Library of Psychology (New York: Oxford University Press, 2015), 89–107.

88. J. Greenberg and E.A. Lind, "The Pursuit of Organizational Justice: From Conceptualization to Implication to Application," in *Industrial and Organizational Psychology: Linking Theory with Practice* ed. C.L. Cooper and E.A. Locke (London: Blackwell, 2000), 72–108 ; C.B. Goldberg, M.A. Clark, and A.B. Henley, "Speaking Up: A Conceptual Model of Voice Responses Following the Unfair Treatment of Others in Non-Union Settings," *Human Resource Management* 50, no. 1 (2011): 75–94; M.R. Bashshur, "When Voice Matters: A Multilevel Review of the Impact of Voice in Organizations," *Journal of Management* 41, no. 5 (2015): 1530–54.

89. R.J. Bies, "Interactional Justice: Looking Backward, Looking Forward," in *The Oxford Handbook of Justice in the Workplace*, ed. R. Cropanzano and M.L. Ambrose, Oxford Library of Psychology (New York: Oxford University Press, 2015), 89–107; R. Cropanzano, J.F. Kirk, and M. Fortin, "How Do We Know When We Are Treated Fairly? Justice Rules and Fairness Judgments," *Research in Personnel and Human Resources Management* 33 (2015): 279–350.

90. J.S. Michel, K. Newness, and K. Duniewicz, "How Abusive Supervision Affects Workplace Deviance: A Moderated-Mediation Examination of Aggressiveness and Work-Related Negative Affect," *Journal of Business and Psychology* 31 (2016): 1–22; J.K. Oh and C.I.C. Farh, "An Emotional Process Theory of How Subordinates Appraise, Experience, and Respond to Abusive Supervision over Time," *Academy of Management Review* 42 (2017): 207–32.

91. D.T. Miller, "Disrespect and the Experience of Injustice," *Annual Review of Psychology* 52 (2001): 527–53; R. Vermunt and H. Steensma, "Procedural Justice," in *Handbook of Social Justice Theory and Research*, ed. C. Sabbagh and M. Schmitt (New York: Springer New York, 2016), 219–36, https://doi.org/10.1007/978-1-4939-3216-0_12; K.A. DeCelles and K. Aquino, "Dark Knights: When and Why an Employee Becomes a Workplace Vigilante," *Academy of Management Review*, February 15, 2019, https://doi.org/10.5465/amr.2017.0300.

92. M.L. Ambrose, M.A. Seabright, and M. Schminke, "Sabotage in the Workplace: The Role of Organizational Injustice," *Organizational Behavior and Human Decision Processes* 89, no. 1 (2002): 947–65.

93. M.A. Campion et al., "Work Redesign: Eight Obstacles and Opportunities," *Human Resource Management* 44, no. 4 (2005): 367–90; S.-J. Cullinane et al., "Job Design under Lean Manufacturing and Its Impact on Employee Outcomes," *Organizational Psychology Review* 3, no. 1 (2013): 41–61.

94. A. Shinnar et al., "Survey of Ergonomic Features of Supermarket Cash Registers," *International Journal of Industrial Ergonomics* 34, no. 6 (2004): 535–41; V. O'Connell, "Stores Count Seconds to Trim Labor Costs," *The Wall Street Journal*, November 13, 2008; A. Kihlstedt and G.M. Hägg, "Checkout Cashier Work and Counter Design—Video Movement Analysis, Musculoskeletal Disorders and Customer Interaction," *International Journal of Industrial Ergonomics* 41, no. 3 (2011): 201–07; "One Checkout Item Every Three Seconds," *Mail Online* (London), July 8, 2012. Average scanning times vary considerably with the scanning technology, product standardization, and ergonomic design of the cashier station.

95. S. Leroy, "Why Is It So Hard to Do My Work? The Challenge of Attention Residue When Switching between Work Tasks," *Organizational Behavior and Human Decision Processes* 109 (2009): 168–81; S. Leroy and T.M. Glomb, "Tasks Interrupted: How Anticipating Time Pressure on Resumption of an Interrupted Task Causes Attention Residue and Low Performance on Interrupting Tasks and How a 'Ready-to-Resume' Plan Mitigates the Effects," *Organization Science* 29 (2018): 380–97.

96. H. Fayol, *General and Industrial Management*, trans. C. Storrs (London: Pitman, 1949); E.E. Lawler III, *Motivation in Work Organizations* (Monterey, CA: Brooks/Cole, 1973), Chap. 7; M.A. Campion, "Ability Requirement Implications of Job Design: An Interdisciplinary Perspective," *Personnel Psychology* 42 (1989): 1–24.

97. A. Smith, *An Inquiry into the Nature and Causes of the Wealth of Nations*, 1st ed., 2 vols. (London: W. Strahan and T. Cadell, 1776), pp. 6–7. Although Smith's general premise is true in most cases, the estimates he provided were speculated, not empirically tested. He even suggested that the 10 pin makers couldn't complete one pin per day, but he also stipulated that is "without any of them having been educated to this peculiar business."

98. F.W. Taylor, *The Principles of Scientific Management* (New York: Harper & Row, 1911); R. Kanigel, *The One Best Way: Frederick Winslow Taylor and the Enigma of Efficiency* (New York: Viking, 1997); M. Derksen, "Turning Men into Machines? Scientific Management, Industrial Psychology, and the 'Human Factor,'" *Journal of the History of the Behavioral Sciences* 50, no. 2 (2014): 148–65.

99. W.F. Dowling, "Job Redesign on the Assembly Line: Farewell to Blue-Collar Blues?" *Organizational Dynamics* (1973): 51–67; J.A. Häusser et al., "Experimental Evidence for the Effects of Task Repetitiveness on Mental Strain and Objective Work Performance," *Journal of Organizational Behavior* 35 (2014): 705–21; E.A.J. van Hooft and M.L.M. van Hooff, "The State of Boredom: Frustrating or Depressing?" *Motivation and Emotion* 42 (2018): 931–46; W. Han et al., "Assessing the Brain 'on the Line': An Ecologically-Valid Assessment of the Impact of Repetitive Assembly Line Work on Hemodynamic Response and Fine Motor Control Using FNIRS," *Brain and Cognition* 136 (2019): 103613, https://doi.org/10.1016/j.bandc.2019.103613.

100. R. Moorhead, "Lawyer Specialization—Managing the Professional Paradox," *Law & Policy* 32, no. 2 (2010): 226–59.

101. J.R. Hackman and E.E. Lawler, "Employee Reactions to Job Characteristics," *Journal of Applied Psychology* 55, no. 3 (1971): 259–86; J.R. Hackman and G.R. Oldham, "The Job Diagnostic Survey: An Instrument for the Diagnosis of Jobs and the Evaluation of Job Redesign Projects" (New Haven, CT: Department of Administrative Sciences, Yale University, May 1974); J.R. Hackman and G.R. Oldham, "Motivation through the Design of Work: Test of a Theory," *Organizational Behavior and Human Performance* 16, no. 2 (1976): 250–79; J.R. Hackman and G. Oldham, *Work Redesign* (Reading, MA: Addison-Wesley, 1980).

102. R.W. Buell, T. Kim, and C.-J. Tsay, "Creating Reciprocal Value Through Operational Transparency," *Management Science* 63 (2017): 1673–95; R.W. Buell, "Operational Transparency," *Harvard Business Review* 97 (March–April 2019): 102–13.

103. M. Gagné and D. Bhave, "Autonomy in the Workplace: An Essential Ingredient to Employee Engagement and Well-Being in Every Culture," in *Human Autonomy in Cross-Cultural Context,* ed. V.I. Chirkov, R.M. Ryan, and K.M. Sheldon, *Cross-Cultural Advancements in Positive Psychology* (Springer: Netherlands, 2011), 163–87.

104. "Toluyemi Nathaniel Talks about Being a Woman in the Tech Space with Softcom," *BellaNaija* (blog), July 2, 2018; Y. Ogunlami, "Nigerian Engineers in Hijabs," *Pulse Nigeria*, August 3, 2018; "75 Softcomers Were Broken into 7 Hackathon Teams," Twitter (Lagos, Nigeria: Softcom, January 24, 2019), https://twitter.com/SoftcomNG/status/1088474546041208832; D.I. Adeleke, "I Visited a Young Nigerian Tech Company Generating Millions in Revenue and This Is What I Learned," *Pulse Nigeria*, January 29, 2019. Some information and quotations are also from Softcom's website: https://softcom.ng/.

105. Maslow introduced or popularized the notion of "growth" to human motivation, and his writing suggests that it is the same as self-actualization. However, a few others suggest that "growth need strength" in the Hackman/Oldham model is a permanent (trait) characteristic. See A.H. Maslow, *Motivation and Personality* (New York: Harper & Row, 1954); J.B. Miner, *Organizational Behavior: Integrated Theory Development and the Role of the Unconscious*, vol. 6 (Armonk, NY: M.E. Sharpe, 2011), 32-33.

106. R.B. Tiegs, L.E. Tetrick, and Y. Fried, "Growth Need Strength and Context Satisfactions as Moderators of the Relations of the Job Characteristics Model," *Journal of Management* 18, no. 3 (1992): 575–93; J.E. Champoux, "A Multivariate Test of the Job Characteristics Theory of Work Motivation," *Journal of Organizational Behavior* 12, no. 5 (1991): 431–46.

107. G.R. Oldham and J.R. Hackman, "Not What It Was and Not What It Will Be: The Future of Job Design Research," *Journal of Organizational Behavior* 31, no. 2–3 (2010): 463–79; A.M. Grant, Y. Fried, and T. Juillerat, "Work Matters: Job Design in Classic and Contemporary Perspectives," in *APA Handbook of Industrial and Organizational Psychology,* ed. S. Zedeck (Washington, DC: American Psychological Association, 2011), 417–53. A very early version of the job characteristics model included social interaction but was later excluded.

108. C. Perrow, "A Framework for the Comparative Analysis of Organizations," *American Sociological Review* 32 (1967): 194–208; R.L. Daft and N.B. Macintosh, "A Tentative Exploration into the Amount and Equivocality of Information Processing in Organizational Work Units," *Administrative Science Quarterly* 26 (1981): 207–24. Job analyzability and variability are embedded in "job complexity," but the latter is a much broader concept that has suffered from many diverse interpretations. See P. Liu and Z. Li, "Task Complexity: A Review and Conceptualization Framework," *International Journal of Industrial Ergonomics* 42 (2012): 553–68; S.Y. Sung, A. Antefelt, and J.N. Choi, "Dual Effects of Job Complexity on Proactive and Responsive Creativity: Moderating Role of Employee Ambiguity Tolerance," *Group & Organization Management* 42 (2017): 388–418.

109. M.M. Coşgel and T.J. Miceli, "Job Rotation: Cost, Benefits, and Stylized Facts," *Journal of Institutional and Theoretical Economics* 155 (1999): 301–20; D. Rissén et al., "Psychophysiological Stress Reactions, Trapezius Muscle Activity, and Neck and Shoulder Pain among Female Cashiers before and after Introduction of Job Rotation," *Work & Stress* 16, no. 2 (2002): 127–37; S. Gallagher et al., "Job Rotation as a Technique for the Control of MSDs: A Fatigue Failure Perspective," *Proceedings of the Human Factors and Ergonomics Society Annual Meeting* 61 (September 1, 2017): 993–94; R.S. Padula et al., "Job Rotation Designed to Prevent Musculoskeletal Disorders and Control Risk in Manufacturing Industries: A Systematic Review," *Applied Ergonomics* 58 (2017): 386–97.

110. J.R. Hackman et al., "A New Strategy for Job Enrichment," *California Management Review* 17, no. 4 (1975): 57–71; R.W. Griffin, *Task Design: An Integrative Approach* (Glenview, IL: Scott Foresman, 1982).

111. P.E. Spector and S.M. Jex, "Relations of Job Characteristics from Multiple Data Sources with Employee Affect, Absence, Turnover Intentions, and Health," *Journal of Applied Psychology* 76 (1991): 46–53; P. Osterman, "How Common Is Workplace Transformation and Who Adopts It?" *Industrial and Labor Relations Review* 47 (1994): 173–88; R. Saavedra and S. K. Kwun, "Affective States in Job Characteristics Theory," *Journal of Organizational Behavior* 21 (2000): 131–46.

112. J.R. Hackman and G. Oldham, *Work Redesign* (Reading, MA: Addison-Wesley, 1980), 137–38.

6 Decision Making and Creativity

Brian A Jackson/Shutterstock

Learning Objectives

After you read this chapter, you should be able to:

LO6-1 Describe the elements of rational choice decision making.

LO6-2 Explain why people don't apply rational choice decision making when identifying problems/opportunities, evaluating/choosing alternatives, and evaluating decision outcomes.

LO6-3 Discuss the roles of emotions and intuition in decision making.

LO6-4 Describe employee characteristics, workplace conditions, and specific activities that support creativity.

LO6-5 Describe the benefits of employee involvement and identify four contingencies that affect the optimal level of employee involvement.

decision making the conscious process of making choices among alternatives with the intention of moving toward some desired state of affairs

rational choice decision making the process of using pure logic and all available information about all alternatives to choose the alternative with the highest value

Everyone who works in organizations makes decisions. But at Estée Lauder, employees are expected to make better decisions by applying creativity. "Creativity is about solving problems, and who doesn't solve problems on a daily basis? Therefore, everybody by virtue of their innate problem-solving skills, is creative," says Mark Polson, vice president of Creativity and Business Innovation at the New York–based cosmetics and skin care firm. "Whatever domain that you're in—be it supply chain, be it sales, be it finance, even procurement, you have the ability to be creative in that role."

This view is echoed by John Demsey, Estée Lauder's executive group president. "I believe in creative minds in every discipline," says Demsey, who led the growth of M.A.C. and Tom Ford (among others) into world-leading brands. "Creativity isn't just about creative directors or copywriters or store designers. It's the ability, initiative, and the self-actualization to reimagine possibilities and to think differently."

Mark Polson explains that Estée Lauder supports creative decision making partly by "creating an environment that doesn't punish failure, but looks to learn from the lessons of failure." Employees also attend training programs and activities that generate more creative thinking. For instance, the company's innovation lab in Queens, New York, hosts design thinking sessions with product developers, engineers, customer-facing employees, and other groups. "We bring them together, put the problem on the table, break them into teams, and just let them come up with ideas and put prototypes together. Then we evaluate them, and iterate and do more prototypes," Polson explains.[1]

Estée Lauder and every other organization rely on effective decision making–from problem finding to developing creative solutions. All organizations depend on employees to foresee and correctly identify problems or opportunities, to consider the full range of alternatives, to pick the best alternative based on several relevant factors, and to execute and evaluate those decisions effectively and objectively. Decision making is not only a critical management skill; it is also a core activity for all staff members directly in their jobs and through employee involvement.

This chapter examines each of these themes. It begins by describing the rational choice view of decision making. Next, the human limitations of rational choice–we call it imperfect rationality–are discussed in the context of how human beings actually make decisions. We also examine the emerging view that decisions consist of a complex interaction of logic and emotion. The latter part of this chapter focuses on two topics that intertwine with decision making: creativity and employee involvement.

LO6-1 Describe the elements of rational choice decision making.

RATIONAL CHOICE DECISION MAKING

Decision making is the process of making choices among alternatives with the intention of moving toward some desired state of affairs.[2] How can we make effective decisions in organizations? This chapter answers this question by describing different ways of thinking about decision making and by examining several issues at each stage of the decision-making process. We begin this journey by discussing the earliest perspective–**rational choice decision making**–which is the process of using pure logic and all available information about all alternatives to choose the alternative with the highest value. Choices with the highest value might have the highest expected profitability,

Rational choice decision making selects the best alternative by calculating the probability that various outcomes will occur from the choices and the expected satisfaction (valences) from each of those outcomes.
ESB Professional/Shutterstock

> **I am not a product of my circumstances. I am a product of my decisions.[3]**
>
> —Stephen R. Covey, author and educator

customer satisfaction, employee well-being, or some combination of these outcomes.

For most of written history, Western societies have characterized rational choice as an ideal state of decision making.[4] The rational choice view was established 2,500 years ago when Plato and his contemporaries in ancient Greece raised logical debate and reasoning to a fine art. About 400 years ago, Descartes and other European philosophers argued that the ability to make logical decisions is one of the most important accomplishments of human beings. In the 1700s, Scottish philosophers refined the notion that the best choice is the one that offers the greatest expected satisfaction. As we shall discover, these views of rational choice decision making are flawed, but this approach provides a useful foundation to understand this topic.

Rational choice decisions often involve complex calculations of data using a formula that points to the best choice. Basically, this formula determines the best alternative by computing the probability that various outcomes will occur from the choices and the expected satisfaction (valences) from each of those outcomes.[5] We have already described similar applications of probability and valences in organizational behavior theories presented earlier in this book, notably the attitude model in Chapter 4 and expectancy theory of motivation in Chapter 5.

To illustrate the rational choice calculation, consider the example in Exhibit 6.1.[6] Suppose that you are given the task of choosing a new supplier of a specific raw material used in the company's products. From experience, you estimate that the preferred supplier should provide a high-quality product (+9) with low prices (+6) and on-time delivery (+4).[7] The numbers, which are on a plus or minus 10-point scale in this example, indicate each outcome's valence—that is, its expected satisfaction or importance. You estimate that supplier A has excellent on-time delivery (about 90 percent probability of exceeding the company's expectations), an 80 percent likelihood of offering low prices, and a 70 percent probability of reliably providing a product with exceptional quality. Supplier B has a 90 percent chance of providing very high product quality but a lower likelihood of on-time delivery (60 percent) and of offering low prices (40 percent).

Exhibit 6.1 Rational Choice Decision-Making Example

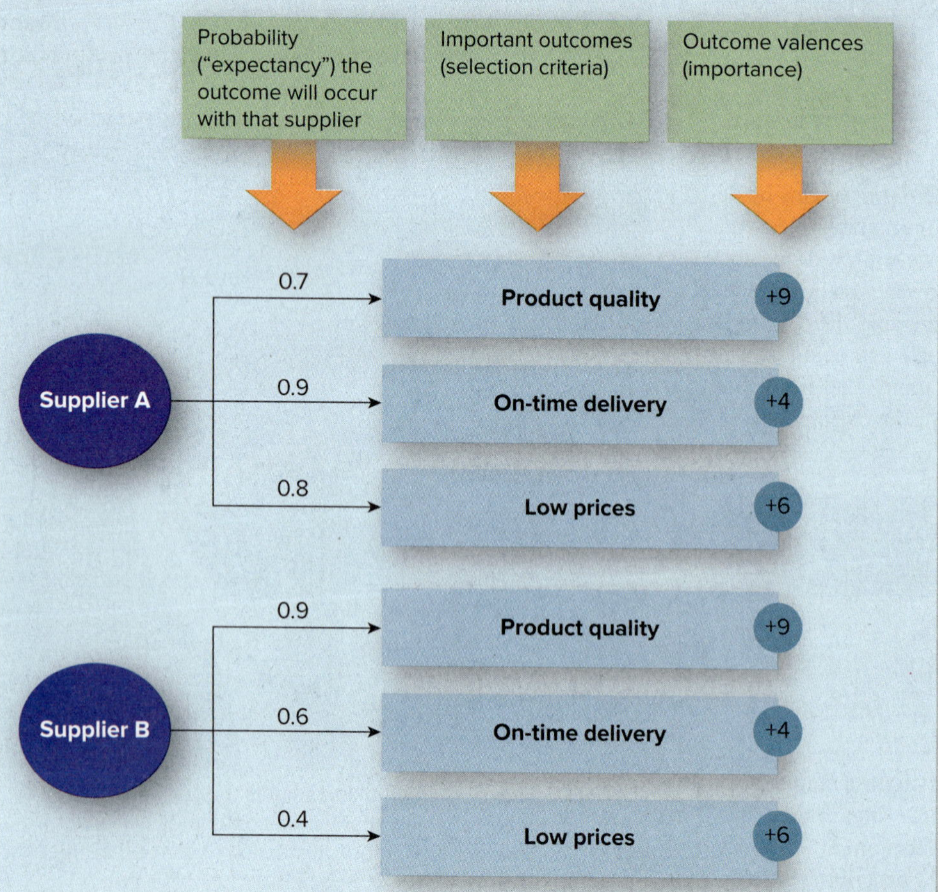

Which of these two suppliers should be selected? A rational choice decision maker would choose Supplier A because that company would produce the highest expected satisfaction. This composite valence is calculated by multiplying the valence of each outcome by the probability of that outcome occurring, then add those results across all three outcomes. The supplier with the higher score is the better choice, given available information. The key point from this example is that all rational decisions rely primarily on two pieces of information: (1) the probability that each outcome will occur and (2) the valence or expected satisfaction of each outcome.

Rational Choice Decision Process

Calculating the best alternative is at the heart of rational choice decision making, but it goes hand-in-hand with the systematic decision process illustrated in Exhibit 6.2.[8] The first step is to identify the problem or recognize an opportunity. A *problem* is a deviation between the current and the desired situation–the gap between "what is" and "what ought to be." This deviation is a symptom of more fundamental causes that need to be corrected. The "ought to be" refers to goals or performance expectations, and these goals later help evaluate the selected choice.[9] For instance, if a customer contact center's goal is to answer incoming client calls within 30 seconds, the problem is the gap between that goal and the actual time the contact center takes to answer most client calls. An *opportunity* is a deviation between current expectations and a potentially better situation that was not previously expected. In other words, an opportunity exists when decision makers discover that some choices may produce better results than current goals or expectations.

The second step involves choosing the best decision process. This step is really a meta-decision–deciding how to decide–because it refers to choosing among the different approaches and processes to make the decision.[10] One meta-decision is whether to solve the problem alone or involve others in the process. We'll examine the contingencies of employee involvement in decision making in the last section of this chapter. Another factor in choosing the best decision process is whether to assume the decision is programmed or nonprogrammed. *Programmed decisions* follow standard operating procedures; they have been resolved in the past, so the optimal solution has already been identified and documented. In contrast, *nonprogrammed decisions* require all steps in the decision model because the problems are new, complex, or ill-defined.

The third step in the rational choice decision process is to identify and/or develop a list of possible choices. This usually begins by searching for ready-made solutions, such as practices that have worked well on similar problems. If none of the existing solutions is acceptable, then decision makers need to design a custom-made solution or modify an existing one.

The fourth step is to select the best choice by applying the rational choice calculation we described in Exhibit 6.1. To choose the alternative with the greatest expected satisfaction, the decision maker must have information about all possible alternatives and their outcomes. That condition is usually impossible, but the rational choice view of decision making assumes this can be accomplished with ease.

The fifth step in the rational choice decision-making process is to implement the selected alternative. The rational choice view has little to say about this step because it assumes that implementation occurs without any problems. The final step is to evaluate whether the gap has narrowed between "what is" and "what ought to be." Ideally, this information should come from systematic benchmarks so that relevant feedback is objective and easily observed.

Exhibit 6.2 Rational Choice Decision Process

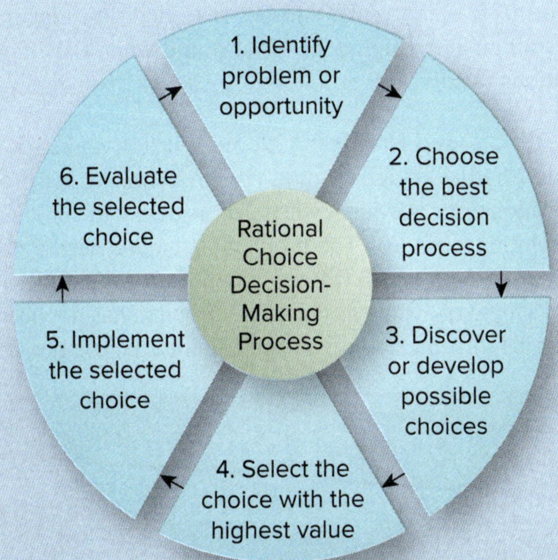

Problems with Rational Choice Decision Making

The rational choice view of decision making seems so logical, yet there are several reasons why it is impossible to apply in reality.[11] Therefore, we need to understand why people have imperfect rationality. Over the next several pages, we reexamine each step in the rational choice decision-making process, but with more detail about what really happens through the lens of "imperfect rationality."

LO6-2 Explain why people don't apply rational choice decision making when identifying problems/opportunities, evaluating/choosing alternatives, and evaluating decision outcomes.

IDENTIFYING PROBLEMS AND OPPORTUNITIES

Some sources suggest that when Albert Einstein was asked how he would save the world in one hour, he replied that most of that time should be spent defining the problem and the rest of that hour solving the problem.[12] Whether Einstein or someone else uttered this advice, it makes the important point that problem identification is not just the first step in decision making; it is arguably the most important step. But problems and opportunities are not clearly labeled objects that appear on our desks.

Instead, they are conclusions that we form from ambiguous and conflicting information.[13]

Problems with Problem Identification

Only by forming an accurate understanding of the problem can we move toward a meaningful solution. Unfortunately, the problem identification stage is, itself, filled with problems. Here are five of the most widely recognized concerns.

Mental Models Decision makers are victims of their own problem framing due to existing mental models. **Mental models** are knowledge structures that we develop to describe, explain, and predict the world around us.[14] These visual or relational images of the external world fill in information that we don't immediately see, which satisfies our need to understand and navigate the surrounding environment (see Chapter 3). Many mental images are also prototypes of ideal conditions–they represent models of how things should be. Unfortunately, these mental models can blind us from seeing unique problems or opportunities because they produce a negative evaluation of things that deviate from the mental model. If an idea doesn't fit the existing mental model of how things should work, then it is quickly dismissed as unworkable or undesirable.

Decisive Leadership Various studies have found that executives are valued for their decisiveness, including how quickly they determine that the situation is a problem, opportunity, or nothing worth their attention.[16] Consequently, many leaders announce problems or opportunities before having a chance to logically assess the situation. The result is often a misguided effort to solve an ill-defined problem or resources wasted on a poorly identified opportunity.

Stakeholder Framing Employees, suppliers, customers, and other stakeholders provide (or hide) information in ways that makes the decision maker see the situation as a problem, opportunity, or steady sailing.[17] Employees point to external factors rather than their own imperfections as the cause of production delays. Suppliers market their new products as unique opportunities and competitor products as risky choices. Many other stakeholders also frame the situation in ways that decision makers will view as a problem or otherwise. Decision makers fall prey to these constructed realities because they have a need to simplify the daily bombardment of complex and often ambiguous information.

Perceptual Defense Under some conditions, decision makers either fail to recognize or quickly forget information that threatens the situation. The tendency to engage in perceptual defense (or its variation, called repressive coping) is a coping mechanism. It is more likely to occur in decision makers with higher trait anxiety (high neuroticism) and when they have limited options to solve the problem.[18]

Solution-Focused Problems Some decision makers jump to a solution before understanding the problem.[19] This problem-identification error is evident when people define the problem as a veiled solution, such as: "The problem is that we need more control over our suppliers." This statement is a proposed solution (control suppliers), whereas the actual problem has not been diagnosed or identified. Decision makers fall into the solution-focused

OB THEORY TO PRACTICE

Mental Model Myopia Almost Rejected *Seinfeld*[15]

Seinfeld was one of the most successful situational comedies (sitcoms) in history, yet it was soundly rejected by executives at Fox network and almost had the same fate at NBC, which aired the pilot episode. The show's near-miss with success occurred because it was a new form of television comedy, one that was profoundly different from the deeply reinforced mental models that network executives relied on to identify future program gems.

NBC executive Rick Ludwin is widely credited with saving *Seinfeld* from the dustbin. As a former stand-up comedian, Ludwin recognized the potential of *Seinfeld*'s unique format for humor. Also, he was responsible for late-night programming, not sitcoms, so he didn't rely on the outdated mental models that blinkered sitcom executives regarding what a successful program should look like. *Seinfeld* scriptwriters Larry David and Jerry Seinfeld also lacked experience in the sitcom industry, which enabled them to produce scripts that forged new territory.

"Larry and Jerry had never written a sitcom, and my department had never developed one," says Rick Ludwin. "We were a good match, because we didn't know what rules weren't supposed to be broken."

STLE ROCK/WEST-SHAPIRO/Album/Alamy Stock Photo

> I suppose it is tempting, if the only tool you have is a hammer, to treat everything as if it were a nail.[20]
>
> —Abraham Maslow, psychologist and scholar

mental models knowledge structures that we develop to describe, explain, and predict the world around us

bounded rationality the view that people are bounded in their decision-making capabilities, including access to limited information, limited information processing, and tendency toward satisficing rather than maximizing when making choices

OB THEORY TO PRACTICE

Identifying Problems and Opportunities More Effectively

- Be aware of the problem identification biases.
- Resist the temptation to look decisive.
- Have an aversion to complacency (practice divine discontent).
- Discuss the situation with others.

problem trap because they have been reinforced by past successes with that solution. When new problems arise, the solution that worked in the past quickly comes to mind before proper problem diagnosis occurs. A second reason for the solution-focused problem identification error is that decision makers are comforted by closure to problems, so they nonconsciously embed a solution in their problem definition. Unfortunately, this solution-focused situation fails to fully diagnose the underlying causes that need to be addressed.

Identifying Problems and Opportunities More Effectively

Recognizing problems and opportunities will always be a challenge, but one way to improve the process is by becoming aware of the five problem identification biases just described. For example, by recognizing that mental models restrict a person's perspective of the world, decision makers are more motivated to consider other perspectives of reality. Along with increasing their awareness of problem identification flaws, leaders require considerable willpower to resist the temptation of looking decisive when a more thoughtful examination of the situation is warranted.

A third way to improve problem identification is to create a norm of "divine discontent." Decision makers with this mindset are never satisfied with current conditions no matter how successful that situation may be, so they more actively search for problems and opportunities.[21] Fourth, problem identification errors can be minimized by discussing the situation with other people, particularly those with different experiences and backgrounds. It is much easier to discover blind spots in problem identification when listening to how others perceive the situation. Opportunities also become apparent when outsiders explore this information from their different mental models.

SEARCHING FOR, EVALUATING, AND CHOOSING ALTERNATIVES

The rational choice view of decision making assumes that decision makers rely on logic to evaluate and choose alternatives. It also assumes that they have well-articulated and agreed-upon organizational goals, that they efficiently and simultaneously process facts about all alternatives and the consequences of those alternatives, and that they choose the alternative with the most favorable outcomes.

Nobel Prize–winning organizational scholar Herbert Simon questioned these assumptions a half century ago. He argued that people engage in **bounded rationality** because they process limited and imperfect information, and they rarely try to select the best choice.[22] Bounded rationality is the most widely known theory questioning the rational choice view, but it is not alone. Other *imperfect rationality* theories identify imperfections in how people form preferences, how they short-circuit the decision-making process, and how their choices are distorted by faulty heuristics and other perceptual biases.[23] Overall, as Exhibit 6.3 illustrates, organizational behavior theories identify several ways that human decision making differs from rational choice assumptions. Let's look at these differences in terms of goals, information processing, and maximization.

Problems with Goals

Goals are a critical component of all decisions because they establish "what ought to be" and, therefore, provide a standard against which each alternative is evaluated. The rational choice view assumes that organizational goals are clear and agreed on, yet in reality they are often ambiguous or in conflict with each other.[24] Ambiguous goals make it difficult to know if a particular choice has greater value to the organization. For example, "satisfy customer needs" may refer to providing efficient service, a variety of services, more personalized service, and other possibilities. Conflicting goals also create havoc with rational decision making. When goals conflict, decision makers need to determine which goal gets priority. Unfortunately, they rarely have a guide map to determine which goals take precedence.

Problems with Information Processing

The rational choice approach assumes that decision makers evaluate all alternatives and all of their features and outcomes simultaneously using unbiased estimates of valences and outcome probabilities (illustrated earlier in Exhibit 6.1). In reality, people sequentially (not all at the same time) evaluate only a few alternatives and only a handful of characteristics.[25] For example, there are hundreds of smartphone models on the market and dozens of features to consider in each model, yet smartphone purchasers typically pay attention to a small subset of phones and a handful of characteristics or expected outcomes of those products.

Furthermore, purchasers rarely line up all of their limited range of alternatives to select the best smartphone. Instead, they

implicit favorite a preferred alternative that the decision maker uses repeatedly as a comparison with other choices

typically evaluate alternatives sequentially using an **implicit favorite**. An implicit favorite is a preferred alternative that becomes the benchmark against which other choices are compared. The preferred alternative is called "implicit" because decision makers don't explicitly decide this initial preference and often aren't even aware of their favoritism.[27]

There are several reasons why decision makers follow a sequential evaluation process using an implicit favorite. First, it is often difficult to have all alternatives available at the same time.[28] It is impossible to collect information about every smartphone product all at once, so the most favorable phone found early in your search becomes the implicit favorite when considering phones that you investigate later. Second, human beings have a natural preference for comparing two choices rather than systematically evaluating many alternatives at the same time.[29] An implicit favorite assists this process by serving as an anchor comparator for evaluating the other choices. Third, people are cognitive misers. They minimize mental effort by quickly forming a preferred alternative (their implicit favorite) and then looking mainly for evidence that supports the preferred choice. In other words, they engage in **confirmation bias**, which we discussed in Chapter 3.[30]

The fourth reason for comparing alternatives sequentially against an implicit favorite is the human need for cognitive consistency and coherence. People want to ensure that their choice is the emotional preference (implicit favorite) as well as the best logical choice. This occurs most easily through sequential analysis of alternatives against an implicit favorite because decision makers subtly change valences and probabilities. Specifically,

> **Some problems are so complex that you have to be highly intelligent and well-informed just to be undecided about them.[26]**
>
> —Laurence J. Peter, educational scholar and author

Exhibit 6.3 Rational Choice Assumptions versus Organizational Behavior Findings about Choosing Alternatives

Rational choice assumptions	Observations from organizational behavior
Goals are clear, compatible, and agreed upon.	Goals are ambiguous, are in conflict, and lack full support.
Decision makers can calculate all alternatives and their outcomes.	Decision makers have limited information-processing abilities.
Decision makers evaluate all alternatives simultaneously.	Decision makers evaluate alternatives sequentially.
Decision makers use absolute standards to evaluate alternatives.	Decision makers evaluate alternatives against an implicit favorite.
Decision makers use factual information to choose alternatives.	Decision makers process perceptually distorted information.
Decision makers choose the alternative with the highest payoff.	Decision makers choose the alternative that is good enough (satisficing).

confirmation bias the process of screening out information that is contrary to our values and assumptions, and to more readily accept confirming information

anchoring and adjustment heuristic a natural tendency for people to be influenced by an initial anchor point such that they do not sufficiently move away from that point as new information is provided

availability heuristic a natural tendency to assign higher probabilities to objects or events that are easier to recall from memory, even though ease of recall is also affected by nonprobability factors (e.g., emotional response, recent events)

representativeness heuristic a natural tendency to evaluate probabilities of events or objects by the degree to which they resemble (are representative of) other events or objects rather than on objective probability information

satisficing selecting an alternative that is satisfactory or "good enough," rather than the alternative with the highest value (maximization)

Decision makers have an implicit favorite because of their need to form preferences quickly, compare options, and maintain consistency between their decision and attitudes.
Mirexon/Shutterstock

they nonconsciously ignore or underweight positive features of the alternatives relative to the implicit favorite, and change the importance of factors to support the favorite. If you discover that the camera on another smartphone has somewhat more positive reviews than the camera on the phone your prefer to buy (your implicit favorite), you nonconsciously make camera quality less important (at least while making the decision) and discount the accuracy of the reviews about camera quality. Ultimately, you distort valences (importance of camera quality) and probabilities (likelihood that the other phone's camera is superior) so your implicit favorite remains the rational best choice.[31]

Biased Decision Heuristics The cornerstone of rational choice decision making is to calculate the alternative with the highest expected satisfaction. However, psychologists Amos Tversky and Daniel Kahneman discovered that human beings have built-in *decision heuristics* that automatically distort those calculations. Three of the most widely studied heuristic biases are anchoring and adjustment, availability, and representativeness:[32]

- **Anchoring and adjustment heuristic**. This heuristic states that we are influenced by an initial anchor point and do not sufficiently move away from that point as new information is provided.[33] The anchor point might be an initial offer price, initial opinion of someone, or initial estimated probability that something will occur. This bias is associated with the problem we described a few paragraphs ago, namely that human beings tend to compare alternatives rather than evaluate them purely against objective criteria. Therefore, if someone requests a high initial price for a car we want to buy, we naturally compare—and thereby anchor—our alternative offer against that high initial price.
- **Availability heuristic**. The availability heuristic is the tendency to estimate the probability of something occurring by how easily we can recall that event. Unfortunately, how easily we recall something is due to several factors, not just how often it occurs (probability).[34] For instance, we overestimate the probability or frequency of recent events as well as emotional events (such as earthquakes and shark attacks) because they are easily remembered.
- **Representativeness heuristic**. This heuristic states that we pay more attention to whether something resembles (is representative of) something else than to more precise statistics about its probability.[35] Suppose that one-fifth of the students in your class are in engineering and the others are business majors. Statistically, there is a 20 percent chance that any individual in that class is an engineering student. Yet, if one student looks and acts like a stereotype of an engineer, we tend to believe the person is an engineer even though there is much stronger and more reliable statistical evidence that he/she is a business major.

Problems with Maximization

One of the main assumptions of rational choice decision making is that people are both motivated and able to identify and select the best alternative (maximization). Yet rather than aiming for maximization, people engage in **satisficing**—they choose the first alternative that exceeds a standard of acceptance for their needs and preferences.[36] In short, they choose an alternative that is "good enough."

Satisficing is usually necessary because choosing the absolutely best choice (maximization) requires complete and perfect information. This is impossible in reality because information is imperfect, costly, or can't be found at all when the decision is made. Hypothetically, even if decision makers could receive complete and perfect information, they wouldn't have the time or cognitive capacity to input and analyze the mammoth amount of complex data. For example, it is difficult to choose the best possible smartphone because of the large number of choices, the many features to consider for each choice, the numerous consequences of each choice (time to first breakdown, system update limits, etc.), and the ambiguous information about many of those features and outcomes. Under those conditions, maximization leads to a spiral of endless trade-offs among the various choices, which can actually result in worse decisions and less satisfied decision makers.[37]

Studies report that people like to have choices, but deciding from among dozens of alternatives and many outcomes for each alternative is cognitively and emotionally draining. Consequently, decision makers satisfice as a way to minimize cognitive effort.[38] They also reduce cognitive effort by discarding a large selection of alternatives using easily identifiable factors (color, size, etc.) and by evaluating them using only a handful of possible outcomes (selection criteria).

> People faced with a large number of alternatives often opt for the least cognitive draining decision strategy: They don't make any decision at all!

People who face a large number of alternatives often opt for a decision strategy that is even less cognitively challenging than satisficing: They don't make any decision at all! In one study, grocery store customers saw one of two jam-tasting booths. Thirty percent of consumers who visited the booth displaying six types of jam purchased one of those products. In contrast, only 3 percent of customers who saw the booth displaying 24 types of jam made a purchase. The larger number of choices discouraged them from making any decision. Other studies revealed similar results in decisions about chocolates, term essays, and pension plan investment options.[39]

Evaluating Opportunities

Opportunities are just as important as problems, but the process of acting on an opportunity differs from the process of solving a problem. Decision makers seldom evaluate several alternatives when they find an opportunity; after all, the opportunity *is* the solution, so why look for others! An opportunity is usually experienced as an exciting and rare revelation, so decision makers tend to have an emotional attachment to the opportunity. Unfortunately, this emotional preference motivates decision makers to apply the opportunity and short-circuit any detailed assessment of its likely benefits. Furthermore, studies indicate that decision makers tend to personalize an opportunity (i.e., it belongs to them) rather than remain impartial evaluators of the opportunity. This ownership mindset makes impersonal analysis of the opportunity even more difficult.[40]

LO6-3 Discuss the roles of emotions and intuition in decision making.

EMOTIONS AND INTUITION IN DECISION MAKING

Emotions and Making Choices

The previous sections of this chapter explained why people are far from perfect at rational decision making. However, Herbert Simon and other scholars who studied imperfect rationality neglected to mention another problem: the rational choice model completely ignores the effect of emotions in human decision making. Just as both the rational and emotional brain centers alert us to problems, they also influence our choice of alternatives.[41] Emotions affect the evaluation of alternatives in three ways.

Emotions Form Early Preferences

The emotional marker process described earlier in this book (Chapters 3, 4, and 5) shapes our preferences for alternatives before we consciously evaluate them. Our brain very quickly attaches specific emotions to information about each alternative, and our preferred alternative is strongly influenced by those initial emotional markers.[42] Of course, logical analysis also influences which alternative we choose, but it requires strong logical evidence to change our initial preferences (initial emotional markers). Yet even logical analysis depends on emotions to sway our decision. Specifically, neuroscientific evidence says that information produced from logical analysis is tagged with emotional markers, and it is those emotional markers, not logical analysis, that motivate us to choose or avoid a particular alternative. In other words, emotions, not rational logic, energize us to make the preferred choice. In fact, people with damaged emotional brain centers have difficulty making choices.

Emotions Influence the Decision Evaluation Process

Moods and specific emotions influence the *process* of evaluating alternatives.[43] For instance, we pay more attention to details when in a negative mood, possibly because a negative mood signals that there is something wrong that requires careful scrutiny. When in a positive mood, on the other hand, we pay less attention to details and rely on a more programmed decision routine. This phenomenon explains why executive teams are often less vigilant about competitors and other environmental threats after they have experienced successful events.[44] Research also

Decision makers tend to pay more attention to details when in a negative mood, and are less vigilant about external threats when in a positive mood.
fizkes/Shutterstock

suggests that when angry, decision makers rely on stereotypes and other shortcuts to speed up the choice process. Anger also makes them more optimistic about the success of risky alternatives, whereas the emotion of fear tends to make them less optimistic. Overall, emotions shape *how* we evaluate information, not just which alternative we select.

Emotions Serve as Information When We Evaluate Alternatives The third way that emotions influence the evaluation of alternatives is through a process called "emotions as information." This refers to the idea that we listen in on our emotions to acquire guidance when making choices.[45] The emotions-as-information effect is similar to having a temporary improvement in emotional intelligence. Most emotional experiences remain below the level of conscious awareness, but people actively try to be more sensitive to these subtle emotions when making a decision.

When buying a new car, for example, you not only logically evaluate each vehicle's features; you also try to gauge your emotions when visualizing what it would be like to own each of the cars on your list of choices. Even when you have information about each vehicle (purchase price, fuel efficiency, maintenance costs, resale value, etc.), you are swayed by your emotional reaction and actively try to sense those emotional responses when thinking about the decision. Everyone pays attention to their emotions to some degree when choosing alternatives. This phenomenon ties directly into our next topic, intuition.

Intuition and Making Choices

Do you get a gut feeling when something isn't quite right? Or perhaps a different emotional experience occurs when you sense an opportunity? These emotional events potentially (but not necessarily) indicate your **intuition**—the ability to know when a problem or opportunity exists and to select the best course of action without conscious reasoning.[46] Some people pay more attention to their gut feelings, whereas others are more comfortable with decisions based on logic and data analysis. However, intuition and logical analysis are not opposites and never completely replace each other. Emotions are always present in human decision making.[47]

Intuition is both an emotional experience and a rapid nonconscious analytic process. The gut feelings we experience are emotional signals that have enough intensity to make us consciously aware of them. These signals warn us of impending danger or motivate us to take advantage of an opportunity. Some intuition also directs us to preferred choices relative to other alternatives in the situation.

All gut feelings are emotional signals, but not all emotional signals are intuition. Emotional signals are valid intuition when they rely on mental models that reasonably and accurately depict the situation where we sense the problem or opportunity. Intuition involves rapidly comparing our observations with these "templates of the mind." Positive or negative emotions are produced, depending on how well that situation fits our mental model.[48] For example, when chess masters quickly scan a chessboard, they experience emotional signals that the chess configuration poses an opportunity or threat. These emotional signals motivate closer observation to logically confirm the situation and to act on it. Thus, intuition signals that a problem or opportunity exists long before conscious rational analysis has occurred.

intuition the ability to know when a problem or opportunity exists and to select the best course of action without conscious reasoning

However, not all emotional signals are intuition because they are not always based on well-grounded mental models. Instead, we sometimes compare the current situation to more remote templates, which may or may not be relevant. A new employee might feel confident about relations with a supplier, whereas an experienced employee senses potential problems. The difference is that the new employee relies on poorly developed or more remote templates from other experiences that might not fit this situation. Thus, the extent to which our gut feelings in a situation represent intuition depends on our level of experience in that situation. The key message here is that some emotional signals are not intuition, so gut feelings alone shouldn't guide our decisions.

So far, we have described intuition as an emotional experience (gut feeling) and a process in which we compare the current situation with well-established templates of the mind. Intuition also relies on *action scripts* that speed up our response to pattern matches or mismatches.[49] Action scripts are programmed decisions; they shorten the decision-making process by jumping from problem identification to selection of a solution. Action scripts are also generic, so we need to consciously adapt them to the specific situation.

Making Choices More Effectively

It is very difficult to get around the human limitations of making choices, but a few strategies can minimize these problems. One important discovery is that decisions tend to have a higher success rate when leaders are more contemplative rather than decisive about the available options. Of course, decisions can also be ineffective when leaders procrastinate in decision making, but research indicates that a lack of logical evaluation of alternatives is a greater concern.

An associated recommendation is to rely on logical analysis, not just intuition (the latter of which dominates in decisive decisions). This advice does not suggest that you ignore intuition; rather, it should be considered only in combination with careful analysis of relevant information. By systematically assessing alternatives against relevant factors, decision makers minimize the implicit favorite and

Mc Graw Hill connect

SELF-ASSESSMENT 6.1: What is Your Preferred Decision-Making Style?

scenario planning a systematic process of thinking about alternative futures and what the organization should do to anticipate and react to those environments

escalation of commitment the tendency to repeat an apparently bad decision or allocate more resources to a failing course of action

self-enhancement a person's inherent motivation to have a positive self-concept (and to have others perceive him or her favorably), such as being competent, attractive, lucky, ethical, and important

prospect theory effect a natural tendency to feel more dissatisfaction from losing a particular amount than satisfaction from gaining an equal amount

satisficing problems that occur when they rely on general, subjective judgments.[51]

Another recommendation is to revisit important problems and opportunities at another time so information is reviewed when decision makers are in different moods and have allowed time for their initial emotions to subside. For example, if you sense that your team is feeling too confident when making an important decision, you might decide to have the committee revisit the decision a few days later when its members are thinking more critically.

Another strategy is **scenario planning**, which is a disciplined method for imagining possible futures.[52] It typically involves thinking about what would happen if a significant environmental condition changed and what the organization should do to anticipate and react to such an outcome. Scenario planning is a useful vehicle for choosing the best solutions under possible scenarios long before they occur, because alternative courses of action are evaluated without the pressure and emotions that occur during real emergencies.

OB THEORY TO PRACTICE

Making Choices More Effectively

- Be more contemplative than decisive for complex problems.
- Use intuition only in combination with logical analysis.
- Revisit decisions that were made when feeling overly positive and confident.
- Practice scenario planning.

IMPLEMENTING AND EVALUATING DECISIONS

Implementing Decisions

Implementing decisions is often skipped over in most writing about decision making. Yet leading business writers emphasize that execution—translating decisions into action—is one of the most important and challenging tasks in the decision-making process.[53] Implementing decisions is mainly about organizational change, which we discuss in Chapter 14, but also relates to motivation (Chapter 5), influence processes (Chapter 9), leadership (Chapter 11), and several other topics throughout this book.

Evaluating Decisions

Contrary to the rational choice view, decision makers aren't completely honest with themselves when evaluating the effectiveness of their decisions. Earlier in this chapter, we explained that decision makers engage in *confirmation bias* to support their implicit favorite and to maintain consistency in their preference and decision. This bias continues long after the decision has been made; during the evaluation stage it is also known as *postdecisional justification*.[54] Decision makers ignore or underemphasize negative outcomes of the choice they made and overemphasize new information about its positive features. Postdecisional justification gives people an excessively optimistic evaluation of their decisions, but only until they receive very clear and undeniable information to the contrary.

Intuition versus Data Analysis: Crunch Your Hunch[50]

63% of 1,048 U.S. senior managers do not believe their companies are analytics-driven.

78% of 250 senior business leaders in Canada agree or somewhat agree that a business leader must go with his or her gut and intuition when an important decision needs to be made quickly.

46% of 3,750 U.S. and European knowledge workers believe that business decisions are made based on data.

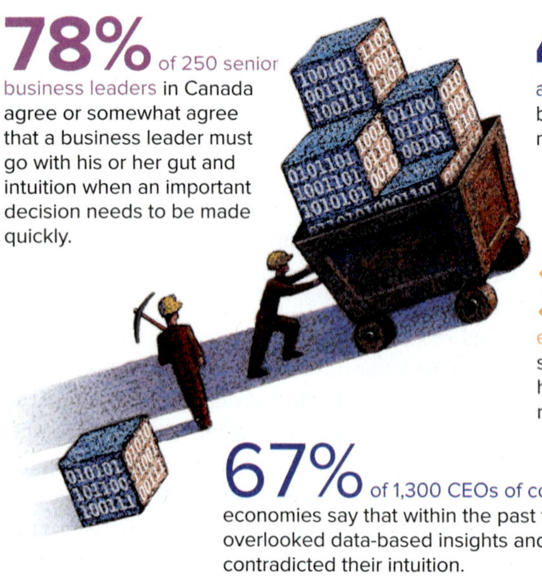

39% of 2,106 senior executives surveyed globally say their decision making is highly data driven (8% say it is rarely data-driven).

67% of 1,300 CEOs of companies in the 11 largest economies say that within the past three years they have overlooked data-based insights and models because they contradicted their intuition.

(photo): Jonathan Evans/Photographer's Choice RF/Getty Images

Escalation of Commitment

Another reason decision makers don't evaluate their decisions very well is due to **escalation of commitment**—the tendency to repeat an apparently bad decision or allocate more resources to a failing course of action.[55] Why are decision makers led deeper and deeper into failing projects? Several explanations have been identified and discussed over the years, but the four main influences are self-justification effect, self-enhancement effect, prospect theory effect, and sunk costs effect.

Self-Justification Effect People try to convey a positive public image of themselves. In decision making, this self-justification typically involves appearing to be rational and competent. Decision makers are therefore motivated to demonstrate that their choices will be successful, which includes continuing to support a decision even when it is not having the desired outcomes. In contrast, pulling the plug symbolizes the project's failure and the decision maker's incompetence. This self-justification effect is particularly evident when decision makers are personally identified with the project, have staked their reputations to some extent on the project's success, and have low self-esteem.[56]

Self-Enhancement Effect People have a natural tendency to feel good about themselves—to feel luckier, more competent, and more successful than average—regarding things that are important to them (see Chapter 3).[57] This **self-enhancement** supports a positive self-concept, but it also increases the risk of escalation of commitment. When presented with evidence that a project is in trouble, self-enhancement biases our interpretation of the information as a temporary aberration from an otherwise positive trend line. And when we eventually realize that the project isn't going as well as planned, we continue to invest in the project because our self-enhancement overestimates the probability that we can rescue the project. Self-justification and self-enhancement often occur together, but they are different mechanisms. Self-justification is a deliberate attempt to maintain a favorable public image, whereas self-enhancement nonconsciously distorts our perceptions so problems are recognized later and our probabilities of success are biased so we continue to invest in the losing project.[58]

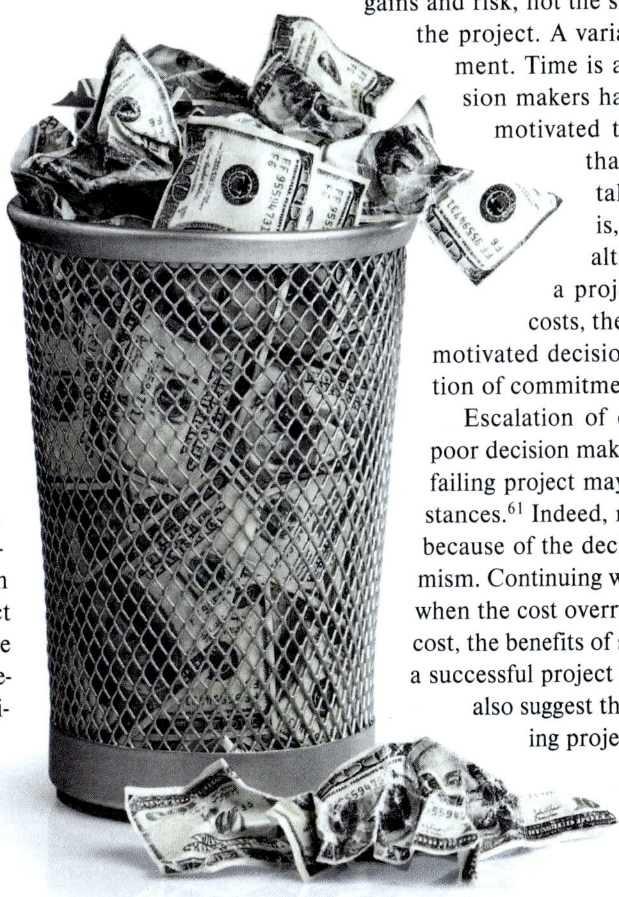

Escalation of commitment occurs partly because people are motivated to invest resources in projects with high sunk costs (large amounts already spent), whereas they should consider only the additional investment's expected future gains.
pogonici/Shutterstock

Prospect Theory Effect **Prospect theory effect** is the tendency to experience stronger negative emotions when losing something of value than positive emotions when gaining something of equal value. This is also known as *loss aversion* because we have a stronger motivation to avoid losses than to risk receiving equally valuable gains. The stronger negative valence of a potential loss motivates escalation of commitment because stopping a project is a certain loss, which evokes more negative emotions to most people than the uncertainty of success associated with continuing to fund the project. Given the choice, decision makers choose escalation of commitment, which is the less painful option at the time.[59]

Sunk Costs Effect People inherently feel motivated to invest more resources in projects that have high sunk costs—the value of resources already invested in the decision.[60] This contrasts with the rational choice view, which states that investing resources should be determined by expected future gains and risk, not the size of earlier resources invested in the project. A variation of sunk costs is time investment. Time is a resource, so the more time decision makers have devoted to a project, the more motivated they are to continue investing in that project. Finally, sunk costs can take the form of closing costs, that is, the financial or nonfinancial penalties associated with shutting down a project. As with other forms of sunk costs, the higher the closing costs, the more motivated decision makers are to engage in escalation of commitment.

Escalation of commitment is usually framed as poor decision making, but adding more resources to a failing project may be beneficial under some circumstances.[61] Indeed, many breakthroughs have occurred because of the decision maker's persistence and optimism. Continuing with a losing project may be prudent when the cost overruns are small relative to the project cost, the benefits of success are high, and the rewards of a successful project are received quickly. Some experts also suggest that throwing more money into a failing project is sometimes a logical attempt to further understand an ambiguous situation. By adding more resources, the decision maker gains new information about the project's development, which provides more feedback about the project's future success. This strategy is particularly common where the project has high closing costs.

creativity the development of original ideas that make a socially recognized contribution

divergent thinking reframing a problem in a unique way and generating different approaches to the issue

Evaluating Decision Outcomes More Effectively

There are several ways to evaluate decisions with less bias.[62] Self-justification effect is minimized by ensuring that the people who made the original decision are not the same people who later evaluate that decision. A second strategy is to publicly establish a preset level at which the decision is abandoned or reevaluated. This action forces the decision maker to abandon the investment if its value falls or cost overruns increase too much, although determining the best stop loss point can be difficult.

Third, decision evaluators should seek out factual and social feedback about the project. Even the strongest escalation and confirmation bias effects collapse when the decision maker is faced with systematic and clear feedback about the project's failings. In addition, decision evaluators can become aware of problems earlier by seeking ongoing feedback from several (preferably impartial) people. Finally, recent evidence suggests that decision evaluators are less likely to engage in escalation of commitment if they change their mindset away from the negative consequences of project failure and focus more on future opportunities to grow the business.

OB THEORY TO PRACTICE

Evaluating Decision Outcomes More Effectively

- *Change the decision maker*. Ensure that the decision evaluators are not the same people who made the decision.
- *Create a stop-loss*. Publicly establish a preset level at which the decision is abandoned or reevaluated.
- *Seek out factual and social feedback*. Develop accessible sources of systematic and clear evidence about the project's development, and receive ongoing feedback about the project from several (preferably impartial) people.
- *Change the decision evaluator's mindset*. Apply interventions that refocus decision evaluator's away from the negative emotions of past financial losses and toward the positive emotions of future growth opportunities.

LO6-4 Describe employee characteristics, workplace conditions, and specific activities that support creativity.

CREATIVITY

The entire decision-making process described over the preceding pages depends on **creativity**—the development of original ideas that make a socially recognized contribution.[63] Creativity enables us to imagine opportunities, such as discovering new products or services, or recognizing problems that are not easily apparent from traditional perspectives. It helps us to develop and choose alternatives by visualizing the future in different ways and figuring out how each choice might be useful or a liability in those scenarios. In short, creativity is valuable throughout the decision-making process.

The Creative Process

How does creativity occur? That question has puzzled experts for centuries and has fascinated scientists who saw how creative thinking led to their own important discoveries. Notably, more than a century ago, German physicist Hermann von Helmholtz gave a public talk in which he described the process that led to his innovations (energy physics, instruments for examining eyes, and many others). A few decades later, London School of Economics professor Graham Wallas built on Helmholtz's ideas to construct the four-stage model shown in Exhibit 6.4.[64] To this day, this model is still considered the most elegant representation of the creative process.

The first stage is *preparation*—the process of investigating the problem or opportunity. Preparation involves developing a clear understanding of what you are trying to achieve through a novel solution and then actively studying information seemingly related to the topic. It is a process of developing knowledge and possibly skills about the topic. The second stage, called *incubation*, is the period of reflective thought. We put the problem aside, but our mind is still working on it in the background.[65] The important condition here is to maintain a low-level awareness by frequently revisiting the problem.

Incubation assists **divergent thinking**—reframing the problem in a unique way and generating different approaches to the issue. Divergent thinking breaks us away from existing mental models so that we can apply concepts or processes from completely different areas of life. This contrasts with *convergent thinking*, which involves calculating the conventionally accepted "right answer" to a logical problem.

Illumination (also called *insight*), the third stage of creativity, refers to the experience of suddenly becoming aware of a unique idea.[66] Wallas and others suggest that this stage begins with a "fringe" awareness before the idea fully enters our consciousness. Illumination is often visually depicted as a lightbulb, but a better image would be a flash of

McGraw Hill connect

SELF-ASSESSMENT 6.2: How Well Do You Engage in Divergent Thinking?

Exhibit 6.4 The Creative Process Model

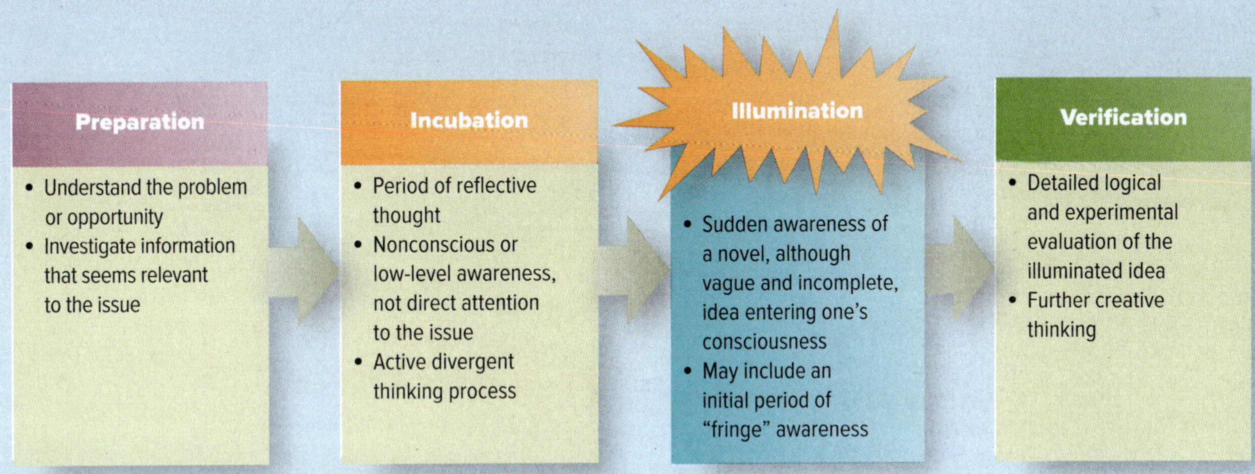

Source: Based on G. Wallas, *The Art of Thought* (London: Jonathan Cape, 1926), Chap. 4.

light or perhaps a briefly flickering candle—these bits of inspiration are fleeting and can be quickly lost if not documented. For this reason, many creative people keep a journal or notebook nearby so they can jot down their ideas before they disappear. Also, flickering ideas don't keep a particular schedule; they might come to you at any time of day or night.

Illumination presents ideas that are usually vague, roughly drawn, and untested. Therefore, the essential final stage of creativity is *verification*, whereby we flesh out the illuminated ideas and subject them to detailed experimentation and evaluation. This stage often calls for further creativity as the ideas evolve into finished products or services. Thus, although verification is labeled the final stage of creativity, it is really the beginning of a long process of creative decision making toward development of an innovative product or service.

Characteristics of Creative People

Everyone is creative, but some people have a higher potential for creativity. Four of the main characteristics that give individuals more creative potential are intelligence, persistence, knowledge and experience, and a cluster of personality traits and values representing independent imagination (see Exhibit 6.5).

- *Cognitive and practical intelligence.* Creative people have above-average intelligence to synthesize information, analyze ideas, and apply their ideas.[67] They recognize the significance of small bits of information and are able to connect them in ways that few others can imagine. They also have *practical intelligence*—the capacity to evaluate the potential usefulness of their ideas.
- *Persistence.* Creative people have persistence, which is based on a high need for achievement, a strong motivation from the task itself, and a moderate or higher self-esteem. Persistence is vital because people need this motivation to continue working on and investing in a project in spite of failures and advice from others to quit. In fact, human beings have a general tendency to dismiss or criticize new ideas, so creative people need persistence to withstand these negative social forces.[68]
- *Knowledge and experience.* Creative people require a foundation of knowledge and experience to discover or acquire new knowledge.[69] However, this expertise is a double-edged sword. As individuals acquire specific knowledge and experience, their mental models about that topic tend to become more rigid. They are less adaptable to new information or rules about that knowledge domain. Some writers suggest that expertise also increases "mindless behavior" because expertise reduces the tendency to question why things happen.[70] To overcome the limitations of expertise, some corporate leaders like to hire people from other industries and specializations.
- *Independent imagination.* Creative people possess a cluster of personality traits and values that support an independent imagination: high openness to experience, moderately low need for affiliation, and strong values around self-direction and stimulation.[71] Openness to experience is a Big Five personality dimension representing the extent to which a person is imaginative, curious, sensitive, open-minded, and original (see Chapter 2). Creative people have a moderately low need for affiliation so they are less embarrassed when making mistakes. Self-direction includes the values of creativity and independent thought; stimulation includes the values of excitement and challenge. Together, these values form openness to change—representing the motivation to pursue innovative ways (see Chapter 2).

McGraw Hill connect

SELF-ASSESSMENT 6.3: Do You Have a Creative Personality?

Exhibit 6.5 Characteristics of Creative People

Characteristics of Creative People

Independent Imagination
- High openness to experience
- Moderately low need for affiliation
- Strong self-direction value
- Strong stimulation value

Cognitive and Practical Intelligence
- Ability to synthesize, analyze, and apply ideas
- Ability to evaluate potential usefulness of ideas

Knowledge and Experience
- Prerequisite knowledge and experience
- Not locked into a fixed knowledge mindset

Persistence
- High need for achievement
- Strong task motivation
- Moderately high self-esteem and optimism

Organizational Conditions Supporting Creativity

Intelligence, persistence, expertise, and independent imagination represent a person's creative potential, but the extent to which these characteristics produce more creative output depends on how well the work environment supports the creative process.[72] Several job and workplace characteristics have been identified in the literature, and different combinations of situations can equally support creativity; there isn't one best work environment.

One of the most important conditions for creativity is a **learning orientation**.[74] A learning orientation is a set of collective beliefs

The Creativity Challenge[73]

44% of U.S. federal government employees say that creativity and innovation are rewarded in their department or agency (increased every year from 37% five years earlier).

58% of 2,010 American knowledge workers in large firms say they are so swamped getting day-to-day work done that they don't have time for creative thinking.

39% of 164,000 workers across 28 countries say their ideal work environment has a culture of innovation and creativity where the status quo is challenged.

61% of 16,571 American employees agree or strongly agree that they are expected to be creative or think of new ways of doing things at work.

27% of 2,606 U.S. workers polled say their organization does nothing to encourage employee creativity (support employee curiosity).

89% of 482 executives surveyed across several countries agree that for a business to be successful, new ideas must come from everyone (senior executives to frontline employees).

(photo): ImageFlow/Shutterstock

learning orientation a set of collective beliefs and norms that encourage people to question past practices, learn new ideas, experiment putting ideas into practice, and view mistakes as part of the learning process

and norms that encourage employees to question past practices, to learn new ideas, to experiment putting ideas into practice, and to view mistakes as part of the learning process. Job characteristics, specifically task significance and autonomy, also contribute to creativity. People are more creative when they believe their work improves the organization or society and when they have the freedom to pursue novel ideas without bureaucratic delays.[75] Creativity is about changing things, and change is possible only when employees have autonomy and the authority to experiment.

Along with a learning orientation and enriched jobs, creativity blossoms through open communication (enabling employees to share ideas and information) and sufficient resources. Organizations also nurture creativity by providing a comfortable degree of job security, which explains why creativity suffers during times of downsizing and corporate restructuring.[76] Some companies also support creativity by designing nontraditional workspaces, such as unique building design or unconventional office areas.[77]

To some degree, creativity also improves with support from leaders and coworkers.[78] Generally, creativity thrives when leaders have an appealing vision of the future and encourage employees to experiment with new ways to achieve that vision (see transformational leadership in Chapter 11). Coworker support can improve creativity, but a few studies suggest that competition among coworkers improves creativity under some conditions. Similarly, it isn't clear how much pressure should be exerted on employees to produce creative ideas. Extreme time pressures are well-known creativity inhibitors, but lack of pressure doesn't seem to produce the highest creativity, either.

Activities That Encourage Creativity

We have described two cornerstones of creativity in organizations: employing people with strong creative potential and providing a work environment that supports creativity. The third cornerstone is activities that help employees think more creatively. Four types of creativity-building activities are: redefine the problem, associative play, cross-pollination, and design thinking.

Redefine the Problem Redefining the problem is a potentially powerful way to unleash creative thinking. One approach is to revisit projects that have been set aside. After a period of neglect, these projects might be seen in new ways.[79] You can also see the problem from different perspectives by asking coworkers unfamiliar with the issue to explore the problem. You state the objectives and give some facts and then let the other person ask questions to further understand the situation. By verbalizing the problem, listening to questions, and hearing what others think, you are more likely to form new perspectives on the issue.[80]

Associative Play Associative play literally involves playing games or being challenged in unusual ways.[81] One form of associative play is to engage in playful activities, particularly with unusual twists to the traditional equipment or rules. Creative thinking emerges naturally from these playful activities and then carries over to work-related problem solving. A second variation is challenging participants to create something new with a specific purpose (e.g., cleaning cutlery) using existing unrelated products (e.g., blow dryer and electric toothbrush). These activities exercise the mind to break out of traditional mental models about existing products and services.

A third variation of associative play, called *morphological analysis*, involves systematically investigating all combinations of characteristics of a product, service, or event, and then looking at the feasibility of each combination.[82] This exercise encourages people to carefully examine combinations that initially seem nonsensical. For instance, employees at a dairy company might look at all combinations of yogurt-based products by considering the contents (fruit, low fat, etc.), occasion (breakfast, dessert, etc.), target group (children, older adults, etc.), size, and packaging. A novel, yet commercially successful, innovation may emerge from the resulting list.

Cross-Pollination Cross-pollination occurs when people from different areas of the organization exchange ideas or when new people are brought into an existing team.[83] This may occur by arranging formal social gatherings, encouraging happenstance interactions with people from other work areas or, as a few firms do, asking employees to move their desks every few months to another location with employees who are only acquaintances. Cross-pollination highlights the fact that creativity rarely occurs alone. Some creative people may be individualistic, but most creative ideas are generated through teams and informal social interaction.

Along with hiring people with strong creative potential and providing a work environment that supports creativity, companies rely on activities that stimulate creative thinking.
Olena Yakobchuk/Shutterstock

Exhibit 6.6 Four Rules of Design Thinking

Design Thinking Rule	Description
Human rule	• Involve several people so the issue and possible solutions are viewed from several angles. • Include clients and end users to enable an iterative process of problem identification and solution development.
Ambiguity rule	• Preserve ambiguity rather than seek clarity too quickly. • Question and refine the stated problem. • Develop more than one solution to the problem.
Re-design rule	• Review past solutions to understand how those inventions tried to satisfy human needs. • Use foresight tools to imagine better solutions for the future.
Tangible rule	• Build several low-cost prototypes to test ideas. • Don't analyze alternatives at a purely conceptual level. • Tolerate failure; embrace a learning orientation.

Source: Based on information in C. Meinel and L. Leifer, "Introduction—Design Thinking Is Mainly about Building Innovators," in *Design Thinking Research: Building Innovators*, ed. H. Plattner, C. Meinel, and L. Leifer (Cham, Switzerland: Springer International, 2015), 1–11.

Design Thinking **Design thinking** is a human-centered, solution-focused creative process that applies both intuition and analytical thinking to clarify problems and generate innovative solutions. It is a framework with four sets of practices to improve creativity and development of new products and services (see Exhibit 6.6).[84]

The Human Rule emphasizes the need for collaboration and empathy with several stakeholders who bring diverse knowledge and experiences so the issue and its possible solutions are viewed from several angles. The Ambiguity Rule identifies the need to continually question possible solutions and to avoid defining the problem too early in the process. The Re-design Rule highlights the need to understand and learn from past solutions as well as to notice trends that might guide possible future states. The Tangible Rule encourages design thinkers to spend more time trying out ideas with low-cost prototypes, rather than analyzing those ideas at a purely conceptual level. It calls for "fail fast, fail often," meaning that prototypes are made quickly and frequently along the journey to the final result.

LO6-5 Describe the benefits of employee involvement and identify four contingencies that affect the optimal level of employee involvement.

EMPLOYEE INVOLVEMENT IN DECISION MAKING

Employee involvement refers to situations in which employees participate in and influence decisions about their jobs, work units, or organization.[85] This involvement is more than just giving workers a voice in decisions; it exists when they actually influence decisions to some degree. There are several levels of employee involvement.[86] A low level of involvement occurs when employees are individually asked for specific information but the problem is not described to them. Somewhat higher involvement occurs when the problem is described and employees are asked individually or collectively for information relating to that problem.

Moving further up the involvement scale, the problem is described to employees, who are collectively given responsibility for developing recommendations. However, the decision maker is not bound to accept those recommendations. At the highest level of involvement, the entire decision-making process is handed over to employees. They identify the problem, discover alternative solutions, choose the best alternative, and implement that choice.

Employee involvement potentially improves problem identification, the number and quality of solutions generated, the evaluation of alternatives, and employee commitment to implementing the selected solution.
stockbroker/123RF

The original decision maker serves only as a facilitator to guide the team's decision process and keep everyone on track.

Benefits of Employee Involvement

For the past half century, organizational behavior experts have advised that employee involvement potentially improves organizational decision making.[87] To begin with, it improves the identification of problems and opportunities. Employees are, in many respects, the sensors of the organization's environment. When the organization's activities misalign with customer expectations, employees are usually the first to know. Employee involvement provides a conduit for organizational leaders to be alerted to such problems. Employee involvement can also potentially improve the number and quality of solutions generated. In a well-managed meeting, team members create synergy by pooling their knowledge to form new alternatives. In other words, several people working together can potentially generate better solutions than the same people working alone.

A third benefit of employee involvement is that, under specific conditions, it improves the evaluation of alternatives. Numerous studies on participative decision making, task conflict, and team dynamics have found that involvement brings out more diverse perspectives, tests ideas, and provides more valuable knowledge, all of which help the decision maker select the best alternative.[88] A mathematical theorem introduced in 1785 by the Marquis de Condorcet states that the alternative selected by the team's majority is more likely to be correct than is the alternative selected by any team member individually.[89]

design thinking a human-centered, solution-focused creative process that applies both intuition and analytical thinking to clarify problems and generate innovative solutions

Along with improving decision quality, involvement tends to strengthen employee commitment to the decision. Rather than viewing themselves as agents of someone else's decision, those who participate in a decision feel personally responsible for its success. Involvement also has positive effects on employee motivation, satisfaction, and turnover. Furthermore, it increases skill variety, felt autonomy, and task identity, all of which increase job enrichment and potentially employee motivation. Participation is also a critical practice in organizational change because employees are more motivated to implement the decision and less likely to resist changes resulting from the decision.[91]

Contingencies of Employee Involvement

If employee involvement is so wonderful, why don't leaders leave all decisions to employees? The answer is that the optimal level of employee involvement depends on the situation. The employee involvement model shown in Exhibit 6.7 lists four contingencies: decision structure, source of decision knowledge, decision commitment, and risk of conflict in the decision process.[93]

- *Decision structure.* At the beginning of this chapter, we learned that some decisions are programmed whereas others are nonprogrammed. Programmed decisions are less likely to need employee involvement because the solutions are already worked out from past incidents. In other words, the benefits of employee involvement increase with the novelty and complexity of the problem or opportunity.
- *Source of decision knowledge.* Subordinates should be involved in some level of decision making when the leader lacks sufficient knowledge and subordinates have additional information to improve decision quality. In many cases, employees are closer to customers and production activities, so they often know where the company can save money, improve product or service quality, and realize opportunities. This is particularly true for complex decisions where employees are more likely to possess relevant information.
- *Decision commitment.* Participation tends to improve employee commitment to the decision. If employees are unlikely to accept a decision made without their involvement, some level of participation is usually necessary.

> **Tell me and I will forget; show me and I will remember; involve me and I will understand.[90]**
>
> —Variation of a proverb by Chinese Confucian philosopher Xun Kuang

OB THEORY TO PRACTICE

High Involvement in IBM's Cognitive Build[92]

Watson, IBM's cognitive technology platform, received a substantial boost when the company launched Cognitive Build, a three-month event that relied on various forms of employee involvement to determine how Watson's artificial intelligence can assist a myriad of corporate and societal objectives. More than 8,000 teams of IBM employees explored the technology's application for data security, air quality monitoring, anti-bullying, social banking, and other themes. One-third of those teams progressed to Cognitive Build's next stage of a completed proposal with some prototyping. IBM employees each received $2,000 in virtual money through the company's internal funding system to "invest" in one or more projects. In effect, they voted on the best projects. The 50 teams with the most virtual investment dollars were given three weeks to build their prototypes, which were then presented to a panel of experts.

Exhibit 6.7 Model of Employee Involvement in Decision Making

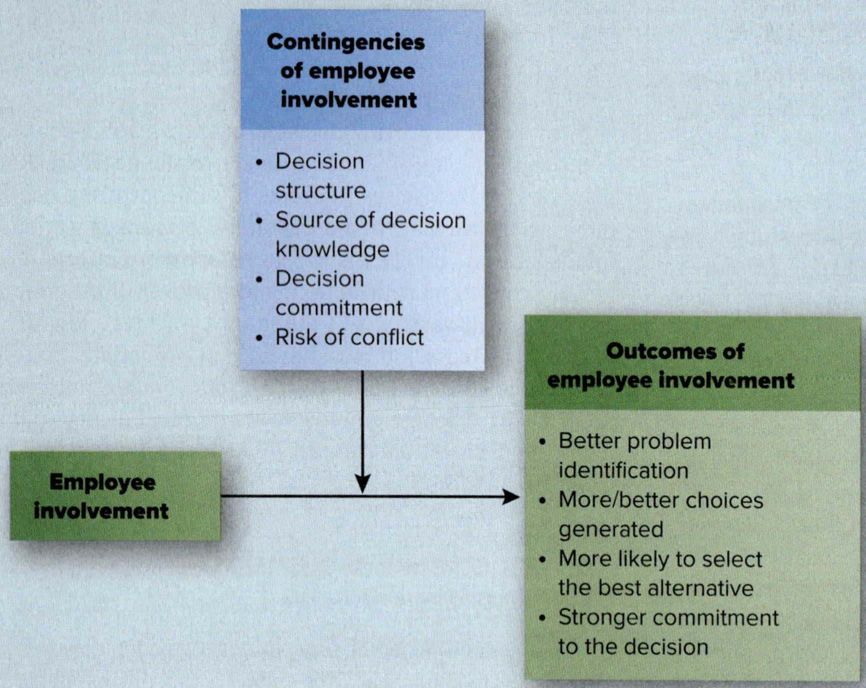

- *Risk of conflict.* Two types of conflict undermine the benefits of employee involvement. First, if employee goals and norms conflict with the organization's goals, only a low level of employee involvement is advisable. Second, the degree of involvement depends on whether employees will agree with one another on the preferred solution. If conflict is likely to occur, high involvement (i.e., employees make the decision) would be difficult to achieve.

Employee involvement is an important component of the decision-making process. To make the best decisions, we need to involve people who have valuable information and who will be more motivated to implement the decision. Employee involvement is a formative stage of team dynamics, so it carries many of the benefits and challenges of working in teams. The next chapter provides a closer look at team dynamics, including processes for making decisions in teams.

Study Checklist

Connect® is available for *M Organizational Behavior*. Additional resources include:

✓ Exercises:

- **Case Analysis:** Apply concepts within the context of a real-world situation.
- **Click and Drag:** Helps make the connection between theory and application through matching, ranking, or grouping activities.
- **Video Case:** See management in action through interactive videos.
- **Self-Assessment:** Designed to promote student self-awareness and reflection, these research-based surveys contain detailed feedback for students.
- **Application-Based Activities:** These highly interactive, application- and analysis-based exercises allow students to take on specific roles to complete management-related tasks within a real-world context.

✓ **SmartBook 2.0™**—Smartbook 2.0 is an adaptive learning solution that provides personalized learning to individual student needs, continually adapts to pinpoint knowledge gaps and focuses learning on concepts requiring additional study. It fosters more productive learning, takes the guesswork out of what to study, and helps students better prepare for class.

Notes

1. L. Hayes, "You're Too Creative to Be an Engineer—and Other Myths . . . ," *Huffington Post (UK)*, October 5, 2016; "Aurecon Appoints Maureen Thurston," news release (Sydney: Aurecon, February 16, 2016); O. Fair, "How to Train Your Dragon," *justimagine*, Aurecon, September 5, 2017, https://justimagine.aurecongroup.com; "Liam Hayes: A Human-Centric HR Leader," *Human Resources Director Australia*, January 9, 2018.
2. F.A. Shull Jr., A.L. Delbecq, and L.L. Cummings, *Organizational Decision Making* (New York: McGraw-Hill, 1970), 31.
3. S.R. Covey, *The Wisdom and Teachings of Stephen R. Covey* (New York: Free Press, 2012).
4. Harvard Business School, *Decision Making: 5 Steps to Better Results* (Cambridge, MA: Harvard Business School Press 2006), Chap. 1; D. Baltzly, "Stoicism" (*Stanford Encyclopedia of Philosophy*, 2008), http://plato.stanford.edu/entries/stoicism/ (accessed March 30, 2008); I. Pownall, *Effective Management Decision Making* (Holstebro, DK: Ventus Publishing, 2012), Chap. 1; C.P. Webel, *The Politics of Rationality: Reason through Occidental History* (New York: Routledge, 2014), Chaps. 1 and 3.

5. J.G. March and H.A. Simon, *Organizations* (New York: Wiley, 1958); K. Manktelow, *Thinking and Reasoning: An Introduction to the Psychology of Reason, Judgment and Decision Making* (Hoboken, NJ: Taylor & Francis, 2012), Chap. 8. Recent neuroscience theory and research suggest that the calculation of probabilities and valences for each alternative is an iterative process of repeatedly sampling memory and available information (because, in reality, information isn't perfect) until the decision maker is sufficiently confident in the estimated composite valence of each choice. See: J.W. Kable and P.W. Glimcher, "The Neurobiology of Decision: Consensus and Controversy," *Neuron* 63, no. 6 (2009): 733–45, https://doi.org/10.1016/j.neuron.2009.09.003; S.B.M. Yoo and B.Y. Hayden, "Economic Choice as an Untangling of Options into Actions," *Neuron* 99, no. 3 (2018): 434–47, https://doi.org/10.1016/j.neuron.2018.06.038; R.G. O'Connell et al., "Bridging Neural and Computational Viewpoints on Perceptual Decision-Making," *Trends in Neurosciences* 41, no. 11 (2018): 838–52, https://doi.org/10.1016/j.tins.2018.06.005.

6. This example differs from the game theory model in classic economic theory. In classic economic theory, the "outcomes" are alternatives, so the probabilities must add up to 1.0. For example, if there is a 30 percent probability that your company will choose supplier A, then there is necessarily a 70 percent chance that the company will choose supplier B (if those are the only choices). The current example, which is much more relevant to business decisions, differs because it calculates each alternative's composite valence from a set of criteria (outcomes) associated with all alternatives. These probabilities do not add up to 1.0 because they refer to entities that are not perfectly correlated (e.g., both suppliers might have a high probability of offering low prices).

7. These criteria are commonly used in supplier selection modeling. See, for example, H. Karimi and A. Rezaeinia, "Supplier Selection Using Revised Multi-Segment Goal Programming Model," *International Journal of Advanced Manufacturing Technology* 70, no. 5/8 (2014): 1227–34.

8. This model is adapted from several sources, including H.A. Simon, *The New Science of Management Decision* (New York: Harper & Row, 1960); H. Mintzberg, D. Raisinghani, and A. Théorêt, "The Structure of 'Unstructured' Decision Processes," *Administrative Science Quarterly* 21 (1976): 246–75; W.C. Wedley and R.H.G. Field, "A Predecision Support System," *Academy of Management Review* 9 (1984): 696–703.

9. P.F. Drucker, *The Practice of Management* (New York: Harper & Brothers, 1954), 353–57; B.M. Bass, *Organizational Decision Making* (Homewood, IL: Irwin, 1983), Chap. 3; H.E. Posen et al., "Renewing Research on Problemistic Search–A Review and Research Agenda," *Academy of Management Annals* 12, no. 1 (2017): 208–51.

10. L.R. Beach and T.R. Mitchell, "A Contingency Model for the Selection of Decision Strategies," *Academy of Management Review* 3 (1978): 439–49; I.L. Janis, *Crucial Decisions* (New York: Free Press, 1989), 35–37; W. Zhongtuo, "Meta-Decision Making: Concepts and Paradigm," *Systematic Practice and Action Research* 13, no. 1 (2000): 111–15; Y.-L. Boureau, P. Sokol-Hessner, and N.D. Daw, "Deciding How To Decide: Self-Control and Meta-Decision Making," *Trends in Cognitive Sciences* 19, no. 11 (2015): 700–710.

11. J. de Jonge, *Rethinking Rational Choice Theory: A Companion on Rational and Moral Action* (Basingstoke, UK: Palgrave Macmillan, 2011).

12. There are a few variations of this quotation, and no direct evidence that Einstein actually offered this advice. Among the earliest citations is a similar quotation allegedly uttered by the head of industrial engineering at Yale University in the 1940s or 1950s. See R.E. Finley and H.R. Ziobro, eds., *The Manufacturing Man and His Job* (New York: American Management Association, 1966), 18; "I Would Spend 55 Minutes Defining the Problem and Then Five Minutes Solving It–Quote Investigator," accessed April 17, 2019, https://quoteinvestigator.com/2014/05/22/solve/.

13. M.A. Roberto, *Know What You Don't Know: How Great Leaders Prevent Problems before They Happen* (Saddle River, NJ: Wharton School Publishing, 2009); M. Meckler and K. Boal, "Decision Errors, Organizational Iatrogenesis and Errors of the 7th Kind," *Academy of Management Perspectives*, October 15, 2018, https://doi.org/10.5465/amp.2017.0144.

14. M.S. Gary and R.E. Wood, "Mental Models, Decision Rules, and Performance Heterogeneity," *Strategic Management Journal* 32, no. 6 (2011): 569–94, https://doi.org/10.1002/smj.899.

15. P. Rosenthal, "NBC Executive Stands Apart by Taking Stands," *Chicago Tribune*, August 21, 2005; L. Mellor, "Seinfeld's Journey from Flop to Acclaimed Hit," *Den of Geek* (London, November 7, 2014), http://www.denofgeek.com (accessed March 6, 2018); S. Austerlitz, "How 'Seinfeld' Revolutionized the Sitcom," *IndieWire* (February 28, 2014), http://www.indiewire.com (accessed March 7, 2018); N.J. Nigro, *Seinfeld FAQ: Everything Left to Know about the Show about Nothing* (Milwaukee: Applause Theatre and Cinema Books, 2015); A. Grant, *Originals: How Non-Conformists Change the World* (New York: Viking, 2016), 44–46.

16. P.C. Nutt, *Why Decisions Fail* (San Francisco: Berrett-Koehler, 2002); S. Finkelstein, *Why Smart Executives Fail* (New York: Viking, 2003); G. Bhardwaj et al., "Alleviating the Plunging-In Bias, Elevating Strategic Problem-Solving," *Academy of Management Learning & Education* 17, no. 3 (September 2018): 279–301, https://doi.org/10.5465/amle.2017.0168.

17. P.C. Nutt, "Framing Strategic Decisions," *Organization Science* 9, no. 2 (1998): 195–216; S. Kaplan, "Framing Contests: Strategy Making Under Uncertainty," *Organization Science* 19, no. 5 (2008): 729–52.

18. M. Hock and H.W. Krohne, "Coping with Threat and Memory for Ambiguous Information: Testing the Repressive Discontinuity Hypothesis," *Emotion* 4, no. 1 (2004): 65–86; J. Brandtstadter, A. Voss, and K. Rothermund, "Perception of Danger Signals: The Role of Control," *Experimental Psychology* 51, no. 1 (2004): 24–32.

19. E. Witte, "Field Research on Complex Decision-Making Processes–The Phase Theorum," *International Studies of Management and Organization*, no. 56 (1972): 156–82; J.A. Bargh and T.L. Chartrand, "The Unbearable Automaticity of Being," *American Psychologist* 54, no. 7 (1999): 462–79.

20. A.H. Maslow, *The Psychology of Science: A Reconnaissance* (Chapel Hill, NC: Maurice Bassett Publishing, 2002).

21. Various sources suggest that the phrase "divine discontent" may have originated with unspecified writing by either of the poets John Milton (1608–1674) or Alexander Pope (1688–1744). Alternatively, it may have been inspired later based on John Stuart Mill's famous quotation in *Utilitarianism* (1863): "It is better to be a human being dissatisfied than a pig satisfied; better to be Socrates dissatisfied than a fool satisfied." Divine discontent became a particularly popular phrase during a couple of decades from the 1890s. It appeared in various books (e.g., Robert Bury, *The Symposium of Plato*, 1909, xlii) as well as in articles in a wide array of magazines and newspapers, including *The Athenaeum Journal* (1896), *Punch Magazine* (1894), *Edinburgh Review* (1900), and frequently in *The Independent* (New York). The phrase is commonly used in reference to the valuable effect of education on the mind (see, e.g., J.L. Spalding, *Education and the Higher Life*, 1900, 167; M. Mead, *Male and Female*, 1949, 160).

22. H.A. Simon, *Administrative Behavior*, 2nd ed. (New York: Free Press, 1957); H.A. Simon, "Rational Decision Making in Business Organizations," *American Economic Review* 69, no. 4 (1979): 493–513; M. Cristofaro, "Herbert Simon's Bounded Rationality: Its Historical Evolution in Management and Cross-Fertilizing Contribution," *Journal of Management History* 23, no. 2 (2017): 170–90.

23. Here are a few of the prominent studies among the dozens that demonstrate imperfect rationality in decision making: E. Witte, N. Joost, and A.L. Thimm, "Field Research on Complex Decision-Making Processes–The Phase Theorem," *International Studies of Management & Organization* 2, no. 2 (1972): 156–82; H. Mintzberg, D. Raisinghani, and A. Théorêt, "The Structure of 'Unstructured' Decision Processes," *Administrative Science Quarterly* 21, no. 2 (1976): 246–75, https://doi.org/10.2307/2392045; T. Gilovich, D. Griffin, and D. Kahneman, *Heuristics and Biases: The Psychology of Intuitive Judgment* (Cambridge: Cambridge University Press, 2002); S. Finkelstein, *Why Smart Executives Fail: And What You Can Learn from Their Mistakes* (New York: Penguin, 2004).

24. M.D. Cohen, J.G. March, and J.P. Olsen, "A Garbage Can Model of Organizational Choice," *Administrative Science Quarterly* 17, no. 1 (1972): 1–25; R.A. Ferrer, E. Orehek, and L.S. Padgett, "Goal Conflict when Making Decisions for Others," *Journal of Experimental Social Psychology* 78 (2018): 93–103.

25. H.A. Simon, *Administrative Behavior*, 2nd ed. (New York: Free Press, 1957), xxv, 80–84.

26. L.J. Peter, *Peter's Almanac* (New York: Morrow, 1982).

27. Current researchers refer to implicit favorite as "predecision information distortion" and the "coherence effect," but these theories are essentially implicit favorite bias. P.O. Soelberg, "Unprogrammed Decision Making," *Industrial Management Review* 8 (1967): 19–29; K.H. Ehrhart and J.C. Ziegert, "Why Are Individuals Attracted to Organizations?" *Journal of Management* 31, no. 6 (2005): 901–19; J.E. Russo, "The Predecisional Distortion of Information," in *Neuroeconomics, Judgment, and Decision Making*, ed. E.A. Wilhelms and V.F. Reyna, *Frontiers of Cognitive Psychology* (New York: Psychology Press, 2015), 91–110.

28. S. Sacchi and M. Burigo, "Strategies in the Information Search Process: Interaction among Task Structure, Knowledge, and Source," *Journal of General Psychology* 135, no. 3 (2008): 252–70.

29. Milton Rokeach famously stated, "Life is ipsative, because decisions in everyday life are inherently and phenomenologically ipsative decisions." *Ipsative* is a process of comparing (usually two) things side-by-side. M. Rokeach, "Inducing Changes and Stability in Belief Systems and Personality Structures," *Journal of Social Issues* 41, no. 1 (1985): 153–71.

30. R.S. Nickerson, "Confirmation Bias: A Ubiquitous Phenomenon in Many Guises," *Review of General Psychology* 2, no. 2 (1998): 175–220; O. Svenson, I. Salo, and T. Lindholm, "Post-Decision Consolidation and Distortion of Facts," *Judgment and Decision Making* 4, no. 5 (2009): 397–407; A.M. Scherer, P.D. Windschitl, and A.R. Smith, "Hope to Be Right: Biased Information Seeking Following Arbitrary and Informed Predictions," *Journal of Experimental Social Psychology* 49, no. 1 (2013): 106–12.

31. A.L. Brownstein, "Biased Predecision Processing," *Psychological Bulletin* 129, no. 4 (2003): 545–68; M. Nurek, O. Kostopoulou, and Y. Hagmayer, "Predecisional Information Distortion in Physicians' Diagnostic Judgments: Strengthening a Leading Hypothesis or Weakening Its Competitor?" *Judgment and Decision Making* 9, no. 6 (2014): 572–85; D. Simon, D. Stenstrom, and S. Read, "The Coherence Effect: Blending Cold and Hot Cognitions," *Journal of Personality & Social Psychology* 109, no. 3 (2015): 369–94; M.L. DeKay, "Predecisional Information Distortion and the Self-Fulfilling Prophecy of Early Preferences in Choice," *Current Directions in Psychological Science* 24, no. 5 (2015): 405–11.

32. T. Gilovich, D. Griffin, and D. Kahneman, *Heuristics and Biases: The Psychology of Intuitive Judgment* (Cambridge: Cambridge University Press, 2002); D. Kahneman, "Maps of Bounded Rationality: Psychology for Behavioral Economics," *American Economic Review* 93, no. 5 (2003): 1449–75; J.S. Blumenthal-Barby and H. Krieger, "Cognitive Biases and Heuristics in Medical Decision Making: A Critical Review Using a Systematic Search Strategy," *Medical Decision Making* 35, no. 4 (2015): 539–57, https://doi.org/10.1177/0272989X14547740; M. Richie and S.A. Josephson, "Quantifying Heuristic Bias: Anchoring, Availability, and Representativeness," *Teaching and Learning in Medicine* 30, no. 1 (2018): 67–75, https://doi.org/10.1080/10401334.2017.1332631.

33. A. Tversky and D. Kahneman, "Judgment under Uncertainty: Heuristics and Biases," *Science* 185, no. 4157 (1974): 1124–31; I. Ritov, "Anchoring in Simulated Competitive Market Negotiation," *Organizational Behavior and Human Decision Processes* 67, no. 1 (1996): 16; J.D. Jasper and S.D. Christman, "A Neuropsychological Dimension for Anchoring Effects," *Journal of Behavioral Decision Making* 18 (2005): 343–69; M.H. Jung, H. Perfecto, and L.D. Nelson, "Anchoring in Payment: Evaluating a Judgmental Heuristic in Field Experimental Settings," *Journal of Marketing Research* 53, no. 3 (2016): 354–68, https://doi.org/10.1509/jmr.14.0238.

34. A. Tversky and D. Kahneman, "Availability: A Heuristic for Judging Frequency and Probability," *Cognitive Psychology* 5 (1973): 207–32; A. Kudryavtsev, "The Availability Heuristic and Reversals Following Large Stock Price Changes," *Journal of Behavioral Finance* 19, no. 2 (2018): 159–76, https://doi.org/10.1080/15427560.2017.1374276.

35. D. Kahneman and A. Tversky, "Subjective Probability: A Judgment of Representativeness," *Cognitive Psychology* 3, no. 3 (1972): 430; S.S. Kulkarni et al., "Defining the Representativeness Heuristic in Trauma Triage: A Retrospective Observational Cohort Study," *PLOS ONE* 14, no. 2 (February 8, 2019): e0212201, https://doi.org/10.1371/journal.pone.0212201.

36. H.A. Simon, "Rational Choice and the Structure of Environments," *Psychological Review* 63 (1956): 129–38; B. Schwartz, "On the Meaning and Measurement of Maximization," *Judgment and Decision Making* 11, no. 2 (2016): 126–46.

37. K. Jain, J.N. Bearden, and A. Filipowicz, "Do Maximizers Predict Better Than Satisficers?" *Journal of Behavioral Decision Making* 26, no. 1 (2013): 41–50; W. Mao, "When One Desires Too Much of a Good Thing: The Compromise Effect under Maximizing Tendencies," *Journal of Consumer Psychology* 26, no. 1 (2016): 66–80.

38. S. Botti and S.S. Iyengar, "The Dark Side of Choice: When Choice Impairs Social Welfare," *Journal of Public Policy and Marketing* 25, no. 1 (2006): 24–38; K.D. Vohs et al., "Making Choices Impairs Subsequent Self-Control: A Limited-Resource Account of Decision Making, Self-Regulation, and Active Initiative," *Journal of Personality and Social Psychology* 94, no. 5 (2008): 883–98.

39. S. Iyengar, *The Art of Choosing* (New York: Hachette, 2010), 177–95; A. Chernev, U. Böckenholt, and J. Goodman, "Choice Overload: A Conceptual Review and Meta-Analysis," *Journal of Consumer Psychology* 25, no. 2 (2015): 333–58.

40. P.C. Nutt, "Search During Decision Making," *European Journal of Operational Research* 160 (2005): 851–76; M.S. Wood, A. McKelvie, and J.M. Haynie, "Making It Personal: Opportunity Individuation and the Shaping of Opportunity Beliefs," *Journal of Business Venturing* 29 (2014): 252–72; Y. Chandra, "A Time-Based Process Model of International Entrepreneurial Opportunity Evaluation," *Journal of International Business Studies* 48 (2017): 423–51.

41. P. Winkielman et al., "Affective Influence on Judgments and Decisions: Moving Towards Core Mechanisms," *Review of General Psychology* 11, no. 2 (2007): 179–92; J.S. Lerner et al., "Emotion and Decision Making," *Annual Review of Psychology* 66, no. 1 (2015): 799–823, https://doi.org/10.1146/annurev-psych-010213-115043; G. Loewenstein, T. O'Donoghue, and S. Bhatia, "Modeling the Interplay between Affect and Deliberation," *Decision* 2, no. 2 (2015): 55–81, https://doi.org/10.1037/dec0000029; T. Poppa and A. Bechara, "The Somatic Marker Hypothesis: Revisiting the Role of the 'Body-Loop' in Decision-Making," *Current Opinion in Behavioral Sciences*, 19 (2018): 61–66, https://doi.org/10.1016/j.cobeha.2017.10.007; C.A. Trujillo, "The Complementary Role of Affect-Based and Cognitive Heuristics to Make Decisions under Conditions of Ambivalence and Complexity," *PLOS ONE* 13, no. 11 (November 9, 2018): e0206724, https://doi.org/10.1371/journal.pone.0206724.

42. A. Bechara and A.R. Damasio, "The Somatic Marker Hypothesis: A Neural Theory of Economic Decision," *Games and Economic Behavior* 52, no. 2 (2005): 336–72; T.S. Saunders and M.J. Buehner, "The Gut Chooses Faster Than the Mind: A Latency Advantage of Affective over Cognitive Decisions," *Quarterly Journal of Experimental Psychology* 66, no. 2 (2013): 381–88; A. Moors, "Automaticity: Componential, Causal, and Mechanistic Explanations," *Annual Review of Psychology* 67, no. 1 (2016): 263–87; T. Poppa and A. Bechara, "The Somatic Marker Hypothesis: Revisiting the Role of the 'Body-Loop' in Decision-Making," *Current Opinion in Behavioral Sciences* 19 (2018): 61–66.

43. J.P. Forgas and J.M. George, "Affective Influences on Judgments and Behavior in Organizations: An Information Processing Perspective," *Organizational Behavior and Human Decision Processes* 86 (2001): 3–34; M.T. Pham, "Emotion and Rationality: A Critical Review and Interpretation of Empirical Evidence," *Review of General Psychology* 11, no. 2 (2007): 155–78; J.P. Forgas and A.S. Koch, "Mood Effects on Cognition," in *Handbook of Cognition and Emotion*, ed. M.D. Robinson, E.R. Watkins, and E. Harmon-Jones (New York: Guilford, 2013), 231–51; J.M. George and E. Dane, "Affect, Emotion, and Decision Making," *Organizational Behavior and Human Decision Processes*, Celebrating Fifty Years of Organizational Behavior and Decision Making Research (1966–2016), 136 (2016): 47–55; A. Prinz, V. Bergmann, and J. Wittwer, "Happy but Overconfident: Positive Affect Leads to Inaccurate Metacomprehension," *Cognition and Emotion* 33, no. 3 (2019): 606–15.

44. D. Miller, *The Icarus Paradox* (New York: HarperBusiness, 1990); D. Miller, "What Happens after Success: The Perils of Excellence," *Journal of Management Studies* 31, no. 3 (1994): 325–68; A.C. Amason and A.C. Mooney, "The Icarus Paradox Revisited: How Strong Performance Sows the Seeds of Dysfunction in Future Strategic Decision-Making," *Strategic Organization* 6, no. 4 (2008): 407–34.

45. M.T. Pham, "The Logic of Feeling," *Journal of Consumer Psychology* 14 (2004): 360–69; N. Schwarz, "Feelings-as-Information Theory," in *Handbook of Theories of Social Psychology*, ed. P. Van Lange, A. Kruglanski, and E.T. Higgins (London: Sage, 2012), 289–308; A.I. Tiba, "Feelings-as-Embodied Information: Studying the Role of Feelings as Images in Emotional Disorders," *Frontiers in Psychology* 9 (2018), https://doi.org/10.3389/fpsyg.2018.00186.

46. O. Behling and N.L. Eckel, "Making Sense out of Intuition," *Academy of Management Executive* 5(1991): 46–54; R.M. Hogarth, "Intuition: A Challenge for Psychological Research on Decision Making," *Psychological Inquiry* 21, no. 4 (2010): 338–53; S. Epstein, "Demystifying Intuition: What It Is, What It Does, and How It Does It," *Psychological Inquiry* 21, no. 4 (2010): 295–312; G.P. Hodgkinson and E. Sadler-Smith, "The Dynamics of Intuition and Analysis in Managerial and Organizational Decision Making," *Academy of Management Perspectives* 32, no. 4 (2018): 473–92, https://doi.org/10.5465/amp.2016.0140.

47. L. Sjöberg, "Intuitive vs. Analytical Decision Making: Which Is Preferred?" *Scandinavian Journal of Management* 19 (2003): 17–29; K. Hamilton, S.-I. Shih, and S. Mohammed, "The Development and Validation of the Rational and Intuitive Decision Styles Scale," *Journal of Personality Assessment* 98, no. 5 (2016): 523–35, https://doi.org/10.1080/00223891.2015.1132426; Y. Wang et al., "Meta-Analytic Investigations of the Relation between Intuition and Analysis," *Journal of Behavioral Decision Making* 30, no. 1 (2017): 15–25, https://doi.org/10.1002/bdm.1903.

48. W.G. Chase and H.A. Simon, "Perception in Chess," *Cognitive Psychology* 4, no. 1 (1973): 55–81; G. Klein, *Intuition at Work* (New York: Currency/Doubleday, 2003); E. Dane, K.W. Rockmann, and M.G. Pratt, "When Should I Trust My Gut? Linking Domain Expertise to Intuitive Decision-Making Effectiveness," *Organizational Behavior and Human Decision Processes* 119, no. 2 (2012): 187–94; A. Linhares and D.M. Chada, "What Is the Nature of the Mind's Pattern-Recognition Process?" *New Ideas in Psychology* 31, no. 2 (2013): 108–21.

49. G. Klein, *Intuition at Work* (New York: Currency/Doubleday, 2003), 12–13, 16–17; G. Kefalidou, D. Golightly, and S. Sharples, "Identifying Rail Asset Maintenance Processes: A Human-Centric and Sensemaking Approach," *Cognition, Technology & Work* 20, no. 1 (2018): 73–92, https://doi.org/10.1007/s10111-017-0452-0.

50. D. Kiron, K. Prentice, and R. B. Ferguson, *The Analytics Mandate* (Cambridge, MA: MIT Sloan Management Review and SAS Institute, May 12, 2014); "PwC's Data and Analytics Survey 2016 Big Decisions" (London: PricewaterhouseCoopers, 2016); "PitchBook Survey Finds Only 38% of Venture Capital Investors Currently Use Data to Source and Evaluate All Investments Opportunities," News release (Seattle: Pitchbook, February 14, 2019); "Study Shows Many Senior Managers Distrust Big Data," news release (New Zealand: Massey University, April 12, 2019).

51. Y. Ganzach, A.H. Kluger, and N. Klayman, "Making Decisions from an Interview: Expert Measurement and Mechanical Combination," *Personnel Psychology* 53 (2000): 1–20; A.M. Hayashi, "When to Trust Your Gut," *Harvard Business Review* 79 (2001): 59–65. Evidence of high failure rates from quick decisions is reported in P.C. Nutt, *Why Decisions Fail* (San Francisco, CA: Berrett-Koehler, 2002); P.C. Nutt, "Search during Decision Making," *European Journal of Operational Research* 160 (2005): 851–76; P.C. Nutt, "Investigating the Success of Decision Making Processes," *Journal of Management Studies* 45, no. 2 (2008): 425–55.

52. R. Bradfield et al., "The Origins and Evolution of Scenario Techniques in Long Range Business Planning," *Futures* 37, no. 8 (2005): 795–812; T.J. Chermack, *Scenario Planning in Organizations* (San Francisco: Berrett-Koehler, 2011); S. Phadnis et al., "Effect of Scenario Planning on Field Experts' Judgment of Long-Range Investment Decisions," *Strategic Management Journal* 36, no. 9 (2015): 1401–11, https://doi.org/10.1002/smj.2293; G. Bowman, "The Practice of Scenario Planning: An Analysis of Inter- and Intra-Organizational Strategizing," *British Journal of Management* 27, no. 1 (2016): 77–96, https://doi.org/10.1111/1467-8551.12098; J.J. Oliver and E. Parrett, "Managing Uncertainty: Harnessing the Power of Scenario Planning," *Strategic Direction* 33, no. 1 (2016): 5–6, https://doi.org/10.1108/SD-09-2016-0131.

53. J. Pfeffer and R.I. Sutton, "Knowing 'What' to Do Is Not Enough: Turning Knowledge into Action," *California Management Review* 42, no. 1 (1999): 83–108; R. Charan, C. Burke, and L. Bossidy, *Execution: The Discipline of Getting Things Done* (New York: Crown Business, 2002); S.A. Kreindler, "What If Implementation Is Not the Problem? Exploring the Missing Links between Knowledge and Action," *The International Journal of Health Planning and Management* 31, no. 2 (2016): 208–26, https://doi.org/10.1002/hpm.2277.

54. C.A. O'Reilly and D.F. Caldwell, "The Commitment and Job Tenure of New Employees: Some Evidence of Postdecisional Justification," *Administrative Science Quarterly* 26, no. 4 (1981): 597–616. Postdecisional justification is the flip side of postdecisional dissonance. For example, see S.W.S. Lee and N. Schwarz, "Washing Away Postdecisional Dissonance," *Science* 328, no. 5979 (2010): 709.

55. B.M. Staw and J. Ross, "Behavior in Escalation Situations: Antecedents, Prototypes, and Solutions," in *Research in Organizational Behavior*, ed. L.L. Cummings and B.M. Staw (Greenwich, CT: JAI, 1987), 39–78; J. Brockner, "The Escalation of Commitment to a Failing Course of Action: Toward Theoretical Progress," *Academy of Management Review* 17, no. 1 (1992): 39–61; D.J. Sleesman et al., "Cleaning up the Big Muddy: A Meta-Analytic Review of the Determinants of Escalation of Commitment," *Academy of Management Journal* 55, no. 3 (2012): 541–62.

56. B.M. Staw, "Knee-Deep in the Big Muddy: A Study of Escalating Commitment to a Chosen Course of Action," *Organizational Behavior and Human Performance* 16, no. 1 (1976): 27–44; D. Steinkühler, M.D. Mahlendorf, and M. Brettel, "How Self-Justification Indirectly Drives Escalation of Commitment–a Motivational Perspective,"

Schmalenbach Business Review: ZFBF 66, no. 2 (2014): 191–222; E.A. Lofquist and R. Lines, "Keeping Promises: A Process Study of Escalating Commitment Leading to Organizational Change Collapse," *The Journal of Applied Behavioral Science* 53, no. 4 (December 1, 2017): 417–45, https://doi.org/10.1177/0021886317711892.

57. C.L. Guenther and M.D. Alicke, "Deconstructing the Better-Than-Average Effect," *Journal of Personality and Social Psychology* 99, no. 5 (2010): 755–70; S. Loughnan et al., "Universal Biases in Self-Perception: Better and More Human Than Average," *British Journal of Social Psychology* 49 (2010): 627–36.

58. M. Keil, G. Depledge, and A. Rai, "Escalation: The Role of Problem Recognition and Cognitive Bias," *Decision Sciences* 38, no. 3 (2007): 391–421; R. Ronay et al., "Pride before the Fall: (Over)Confidence Predicts Escalation of Public Commitment," *Journal of Experimental Social Psychology* 69 (2017): 13–22, https://doi.org/10.1016/j.jesp.2016.10.005.

59. G. Whyte, "Escalating Commitment in Individual and Group Decision Making: A Prospect Theory Approach," *Organizational Behavior and Human Decision Processes* 54 (1993): 430–55; D. Kahneman and J. Renshon, "Hawkish Biases," in *American Foreign Policy and the Politics of Fear: Threat Inflation since 9/11*, ed. T. Thrall and J. Cramer (New York: Routledge, 2009), 79–96.

60. D.J. Sleesman et al., "Cleaning up the Big Muddy: A Meta-Analytic Review of the Determinants of Escalation of Commitment," *Academy of Management Journal* 55, no. 3 (2012): 541–62; B.M. Sweis et al., "Sensitivity to 'Sunk Costs' in Mice, Rats, and Humans," *Science* 361, no. 6398 (2018): 178–81, https://doi.org/10.1126/science.aar8644.

61. J.D. Bragger et al., "When Success Breeds Failure: History, Hysteresis, and Delayed Exit Decisions," *Journal of Applied Psychology* 88, no. 1 (2003): 6–14; H. Drummond, "Escalation of Commitment: When to Stay the Course?" *The Academy of Management Perspectives* 28, no. 4 (2014): 430–46.

62. I. Simonson and B.M. Staw, "De-Escalation Strategies: A Comparison of Techniques for Reducing Commitment to Losing Courses of Action," *Journal of Applied Psychology* 77 (1992): 419–26; W. Boulding, R. Morgan, and R. Staelin, "Pulling the Plug to Stop the New Product Drain," *Journal of Marketing Research*, no. 34 (1997): 164–76; B.M. Staw, K.W. Koput, and S.G. Barsade, "Escalation at the Credit Window: A Longitudinal Study of Bank Executives' Recognition and Write-Off of Problem Loans," *Journal of Applied Psychology* 82, no. 1 (1997): 130–42; D. Ghosh, "De-Escalation Strategies: Some Experimental Evidence," *Behavioral Research in Accounting* 9 (1997): 88–112; M. Keil and D. Robey, "Turning around Troubled Software Projects: An Exploratory Study of the Deescalation of Commitment to Failing Courses of Action," *Journal of Management Information Systems* 15 (1999): 63–87; B.C. Gunia, N. Sivanathan, and A.D. Galinsky, "Vicarious Entrapment: Your Sunk Costs, My Escalation of Commitment," *Journal of Experimental Social Psychology* 45, no. 6 (2009): 1238–44; A.C. Hafenbrack, Z. Kinias, and S.G. Barsade, "Debiasing the Mind through Meditation: Mindfulness and the Sunk-Cost Bias," *Psychological Science* 25, no. 2 (2014): 369–76, https://doi.org/10.1177/0956797613503853.

63. M.I. Stein, "Creativity and Culture," *Journal of Psychology* 36 (1953): 311–22; M.A. Runco and G.J. Jaeger, "The Standard Definition of Creativity," *Creativity Research Journal* 24, no. 1 (2012): 92–96.

64. G. Wallas, *The Art of Thought* (London: Jonathan Cape, 1926). For recent applications of Wallas's classic model, see T. Kristensen, "The Physical Context of Creativity," *Creativity and Innovation Management* 13, no. 2 (2004): 89–96; U.E. Haner, "Spaces for Creativity and Innovation in Two Established Organizations," *Creativity and Innovation Management* 14, no. 3 (2005): 288–98.

65. R.S. Nickerson, "Enhancing Creativity," in *Handbook of Creativity,* ed. R.J. Sternberg (New York: Cambridge University Press, 1999), 392–430.

66. R.J. Sternberg and J.E. Davidson, *The Nature of Insight* (Cambridge, MA: MIT Press, 1995); W. Shen et al., "Feeling the Insight: Uncovering Somatic Markers of the 'Aha' Experience," *Applied Psychophysiology and Biofeedback*, September 19, 2017, https://doi.org/10.1007/s10484-017-9381-1.

67. R.J. Sternberg and L.A. O'Hara, "Creativity and Intelligence," in *Handbook of Creativity*, ed. R.J. Sternberg (New York: Cambridge University Press, 1999), 251–72; S. Taggar, "Individual Creativity and Group Ability to Utilize Individual Creative Resources: A Multilevel Model," *Academy of Management Journal* 45 (2002): 315–30; R.J. Sternberg, "Successful Intelligence: A Model for Testing Intelligence beyond IQ Tests," *European Journal of Education and Psychology* 8, no. 2 (2015): 76–84, https://doi.org/10.1016/j.ejeps.2015.09.004.

68. G.J. Feist, "The Influence of Personality on Artistic and Scientific Creativity," in *Handbook of Creativity*, ed. R.J. Sternberg (New York: Cambridge University Press, 1999), 273–96; T. Åsterbro, S.A. Jeffrey, and G.K. Adomdza, "Inventor Perseverance after Being Told to Quit: The Role of Cognitive Biases," *Journal of Behavioral Decision Making* 20 (2007): 253–72; J.S. Mueller, S. Melwani, and J.A. Goncalo, "The Bias against Creativity: Why People Desire but Reject Creative Ideas," *Psychological Science* 23, no. 1 (2012): 13–17.

69. R.W. Weisberg, "Creativity and Knowledge: A Challenge to Theories," in *Handbook of Creativity*, ed. R.J. Sternberg (New York: Cambridge University Press, 1999), 226–50.

70. R.I. Sutton, *Weird Ideas That Work* (New York: Free Press, 2002), 53–54, 121; E. Dane, "Reconsidering the Trade-Off between Expertise and Flexibility: A Cognitive Entrenchment Perspective," *Academy of Management Review* 35, no. 4 (2010): 579–603.

71. G.J. Feist, "The Influence of Personality on Artistic and Scientific Creativity," in *Handbook of Creativity*, ed. R.J. Sternberg (New York: Cambridge University Press, 1999), 273–96; C.E. Shalley, J. Zhou, and G.R. Oldham, "The Effects of Personal and Contextual Characteristics on Creativity: Where Should We Go from Here?" *Journal of Management* 30, no. 6 (2004): 933–58; S.J. Dollinger, K.K. Urban, and T.A. James, "Creativity and Openness to Experience: Validation of Two Creative Product Measures," *Creativity Research Journal* 16, no. 1 (2004): 35–47; T.S. Schweizer, "The Psychology of Novelty-Seeking, Creativity and Innovation: Neurocognitive Aspects within a Work-Psychological Perspective," *Creativity and Innovation Management* 15, no. 2 (2006): 164–72; S. Acar and M.A. Runco, "Creative Abilities: Divergent Thinking," in *Handbook of Organizational Creativity*, ed. M. Mumford (Waltham, MA: Academic Press, 2012), 115–39.

72. C.E. Shalley, J. Zhou, and G.R. Oldham, "The Effects of Personal and Contextual Characteristics on Creativity: Where Should We Go from Here?" *Journal of Management* 30, no. 6 (2004): 933–58; S.T. Hunter, K.E. Bedell, and M.D. Mumford, "Climate for Creativity: A Quantitative Review," *Creativity Research Journal* 19, no. 1 (2007): 69–90; N. Anderson, K. Potočnik, and J. Zhou, "Innovation and Creativity in Organizations: A State-of-the-Science Review, Prospective Commentary, and Guiding Framework," *Journal of Management* 40, no. 5 (2014): 1297–1333, https://doi.org/10.1177/0149206314527128.

73. M. Hvisdos, "How to Foster Curiosity and Creativity in the Workplace," *Training*, 8 June 2016; "The Collaborative Work Environment" (Troy, MI: Kelly Services, June 2016); "The State of Work," 2018-2019 U.S. Edition (Lehi, Utah: Workfront, August 29, 2018); B. Wigert and J. Robison, "Fostering Creativity at Work: Do Your Managers Push or Crush Innovation?," Gallup Workplace, December 19, 2018; "Innovation Ecosystems: How to Foster Business Success," *Harvard Business Review Analytic Services*, August 16, 2019; Office of Personnel Management, "2019 Federal Employee Viewpoint Survey" (Washington, DC: United States Government, October 2019).

74. Learning orientation has multiple meanings. Rather than the "learning goal orientation" definition, we are referring to the marketing-based definition associated with organizational learning. See, for example, W.E. Baker and J.M. Sinkula, "The Synergistic Effect of Market Orientation and Learning Orientation on Organizational Performance," *Journal of the Academy of Marketing Science* 27, no. 4 (1999): 411–27, https://doi.org/10.1177/0092070399274002; O. Pesämaa et al., "How a Learning Orientation Affects Drivers of Innovativeness and Performance in Service Delivery," *Journal of Engineering and Technology Management* 30, no. 2 (2013): 169–87, https://doi.org/10.1016/j.jengtecman.2013.01.004; J.C. Real, J.L. Roldán, and A. Leal, "From Entrepreneurial Orientation and Learning Orientation to Business Performance: Analysing the Mediating Role of Organizational Learning and the Moderating Effects of Organizational Size," *British Journal of Management* 25, no. 2 (2014): 186–208, https://doi.org/10.1111/j.1467-8551.2012.00848.x.

75. A. Cummings and G.R. Oldham, "Enhancing Creativity: Managing Work Contexts for the High Potential Employee," *California Management Review*, no. 40 (1997): 22–38; F. Coelho and M. Augusto, "Job Characteristics and the Creativity of Frontline Service Employees," *Journal of Service Research* 13, no. 4 (2010): 426–38; G. Hirst et al., "How Does Bureaucracy Impact Individual Creativity? A Cross-Level Investigation of Team Contextual Influences on Goal Orientation–Creativity Relationships," *Academy of Management Journal* 54, no. 3 (June 2011): 624–41, https://doi.org/10.5465/amj.2011.61968124; W. Zhang et al., "Exploring the Effects of Job Autonomy on Engagement and Creativity: The Moderating Role of Performance Pressure and Learning Goal Orientation," *Journal of Business and Psychology* 32, no. 3 (2017): 235–51, https://doi.org/10.1007/s10869-016-9453-x.

76. T.M. Amabile, "Changes in the Work Environment for Creativity during Downsizing," *Academy of Management Journal* 42 (1999): 630–40.

77. J. Moultrie et al., "Innovation Spaces: Towards a Framework for Understanding the Role of the Physical Environment in Innovation," *Creativity & Innovation Management* 16, no. 1 (2007): 53–65.

78. C.E. Shalley, J. Zhou, and G.R. Oldham, "The Effects of Personal and Contextual Characteristics on Creativity: Where Should We Go from Here?" *Journal of Management* 30, no. 6 (2004): 933–58; S. Powell, "The Management and Consumption of Organisational Creativity," *Journal of Consumer Marketing* 25, no. 3 (2008): 158–66; D.J. Hughes et al., "Leadership, Creativity, and Innovation: A Critical Review and Practical Recommendations," *The Leadership Quarterly* 29, no. 5 (2018): 549–69, https://doi.org/10.1016/j.leaqua.2018.03.001.

79. A. Hiam, "Obstacles to Creativity–and How You Can Remove Them," *Futurist* 32 (1998): 30–34.

80. M.A. West, *Developing Creativity in Organizations* (Leicester, UK: BPS Books, 1997), 33–35.

81. S. Brown, *Play: How It Shapes the Brain, Opens the Imagination, and Invigorates the Soul* (New York: Avery, 2009); C. Mainemelis and D.D. Dionysiou, "Play, Flow, and Timelessness," in *The Oxford Handbook of Creativity, Innovation, and Entrepreneurship*, ed. C. Shalley, M. Hitt, and J. Zhou (New York: Oxford University Press, 2015), 121–40; C.A. Petelczyc et al., "Play at Work: An Integrative Review and Agenda for Future Research," *Journal of Management* 44, no. 1 (2018): 161–90, https://doi.org/10.1177/0149206317731519.

82. T. Ritchey, *Wicked Problems–Social Messes: Decision Support Modelling with Morphological Analysis, Risk, Governance and Society* (Berlin: Springer-Verlag, 2011); S. Seidenstricker and C. Linder, "A Morphological Analysis-Based Creativity Approach to Identify and Develop Ideas for BMI: A Case Study of a High-Tech Manufacturing Company," *International Journal of Entrepreneurship and Innovation Management* 18, no. 5-6 (2014): 409–24.

83. A. Hargadon and R.I. Sutton, "Building an Innovation Factory," *Harvard Business Review* 78 (2000): 157–66; T. Kelley, *The Art of Innovation* (New York: Currency Doubleday, 2001), 158–62; P.F. Skilton and K.J. Dooley, "The Effects of Repeat Collaboration on Creative Abrasion," *Academy of Management Review* 35, no. 1 (2010): 118–34.

84. E. Köppen and C. Meinel, "Empathy via Design Thinking: Creation of Sense and Knowledge," in *Design Thinking Research: Building Innovators*, ed. H. Plattner, C. Meinel, and L. Leifer (Cham, Switzerland: Springer International, 2015), 15–28; K.D. Elsbach and I. Stigliani, "Design Thinking and Organizational Culture: A Review and Framework for Future Research," *Journal of Management* 44, no. 6 (2018): 2274–2306, https://doi.org/10.1177/0149206317744252.

85. M. Fenton-O'Creevy, "Employee Involvement and the Middle Manager: Saboteur or Scapegoat?" *Human Resource Management Journal*, no. 11 (2001): 24–40. Also see V.H. Vroom and A.G. Jago, *The New Leadership: Managing Participation in Organizations* (Englewood Cliffs, NJ: Prentice Hall, 1988).

86. V.H. Vroom and A.G. Jago, *The New Leadership: Managing Participation in Organizations* (Englewood Cliffs, NJ: Prentice Hill, 1988).

87. Some of the early OB writing on employee involvement includes C. Argyris, *Personality and Organization* (New York: Harper & Row, 1957); D. McGregor, *The Human Side of Enterprise* (New York: McGraw-Hill, 1960); R. Likert, *New Patterns of Management* (New York: McGraw-Hill, 1961).

88. R.J. Ely and D.A. Thomas, "Cultural Diversity at Work: The Effects of Diversity Perspectives on Work Group Processes and Outcomes," *Administrative Science Quarterly* 46 (2001): 229–73; E. Mannix and M.A. Neale, "What Differences Make a Difference? The Promise and Reality of Diverse Teams in Organizations," *Psychological Science in the Public Interest* 6, no. 2 (2005): 31–55.

89. D. Berend and J. Paroush, "When Is Condorcet's Jury Theorem Valid?" *Social Choice and Welfare* 15, no. 4 (1998): 481–88.

90. This quotation has a long and convoluted history. It has been attributed (incorrectly) to Benjamin Franklin and to Native Americans. The quotation stated here was popular in education during the 1960s and is cited in the 1975 source below. However, this quotation is almost certainly an adaptation of writing by Chinese Confucian philosopher Xun Kuang (circa 250 BC). A simplified version of his original statement is: "I hear and I forget; I see and I remember; I do and I understand." R. E. Keeton, "Tell Me, Show Me, Involve Me," *Learning and the Law* 2 (1975): 16–21, 64–65.

91. K.T. Dirks, L.L. Cummings, and J.L. Pierce, "Psychological Ownership in Organizations: Conditions under Which Individuals Promote and Resist Change," *Research in Organizational Change and Development*, no. 9 (1996): 1–23; J.P. Walsh and S.F. Tseng, "The Effects of Job Characteristics on Active Effort at Work," *Work & Occupations* 25, no. 1 (1998): 74–96; B. Scott-Ladd and V. Marshall, "Participation in Decision Making: A Matter of Context?" *Leadership & Organization Development Journal* 25, no. 8 (2004): 646–62.

92. V. van de Vliet, "How to Become a True Cognitive Enterprise," *Inspire Beyond Today's Technology* (Amsterdam: IBM, 2016), https://www.ibm.com/systems/be/inspire/ibm-cognitive-build (accessed 9 March 2018); "Internal Communications Interview with IBM," podcast in *csuite podcast* (Audere Communications, 12 December 2016); "Cognitive Build Hits World of Watson," *Medium*, October 28, 2016; "Best in Internal Communications 2017," *PR Week*, March 17, 2017.

93. V.H. Vroom and A.G. Jago, *The New Leadership: Managing Participation in Organizations* (Englewood Cliffs, NJ: Prentice Hall, 1988).

PART 3

7 Team Dynamics

Kaiskynet Studio/Shutterstock

Learning Objectives

After you read this chapter, you should be able to:

LO7-1 Define teams and informal groups and explain why employees join informal groups.

LO7-2 Discuss the benefits and limitations of teams.

LO7-3 Outline the team effectiveness model and discuss how task characteristics, team size, and team composition influence team effectiveness.

LO7-4 Discuss how the six team processes—team development, norms, roles, cohesion, trust, and mental models—influence team effectiveness.

LO7-5 Discuss the characteristics and factors required for the success of self-directed teams and remote teams.

LO7-6 Identify four constraints on team decision making and discuss ways to improve decision making and creativity in teams.

teams groups of two or more people who interact with and influence each other, are mutually accountable for achieving common goals associated with organizational objectives, and perceive themselves as a social entity within an organization

Executives at RBC Capital Markets identify teamwork as a key reason for their success as a top-ranked investment bank. The company carefully selects job applicants who are "understated and team-oriented." Big-ego Masters of the Universe financiers are not welcome, warns a senior executive. Teamwork is vital because no individual has sufficient expertise to provide the investment bank's complex services. RBC Capital Markets chief executive Derek Neldner gives this example: "If you are going to offer serious coverage to a health care client, you need an analyst who can talk authoritatively on medical devices, an expert on pharmaceuticals, one on biotech, and so on."

The shift from individual stars to high-performing teams is also evident at Merrill Lynch Wealth Management. A decade ago, most of the company's 15,000 financial advisors worked alone with their clients. Today, 77 percent of Merrill Lynch's advisors work in teams. These teams offer greater expertise across a broader range of asset classes (stocks, bonds, derivatives, cash management, etc.) as well as expertise across regions of the world.

"It's exceedingly rare that a single individual could deliver everything a client needs today," says Merrill Lynch Wealth Management president Andy Sieg. "When you look at what clients need—comprehensive advice across their financial lives—it very quickly becomes obvious that the only way to deliver that is through a team."[1]

Investment analysts, financial advisors, and others in the finance industry increasingly work in teams rather than alone. Why are teams becoming so important, and how can organizations improve team effectiveness? We find the answers to these and other questions in this chapter on team dynamics. This chapter begins by defining teams, examining the reasons organizations rely on teams, and explaining why people join informal groups in organizational settings. A large segment of this chapter examines a model of team effectiveness, which includes team and organizational environment, team design, and team processes (team development, norms, roles, cohesion, trust, and mental models). We then turn our attention to two specific types of teams: self-directed teams and remote teams. The final section of this chapter looks at the challenges and strategies for making better decisions in teams.

LO7-1 Define teams and informal groups and explain why employees join informal groups.

TEAMS AND INFORMAL GROUPS

Teams are groups of two or more people who interact with and influence each other, are mutually accountable for achieving common goals associated with organizational objectives, and perceive themselves as a social entity within an organization.[2] This definition has a few important components worth repeating. First, all teams exist to fulfill some purpose, such as providing wealth management services, repairing electric power lines, designing a new educational program, or making an important executive decision. Second, team members are held together by their interdependence and need for collaboration to achieve common goals. All teams require some form of communication so that members can coordinate, share information, and develop a common mindset regarding their purpose and objectives. Third, team members influence each other, although some members may be more influential than others regarding the team's goals and activities. Finally, a team exists when its members perceive themselves to be a team. They feel connected to each other through a common interest or purpose.

There are many types of teams in organizations, and each type can be distinguished by three characteristics: team permanence, skill diversity, and authority dispersion (see Exhibit 7.1).[3] Team permanence refers to how long that type of team usually exists. Accounting, marketing, and other departments are usually long-lasting structures, so these teams have high permanence. In contrast, task forces and project teams usually have low permanence because most are formed temporarily to solve a problem, realize an opportunity, or design a product or service.

A second distinguishing characteristic is the team's skill diversity. A team has high skill diversity when its members possess different skills and knowledge, whereas low diversity exists when team members have similar abilities and, therefore, are interchangeable. Most functional departments have low skill diversity because they organize employees around their common skill sets (e.g., people with accounting expertise are located in the accounting department). In contrast, financial advisory team members have diverse expertise in different asset classes (stocks, bonds, etc.) or economic regions.

Authority dispersion, the third distinguishing characteristic of teams, refers to the degree that decision-making responsibility is distributed throughout the team (high dispersion) or is

Exhibit 7.1 Team Permanence, Skill Diversity, and Authority Dispersion for Selected Team Types

Team Type	Description	Typical Characteristics
Departmental teams	Teams that consist of employees who have similar or complementary skills and are located in the same unit of a functional structure; usually have minimal task interdependence because each person works with clients or with employees in other departments.	*Team permanence:* High—departments continue indefinitely. *Skill diversity:* Low to medium—departments are often organized around common skills (e.g., accounting staff located in the accounting department). *Authority dispersion:* Low—departmental power is usually concentrated in the departmental manager.
Self-directed teams	Teams whose members are organized around work processes that complete an entire piece of work requiring several interdependent tasks and have substantial autonomy over the execution of those tasks (i.e., they usually control inputs, flow, and outputs with little or no supervision).	*Team permanence:* High—teams are usually assigned indefinitely to a specific cluster of production or service activities. *Skill diversity:* Medium to high—members typically perform different tasks requiring diverse skill sets, but cross-training can somewhat reduce skill diversity. *Authority dispersion:* High—team members share power, usually with limited hierarchical authority.
Task force (project) teams	Cross-functional teams whose members are usually drawn from several disciplines to solve a specific problem, realize an opportunity, or design a product or service.	*Team permanence:* Low—teams typically disband on completion of a specific project. *Skill diversity:* Medium to high—members are typically drawn from several functional specializations associated with the complexity of the problem or opportunity. *Authority dispersion:* Medium—teams often have someone with formal authority (project leader), but members also have moderate power due to their expertise and functional representation.

vested in one or a few members of the team (low dispersion). Departmental teams tend to have low authority dispersion because power is somewhat concentrated in a formal manager. Self-directed teams usually have high authority dispersion because the entire team makes key decisions and hierarchical authority is limited.

Informal Groups

This chapter mainly focuses on formal teams, but employees also belong to informal groups. All teams are groups but many groups do not satisfy our definition of teams. Groups include people assembled together, whether or not they have any interdependence or organizational objective. The friends you meet for lunch are an *informal group*, but they wouldn't be called a team because they have little or no interdependence (each person could just as easily eat lunch alone) and no organizationally mandated purpose. Instead, an informal group exists primarily for the benefit of their members.

Why do informal groups exist? One reason is that human beings are social animals. Our drive to bond is hardwired through evolutionary development, creating a need to belong to informal groups.[4] This is evident by the fact that people invest considerable time and effort forming and maintaining social relationships without any special circumstances or ulterior motives. A second reason people join informal groups is provided by social identity theory, which states that individuals define themselves by their group affiliations (see Chapter 3). Thus, we join groups—particularly those that are viewed favorably by others and have values similar to our own—because they shape and reinforce our self-concept.[5]

A third reason informal groups exist is that they accomplish personal objectives that cannot be achieved by individuals

Informal groups exist in organizations because people have a drive to bond, define themselves partly by their social identity, need others to help accomplish nontask goals, and rely on social interaction to minimize stress.
Jetta Productions/Getty Images

working alone. For example, employees will sometimes congregate to support or oppose organizational changes because this collective effort has more power than individuals who try to bring about change alone. These informal groups, called coalitions, are discussed in Chapter 9. A fourth explanation for informal groups is that we are comforted by the mere presence of other people and are therefore motivated to be near them in stressful situations. When in danger, people congregate near each other even though doing so serves no protective purpose. Similarly, employees tend to mingle more often after hearing rumors that the company might be acquired by a competitor. As Chapter 4 explained, this social support minimizes stress by providing emotional and/or informational resources to buffer the stress experience.[6]

Informal Groups and Organizational Outcomes Informal groups are not created to serve corporate objectives, yet they have a profound influence on the organization and its employees. Informal groups potentially minimize employee stress because, as mentioned, group members provide emotional and informational social support. This stress-reducing capability of informal groups improves employee well-being, which potentially increases organizational effectiveness. Informal groups are also the backbone of **social networks**, which are important sources of trust building, information sharing, power, influence, and employee well-being in the workplace.[7] Chapter 9 explains how social networks are a source of influence in organizational settings. Employees with strong informal networks tend to have more power and influence because they receive better information and preferential treatment from others and their talent is more visible to key decision makers.

LO7-2 Discuss the benefits and limitations of teams.

BENEFITS AND LIMITATIONS OF TEAMS

Why are teams important at RBC Capital Markets, Merrill Lynch Wealth Management, and so many other organizations around the world? The answer to this question has a long history.[8] Early research on British coal mining in the 1940s, the Japanese economic miracle of the 1970s, and a huge number of investigations since then have revealed that *under the right conditions*, teams make better decisions, develop better products and services, and create a more engaged workforce than do employees working alone.[9] Similarly, team members can quickly share information and coordinate tasks, whereas these processes are slower and prone to more errors in traditional departments led by supervisors. Teams typically provide superior customer service because they offer clients a greater breadth of knowledge and expertise than do individual "stars" working alone.

social networks social structures of individuals or social units that are connected to each other through one or more forms of interdependence

process losses resources (including time and energy) expended toward team development and maintenance rather than the task

Another benefit of teams is that, in many situations, their members are more motivated than when working alone.[11] Teams generate three motivating forces. First, employees have a drive to bond and are motivated to fulfill the goals of groups to which they belong. This felt obligation is particularly strong when the employee's social identity is connected to the team. Second, employees have high accountability to fellow team members, who monitor performance more closely than a traditional supervisor. This accountability is particularly strong when the team's performance depends on the worst performer, such as on an assembly line. Third, each team member creates a moving performance standard for the others. Employees are also motivated to work harder because of apprehension that their performance will be compared to the performance of others. When a few employees complete tasks faster, other team members recognize that they could work faster—and that they should work faster.

> **Talent wins games, but teamwork and intelligence win championships.[10]**
>
> —Michael Jordan, professional basketball player and sports executive

The Challenges of Teams

Teams are potentially very productive, but they are not always as effective as individuals working alone.[13] The main problem is that teams have additional costs called **process losses**—resources (including time and energy) expended on team development and maintenance rather than on directly toward task performance.[14] Team members need time and effort to develop mutual understanding of their goals, determine the best strategy for accomplishing those goals, negotiate their specific roles, agree on informal rules of conduct, and resolve their disagreements. An employee working alone on a project does not have these misunderstandings, divergent viewpoints, disagreements,

> **If I could solve all the problems myself, I would.**[17]
>
> —Thomas Edison, inventor, when asked why he needed a team of 21 assistants

OB THEORY TO PRACTICE

What Organizations Say about Teamwork[12]

Company	What They Say about Teamwork
Audi Hungaria Motor (Hungarian division of the German automobile manufacturer)	"Employees in administration and production always work in teams. Personnel selection takes account not only of specialist qualifications and work experience, but also of team capabilities, language knowledge and social competence."
National Aeronautics and Space Administration	"NASA's most powerful tool for achieving mission success is a multi-disciplinary team of diverse competent people across all NASA Centers. Our approach to teamwork is based on a philosophy that each team member brings unique experience and important expertise to project issues."
Amgen	"Our teams work quickly to move scientific breakthroughs from the lab through the clinic to the marketplace and to support other aspects of our business. Diverse teams working together generate the best decisions for patients, staff and stockholders. Our team structure provides opportunities for Amgen staff to impact the direction of the organization, to gain broader perspective about other functions within Amgen and to reach their full potential."
General Dynamics Mission Systems–Canada	"At General Dynamics Mission Systems–Canada, teamwork is not a buzzword, it is the foundation of everything we do. Our collaborative, multi-function, dialogue-driven, teams create the innovations that enable us to succeed with our customers."

or coordination problems (at least, not nearly as much as with other people). When the work is so complex that it requires knowledge and skills from several people, a team-based structure is usually required. But when the work can be performed by one person, process losses can make a team much less effective than an individual working alone.

Process losses tend to increase with the team's diversity and size.[15] A diverse team has a range of beliefs and values, which can slow development toward a high-performance unit. Conflicts about the team's purpose, roles, and coordination routines are more likely to flare up and take longer to resolve. Larger teams have higher process losses because understanding, agreeing with, and synchronizing work with many people is more difficult than with a few people. Larger teams also require more time for each member to be meaningfully involved in the team's decisions.

Process losses are also amplified, at least temporarily, when adding new members to an existing team. The new team members consume time and effort figuring out how to work well with other team members. Performance also suffers among current team members while their attention is diverted from task performance to accommodating and integrating the newcomer. The software industry even has a name for the problems of adding people to a team: **Brooks's law** says that adding more people to a late software project only makes it later![16]

Social Loafing The process losses just described mainly refer to coordination challenges, but teams also suffer from motivational process losses. The best-known motivational process loss is **social loafing**, which occurs when people exert less effort (and usually perform at a lower level) in teams than when working alone.[18]

Social loafing is more pervasive under several conditions.[19] It is more likely to occur when individual performance is hidden or difficult to distinguish from the performance of other team members. Individual performance is less visible in larger rather than smaller teams. It is also hidden when the team produces a

Social loafing is more likely to occur when individual performance is hidden or difficult to distinguish from the performance of other team members.
Westend61/Getty Images

single output (e.g., solving a client's problem) rather than separate outputs for each team member (e.g., each member reviews several accounting reports per day). Second, social loafing is more common when the work is boring or the team's overall task has low task significance (see Chapter 5). Third, social loafing is more prevalent among team members with low conscientiousness and low agreeableness personality traits as well as low collectivist values.

Fourth, social loafing is more widespread when employees aren't motivated to help the team achieve its goals. Individual members are less motivated when they have low social identity with the team. Motivation is also lower when employees believe other team members aren't pulling their weight. In other words, social loafers provide only as much effort as they believe others will provide, which is their way of maintaining equity in work allocation. Employees also lack motivation to help the team when they believe they have little control over the team's success, such as when the team is large (their contribution has minimal effect on the team's performance) and when the team is dependent on other members with known performance problems.

Overall, teams can be very powerful forces for competitive advantage, or they can be much more trouble than they are worth. To understand when teams are better than individuals working alone, we need to more closely examine the conditions that make teams effective or ineffective. The next few sections of this chapter discuss the model of team effectiveness.

Brooks's law the principle that adding more people to a late software project only makes it later

social loafing the problem that occurs when people exert less effort (and usually perform at a lower level) when working in teams than when working alone

OB THEORY TO PRACTICE

Minimizing Social Loafing[20]

- *Form smaller teams*—Splitting the team into several smaller groups reduces social loafing because each person's performance becomes more noticeable and important for team performance. Individuals also tend to develop stronger commitment to and identify with smaller than larger teams.
- *Measure individual performance*—Social loafing is minimized when each member's contribution is measured. This is possible when each member can perform parallel tasks, such as serving different customers. But measuring individual performance is difficult to implement when the team produces a single output, such as solving one client's problem.
- *Specialize tasks*—It is easier to measure individual performance when each team member performs a different work activity. For example, rather than pooling their effort for all incoming customer inquiries, each customer service representative might be assigned a particular type of client.
- *Increase job enrichment*—Social loafing is minimized when each team member's job is high motivating, such as when the work has high task significance or is sufficiently varied and challenging rather than boring.
- *Increase mindfulness of team obligations*—Social loafing can be minimized by alerting team members to this problem and asking them to declare their commitment to the team's performance objectives. This relates to the discussion in Chapter 2 on increasing employee awareness of values and ethics.
- *Select motivated, team-oriented employees*—Employees are less susceptible to social loafing when they are self-motivated, have moderately high conscientiousness and agreeableness personality traits, have a somewhat collectivist value orientation, and develop a strong social identity with the team.

LO7-3 Outline the team effectiveness model and discuss how task characteristics, team size, and team composition influence team effectiveness.

A MODEL OF TEAM EFFECTIVENESS

Why are some teams effective while others fail? To answer this question, we first need to clarify the meaning of team effectiveness. A team is effective when it benefits the organization and its members, and survives long enough to accomplish its mandate.[21] First, teams exist to serve some organizational purpose, so effectiveness is partly measured by the achievement of that objective. Second, a team's effectiveness relies on the satisfaction and well-being of its members. People join groups to fulfill their personal needs, so effectiveness is partly measured by this need fulfillment. Third, team effectiveness includes the ability and motivation of team members to remain together long enough to accomplish the assigned goals. Even teams that exist for only a few days could fall apart literally (people refuse to join or stay with the team) or cognitively (members become emotionally disengaged from the team).

Researchers have developed several models over the years to identify the features, conditions, and processes that make some teams more effective than others.[22] Exhibit 7.2 integrates the main components of these team effectiveness models. This exhibit is a meta-model because each component (team development, team cohesion, etc.) includes its own set of theories and models to explain how that component operates. Over the next two sections, we discuss theories for each part of this model.

The organizational and team environment refers to the context surrounding the team, such as its physical work space and organizational leadership. Team design refers to variables that, for the most part, are assigned to the team when it is created and altered throughout its existence. The number of people assigned to the team (team size) and the personal attributes these members bring to the team (team composition) are elements of team design, for example. Team processes are the cognitive and

Exhibit 7.2 Team Effectiveness Model

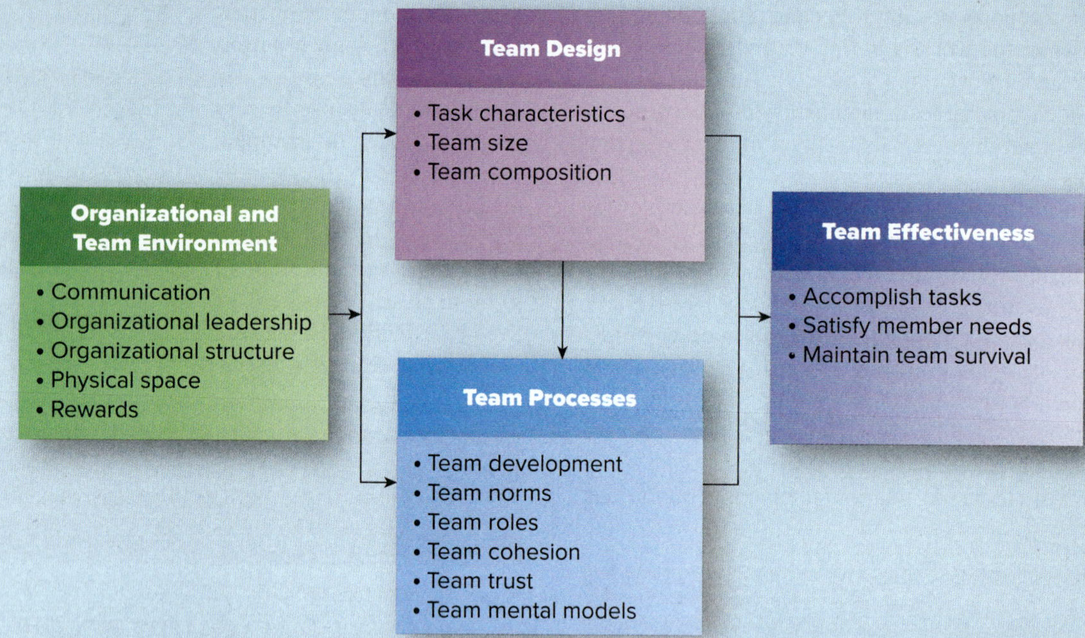

emotional dynamics of the team that continually change with its development. These processes center around the team's development and the associated variables of team norms, roles, cohesion, trust, and shared/complementary mental models.[23]

Organizational and Team Environment

The organizational and team environment represents all conditions surrounding the team that influence its effectiveness.[24] Teams thrive where the physical workspace encourages collaborative interaction, information systems support team coordination, organizational leaders instill a culture of teamwork, and the reward system reinforces collaboration rather than competition among team members. Team effectiveness also benefits from an organizational structure that clusters work activities within the team and creates fairly distinct boundaries between the team and other work units.[25]

OB THEORY TO PRACTICE

Obeya Room Strengthens Team Performance[26]

Many years ago, Toyota Motor Company discovered that it could speed up new car design by forming a cross-functional team and having the team members meet regularly in an "obeya"—Japanese for "large room."

Many European companies have recently introduced obeya rooms to improve team performance on complex problems through face-to-face interaction. For example, ING Bank created obeya rooms in several European countries so operations teams can speed up communication and decision making as the company moves toward a more agile work culture.

"This is the heart of ING's transformation," ING chief operating and transformation officer Roel Louwhoff says proudly during a tour of ING's obeya room in Amsterdam. "The purpose is simple: having the full overview of the status of all projects and solving issues quickly. . . . You immediately see how everything fits together."

Sam Edwards/OJO Images/Getty Images

task interdependence
the extent to which team members must share materials, information, or expertise in order to perform their jobs

TEAM DESIGN ELEMENTS

Even in a team-friendly environment, the team's effectiveness will fall short of its potential if the task characteristics, team size, and team composition are poorly designed for the team's objectives and functioning.

Task Characteristics

Teams are more effective than individuals in specific types of tasks.[27] They are better for work that is too complex for any individual to perform, such as launching the business in a new market, developing a computer operating system, or constructing a bridge. Complex work requires skills and knowledge beyond one person's abilities. Teams are particularly well suited for complex work that can be divided into more specialized roles, particularly when team members in those specialized roles are able to coordinate frequently with each other.

Task complexity demands teamwork, but teams perform better when the work is well structured and predictable rather than ambiguous and unpredictable. Team members on an automobile assembly line have well-structured and predictable tasks. They perform the same set of tasks each day (low *task variability*–see Chapter 5)–and the work is predictable enough for well-established procedures (high *task analyzability*). The main benefit of well-structured tasks is that it is easier to coordinate the work among several people.

In contrast, ambiguous and unpredictable tasks are more difficult to coordinate among team members, which leads to higher process losses and errors. Fortunately, teams can still perform these less-structured and less predictable tasks reasonably well when members are experienced in well-defined broader roles. During surgery, for example, medical team members know generally what to expect of each other even when unique problems arise.[28]

Task Interdependence Another task-related influence on team effectiveness is **task interdependence**–the extent to which team members must share materials, information, or expertise to perform their jobs.[29] Apart from complete independence, there are three levels of task interdependence, as illustrated in Exhibit 7.3.[30] The lowest level, called *pooled interdependence*, occurs when an employee or work unit shares machinery, technical support, financial support, or other common (pooled) resources, but otherwise operates independently from other employees or work units. A higher level of interdependence occurs when the output of one person or work unit becomes the direct input for another person or unit. This *sequential interdependence* typically occurs on an assembly line because each team member's output is forwarded to the next person on the line for further assembly of the product or service.

Reciprocal interdependence, in which work output is exchanged back and forth among individuals or work units, produces the highest level of interdependence. People who design a new product or service would typically have reciprocal interdependence because their design decisions affect others involved in the design process. Any decision made by the design engineers would influence the work of the manufacturing engineers and purchasing specialists, and vice versa. Employees with reciprocal interdependence should be organized into teams to facilitate coordination in their interwoven relationship.

As a rule, the higher the level of task interdependence, the greater the need to organize people into teams rather than have them work alone.[31] Higher task interdependence usually requires more intense coordination, and team structures enable better interpersonal communication than when employees work independently from each other or in different departments. High task interdependence also motivates most people to be part of the team and to coordinate with each other.

However, this rule has one important condition: employees with high interdependence should be formed into teams *only* when they have the same task goals, such as serving the same clients or collectively assembling the same product. In contrast, a team structure may lead to dysfunctional conflict when each member has unique goals (such as serving different clients) but these employees are dependent on each other to achieve those distinct goals. Under these conditions, the company should try to reduce the level of interdependence or rely on supervision as a buffer or mediator among employees.

Task complexity demands teamwork, but teams perform better when the work is well structured rather than ambiguous and unpredictable.
Kristy-Anne Glubish/Design Pics

Team Size

Teams need to be large enough to provide the necessary abilities and viewpoints to perform the assigned work, yet small enough to maintain efficient coordination and meaningful involvement of each member.[32] The ideal team size varies with the type of team, the tasks it is expected to perform, and the available forms of coordination (see Chapter 12). Smaller teams (say, a half-dozen members) operate more effectively than larger teams because they have less process loss (easier coordination, less conflict, less time to make decisions, etc.). Members of smaller teams also tend to feel more engaged in teamwork because they

Exhibit 7.3 Levels of Task Interdependence

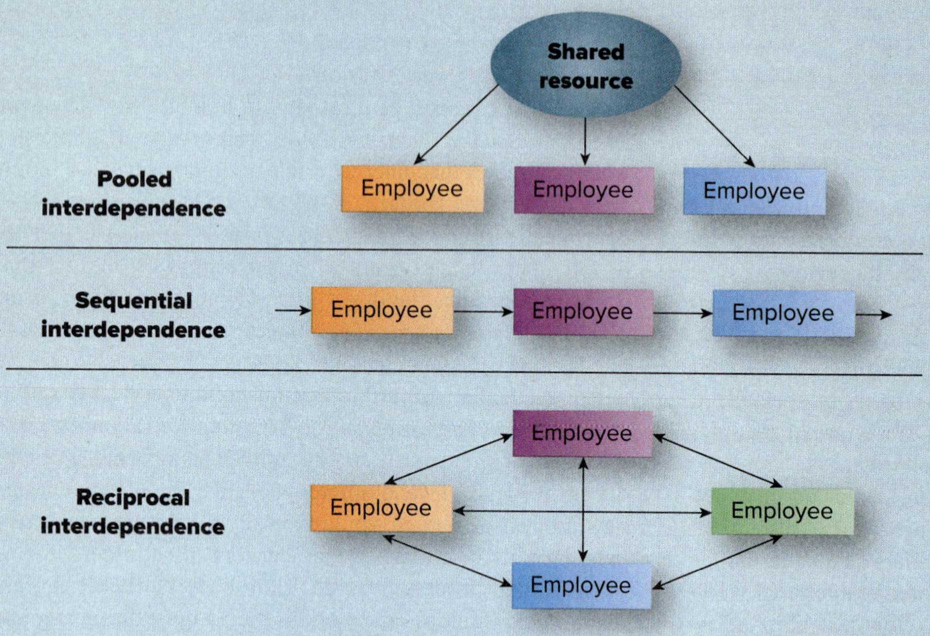

have more influence on the group's norms and goals and feel more responsible for its successes and failures. Also, members of smaller teams get to know one another better, which improves mutual trust as well as perceived support, help, and assistance from those team members.[33]

> Teams need to be large enough to accomplish the assigned work, yet small enough to maintain efficient coordination and meaningful involvement of each member.

Should companies have 100-person teams if the task is highly complex? The answer is that a group this large probably isn't a team, even if management calls it one. A team exists when its members interact and influence each other, are mutually accountable for achieving common goals associated with organizational objectives, and perceive themselves as a social entity within an organization. It is very difficult for everyone in a 100-person work unit to influence each other and perceive themselves as members of the same team. However, such complex tasks can usually be divided into several teams.

Team Composition

Team effectiveness depends on the qualities of the people who are members of those teams.[34] To begin with, a team's performance depends on how well its members engage in *taskwork*—that is, perform task-related behaviors toward the achievement of the team's objectives. Taskwork requires team members who are highly motivated, possess the required abilities, and have clear role perceptions about how and when to perform the assigned work (see the MARS model in Chapter 1).

But effective teams demand more than just individuals who perform their own jobs well. They also need members who are motivated, able, and have clear role perceptions about engaging in *teamwork* behaviors.[35] Teamwork behaviors maintain the team's existence and functioning. In other words, the best performing teams have members who are effective at performing their tasks and effective at supporting the team's dynamics.

The most frequently mentioned teamwork behaviors are depicted in the "Five Cs" model illustrated in Exhibit 7.4. Coordinating, communicating, and cooperating are mainly (but not entirely) about supporting team members on their task, whereas comforting and conflict resolving primarily maintain healthy psychological and interpersonal dynamics in the team.[36]

- *Cooperating.* Effective team members are willing and able to work with others. This includes sharing resources and being sufficiently flexible to accommodate the needs of other team members.
- *Coordinating.* Effective team members actively manage the team's work so it is performed efficiently and harmoniously. This includes keeping the team on track and helping to integrate the work performed by different members. To effectively coordinate, team members must know the other team members' work to some extent, not just their own.
- *Communicating.* Effective team members transmit information freely (rather than reluctantly), efficiently (using the best channel and symbols), and respectfully (minimizing arousal of negative emotions).[37] They also listen actively to coworkers.

Exhibit 7.4 Five Cs of Effective Team Member Behavior

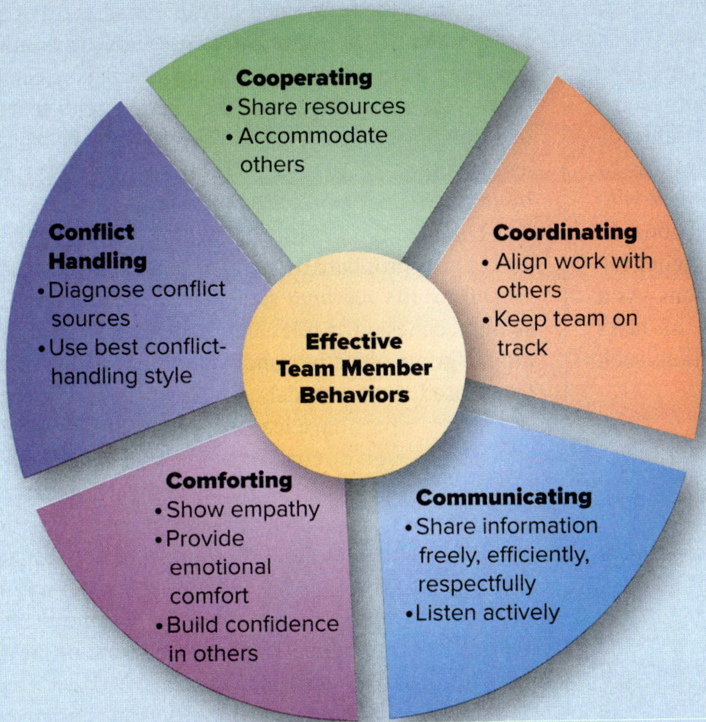

Sources: Based on information in V. Rousseau, C. Aubé, and A. Savoie, "Teamwork Behaviors: A Review and an Integration of Frameworks," *Small Group Research* 37, no. 5 (2006), 540–70; M.L. Loughry, M.W. Ohland, and D.D. Moore, "Development of a Theory-Based Assessment of Team Member Effectiveness," *Educational and Psychological Measurement* 67, no. 3 (2007), 505–24; E. Salas et al., "Understanding and Improving Teamwork in Organizations: A Scientifically Based Practical Guide," *Human Resource Management* 54, no. 4 (2015): 599–622.

- *Comforting.* Effective team members help coworkers maintain a positive and healthy psychological state. They show empathy, provide emotional comfort, and build coworker feelings of confidence and self-worth.
- *Conflict handling.* Conflict is inevitable in social settings, but effective team members have the skills and motivation to resolve disagreements within the group. This involves using appropriate conflict-handling styles as well as diagnostic skills to identify and resolve the structural sources of conflict.

Team Diversity Diversity, another aspect of team composition, has both advantages and challenges for team effectiveness.[39] One advantage of diverse teams is that people from dissimilar backgrounds tend to see a problem or opportunity from different angles. Team members have varied mental models, which increases their likelihood of identifying viable solutions to difficult problems. A second advantage is that diverse team members have a broader pool of technical abilities to serve clients or design new products.

Third, diverse teams often provide better representation of the team's constituents, such as other departments or clients from similarly diverse backgrounds. This representation not only brings different viewpoints to the decision; it also gives stakeholders a belief that they have a voice in that decision process. As we learned in Chapter 5, voice is an important ingredient in procedural justice, so stakeholders are more likely to believe the team's decision is fair when the team mirrors the surface or deep-level diversity of its constituents.

Team diversity also presents a number of challenges. Employees with diverse backgrounds take longer to become a high-performing team. This occurs partly because people with varied worldviews take longer to reach agreement on team goals, operational procedures, and informal team dynamics (norms, roles, etc.). The team development process is also slower because it takes longer to

Rating Teamwork Skills in College Graduates and Coworkers[38]

85% of 4,213 senior (graduating) students at American universities and colleges say they are very or extremely proficient in teamwork/collaboration.

51% of 1,021 hiring managers say that being team-oriented is a top soft skill they assess in job applicants.

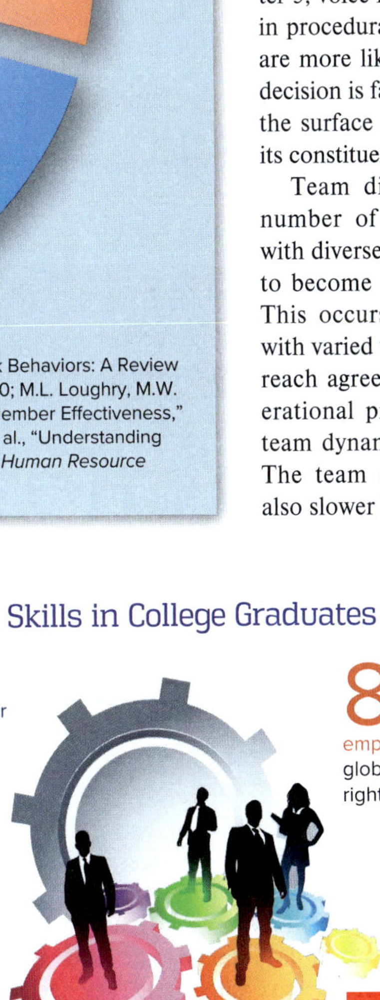

81% of 25,000 employees in 1,000 companies globally believe they have the right people on their team.

77% of 201 American employers rate recent college graduates as very or extremely proficient in teamwork/collaboration.

27% of 25,000 employees in 1,000 companies globally rate the organization's team-building efforts as very good (35% rate them as poor).

solarseven/Shutterstock

norms the informal rules and shared expectations that groups establish to regulate the behavior of their members

build trust with coworkers whose personal characteristics, experiences, and beliefs are different from ours.

A related challenge is that diverse teams are susceptible to "faultlines"—hypothetical dividing lines that may split a team into subgroups along gender, ethnic, professional, or other dimensions.[40] These faultlines undermine team effectiveness by reducing the motivation to communicate and coordinate with teammates on the other side of the hypothetical divisions. In contrast, members of homogenous teams experience higher satisfaction, less conflict, and better interpersonal relations. As a result, homogeneous teams tend to be more effective on tasks requiring a high degree of cooperation and coordination, such as emergency response teams.

Mc Graw Hill connect

SELF-ASSESSMENT 7.1: Are You a Team Player?

LO7-4 Discuss how the six team processes—team development, norms, roles, cohesion, trust, and mental models—influence team effectiveness.

TEAM PROCESSES

The third set of elements in the team effectiveness model are *team processes*, which include team development, norms, roles, cohesion, trust, and team mental models. These are the cognitive and emotional dynamics of the team that continually change with its development. In other words, this section looks at the continuously evolving collective beliefs, expectations, and feelings of the team as well as how those team dynamics influence team effectiveness.

Team Development

Team development is at the heart of team processes because the other dynamics—shaping norms, roles, cohesion, trust, and mental models—are embedded in team development. Team members resolve several issues and pass through several stages of development before emerging as an effective work unit. They need to get to know and trust one another, understand and agree on their respective roles, discover appropriate and inappropriate behaviors (norms), develop mutual understanding of the team's objectives and their coordination in that process (team mental models), and develop a strong bond with the team and its members (cohesion).

A popular model that captures most team development activities is illustrated in Exhibit 7.5.[41] The diagram shows teams moving systematically from one stage to the next, while the dashed lines indicate that teams might—and often do—fall back to an earlier stage of development as new members join or other conditions disrupt the team's maturity. *Forming*, the first stage of team development, is a period of testing and orientation in which members learn about each other and evaluate the benefits and costs of continued membership. People tend to be polite, will defer to authority, and try to find out what is expected of them and how they will fit into the team. The *storming* stage is marked by interpersonal conflict as members become more proactive and compete for various team roles. Members try to establish norms of appropriate behavior and performance standards.

During the *norming* stage, the team develops its first real sense of cohesion as roles are established and a consensus forms around group objectives and common as well as complementary team-based mental models. By the *performing* stage, team members have learned to efficiently coordinate and resolve conflicts. In high-performance teams, members are highly cooperative, have a high level of trust in one another, have functional shared mental models of group objectives and work processes, and identify with the team. Finally, the *adjourning* stage occurs when the team is about to disband. Team members shift their attention away from task orientation to a relationship focus.

This model depicts team development fairly well because it identifies and incorporates all of the other team processes. It recognizes that team members become cohesive, develop norms to guide behavior, assign roles, form team mental models, and develop trust in one another. However, the model is not a perfect representation of team development.[42] It does not show that some teams remain in a particular stage longer than others and does not explain why teams sometimes regress back to earlier stages of development. Perhaps most important, this model does not explain the intricacies of how norms, cohesion, mental models, and other team dynamics evolve (sometimes rapidly, sometimes slowly) over time. Fortunately, these team processes are explained by separate theories. The remainder of this section describes each of these, beginning with team norms.

Team Norms

Norms are the informal rules and shared expectations that groups establish to regulate the behavior of their members. Norms apply only to behavior, not to private thoughts or feelings. Furthermore, norms exist only for behaviors that are important to the team.[43] The team development model in Exhibit 7.5 suggests that team norms develop during storming stage, likely because conflict often occurs when members try to reach agreement on what behavior is expected or forbidden. However, it is more accurate to say that norms begin as soon as the team forms and that some norms continue to change over the team's lifespan.

Teams develop norms for a few reasons. First, most norms develop when members associate these behaviors with the team's performance or the well-being of its members. The perceived value of norms motivates members to enact them as well as influence others to do the same.[44] Some norms originate from

Exhibit 7.5 Stages of Team Development

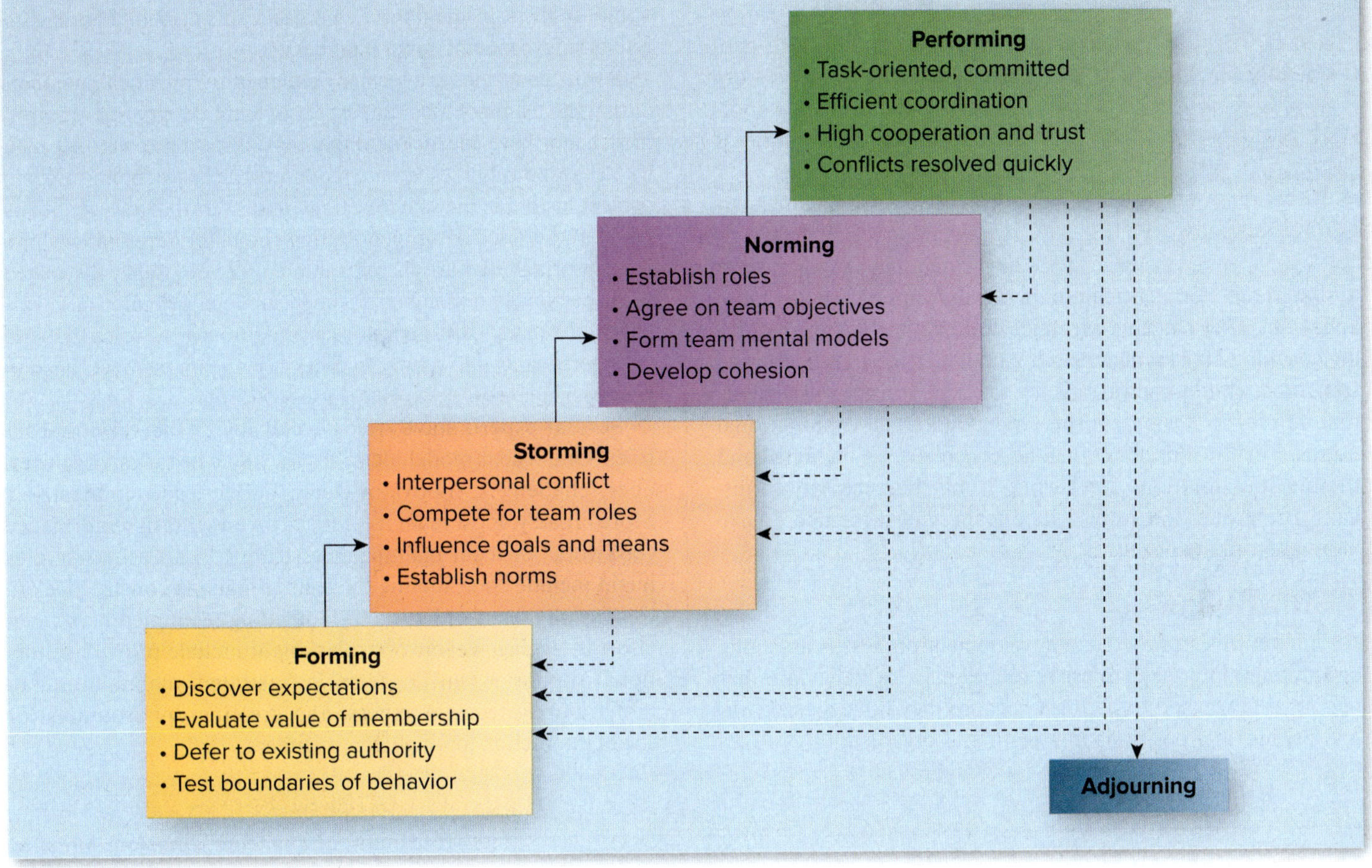

a critical incident; for instance, a norm of wearing safety glasses emerges after a team member is seriously hurt from not wearing them. Other norms are brought into the team due to experiences that some members have had in previous teams.[45]

Second, team norms develop because they improve predictability and conflict-avoidance in coworker relations. Newcomers, for instance, try to fit in with the group by actively discovering and behaving consistently with the team's norms. Third, teams develop norms to routinize behavior with minimal cognitive effort, which improves social order and coordination among team members. This explains why norms often develop regarding seemingly minor issues, such as where people sit in meetings.

An important feature of team norms is that they are enforced.[46] Coworkers display their displeasure if we are absent from work too often or don't have our part of a project completed on time. Norms are also directly reinforced through praise from high-status members and easier access to valued resources. These forms of peer pressure and reinforcement can occur even when team members work remotely from one another. But team members often conform to prevailing norms without direct reinforcement or punishment because they identify with the group and want to align their behavior with the team's expectations. The more closely the person's social identity is connected to the group, the more the individual is motivated to obey the team's norms.[47]

Managing Team Norms The two best ways to establish desired norms in new teams are to select team members whose values and past behavior are compatible with those norms and to clearly state the norms when those people are assigned to the

Team norms improve predictability and conflict-avoidance in coworker relations; they also improve social order and coordination among team members.
Larry Williams/Getty Images

role a set of behaviors that people are expected to perform because they hold specific formal or informal positions in a team and organization

team cohesion the degree of attraction people feel toward the team and their motivation to remain members

team. As an example, if organizational leaders want their teams to have strong safety norms, they should hire people who already value safety and clearly state the importance of safety during one of the team's first meetings.

For existing teams, research indicates that leaders have the capacity to remove dysfunctional norms by cautioning team members against these behaviors. They can also introduce desired norms through ongoing coaching of team members.[48] Another suggestion that works sometimes (but not always) is to introduce team-based rewards that reinforce desired norms and counteract dysfunctional norms. Finally, if dysfunctional norms are deeply ingrained and the previous solutions don't work, it may be necessary to disband the group and form a new team whose members have more appropriate norms.

Team Roles

An inherent part of the team development process is assigning and maintaining team roles. A **role** is a set of behaviors that people are expected to perform because they hold specific formal or informal positions in a team and organization.[49] Roles are similar to norms in the sense that they both establish and reinforce expected patterns of behavior. However, most norms apply to all team members, whereas a role typically applies to one or a few specific team members.

Some team roles are formally assigned to individual members during the team composition aspect of team design. For example, most teams have a leader, and that person is expected to help clarify task responsibilities, ensure that everyone has an opportunity to present his or her views in meetings, and so forth. However, many roles are adopted informally during the team development process. Informal roles are shared, but many are eventually associated with specific team members through subtle positioning and negotiation. In many cases, employees are attracted to roles that suit their personality and values. In other cases, team members encourage specific coworkers to take on selected roles.

Several experts have tried to categorize the various team roles. One recent model identifies six role categories: organizer, doer, challenger, innovator, team builder, and connector.[50] More broadly, most team roles focus on either task performance (taskwork) or team maintenance (teamwork). Taskwork roles might include coordinating the team, providing constructive critique of the team's plans, and motivating team members when effort is lagging. Teamwork roles might include providing emotional support when the team is frustrated, maintaining harmony among team members, and creating opportunities for social interaction among team members.

McGraw Hill connect

SELF-ASSESSMENT 7.2: What Team Roles Do You Prefer?

Team Cohesion

Another team process is **team cohesion**, which refers to the degree of attraction people feel toward the team and their motivation to remain members. A team has high cohesion when its members are attracted to the team, take ownership of the team's success, make the team part of their self-concept, are committed to the team's goals or tasks, and feel a collective sense of team pride.[51] Thus, team cohesion is an emotional experience, not just a calculation of whether to stay or leave the team.

Influences on Team Cohesion Six of the most important influences on team cohesion are described below. Some of these conditions strengthen the individual's identity with the team; others strengthen the individual's belief that team membership will fulfill personal needs.

- *Member similarity.* A well-established research finding is that we are attracted more to coworkers who are similar to us.[52] This similarity-attraction effect occurs because we assume that people are more trustworthy and more likely to accept us if they look and act like us. We also believe that these similar others will create fewer conflicts and violations of our expectations. Thus, teams have higher cohesion or become cohesive more quickly when members are similar to each other. In contrast, high cohesion is more difficult and takes longer in teams with diverse members. This difficulty varies with the form of diversity, however.[53]
- *Team size.* Smaller teams tend to have more cohesion than larger teams. One reason is that it is easier for a few people to agree on goals

OB THEORY TO PRACTICE

Managing Norms in New and Established Teams

For New Teams

- Select team members whose values and past behavior are compatible with the desired norms.
- Clearly state desired norms to incoming team members.

For Established Teams

- Remove dysfunctional norms by cautioning team members against these behaviors.
- Introduce desired norms through ongoing coaching of team members.
- Introduce team-based rewards that reinforce desired norms and counteract dysfunctional norms.
- If the above actions fail: Disband the group and form a new team whose members have more appropriate norms.

and coordinate work activities. Another reason is that members have more influence in smaller teams, so they feel a greater sense of involvement and ownership in the team. However, small teams have less cohesion when they lack enough qualified members to perform the required tasks.

- *Member interaction.* Teams tend to have more cohesion when their members interact with each other fairly regularly. More frequent interaction occurs when team members perform highly interdependent tasks and work in the same physical area or at least communicate remotely through channels with high social presence.
- *Somewhat difficult entry.* Teams tend to have more cohesion when entry to the team is restricted. The more elite the team, the more prestige it confers on its members, and the more they tend to value their membership in the unit. At the same time, research suggests that severe initiations can weaken team cohesion because of the adverse effects of humiliation, even for those who successfully endure the initiation.[54]
- *Team success.* Team cohesion increases with the team's success because people are attracted to groups that fulfill their needs and goals.[55] Furthermore, individuals are more likely to identify with successful teams than with teams that often fail to achieve their goals.
- *External competition and challenges.* Teams tend to have more cohesion when they face external competition or a challenging objective that is important. Employees value their membership on the team because of its ability to overcome the threat or competition and as a form of social support. However, cohesion can dissipate when external challenges overwhelm the team and threaten its success or viability.[56]

Members of highly cohesive teams spend more time together, share information more frequently, and are more satisfied with each other.
Peopleimages/Getty Images

Consequences of Team Cohesion Teams with higher cohesion tend to perform better than those with low cohesion.[57] In fact, the team's existence depends on some level of cohesion because it motivates team members to remain members and help the team achieve its objectives. Members of highly cohesive teams spend more time together, share information more frequently, and are more satisfied with each other. They give each other more social support in stressful situations and work to minimize dysfunctional conflict.[58] When conflict does arise, members of highly cohesive teams tend to resolve their differences swiftly and effectively.

The relationship between team cohesion and team performance depends on two conditions, however. First, team cohesion has less effect on team performance when the team has low task interdependence.[59] High cohesion motivates employees to coordinate and cooperate with other team members. But cooperation and coordination are less critical when the team members don't depend on each other to perform their jobs (i.e., low task interdependence), so the motivational effect of high cohesion is less relevant under those conditions.

Second, the effect of cohesion on team performance depends on whether the team's norms are aligned or conflict with organizational objectives.[60] As Exhibit 7.6 illustrates, teams with high cohesion perform better when their norms support the company's goals, whereas higher cohesion can potentially reduce team performance when norms are counterproductive. This effect occurs because cohesion motivates employees to perform at a level more consistent with team norms. If a team's norm tolerates or encourages absenteeism, employees will be more motivated to take unjustified sick leave. If the team's norm discourages absenteeism, employees are more motivated to avoid taking sick leave.

Exhibit 7.6 Effect of Team Cohesion on Task Performance

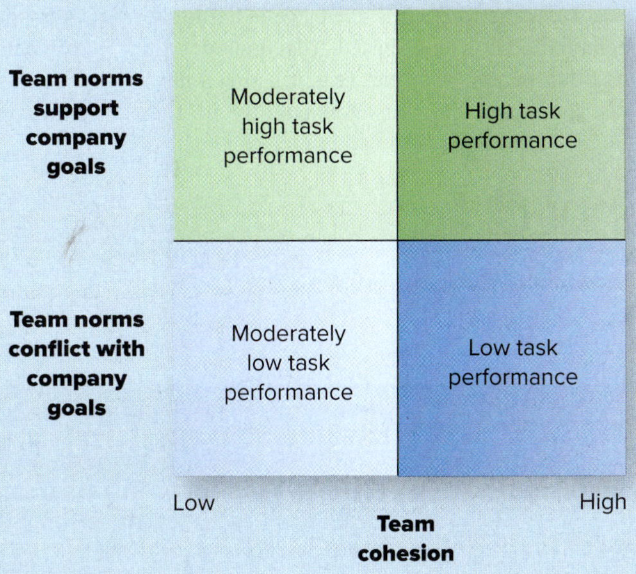

trust positive expectations one person has toward another person in situations involving risk

mental models knowledge structures that we develop to describe, explain, and predict the world around us

One last comment about team cohesion and performance: A few paragraphs ago we stated that team performance (success) causes cohesion, whereas we are now saying that team cohesion causes team performance. Both statements are correct. Teams with higher cohesion perform better, and teams with better performance become more cohesive. Which direction is stronger? A major review of past studies reported that in established teams (i.e., typical of teams in most organizations), cohesion has a much stronger effect on team performance than the effect of team performance on team cohesion. Only lab experiments that studied short-lived student teams found that both directions were equal. Student teams typically have fairly low cohesion due to their brief existence and non-essential purpose to most members.[61]

Team Trust

Any relationship—including the relationship among team members—depends on a certain degree of trust.[62] **Trust** refers to positive expectations one person has toward another person in situations involving risk (see Chapter 4). Trust is ultimately perceptual; we trust others on the basis of our beliefs about their ability, integrity, and benevolence. Trust is also emotional; we experience positive feelings toward those we trust.[63]

Trust is built on three foundations in a hierarchy from lowest to highest: calculus, knowledge, and identification.[64] *Calculus-based trust* represents a logical calculation that other team members will act appropriately because they face sanctions if their actions violate reasonable expectations.[65] It offers the lowest potential trust and is easily broken by a violation of expectations. *Knowledge-based trust* is based on the predictability of another team member's behavior. This predictability refers only to "positive expectations," as the definition of trust states, because you would not trust someone who tends to engage in harmful or dysfunctional behavior. Knowledge-based trust includes our confidence in the other person's abilities (e.g., trusting a physician) as well as someone who acts consistently in their performance toward team goals.[66] Knowledge-based trust offers a higher potential level of trust and is more stable because it develops over time.

Identification-based trust is based on mutual understanding and an emotional bond among team members. It occurs when team members think, feel, and act like one another. High-performance teams exhibit this level of trust because they share the same values and mental models. Identification-based trust is potentially the strongest and most robust of all three types of trust.[67] The individual's self-concept is based partly on membership in the team whose members hold similar values, so any transgressions by other team members are quickly forgiven. People are more reluctant to acknowledge a violation of this high-level trust because it strikes at the heart of their self-concept.

Dynamics of Team Trust Employees typically join a team with a moderate or high level—not a low level—of trust in their new coworkers.[68] The main explanation why people have high trust (called *swift trust*) at the outset is that they usually believe fellow team members are reasonably competent (knowledge-based trust) and they tend to develop some degree of social identity with the team (identification-based trust). Even when working with strangers, most employees display some level of trust, if only because it supports their self-view of being a good person. However, trust is fragile in new relationships because it is based on assumptions rather than well-established experience. Studies report that trust tends to decrease rather than increase over time.[69]

Team Mental Models

Mental models are visual or relational images in our mind that we develop to describe, explain, and predict the world around us (see Chapter 3). Team mental models are cognitive images that team members form about the team's tasks, relationship dynamics, and knowledge repository.[70] Team members have both shared and complementary mental models. As a team matures, its members form shared mental models, meaning that they develop similar images and expectations about the team's objectives, shared values, behavior norms, and work style, as well as a general picture of how each member participates in the work process.

Complementary mental models are cognitive images held by specific (rather than all) team members but that are compatible with the mental models held by other team members. Each team member has a unique background and is located in different parts of the work process. Consequently,

McGraw Hill connect

SELF-ASSESSMENT 7.3: How Trusting Are You?

> As a team matures, its members form shared mental models—similar images and expectations about the team's objectives, values, norms, work process, etc.

each member has unique perceptions about how the team operates. For example, engineering team members would view customers somewhat differently from how marketing members of that team view customers. In successful teams, each member's mental model operates in harmony with the unique mental models of other team members.

Shared and complementary mental models enable team members to establish effective coordinating routines.[71] In high-performing teams, each member develops habitual work practices that coordinate almost automatically with the behaviors and expectations of other members. This alignment of mental images and predictions also support the perception that the group is a functioning social entity with meaningful purpose and performance capabilities.

Team mental models also help team members to know where knowledge is located within the team.[72] Members of cross-functional teams, for instance, have diverse knowledge and skills (production, legal, marketing, technology, etc.) that are collectively applied to achieve the team's objectives. To make better decisions or serve clients well, team members often need to consult with coworkers who possesses specific skills and knowledge. This awareness of the team's diverse knowledge repository is therefore a vital part of team mental models.

Improving Team Processes through Team Building

Teams require time to become cohesive, form productive norms, assign roles, build knowledge and identification-level trust, and form functioning shared and complementary mental models. Team building consists of activities that attempt to speed up or improve these team development processes.[73]

As we have emphasized throughout this section, team development consists of several diverse team processes. Therefore, not surprisingly, there are several types of team building to serve those processes. Some team-building interventions are task-focused. They clarify the team's performance goals, increase the team's motivation to accomplish these goals, and establish a mechanism for systematic feedback on the team's goal performance. A second type of team building focuses on improving the team's problem-solving skills.

A third team building category clarifies and reconstructs each member's perception of her or his role as well as the role expectations that member has of other team members. Role definition team building also helps the team to develop shared and complementary mental models, such as how to interact with clients, maintain machinery, and engage in meetings.[74] A fourth—and likely the most popular—type of team building is aimed at helping team members to improve interpersonal relations, such as building trust in each other and becoming a more cohesive team.[75] Popular interventions such as wilderness team activities, paintball wars, and obstacle-course challenges are intended to support these team processes.

Some team building interventions work better than others and in some situations more than others.[77] Goal setting tends to be the most successful type of team building, although role clarification and adventure programs (to improve interpersonal relations) are also effective to some extent. Interventions are also more successful when they focus on one rather than multiple team-building objectives.

However, many team-building activities fall short of their potential.[78] One problem is that these activities are often applied as a general solution without adequately diagnosing the specific issues that need to be addressed to improve team effectiveness. Team building also tends to be applied as a one-shot jump start for a newly-formed team, whereas it should be an ongoing process throughout the team's existence. Finally, we must remember that team building occurs on the job, not just on an obstacle course or in a national park. Organizations should encourage team members to reflect on their work experiences and to experiment with just-in-time learning for team development.

OB THEORY TO PRACTICE

Popular Team-Building Activities[76]

Team-Building Activity	Description	Example
Team volunteering events	Teams of employees spend a day providing a public service to the community.	Nicor Gas employees in Illinois volunteer their time in teams to help the community, such as building a house for Habitat for Humanity.
Team scavenger hunt or treasure hunt events	Teams follow instructions to find clues or objects collected throughout the building or community.	Employees at Treatwell, Europe's largest hair salon booking website, engaged in a scavenger hunt around Barcelona, Spain, with teams comprising staff from the firm's 10 countries.
Team sports or exercise events	Team members engage in a wide variety of sports or health activities, such as sports tournaments across departments.	Employee teams at SmartBiz Loans in San Francisco compete in ring-toss, egg relay, touch football, and other activities during the company's annual SmartBiz Olympics.
Team cooking events	Team members either learn how to cook a quality meal or several teams compete in teams to make the best dish with given ingredients.	Employee teams at software company Cobalt participated in an Iron Chef competition, where they had one hour to make the best dish that incorporated a themed ingredient.

LO7-5 Discuss the characteristics and factors required for the success of self-directed teams and remote teams.

SELF-DIRECTED AND REMOTE (VIRTUAL) TEAMS

This chapter began by noting that there are many types of teams in organizations. This section highlights two increasingly important types of teams in the workplace: self-directed teams and remote teams.

Self-Directed Teams

Self-directed teams (SDTs) are cross-functional groups organized around work processes that complete an entire piece of work requiring several interdependent tasks and have substantial autonomy over the execution of those tasks.[79] This definition captures two distinct features of SDTs. First, these teams complete an entire piece of work requiring several interdependent tasks. Employees within the team are clustered together with minimal interdependence or interaction with people outside the team. The result is a close-knit group of employees who depend on each other to accomplish the team's work objectives. The second distinctive feature of SDTs is that they have substantial autonomy over the execution of their tasks. In particular, these teams plan, organize, and control work activities with little or no direct involvement of a higher-status supervisor.

Success Factors for Self-Directed Teams Self-directed teams are found in several industries, ranging from petrochemical plants to aircraft parts manufacturing. Most of the top-rated manufacturing firms in North America apparently rely on SDTs.[80] Indeed, self-directed teams have become such a popular way to organize employees that many companies don't realize they have them.

The popularity of SDTs is consistent with research indicating that they potentially increase both productivity and job satisfaction.[81] However, the success of self-directed teams depends on several factors.[82] SDTs should be responsible for an entire work process, such as making an entire product or providing a service. This structure keeps each team sufficiently independent from other teams, yet it demands a relatively high degree of interdependence among employees within the team.[83] In addition, SDTs should have sufficient autonomy to organize and coordinate their work. Autonomy allows them to respond more quickly and effectively to client and stakeholder demands. It also increases intrinsic motivation among team members. Finally, SDTs are more successful when the work site and technology support coordination and communication among team members. Too often, management calls a group of employees a "team," yet the work layout, assembly-line structure, and other technologies isolate the employees from one another.

> **OB THEORY TO PRACTICE**
>
> ### Building Successful Self-Directed Teams at Buurtzorg Nederland[84]
>
> Buurtzorg Nederland employs almost 15,000 professionals (mostly registered nurses) in more than 1,000 self-directed teams across the Netherlands and other countries. "Self-managing teams have professional freedom with responsibility," says Buurtzorg's website.
>
> Each self-directed team consists of up to 12 nurses responsible for between 50 and 60 home care patients, most of whom are elderly, disabled, or terminally ill. The team members have autonomy to organize the work, make decisions, and build their own caseload of new clients. Performance is measured at the team level, including patient satisfaction, work efficiency, and cost savings.
>
> Independent studies report that Buurtzorg's self-directed teams are significantly more cost-efficient than traditional (mostly non-team) services by competitors. Employees also enjoy the team structure. The company has been the top employer in the Netherlands for several consecutive years.

Remote (Virtual) Teams

Chapter 1 described how *remote work*—performing work from home or other nonbusiness site—has become a common arrangement in most organizations. However, the COVID-19 pandemic made remote work more appealing and necessary as a productive way to apply social distancing and self-isolation practices. Most employees work in teams for some or all of their tasks, so the increasing popularity of remote work has produced more remote teams.

Remote teams (also known as *virtual* or *distributed teams*) are teams whose members operate across space, time, and organizational boundaries and are linked through information technologies to achieve organizational tasks.[85] Remote teams differ from traditional teams in two ways: (1) One or more members work remotely at least some of the time rather than always being colocated (working in the same physical area as coworkers), and (2) due to their lack of colocation, members of remote teams depend primarily on information technologies in addition to or instead of face-to-face interaction to communicate and coordinate their work effort.

Teams vary in their degree of remoteness (or *virtuality*). Team remoteness increases with the geographic dispersion of team members, percentage of members who work apart, and percentage of time that members work apart.[86] For example, a team has minimal remoteness when most of its members work in the same physical location most days and only one or two work from home occasionally. High remoteness exists when team members are spread around the world and few members have met the others face-to-face.

A team's remoteness depends on the geographic dispersion of its members, percentage of members who work apart, and percentage of time that members work apart.
Ariel Skelley/Getty Images

self-directed teams (SDTs) cross-functional work groups that are organized around work processes, complete an entire piece of work requiring several interdependent tasks, and have substantial autonomy over the execution of those tasks

remote teams teams whose members operate across space, time, and organizational boundaries and are linked through information technologies to achieve organizational tasks

human capital the knowledge, skills, abilities, creative thinking, and other valued resources that employees bring to the organization

The social distancing and self-isolation requirements in the COVID-19 pandemic have made remote teams more commonplace. However, these teams were gaining popularity in organizations many years earlier. One factor is that an increasing percentage of employees perform knowledge work (rather than physical production work), which enables them to do their job from almost anywhere. Second, information technologies have made it easier than ever to communicate and coordinate remotely with other knowledge workers.[87] A third factor is the increasing recognition that the organization's competitive advantage is its **human capital**—the knowledge, skills, abilities, creativity, and other valued resources that employees bring to the organization. Leveraging the potential of human capital typically occurs through teams, many of which have degrees of remoteness because staff members are distributed across several cities and countries.

Success Factors for Remote Teams Remote teams face all the challenges of traditional teams, as well as the issues arising from time and distance. These challenges increase with the team's remoteness, particularly when the team exists for only a short time.[88] Fortunately, OB research has identified the following strategies to minimize most remote team problems.[89] First, remote team members need to apply the effective team behaviors (five Cs) described earlier in this chapter. They also require good communication technology skills, self-leadership skills to motivate and guide their behavior without peers or bosses nearby, and emotional intelligence to decipher the feelings of other team members from text messages and other limited communication media.

Second, remote teams should have a toolkit of communication channels (messaging, online whiteboards, video conferencing, etc.) as well as the freedom to choose the channels that work best for them.[90] This recommendation may seem obvious, but unfortunately senior management tends to impose technology on remote teams, often based on advice from external consultants, and expects team members to use the same communication technology throughout their work. In contrast, research suggests that communication channels gain and lose importance over time, depending on the task and level of trust.

> Remote teams need plenty of structure, such as clear operational objectives, documented work processes, and agreed-on roles and responsibilities.

Third, remote teams need plenty of structure, such as clear operational objectives, documented work processes, and agreed-on roles and responsibilities.[91] The final recommendation is that remote team members should meet face-to-face fairly early in the team development process. This idea may seem contradictory to the entire notion of remote teams, but so far, no technology has replaced face-to-face interaction for high-level bonding and mutual understanding.[92]

> Creative ideas often sound bizarre or illogical when first presented, so evaluation apprehension tends to discourage employees from mentioning them in front of coworkers.

LO7-6 Identify four constraints on team decision making and discuss ways to improve decision making and creativity in teams.

TEAM DECISION MAKING

Self-directed teams, remote teams, and practically all other groups are expected to make decisions. Teams are potentially more effective than individuals at identifying problems, choosing alternatives, and evaluating their decisions. To leverage these benefits, however, we first need to understand the constraints on effective team decision making. Then, we look at specific team structures that try to overcome these constraints.

Constraints on Team Decision Making

Anyone who has spent enough time in the workplace can recite several ways in which teams stumble in decision making. The four most common problems are time constraints, evaluation apprehension, pressure to conform, and overconfidence.

Time Constraints Committees keep minutes and waste hours. This popular saying captures the fact that teams take longer than individuals to make decisions.[93] Teams consume time organizing, coordinating, and maintaining relationships (i.e., process losses). Team members require time to build rapport, agree on rules and norms of behavior in the decision process, and understand each other's ideas.

Another time-related constraint in most team structures is that only one person can speak at a time.[94] This problem, known as **production blocking**, undermines idea generation in a few ways. First, team members need to listen in on the conversation to find an opportune time to speak up, but this monitoring makes it difficult for them to concentrate on their own ideas. Second, ideas are fleeting, so the longer participants wait to speak, the more likely their flickering ideas will die out. Third, team members might remember their fleeting thoughts by concentrating on them, but this causes them to pay less attention to the conversation. By ignoring what others are saying, team members miss other potentially good ideas.

> Insanity in individuals is something rare—but in groups, parties, nations, and epochs, it is the rule.[98]
>
> —Friedrich Nietzsche, 1800s German philosopher

Evaluation Apprehension Team members are often reluctant to mention ideas that seem silly because they believe (often correctly) that other team members are silently evaluating them.[95] This **evaluation apprehension** is based on the individual's desire to create a favorable public image and need to protect self-esteem. It is most common when meetings are attended by people with different levels of status or expertise or when members formally evaluate each other's performance throughout the year. Creative ideas often sound bizarre or illogical when first presented, so evaluation apprehension tends to discourage employees from mentioning them in front of coworkers.

Pressure to Conform Team cohesion leads employees to conform to the team's norms. This control keeps the group organized around common goals, but it also may cause team members to suppress their dissenting opinions, particularly when a strong team norm is related to the issue. When someone does state a point of view that violates the majority opinion, other members might punish the violator or try to persuade him or her that the opinion is incorrect. Conformity also can be subtle. To some extent, we depend on the opinions that others hold to validate our own views. If coworkers don't agree with us, we begin to question our own opinions even without overt peer pressure.

Overconfidence (Inflated Team Efficacy) To some degree, teams are more successful when their members have collective confidence in how well they work together and the likely success of their team effort.[96] This **team efficacy** is similar to individual self-efficacy, which we discussed in Chapter 3. High-efficacy teams set more challenging goals and are more motivated to achieve them, both of which increase team performance.

Unfortunately, there is a curvilinear relationship between team efficacy and the quality of team decisions (as well as other forms of team performance). In other words, teams make worse decisions when they are overconfident as well as underconfident.[97] Overconfident teams are less vigilant when making decisions, partly because they have more positive than negative emotions and moods during these events. They also engage in less constructive debate and are less likely to seek out or accept information located outside the team, both of which undermine the quality of team decisions.

Why do teams become overconfident? The main reason is a team-level variation of self-enhancement (see Chapter 3). Team members have a natural motivation to believe that the team's capabilities are above average. Overconfidence is more common in highly cohesive teams because self-enhancement occurs for things that are important. By definition, members of cohesive teams value their association with the team. Overconfidence is also stronger when the team has external threats or competition because these adversaries generate "us versus them" differentiation. Team efficacy is further inflated by the mutually reinforcing beliefs of the team. Employees develop a clearly and higher opinion of their team when other team members echo that opinion.

Improving Decision Making and Creativity in Teams

Team decision making is fraught with problems, but there are several ways to minimize these pitfalls. Checks and balances need to be in place to prevent the leader or other individuals from dominating the discussion. The team should also be large enough to possess the collective knowledge to resolve the problem yet small enough to avoid consuming too much time or restrict individual input. Team members should be confident in their decision making but also be wary about being overconfident. This calls for team team membership with sufficient diversity as well as team norms that encourage critical thinking.

Another important ingredient for effective team decision making is an environment in which team members have psychological safety.[99] **Psychological safety** is a shared belief that engaging in interpersonal risk-taking will not have adverse consequences. This belief exists when employees are confident that they can constructively disagree with the majority, present weird ideas, or experiment with novel behaviors without fear that coworkers will belittle them or that the company will limit their career progress. Psychological safety requires team norms that encourage employees to respect and value one another, demonstrate interest in one another, be open-minded about and tolerant with coworkers' opinions, and show positive intentions toward one another. Showing positive intentions involves displaying positive emotions and nonthreatening behavior when discussing different points of view.

Brainstorming rules potentially increase divergent thinking and minimize evaluation apprehension, but field research indicates that these benefits require an experienced facilitator and confident employees who work in a collaborative learning orientation culture that prioritizes psychological safety.
wavebreakmedia/Shutterstock

These recommendations improve most types of team-level decisions. OB studies have also identified four team structures that encourage creativity in a team setting: brainstorming, brainwriting, electronic brainstorming, and nominal group technique.

- **Brainstorming.** This team event encourages participants to think up many ideas for the ultimate objective of generating the most creative ideas.[100] The process consists of four rules: (1) Speak freely—describe even the craziest ideas, (2) don't criticize others or their ideas, (3) provide as many ideas as possible—the quality of ideas increases with the quantity of ideas, and (4) build on the ideas that others have presented. Brainstorming rules potentially increase divergent thinking and minimize evaluation apprehension, but field research indicates that these benefits require an experienced facilitator and confident employees who work in a collaborative learning orientation culture that prioritizes psychological safety.[101]
- **Brainwriting.** This is a variation of brainstorming that minimizes the problem of production blocking by removing conversation during idea generation.[102] There are many forms of brainwriting, but they all have the common feature that individuals write down their ideas rather than verbally describe them. In one version, participants write their ideas on cards and place them in the center of the table. At any time, participants can pick up one or more cards in the center to spark their thinking or further build (piggyback) on those ideas. The limited research on brainwriting suggests that it produces more and better quality ideas than brainstorming due to the lack of production blocking.

production blocking a time constraint in team decision making due to the procedural requirement that only one person may speak at a time

evaluation apprehension a decision-making problem that occurs when individuals are reluctant to mention ideas that seem silly because they believe (often correctly) that other team members are silently evaluating them

team efficacy the collective belief among team members in the team's capability to successfully complete a task

psychological safety a shared belief that it is safe to engage in interpersonal risk-taking; specifically, that presenting unusual ideas, constructively disagreeing with the majority, and experimenting with new work behaviors will not result in coworkers posing a threat to their self-concept, status, or career

brainstorming a freewheeling, face-to-face meeting where team members aren't allowed to criticize but are encouraged to speak freely, generate as many ideas as possible, and build on the ideas of others

brainwriting a variation of brainstorming whereby participants write (rather than speak about) and share their ideas

electronic brainstorming a form of brainstorming that relies on networked computers for submitting and sharing creative ideas

nominal group technique a variation of brainwriting consisting of three stages in which participants (1) silently and independently document their ideas, (2) collectively describe these ideas to the other team members without critique, and then (3) silently and independently evaluate the ideas presented

- **Electronic brainstorming**. This activity is similar to brainwriting but uses digital networks rather than handwritten cards to document and share ideas. After receiving the question or issue, participants enter their ideas using special digital software. The ideas are distributed anonymously to other participants, who are encouraged to piggyback on those ideas. Team members eventually vote electronically on the ideas presented. Face-to-face discussion usually follows. Electronic brainstorming can be quite effective at generating creative ideas with minimal production blocking, evaluation apprehension, or conformity problems.[103] Yet, this activity is seldom used because it tends to be too structured and technology-bound.
- **Nominal group technique**. This is another variation of brainwriting, but adds a verbal element to the process.[104] The problem is described, team members silently and independently write down as many solutions as they can, then they describe their solutions to the other team members, usually in a round-robin format. As with brainstorming, there is no criticism or debate, just clarification. Finally, participants silently and independently rank-order or vote on each proposed solution. Nominal group technique has been used in real-world decisions and tends to improve the quality of ideas generated. However, production blocking and evaluation apprehension still occur to some extent. Training improves this structured approach to team decision making.[105]

Study Checklist

Connect® is available for *M Organizational Behavior*. Additional resources include:

✓ Exercises:

- **Case Analysis:** Apply concepts within the context of a real-world situation.
- **Click and Drag:** Helps make the connection between theory and application through matching, ranking, or grouping activities.
- **Video Case:** See management in action through interactive videos.
- **Self-Assessment:** Designed to promote student self-awareness and reflection, these research-based surveys contain detailed feedback for students.
- **Application-Based Activities:** These highly interactive, application- and analysis-based exercises allow students to take on specific roles to complete management-related tasks within a real-world context.

✓ **SmartBook 2.0™**—Smartbook 2.0 is an adaptive learning solution that provides personalized learning to individual student needs, continually adapts to pinpoint knowledge gaps and focuses learning on concepts requiring additional study. It fosters more productive learning, takes the guesswork out of what to study, and helps students better prepare for class.

Notes

1. S. Garmhausen, "Why Teams Dominate at the Top Financial Advisors," *Barron's*, April 19, 2019; A. Willis, "Why RBC Is Becoming the New England Patriots of Bay Street," *Globe & Mail*, April 24, 2019; "Canada's Best Investment Bank 2019: RBC Capital Markets," *Euromoney*, July 10, 2019.
2. M.E. Shaw, *Group Dynamics*, 3rd ed. (New York: McGraw-Hill, 1981), 8; E. Sundstrom, "The Challenges of Supporting Work Team Effectiveness," in *Supporting Work Team Effectiveness* ed. E. Sundstrom and Associates (San Francisco, CA: Jossey-Bass, 1999), 6–9; L.E. Benishek and E.H. Lazzara, "Teams in a New Era: Some Considerations and Implications," *Frontiers in Psychology* 10 (2019), https://doi.org/10.3389/fpsyg.2019.01006. Even though a distinct social entity, a team's boundaries (who is and who is not a member) may be fuzzier than previously assumed. See M. Mortensen and M.R. Haas, "Perspective–Rethinking Teams: From Bounded Membership to Dynamic Participation," *Organization Science* 29 (2018): 341–55.
3. J.R. Hollenbeck, B. Beersma, and M.E. Schouten, "Beyond Team Types and Taxonomies: A Dimensional Scaling Conceptualization for Team Description," *Academy of Management Review* 37, no. 1 (2012): 82–106. This article uses the term *skill differentiation*, whereas we use *skill diversity*, which is a more common label to describe variations among team members; skill differences represent a form of deep-level diversity. The original article also uses the label *authority differentiation*, whereas we believe that *authority dispersion* is more consistent with power variations, such as in decentralization of organizational structures.
4. J.R. Spoor and J.R. Kelly, "The Evolutionary Significance of Affect in Groups: Communication and Group Bonding," *Group Processes & Intergroup Relations* 7 (2004): 398–412; W.S. Jansen et al., "Inclusion: Conceptualization and Measurement," *European Journal of Social Psychology* 44 (2014): 370–85.
5. S.A. Haslam and N. Ellemers, "Identity Processes in Organizations," in *Handbook of Identity Theory and Research*, ed. J.S. Schwartz, K. Luyckx, and L.V. Vignoles (New York: Springer New York, 2011), 715–44; R. Spears, "Group Identities: The Social Identity Perspective," in *Handbook of Identity Theory and Research*, ed. S.J. Schwartz, K. Luyckx, and V.L. Vignoles (New York: Springer New York, 2011), 201–24; S.K. Kang and G.V. Bodenhausen, "Multiple Identities in Social Perception and Interaction: Challenges and Opportunities," *Annual Review of Psychology* 66 (2015): 547–74.

6. S. Cohen, "The Pittsburgh Common Cold Studies: Psychosocial Predictors of Susceptibility to Respiratory Infectious Illness," *International Journal of Behavioral Medicine* 12, no. 3 (2005): 123–31; S.Y. Shin and S.G. Lee, "Effects of Hospital Workers? Friendship Networks on Job Stress," *PLoS ONE* 11, no. 2 (2016): e0149428.

7. R. Cross and R.J. Thomas, *Driving Results through Social Networks: How Top Organizations Leverage Networks for Performance and Growth* (San Francisco: Jossey-Bass, 2009); R. McDermott and D. Archibald, "Harnessing Your Staff's Informal Networks," *Harvard Business Review* 88, no. 3 (2010): 82–89; J.R. Methot, E.H. Rosado-Solomon, and D.G. Allen, "The Network Architecture of Human Capital: A Relational Identity Perspective," *Academy of Management Review* 43 (2018): 723–48.

8. M. Moldaschl and W. Weber, "The 'Three Waves' of Industrial Group Work: Historical Reflections on Current Research on Group Work," *Human Relations* 51 (1998): 347–88. Several popular books in the 1980s encouraged teamwork, based on the Japanese economic miracle. These books include W. Ouchi, *Theory Z: How American Management Can Meet the Japanese Challenge* (Reading, MA: Addison-Wesley, 1981); R. T. Pascale and A. G. Athos, *Art of Japanese Management* (New York: Simon & Schuster, 1982).

9. C.R. Emery and L.D. Fredenhall, "The Effect of Teams on Firm Profitability and Customer Satisfaction," *Journal of Service Research* 4 (2002): 217–29; J.R. Hackman, *Collaborative Intelligence: Using Teams to Solve Hard Problems* (San Francisco: Berrett-Koehler Publishers, 2011); E. Salas, D.L. Reyes, and S.H. McDaniel, "The Science of Teamwork: Progress, Reflections, and the Road Ahead.," *American Psychologist* 73 (2018): 593–600.

10. M. Jordan, *I Can't Accept Not Trying: Michael Jordan on the Pursuit of Excellence* (San Francisco: Harper, 1994), 24.

11. R.E. Baumeister and M.R. Leary, "The Need to Belong: Desire for Interpersonal Attachments as a Fundamental Human Motivation," *Psychological Bulletin* 117 (1995): 497–529; J.M. Feinberg and J.R. Aiello, "Social Facilitation: A Test of Competing Theories," *Journal of Applied Social Psychology* 36, no. 5 (2006): 1087–109; A.M. Grant, "Relational Job Design and the Motivation to Make a Prosocial Difference," *Academy of Management Review* 32, no. 2 (2007): 393–417; N.L. Kerr and D.H. Seok, "'. . . with a Little Help from My Friends': Friendship, Effort Norms, and Group Motivation Gain," *Journal of Managerial Psychology* 26, no. 3 (2011): 205–18; D. Herbst and A. Mas, "Peer Effects on Worker Output in the Laboratory Generalize to the Field," *Science* 350, no. 6260 (2015): 545–49.

12. This information is from the websites of these companies, mostly on their "Careers" or "Our Values" pages.

13. E.A. Locke et al., "The Importance of the Individual in an Age of Groupism," in *Groups at Work: Theory and Research*, ed. M.E. Turner (Mahwah, NJ: Erlbaum, 2001), 501–28; N.J. Allen and T.D. Hecht, "The 'Romance of Teams': Toward an Understanding of Its Psychological Underpinnings and Implications," *Journal of Occupational and Organizational Psychology* 77 (2004): 439–61.

14. I.D. Steiner, *Group Process and Productivity* (New York: Academic Press, 1972); S. Coyle, K. Conboy, and T. Acton, "Group Process Losses in Agile Software Development Decision Making," *International Journal of Intelligent Information Technologies* 9, no. 2 (2013): 38–53; K. Srikanth, S. Harvey, and R. Peterson, "A Dynamic Perspective on Diverse Teams: Moving from the Dual-Process Model to a Dynamic Coordination-Based Model of Diverse Team Performance," *Academy of Management Annals* 10 (2016): 453–93.

15. G.K. Stahl et al., "Unraveling the Effects of Cultural Diversity in Teams: A Meta-Analysis of Research on Multicultural Work Groups," *Journal of International Business Studies* 41 (2010): 690–709; M.W. McCarter and R.M. Sheremeta, "You Can't Put Old Wine in New Bottles: The Effect of Newcomers on Coordination in Groups," *PLoS ONE* 8, no. 1 (2013): e55058.

16. F.P. Brooks, ed. *The Mythical Man- Month: Essays on Software Engineering*, Second ed. (Reading, MA: Addison-Wesley, 1995); B.R. Staats, K.L. Milkman, and C.R. Fox, "The Team Scaling Fallacy: Underestimating the Declining Efficiency of Larger Teams," *Organizational Behavior and Human Decision Processes* 118, no. 2 (2012): 132–42; T. van Balen and M. Tarakci, "Never Change a Winning Team?," SSRN Scholarly Paper (Rochester, NY: Social Science Research Network, May 4, 2017).

17. The origin of this quotation remains unknown. The earliest publication of this quotation that we could find is in *Madison (WI) Magazine* 43 (2001): 62.

18. S.J. Karau and K.D. Williams, "Social Loafing: A Meta-Analytic Review and Theoretical Integration," *Journal of Personality and Social Psychology* 65 (1993): 681–706; R.C. Liden et al., "Social Loafing: A Field Investigation," *Journal of Management* 30 (2004): 285–304.

19. B. Latane, K. Williams, and S. Harkins, "Many Hands Make Light the Work: The Causes and Consequences of Social Loafing," *Journal of Personality & Social Psychology* 37 (1979): 822–32; U.-C. Klehe and N. Anderson, "The Moderating Influence of Personality and Culture on Social Loafing in Typical versus Maximum Performance Situations," *International Journal of Selection and Assessment* 15 (2007): 250–62; R. B. Lount and S. L. Wilk, "Working Harder or Hardly Working? Posting Performance Eliminates Social Loafing and Promotes Social Laboring in Workgroups," *Management Science* 60 (2014): 1098–106; M. C. Schippers, "Social Loafing Tendencies and Team Performance: The Compensating Effect of Agreeableness and Conscientiousness," *Academy of Management Learning & Education* 13 (2014): 62–81; B. Meyer, C. C. Schermuly, and S. Kauffeld, "That's Not My Place: The Interacting Effects of Faultlines, Subgroup Size, and Social Competence on Social Loafing Behaviour in Work Groups," *European Journal of Work and Organizational Psychology* 25 (2016): 31–49.

20. C. Lam, "The Role of Communication and Cohesion in Reducing Social Loafing in Group Projects," *Business and Professional Communication Quarterly* 78 (2015): 454–75; S.H. Czyż et al., "Participation in Team Sports Can Eliminate the Effect of Social Loafing," *Perceptual and Motor Skills* 123 (2016): 754–68; V. Peñarroja, V. Orengo, and A. Zornoza, "Reducing Perceived Social Loafing in Virtual Teams: The Effect of Team Feedback with Guided Reflexivity," *Journal of Applied Social Psychology* 47 (2017): 424–35; I. Fronza and X. Wang, "Towards an Approach to Prevent Social Loafing in Software Development Teams," in *11th ACM/IEEE International Symposium on Empirical Software Engineering and Measurement (Esem 2017)* (New York: IEEE, 2017), 241–46; A.A. Curcio and M.A. Lynch, "Addressing Social Loafing on Faculty Committees," *Journal of Legal Education* 67 (2017): 242–62.

21. E. Sundstrom, K.P. De Meuse, and D. Futrell, "Work Teams: Applications and Effectiveness," *American Psychologist, Organizational Psychology*, 45, no. 2 (1990): 120–33; J.R. Hackman et al., "Team Effectiveness in Theory and in Practice," in *Industrial and Organizational Psychology: Linking Theory with Practice*, ed. C.L. Cooper and E.A. Locke (Oxford, UK: Blackwell, 2000), 109–29. Recent literature has focused mainly on the first two functions, but team survival is also an important outcome. See J.E. Mathieu et al., "Embracing Complexity: Reviewing the Past Decade of Team Effectiveness Research," *Annual Review of Organizational Psychology and Organizational Behavior* 6 (2019): 17–46.

22. M. A. West, C. S. Borrill, and K. L. Unsworth, "Team Effectiveness in Organizations," *International Review of Industrial and Organizational Psychology* 13 (1998): 1-48; M. A. Marks, J. E. Mathieu, and S. J. Zaccaro, "A Temporally Based Framework and Taxonomy of Team Processes," *Academy of Management Review* 26, no. 3 (2001): 356-76; J. E. McGrath, H. Arrow, and J. L. Berdahl, "The Study of Groups: Past, Present, and Future," *Personality & Social Psychology Review* 4, no. 1 (2000): 95-105.

23. Team process variables are sometimes labeled as "emergent states" of the team, but this confuses processes with momentary snapshots of the team. McGrath recommended that team models and studies should focus on team processes rather than the snapshot "series of states" that emerge from those processes. He explained that the processes generating team states are logically more important for understanding team dynamics. Unfortunately, recent writers on teams have neglected that advice. See J.E. McGrath, "Studying Groups at Work: Ten Critical Needs for Theory and Practice," in *Designing Effective Work Groups*, ed. P.S. Goodman and and Associates (San Francisco: Jossey-Bass, 1986), 362-92.

24. M. Kouchaki et al., "The Treatment of the Relationship between Groups and Their Environments: A Review and Critical Examination of Common Assumptions in Research," *Group & Organization Management* 37, no. 2 (2012): 171-203.

25. E. Sundstrom, "The Challenges of Supporting Work Team Effectiveness," in *Supporting Work Team Effectiveness*, ed. E. Sundstrom and Associates (San Francisco, CA: Jossey-Bass, 1999), 6-9; G.L. Stewart, "A Meta-Analytic Review of Relationships between Team Design Features and Team Performance," *Journal of Management* 32, no. 1 (2006): 29-54; H. Huettermann, S. Doering, and S. Boerner, "Leadership and Team Identification: Exploring the Followers' Perspective," *Leadership Quarterly* 25, no. 3 (2014): 413-32; J.E. Mathieu, L. D'Innocenzo, and M.R. Kukenberge, "Contextual Issues in Project Performance: A Multilevel Perspective," in *The Psychology and Management of Project Teams: An Interdisciplinary Perspective*, ed. B. Hobbs, E.K. Kelloway, and F. Chiocchio (New York: Oxford University Press, 2015), 101-36; F. Schölmerich, C.C. Schermuly, and J. Deller, "How Leaders' Diversity Beliefs Alter the Impact of Faultlines on Team Functioning," *Small Group Research* 47, no. 2 (2016): 177-206; S.A. Conroy and N. Gupta, "Team Pay-for-Performance: The Devil Is in the Details," *Group & Organization Management* 41, no. 1 (2016): 32-65.

26. "The Olympian Task of Transforming ING," news release (ING Bank, Amsterdam, February 16, 2017); S. Arlt, "Schöne, neue Arbeitswelt (Beautiful, New Working Environment)," *Deutschlandfunk Kultur*, November 7, 2017; M. Korytowska, "Obeya Room in Portfolio Management," *LinkedIn Pulse*, February 11, 2019; J.M. Morgan and J.K. Liker, *Designing the Future: How Ford, Toyota, and Other World-Class Organizations Use Lean Product Development to Drive Innovation and Transform Their Business* (New York: McGraw-Hill Professional, 2019), 93-109.

27. J.E. Mathieu et al., "Embracing Complexity: Reviewing the Past Decade of Team Effectiveness Research," *Annual Review of Organizational Psychology and Organizational Behavior* 6 (2019): 17-46.

28. M.A. Campion, E.M. Papper, and G.J. Medsker, "Relations between Work Team Characteristics and Effectiveness: A Replication and Extension," *Personnel Psychology* 49 (1996): 429-52; N. Sivasubramaniam, S.J. Liebowitz, and C.L. Lackman, "Determinants of New Product Development Team Performance: A Meta-Analytic Review," *Journal of Product Innovation Management* 29, no. 5 (2012): 803-20; M.A. Valentine and A.C. Edmondson, "Team Scaffolds: How Mesolevel Structures Enable Role-Based Coordination in Temporary Groups," *Organization Science* 26, no. 2 (2015): 405-22.

29. G. Van der Vegt and E. Van de Vliert, "Intragroup Interdependence and Effectiveness: Review and Proposed Directions for Theory and Practice," *Journal of Managerial Psychology* 17, no. 1/2 (2002): 50-67; J. Lyubovnikova et al., "24-Karat or Fool's Gold? Consequences of Real Team and Co-Acting Group Membership in Healthcare Organizations," *European Journal of Work and Organizational Psychology* 24, no. 6 (2015): 929-50; S. H. Courtright et al., "Structural Interdependence in Teams: An Integrative Framework and Meta-Analysis," *Journal of Applied Psychology* 100, no. 6 (2015): 1825-46.

30. J.D. Thompson, *Organizations in Action* (New York: McGraw-Hill, 1967), 54-55; F.M. Barbibi and G. Masino, *J.D. Thompson's Organizations In Action 50Th Anniversary: A Reflection* (Bologna. Italy: TAO Digital Library, 2017), Chap. 1. A slight variation of Thompson's model is also applied to understand interdependence in multi-team systems. See: R. Rico et al., "Structural Influences upon Coordination and Performance in Multiteam Systems," *Human Resource Management Review* 28 (2018): 332-46.

31. J.D. Thompson, *Organizations in Action* (New York: McGraw-Hill, 1967), 55-59.

32. J.R. Katzenbach and D.K. Smith, *The Wisdom of Teams: Creating the High-Performance Organization* (Boston: Harvard University Press, 1993), 45-47; C. Aube, V. Rousseau, and S. Tremblay, "Team Size and Quality of Group Experience: The More the Merrier?" *Group Dynamics: Theory Research and Practice* 15, no. 4 (2011): 357-75; J.S. Mueller, "Why Individuals in Larger Teams Perform Worse," *Organizational Behavior and Human Decision Processes* 117, no. 1 (2012): 111-24; Y.-N. Lee, J.P. Walsh, and J. Wang, "Creativity in Scientific Teams: Unpacking Novelty and Impact," *Research Policy* 44, no. 3 (2015): 684-97.

33. J.S. Mueller, "Why Individuals in Larger Teams Perform Worse," *Organizational Behavior and Human Decision Processes* 117, no. 1 (2012): 111-24.

34. J.E. Mathieu et al., "A Review and Integration of Team Composition Models: Moving toward a Dynamic and Temporal Framework," *Journal of Management* 40, no. 1 (2014): 130-60; N.J. Allen and T. O'Neill, "Team Composition and Performance: Considering the Project-Team Challenge," in *The Psychology and Management of Project Teams: An Interdisciplinary Perspective*, ed. B. Hobbs, E.K. Kelloway, and F. Chiocchio (New York: Oxford University Press, 2015), 301-28.

35. Taskwork and teamwork have varied definitions in the literature (e.g., behaviors versus competencies; individual- versus team-level phenomena). Our definition, which refers to individual-level behaviors focused on task performance versus team maintenance, is similar to the conceptualizations by Eduardo Salas and his colleagues, as well as to Lewin's seminal ideas about locomotion versus maintenance in groups. See, for example, J.E. Driskell, E. Salas, and T. Driskell, "Foundations of Teamwork and Collaboration," *American Psychologist* 73, no. 4 (2018): 334-48; E. Salas et al., "Can Teamwork Promote Safety in Organizations?" *Annual Review of Organizational Psychology and Organizational Behavior* 7 (2020): 283-313.

36. F.P. Morgeson, M.H. Reider, and M.A. Campion, "Selecting Individuals in Team Settings: The Importance of Social Skills, Personality Characteristics, and Teamwork Knowledge," *Personnel Psychology* 58, no. 3 (2005): 583-611; V. Rousseau, C. Aubé, and A. Savoie, "Teamwork Behaviors: A Review and an Integration of Frameworks," *Small Group Research* 37, no. 5 (2006): 540-70; M.L. Loughry, M.W. Ohland, and D.D. Moore, "Development of a Theory-Based Assessment of Team Member Effectiveness," *Educational and Psychological Measurement* 67, no. 3 (2007): 505-24; E. Salas et al., "Understanding and Improving Teamwork in Organizations: A Scientifically Based Practical Guide," *Human Resource Management* 54, no. 4 (2015): 599-622.

37. S. McComb et al., "The Five Ws of Team Communication," *Industrial Management* 54, no. 5 (2012): 10–13.

38. TINYpulse, *7 Vital Trends Disrupting Today's Workplace*, 2013 TINYpulse Employee Engagement Survey (Seattle: TINYpulse, December 2013); CareerBuilder, "Overwhelming Majority of Companies Say Soft Skills Are Just as Important as Hard Skills, According to a New Careerbuilder Survey," news release (Chicago: CareerBuilder, April 10, 2014); Association of American Colleges & Universities, *Falling Short? College Learning and Career Success* (Washington, DC: Hart Research Associates, January 20, 2015); *The Class of 2016 Student Survey Report* (Bethlehem, PA: National Association of Colleges and Employers, October 2016).

39. D. van Knippenberg, C.K.W. De Dreu, and A.C. Homan, "Work Group Diversity and Group Performance: An Integrative Model and Research Agenda," *Journal of Applied Psychology* 89, no. 6 (2004): 1008–22; E. Mannix and M.A. Neale, "What Differences Make a Difference? The Promise and Reality of Diverse Teams in Organizations," *Psychological Science in the Public Interest* 6, no. 2 (2005): 31–55; L.M. Shore et al., "Inclusion and Diversity in Work Groups: A Review and Model for Future Research," *Journal of Management* 37, no. 4 (2011): 1262–89; S.K. Horwitz, "Functional Diversity in Project Teams: Working across Boundaries," in *The Psychology and Management of Project Teams: An Interdisciplinary Perspective*, ed. B. Hobbs, E.K. Kelloway, and F. Chiocchio (New York: Oxford University Press, 2015), 329–63.

40. D.C. Lau and J.K. Murnighan, "Interactions within Groups and Subgroups: The Effects of Demographic Faultlines," *Academy of Management Journal* 48, no. 4 (2005): 645–59; S.M.B. Thatcher and P.C. Patel, "Group Faultlines: A Review, Integration, and Guide to Future Research," *Journal of Management* 38, no. 4 (2012): 969–1009; M. Shemla et al., "A Review of Perceived Diversity in Teams: Does How Members Perceive Their Team's Composition Affect Team Processes and Outcomes?" *Journal of Organizational Behavior* 37 (2016): S89–S106.

41. B.W. Tuckman and M.A.C. Jensen, "Stages of Small-Group Development Revisited," *Group and Organization Studies* 2 (1977): 419–42; B.W. Tuckman, "Developmental Sequence in Small Groups," *Group Facilitation* (2001): 66–81; D.A. Bonebright, "40 Years of Storming: A Historical Review of Tuckman's Model of Small Group Development," *Human Resource Development International* 13, no. 1 (2010): 111–20.

42. G.R. Bushe and G.H. Coetzer, "Group Development and Team Effectiveness: Using Cognitive Representations to Measure Group Development and Predict Task Performance and Group Viability," *Journal of Applied Behavioral Science* 43, no. 2 (2007): 184–212.

43. D.C. Feldman, "The Development and Enforcement of Group Norms," *Academy of Management Review* 9 (1984): 47–53; E. Fehr and U. Fischbacher, "Social Norms and Human Cooperation," *Trends in Cognitive Sciences* 8, no. 4 (2004): 185–90; B.A. De Jong, K.M. Bijlsma-Frankema, and L.B. Cardinal, "Stronger Than the Sum of Its Parts? The Performance Implications of Peer Control Combinations in Teams," *Organization Science* 25 (2014): 1703–21.

44. J.M. Nolan, "Social Norms and Their Enforcement," in *The Oxford Handbook of Social Influence*, ed. S.G. Harkins, K.D. Williams, and J. Burger (New York: Oxford University Press, 2015); A. Diekmann and W. Przepiorka, "'Take One for the Team!' Individual Heterogeneity and the Emergence of Latent Norms in a Volunteer's Dilemma," *Social Forces* 94 (2016): 1309–33.

45. K.D. Opp, "How Do Norms Emerge? An Outline of a Theory," *Mind & Society* 2, no. 1 (2001): 101–28.

46. J.M. Nolan, "Social Norms and Their Enforcement," in *The Oxford Handbook of Social Influence*, ed. S.G. Harkins, K.D. Williams, and J. Burger (New York: Oxford University Press, 2015); B. Manata, "The Structural Effects of Team Density and Normative Standards on Team Member Performance," *Human Communication Research* 45 (2019): 309–33.

47. N. Ellemers and F. Rink, "Identity in Work Groups: The Beneficial and Detrimental Consequences of Multiple Identities and Group Norms for Collaboration and Group Performance," *Advances in Group Processes* 22 (2005): 1–41. For research on norm development and reinforcement in virtual teams, see K. Moser and C. Axtell, "The Role of Norms in Virtual Work: A Review and Agenda for Future Research," *Journal of Personnel Psychology* 12 (2013): 1–6.

48. S. Taggar and R. Ellis, "The Role of Leaders in Shaping Formal Team Norms," *Leadership Quarterly* 18, no. 2 (2007): 105–20; B.A. De Jong, K.M. Bijlsma-Frankema, and L.B. Cardinal, "Stronger Than the Sum of Its Parts? The Performance Implications of Peer Control Combinations in Teams," *Organization Science* 25, no. 6 (2014): 1703–21.

49. A.P. Hare, "Types of Roles in Small Groups: A Bit of History and a Current Perspective," *Small Group Research* 25 (1994): 443–48; A. Aritzeta, S. Swailes, and B. Senior, "Belbin's Team Role Model: Development, Validity and Applications for Team Building," *Journal of Management Studies* 44, no. 1 (2007): 96–118.

50. J.E. Mathieu et al., "Team Role Experience and Orientation: A Measure and Tests of Construct Validity," *Group & Organization Management* 40, no. 1 (2015): 6–34. Also see J.K. Summers, S.E. Humphrey, and G.R. Ferris, "Team Member Change, Flux in Coordination, and Performance: Effects of Strategic Core Roles, Information Transfer, and Cognitive Ability," *Academy of Management Journal* 55, no. 2 (2012): 314–38; N. Lehmann-Willenbrock, S.J. Beck, and S. Kauffeld, "Emergent Team Roles in Organizational Meetings: Identifying Communication Patterns via Cluster Analysis," *Communication Studies* 67, no. 1 (2016): 37–57.

51. D.J. Beal et al., "Cohesion and Performance in Groups: A Meta-Analytic Clarification of Construct Relations," *Journal of Applied Psychology* 88, no. 6 (2003): 989–1004; S.W.J. Kozlowski and D.R. Ilgen, "Enhancing the Effectiveness of Work Groups and Teams," *Psychological Science in the Public Interest* 7, no. 3 (2006): 77–124.

52. R.M. Montoya, R.S. Horton, and J. Kirchner, "Is Actual Similarity Necessary for Attraction? A Meta-Analysis of Actual and Perceived Similarity," *Journal of Social and Personal Relationships* 25, no. 6 (2008): 889–922; M.T. Rivera, S.B. Soderstrom, and B. Uzzi, "Dynamics of Dyads in Social Networks: Assortative, Relational, and Proximity Mechanisms," *Annual Review of Sociology* 36 (2010): 91–115.

53. D. van Knippenberg, C.K.W. De Dreu, and A.C. Homan, "Work Group Diversity and Group Performance: An Integrative Model and Research Agenda," *Journal of Applied Psychology* 89, no. 6 (2004): 1008–22; K.A. Jehn, G.B. Northcraft, and M.A. Neale, "Why Differences Make a Difference: A Field Study of Diversity, Conflict, and Performance in Workgroups," *Administrative Science Quarterly* 44, no. 4 (1999): 741–63. For evidence that diversity/similarity does not always influence cohesion, see S.S. Webber and L.M. Donahue, "Impact of Highly and Less Job-Related Diversity on Work Group Cohesion and Performance: A Meta-Analysis," *Journal of Management* 27, no. 2 (2001): 141–62.

54. E. Aronson and J. Mills, "The Effects of Severity of Initiation on Liking for a Group," *Journal of Abnormal and Social Psychology* 59 (1959): 177–81; J.E. Hautaluoma and R.S. Enge, "Early Socialization into a Work Group: Severity of Initiations Revisited," *Journal of Social Behavior & Personality* 6 (1991): 725–48.

55. B. Mullen and C. Copper, "The Relation between Group Cohesiveness and Performance: An Integration," *Psychological Bulletin* 115 (1994): 210–27; C.J. Fullagar and D.O. Egleston, "Norming and Performing: Using Microworlds to Understand the Relationship between Team Cohesiveness and Performance," *Journal of Applied Social Psychology* 38, no. 10 (2008): 2574–93; R. Wageman et al., *Senior Leadership Teams* (Boston: Harvard Business School Press, 2008): 69–70.

56. M. Rempel and R.J. Fisher, "Perceived Threat, Cohesion, and Group Problem Solving in Intergroup Conflict," *International Journal of Conflict Management* 8 (1997): 216–34; M.E. Turner and T. Horvitz, "The Dilemma of Threat: Group Effectiveness and Ineffectiveness under Adversity," in *Groups at Work: Theory and Research*, ed. M.E. Turner (Mahwah, NJ: Erlbaum, 2001), 445–70.

57. A.V. Carron et al., "Cohesion and Performance in Sport: A Meta-Analysis," *Journal of Sport and Exercise Psychology* 24 (2002): 168–88; D.J. Beal et al., "Cohesion and Performance in Groups: A Meta-Analytic Clarification of Construct Relations," *Journal of Applied Psychology* 88, no. 6 (2003): 989–1004; L.A. DeChurch and J.R. Mesmer-Magnus, "The Cognitive Underpinnings of Effective Teamwork: A Meta-Analysis," *Journal of Applied Psychology* 95, no. 1 (2010): 32–53; S.M. Gully, D.J. Devine, and D.J. Whitney, "A Meta-Analysis of Cohesion and Performance: Effects of Level of Analysis and Task Interdependence," *Small Group Research* 43, no. 6 (2012): 702–25.

58. W. Piper et al., "Cohesion as a Basic Bond in Groups," *Human Relations* 36 (1983): 93–108; S.Y. Shin and S.G. Lee, "Effects of Hospital Workers? Friendship Networks on Job Stress," *PLoS ONE* 11, no. 2 (2016): e0149428.

59. S.M. Gully, D.J. Devine, and D.J. Whitney, "A Meta-Analysis of Cohesion and Performance: Effects of Level of Analysis and Task Interdependence," *Small Group Research* 43, no. 6 (2012): 702–25.

60. K.L. Gammage, A.V. Carron, and P.A. Estabrooks, "Team Cohesion and Individual Productivity: The Influence of the Norm for Productivity and the Identifiability of Individual Effort," *Small Group Research* 32 (2001): 3–18; C. Langfred, "Is Group Cohesiveness a Double-Edged Sword? An Investigation of the Effects of Cohesiveness on Performance," *Small Group Research* 29 (1998): 124–43; N.L. Jimmieson, M. Peach, and K.M. White, "Utilizing the Theory of Planned Behavior to Inform Change Management," *Journal of Applied Behavioral Science* 44, no. 2 (2008): 237–62. Concerns about existing research on cohesion-performance are discussed in M. Casey-Campbell and M.L. Martens, "Sticking It All Together: A Critical Assessment of the Group Cohesion–Performance Literature," *International Journal of Management Reviews* 11, no. 2 (2009): 223–46.

61. J. Mathieu et al., "Modeling Reciprocal Team Cohesion-Performance Relationships, as Impacted by Shared Leadership and Members' Competence," *Journal of Applied Psychology* 100, no. 3 (2015): 713–34.

62. D.M. Rousseau et al., "Not So Different after All: A Cross-Discipline View of Trust," *Academy of Management Review* 23 (1998): 393–404; I. Yang, "What Makes an Effective Team? The Role of Trust (Dis)Confirmation in Team Development," *European Management Journal* 32 (2014): 858–69; A.C. Costa, C.A. Fulmer, and N.R. Anderson, "Trust in Work Teams: An Integrative Review, Multilevel Model, and Future Directions," *Journal of Organizational Behavior* 39 (2018): 169–84.

63. D.J. McAllister, "Affect- and Cognition-Based Trust as Foundations for Interpersonal Cooperation in Organizations," *Academy of Management Journal* 38, no. 1 (1995): 24–59; M. Williams, "In Whom We Trust: Group Membership as an Affective Context for Trust Development," *Academy of Management Review* 26, no. 3 (2001): 377–96; M. Pirson and D. Malhotra, "Foundations of Organizational Trust: What Matters to Different Stakeholders?" *Organization Science* 22, no. 4 (2011): 1087–104.

64. R.J. Lewicki, E.C. Tomlinson, and N. Gillespie, "Models of Interpersonal Trust Development: Theoretical Approaches, Empirical Evidence, and Future Directions," *Journal of Management* 32, no. 6 (2006): 991–1022.

65. R.J. Lewicki, E.C. Tomlinson, and N. Gillespie, "Models of Interpersonal Trust Development: Theoretical Approaches, Empirical Evidence, and Future Directions," *Journal of Management* 32 (2006): 991–1022; N. Zhao et al., "The Impact of Traditionality/Modernity on Identification- and Calculus-Based Trust," *International Journal of Psychology* 54 (2019): 237–46.

66. E.M. Whitener et al., "Managers as Initiators of Trust: An Exchange Relationship Framework for Understanding Managerial Trustworthy Behavior," *Academy of Management Review* 23 (1998): 513–30; T. Simons et al., "How Leader Alignment of Words and Deeds Affects Followers: A Meta-Analysis of Behavioral Integrity Research," *Journal of Business Ethics* 132 (2015): 831–44.

67. H. Akrout and M.F. Diallo, "Fundamental Transformations of Trust and Its Drivers: A Multi-Stage Approach of Business-to-Business Relationships," *Industrial Marketing Management* 66 (2017): 159–71; A.C. Costa, C.A. Fulmer, and N.R. Anderson, "Trust in Work Teams: An Integrative Review, Multilevel Model, and Future Directions," *Journal of Organizational Behavior* 39 (2018): 169–84.

68. C.B. Crisp and S.L. Jarvenpaa, "Swift Trust in Global Virtual Teams: Trusting Beliefs and Normative Actions," *Journal of Personnel Psychology* 12 (2013): 45–56; O. Schilke and L. Huang, "Worthy of Swift Trust? How Brief Interpersonal Contact Affects Trust Accuracy," *Journal of Applied Psychology* 103 (2018): 1181–97.

69. K.T. Dirks and D.L. Ferrin, "The Role of Trust in Organizations," *Organization Science* 12 (2004): 450–67; I. Yang, "What Makes an Effective Team? The Role of Trust (Dis)Confirmation in Team Development," *European Management Journal* 32 (2014): 858–69.

70. L.A. DeChurch and J.R. Mesmer-Magnus, "The Cognitive Underpinnings of Effective Teamwork: A Meta-Analysis," *Journal of Applied Psychology* 95 (2010): 32–53; C. Aubé, V. Rousseau, and S. Tremblay, "Perceived Shared Understanding in Teams: The Motivational Effect of Being 'on the Same Page,'" *British Journal of Psychology* 106 (2015): 468–86; J.M. Schmidtke and A. Cummings, "The Effects of Virtualness on Teamwork Behavioral Components: The Role of Shared Mental Models," *Human Resource Management Review* 27 (2017): 660–77.

71. R. Rico, M. Sánchez-Manzanares, and C. Gibson, "Team Implicit Coordination Processes: A Team Knowledge-Based Approach," *Academy of Management Review* 33 (2008): 163–84; J.C. Gorman, "Team Coordination and Dynamics: Two Central Issues," *Current Directions in Psychological Science* 23 (2014): 355–60; J. Schmutz et al., "Effective Coordination in Medical Emergency Teams: The Moderating Role of Task Type," *European Journal of Work and Organizational Psychology* 24 (2015): 761–76.

72. L. Argote, B.L. Aven, and J. Kush, "The Effects of Communication Networks and Turnover on Transactive Memory and Group Performance," *Organization Science* 29 (2018): 191–206.

73. C.A. Beatty and B.A. Barker, *Building Smart Teams: Roadmap to High Performance* (Thousand Oaks, CA: Sage, 2004); W.G. Dyer, J.H. Dyer, and W.G. Dyer, *Team Building: Proven Strategies for Improving Team Performance*, 5th ed. (San Francisco: Jossey-Bass, 2013); C.N. Lacerenza et al., "Team Development Interventions: Evidence-Based Approaches for Improving Teamwork," *American Psychologist* 73 (2018): 517–31.

74. J. Langan-Fox and J. Anglim, "Mental Models, Team Mental Models, and Performance: Process, Development, and Future Directions," *Human Factors and Ergonomics in Manufacturing* 14 (2004): 331–52; J.E. Mathieu et al., "Scaling the Quality of Teammates' Mental Models: Equifinality and Normative Comparisons," *Journal of Organizational Behavior* 26 (2005): 37–56.

75. D.R. Seibold and R.A. Meyers, "Interventions in Groups: Methods for Facilitating Team Development," in *Research Methods for Studying Groups and Teams: A Guide to Approaches, Tools, and Technologies*, ed. A. Hollingshead and M.S. Poole (New York: Routledge, 2012), 418–41; A. Hämmelmann and R. van Dick, "Building the Team: Effect on the Individual—An Evaluation of Team Building Interventions (Entwickeln Im Team—Effekte Für Den Einzelnen: Eine Evaluation Von Teamentwicklungsmaßnahmen)," *Gruppendynamik und Organisationsberatung* 44, no. 2 (2013): 221–38.

76. K. Scott, "Treatwell Flies Global Workforce to Barcelona for Team-Building Exercise," *Employee Benefits (London, UK)*, September 14, 2016; "Local Faith Communities Start Aurora Habitat for Humanity Home; Nicor Gas Employees Pitch In," *Daily Herald (Arlington Heights, IL)*, May 23, 2017; R. Inman, "Why We Used an Iron Chef Competition as a Team Building Exercise," *Cobalt Blog*, February 2, 2017, http://www.cobalt.net/used-iron-chef-competition-team-building-exercise; "Best Fintechs to Work For," *American Banker*, February 24, 2019.

77. L.J. Martin, A.V. Carron, and S.M. Burke, "Team Building Interventions in Sport: A Meta-Analysis," *Sport & Exercise Psychology Journal* 5, no. 2 (2009): 3–18; C. Klein et al., "Does Team Building Work?" *Small Group Research* 40, no. 2 (2009): 181–222; I. Nadler, P.M. Sanderson, and H.G. Liley, "The Accuracy of Clinical Assessments as a Measure for Teamwork Effectiveness," *Simulation in Healthcare* 6, no. 5 (2011): 260–68; Y.J. Yi, "Effects of Team-Building on Communication and Teamwork among Nursing Students," *International Nursing Review* 63, no. 1 (2016): 33–40; C.N. Lacerenza et al., "Team Development Interventions: Evidence-Based Approaches for Improving Teamwork," *American Psychologist* 73 (2018): 517–31.

78. R.W. Woodman and J.J. Sherwood, "The Role of Team Development in Organizational Effectiveness: A Critical Review," *Psychological Bulletin* 88 (1980): 166–86; C.J. Miller et al., "A Systematic Review of Team-Building Interventions in Non-Acute Healthcare Settings," *BMC Health Services Research* 18, no. 1 (2018): 146, https://doi.org/10.1186/s12913-018-2961-9.

79. S.A. Mohrman, S.G. Cohen, and A.M. Mohrman Jr., *Designing Team-Based Organizations: New Forms for Knowledge Work* (San Francisco: Jossey-Bass, 1995), 39–40; D.E. Yeatts and C. Hyten, *High-Performing Self-Managed Work Teams: A Comparison of Theory and Practice* (Thousand Oaks, CA: Sage, 1998); E.E. Lawler, *Organizing for High Performance* (San Francisco: Jossey-Bass, 2001); R.J. Torraco, "Work Design Theory: A Review and Critique with Implications for Human Resource Development," *Human Resource Development Quarterly* 16, no. 1 (2005): 85–109.

80. P. Panchak, "Production Workers Can Be Your Competitive Edge," *Industry Week*, October 2004, 11; S.K. Muthusamy, J.V. Wheeler, and B.L. Simmons, "Self-Managing Work Teams: Enhancing Organizational Innovativeness," *Organization Development Journal* 23, no. 3 (2005): 53–66.

81. A. Krause and H. Dunckel, "Work Design and Customer Satisfaction: Effects of the Implementation of Semi-Autonomous Group Work on Customer Satisfaction Considering Employee Satisfaction and Group Performance (translated abstract)," *Zeitschrift für Arbeits-und Organisationspsychologie* 47, no. 4 (2003): 182–93; G.L. Stewart, S.H. Courtright, and M.R. Barrick, "Peer-Based Control in Self-Managing Teams: Linking Rational and Normative Influence with Individual and Group Performance," *Journal of Applied Psychology* 97 (2012): 435–47; E.E.M. Maurits et al., "Home-Care Nursing Staff in Self-Directed Teams Are More Satisfied with Their Job and Feel They Have More Autonomy over Patient Care: A Nationwide Survey," *Journal of Advanced Nursing* 73 (2017): 2430–40.

82. J.L. Cordery et al., "The Impact of Autonomy and Task Uncertainty on Team Performance: A Longitudinal Field Study," *Journal of Organizational Behavior* 31 (2010): 240–58; N.C. Magpili and P. Pazos, "Self-Managing Team Performance: A Systematic Review of Multilevel Input Factors," *Small Group Research* 49 (2018): 3–33; M. Renkema, T. Bondarouk, and A. Bos-Nehles, "Transformation to Self-Managing Teams: Lessons Learned: A Look at Current Trends and Data," *Strategic HR Review* 17 (2018): 81–84.

83. E. Ulich and W.G. Weber, "Dimensions, Criteria, and Evaluation of Work Group Autonomy," in *Handbook of Work Group Psychology*, ed. M.A. West (Chichester, UK: Wiley, 1996), 247–82.

84. K. Monsen and J. deBlok, "Buurtzorg Nederland," *American Journal of Nursing* 113, no. 8 (2013): 55–59; J.D. Blok, "Neighbourhood Scheme Transforms Services," *Primary Health Care* 25, no. 2 (2015); B. Gray, D.O. Sarnak, and J. Burgers, *Home Care by Self-Governing Nursing Teams: The Netherlands' Buurtzorg Model*, The Commonwealth Fund (New York: May 29, 2015); "The Buurtzorg Model—Buurtzorg International," Buurtzorg—About Us, accessed May 2, 2019, https://www.buurtzorg.com/about-us/buurtzorgmodel/; L. Gill, "Buurtzorg and the Power of Self-Managed Teams of Nurses," Episode 26, *Leadermorphosis*, December 17, 2018, accessed May 2, 2019, http://leadermorphosis.co/ep-26-buurtzorg-and-the-power-of-self-managed-teams-of-nurses.

85. J. Lipnack and J. Stamps, *Virtual Teams: People Working across Boundaries with Technology* (New York: Wiley, 2001); J.H. Dulebohn and J.E. Hoch, "Virtual Teams in Organizations," *Human Resource Management Review* 27 (2017): 569–74. Some suggest that remote teams differ slightly from distributed teams, where the latter have no physical base location. However, we group them together because they overlap in terms of OB concepts and practices.

86. L. Schweitzer and L. Duxbury, "Conceptualizing and Measuring the Virtuality of Teams," *Information Systems Journal* 20, no. 3 (2010): 267–95; M.K. Foster et al., "Rethinking Virtuality and Its Impact on Teams," *Small Group Research* 46, no. 3 (2015): 267–99; J.M. Schaubroeck and A. Yu, "When Does Virtuality Help or Hinder Teams? Core Team Characteristics as Contingency Factors," *Human Resource Management Review* 27 (2017): 635–47.

87. L.L. Gilson et al., "Virtual Teams Research: 10 Years, 10 Themes, and 10 Opportunities," *Journal of Management* 41, no. 5 (2015): 1313–37.

88. J.L. Cordery and C. Soo, "Overcoming Impediments to Virtual Team Effectiveness," *Human Factors and Ergonomics in Manufacturing & Service Industries* 18 (2008): 487–500; A. Ortiz de Guinea, J. Webster, and D.S. Staples, "A Meta-Analysis of the Consequences of Virtualness on Team Functioning," *Information & Management* 49, no. 6 (2012): 301–08; T.A. O'Neill, L.A. Hambley, and G.S. Chatellier, "Cyberslacking, Engagement, and Personality in Distributed Work Environments," *Computers in Human Behavior* 40 (2014): 152–60.

89. L.L. Martins and M.C. Schilpzand, "Global Virtual Teams: Key Developments, Research Gaps, and Future Directions," *Research in Personnel and Human Resources Management* 30 (2011): 1–72; S. Krumm et al., "What Does It Take to Be a Virtual Team Player? The Knowledge, Skills, Abilities, and Other Characteristics Required in Virtual Teams," *Human Performance* 29, no. 2 (2016): 123–42; J.L. Gibbs, A. Sivunen, and M. Boyraz, "Investigating the Impacts of Team Type and Design on Virtual Team Processes," *Human Resource Management Review* 27 (2017): 590–603.

90. S.L. Marlow, C.N. Lacerenza, and E. Salas, "Communication in Virtual Teams: A Conceptual Framework and Research Agenda," *Human Resource Management Review* 27 (2017): 575–89; L. Handke et al., "Teams, Time, and Technology: Variations of Media Use Over Project Phases," *Small Group Research* 50 (2019): 266–305.

91. G.G. Harwood, "Design Principles for Successful Virtual Teams," in *The Handbook of High-Performance Virtual Teams: A Toolkit for Collaborating across Boundaries*, ed. J. Nemiro and M.M. Beyerlein (San Francisco: Jossey-Bass, 2008), 59–84. Also see H. Duckworth, "How TRW Automotive Helps Global Virtual Teams Perform at the Top of Their Game," *Global Business and Organizational Excellence* 28, no. 1 (2008): 6–16; L. Dubé and D. Robey, "Surviving the Paradoxes of Virtual Teamwork," *Information Systems Journal* 19, no. 1 (2009): 3–30.

92. L. Dubé and D. Robey, "Surviving the Paradoxes of Virtual Teamwork," *Information Systems Journal* 19, no. 1 (2009): 3–30.

93. V.H. Vroom and A.G. Jago, *The New Leadership* (Englewood Cliffs, NJ: Prentice Hall, 1988), 28–29.

94. M. Diehl and W. Stroebe, "Productivity Loss in Idea-Generating Groups: Tracking Down the Blocking Effects," *Journal of Personality and Social Psychology* 61 (1991): 392–403; W. Stroebe, B.A. Nijstad, and E.F. Rietzschel, "Beyond Productivity Loss in Brainstorming Groups: The Evolution of a Question," in *Advances in Experimental Social Psychology*, ed. P.Z. Mark and M.O. James (Academic Press, 2010), 157–203; D.D. Henningsen and M.L.M. Henningsen, "Generating Ideas About the Uses of Brainstorming: Reconsidering the Losses and Gains of Brainstorming Groups Relative to Nominal Groups," *Southern Communication Journal* 78 (2013): 42–55.

95. P. Bordia, B.E. Irmer, and D. Abusah, "Differences in Sharing Knowledge Interpersonally and via Databases: The Role of Evaluation Apprehension and Perceived Benefits," *European Journal of Work and Organizational Psychology* 15, no. 3 (2006): 262–80; L. McGrath, "When Pairing Reduces Scaring: The Effect of Dyadic Ideation on Evaluation Apprehension," *International Journal of Innovation Management* 19, no. 04 (2015): 1550039.

96. A.D. Stajkovic, D. Lee, and A.J. Nyberg, "Collective Efficacy, Group Potency, and Group Performance: Meta-Analyses of Their Relationships, and Test of a Mediation Model," *Journal of Applied Psychology* 94, no. 3 (2009): 814–28; J. Schepers et al., "Fields of Gold: Perceived Efficacy in Virtual Teams of Field Service Employees," *Journal of Service Research* 14, no. 3 (2011): 372–89. OB experts describe team efficacy as efficacy toward a specific task, whereas team potency is the team's general efficacy.

97. D. Miller, *The Icarus Paradox: How Exceptional Companies Bring about Their Own Downfall* (New York: HarperBusiness, 1990); G. Whyte, "Recasting Janis's Groupthink Model: The Key Role of Collective Efficacy in Decision Fiascoes," *Organizational Behavior and Human Decision Processes* 73, no. 2–3 (1998): 185–209; K. Tasa and G. Whyte, "Collective Efficacy and Vigilant Problem Solving in Group Decision Making: A Non-Linear Model," *Organizational Behavior and Human Decision Processes* 96, no. 2 (2005): 119–29; T.L. Rapp et al., "The Role of Team Goal Monitoring in the Curvilinear Relationship between Team Efficacy and Team Performance," *Journal of Applied Psychology* 99 (2014): 976–87; W.-W. Park, M.S. Kim, and S.M. Gully, "Effect of Cohesion on the Curvilinear Relationship Between Team Efficacy and Performance," *Small Group Research* 48 (2017): 455–81.

98. F.W. Nietzsche, *Beyond Good and Evil: Prelude to a Philosophy of the Future*, trans. H. Zimmern (London: G. Allen & Unwin, 1906), Chap. 4, statement 156.

99. A.C. Edmondson and Z. Lei, "Psychological Safety: The History, Renaissance, and Future of an Interpersonal Construct," *Annual Review of Organizational Psychology and Organizational Behavior* 1 (2014): 23–43; A. Newman, R. Donohue, and N. Eva, "Psychological Safety: A Systematic Review of the Literature," *Human Resource Management Review* 27 (2017): 521–35.

100. The term "brainstorm" dates back to a New York murder case in 1907 as one expert's reference to temporary insanity. By the mid-1920s, the meaning of a brainstorm had shifted markedly to a state of creative thinking. Advertising executive Alex Osborn (the *O* in BBDO, a global advertising agency) first described the brainstorming process in the little-known 1942 booklet *How to Think Up* (p. 29). Osborn gave a fuller description of the brainstorming process in his popular 1948 (*Your Creative Power*) and 1953 (*Applied Imagination*) books. See A. F. Osborn, *How to Think Up* (New York: McGraw-Hill, 1942), Chap. 4; A. F. Osborn, *Your Creative Power* (New York: Scribner's Sons, 1948); A. F. Osborn, *Applied Imagination* (New York: Scribner's Sons, 1953).

101. R.I. Sutton and A. Hargadon, "Brainstorming Groups in Context: Effectiveness in a Product Design Firm," *Administrative Science Quarterly* 41 (1996): 685–718; T. Kelley, *The Art of Innovation* (New York: Currency Doubleday, 2001); J.M. Levine et al., "Group Brainstorming: When Regulatory Nonfit Enhances Performance," *Group Processes & Intergroup Relations* 19, no. 2 (2016): 257–71; K.J. Levine, K.B. Heuett, and K.M. Reno, "Re-Operationalizing Established Groups in Brainstorming: Validating Osborn's Claims," *The Journal of Creative Behavior* 51, no. 3 (2017): 252–62; P.B. Paulus and J.B. Kenworthy, "Effective Brainstorming," in *The Oxford Handbook of Group Creativity and Innovation*, ed. P.B. Paulus and B.A. Nijstad (New York: Oxford University Press, 2019), 287–306.

102. P.A. Heslin, "Better Than Brainstorming? Potential Contextual Boundary Conditions to Brainwriting for Idea Generation in Organizations," *Journal of Occupational and Organizational Psychology* 82, no. 1 (2009): 129–45; N. Michinov, "Is Electronic Brainstorming or Brainwriting the Best Way to Improve Creative Performance in Groups? An Overlooked Comparison of Two Idea-Generation Techniques," *Journal of Applied Social Psychology* 42 (2012): E222–E243; M. Litcanu et al., "Brain-Writing Vs. Brainstorming Case Study For Power Engineering Education," *Procedia - Social and Behavioral Sciences* 191 (2015): 387–90.

103. R.B. Gallupe, L.M. Bastianutti, and W.H. Cooper, "Unblocking Brainstorms," *Journal of Applied Psychology* 76 (1991): 137–42; W.H. Cooper et al., "Some Liberating Effects of Anonymous Electronic Brainstorming," *Small Group Research* 29, no. 2 (1998): 147–78; J. Baruah and P.B. Paulus, "The Role of Time and Category Relatedness in Electronic Brainstorming," *Small Group Research* 47 (2016): 333–42; H. Al-Samarraie and S. Hurmuzan, "A Review of Brainstorming Techniques in Higher Education," *Thinking Skills and Creativity* 27 (2018): 78–91.

104. A.L. Delbecq, A.H. Van de Ven, and D.H. Gustafson, *Group Techniques for Program Planning: A Guide to Nominal Group and Delphi Processes* (Middleton, WI: Green Briar Press, 1986).

105. S. Frankel, "NGT + MDS: An Adaptation of the Nominal Group Technique for Ill-Structured Problems," *Journal of Applied Behavioral Science* 23 (1987): 543–51; H. Barki and A. Pinsonneault, "Small Group Brainstorming and Idea Quality: Is Electronic Brainstorming the Most Effective Approach?" *Small Group Research* 32, no. 2 (2001): 158–205; P.P. Lago et al., "Structuring Group Decision Making in a Web-Based Environment by Using the Nominal Group Technique," *Computers & Industrial Engineering* 52, no. 2 (2007): 277–95.

8 Communicating in Teams and Organizations

metamorworks/iStock/Getty Images

Learning Objectives

After you read this chapter, you should be able to:

LO8-1 Explain why communication is important in organizations and discuss four influences on effective communication encoding and decoding.

LO8-2 Compare and contrast the advantages and disadvantages of digital written communication channels, other verbal communication channels, and nonverbal communication.

LO8-3 Discuss the relevance of synchronicity, social presence, social acceptance, and media richness when choosing the preferred communication channel.

LO8-4 Discuss various barriers (noise) to effective communication, including cross-cultural and gender-based differences in communication.

LO8-5 Explain how to get your message across more effectively and summarize the elements of active listening.

LO8-6 Describe effective communication strategies in organizational hierarchies and review the role and relevance of the organizational grapevine.

John Legere has straightforward advice for all leaders. "The most powerful formula for success is three simple steps: 1. Shut up and listen to your customers and employees. 2. Do what they tell you. 3. Repeat." Legere, who recently stepped down as CEO of T-Mobile US, practices what he preaches. His town hall meetings with employees have become legendary. He constantly tweets with customers and staff alike. And he interacts personally—not just remotely—with the people on the front lines. "At T-Mobile, we've cut through the layers—and hierarchy—to listen to employees directly every single day," he says. "I've personally flown over a million miles to visit our call centers and retail stores—because it's so important to cut out all the layers and hear directly from employees."[1]

communication the process by which information is transmitted and *understood* between two or more people

> An organization comes into being when there are persons able to communicate with each other.[3]
>
> —Chester Barnard, pioneering OB scholar and telecommunications CEO

John Legere may be a role model for the future of organizational communication. Many executives continue to rely on formal, impersonal news releases to the public and equally staid emails or reports to employees. Meanwhile, Legere and a handful of other executives rely on a variety of communication channels to represent the social presence, seriousness, urgency, and other attributes that the audience interprets from those channels.

We are experiencing the most significant and disruptive transformation of organizational communication in our lifetimes. Digital real-time group messaging (chat channels), task-management pages, video conferences, text messaging, document repositories, intranet wikis, and other methods barely existed in organizations a decade ago. Indeed, many businesses in the United States and other countries are still struggling with whether—let alone determining how—to incorporate these new ways of interacting in the workplace. Social media and other forms of digital communication offer new methods of information sharing and social bonding. Equally important, employees use these emerging communication channels in their private lives and expect to have them available at work.

Communication refers to the process by which information is transmitted and *understood* between two or more people. We emphasize the word "understood" because communication is effective when the receiver accurately deciphers the sender's message. This chapter begins by discussing the importance of effective communication, outlining the communication process model, and discussing factors that improve communication coding and decoding. Next, we identify types of communication channels, including digital messaging and social media, followed by factors to consider when choosing a communication medium. This chapter then identifies barriers to effective communication. The latter part of this chapter looks at communication in organizational hierarchies and offers insight about the pervasive organizational grapevine.

LO8-1 Explain why communication is important in organizations and discuss four influences on effective communication encoding and decoding.

THE IMPORTANCE OF COMMUNICATION

Effective communication is vital to all organizations, so much so that no company could exist without it. The reason? Recall from Chapter 1 that organizations are defined as groups of people who work interdependently toward some purpose. People work interdependently only when they can communicate with one another. Organizations rely on a variety of coordinating mechanisms (see Chapter 12), but frequent, timely, and accurate communication remains the primary means through which employees and work units effectively synchronize their work.[2]

Communication is also vital for effective decision making. Imagine the challenge of making a decision without any information about the decision context, the alternatives available, the likely outcomes of those options, or the extent to which the decision is achieving its objectives. Communication brings this information from the external environment into the organization and distributes it so employees can solve problems and discover opportunities. For example, airline cockpit crews make much better decisions—and thereby cause far fewer accidents—when the captain encourages the crew to openly share information.[4]

A third function of communication is to change behavior.[5] When conveying information to others, we are often trying to alter their beliefs, feelings, and ultimately their behavior. This influence process might be passive, such as merely describing the situation more clearly and fully, or it might be a deliberate

Effective communication is vital to all organizations because it is the primary means through which employees and work units synchronize their work.
Iam Anupong/Getty Images

attempt to change someone's thoughts and actions. We discuss the topic of persuasion later in this chapter.

A fourth function of communication is to support employee well-being.[6] Communication minimizes stress by conveying knowledge that helps employees better manage their work environment. For instance, research shows that new employees adjust much better to the organization when coworkers communicate subtle nuggets of wisdom, such as how to complete work procedures correctly, find useful resources, handle difficult customers, and avoid office politics.[7] Communication also minimizes stress emotionally; talking with others can be a soothing balm during difficult times. Indeed, people are less susceptible to colds, cardiovascular disease, and other physical and mental illnesses when they have regular social interaction.[8] In essence, people have an inherent drive to bond, to validate their self-worth, and to maintain their social identity. Communication is the means through which these drives and needs are fulfilled.

A MODEL OF COMMUNICATION

The model presented in Exhibit 8.1 provides a useful "conduit" metaphor for thinking about the communication process.[9] According to this model, communication flows through one or more channels (also called *media*) between the sender and receiver. The sender forms a message and encodes it into words, gestures, voice intonations, and other symbols or signs. Next, the encoded message is transmitted to the intended receiver through voice, text, nonverbal cues, or other channels. The receiver senses the incoming message and decodes it into something meaningful. Ideally, the decoded meaning is what the sender had intended.

In most situations, the sender looks for evidence that the other person has received and understood the transmitted message. This feedback may involve the receiver repeating the message back to the sender or demonstrating awareness of the message indirectly through the receiver's subsequent actions. Notice that feedback repeats the communication process. Intended feedback is encoded, transmitted, received, and decoded from the receiver to the sender of the original message.

Exhibit 8.1 The Communication Process Model

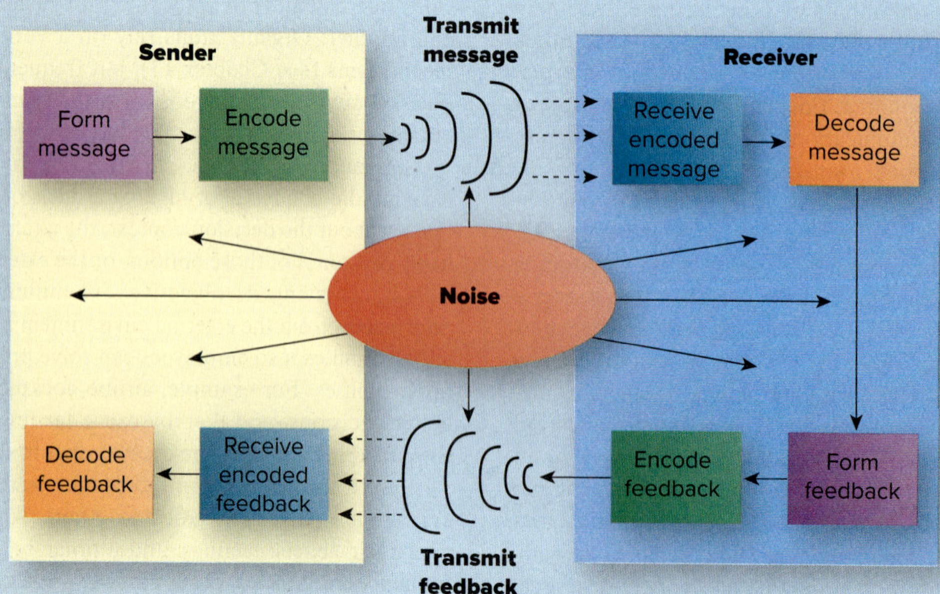

This model recognizes that communication is not a free-flowing conduit. Instead, the transmission of meaning from one person to another is hampered by *noise*—the psychological, social, and structural barriers that distort and obscure the sender's intended message. If any part of the communication process is distorted or broken, the sender and receiver will not have a common understanding of the message.

Influences on Effective Encoding and Decoding

According to the communication process model, effective communication depends on the sender's and receiver's ability, motivation, role clarity, and situational support to efficiently and accurately encode and decode information. Four main factors influence the effectiveness of this encoding-decoding process.[10]

First, the sender and receiver encode and decode more effectively when they have similar "codebooks," which are dictionaries of symbols, language, gestures, idioms, and other tools used to convey information. With similar codebooks, the communication participants assign the same or similar meaning to the transmitted symbols and signs. Communication efficiency also improves because there is less need for redundancy (repeating the message in different ways) and less need for confirmation feedback ("So, you are saying that . . . ?").

Second, the encoding-decoding process improves with the sender's experience at transmitting a message. The more frequently the sender transmits a specific message, particularly to a similar audience, the more she or he learns which words, symbols, voice intonations, and other features transmit the message more clearly and persuasively to others. A third factor is how motivated and able the sender and receiver are at using the selected communication channel(s). Even when the sender and receiver have the same codebooks, the message can get lost in translation when one or both parties use a channel that they dislike using or don't know how to use very well.[11]

Fourth, the encoding-decoding process is more successful when the sender and receiver have shared mental models of the communication context. Mental models are visual or relational images of the communication setting (see Chapter 3). With shared mental models, the sender and receiver have similar images and expectations regarding the location, time, layout, and other features of the context of the information transmitted. These shared mental models potentially increase the accuracy of the message content and reduce the need for communication about that context. For example, it is easier for two people to discuss events that occur in a nuclear plant control room if both of them have detailed mental models of the control room.

People who communicate with similar codebooks are able to encode and decode more accurately because they assign the same or similar meaning to the transmitted symbols and signs.
Jorg Greuel/Getty Images

OB THEORY TO PRACTICE

Encoding and Decoding More Effectively

The message is more likely to be received and understood when

- Both sender and receiver possess similar "codebooks" of symbols, language, gestures, etc.
- The sender has experience encoding the specific message to a specific audience.
- Both sender and receiver have the ability and motivation to use the selected communication channel(s).
- Both sender and receiver have shared mental models of the communication context.

LO8-2 Compare and contrast the advantages and disadvantages of digital written communication channels, other verbal communication channels, and nonverbal communication.

COMMUNICATION CHANNELS

A central feature of the communication model is the channel or medium through which information is transmitted. There are two main types of channels: nonverbal and verbal. Nonverbal communication is any type of communication that does not use words, such as diagrams and hand gestures. Verbal communication uses words, so it includes both spoken and written channels. However, spoken and written communication are quite

> Digital written communication will likely bring about less face-to-face and voice communication and more dialogue with people further up the hierarchy.

different from each other and have different benefits and limitations for transmitting messages, which we discuss later in this section. Also, written communication has traditionally been much slower than spoken communication at transmitting messages, although text messaging, emails, and other digital media have significantly improved written communication efficiency.

Internet and Digital Communication

Text messaging, online chat, virtual whiteboards, and other digital text-based communication channels barely existed in organizations a dozen years ago, whereas they are increasingly integrated into enterprise communication platforms. Email still dominates the corporate landscape, but its popularity is waning. Employees in almost every age group use email more often than any other communication channel, but chat and text messaging have gained popularity in organizations over the past few years. In fact, Generation Z employees—those in their mid-twenties or younger—already use chat and text messages more than email in the workplace.[12]

As Exhibit 8.2 shows, the average person in this large, continuously monitored, sample spent about one hour each work day (18 percent of 5.5 hours of active screen time) communicating via computer. From early 2014 to early 2019, email activity dropped steadily from 75 percent to 56 percent of total computer-mediated communication time. Voice-only communication also dropped (from more than 9 percent to about 3 percent), although some increase in video chat partly offset the voice-only decline. Meanwhile, online chat and instant messaging jumped from 6 percent to 28 percent of total computer-mediated communication over this five-year period.

Why is the preferred type of digital communication changing? One likely explanation is shifting preferences. Younger employees grew up in the era of smartphones, so text messaging, real-time (synchronous) chat, and other emerging digital text-based communication channels are already embedded in their lives. The other likely reason is opportunity. Slack, Microsoft Teams, Workplace from Facebook, Basecamp, and other enterprise collaboration platforms are rapidly being introduced in the workplace. In fact, many of these collaborative communication products didn't exist in 2014! These products rely on chat and messaging, not email, as the primary communication channels.

Exhibit 8.2 Use of Computer-Mediated Communication Channels

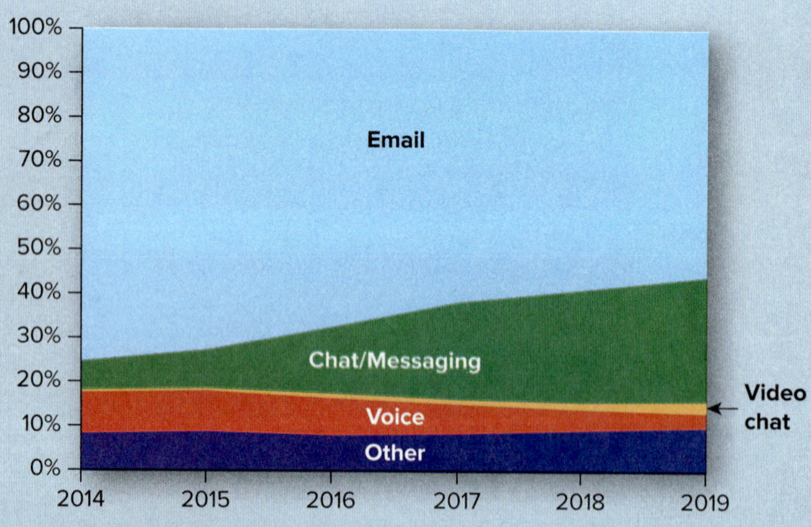

Percentage of total time in computer-mediated communication at work spent actively using each communication channel. Data are for the month of January 2014 to January 2019.

Source: Adapted from information reported in R. Molla, "The Productivity Pit: How Slack Is Ruining Work," Vox, May 1, 2019. Data are from 12,000 RescueTime app users. Data points are from the first month (January) of each year. On average, users actively focused on their screens for 5.5 hours each work day. The data shown here represent the 18 percent (about one hour) of total active screen time spent engaging in communication activity.

Benefits of Digital Written Communication

Almost all workplaces rely heavily on digital text-based communication in one form or another. Email and text messages are the first choice for coordinating work and transmitting well-defined information. They have become more popular than face-to-face meetings (in-person or remote), voice conversations, and other media. Why? Because digital messages can be written, edited, appended, and transmitted quickly to many people. Most digital written communication is also asynchronous (messages are sent and received at different times), so the dialogue does not require timely coordination. Furthermore, email software and many of the new collaborative communication platforms include search engines, which makes these channels convenient filing cabinets.[13]

Communication patterns changed significantly when email entered the workplace, and these changes will likely continue as other digital written channels become more popular. Specifically, it will likely bring about less face-to-face and voice communication and more dialogue with people further up the hierarchy.[14] Digital channels also reduce social and organizational status differences between sender and receiver, mainly because they provide fewer cues of these differences than is evident in face-to-face interaction. However, status differences still exist to some extent, such as when managers reply less quickly and with shorter messages.[15]

Email and other forms of digital written communication potentially reduce stereotyping and prejudice because age, race, and other features of the participants are unknown or less noticeable.[16] Compared to face-to-face interactions, digital communication channels also give the sender more time to craft diplomatic messages. However, these diplomatic efforts usually occur only when the writer is aware of potential conflict or perceived prejudice. Otherwise, as we discuss next, digital text-based communication has a tendency to generate and amplify conflict and reliance on stereotypes.

Problems with Email and Other Digital Message Channels

Email, text messages, and other written digital message channels dominate organizational communication, but they have several limitations. Here are the top four complaints.

Faulty Communication of Emotions People consistently and significantly overestimate the degree to which they understand the emotional meaning of digital messages. The problem is that we rely on facial expressions and other nonverbal cues to interpret the emotional meaning of words, whereas digital text-based communication lacks this parallel channel. Senders try to clarify the emotional tone of their messages by using expressive language ("Wonderful to hear from you!"), highlighting phrases in boldface or quotation marks, and inserting graphic faces (emojis and emoticons) representing the desired emotion. Studies suggest that writers are getting better at using these emotion symbols. Even so, emojis do not replace the full complexity of real facial expressions, voice intonation, and hand movements.[17]

People consistently and significantly overestimate the degree to which they understand the emotional meaning of digital messages.
ESB Professional/Shutterstock

social media digital communication channels that enable people to collaborate in the creation and exchange of user-generated content

Less Politeness and Respectfulness Digital messages are often less diplomatic than written letters. Indeed, the term *flaming* has entered our language to describe digital messages that communicate hostility and other forms of disrespect. One reason is that digital media are more impersonal (less social presence) than most other communication channels, which reduces the sender's empathy and sensitivity when crafting the message. A second reason is that digital messages can be written and transmitted before the sender's emotions subside. Paper-based messages take longer to prepare and deliver, allowing the sender to reflect more calmly on the content before it is dispatched. Receivers are also partly to blame because, on average, they infer a less respectful interpretation of the digital message than was intended by the sender.[18] Fortunately, flaming incidents may be declining as employees improve their skills with digital channels and as more companies establish explicit norms and rules to minimize flaming and cyberbullying.

Inefficient for Ambiguous, Complex, and Novel Situations Digital messages are incredibly efficient for well-defined situations, such as confirming the location of a meeting or giving basic instructions for a routine activity. But this form of communication can be cumbersome and dysfunctional in ambiguous, complex, and novel situations. As we will describe later in this section, these circumstances require communication channels that transmit a larger volume of information with more rapid feedback. In other words, when the issue gets messy, stop emailing or texting and start talking, preferably face-to-face.

Contributes to Information Overload Digital messages contribute to information overload.[19] More than 300 billion business and consumer emails and likely a similar number of text messages are sent and received every day.[20] This glut occurs because these messages are easily created and copied to many people. Text messages are usually much briefer than emails, but they still contribute to information overload because several messages are often transmitted to convey the same information found in fewer emails.

Social Media Communication in the Workplace

The emergence of social media is rapidly changing how people share information. **Social media** refers to digital (i.e., Internet, intranet, mobile, etc.) communication channels that enable people to collaborate in the creation and exchange of user-generated content. User-generated content exists when audience members (users) are partly or completely responsible for the creation or amendment of the content.[21] Social media are called "social" because user-generated content creation is a reciprocally interactive social process.

Unlike social media, traditional forms of organizational communication channels "push" information from the content creator (sender) to the audience. For instance, memos, corporate intranet web pages, policy guidelines, company magazines, and video messages from the CEO provide little or no opportunity for recipients to respond, append, revise, or make any other collaborative contribution to the original message. Even email tends to be a one way exchange, such as when the CEO emails corporate news to employees or an employee notifies coworkers about a meeting.

Most social media activity within organizations initially occurred through Facebook, Twitter, and other public platforms, often without the company's formal approval. These platforms still dominate the workplace, but organizations are quickly introducing enterprise collaborative platforms that are built around social media principles, such as Slack, Microsoft Teams, and Workplace from Facebook. These systems rely heavily on structured chat and instant messaging threads, but they also include shared file space, collaborative document editing, media sharing, group video calls, and shared task scheduling.

Social media exists in many forms. Each social media channel emphasizes specific functions, such as presenting the individual's identity, enabling conversations, sharing information, sensing the presence of others in the virtual space, maintaining relationships, revealing reputation or status, and supporting communities (see Exhibit 8.3).[22] For instance, Facebook has a strong emphasis on maintaining relationships but relatively low emphasis on sharing information or forming communities (groups). Wikis, on the other hand, focus on sharing information or forming communities but have a much lower emphasis on presenting the user's identity or reputation.

Several studies conclude that Slack, Microsoft Teams, and other enterprise collaborative platforms improve knowledge sharing and socializing among employees under some conditions.[23] When a major credit card company introduced one of these platforms, its employees became 31 percent better at finding information and 71 percent better at finding the person with the original information. A large-scale study of Twitter tweets reported that this form of communication aided employees in transmitting knowledge, maintaining collegiality among coworkers, and strengthening their professional network. Many social media platforms enable feedback, which potentially gives employees more voice, particularly where management encourages feedback.

Nonverbal Communication

Nonverbal communication includes facial gestures, voice intonation, physical distance, and even silence.[24] This communication channel is necessary where noise or physical distance prevents effective verbal exchanges and where the need for immediate feedback precludes written communication. But even in quiet face-to-face meetings, most information is communicated nonverbally. Rather like a parallel conversation, nonverbal cues signal subtle information to both parties, such as reinforcing their interest in the verbal conversation or demonstrating their relative status in the relationship.[25]

Nonverbal communication differs from verbal (i.e., written and spoken) communication in a couple of ways. First, it is less

Exhibit 8.3 Functions of Communicating through Social Media

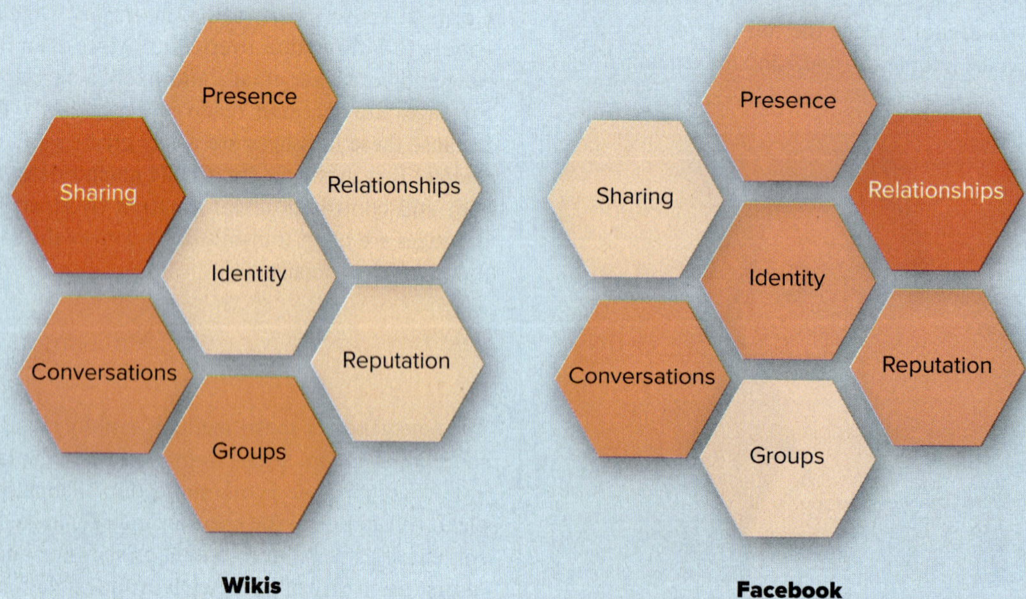

Source: Based on J.H. Kietzmann, K. Hermkens, I.P. McCarthy, and B.S. Silvestre, "Social Media? Get Serious! Understanding the Functional Building Blocks of Social Media," *Business Horizons* 54, no. 3 (2011): 241–51.

Top 10 Body Language Mistakes in Job Interviews[26]

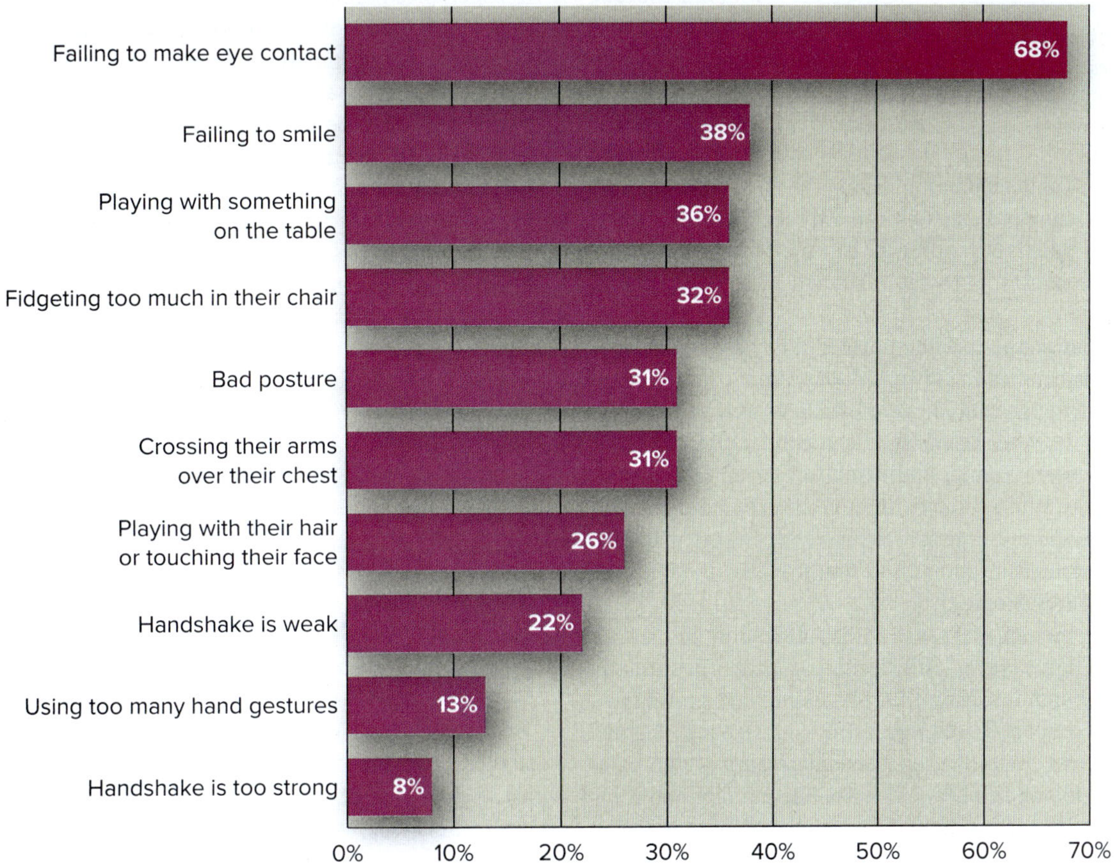

Note: Percentage of more than 1,014 human resource and hiring managers surveyed who identified each of these nonverbal behaviors as the biggest body language mistakes made by job candidates during hiring interviews.

rule-bound than verbal communication. We receive considerable formal training on how to understand spoken words but very little on how to understand the nonverbal signals that accompany those words. Consequently, nonverbal cues are generally more ambiguous and susceptible to misinterpretation. At the same time, many facial expressions (such as smiling) are hardwired and universal, thereby providing the only reliable means of communicating across cultures.

The other difference between verbal and nonverbal communication is that the former is typically conscious, whereas most nonverbal communication is automatic and nonconscious. We normally plan the words we say or write, but we rarely plan every blink, smile, or other gesture during a conversation. Indeed, as we just mentioned, many of these facial expressions communicate the same meaning across cultures because they are hardwired, nonconscious responses to human emotions.[27] For example, pleasant emotions cause the brain center to widen the mouth, whereas negative emotions produce constricted facial expressions (squinting eyes, pursed lips, etc.).

> **The most important thing in communication is hearing what isn't said.[28]**
>
> —Peter Drucker, scholar, consultant, "father" of management theory

emotional contagion the nonconscious process of "catching" or sharing another person's emotions by mimicking that person's facial expressions and other nonverbal behavior

Emotional Contagion One of the most fascinating aspects of nonverbal communication is **emotional contagion**, which is the automatic process of "catching" or sharing another person's emotions by mimicking that person's facial expressions and other nonverbal behavior. Technically, human beings have brain receptors that cause them to mirror what they observe. In other words, to some degree our brain causes us to act as though we are the person we are watching.[29]

Consider what happens when you see a coworker accidentally bang his or her head against a door frame. Chances are, you wince and put your hand on your own head as if you had hit the door. Similarly, while listening to someone describe a positive event, you tend to smile and exhibit other emotional displays of happiness. While some of our nonverbal communication is planned, emotional contagion represents nonconscious behavior—we automatically mimic and synchronize our nonverbal behaviors with other people.[30]

Emotional contagion influences communication and social relationships in three ways.[31] First, mimicry provides continuous feedback, communicating that we understand and empathize with the sender. To consider the significance of this, imagine employees remaining expressionless after watching a coworker bang his or her head! The lack of parallel behavior conveys a lack of understanding or caring. A second function is that we experience stronger emotional meaning when we mimic the nonverbal behaviors that represent the emotional experience someone is describing to us. If a coworker is angry with a client, our tendency to frown and show anger while listening helps us to experience that emotion more fully.

The third function of emotional contagion is to fulfill the drive to bond that we mentioned earlier in this chapter and was introduced in Chapter 5. Bonding develops through each person's awareness of a collective sentiment. Emotional contagion generates that communal experience because those participating in the communication event witness others sharing the same emotions that they feel. This strengthens relations among team members as well as between leaders and followers by providing evidence of their similarity.

LO8-3 Discuss the relevance of synchronicity, social presence, social acceptance, and media richness when choosing the preferred communication channel.

CHOOSING THE BEST COMMUNICATION CHANNEL

Employees have more communication channels to choose from than ever before, ranging from physical and digital forms of face-to-face interaction to a multitude of ways to transmit written messages. Which communication channel is most appropriate in a particular situation? There are many factors to consider, but the four most important are summarized in Exhibit 8.4 and described in this section.

Exhibit 8.4 Factors in Choosing the Best Communication Channel

Channel Choice Factor	Description	Depends on . . .
Synchronicity	The channel requires or allows the sender and receiver to communicate with each other at the same time (synchronous) or at different times (asynchronous).	• Time urgency (immediacy) • Complexity of the topic • Cost of both parties communicating at the same time • Whether receiver should have time to reflect before responding
Social presence	The channel creates psychological closeness to others, awareness of their humanness, and appreciation of the interpersonal relationship.	• Need to empathize with others • Need to influence others
Social acceptance	The channel is approved and supported by others (receiver, team, organization, or society).	• Organizational, team, and cultural norms • Each party's preferences and skills with the channel • Symbolic meaning of the channel
Media richness	The channel has high data-carrying capacity—the volume and variety of information that can be transmitted during a specific time.	• Situation is nonroutine • Situation is ambiguous

Synchronicity

Communication channels vary in their **synchronicity**, that is, the extent to which they require or allow both sender and receiver to be actively involved in the conversation at the same time.[32] Face-to-face conversations are almost always synchronous, whereas most digital text communication can occur with each party participating at different times (asynchronous). Text messaging can be asynchronous, but some forms (online chat) are often applied in practice as synchronous conversation. Synchronous communication is preferred when the information is required quickly (high immediacy) or where the issue is complex and therefore requires the parties to address several related decisions. Asynchronous communication is better when the issue is simple, the issue has low time urgency, getting both parties together at the same time is costly, and/or the receiver would benefit from time to reflect on the message before responding.

Social Presence

Social presence refers to how much the communication channel creates psychological closeness to others, awareness that there is another human being (or several others) in the conversation, and appreciation of the interpersonal relationship.[33] Face-to-face interactions almost always have the highest social presence, whereas low social presence would typically occur when uploading a document where anyone in the organization can retrieve it. Social presence is usually stronger in synchronous communication because the receiver's immediate responses to our messages increase the sense of connectedness with that person. Although social presence is affected mostly by specific channel characteristics, message content also plays a role. For example, social presence is higher when the sender's message style is casual rather than formal and when the message describes personal information about the sender.

A communication channel is valued for its social presence effect when the purpose of the dialogue is to understand and empathize with the other person or group. People are also more willing to listen and help others when there is a degree of interpersonal relationship or feeling of human connectedness. Therefore, channels with high social presence are better when the sender wants to influence the receiver.[34]

A communication channel is valued for its social presence effect when the purpose of the dialogue is to understand and empathize with the other person or group.
Larry Williams/LWA/Blend Images LLC

Social Acceptance

Social acceptance refers to how well the communication medium is approved and supported by coworkers, teams, the organization, and society.[35] One social acceptance factor is the set of norms held by others involved in the communication event. Norms explain why face-to-face meetings are daily events among staff in some firms, whereas video conferences and Twitter tweets are the media of choice in other organizations. National culture also influences preferences for specific communication channels.[36] For instance, emojis populate more business emails and text messages in China than in the United States, likely because people in China prefer conveying emotions indirectly rather than directly (in words) and because they value the complex, ambiguous, and cute symbolism of emojis.[37]

A second social acceptance factor is the sender's and receiver's preferences for specific communication channels.[38] You may have noticed that some coworkers ignore (or rarely check) voicemail, yet they quickly respond to text messages or Twitter tweets. These preferences are due to the individual's personality, values, experience, and previous success with some channels more than others.

A third social acceptance factor is the symbolic meaning of a channel.[39] Many years ago, communications scholar Marshall McLuhan wrote: "The medium is the message." This famous statement has multiple meanings, including the notion that an emerging communication channel (medium) shapes society. However, the statement also highlights the fact that the selected channel communicates a message beyond the content sent through that channel. Some communication channels are viewed as impersonal whereas others are more personal; some are considered professional whereas others are casual; some are seen as "cool" whereas others are old-fashioned. For instance, phone calls and other synchronous communication channels convey a greater sense of urgency than do text messages and other asynchronous channels.

Media Richness

Media richness refers to the communication channel's data-carrying capacity—the volume and variety of information that

synchronicity the extent to which the channel requires or allows both sender and receiver to be actively involved in the conversation at the same time (synchronous) or at different times (asynchronous)

social presence the extent to which a communication channel creates psychological closeness to others, awareness of their humanness, and appreciation of the interpersonal relationship

media richness a medium's data-carrying capacity—that is, the volume and variety of information that can be transmitted during a specific time

OB THEORY TO PRACTICE

The Channel's Symbolic Meaning Is Important When Terminating Employment[40]

The symbolic meaning of a communication channel can be as important as the content of the message transmitted through that channel. The channel's symbolic meaning is perhaps most apparent in stories about managers who use emails and other impersonal channels to inform employees that they have been fired or laid off.

In a recent case involving dismissal by text message, Australia's Fair Work Commission warned employers that digital written communication channels are "unnecessarily callous" and therefore (with rare exceptions) should not be used. The Commission explained that "termination of employment is a matter of such significance that basic human dignity requires that dismissal be conveyed personally."

perfectlab/Shutterstock

can be transmitted during a specific time.[41] Exhibit 8.5 illustrates various communication channels arranged in a hierarchy of richness, with face-to-face interaction at the top and lean data-only reports at the bottom. A communication channel has high richness when it is able to convey multiple cues (such as both verbal and nonverbal information), allows timely feedback from receiver to sender, allows the sender to customize the message to the receiver, and makes use of

Exhibit 8.5 Media Richness Hierarchy

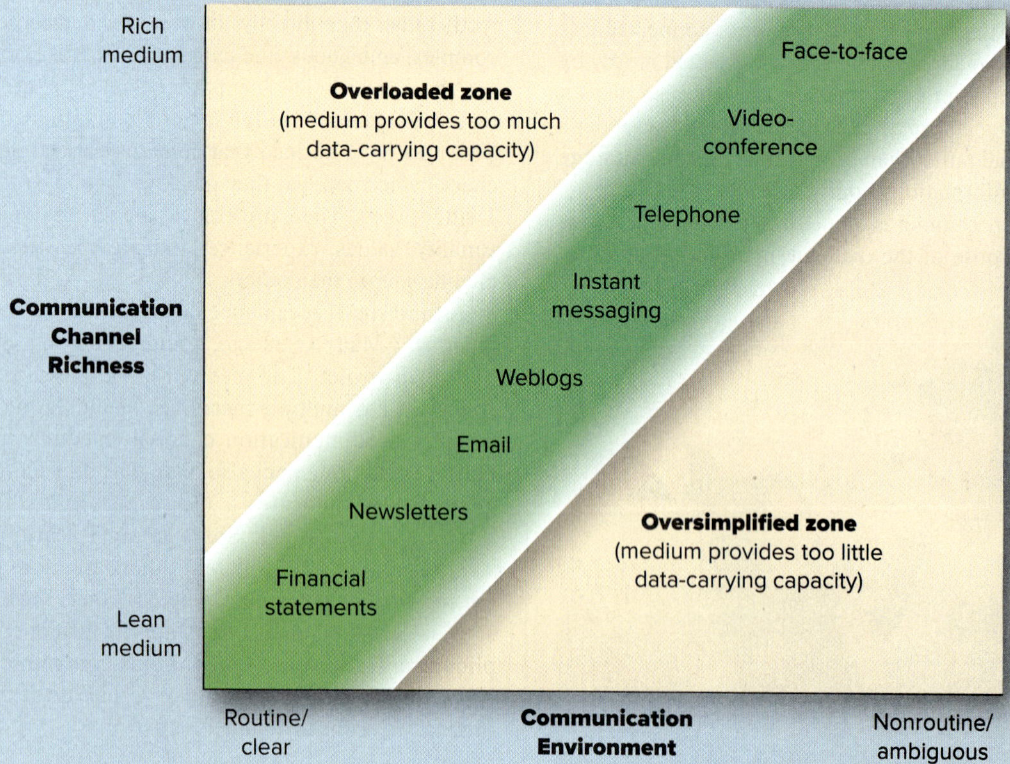

Sources: Based on R.L. Daft and R.H. Lengel, "Information Richness: A New Approach to Managerial Behavior and Organization Design," *Research in Organizational Behavior* 6 (1984): 199; R.H. Lengel and R.L. Daft, "The Selection of Communication Media as an Executive Skill," *Academy of Management Executive* 2, no. 3 (August 1988): 226.

complex symbols (such as words and phrases with multiple meanings).

Face-to-face communication has very high media richness because it allows us to communicate both verbally and nonverbally at the same time, to get feedback almost immediately from the receiver, to quickly adjust our message and style, and to use complex language such as metaphors and idioms (e.g., "spilling the beans"). For example, department and shift teams in many hospitals have brief stand-up daily huddles during which team members share information and expectations about the day's work.[42] Rich media tend to be synchronous and have high social presence, but not always.

Rich media are better than lean media when the communication situation is nonroutine and ambiguous. Under these conditions, the sender and receiver need to transmit a large volume of information with immediate feedback so they can understand the situation and agree on the best way to coordinate. Lean media work well in routine situations because the sender and receiver have shared mental models to understand the situation and determine how to coordinate their work. Using a rich medium—such as holding a special meeting—when the situation is routine and clear would be a waste of time.[43]

Exceptions to the Media Richness Theory Research generally supports media richness theory for traditional channels (face-to-face, written memos, etc.). However, the model doesn't fit reality nearly as well when digital communication channels are studied.[44] Three factors seem to explain why digital channels may have more media richness than media richness theory proposes:

1. *Ability to multicommunicate*. It is usually difficult (as well as rude) to communicate face-to-face with someone while simultaneously transmitting messages to another person using another channel. Most digital communication channels, on the other hand, require less social etiquette and attention, so employees can easily engage in two or more communication events at the same time. In other words, they can multicommunicate.[45] For example, employees tap out text messages to a client while simultaneously listening to a discussion at a large meeting. Research consistently finds that people multitask less efficiently than they assume,[46] but the volume of information transmitted simultaneously through two digital communication channels is sometimes greater than through one high media richness channel.

Digital channels have more media richness than the theory predicts possibly because there is considerable variation in the proficiency with which people can "push" information through these types of channels.
ra2studio/Shutterstock

persuasion the use of facts, logical arguments, and emotional appeals to change another person's beliefs and attitudes, usually for the purpose of changing the person's behavior

2. *Communication proficiency*. Earlier in this chapter we explained that communication effectiveness is partially determined by the sender's ability and motivation to use the selected communication channel. People with higher proficiency can "push" more information through the channel, thereby increasing the channel's information flow. Experienced smartphone users, for instance, can whip through messages in a flash, whereas new users struggle to type notes and organize incoming messages. In contrast, the ability to communicate through casual conversation and other natural channels is less varied, because most of us develop good levels of proficiency throughout life and possibly through hardwired evolutionary development.[47]

3. *Social presence effects*. Channels with high media richness tend to have more social presence.[48] This improves empathy, but it also sensitizes both parties to their relative status and self-presentation, which can distort or divert attention away from the message.[49] During a personal meeting with the company's CEO, for example, you might concentrate more on your image to the CEO than on what the executive is saying to you. In other words, the benefits of channels with high media richness may be offset by social presence distractions, whereas lean media have much less social presence to distract or distort the transmitted information.

Communication Channels and Persuasion

Some communication channels are more effective than others for **persuasion**; that is, using facts, logical arguments, and emotional appeals to change another person's beliefs and attitudes, usually for the purpose of changing behavior. Studies support the long-held view that spoken communication, particularly face-to-face interaction, is more persuasive than emails, websites, and other forms of written communication. There are three main reasons for this persuasive effect.[50] First, spoken communication is typically accompanied by nonverbal communication. People are persuaded more when they receive both emotional and logical messages, and the combination of spoken with nonverbal communication provides this dual punch. A lengthy pause, raised voice tone, and (in face-to-face interaction) animated hand gestures can amplify the emotional tone of the message, thereby signaling the vitality of the issue.

A second reason conversations are more persuasive is that spoken communication offers the sender high-quality, immediate feedback about whether the receiver understands and accepts the message (i.e., is being persuaded). This feedback allows the sender to adjust the content and emotional tone of the message more quickly than with written communication. A third reason is that people are persuaded more under conditions of high social presence than low social presence.

information overload
a condition in which the volume of information received exceeds the person's capacity to process it

Listeners have higher motivation to pay attention and consider the sender's ideas in face-to-face conversations (high social presence). In contrast, persuasive communication through a website, email, and other low social presence channels are less effective due to the higher degree of anonymity and psychological distance from the persuader.

Although spoken communication tends to be more persuasive, written communication also can persuade others to some extent. Written messages have the advantage of presenting more technical detail than can occur through conversation. This factual information is valuable when the issue is important to the receiver. Also, people experience a moderate degree of social presence in written communication with friends and coworkers, so written messages can be persuasive when sent and received with close associates.

LO8-4 Discuss various barriers (noise) to effective communication, including cross-cultural and gender-based differences in communication.

COMMUNICATION BARRIERS (NOISE)

In spite of the best intentions of sender and receiver to communicate, several barriers (called "noise" earlier in Exhibit 8.1) inhibit the effective exchange of information. One barrier is that both sender and receiver have imperfect perceptual processes. As receivers, we don't listen as well as senders assume, and our needs and expectations influence what signals get noticed and ignored. We aren't any better as senders, either. Some studies suggest that we have difficulty stepping out of our own perspectives and stepping into the perspectives of others, so we overestimate how well other people understand the message we are communicating.[51]

Language can be a huge source of communication noise because sender and receiver might not have the same codebook. They might struggle to communicate in a language that neither of them has mastered, or they might come from cultures that assign different meanings for specific words and phrases. The English language (among others) also has built-in ambiguities that cause misunderstandings. Consider the phrase "Can you close the door?" You might assume the sender is asking whether shutting the door is permitted. However, the question might be asking whether you are physically able to shut the door, or possibly whether the door is designed such that it can be shut. In fact, this question might not be a question at all; the person could be politely *directing* you to shut the door.[53]

> The greatest barrier to communication is the illusion that it has been achieved.[52]
>
> —adapted from William H. Whyte (journalist and anthropologist)

The ambiguity of language isn't always dysfunctional noise, however.[54] At times, leaders purposively use obscure language to reflect the ambiguity of the topic or to avoid unwanted emotional responses produced from more specific words. They might use metaphors to represent an abstract vision of the company's future, or use obtuse phrases such as "rightsizing" and "restructuring" to obscure the underlying message that people would be fired or laid off. Studies report that effective communicators also use more abstract words and symbols when addressing diverse or distant (not well known to the speaker) audiences, because abstraction increases the likelihood that the message is understood across a broader range of listeners.

Jargon—specialized words and phrases for specific occupations or groups—potentially improves communication efficiency. However, it is a source of communication noise when transmitted to people who do not possess the jargon codebook. This problem was apparent in one recent study, which reported that physicians used more than two dozen jargon terms, on average, during consultations with parents of children with sleep disorders.[55] Another source of noise in the communication process is the tendency to filter messages. Filtering may involve deleting or delaying negative information or using less harsh words so the message sounds more favorable.[56]

Information Overload

Start with a daily avalanche of email, then add in text messages, PDF file downloads, cell/mobile phone calls, web pages, hard-copy documents, some Twitter tweets, blogs, wikis, and other sources of incoming information. Altogether, you have created a perfect recipe for **information overload**.[57] Information overload occurs whenever the job's information load exceeds the individual's capacity to get through it. Employees have a certain *information-processing capacity*—the amount of information that they are able to process in a fixed unit of time. Meanwhile, jobs have a varying *information load*—the amount of information to be processed per unit of time. Information overload creates noise in the communication system because information gets overlooked or misinterpreted when people can't process it fast enough. The result is poorer-quality decisions as well as higher stress.[58]

Information overload problems can be minimized by increasing our information processing capacity, reducing the job's information load, or through a combination of both. Employees can temporarily increase

Information overload occurs whenever the job's information load exceeds the individual's capacity to get through it.
alphaspirit/Shutterstock

their information processing capacity by reading faster, scanning through documents more efficiently, managing their time use (less wasted time), removing distractions that slow information processing speed, and working longer hours. However, working beyond one's natural capacity is not sustainable for the long term.

Information load can be reduced by buffering, omitting, and summarizing. Buffering involves having incoming communication filtered, usually by an assistant. Omitting occurs when we decide to overlook messages, such as using software rules to redirect emails to folders that we rarely look at. Summarizing involves digesting a condensed version of the complete communication, such as reading an executive summary rather than the full report.

OB THEORY TO PRACTICE

Minimizing Information Overload

Increase information processing capacity by

- Learning to read faster.
- Scanning through documents more efficiently.
- Removing distractions that slow information-processing speed.
- Working longer hours (when overload is temporary).

Reduce information load by

- Buffering—have incoming messages filtered by an assistant (human or automated).
- Omitting—have nonessential messages discarded or redirected somewhere that you might (or might not) view later.
- Summarizing—view only the executive summary or other condensed version of the complete communication.

CROSS-CULTURAL AND GENDER COMMUNICATION

Globalization and increasing cultural diversity have created more cross-cultural communication issues.[59] As mentioned in the previous section, language differences can be a significant source of noise in the communication process. Words are easily misunderstood in verbal communication when those involved have a limited vocabulary (such as when two executives need to communicate in a language that neither of them uses regularly). Even when both are fluent, the sender's accent might distort the usual sound of some words.

Voice intonation is another cross-cultural communication barrier. How loudly, deeply, and quickly people speak varies across cultures, and these voice intonations send secondary messages that have different meaning in each society. Words are also assigned somewhat different meaning across cultures. For example, KPMG staff from the United Kingdom sometimes referred to another person's suggestions as "interesting." They had to clarify to their German colleagues that "interesting" might not be complimenting the idea.[60]

Another cross-cultural dimension of communication is how people interpret conversational gaps (silence) and overlaps. Silence is revered in Japan because it symbolizes respect, indicates that the listener is thoughtfully contemplating what has just been said, and is a way of avoiding overt conflict.[61] Consequently, the informal communication practice in Japan and a few other countries is to let the other person finish speaking and sometimes wait a few seconds before saying anything. In contrast, most people in the United States and similar cultures avoid silence and interpret those incidents as a sign of disagreement. Conversational overlaps are considered rude in Japan, whereas people from Brazil and France are more likely to interpret interruptions and overlaps as evidence of the person's interest and involvement in the conversation. Meetings in countries that expect overlapping conversations can seem like a chaotic cacophony to those from other cultures.

Nonverbal Differences across Cultures

Nonverbal communication represents another potential area for misunderstanding across cultures. Many nonconscious or involuntary nonverbal cues (such as smiling) have the same meaning around the world, but deliberate gestures often have different interpretations. For example, most of us shake our head from side to side to say, "No," but a variation of head shaking means "I understand" to many people in India. Filipinos raise their eyebrows to give an affirmative answer, yet Arabs interpret this expression (along with clicking one's tongue) as a negative response. Most Americans maintain eye contact with the speaker to show interest and respect, whereas some North American native groups learn at an early age to show respect by looking down when an older or more senior person is talking to them.[62]

Exhibit 8.6 Gender Differences in Communication

When Men Communicate	When Women Communicate
1. Report talk—give advice, assert power	1. Rapport talk—relationship building
2. Give advice directly	2. Give advice indirectly
3. Dominant conversation style	3. Flexible conversation style
4. Apologize less often	4. Apologize more often
5. Less sensitive to nonverbal cues	5. More sensitive to nonverbal cues

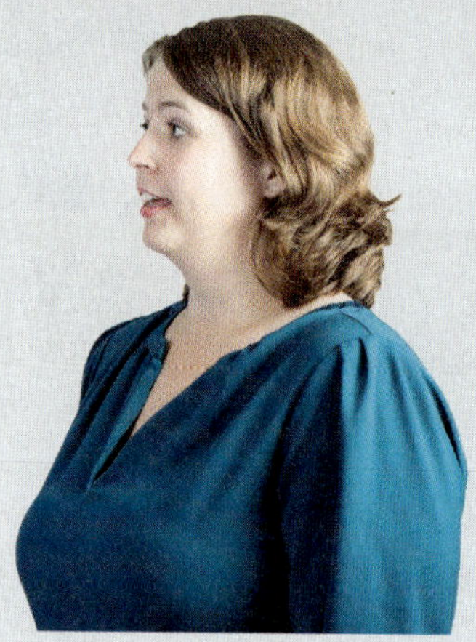

(Photos): Brittany Herbert/McGraw-Hill

Gender Differences in Communication

Men and women have similar communication practices, but there are subtle distinctions that can occasionally lead to misunderstanding and conflict (see Exhibit 8.6).[63] One distinction is that men are more likely than women to view conversations as negotiations of relative status and power. They assert their power by directly giving advice to others (e.g., "You should do the following") and using combative language. There is also evidence that men dominate the talk time in conversations with women, as well as interrupt more and adjust their speaking style less than do women.

Men engage in more "report talk," in which the primary function of the conversation is impersonal and efficient information exchange. However, women engage in more "rapport talk"—verbal and nonverbal communication that builds relationships by showing egalitarian, empathetic support, and engagement with the other person.[64] They also subdue their power in the relationship through more deferential communication, including modifiers ("It might be a good idea . . . "), disclaimers ("I'm not certain, but . . . "), and tag questions ("This works, doesn't it?").

Women tend to make more use of indirect requests ("Do you think you should . . . "), apologize more often, and seek advice from others more quickly than do men. Men also use these speech patterns to some extent, but women use them more frequently as well as across communication channels (conversations, text messages, etc.). Research also reports that women are more sensitive than men to nonverbal cues in face-to-face meetings. Together, these conditions can create communication conflicts. Women who describe problems get frustrated that men offer advice rather than rapport, whereas men become frustrated because they can't understand why women don't appreciate their advice.

LO8-5 Explain how to get your message across more effectively and summarize the elements of active listening.

IMPROVING INTERPERSONAL COMMUNICATION

Effective interpersonal communication depends on the sender's ability to get the message across and the receiver's performance as an active listener. In this section, we outline these two essential features of effective interpersonal communication.

Getting Your Message Across

This chapter began with the statement that effective communication occurs when the other person receives and understands the message. This is more difficult to accomplish than most people believe. To get your message across to the other person, you first need to empathize with the receiver, such as being sensitive to words that may be ambiguous or trigger the wrong emotional response. Second, you should repeat the message, such as by rephrasing the key points a couple of times. Third, your message competes with other messages and noise, so find a time when the receiver is less likely to be distracted by these other matters. Finally, focus on the problem, not the person, if you have negative information to convey. People stop listening when the information attacks their self-concept. Also, suggest things

> Nature gave us one tongue, but two ears, so we may listen twice as much as we speak.[65]
>
> —Epictetus, Greek philosopher

the listener can do to improve, rather than pointing to him or her as the problem.

Active Listening

Active listening is a process of mindfully sensing the sender's signals, evaluating them accurately, and responding appropriately. These three components of active listening–sensing, evaluating, and responding–represent the listener's side of the communication model described at the beginning of this chapter. Listeners receive the sender's signals, decode them as intended, and provide appropriate and timely feedback to the sender (see Exhibit 8.7). Active listeners constantly cycle through sensing, evaluating, and responding during the conversation and engage in various activities to improve these processes.[66]

- *Sensing*. Sensing is the process of receiving signals from the sender and paying attention to them. Active listeners improve sensing in three ways. First, they postpone evaluation by not forming an opinion until the speaker has finished. Second, they avoid interrupting the speaker's conversation. Third, they remain motivated to listen to the speaker.
- *Evaluating*. This component of listening includes understanding the message meaning, evaluating the message, and remembering the message. To improve their evaluation of the conversation, active listeners empathize with the speaker—they try to understand and be sensitive to the speaker's feelings, thoughts, and situation. Evaluation also improves by organizing the speaker's ideas during the communication episode.
- *Responding*. This third component of listening involves providing feedback to the sender, which motivates and directs the speaker's communication. Active listeners accomplish this by maintaining sufficient eye contact and sending back channel signals (e.g., "I see"), both of which show interest. They also respond by clarifying the message—rephrasing the speaker's ideas at appropriate breaks ("So you're saying that . . . ?").

Exhibit 8.7 Active Listening Process and Strategies

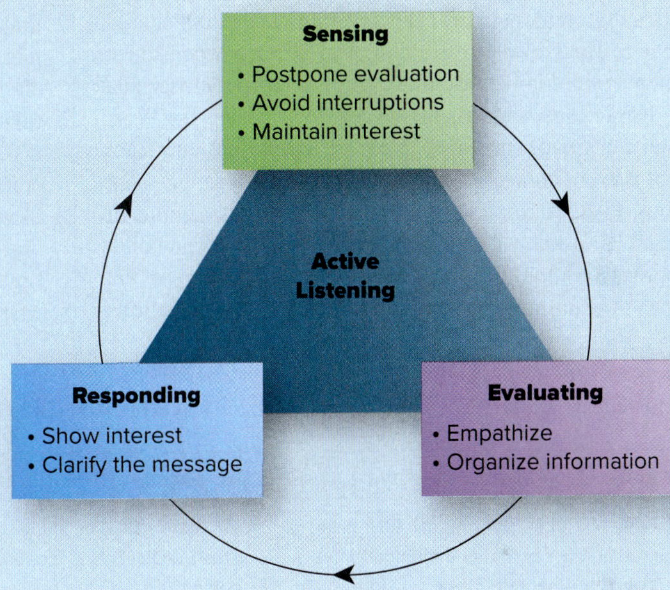

LO8-6 Describe effective communication strategies in organizational hierarchies and review the role and relevance of the organizational grapevine.

IMPROVING COMMUNICATION THROUGHOUT THE HIERARCHY

So far, we have looked at micro-level issues in the communication process, namely, sending and receiving information between two employees or among members of a small team. But in this era where knowledge is competitive advantage, corporate leaders also need to maintain an open flow of communication up, down, and across the entire organization. In this section, we discuss three organizationwide communication strategies:

McGraw Hill connect

SELF-ASSESSMENT 8.1: Are You an Active Listener?

workspace design, digitally-based communication, and direct communication with top management.

Workspace Design

The location and design of hallways, offices, cubicles, and communal areas (cafeterias, elevators) all influence to whom we speak as well as the frequency of that communication.[67] Many organizations have shifted from cubicles to open spaces in the hope that the increased line-of-sight to coworkers will improve information sharing. However, two factors may reverse this trend. First, the COVID-19 pandemic demanded more social distancing to protect employees' health. Some companies fulfilled this requirement by transferring employees from shared work areas to their own private cubicles. Second, open-space arrangements potentially undermine employee productivity due to noise, distractions, and loss of privacy.[68]

Another workspace strategy is to cloister employees into team spaces, but also encourage sufficient interaction with people from other teams. Pixar Animation Studios constructed its campus in Emeryville, California, with these principles in mind. The building encourages communication among team members. At the same time, the campus encourages happenstance interactions with people on other teams. Pixar executives call this the "bathroom effect" because team members must leave their isolated pods to fetch their mail, have lunch, or visit the restroom.[69]

Digitally Based Organizational Communication

For decades, employees received official company news through hard-copy newsletters and magazines. Some firms still use these communication devices, but the traditional company magazine has almost completely been replaced by intranet web pages or PDF format files.

Even so, employees are increasingly skeptical of information that has been screened and packaged by management. Companies are adapting to this skepticism by introducing social media channels through the emerging enterprise collaborative platforms described earlier in this chapter. Along with enabling task-focused message threads, these systems allow users to generate blogs, shared notices, and other news-oriented sites, most of which also allow feedback comments from readers within the organization. In many instances, company magazines have been replaced by real-time text messages directly from employees where the events occur.[70]

The Quality of Direct Communication with Management[72]

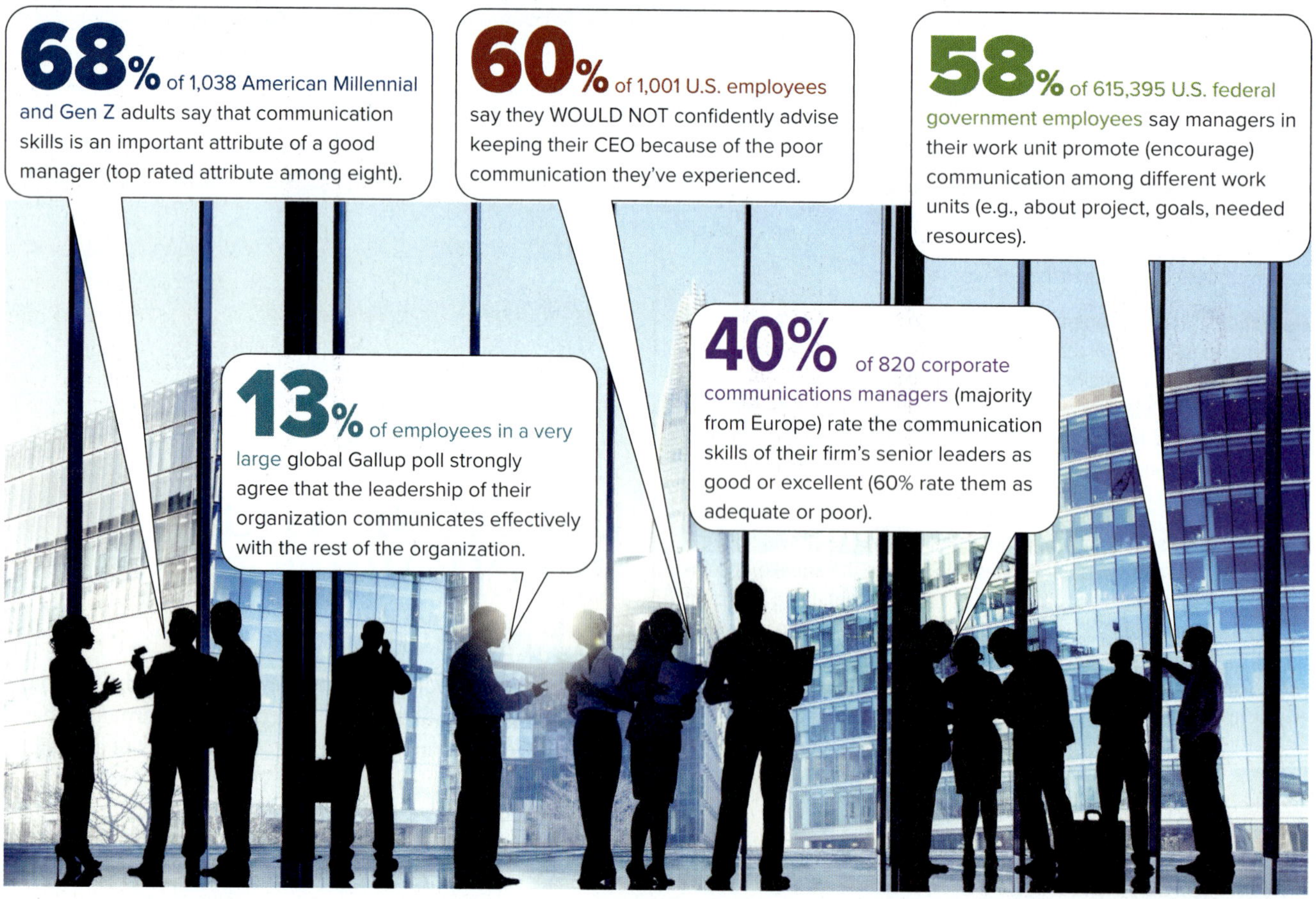

Rawpixel.com/Shutterstock

Wikis are another form of organizational communication, particularly where employees need to share structured documentation that continually changes. Wikis are collaborative digital spaces in which anyone in a group can write, edit, or remove material from the site. *Wikipedia,* the popular online encyclopedia, is a massive public example of a wiki. However, employee involvement in corporate wikis has been lower than expected, likely because wiki involvement takes time and the company does not reward or recognize those who provide this time to wiki development.[71]

Direct Communication with Top Management

Effective organizational communication includes regular interaction directly between senior executives and employees further down the hierarchy. One form of direct communication is through town hall meetings, where executives brief a large gathering of staff on the company's current strategy and results. Although the communication is mostly from executives to employees, town hall meetings are more personal and credible than video or written channels. Also, these events usually provide some opportunity for employees to ask questions. Another strategy is for senior executives to hold roundtable forums with a small representation of employees, mainly to hear their opinions on various issues.

A less formal approach to direct communication is **management by wandering around (MBWA)**. Coined by people at Hewlett-Packard four decades ago, this is the practice of senior executives getting out of their offices and casually chatting with employees on a daily or regular basis.[73] Less information is filtered when executives casually and regularly chat directly with employees. These MBWA conversations also help executives acquire a deeper meaning and quicker understanding of internal organizational problems. A third benefit is that employees potentially develop better empathy for decisions made further up the corporate hierarchy.

COMMUNICATING THROUGH THE GRAPEVINE

Organizational leaders may try their best to quickly communicate breaking news to employees through emails, text messages, and other direct formal channels, but employees still rely to some extent on the corporate **grapevine**. The grapevine is an unstructured and informal network founded on social relationships rather than organizational charts or job descriptions. What do employees think about the grapevine? Surveys have found that almost all employees use the grapevine, but very few of them prefer this source of information. In one survey, only one-third of employees believe grapevine information is credible. In other words, employees turn to the grapevine when they have few other options.[74]

management by wandering around (MBWA) a communication practice in which executives get out of their offices and learn from others in the organization through face-to-face dialogue

grapevine an unstructured and informal communication network founded on social relationships rather than organizational charts or job descriptions

Grapevine Characteristics

Research conducted several decades ago reported that the grapevine transmits information very rapidly in all directions throughout the organization. The typical pattern is a cluster chain, whereby a few people actively transmit information to many others. The grapevine works through informal social networks, so it is more active where employees have similar backgrounds and are able to communicate easily. Many rumors seem to have at least a kernel of truth, possibly because they are transmitted through media-rich communication channels (e.g., face-to-face) and employees are motivated to communicate effectively. Nevertheless, the grapevine distorts information by deleting fine details and exaggerating key points of the story.[75]

Some of these characteristics might still be true, but the grapevine almost certainly has changed as email, text messaging, and social media practices have replaced the traditional water cooler as sources of gossip. For example, several Facebook sites are unofficially themed around specific companies, allowing employees and customers to vent their complaints about the organization. Along with altering the speed and network of corporate grapevines, the Internet has expanded these networks around the globe, not just around the next cubicle.[76]

Grapevine Benefits and Limitations

Should the grapevine be encouraged, tolerated, or quashed? The difficulty in answering this question is that the grapevine has both benefits and limitations.[77] One benefit, as was mentioned earlier, is that employees rely on the grapevine when

> The grapevine works through informal social networks, so it is more active where employees have similar backgrounds and are able to communicate easily.

information is not available through formal channels. It is also the main conduit through which organizational stories and other symbols of the organization's culture are communicated. A third benefit of the grapevine is that this social interaction relieves anxiety. This explains why rumor mills are most active during times of uncertainty.[78] Finally, the grapevine is associated with the drive to bond. Being a recipient of gossip is a sign of inclusion, according to evolutionary psychologists. Trying to quash the grapevine is, in some respects, an attempt to undermine the natural human drive for social interaction.[79]

The grapevine potentially offers these benefits, but it is not a preferred communication medium. Grapevine information is sometimes so distorted that it escalates rather than reduces employee anxiety. Furthermore, employees develop more negative attitudes toward the organization when management is slower than the grapevine in communicating information. What should corporate leaders do with the grapevine? Companies should listen to the grapevine as a signal of employee anxiety, then correct the cause of this anxiety. Leaders also need to advise employees when the grapevine transmits blatant errors and fabrications. Most important, corporate leaders need to view the grapevine as a competitor and meet this challenge by directly informing employees of news before it spreads throughout the grapevine.

Study Checklist

Connect® is available for *M Organizational Behavior*. Additional resources include:

✓ Exercises:

- **Case Analysis:** Apply concepts within the context of a real-world situation.
- **Click and Drag:** Helps make the connection between theory and application through matching, ranking, or grouping activities.
- **Video Case:** See management in action through interactive videos.
- **Self-Assessment:** Designed to promote student self-awareness and reflection, these research-based surveys contain detailed feedback for students.
- **Application-Based Activities:** These highly interactive, application- and analysis-based exercises allow students to take on specific roles to complete management-related tasks within a real-world context.

✓ **SmartBook 2.0**™—Smartbook 2.0 is an adaptive learning solution that provides personalized learning to individual student needs, continually adapts to pinpoint knowledge gaps and focuses learning on concepts requiring additional study. It fosters more productive learning, takes the guesswork out of what to study, and helps students better prepare for class.

Notes

1. J. Legere, "T-Mobile's CEO on Winning Market Share by Trash-Talking Rivals," *Harvard Business Review*, January-February 2017; J. Legere, "Un-Carrier Is from the Inside Out!," September 26, 2017, https://www.t-mobile.com/news/un-carrier-is-from-the-inside-out; M. Davis, "T-Mobile CEO John Legere Met Employees at Sprint Campus Weeks after Negative Report," *Kansas City Star*, October 5, 2018.

2. A.H. Van de Ven, A.L. Delbecq, and R. Koenig Jr., "Determinants of Coordination Modes within Organizations," *American Sociological Review* 41 (1976): 322–38; J.H. Gittell, R. Seidner, and J. Wimbush, "A Relational Model of How High-Performance Work Systems Work," *Organization Science* 21 (2010): 490–506; R. Foy et al., "Meta-Analysis: Effect of Interactive Communication between Collaborating Primary Care Physicians and Specialists," *Annals of Internal Medicine* 152 (2010): 247–58.

3. C. Barnard, *The Functions of the Executive* (Cambridge, MA: Harvard University Press, 1938), 82. Barnard's entire statement also refers to the other features of organizations that we describe in Chapter 1, namely, that (1) people are willing to contribute their effort to the organization and (2) they have a common purpose.

4. J. O'Toole and W. Bennis, "What's Needed Next: A Culture of Candor," *Harvard Business Review* 87, no. 6 (2009): 54–61.

5. W.J.L. Elving, "The Role of Communication in Organisational Change," *Corporate Communications* 10, no. 2 (2005): 129–38; P.M. Leonardi, T.B. Neeley, and E.M. Gerber, "How Managers Use Multiple Media: Discrepant Events, Power, and Timing in Redundant Communication," *Organization Science* 23, no. 1 (2012): 98–117; D.A. Tucker, P. Yeow, and G.T. Viki, "Communicating during Organizational Change Using Social Accounts: The Importance of Ideological Accounts," *Management Communication Quarterly* 27, no. 2 (2013): 184–209.

6. R.E. Baumeister and M.R. Leary, "The Need to Belong: Desire for Interpersonal Attachments as a Fundamental Human Motivation," *Psychological Bulletin* 117 (1995): 497–529; K.H. Greenaway et al., "Social Identities Promote Well-Being because They Satisfy Global Psychological Needs," *European Journal of Social Psychology* 46 (2016): 294–307; N. Steverink et al., "The Associations of Different Social Needs with Psychological Strengths and Subjective Well-Being: An Empirical Investigation Based on Social Production Function Theory," *Journal of Happiness Studies* 21 (2020): 799–824.

7. A.M. Saks, K.L. Uggerslev, and N.E. Fassina, "Socialization Tactics and Newcomer Adjustment: A Meta-Analytic Review and Test of a Model," *Journal of Vocational Behavior* 70, no. 3 (2007): 413–46.
8. S. Cohen, "The Pittsburgh Common Cold Studies: Psychosocial Predictors of Susceptibility to Respiratory Infectious Illness," *International Journal of Behavioral Medicine* 12, no. 3 (2005): 123–31; B.A. Scott et al., "A Daily Investigation of the Role of Manager Empathy on Employee Well-Being," *Organizational Behavior and Human Decision Processes* 113, no. 2 (2010): 127–40; S.Y. Shin and S.G. Lee, "Effects of Hospital Workers' Friendship Networks on Job Stress," *PLoS ONE* 11, no. 2 (2016): e0149428.
9. C.E. Shannon and W. Weaver, *The Mathematical Theory of Communication* (Urbana: University of Illinois Press, 1949); R.M. Krauss and S.R. Fussell, "Social Psychological Models of Interpersonal Communication," in *Social Psychology: Handbook of Basic Principles*, ed. E.T. Higgins and A. Kruglanski (New York: Guilford Press, 1996), 655–701.
10. R. Cross and R.J. Thomas, *Driving Results through Social Networks: How Top Organizations Leverage Networks for Performance and Growth* (San Francisco: Jossey-Bass, 2009); R. McDermott and D. Archibald, "Harnessing Your Staff's Informal Networks," *Harvard Business Review* 88, no. 3 (2010): 82–89; J.R. Methot, E.H. Rosado-Solomon, and D.G. Allen, "The Network Architecture of Human Capital: A Relational Identity Perspective," *Academy of Management Review* 43 (2018): 723–48.
11. Y. van den Boer et al., "Towards a Model of Source and Channel Choices in Business-to-Government Service Interactions: A Structural Equation Modeling Approach," *Government Information Quarterly* 34 (2017): 434–56; R. McColl and M. Michelotti, "Sorry, Could You Repeat the Question? Exploring Video-Interview Recruitment Practice in HRM," *Human Resource Management Journal* 29 (2019): 637–56.
12. "Email Statistics Report, 2019–2023" (Palo Alto, CA: The Radicati Group, February 2019); "Communication Barriers in the Modern Workplace" (London: The Economist Intelligence Unit, March 2018); L. Wright and N. McCullough, "New Survey Explores the Changing Landscape of Teamwork," *Microsoft 365 Blog* (blog), April 19, 2018, https://www.microsoft.com/en-us/microsoft-365/blog/2018/04/19/new-survey-explores-the-changing-landscape-of-teamwork/.
13. N.B. Ducheneaut and L.A. Watts, "In Search of Coherence: A Review of E-Mail Research," *Human-Computer Interaction* 20, no. 1-2 (2005): 11–48; R.S. Mano and G.S. Mesch, "E-Mail Characteristics, Work Performance and Distress," *Computers in Human Behavior* 26, no. 1 (2010): 61–69.
14. W. Lucas, "Effects of E-mail on the Organization," *European Management Journal* 16 (1998): 18–30; D.A. Owens, M.A. Neale, and R.I. Sutton, "Technologies of Status Management Status Dynamics in E-Mail Communications," *Research on Managing Groups and Teams* 3 (2000): 205–30; G. de La Rupelle, C. Guthrie, and M. Kalika, "La relation entre l'intensité perçue d'utilisation de la messagerie électronique et la qualité de la relation hiérarchique," *Relations Industrielles* 70 (2015): 157–85; C.M. Brotheridge, D.J. Neufeld, and B. Dyck, "Communicating Virtually in a Global Organization," *Journal of Managerial Psychology* 30 (2015): 909–24.
15. N. Panteli, "Richness, Power Cues and Email Text," *Information & Management* 40 (2002): 75–86; C.T. Carr and C. Stefaniak, "Sent from My iPhone: The Medium and Message as Cues of Sender Professionalism in Mobile Telephony," *Journal of Applied Communication Research* 40 (2012): 403–24; D.C. DeAndrea, "Advancing Warranting Theory," *Communication Theory* 24 (2014): 186–204; C.M. Brotheridge, D.J. Neufeld, and B. Dyck, "Communicating Virtually in a Global Organization," *Journal of Managerial Psychology* 30 (2015): 909–24.
16. J.B. Walther et al., "Computer-Mediated Communication and the Reduction of Prejudice: A Controlled Longitudinal Field Experiment among Jews and Arabs in Israel," *Computers in Human Behavior* 52 (2015): 550–58.
17. K. Byron, "Carrying Too Heavy a Load? The Communication and Miscommunication of Emotion by Email," *Academy of Management Review* 33 (2008): 309–27; M.A. Riordan and L.A. Trichtinger, "Overconfidence at the Keyboard: Confidence and Accuracy in Interpreting Affect in E-Mail Exchanges," *Human Communication Research* 43 (2017): 1–24; K. Lohmann, S.S. Pyka, and C. Zanger, "The Effects of Smileys on Receivers' Emotions," *Journal of Consumer Marketing* 34 (2017): 489–95; C. Laubert and J. Parlamis, "Are You Angry (Happy, Sad) or Aren't You? Emotion Detection Difficulty in Email Negotiation," *Group Decision and Negotiation* 28 (2019): 377–413.
18. H. Lee, "Behavioral Strategies for Dealing with Flaming in an Online Forum," *The Sociological Quarterly* 46 (2005): 385-403; A.K. Turnage, "Email Flaming Behaviors and Organizational Conflict," *Journal of Computer-Mediated Communication* 13 (2007): 43–59; K. Byron, "Carrying Too Heavy a Load? The Communication and Miscommunication of Emotion by Email," *Academy of Management Review* 33 (2008): 309–27.
19. N. Sobotta and M. Hummel, "A Capacity Perspective on E-Mail Overload: How E-Mail Use Contributes to Information Overload" (paper presented at the 2015 48th Hawaii International Conference on System Sciences, January 5–8, 2015), 692–701; S. Drössler et al., "Informationsüberflutung durch digitale Medien am Arbeitsplatz (Information overload by digital media at the workplace. Systematic review of qualitative studies)," *Zentralblatt für Arbeitsmedizin, Arbeitsschutz und Ergonomie (Central Journal for Occupational Medicine, Occupational Safety and Ergonomics)* 68 (2018): 77–88.
20. "Email Statistics Report, 2019-2023" (Palo Alto, CA: The Radicati Group, February 2019). The daily number of text messages globally could be as much as 300 billion. This is estimated from statistics on Apple iMessages, Whatapp messages, and a recent estimate of 26 billion daily messages in the U.S. in 2018. See "How Many Texts Do People Send Every Day (2018)?, November 2018, https://www.textrequest.com/blog/how-many-texts-people-send-per-day/.
21. Social media definitions in the literature tend to be obtuse, varied, and in many cases, elusive. Our definition is based on two of the more widely cited sources: A.M. Kaplan and M. Haenlein, "Users of the World, Unite! The Challenges and Opportunities of Social Media," *Business Horizons* 53 (2010): 59–68; C.T. Carr and R.A. Hayes, "Social Media: Defining, Developing, and Divining," *Atlantic Journal of Communication* 23 (2015): 46–65.
22. J.H. Kietzmann et al., "Social Media? Get Serious! Understanding the Functional Building Blocks of Social Media," *Business Horizons* 54 (2011): 241–51; J.W. Treem and P.M. Leonardi, "Social Media Use in Organizations: Exploring the Affordances of Visibility, Editability, Persistence, and Association," *Communication Yearbook* 36 (2012): 143–89; C.V. Baccarella et al., "Social Media? It's Serious! Understanding the Dark Side of Social Media," *European Management Journal* 36 (2018): 431–38.

23. W. van Zoonen, T.G.L.A. van der Meer, and J.W.M. Verhoeven, "Employees Work-Related Social-Media Use: His Master's Voice," *Public Relations Review* 40 (2014): 850–52; G. Martin, E. Parry, and P. Flowers, "Do Social Media Enhance Constructive Employee Voice All of the Time or Just Some of the Time?" *Human Resource Management Journal* 25 (2015): 541–62; W. van Zoonen, J.W.M. Verhoeven, and R. Vliegenthart, "How Employees Use Twitter to Talk about Work: A Typology of Work-Related Tweets," *Computers in Human Behavior* 55, Part A (2016): 329–39; P. Leonardi and T. Neeley, "What Managers Need to Know about Social Tools," *Harvard Business Review*, November–December 2017.

24. S. Bonaccio et al., "Nonverbal Behavior and Communication in the Workplace: A Review and an Agenda for Research," *Journal of Management* 42 (2016): 1044–74.

25. L.Z. Tiedens and A.R. Fragale, "Power Moves: Complementarity in Dominant and Submissive Nonverbal Behavior," *Journal of Personality and Social Psychology* 84, no. 3 (2003): 558–68.

26. "The Most Unusual Interview Mistakes and Biggest Body Language Mishaps, According to Annual CareerBuilder Survey," news release (Chicago: CareerBuilder, February 22, 2018).

27. P. Ekman and E. Rosenberg, *What the Face Reveals: Basic and Applied Studies of Spontaneous Expression Using the Facial Action Coding System* (Oxford, UK: Oxford University Press, 1997); P. Winkielman and K.C. Berridge, "Unconscious Emotion," *Current Directions in Psychological Science* 13, no. 3 (2004): 120–23.

28. J. Champy, *What I Learned from Peter Drucker* (Boston: New Word City, 2010), Chap. 4.

29. W.J. Becker and R. Cropanzano, "Organizational Neuroscience: The Promise and Prospects of an Emerging Discipline," *Journal of Organizational Behavior* 31 (2010): 1055–59; S.G. Barsade, C.G.V. Coutifaris, and J. Pillemer, "Emotional Contagion in Organizational Life," *Research in Organizational Behavior* 38 (2018): 137–51.

30. M. Sonnby-Borgstrom, P. Jonsson, and O. Svensson, "Emotional Empathy as Related to Mimicry Reactions at Different Levels of Information Processing," *Journal of Nonverbal Behavior* 27 (2003): 3–23; V. Vijayalakshmi and S. Bhattacharyya, "Emotional Contagion and Its Relevance to Individual Behavior and Organizational Processes: A Position Paper," *Journal of Business and Psychology* 27 (2012): 363–74. However, emotional contagion is not universally automatic. It may depend on social relations between the parties. See M. Wróbel and K.K. Imbir, "Broadening the Perspective on Emotional Contagion and Emotional Mimicry: The Correction Hypothesis," *Perspectives on Psychological Science* 14 (2019): 437–51.

31. T.L. Chartrand and J.L. Lakin, "The Antecedents and Consequences of Human Behavioral Mimicry," *Annual Review of Psychology* 64 (2013): 285–308; E. Prochazkova and M.E. Kret, "Connecting Minds and Sharing Emotions through Mimicry: A Neurocognitive Model of Emotional Contagion," *Neuroscience & Biobehavioral Reviews* 80 (2017): 99–114.

32. A.R. Dennis, R.M. Fuller, and J.S. Valacich, "Media, Tasks, and Communication Processes: A Theory of Media Synchronicity," *MIS Quarterly* 32 (2008): 575–600; S. Taipale, "Synchronicity Matters: Defining the Characteristics of Digital Generations," *Information, Communication & Society* 19 (2016): 80–94; I. Geiger and C. Laubert, "Situational Strategic versus Personal Influences on Negotiation Medium Choice: Media Synchronicity Theory and Affect for Communication Channel," *International Journal of Conflict Management* 29 (2018): 398–423.

33. R.E. Rice, "Media Appropriateness: Using Social Presence Theory to Compare Traditional and New Organizational Media," *Human Communication Research* 19 (1993): 451–84; D. Gooch and L. Watts, "The Impact of Social Presence on Feelings of Closeness in Personal Relationships," *Interacting with Computers* 27 (2015): 661–74; C.S. Oh, J.N. Bailenson, and G. Welch, "A Systematic Review of Social Presence: Definition, Antecedents, and Implications," *Frontiers in Robotics and AI* (October 15, 2018), https://doi.org/10.3389/frobt.2018.00114.

34. N. Walter, K. Ortbach, and B. Niehaves, "Designing Electronic Feedback—Analyzing the Effects of Social Presence on Perceived Feedback Usefulness," *International Journal of Human-Computer Studies* 76 (2015): 1–11; S.C. Srivastava and S. Chandra, "Social Presence in Virtual World Collaboration: An Uncertainty Reduction Perspective Using a Mixed Methods Approach," *MIS Quarterly* 42 (2018): 779–803.

35. J. Fulk, "Social Construction of Communication Technology," *Academy of Management Journal* 36 (1993): 921–50; J.W. Turner et al., "Exploring the Dominant Media: How Does Media Use Reflect Organizational Norms and Affect Performance?" *Journal of Business Communication* 43 (2006): 220–50; J.B. Bayer, S.W. Campbell, and R. Ling, "Connection Cues: Activating the Norms and Habits of Social Connectedness," *Communication Theory* 26 (2016): 128–49.

36. Z. Lee and Y. Lee, "Emailing the Boss: Cultural Implications of Media Choice," *IEEE Transactions on Professional Communication* 52, no. 1 (2009): 61–74; D. Holtbrügge, A. Weldon, and H. Rogers, "Cultural Determinants of Email Communication Styles," *International Journal of Cross Cultural Management* 13, no. 1 (2013): 89–110.

37. "Emojis Gain Hearts, Business in Shy Chinese," *Xinhua News Agency*, August 18, 2016; J. D'Onfro, "13 Rules Regarding Proper Email Etiquette from Around the World," *Mental Floss*, February 20, 2017; Z. Zhang, "WeChat's Exclusive Emojis Express Emotions Western Apps Cannot," *Quartz*, July 19, 2018; O. Surcouf, "Korean Apps Conquer Asia with Cute Emojis," *Asia Times*, March 16, 2019.

38. R.C. King, "Media Appropriateness: Effects of Experience on Communication Media Choice," *Decision Sciences* 28 (1997): 877–910; A. Oeldorf-Hirsch and K.L. Nowak, "There Is Something I Need to Tell You: Balancing Appropriateness and Efficiency in Modality Choice for Interpersonal Disclosures," *Communication Studies* 69 (2018): 125–44.

39. K.K. Stephens, A.K. Barrett, and M.J. Mahometa, "Organizational Communication in Emergencies: Using Multiple Channels and Sources to Combat Noise and Capture Attention," *Human Communication Research* 39 (2013): 230–51; J. Eden and A.E. Veksler, "Relational Maintenance in the Digital Age: Implicit Rules and Multiple Modalities," *Communication Quarterly* 64 (2016): 119–44. Marshall McLuhan's treatise on the medium is the message is found in: M. McLuhan, *Understanding Media: The Extensions of Man* (New York: McGraw-Hill, 1964).

40. *Kurt Wallace v AFS Security 24/7 Pty Ltd*, No. 4292 (Fair Work Commission [Australia], June 28, 2019).

41. R.L. Daft and R.H. Lengel, "Information Richness: A New Approach to Managerial Behavior and Organization Design," *Research in Organizational Behavior* 6 (1984): 191–233; R.H. Lengel and R.L. Daft, "The Selection of Communication Media as an Executive Skill," *Academy of Management Executive* 2 (1988): 225–32.

42. H. Rodriguez et al., "Huddle Up! The Adoption and Use of Structured Team Communication for VA Medical Home Implementation," *Health Care Management Review* 40 (2015): 286–99; R.W. Quinn and J.S. Bunderson, "Could We Huddle on This Project? Participant Learning in Newsroom Conversations," *Journal of Management* 42 (2016): 386–418.

43. R.E. Rice, "Task Analyzability, Use of New Media, and Effectiveness: A Multi-Site Exploration of Media Richness," *Organization Science* 3 (1992): 475–500; V.W. Kupritz and E. Cowell, "Productive Management Communication: Online and Face-to-Face," *Journal of Business Communication* 48 (2011): 54–82.

44. R.F. Otondo et al., "The Complexity of Richness: Media, Message, and Communication Outcomes," *Information & Management* 45, no. 1 (2008): 21–30.

45. N.L. Reinsch Jr., J.W. Turner, and C.H. Tinsley, "Multicommunicating: A Practice Whose Time Has Come?" *Academy of Management Review* 33 (2008): 391–403; A.F. Cameron and J. Webster, "Multicommunicating: Juggling Multiple Conversations in the Workplace," *Information Systems Research* 24 (2013): 352–71; N.L. Reinsch and J.W. Turner, "Multicommunicator Aspirational Stress, Suggestions for Teaching and Research, and Other Insights after 10 Years of Multicommunication Research," *Journal of Business and Technical Communication* 33 (2019): 141–71.

46. S. Xu, Z. Wang, and P. David, "Media Multitasking and Well-Being of University Students," *Computers in Human Behavior* 55, Part A (2016): 242–50; A.-F. Cameron et al., "Multicommunicating in Meetings: Effects of Locus, Topic Relatedness, and Meeting Medium," *Management Communication Quarterly* 32 (2018): 303–36.

47. J.R. Carlson and R.W. Zmud, "Channel Expansion Theory and the Experiential Nature of Media Richness Perceptions," *Academy of Management Journal* 42 (1999): 153–70; N. Kock, "Media Naturalness Theory: Human Evolution and Behaviour towards Electronic Communication Technologies," in *Applied Evolutionary Psychology*, ed. S.C. Roberts (Oxford, UK: Oxford University Press, 2012), 381–98; I. Blau, O. Weiser, and Y. Eshet-Alkalai, "How Do Medium Naturalness and Personality Traits Shape Academic Achievement and Perceived Learning? An Experimental Study of Face-to-Face and Synchronous E-Learning," *Research in Learning Technology* 25 (2017),https://doi.org/10.25304/rlt.v25.1974.

48. L.P. Robert and A.R. Dennis, "Paradox of Richness: A Cognitive Model of Media Choice," *IEEE Transactions on Professional Communication* 48 (2005): 10–21; C. Belletier et al., "Choking under Monitoring Pressure: Being Watched by the Experimenter Reduces Executive Attention," *Psychonomic Bulletin & Review* 22 (2015): 1410–16; C. Belletier, A. Normand, and P. Huguet, "Social-Facilitation-and-Impairment Effects: From Motivation to Cognition and the Social Brain," *Current Directions in Psychological Science* 28 (2019): 260–65.

49. D. Muller, T. Atzeni, and F. Butera, "Coaction and Upward Social Comparison Reduce the Illusory Conjunction Effect: Support for Distraction–Conflict Theory," *Journal of Experimental Social Psychology* 40, no. 5 (2004): 659–65; L.P. Robert and A.R. Dennis, "Paradox of Richness: A Cognitive Model of Media Choice," *IEEE Transactions on Professional Communication* 48, no. 1 (2005): 10–21.

50. E.V. Wilson, "Perceived Effectiveness of Interpersonal Persuasion Strategies in Computer-Mediated Communication," *Computers in Human Behavior* 19, no. 5 (2003): 537–52; K. Sassenberg, M. Boos, and S. Rabung, "Attitude Change in Face-to-Face and Computer-Mediated Communication: Private Self-Awareness as Mediator and Moderator," *European Journal of Social Psychology* 35 (2005): 361–74; P. Di Blasio and L. Milani, "Computer-Mediated Communication and Persuasion: Peripheral vs. Central Route to Opinion Shift," *Computers in Human Behavior* 24, no. 3 (2008): 798–815.

51. J.W. Bang and D. Rahnev, "Stimulus Expectation Alters Decision Criterion but Not Sensory Signal in Perceptual Decision Making," *Scientific Reports* 7, no. 1 (December 6, 2017): 1–12; M.M. Roghanizad and V.K. Bohns, "Ask in Person: You're Less Persuasive than You Think over Email," *Journal of Experimental Social Psychology* 69 (March 2017): 223–26; A. Tapal, Y. Yeshurun, and B. Eitam, "Relevance-Based Processing: Little Role for Task-Relevant Expectations," *Psychonomic Bulletin & Review* 26 (2019): 1426–32.

52. Most sources incorrectly attribute this famous quotation (usually with "accomplished" rather than "achieved") to the Irish playwright and social critic George Bernard Shaw. This specific statement was likely first uttered in the late 1950s by Joe Coffman, president of Tecnifax Corporation and an enthusiast of visual and interpersonal communication. Coffman almost certainly adapted it from the following passage in William H. Whyte's 1950 *Fortune* magazine article on communication, which became one of *Fortune*'s most-read articles: "The great enemy of communication, we find, is the illusion of it." Coffman's statement was originally published in a 1960 article summarizing a public health conference, during which one of the speakers credited Coffman as the originator of this quotation. See W.H. Whyte, "Is Anybody Listening," *Fortune*, September 1950, 77ff; "Web of Mutual Anticipations: Conference Report," *Public Health Reports* 75, no. 10 (1960): 927; D.M. Davis, *A Biased Biography: Mine* (Lincoln, NE: iUniverse, 2004); "The Biggest Problem in Communication Is the Illusion That It Has Taken Place," *Quote Investigator*, August 31, 2014, http://quoteinvestigator.com/2014/08/31/illusion/.

53. R.M. Krauss, "The Psychology of Verbal Communication," in *International Encyclopedia of the Social and Behavioral Sciences*, ed. N. Smelser and P. Baltes (London: Elsevier, 2002), 16161–65.

54. A.M. Carton, C. Murphy, and J.R. Clark, "A (Blurry) Vision of the Future: How Leader Rhetoric about Ultimate Goals Influences Performance," *Academy of Management Journal* 57 (2014): 1544–70; P.D. Joshi et al., "Communicating with Distant Others: The Functional Use of Abstraction," *Social Psychological and Personality Science* 7 (2016): 37–44. Ambiguous language by politicians also increases with the diversity of constituents. See C. Chapp et al., "Going Vague: Ambiguity and Avoidance in Online Political Messaging," *Social Science Computer Review* 37 (2019): 591–610.

55. A.R. Links et al., "Surgeon Use of Medical Jargon with Parents in the Outpatient Setting," *Patient Education and Counseling* 102 (2019): 1111–18.

56. C.E. Connelly et al., "Knowledge Hiding in Organizations," *Journal of Organizational Behavior* 33 (2012): 64–88.

57. T. W. Jackson and P. Farzaneh, "Theory-Based Model of Factors Affecting Information Overload," *International Journal of Information Management* 32, no. 6 (2012): 523–32.

58. A. G. Schick, L. A. Gordon, and S. Haka, "Information Overload: A Temporal Approach," *Accounting, Organizations & Society* 15 (1990): 199–220; A. Edmunds and A. Morris, "The Problem of Information Overload in Business Organisations: A Review of the Literature," *International Journal of Information Management* 20 (2000): 17–28; R. Pennington, "The Effects of Information Overload on Software Project Risk Assessment," *Decision Sciences* 38, no. 3 (2007): 489–526.

59. A.-W. Harzing, K. Köster, and U. Magner, "Babel in Business: The Language Barrier and Its Solutions in the HQ-Subsidiary Relationship," *Journal of World Business* 46 (2011): 279–87; N. Aichhorn and J. Puck, "Bridging the Language Gap in Multinational Companies: Language Strategies and the Notion of Company-Speak," *Journal of World Business* 52 (2017): 386–403; D.E. Welch and L.S. Welch, "Developing Multilingual Capacity: A Challenge for the Multinational Enterprise," *Journal of Management* 44 (2018): 854–69.

60. T. Craig, "Different Strokes," *Personnel Today*, November 25, 2008, 190.

61. D.C. Barnlund, *Communication Styles of Japanese and Americans: Images and Realities* (Belmont, CA: Wadsworth, 1988); H. Yamada, *American and Japanese Business Discourse: A Comparison of Interaction Styles* (Norwood, NJ: Ablex, 1992), Chap. 2; T. Hasegawa and W.B. Gudykunst, "Silence in Japan and the United States," *Journal of Cross-Cultural Psychology* 29 (1998): 668–84; M. Fujio, "Silence during Intercultural Communication: A Case Study," *Corporate Communications* 9 (2004): 331–39.

62. H. Blagg, "A Just Measure of Shame?" *British Journal of Criminology* 37 (1997): 481–501; R.E. Axtell, *Gestures: The Do's and Taboos of Body Language around the World*, rev. ed. (New York: Wiley, 1998); L. Kelly and J.B. Brown, "Listening to Native Patients. Changes in Physicians' Understanding and Behaviour," *Canadian Family Physician* 48 (October 2002): 1645–52; A. McCarthy et al., "Cultural Display Rules Drive Eye Gaze during Thinking," *Journal of Cross-Cultural Psychology* 37 (2006): 717–22; H. Akechi et al., "Attention to Eye Contact in the West and East: Autonomic Responses and Evaluative Ratings," *PLOS ONE* 8, no. 3 (March 13, 2013): e59312.

63. D. Tannen, *You Just Don't Understand: Men and Women in Conversation* (New York: Ballantine Books, 1990); J.L. Locke, *Duels and Duets: Why Men and Women Talk So Differently* (Cambridge, UK: Cambridge University Press, 2011); M.R. Atai and F. Chahkandi, "Democracy in Computer-Mediated Communication: Gender, Communicative Style, and Amount of Participation in Professional Listservs," *Computers in Human Behavior* 28, no. 3 (2012): 881–88; A.B. Hancock and B.A. Rubin, "Influence of Communication Partner's Gender on Language," *Journal of Language and Social Psychology* 34, no. 1 (2015): 46–64.

64. A. Mulac et al., "'Uh-Huh. What's That All About?' Differing Interpretations of Conversational Backchannels and Questions as Sources of Miscommunication across Gender Boundaries," *Communication Research* 25 (1998): 641–68; N.M. Sussman and D.H. Tyson, "Sex and Power: Gender Differences in Computer-Mediated Interactions," *Computers in Human Behavior* 16 (2000): 381–94; C. Leaper and R.D. Robnett, "Women Are More Likely Than Men to Use Tentative Language, Aren't They? A Meta-Analysis Testing for Gender Differences and Moderators," *Psychology of Women Quarterly* 35, no. 1 (2011): 129–42.

65. This quotation is varied slightly from the original translations by E. Carter, *All the Works of Epictetus, Which Are Now Extant*, 3rd ed., vol. 2 (London: J. and F. Rivington, 1768), 333; T.W. Higginson, *The Works of Epictetus* (Boston: Little, Brown, and Company, 1866), 428.

66. L.B. Comer and T. Drollinger, "Active Empathetic Listening and Selling Success: A Conceptual Framework," *Journal of Personal Selling & Sales Management* 19 (1999): 15–29; T. Drollinger, L.B. Comer, and P.T. Warrington, "Development and Validation of the Active Empathetic Listening Scale," *Psychology and Marketing* 23, no. 2 (2006): 161–80; P. JungKun et al., "The Role of Listening in E-Contact Center Customer Relationship Management," *Journal of Services Marketing* 29, no. 1 (2015): 49–58.

67. T.J. Allen, "Architecture and Communication among Product Development Engineers," *California Management Review* 49, no. 2 (2007): 23–41; M.C. Davis, D.J. Leach, and C.W. Clegg, "The Physical Environment of the Office: Contemporary and Emerging Issues," in *International Review of Industrial and Organizational Psychology 2011* (Wiley, 2011), 193–237; J. Kim and R. de Dear, "Workspace Satisfaction: The Privacy-Communication Trade-Off in Open-Plan Offices," *Journal of Environmental Psychology* 36 (2013): 18–26.

68. A. Seddigh et al., "The Association between Office Design and Performance on Demanding Cognitive Tasks," *Journal of Environmental Psychology* 42 (2015): 172–81; M. Yadav et al., "The Irrelevant Speech Effect in Multi-Talker Environments: Applications to Open-Plan Offices," *The Journal of the Acoustical Society of America* 143, no. 3 (2018): 1725; K. Chan, "Cubicle Comeback? Pandemic Will Reshape Office Life for Good," *Chicago Tribune*, May 12, 2020.

69. S.P. Means, "Playing at Pixar," *Salt Lake Tribune* (Utah), May 30, 2003, D1; G. Whipp, "Swimming against the Tide," *Los Angeles Daily News*, May 30, 2003, U6.

70. C.J. Turco, "A New Era of Corporate Conversation," *MIT Sloan Management Review* 58, no. 1 (Fall 2016): 11–12.

71. M.L. Yeo and O. Arazy, "What Makes Corporate Wikis Work? Wiki Affordances and Their Suitability for Corporate Knowledge Work," in *Design Science Research in Information Systems. Advances in Theory and Practice*, ed. K. Peffers, M. Rothenberger, and B. Kuechler, vol. 7286 (Berlin, Heidelberg: Springer Berlin Heidelberg, 2012), 174–90, https://doi.org/10.1007/978-3-642-29863-9_14; H. Hasan and C.C. Pfaff, "An Activity Theory Analysis of Corporate Wikis," *Information Technology & People* 25 (2012): 423–37; E. Bolisani and E. Scarso, "Factors Affecting the Use of Wiki to Manage Knowledge in a Small Company," *Journal of Knowledge Management* 20 (2016): 423–43.

72. "State of the Sector 2019: The Definitive Global Survey of the Internal Communication Profession" (London: Gatehouse, February 2019); "Dynamic Signal Study Finds U.S. Workforce Stressed and Ready to Quit, Compounding Concerns from Tight Labor Market and Possible Economic Downturn," news release (San Bruno, CA: Dynamic Signal, March 20, 2019); Office of Personnel Management, "2019 Federal Employee Viewpoint Survey" (Washington, DC: U.S. Government, October 2019); "Millennials Are Managers Now," *Zapier* (blog), March 10, 2020, https://zapier.com/blog/millennial-managers-report/; S.M. O'Keefe and J. Buono, "Crisis Communication: How Great Leaders Stop Rumors before They Start," *Gallup Workplace*, April 3, 2020.

73. W. Ouchi, *Theory Z* (New York: Avon Books, 1981), 176–77; T. Peters and R. Waterman, *In Search of Excellence* (New York: Harper and Row, 1982), 122.

74. R. Rousos, "Trust in Leaders Lacking at Utility," *The Ledger* (Lakeland, FL), July 29, 2003, B1; B. Whitworth and B. Riccomini, "Management Communication: Unlocking Higher Employee Performance," *Communication World*, March/April 2005, 18–21.

75. K. Davis, "Management Communication and the Grapevine," *Harvard Business Review* 31 (1953): 43–49; W.L. Davis and J.R. O'Connor, "Serial Transmission of Information: A Study of the Grapevine," *Journal of Applied Communication Research* 5 (1977): 61–72.

76. G. Dalziel, *Rumor and Communication in Asia in the Internet Age* (New York: Routledge, 2013); K.L. Robinson and P.D. Thelen, "What Makes the Grapevine So Effective? An Employee Perspective on Employee- Organization Communication and Peer-to-Peer Communication," *Public Relations Journal*12, no. 2 (2018).

77. S.R. Clegg and A. van Iterson, "Dishing the Dirt: Gossiping in Organizations," *Culture and Organization* 15 (2009): 275–89; C. Mills, "Experiencing Gossip: The Foundations for a Theory of Embedded Organizational Gossip," *Group & Organization Management* 35 (2010): 213–40; T.J. Grosser et al., "Hearing It through the Grapevine: Positive and Negative Workplace Gossip," *Organizational Dynamics* 41 (2012): 52–61.

78. R.L. Rosnow, "Inside Rumor: A Personal Journey," *American Psychologist* 46 (1991): 484–96; P. Bordia et al., "Management Are Aliens! Rumors and Stress during Organizational Change," *Group & Organization Management* 31 (2006): 601–21; K. Smet et al., "The Explanatory Role of Rumours in the Reciprocal Relationship between Organizational Change Communication and Job Insecurity: A Within-Person Approach," *European Journal of Work and Organizational Psychology* 25 (2016): 631–44.

79. N. Nicholson, "Evolutionary Psychology: Toward a New View of Human Nature and Organizational Society," *Human Relations* 50 (1997): 1053–78; E.K. Foster, "Research on Gossip: Taxonomy, Methods, and Future Directions," *Review of General Psychology* 8, no. 2 (2004): 78–99; B. Beersma and G.A. Van Kleef, "Why People Gossip: An Empirical Analysis of Social Motives, Antecedents, and Consequences," *Journal of Applied Social Psychology* 42, no. 11 (2012): 2640–70.

9 Power and Influence in the Workplace

Compassionate Eye Foundation/Mark Langridge/Getty Images

Learning Objectives

After you read this chapter, you should be able to:

LO9-1 Describe the dependence model of power and the five sources of power in organizations.

LO9-2 Discuss the four contingencies of power.

LO9-3 Explain how people and work units gain power through social networks.

LO9-4 Describe eight types of influence tactics, three consequences of influencing others, and three contingencies to consider when choosing an influence tactic.

LO9-5 Identify the organizational conditions and personal characteristics associated with organizational politics, as well as ways to minimize organizational politics.

power the capacity of a person, team, or organization to influence others

One of the most popular topics in organizational behavior classes is about managing your boss. The theme may sound manipulative, but managing your boss is actually a valuable process of gaining power and using influence for the benefit of the organization. Most executives say it is a key factor in everyone's career success.

"Managing up is about setting boundaries and rules on how you and your manager work together," explains Tomas Kucera, vice president of business operations at SolarWinds, the Austin, Texas, firm that develops enterprise information technology infrastructure management software. "It is about understanding the needs of the other person and helping them to achieve their goals."

There are many ways to manage your boss—or anyone else in and around organizations—such as aligning communication and work styles, becoming a valuable resource, being solution-oriented rather than problem-oriented, and supporting your manager's career success by performing your own job well. These and other practices develop power bases and apply influence tactics that ultimately change (or stabilize) the behavior of others. These activities are not unusual. On the contrary, OB experts point out that power and influence are inherent in all organizations. They exist in every business and in every decision and action.[1]

This chapter unfolds as follows: First, we define power and present a basic model depicting the dynamics of power in organizational settings. The chapter then discusses the five bases of power. Next, we look at the contingencies necessary to translate those sources into meaningful power. Our attention then turns to social networks and how they provide power to members through social capital. The latter part of this chapter examines the various types of influence in organizational settings as well as the contingencies of effective influence strategies. The final section of this chapter looks at situations in which influence becomes organizational politics, as well as ways of minimizing political behavior.

LO9-1 Describe the dependence model of power and the five sources of power in organizations.

THE MEANING OF POWER

Power is the capacity of a person, team, or organization to influence others.[2] There are a few important features of this definition. First, power is not the act of changing someone's attitudes or behavior; it is only the *potential* to do so. People frequently have power they do not use; they might not even know they have power. Second, power is based on the target's *perception* that the power holder controls (i.e., possesses, has access to, or regulates) a valuable resource that can help to achieve the target person's goals.[3] An employee might have valuable expertise, yet this power base doesn't translate into actual power because others in the organization don't know about or understand the value of this expertise. However, power is not your own perception or feeling of power; it exists only when others believe you have power.

Third, power involves asymmetric (unequal) *dependence* of one party on another party.[4] This dependent relationship is illustrated in Exhibit 9.1. The line from Person B to the goal shows that he or she believes Person A controls a resource that can help or hinder Person B in achieving that goal. Person A—the dominant power holder in this illustration—might have power over Person B by controlling a desired job assignment, useful information, rewards, or even the privilege of being associated with Person A! For example, if you believe a coworker has expertise (the resource) that would substantially help you write a better report (your goal), then that coworker has some

Exhibit 9.1 Dependence Model of Power

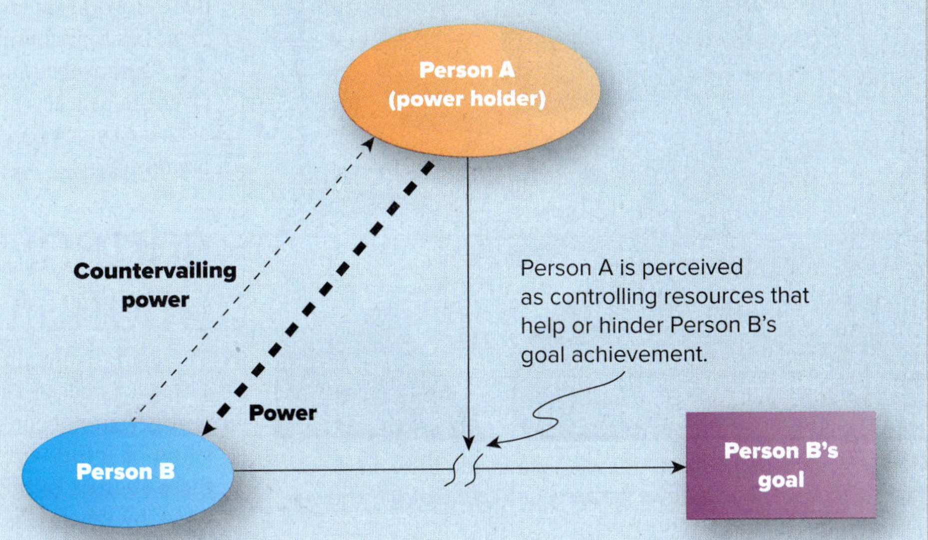

countervailing power the capacity of a person, team, or organization to keep a more powerful person or group in the exchange relationship

legitimate power an agreement among organizational members that people in certain roles can request certain behaviors of others

norm of reciprocity a felt obligation and social expectation of helping or otherwise giving something of value to someone who has already helped or given something of value to you

power over you because you value that expertise to achieve your goal. Whatever the resource is, Person B perceives a dependence on Person A (the power holder) to provide the resource so Person B can reach his or her goal.

Although dependence is a key element of power relationships, we use the phrase *asymmetric dependence* because the less powerful party also has some power—called **countervailing power**—over the more powerful party. In Exhibit 9.1, Person A dominates the power relationship, but Person B has enough countervailing power to keep Person A in the exchange relationship and ensure that person uses his or her dominant power judiciously. For example, although managers have power over subordinates in many ways (e.g., control of job security and preferred work assignments), those employees have countervailing power by possessing skills and knowledge to keep production humming and customers happy, something that management can't accomplish alone.

Power involves asymmetric dependence of one party on another party because the less powerful party has countervailing power over the stronger power holder.
Image Source/Getty Images

One other key feature is that all power relationships depend on some minimum level of trust. Trust indicates a level of expectation that the more powerful party will deliver the resource. For example, you trust your employer to give you a paycheck at the end of each pay period. Even those in extremely dependent situations will usually walk away from the relationship if they lack a minimum level of trust in the more powerful party.

Let's look at this power dependence model in the employee-manager relationship. You depend on your boss to support your continued employment, satisfactory work arrangements, and other valued resources. At the same time, the manager depends on you to complete required tasks and to work effectively with others in the completion of their work. Managers (and the companies they represent) typically have more power, whereas employees have weaker countervailing power. But sometimes employees do have more power than their bosses in the employment relationship. The extent that your source of power (such as expertise) actually generates power depends on several factors, such as the employer's awareness of your source of power and how many other employees have that source of power. Finally, trust is an essential ingredient in this relationship. Even with strong power, the employee-manager relationship comes apart when one party no longer sufficiently trusts the other.

The dependence model reveals only the core features of power dynamics between people and work units in organizations. We also need to learn about the specific sources of power and contingencies that support or inhibit those power bases. As Exhibit 9.2 illustrates, power is derived from five sources: legitimate, reward, coercive, expert, and referent. The model also identifies four contingencies of power: the employee's or department's nonsubstitutability, centrality, visibility, and discretion. Over the next few sections of this chapter, we will discuss each of these sources and contingencies of power in the context of organizations.

SOURCES OF POWER IN ORGANIZATIONS

There are five main sources of power in human interactions.[5] Three of these—legitimate, reward, and coercive—originate mostly (but not completely) from the power holder's formal position or informal role. In other words, the person is granted these sources of power formally by the organization or informally by coworkers. Two other sources of power—expert and referent—originate mainly from the power holder's own

Exhibit 9.2 Sources and Contingencies of Power

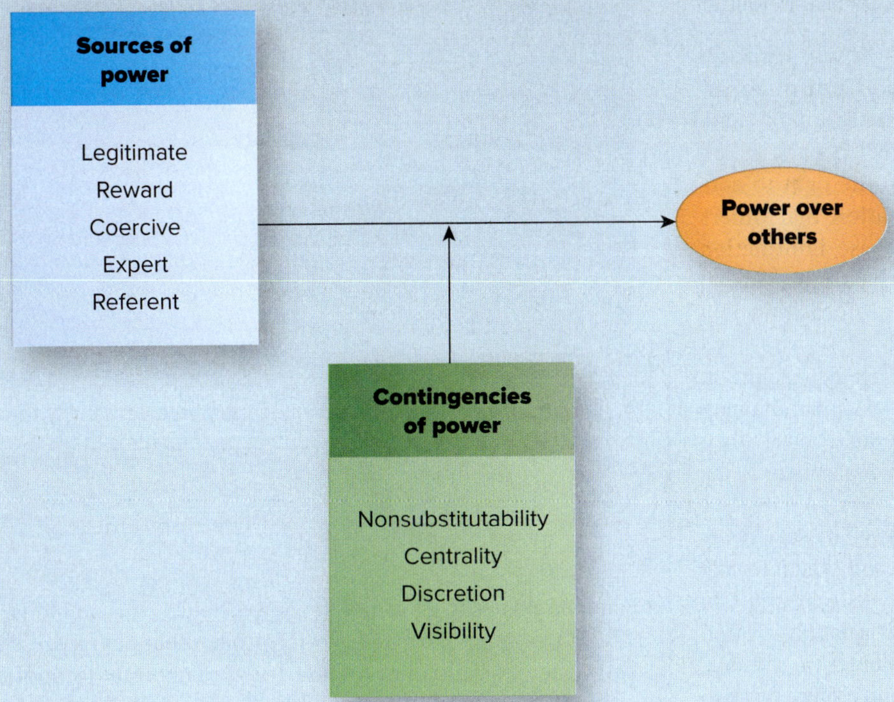

characteristics; in other words, people carry these power bases around with them. However, even personal sources of power are not completely within the person because they depend on how others perceive them.

Legitimate Power

Legitimate power is an agreement among organizational members that people in certain roles can request a set of behaviors from others. This perceived right or obligation originates from formal job descriptions as well as informal rules of conduct. It is usually the most important source of power in organizational settings, particularly between employees and managers.[6] For example, managers have a legitimate right to tell employees what tasks to perform, whom to work with, what company resources they can use, and so forth. Employees follow the boss's requests because they have agreed to follow a range of requests from people in positions of higher authority. Employee motivation to comply with these requests occurs separately from the manager's ability to reward or punish employees.

Legitimate power has restrictions; it gives the power holder only the right to ask others to perform a limited domain of behaviors, known as the "zone of indifference."[7] Although most employees accept the boss's right to deny them access to Facebook during company time, some might draw the line when the boss asks them to work several hours beyond the regular workday. They either overtly refuse to follow orders or engage in delaying and other evasive tactics.

Several factors influence the size of the zone of indifference and, consequently, the magnitude of legitimate power. Highly trusted power holders have a larger zone of indifference. Employees are more willing to abide by the requests of trusted leaders even when those requests are unusual or on the periphery of expected job duties. Some people are more obedient to authority due to their values and personality traits. Specifically, those who value conformity and tradition as well as have high power distance (i.e., they accept an unequal distribution of power) tend to give their bosses a larger zone of indifference. The organization's culture represents another influence on the willingness of employees to follow orders.[8]

Managers are not the only people with legitimate power in organizations. Employees also have legitimate power over their bosses and coworkers through legal and administrative rights as well as informal norms.[9] An organization might give employees the right to request information that is required for their job. Laws give employees the right to refuse to work in unsafe conditions. More subtle forms of legitimate power also exist. Human beings have a **norm of reciprocity**—a felt obligation and social expectation of helping or otherwise giving something of value to someone who has already helped or given something of value to you.[10] If a coworker previously helped you resolve a difficult problem with a client, that coworker has power because you feel an obligation to help the coworker on something of similar value in the future. The norm of reciprocity is a form of

> **Legitimate power gives the power holder only the right to ask others to perform a limited domain of behaviors, known as the "zone of indifference."**

referent power the capacity to influence others on the basis of an identification with and respect for the power holder

charisma a set of self-presentation characteristics and nonverbal communication behaviors (i.e. signaling) that generate interpersonal attraction and referent power over others as well as deference to the charismatic person

legitimate power because it is an informal rule of conduct that we are expected to follow.

Legitimate Power through Information Control A particularly potent form of legitimate power occurs when people have the right to control information that others receive.[11] These information gatekeepers have power in two ways. First, information is a resource, so those who need information are dependent on the gatekeeper to provide that resource. For example, the map department of a mining company has considerable power when other departments are dependent on the map department to deliver maps required for exploration projects.

Second, information gatekeepers gain power by selectively distributing information such that those receiving the information perceive the situation in a specific way.[12] As we learned in the previous chapter on communication, information is often filtered as it flows up the hierarchy, which enables those transmitting the information to frame the situation in a more positive light. This framing allows the information gatekeeper to steer the decision maker toward one decision rather than another.

Reward Power

Reward power is derived from the person's ability to control the allocation of rewards valued by others and to remove negative sanctions (i.e., negative reinforcement). Managers have formal authority that gives them power over the distribution of organizational rewards such as pay, promotions, time off, vacation schedules, and work assignments. Employees have reward power over coworkers through organizational citizenship behaviors, such as lending work resources or coaching others. They also have reward power over their bosses through feedback they provide to the company about the boss's leadership.

Coercive Power

Coercive power is the ability to apply punishment. Managers usually have considerable coercive power, ranging from showing disapproval to firing employees. Employees also have coercive power, such as when coworkers use peer pressure to change another employee's behavior. In fact, one recent study found that hospital employees were more likely to follow prescribed hygienic activity (wash their hands) when faced with peer pressure than when the hospital rewarded this behavior with a large financial incentive.[13]

Expert Power

Legitimate, reward, and coercive power originate mostly from an organizational position or role.[14] Expert power, on the other hand, originates from within the power holder. It is an individual's or work unit's capacity to influence others by possessing knowledge or skills valued by others. An important form of expert power is the perceived ability to manage uncertainties in the business environment. Organizations are more effective when they operate in predictable environments, so they value people who can cope with turbulence in consumer trends, societal changes, unstable supply lines, and so forth. Expertise can help companies cope with uncertainty in three ways: through prevention, forecasting, and absorption. These coping strategies are arranged in a hierarchy of importance, with prevention being the most powerful:[15]

An important form of expert power is the perceived ability to prevent, forecast, or absorb disruptive uncertainties in the business environment.
Darren Greenwood/Design Pics

- *Prevention*—The most effective strategy is to prevent environmental changes from occurring. For example, financial experts acquire power by preventing the organization from experiencing a cash shortage or defaulting on loans.
- *Forecasting*—The next best strategy is to predict environmental changes or variations. In this respect, trendspotters and other marketing specialists gain power by predicting changes in consumer preferences.
- *Absorption*—People and work units also gain power by absorbing or neutralizing the impact of environmental shifts as they occur. An example is the ability of maintenance crews to come to the rescue when machines break down.

Referent Power

People have **referent power** when others identify with them, like them, or otherwise respect them. As with expert power, referent power originates within the power holder. It is largely a function of the person's interpersonal skills. Referent power is also associated with **charisma**. Experts have difficulty agreeing on the meaning of charisma. Some describe charisma as a special "gift" or trait within the charismatic person, while others say

> **Blind respect for authority is the greatest enemy of the truth.[18]**
>
> —Albert Einstein, theoretical physicist

it is mainly in the eyes of the beholder. It may be best described as a set of self-presentation characteristics and nonverbal communication behaviors (i.e. signaling) that generate interpersonal attraction and referent power over others as well as deference to the charismatic person.[16]

Deference to Power

One of the most troubling observations about power in organizations is the human tendency to mindlessly follow the guidance of people who are charismatic (i.e., have referent power) or claim to have legitimate or expert power. Deferential followers rarely evaluate the appropriateness of the requested behavior or the power holder's right to make this request. They don't even investigate whether the power holder's legitimate authority or expertise really exists.[17]

Consider this recent example: Before the instructor of an undergraduate course arrived for class, two casually dressed people (a 29-year-old Black male and a 50-year-old Caucasian female) entered and set their belongings down at the front of the classroom. Without introduction, one of them said to the students: "I need you to put your cell phones in this box." One of them then walked around the classroom with a box to collect the students' phones. If any student questioned this task, they were authoritatively told, "It is important for you to follow instructions and put your phone in the box." The two also said (when asked) that they did not know where the instructor was at that time. Most students cherish their cell/mobile phones, yet an average of 85 percent of students across five small classes surrendered their phones to these strangers without receiving any explanation or assurance! Fortunately, these two people were confederates of the instructor and all phones were returned after the confederates had collected and counted them.[19]

This example was an experimental event in a classroom, but deference to power sometimes has tragic consequences. Not long ago, the Canadian justice system discovered that one of its "star" expert witnesses—a forensic child pathology expert—had provided inaccurate cause of death evaluations in at least 20 cases. A dozen of those cases resulted in wrongful or highly questionable criminal convictions. The pathologist's reputation as a renowned authority was the main reason why his often-weak evidence was accepted without question. "Experts in a courtroom—we give great deference to experts," admits a Canadian defense lawyer familiar with the situation.[20]

LO9-2 Discuss the four contingencies of power.

CONTINGENCIES AND CONSEQUENCES OF POWER

Contingencies of Power

Suppose that you have valuable expertise that can give the organization significant competitive advantage over rivals. Does this expertise mean that you are influential? Not necessarily. As was illustrated earlier in Exhibit 9.2, sources of power generate power only under some conditions. Four important contingencies of power are nonsubstitutability, centrality, visibility, and discretion.[21]

Nonsubstitutability Individuals and work units have more power when the resource they offer is nonsubstitutable. If you have expertise that is valuable to the organization and that no other employee can provide, you would be more powerful than if several people in your company possess this valued knowledge. Conversely, power decreases as the number of alternative sources of the resource increases. Substitutability refers not only to other sources that offer the resource; it also refers to substitutions of the resource itself. You might be the only person with specialized knowledge about a topic, but that knowledge becomes substitutable if technology or documented procedures provide similar guidance.

One strategy to increase nonsubstitutability is controlling access to the resource. Several professions leverage their expert power by restricting access to the profession and often to the educational programs that train people into that profession. Employees are also less substitutable when they operate special equipment or possess other knowledge that remains undocumented.

A second strategy is differentiating the resource from the alternatives. Consulting firms sometimes use this tactic. They take skills and knowledge that many competitors can also provide and wrap them into a package (with the latest buzz words, of course) so it looks like a service that no one else can offer.

Nonsubstitutability through differentiation is also recommended when developing our *personal brand*. Our public image and reputation should be authentic (who we really are and what we can deliver) and valuable to employers. But it also needs to be

centrality a contingency of power pertaining to the degree and nature of interdependence between the power holder and others

unique, which leverages the power of nonsubstitutability. "Be unique about something. Be a specialist in something. Be known for something. Drive something," advises Barry Salzberg, the former global CEO of Deloitte Touche Tohmatsu Limited. "That's very, very important for success in leadership because there are so many highly talented people. What's different about you—that's your personal brand."[22]

Centrality **Centrality** refers to the power holder's importance based on the degree and nature of interdependence with others.[24] Centrality increases with the number of people dependent on you as well as how quickly and severely they are affected by that dependence. Think about your own centrality for a moment: If you decided not to show up for work or school tomorrow, how many people would have difficulty performing their jobs because of your absence? How soon after they arrive at work would these coworkers have to adjust their tasks and work schedule as a result of your absence? If you have high centrality, many people in the organization would be adversely affected by your absence, and they would be affected quickly.

Visibility Power does not flow to unknown people in the organization. Instead, employees gain power when their talents remain in the forefront of the minds of their boss, coworkers, and others. In other words, power increases with visibility. This visibility can occur, for example, by taking on people-oriented jobs and projects that require frequent interaction with senior executives. Employees also gain visibility by being, quite literally, visible. Some people strategically locate themselves in more visible work areas, such as those closest to the boss or where other employees frequently pass by.

People often use public symbols as subtle (and not-so-subtle) cues to make their power sources known to others. Some display their educational diplomas and awards on office walls to remind visitors of their expertise. Medical professionals wear white coats with stethoscopes around their necks to symbolize their legitimate and expert power in hospital settings. Other people play the game of "face time"—spending more time in the office and showing that they are working productively.

Discretion Another important contingency of power in organizations is the freedom to exercise judgment. This discretion involves making decisions without referring to a specific rule or receiving permission from someone else.[25] Employees have more power due to increased discretion when they are given more autonomy over their work (see Chapter 5). In contrast, an employee's discretion to apply their legitimate, reward, and coercive power is often curtailed by rules and higher authorities.[26]

Consequences of Power

How does power affect the power holder? The answer depends to some extent on the type of power.[27] When people feel empowered (high self-determination, meaning, competence, and impact), they believe they have power over themselves and freedom from being influenced by others. Empowerment tends to increase motivation, job satisfaction, organizational commitment, and job performance. However, this feeling of being in control and free from others' authority also increases automatic rather than mindful thinking. In particular, people who feel powerful usually are more likely to rely on stereotypes, have difficulty empathizing, and generally have less accurate perceptions compared with people who have less power.[28]

The other type of power is one in which an individual has power *over others*, such as the legitimate, reward, and coercive power that managers have over employees in the workplace. This type of power produces a sense of duty or responsibility for the people over whom the power holder has authority. Consequently, people who have power over others tend to be more mindful of their actions and engage in less stereotyping. Even when people feel empowered, they can shift their focus from self to others, so the power becomes viewed more as one of social responsibility than enjoyable for its own sake.[29]

OB THEORY TO PRACTICE

The Power of Your Personal Brand[23]

One of the top drivers of career success is your personal brand—what makes you unique and valuable. "Nurturing and enhancing your professional 'brand' should be up there with performance as top priorities in your career journey," says public relations executive Curtis Sparrer.

The power of your personal brand increases with its nonsubstitutability—how much it differentiates you from others. Furthermore, personal brand power increases with visibility. "In order for your great performance to be appreciated, it needs to be visible," says university professor Jeffrey Pfeffer, a leading expert on power in organizations.

Rita Mitjans adds that you need to actively manage your public image. "Make sure that you are able to articulate and present the brand that you want others to see," advises the chief diversity and corporate social responsibility officer at payroll and tax services firm ADP.

Artem Furman/Shutterstock

social networks social structures of individuals or social units that are connected to each other through one or more forms of interdependence

social capital the knowledge, opportunities, and other resources available to members of a social network, along with the mutual support, trust, reciprocity, and coordination that facilitate sharing of those resources

LO9-3 Explain how people and work units gain power through social networks.

THE POWER OF SOCIAL NETWORKS

"It's not what you know, but who you know that counts!" This often-heard statement reflects the idea that employees get ahead not just by developing their competencies, but by locating themselves within **social networks**—social structures of individuals or social units (e.g., departments, organizations) that are connected to each other through one or more forms of interdependence.[30] Some networks are held together due to common interests, such as when employees who exercise over their lunch hours spend more time together. Other networks form around common status, expertise, kinship, or physical proximity. For instance, employees are more likely to form networks with coworkers who have common educational backgrounds and occupational interests.[31]

Social networks exist everywhere because people have a drive to bond. Cultural norms also seem to influence active network involvement. Social networking may be more of a central life activity in Asian cultures that emphasize *guanxi*, a Chinese term referring to an individual's network of social connections. Guanxi is an expressive activity because being part of a close-knit network of family and friends reinforces one's self-concept. It is also an instrumental activity for receiving favors and opportunities from others. Guanxi is sometimes so pervasive, however, that several experts warn it can undermine the organization's effectiveness.[32]

Social networks potentially enhance and maintain the power of its members through three resources: information, visibility, and referent power.
Helder Almeida/Shutterstock

Social Capital and Sources of Power

Social networks generate power through **social capital**—the knowledge, opportunities, and other resources available to members of a social network as well as the mutual support, trust, reciprocity, and coordination that facilitate sharing of those resources.[33] Compared to nonmembers, members within a social network are more motivated and able to communicate, distribute, or otherwise provide resources within their power to others in that community.

Social networks potentially enhance and maintain the power of its members through three resources: information, visibility, and referent power. Probably the best-known resource is information from other network members, which improves the individual's expert power.[34] The goodwill of social capital opens communication pipelines among those within the network. Network members receive valuable knowledge more easily and more quickly from fellow network members than do people outside that network.[35] With better information access and timeliness, members have more power because their expertise is a scarce resource; it is not widely available to people outside the network.

Increased visibility is a second social network resource that enhances a person's power. When asked to recommend someone who has a particular expertise, other network members more readily think of you than of people outside the network. A third resource from social networks is increased referent power. People tend to gain referent power through networking because members of the network identify with or at least have greater trust in each other. Referent power is also apparent by the fact that reciprocity increases among network members as they become more embedded in the network.[36]

Social networks are often viewed as free spirits, yet they can be orchestrated to some extent through organizational structures and other practices.[37] Whether or not you try to manage social networks, you need to be aware of them. Indeed, people gain power in organizations by knowing what the social networks around them look like.[38]

McGraw Hill connect

SELF-ASSESSMENT 9.1: Do you have a guanxi orientation?

Gaining Power through Social Networks

How do individuals (and teams and organizations) gain social capital from social networks? To answer this question, we need to consider the number, depth, variety, and centrality of connections that people have in their networks.

Strong Ties, Weak Ties, Many Ties The volume of information, opportunities, and other social capital that we receive from networks depends on strong ties, weak ties, and many ties. Strong ties are close-knit relationships, which are evident from how often we interact with specific people, how much we share resources with them, and whether we have multiple or single-purpose relationships with them (e.g., friend, coworker, sports partner). Strong ties are valuable because they offer resources more quickly and usually more plentifully than are available from weak ties (i.e., acquaintances). Strong ties also offer greater social support and greater cooperation for favors and assistance.[39]

Strong connections aren't necessarily the most valuable ties. Instead, having weak ties (i.e., being merely acquaintances) with people from diverse networks can be equally or more valuable than having only strong ties (i.e., having close friendships) with people in similar networks.[40] Why is this so? Strong ties—our close-knit circle of friends—tend to be similar to us and to each other. Consequently, they provide much of the same information and other resources that we already have or that other strong ties provide.[41] Weak ties, on the other hand, are acquaintances who are different from us and therefore more likely to offer unique opportunities, connections, and other resources not available from our strong ties. Weak ties exist when we serve as a "bridge" across several unrelated networks.

Having weak ties (acquaintances) with people from diverse networks can be more valuable than having strong ties (close friendships) with people in similar networks.
Dimitri Vervitsiotis/Getty Images

The value of weak ties is most apparent in job hunting and career development.[42] People with diverse networks tend to be more successful job seekers because they have a wider net to catch new job opportunities. In contrast, people who belong to similar overlapping networks tend to receive fewer leads, many of which they already knew about. Careers are increasingly expanding across many organizations and industries. Therefore, you need to establish connections with people from a diverse range of industries, professions, and other spheres of life.

Finally, our power and social capital increase with many ties—the number of people connected to you in a social network. The more people you know, the more network resources are available to you. Generally, as your social network grows, you have less time and energy to maintain strong ties. However, some people have an amazing capacity to support relatively active and frequent connections to many people. Emerging social media (Twitter, Facebook, LinkedIn, etc.) have further amplified this capacity to maintain numerous connections at a fairly strong level.[43]

Social Network Centrality Earlier in this chapter, we explained that centrality is an important contingency of power. This contingency also applies to social networks.[44] The more central a person (or team or organization) is located in the network, the more social capital and therefore more power he or she acquires. Centrality is your importance in that network.

Three factors determine your centrality in a social network. One factor is "betweenness," which literally refers to how much you are located between others in the network. In Exhibit 9.3, Person A has high betweenness centrality because he or she is a gatekeeper who controls the flow of information to and from many other people in the network. Person H has less betweenness, whereas Person F and several other network members in the diagram have no betweenness. The more betweenness you have, the more you control the distribution of information and other resources to people on either side of you.

A second factor in centrality is the number or percentage of connections you have to others in the network (called *degree centrality*). The network resources (information, favors, etc.) available to you increases with the number of people connected to you. The number of connections also increases centrality because you are more visible to other members of the network. Although being a member of a network gives you access to resources in that network, having a direct connection to more people within the network makes that resource sharing more fluid.

A third factor in centrality is the "closeness" of the relationship with others in the network. High closeness refers to strong ties. It is depicted by shorter, more direct, and efficient paths or connections with others in the network. For example, Person A

structural hole an area between two or more dense social network areas that lacks network ties

Exhibit 9.3 Centrality in Social Networks

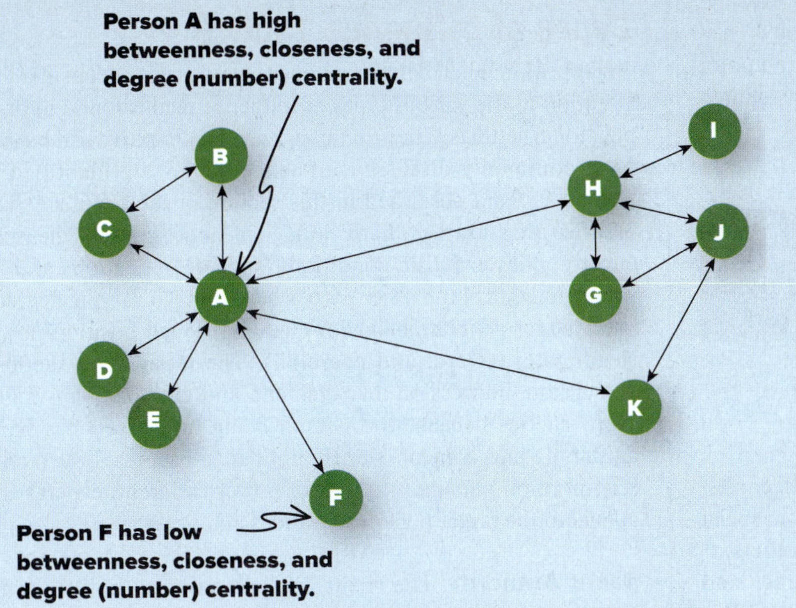

has fairly high closeness centrality because he or she has direct paths to most of the network. Also, many of these paths are short, which implies efficient and high quality communication links. Your centrality increases with your closeness to other network members because they are affected more quickly and significantly by you.

One last observation is that Exhibit 9.3 illustrates two clusters of people in the network. The gap between these two clusters is called a **structural hole**.[45] Notice that Person A provides the main bridge across this structural hole (connecting to H and K in the other cluster). This bridging role gives Person A additional power in the network. By bridging this gap, Person A becomes a broker–someone who connects two independent networks and controls information flow between them. Research shows that the more brokering relationships you have, the more likely you are to get early promotions and higher pay.

The Dark Side of Social Networks Social networks occur naturally in all organizations, yet they can create a formidable barrier to those who are not actively connected to them.[46] Women are often excluded from social networks in male-dominated jobs and industries because people tend to network with others with similar characteristics and backgrounds. These gendered networks can be a liability for women because they limit referrals,

OB THEORY TO PRACTICE

Introverts Can Be Effective Networkers, Too[47]

Networking requires communication and the confidence to introduce yourself to strangers. These practices come more naturally to extraverts, but networking experts say that introverts also can be good at networking. Here's how:

Networking is about listening, not just talking. Networking is two-way communication, which means that you need to listen to and develop empathy with others in your network. Introverts have a stronger preference than extroverts to listen, so it is an advantage they can use. Good listeners more quickly identify the needs of people they meet and therefore are more likely to convey information of value to others in the network.

Networking is personal, not mass production. People make the mistake of assuming that they need to "work the room" by introducing themselves to as many people as possible. But networking is about personal relationships, so it's fine to meet only a handful of people at a particular event. That deeper interaction could produce clearer understanding of the potential relationship and the means to strengthen that relationship.

Network rejection is about misalignment, not personal fault. Some people you meet don't want to continue the conversation. Introverts take these networking failures more personally than do extroverts, who just move on to the next social opportunity. While we always need to reflect and learn from life's events, introverts in particular need to recognize that social interaction rejections are usually misalignments of interests, not evidence of a personal fault.

Networking is a skill, not a personality trait. Introversion is a preference and behavioral tendency, not an innate lack of ability to interact with other people. Some very notable public speakers, politicians, and business leaders are very good at the intense social interaction because they have developed appropriate skills and knowledge. While introverts might not enjoy social interaction as much as do extraverts, they can learn how to effectively meet strangers and form initial social bonds that lead to network relationships.

Networking is (partly) online, not just face-to-face. The Internet has created the best of both worlds for introverts. They can engage in effective networking without the stress or awkwardness of social interaction. At the same time, introverts can't always hide behind an Internet connection. Networking ultimately thrives on plenty of face-to-face interaction, not just emails, text messaging, and social media links. "People remember faces and conversations more than the written word," advises the CEO of one careers company.

Networking can be structured, to some extent. Some experts suggest that networking isn't completely impromptu conversation. This is good news for introverts because they prefer structured social interaction. Before meeting people, introverts can think about specific questions to ask, practice ways to deliver those questions casually (not as a wooden interviewer), and practice answers to common questions that others will ask. And when someone does ask an unexpected question, a short answer can be fine when followed by asking that question or another one back to the other person.

knowledge, and other forms of career-enhancing resources that networks provide. Many organizations today try to leverage the power of social networks by supporting several surface-level and deep-level diversity employee groups. Even so, "old boys' networks," as well as mono-ethnic networks, are difficult to uproot in organizations because of the natural human tendency to interact more with people who have similar characteristics.

LO9-4 Describe eight types of influence tactics, three consequences of influencing others, and three contingencies to consider when choosing an influence tactic.

INFLUENCING OTHERS

So far, this chapter has focused on the sources, contingencies, and consequences of power as well as power derived from social networks. But power is only the *capacity* to influence others. It represents the potential to change someone's attitudes and behavior. **Influence**, on the other hand, is power in motion. It applies one or more sources and contingencies of power in an attempt to alter another person's beliefs, feelings, and behavior.[48] Consequently, the remainder of this chapter looks at how people use power to influence others.

Influence tactics are woven throughout the social fabric of all organizations. Influence is an essential process through which people coordinate their effort and act in concert to achieve organizational objectives. It is central to the definition of leadership. Influence operates down, across, and up the corporate hierarchy. Executives ensure that subordinates complete required tasks. Employees influence coworkers to help them with their job assignments.

Types of Influence Tactics

Organizational behavior researchers have devoted considerable attention to the various types of influence tactics found in organizational settings. They do not agree on a definitive list, but the most commonly discussed influence tactics are identified in Exhibit 9.4 and described in this section of the chapter.[49] The first five are known as "hard" influence tactics because the influencer applies extrinsic conditions, such as obligations and rewards, to control the other party's behavior. To varying degrees, hard tactics generate behavior change through position power (legitimate, reward, and coercion). The latter three tactics—persuasion, impression management, and exchange—are called "soft" tactics because the person being influenced has more autonomy and control over the influence process. Soft tactics rely more on personal sources of power (referent, expert) and appeal to the target person's attitudes and needs.[50]

Silent Authority The silent application of authority occurs when someone complies with a request because of the requester's legitimate power as well as the role expectations of the person receiving the request.[51] Essentially, this is deference to authority, which we discussed earlier in this chapter. It occurs when you comply with your boss's request to complete a particular task. If the task is within your job scope and your boss has the right to make this request, then this influence strategy operates without negotiation, threats, persuasion, or other tactics. Experts suggest that every organization requires this influence strategy to operate. Silent authority is the most common form of influence in high power distance cultures.[52]

> **Nothing more enhances authority than silence.**[53]
>
> —Charles de Gaulle, former French president and military leader

Exhibit 9.4 Types of Influence Tactics in Organizations

Influence Tactic	Description
Silent authority	Influencing behavior through legitimate power without explicitly referring to that power base.
Assertiveness	Actively applying legitimate and coercive power by applying pressure or threats.
Information control	Explicitly manipulating someone else's access to information for the purpose of changing his or her attitudes and/or behavior.
Coalition formation	Forming a group that attempts to influence others by pooling the resources and power of its members.
Upward appeal	Relying symbolically or in reality on people with higher authority or expertise to support our position.
Persuasion	Using logical arguments, factual evidence, and emotional appeals to convince people of the value of a request.
Impression management	Actively shaping, through self-presentation and other means, the perceptions and attitudes that others have of us. Includes ingratiation, which refers to the influencer's attempt to be more liked by the targeted person or group.
Exchange	Promising benefits or resources in exchange for the target person's compliance.

Dysfunctional Influence through Assertiveness[54]

29% of 3,420 American employees surveyed say they have been bullied at work.

23% of 2,000 UK-based employees say they have been bullied at work.

31% of 266,535 individual employee–employer disputes submitted in the most recent year to the Japanese government were about bullying and other abusive behavior.

20% of 2,951 employees surveyed across 733 fire departments in Japan say they have experienced power harassment—a form of workplace bullying (28% of female and 17.5% of male fire department staff).

13% of 147,237 Australian Public Service (APS) employees believe they have been subjected to bullying or harassment at work within the previous 12 months.

SteveLuker/Getty Images

influence any behavior that attempts to alter someone's attitudes or behavior

coalition a group that attempts to influence people outside the group by pooling the resources and power of its members

upward appeal a type of influence in which someone with higher authority or expertise is relied on in reality or symbolically to support the influencer's position

Assertiveness Assertiveness might be called "vocal authority" because it more explicitly applies legitimate and coercive power to influence others. This includes persistently reminding the target of his or her obligations, frequently checking the target's work, confronting the target, and using threats of sanctions to force compliance. Workplace bullying is an extreme form of assertiveness because it involves explicit threats of punishment.

Information Control Earlier in this chapter we explained that people gain power when they have legitimate power or social network centrality to control how much and what type of information others receive. This power translates into influence when the power holder's selective distribution of information reframes how others perceive the situation and consequently alters their attitudes and/or behavior. For example, research has found that CEOs influence their board of directors by selectively feeding and withholding information.[55]

Coalition Formation When someone acting alone lacks sufficient power to influence others, he or she might be able to do so by forming a **coalition** of people who support the proposed change.[56] A coalition is influential in three ways. First, it pools the power and resources of many people, so the coalition potentially has more influence than its members have if they operated alone. Second, the coalition's mere existence can influence others by symbolizing the legitimacy of the issue. In other words, a coalition creates a sense that the issue deserves attention because it has broad support. Third, a coalition increases the confidence and motivation of its members through social identity theory (see Chapter 3). This motivation occurs because a coalition consists of like-minded people, so its members identify with the group and feel more confident in supporting the coalition's mandate.[57]

Upward Appeal **Upward appeal** is a type of influence whereby someone with higher authority or expertise is relied on in reality or symbolically to support the influencer's position. It occurs when an employee says, "The boss likely agrees with me on this matter; let's find out!" Upward appeal also occurs when relying on the authority of the firm's policies or values. By reminding others that your request is consistent with the organization's overarching goals, you are implying support from senior

> A coalition pools the power and resources of many people, demonstrates broad support for the issue, and increases the confidence and motivation of coalition members.

persuasion the use of facts, logical arguments, and emotional appeals to change another person's beliefs and attitudes, usually for the purpose of changing the person's behavior

inoculation effect a persuasive communication strategy of warning listeners that others will try to influence them in the future and that they should be wary of the opponent's arguments

executives without formally involving them.

Persuasion The influence tactics described so far are called "hard" influence tactics because the influencer attempts to control the other party's behavior through position power. The three remaining categories—persuasion, impression management, and exchange—are "soft" influence strategies because the person being influenced has more autonomy and control over the influence process. The first of these, **persuasion**, involves the use of facts, logical arguments, and emotional appeals to change another person's beliefs and attitudes, usually for the purpose of changing his or her behavior. This is the most widely used and accepted influence strategy in organizations. It is a quality of effective leaders and, in many societies, a noble skill.

The effectiveness of persuasion as an influence tactic depends on characteristics of the persuader, message content, communication channel, and the audience being persuaded (see Exhibit 9.5).[58] People are more persuasive when they are perceived to have expertise and credibility. Persuaders have more credibility when they do not seem to profit from the persuasion attempt, they acknowledge limitations with their position, and they note minor positive features of the alternative choices.

Several characteristics of message content increase your ability to persuade others, particularly when the issue is important to the audience.[59] The speaker's message is more persuasive when it acknowledges several points of view. This increases the speaker's credibility and avoids having the audience feel boxed in by the persuasion attempt. The message should also be limited to a few strong arguments, which are repeated a few times, but not too frequently. The message should use emotional appeals (such as graphically showing the unfortunate consequences of a bad decision), but only in combination with logical arguments and specific recommendations to overcome the threat. Finally, message content is more persuasive when the audience is warned about opposing arguments. This **inoculation effect** causes listeners to

Persuasion tends to work best through communication channels with high social presence and media-richness, such as in face-to-face conversations.
Monkey Business Images/Shutterstock

Exhibit 9.5 Elements of Persuasion

Persuasion Element	Characteristics of Effective Persuasion
Persuader characteristics	• Expertise • Credibility • No apparent profit motive • Appears somewhat neutral (acknowledges strengths of alternative choices)
Message content	• Multiple viewpoints (not exclusively supporting the preferred option) • Limited to a few strong arguments (not many arguments) • Repeats arguments, but not excessively • Uses emotional appeals in combination with logical arguments • Offers specific solutions to overcome the stated problems • Inoculation effect—audience warned of counterarguments that opponents will present
Communication channel	• Channels with high media-richness and social presence are usually more persuasive
Audience characteristics	Persuasion is LESS effective when the audience • Has higher self-esteem • Has higher intelligence • Has a self-concept tied to an opposing position

generate counterarguments to the anticipated persuasion attempts, which makes the opponent's subsequent persuasion attempts less effective.[60]

Two other considerations when persuading people are the communication channel and characteristics of the audience. Generally, persuasion works best through communication channels with high social presence and media-richness, such as in face-to-face conversations (see Chapter 8). The human presence of face-to-face communication increases the persuader's credibility, and the richness of this channel provides faster feedback that the influence strategy is working. With respect to audience characteristics, it is more difficult to persuade people who have high self-esteem and intelligence, as well as a self-concept that is strongly tied to the opposing viewpoint.[61]

Impression Management The softest of the soft influence tactics is **impression management**—actively shaping the perceptions and attitudes that others have of us.[62] Impression management mostly occurs through self-presentation. Employees routinely engage in pleasant impression management behaviors to satisfy social norms, such as the way they dress and how they behave toward colleagues and customers. People sometimes craft their public image to depict their importance and expertise, which affects their influence under some circumstances. For this reason, impression management plays a significant role in an individual's personal brand—forming and displaying an accurate impression of that person's own distinctive, competitive advantage.[63]

impression management actively shaping through self-presentation and other means the perceptions and attitudes that others have of us

One subcategory of impression management is *ingratiation*, which is any attempt to increase liking by, or perceived similarity to, some targeted person.[64] Ingratiation includes flattering your boss, demonstrating similar views as your boss (e.g., agreeing with the boss's suggestions), or asking your boss for advice. Ingratiation is one of the more effective influence tactics at boosting a person's career success. However, people who engage in high levels of ingratiation are less (not more) influential and less likely to get promoted because too much ingratiation is viewed as insincere and self-serving.[65]

OB THEORY TO PRACTICE

Impression Management in Job Interviews[66]

Interviewer Question	Impression Management Principle	Do Say . . .	Don't Say . . .
Why are you interested in this job?	Demonstrate that you researched the job and firm, are motivated, and see alignment with your career.	"This job gives me greater opportunity to apply my current skills (name some) and develop others. This firm also has a great reputation for rewarding successful teams."	"I wondered about that, too, but hopefully I'll be able to get some sort of new skills I can use."
Describe a situation in which you had to deal with a professional disagreement or conflict.	Demonstrate that you are a good team player who is diplomatic, honest, and forthright at conflict handling and problem solving.	"My coworker and I once disagreed on (describe situation). We discussed our different methods and came up with a better way that combined the best of each of our methods."	"I avoid disagreements as much as possible. Better to steer clear of them and hope they go away."
Where do you see yourself in five years' time?	Demonstrate that you are goal-oriented and think about your career (not just current work), how it will benefit the company, and how the job opening is part of that future.	"I want to help the company's bottom line by becoming an expert in (name one of the job's competencies), as well as mentor junior staff as I move into leadership roles."	"I want to be a millionaire before I turn 30 by trading stock market derivatives when I'm not doing this job."
Why do you want to leave your current job?	Demonstrate sensible and justifiable factors that would not be a concern in the new job. Avoid dwelling on personalities and bad experiences.	"I very much enjoy my current job and coworkers, but the company was just acquired by a larger firm and there is a good chance that the entire department will be shut down."	"Everybody hates working at that company. Top management is clueless. Also, I don't like my boss. She always asks me to redo my work because of trivial errors in my calculations."
How many times do a clock's hands overlap in a day?	Demonstrate your process of thinking logically through unexpected problems and your can-do attitude toward solving problems.	"Let's see, there are 24 hours in a day and every time on the clock happens twice, so . . ."	"Gosh, I have no idea. I'm not that good at math."

connect

SELF-ASSESSMENT 9.2: What Is Your Approach to Influencing Coworkers?

Exchange Exchange activities involve the promise of benefits or resources in exchange for the target person's compliance with your request. Negotiation is an integral part of exchange influence activities. For instance, you might negotiate with your boss for a day off in return for working a less desirable shift at a future date. Exchange also includes applying the norm of reciprocity that we described earlier, such as reminding the target of past benefits or favors, with the expectation that the target will now make up for that debt. The norm of reciprocity also influences others in social networks. Active networkers build up "exchange credits" by helping colleagues in the short term for reciprocal benefits in the long term.

Consequences and Contingencies of Influence Tactics

Faced with a variety of influence strategies, you are probably asking: Which ones are best? To answer this question, we first need to describe the three ways that people respond to influence: resistance, compliance, or commitment (see Exhibit 9.6).[67] *Resistance* occurs when people or work units oppose the behavior desired by the influencer. At the extreme, they refuse to engage in the behavior. However, there are degrees of resistance, such as when people do what the power holder has requested yet maintain their opposition by performing the tasks poorly or continuing to complain about the imposed work.

Compliance occurs when people are extrinsically motivated to implement the influencer's request (see Chapter 5). They perform the requested task for purely instrumental reasons. Compliance usually involves engaging in the behavior with no more effort than is required. Furthermore, compliance usually stops—employees no longer perform the requested behavior—when the extrinsic source of motivation is removed. The strongest outcome of influence is *commitment*. This occurs when people identify with the influencer's request and are highly motivated to implement it even when extrinsic sources of motivation are not present.

People usually react more favorably to soft tactics than to hard tactics. Soft influence tactics rely on personal sources of power (expert and referent power), which tend to build commitment to the influencer's request. In contrast, hard tactics rely on position power (legitimate, reward, and coercion), so they tend to produce compliance or, worse, resistance. Hard tactics also tend to undermine trust, which can hurt future relationships.

Exhibit 9.6 Consequences of Hard and Soft Influence Tactics

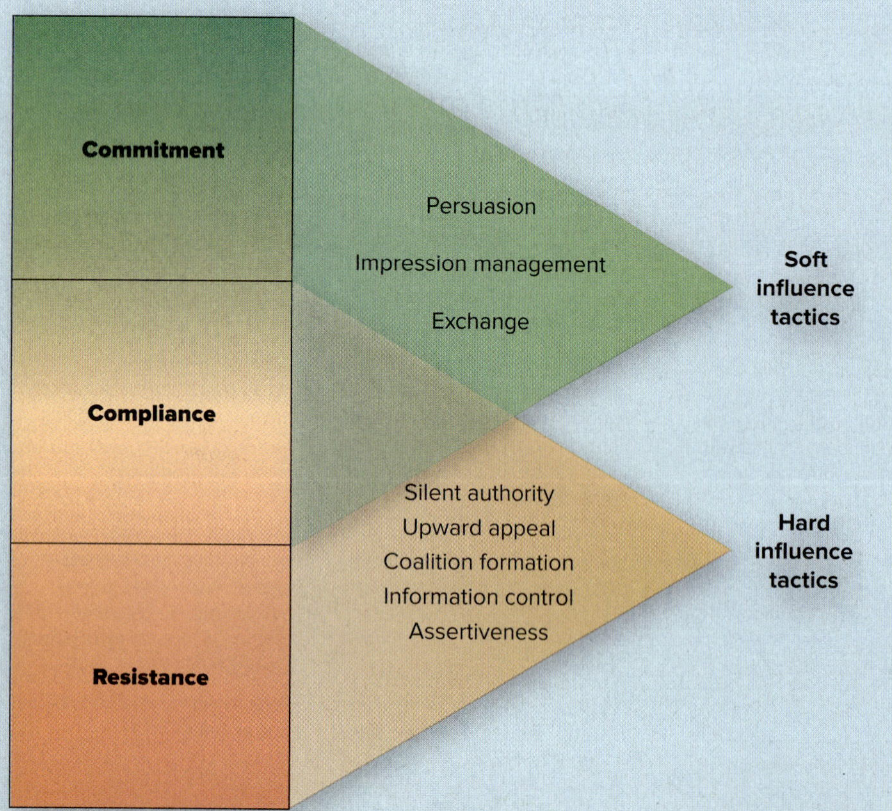

The most appropriate influence strategy depends on a few contingencies.[68] One obvious factor is the influencer's strongest sources of power. Those with expertise tend to have more influence using persuasion, whereas those with a strong legitimate power base may be more successful applying silent authority. A second contingency is whether the person being influenced is higher, lower, or at the same level in the organization. As an example, employees may face adverse career consequences by being too assertive with their boss. Meanwhile, supervisors who engage in ingratiation and some other forms of impression management tend to lose the respect of their staff.

Finally, the most appropriate influence tactic depends on personal, organizational, and cultural values.[69] People with a strong power orientation might feel more comfortable using assertiveness, whereas those who value conformity might feel more comfortable with upward appeals. At an organizational level, firms with a competitive culture might encourage more use of information control and coalition formation, whereas companies with a more collegial culture would likely encourage more influence through persuasion. The preferred influence tactics also vary across societal cultures. Research indicates that ingratiation is much more common among managers in the United States than in Hong Kong. One explanation is that this tactic is incompatible with the more distant roles that managers and employees expect in high power distance cultures.

LO9-5 Identify the organizational conditions and personal characteristics associated with organizational politics, as well as ways to minimize organizational politics.

ORGANIZATIONAL POLITICS

Organizational politics goes hand-in-hand with the topics of organizational power and influence. Unfortunately, the meaning of organizational politics is quite muddled. The most widely held view among scholars, which this book adopts, is that **organizational politics** is the use of influence tactics for personal gain at the perceived expense of others and the organization.[70] This definition recognizes that all political behaviors apply one or more influence tactics. However, influence activities are organizational politics only when the perpetrator is apparently motivated by self-interest and the action is likely to have an adverse effect on others and the organization. Organizational politics is necessarily a perceptual interpretation of events because it is very difficult to know the political actor's motives or awareness of how their actions affect others.

This definition is consistent with the public view that organizational politics is self-serving behavior. Although many employees admit that they have engaged in politics to benefit their career advancement, they do not claim it is good for the organization. On the contrary, employees consistently identify "office politics" as one of the top reasons for their work-related stress, suboptimal performance, and motivation to leave the company.[72]

Some popular press writers (as well as a few scholars) claim that organizational politics can be beneficial.[73] These "positive politics" sources suggest that "politics is an essential skill in managers who wish to get things done" and that it is "an indispensable component of organizational life." The problem with the positive politics view is that it labels almost all influence activities as political tactics. For example, they define organizational politics as "power in action, using a range of techniques and tactics." Yet, as we stated earlier in the chapter, *influence* is defined as power in action. Organizational politics and influence are not the same concept.

Meanwhile, numerous studies have documented the adverse consequences of organizational politics.[74] Employees who observe or experience organizational politics from others have lower job satisfaction, organizational commitment, organizational citizenship, and task performance, as well as higher levels of work-related stress and motivation to leave the organization. And because political tactics serve individuals rather than organizations, they potentially divert resources away from the organization's effective functioning and may threaten its survival.

organizational politics
the use of influence tactics for personal gain at the perceived expense of others and the organization

Office Politics by the Numbers[75]

65% of 3,000 employees say they would be more productive working from home due to minimal office politics compared to an office.

63% of 2,843 professionals identify work politics/colleagues as one of their top five drivers of stress at work.

58% of 763 American employees say they have left jobs, or are considering leaving, because of office politics.

39% of 1,700 18–34 year-old employees in India identify office politics as a major barrier to working effectively (second highest barrier, following excessive workload).

25% of 1,000 professional adults identify workplace politics as one of their major career struggles (fourth highest on the list of 10 struggles).

SchulteProductions/Getty Images

> Keep your friends close and your enemies closer.[71]
>
> —Attributed to Sun-Tzu, Chinese general, circa 500 B.C.

dark triad a cluster of three socially undesirable (dark) personality traits: Machiavellianism, narcissism, and psychopathy

Individual Differences in Organizational Politics

Some people are more likely than others to engage in organizational politics.[76] Employees with a strong need for personalized power seek power for its own sake and try to acquire more power. This contrasts with people with a strong need for socialized power; they seek power as an instrument to accomplish organizationally beneficial objectives.

Individuals with **dark triad** personality characteristics are also more likely to engage in organizational politics (see Chapter 2).[77] These people routinely engage in deceit and malevolently undermine others to maximize their own gains. They believe that using lies, manipulation, exploitation, and other undesirable influence tactics are acceptable ways to achieve their personal goals (*Machiavellianism*). They arrogantly exploit coworkers for personal aggrandizement and take pleasure in others' misfortune (*narcissism*). They are also selfish self-promoters who manipulate others and engage in antisocial, impulsive, and often fraudulent thrill-seeking behavior without feelings of remorse (*psychopathy*).

Mc Graw Hill connect

SELF-ASSESSMENT 9.3: How Politically Charged Is Your School?

Minimizing Organizational Politics

Several conditions encourage organizational politics, so countervailing strategies can keep political activities to a minimum.[78] First, when budgets or other scarce resources are slashed, people rely on political tactics to safeguard their resources and maintain the status quo. Understandably, it is difficult to add resources, but sometimes this action is less costly than the consequences of organizational politics.

Second, people rely more on political tactics to get what they want when organizational resource allocation decisions have ambiguous or missing rules. Therefore, companies need to establish clear guidelines for allocation of scarce resources. Third, organizational change tends to bring out more organizational politics, mainly because change creates ambiguity and threatens the employee's power and other valued resources. Consequently, leaders need to apply the organizational change strategies that we describe in Chapter 14, particularly through communication, learning, and involvement.

Fourth, political behavior is more common in work units and organizations where it is tolerated and reinforced. Some companies seem to nurture self-serving behavior through reward systems and the role modeling of organizational leaders. To minimize political norms, the organization needs to diagnose and alter systems and role modeling that support self-serving behavior. One of the most important strategies is for leaders to become role models of organizational citizenship rather than symbols of dark triad people who are rewarded for their manipulative and exploitive behavior.

Study Checklist

Connect® is available for *M Organizational Behavior*. Additional resources include:

✓ Exercises:

- **Case Analysis:** Apply concepts within the context of a real-world situation.
- **Click and Drag:** Helps make the connection between theory and application through matching, ranking, or grouping activities.
- **Video Case:** See management in action through interactive videos.
- **Self-Assessment:** Designed to promote student self-awareness and reflection, these research-based surveys contain detailed feedback for students.
- **Application-Based Activities:** These highly interactive, application- and analysis-based exercises allow students to take on specific roles to complete management-related tasks within a real-world context.

✓ **SmartBook 2.0™**—Smartbook 2.0 is an adaptive learning solution that provides personalized learning to individual student needs, continually adapts to pinpoint knowledge gaps and focuses learning on concepts requiring additional study. It fosters more productive learning, takes the guesswork out of what to study, and helps students better prepare for class.

Notes

1. J.J. Gabarro and J.P. Kotter, "Managing Your Boss," *Harvard Business Review* 58, no. 1 (1980): 92–100; B. Tulgan, *It's Okay to Manage Your Boss* (San Francisco: Jossey-Bass, 2010); T. Kucera, "How to Manage Your Manager," *LinkedIn Pulse*, March 5, 2017.
2. J.R. French and B. Raven, "The Bases of Social Power," in *Studies in Social Power*, ed. D. Cartwright (Ann Arbor: University of Michigan Press, 1959), 150–67; A.D. Galinsky et al., "Power and Perspectives Not Taken," *Psychological Science* 17, no. 12 (2006): 1068–74. Also see H. Mintzberg, *Power in and around Organizations* (Englewood Cliffs, NJ: Prentice Hall, 1983), Chap. 1; J. Pfeffer, *Managing with Power: Politics and Influence in Organizations* (Boston: Harvard Business School Press, 1992), 17, 30; A. Guinote and T.K. Vescio, "Introduction: Power in Social Psychology," in *The Social Psychology of Power*, ed. A. Guinote and T.K. Vescio (New York: Guilford Press, 2010), 1–18.
3. R.A. Dahl, "The Concept of Power," *Behavioral Science* 2 (1957): 201–18; R.M. Emerson, "Power-Dependence Relations," *American Sociological Review* 27 (1962): 31–41; A.M. Pettigrew, *The Politics of Organizational Decision-Making* (London: Tavistock, 1973).
4. J. Pfeffer and G.R. Salancik, *The External Control of Organizations* (New York: Harper & Row, 1978), 52–54; K. Cowan, A.K. Paswan, and E. Van Steenburg, "When Inter-Firm Relationship Benefits Mitigate Power Asymmetry," *Industrial Marketing Management* 48 (2015): 140–48.
5. J.R. French and B. Raven, "The Bases of Social Power," in *Studies in Social Power*, ed. D. Cartwright (Ann Arbor: University of Michigan Press, 1959), 150–67; P.M. Podsakoff and C. Schreisheim, "Field Studies of French and Raven's Bases of Power: Critique, Analysis, and Suggestions for Future Research," *Psychological Bulletin* 97 (1985): 387–411; P.P. Carson and K.D. Carson, "Social Power Bases: A Meta-Analytic Examination of Interrelationships and Outcomes," *Journal of Applied Social Psychology* 23 (1993): 1150–69. Most alternative models of power bases parallel French and Raven's list. See P. Heinemann, *Power Bases and Informational Influence Strategies: A Behavioral Study on the Use of Management Accounting Information* (Wiesbaden, Germany: Deutscher Universitäts-Verlag, 2008). Raven subsequently proposed information power as a sixth source of power. We present information power as forms of legitimate and expert power rather than as a distinct sixth power base.
6. Legitimate power and expert power are also consistently the strongest sources of power that coaches have over players in sports. See P. Rylander, "Coaches' Bases of Power: Developing Some Initial Knowledge of Athletes' Compliance with Coaches in Team Sports," *Journal of Applied Sport Psychology* 27, no. 1 (2015): 110–21.
7. C. Barnard, *The Function of the Executive* (Cambridge, MA: Harvard University Press, 1938), 167–70; B.J. Tepper, "What Do Managers Do When Subordinates Just Say, 'No'? An Analysis of Incidents Involving Refusal to Perform Downward Requests," in *Power and Influence in Organizations*, ed. L. L. Neider and C.A. Schreisheim (Charlotte, NC: IAP/Information Age Publishing, 2006), 1–20.
8. A.I. Shahin and P.L. Wright, "Leadership in the Context of Culture: An Egyptian Perspective," *Leadership & Organization Development Journal* 25, no. 5/6 (2004): 499–511; Y.J. Huo et al., "Leadership and the Management of Conflicts in Diverse Groups: Why Acknowledging versus Neglecting Subgroup Identity Matters," *European Journal of Social Psychology* 35, no. 2 (2005): 237–54.
9. B.H. Raven, "Kurt Lewin Address: Influence, Power, Religion, and the Mechanisms of Social Control," *Journal of Social Issues* 55 (1999): 161–86.
10. A.W. Gouldner, "The Norm of Reciprocity: A Preliminary Statement," *American Sociological Review* 25 (1960): 161–78.
11. G. Yukl and C.M. Falbe, "Importance of Different Power Sources in Downward and Lateral Relations," *Journal of Applied Psychology* 76 (1991): 416–23; B.H. Raven, "Kurt Lewin Address: Influence, Power, Religion, and the Mechanisms of Social Control," *Journal of Social Issues* 55 (1999): 161–86.
12. A.M. Pettigrew, "Information Control as a Power Resource," *Sociology* 6, no. 2 (1972): 187–204; P.L. Dawes, D.Y. Lee, and G.R. Dowling, "Information Control and Influence in Emergent Buying Centers," *Journal of Marketing* 62, no. 3 (1998): 55–68; J. Webster et al., "Beyond Knowledge Sharing: Withholding Knowledge at Work," *Research in Personnel and Human Resources Management* 27 (2008): 1–37; C.E. Connelly et al., "Knowledge Hiding in Organizations," *Journal of Organizational Behavior* 33, no. 1 (2012): 64–88.
13. S.L. Robinson, J. O'Reilly, and W. Wang, "Invisible at Work: An Integrated Model of Workplace Ostracism," *Journal of Management* 39 (2013): 203–31; S. Gallani, "Incentives Don't Help People Change, but Peer Pressure Does," *Harvard Business Review*, March 23, 2017.
14. J.M. Peiro and J.L. Melia, "Formal and Informal Interpersonal Power in Organisations: Testing a Bifactorial Model of Power in Role-Sets," *Applied Psychology* 52, no. 1 (2003): 14–35.
15. C.R. Hinings et al., "Structural Conditions of Intraorganizational Power," *Administrative Science Quarterly* 19 (1974): 22–44. Also see C.S. Saunders, "The Strategic Contingency Theory of Power: Multiple Perspectives," *Journal of Management Studies* 27 (1990): 1–21.
16. W.H. Friedland, "For a Sociological Concept of Charisma," *Social Forces* 43, no. 1 (1964): 18–26; K. Miyahara, "Charisma: From Weber to Contemporary Sociology," *Sociological Inquiry* 53, no. 4 (1983): 368–88; J.D. Kudisch and M.L. Poteet, "Expert Power, Referent Power, and Charisma: Toward the Resolution of a Theoretical Debate," *Journal of Business & Psychology* 10 (1995): 177- 95; K.O. Tskhay, R. Zhu, and N.O. Rule, "Perceptions of Charisma from Thin Slices of Behavior Predict Leadership Prototypicality Judgments," *Leadership Quarterly*, 28 (2017): 555–62. One recent review analyzes various definitions and concludes that charisma "is values-based, symbolic, and emotion-laden leader signaling." Although a useful development, even this definition may miss the mark somewhat because all interactions generate emotions, and people can be charismatic by their mere presence (signaling) without conversation and therefore perhaps without values-based interaction. See J. Antonakis et al., "Charisma: An Ill-Defined and Ill-Measured Gift," *Annual Review of Organizational Psychology and Organizational Behavior* 3 (2016): 293–319.
17. R.B. Cialdini and N.J. Goldstein, "Social Influence: Compliance and Conformity," *Annual Review of Psychology* 55 (2004): 591–621.
18. A. Einstein, *The Ultimate Quotable Einstein*, ed. A. Calaprice (Princeton, NJ: Princeton University Press, 2011), 161. Originally in a letter to Swiss teacher Jost Winteler on July 8, 1901.
19. S.D. Farley, D.H. Carson, and T.J. Pope, "'I Would Never Fall for That': The Use of an Illegitimate Authority to Teach Social Psychological Principles," *Teaching of Psychology* 46, no. 2 (2019): 146–52.

20. C. Perkel, "It's Not CSI," *Canadian Press*, November 10, 2007; "Dr. Charles Smith: The Man behind the Public Inquiry," *CBC News* (Toronto), August 10, 2010; J. Chipman, *Death in the Family* (Toronto: Doubleday Canada, 2017). The broader problem of judicial deference to medical experts is discussed in C. Foster, "The Dangers of Deferring to Doctors | Practical Ethics," *Oxford University-Practical Ethics* (blog), July 30, 2018, http://blog.practicalethics.ox.ac.uk/2018/07/the-dangers-of-deferring-to-doctors/.

21. D.J. Hickson et al., "A Strategic Contingencies' Theory of Intraorganizational Power," *Administrative Science Quarterly* 16 (1971): 216–27; C.R. Hinings et al., "Structural Conditions of Intraorganizational Power," *Administrative Science Quarterly* 19 (1974): 22–44; R.M. Kanter, "Power Failure in Management Circuits," *Harvard Business Review* (1979): 65–75.

22. A. Bryant, "The Right Job? It's Much Like the Right Spouse," *The New York Times*, May 22, 2011, 2.

23. J. Pfeffer, *Power: Why Some People Have It–and Others Don't* (New York: Harper Collins, 2010), 26–27; C. Sparrer, "Establish Your Personal Brand for Workplace Success," *Forbes*, January 7, 2019; L. Blanco, "How to Become Visible through Personal Branding in the Social Age," *Black Enterprise*, March 7, 2019.

24. D.J. Hickson et al., "A Strategic Contingencies' Theory of Intraorganizational Power," *Administrative Science Quarterly* 16 (1971): 219–21; J.D. Hackman, "Power and Centrality in the Allocation of Resources in Colleges and Universities," *Administrative Science Quarterly* 30 (1985): 61–77; D.J. Brass and M.E. Burkhardt, "Potential Power and Power Use: An Investigation of Structure and Behavior," *Academy of Management Journal* 36 (1993): 441–70.

25. A. Caza, "Typology of the Eight Domains of Discretion in Organizations," *Journal of Management Studies* 49, no. 1 (2012): 144–77.

26. B.E. Ashforth, "The Experience of Powerlessness in Organizations," *Organizational Behavior and Human Decision Processes* 43 (1989): 207–42; D.B. Wangrow, D.J. Schepker, and V.L. Barker, "Managerial Discretion: An Empirical Review and Focus on Future Research Directions," *Journal of Management* 41, no. 1 (2015): 99–135.

27. J. Lammers, J.I. Stoker, and D.A. Stapel, "Differentiating Social and Personal Power: Opposite Effects on Stereotyping, but Parallel Effects on Behavioral Approach Tendencies," *Psychological Science* 20, no. 12 (2009): 1543–49.

28. J. Lammers et al., "Power and Morality," *Current Opinion in Psychology* 6 (2015): 15–19.

29. A.D. Galinsky et al., "Acceleration with Steering: The Synergistic Benefits of Combining Power and Perspective-Taking," *Social Psychological and Personality Science* 5, no. 6 (2014): 627–35.

30. S. Wasserman and K. Faust, *Social Network Analysis: Methods and Applications*, Structural Analysis in the Social Sciences (Cambridge, UK: Cambridge University Press, 1994), Chap. 1; D.J. Brass et al., "Taking Stock of Networks and Organizations: A Multilevel Perspective," *Academy of Management Journal* 47, no. 6 (2004): 795–817.

31. M. Grossetti, "Where Do Social Relations Come From? A Study of Personal Networks in the Toulouse Area of France," *Social Networks* 27, no. 4 (2005): 289–300.

32. R.J. Taormina and J.H. Gao, "A Research Model for Guanxi Behavior: Antecedents, Measures, and Outcomes of Chinese Social Networking," *Social Science Research* 39, no. 6 (2010): 1195–212; J. Barbalet, "Guanxi, Tie Strength, and Network Attributes," *American Behavioral Scientist* 59, no. 8 (2015): 1038–50; X.-A. Zhang, N. Li, and T.B. Harris, "Putting Non-Work Ties to Work: The Case of Guanxi in Supervisor–Subordinate Relationships," *Leadership Quarterly* 26, no. 1 (2015): 37–54. For problems with guanxi, see W.R. Vanhonacker, "When Good Guanxi Turns Bad," *Harvard Business Review* 82, no. 4 (2004): 18–19; F. Yang, "Guanxi Human Resource Management Practices as a Double-Edged Sword: The Moderating Role of Political Skill," *Asia Pacific Journal of Human Resources* 52, no. 4 (2014): 496–510.

33. A. Portes, "Social Capital: Its Origins and Applications in Modern Society," *Annual Review of Sociology* 24 (1998): 1–24; P. S. Adler and S. W. Kwon, "Social Capital: Prospects for a New Concept," *Academy of Management Review* 27, no. 1 (2002): 17–40; R. Lee, "Social Capital and Business and Management: Setting a Research Agenda," *International Journal of Management Reviews* 11, no. 3 (2009): 247–73.

34. R. Chisholm, *Developing Network Organizations: Learning from Practice and Theory* (Reading, MA: Addison-Wesley Longman, 1998); W.S. Chow and L.S. Chan, "Social Network, Social Trust and Shared Goals in Organizational Knowledge Sharing," *Information & Management* 45, no. 7 (2008): 458–65.

35. R.S. Burt, *Structural Holes: The Social Structure of Competition* (Cambridge, MA: Harvard University Press, 1992).

36. M.T. Rivera, S.B. Soderstrom, and B. Uzzi, "Dynamics of Dyads in Social Networks: Assortative, Relational, and Proximity Mechanisms," *Annual Review of Sociology* 36 (2010): 91–115.

37. R. Cross and R.J. Thomas, *Driving Results through Social Networks: How Top Organizations Leverage Networks for Performance and Growth* (San Francisco: Jossey-Bass, 2009); R. McDermott and D. Archibald, "Harnessing Your Staff's Informal Networks," *Harvard Business Review* 88, no. 3 (2010): 82–89.

38. M. Kilduff and D. Krackhardt, *Interpersonal Networks in Organizations: Cognition, Personality, Dynamics, and Culture* (New York: Cambridge University Press, 2008).

39. D.J. Brass et al., "Taking Stock of Networks and Organizations: A Multilevel Perspective," *Academy of Management Journal* 47, no. 6 (2004): 795–817; D. Melamed and B. Simpson, "Strong Ties Promote the Evolution of Cooperation in Dynamic Networks," *Social Networks* 45 (2016): 32–44.

40. M.S. Granovetter, "The Strength of Weak Ties," *American Journal of Sociology* 78 (1973): 1360–80; B. Erickson, "Social Networks," in *The Blackwell Companion to Sociology*, ed. J.R. Blau (Malden, MA: Blackwell, 2004), 314–26.

41. B. Uzzi and S. Dunlap, "How to Build Your Network," *Harvard Business Review* 83, no. 12 (2005): 53–60.

42. S.C. de Janasz and M.L. Forret, "Learning the Art of Networking: A Critical Skill for Enhancing Social Capital and Career Success," *Journal of Management Education* 32, no. 5 (2008): 629–50; Y. Zenou, "A Dynamic Model of Weak and Strong Ties in the Labor Market," *Journal of Labor Economics* 33, no. 4 (2015): 891–932.

43. C.C. Su and N.K. Chan, "Predicting Social Capital on Facebook: The Implications of Use Intensity, Perceived Content Desirability, and Facebook-Enabled Communication Practices," *Computers in Human Behavior* 72 (2017): 259–68.

44. C. Phelps, R. Heidl, and A. Wadhwa, "Knowledge, Networks, and Knowledge Networks: A Review and Research Agenda," *Journal of Management* 38, no. 4 (2012): 1115–66.

45. R.S. Burt, *Structural Holes: The Social Structure of Competition* (Cambridge, MA: Harvard University Press, 1992); D.J. Brass and D.M. Krackhardt, "Power, Politics, and Social Networks in Organizations," in *Politics in Organizations: Theory and Research Considerations*, ed. G.R. Ferris and D.C. Treadway (New York: Routledge, 2012), 355–75.

46. B.R. Ragins and E. Sundstrom, "Gender and Power in Organizations: A Longitudinal Perspective," *Psychological Bulletin* 105 (1989): 51–88; S. McDonald et al., "Frontiers of Sociological Research on Networks, Work, and Inequality," in *Networks, Work and Inequality*, ed. S. McDonald, Research in the Sociology of Work (Bingley, UK: Emerald Group Publishing Limited, 2013), 1–41.

47. Y. Amichai-Hamburger, G. Wainapel, and S. Fox, "'On the Internet No One Knows I'm an Introvert': Extroversion, Neuroticism, and Internet Interaction," *CyberPsychology & Behavior* 5, no. 2 (2002): 125–28; K. Brooks, "Networking 101 for Introverts," *Psychology Today* (2010); D. Zack, *Networking for People Who Hate Networking* (San Francisco: Berret-Koehler, 2010).

48. S. Lee et al., "How Do I Get My Way? A Meta-Analytic Review of Research on Influence Tactics," *The Leadership Quarterly* 28 (2017): 210–28.

49. D. Kipnis, S.M. Schmidt, and I. Wilkinson, "Intraorganizational Influence Tactics: Explorations in Getting One's Way," *Journal of Applied Psychology* 65 (1980): 440–52; G. Yukl, "Power and the Interpersonal Influence of Leaders," in *Power and Interdependence in Organizations*, ed. D. Tjosvold and B. Wisse (New York: Cambridge University Press, 2009), 207–23. A recent review includes these influence tactics but divides some of them into narrower subcategories. See S. Lee et al., "How Do I Get My Way? A Meta-Analytic Review of Research on Influence Tactics," *The Leadership Quarterly* 28 (2017): 210–28.

50. B. van Knippenberg, R. van Eijbergen, and H. Wilke, "The Use of Hard and Soft Influence Tactics in Cooperative Task Groups," *Group Processes & Intergroup Relations* 2 (1999): 231–44.

51. R.B. Cialdini and N.J. Goldstein, "Social Influence: Compliance and Conformity," *Annual Review of Psychology* 55, (2004): 591–621; A. Bourgoin, N. Bencherki, and S. Faraj, "'And Who Are You?' A Performative Perspective on Authority in Organizations," *Academy of Management Journal*, July 25, 2019.

52. The most widely applied model or power excludes silent authority. Its closest category is "legitimating tactics," which is an active attempt to demonstrate one's right to the request based on rules or contracts. See G. Yukl, C.F. Seifert, and C. Chavez, "Validation of the Extended Influence Behavior Questionnaire," *The Leadership Quarterly* 19 (2008): 609–21. Several studies identify the importance of silent authority in high power distance cultures. For example, see Y. Zhai, "Values of Deference to Authority in Japan and China," *International Journal of Comparative Sociology* 58, no. 2 (April 2017): 120–39.

53. C. de Gaulle, *The Edge of the Sword (Le fil de l'epée)*, trans. G. Hopkins (London: Faber, 1960), 59.

54. "Workplace Bullying Widespread at Fire Departments, Survey Shows," *Japan Times*, March 29, 2017; R. Nauen, "3 in 10 Workers Report Feeling Bullied at Work," news release (Chicago: CareerBuilder, October 19, 2017); "Survey Finds Harassment a Problem for One in Three Japanese Workers," *Nippon.com*, July 23, 2019; L. Rosling, "Bullying in the Workplace–Statistics for the UK," *SME Loans* (blog), July 31, 2019, https://smeloans.co.uk/bullying-in-the-workplace-statistics-uk/; "State of the Service Report 2018–19" (Canberra: Australian Government, Australian Public Service Commission, November 2019).

55. S. Maitlis, "Taking It from the Top: How CEOs Influence (and Fail to Influence) Their Boards," *Organization Studies* 25, no. 8 (2004): 1275–311. This type of influence is a form of manipulation. See P. Fleming and A. Spicer, "Power in Management and Organization Science," *The Academy of Management Annals* 8, no. 1 (2014): 237–98.

56. J.K. Murnighan, "Organizational Coalition Formation: Process, Consequences and Dominant Coalitions," BEBR faculty working paper, 1985; W.B. Stevenson, J.L. Pearce, and L.W. Porter, "The Concept of 'Coalition' in Organization Theory and Research," *Academy of Management Review* 10, no. 2 (1985): 256–68; F. Liu, O. Dedehayir, and B. Katzy, "Coalition Formation during Technology Adoption," *Behaviour & Information Technology* 34 (2015): 1186–99.

57. A.T. Cobb, "Toward the Study of Organizational Coalitions: Participant Concerns and Activities in a Simulated Organizational Setting," *Human Relations* 44 (1991): 1057–79; E.A. Mannix, "Organizations as Resource Dilemmas: The Effects of Power Balance on Coalition Formation in Small Groups," *Organizational Behavior and Human Decision Processes* 55 (1993): 1–22; K. Rangus and M. Černe, "The Impact of Leadership Influence Tactics and Employee Openness toward Others on Innovation Performance: Leadership Influence Tactics and Employee Openness," *R&D Management* 49, no. 2 (2019): 168–79.

58. A.P. Brief, *Attitudes in and around Organizations* (Thousand Oaks, CA: Sage, 1998), 69–84; D.J. O'Keefe, *Persuasion: Theory and Research* (Thousand Oaks, CA: Sage, 2002); R.H. Gass and J.S. Seiter, *Persuasion: Social Influence and Compliance Gaining*, 5th ed. (New York: Routledge, 2014).

59. These and other features of message content in persuasion are detailed in R. Petty and J. Cacioppo, *Attitudes and Persuasion: Classic and Contemporary Approaches* (Dubuque, IA: W.C. Brown, 1981); D.J. O'Keefe, *Persuasion: Theory and Research* (Thousand Oaks, CA: Sage, 2002), Chap. 9; G. Van Kleef, H. van den Berg, and M. Heerdink, "The Persuasive Power of Emotions: Effects of Emotional Expressions on Attitude Formation and Change," *Journal of Applied Psychology* 100 (2015): 1124–42; E. Falk and C. Scholz, "Persuasion, Influence, and Value: Perspectives from Communication and Social Neuroscience," *Annual Review of Psychology* 69 (2018): 329–56; D. Albarracin and S. Shavitt, "Attitudes and Attitude Change," *Annual Review of Psychology* 69 (2018): 299–327.

60. J.A. Banas and S.A. Rains, "A Meta-Analysis of Research on Inoculation Theory," *Communication Monographs* 77, no. 3 (2010): 281–311; B. Ivanov et al., "Beyond Simple Inoculation: Examining the Persuasive Value of Inoculation for Audiences with Initially Neutral or Opposing Attitudes," *Western Journal of Communication* 81, no. 1 (2017): 105–26.

61. Y. Lim and R.J. Lee-Won, "When Retweets Persuade: The Persuasive Effects of Dialogic Retweeting and the Role of Social Presence in Organizations' Twitter-Based Communication," *Telematics and Informatics* 34, no. 5 (2017): 422–33; P. Briñol and R.E. Petty, "The Impact of Individual Differences on Attitudes and Attitude Change," in *The Oxford Handbook of Personality and Social Psychology*, ed. D. Albarracín and B. Johnson, 2nd ed., vol. 1 (New York: Oxford University Press, 2019), 520–56.

62. M. Bolino, D. Long, and W. Turnley, "Impression Management in Organizations: Critical Questions, Answers, and Areas for Future Research," *Annual Review of Organizational Psychology and Organizational Behavior* 3 (2016): 377–406.

63. T. Peters, "The Brand Called You," *Fast Company*, August 1997; C. Johnson, *Platform: The Art and Science of Personal Branding* (New York: Penguin Random House, 2019); L.A. King, *Just Do You: Authenticity, Leadership, and Your Personal Brand* (Toronto: Ingenium Books, 2019).

64. D. Strutton and L.E. Pelton, "Effects of Ingratiation on Lateral Relationship Quality within Sales Team Settings," *Journal of Business Research* 43 (1998): 1–12; R. Vonk, "Self-Serving Interpretations of Flattery: Why Ingratiation Works," *Journal of Personality and Social Psychology* 82 (2002): 515–26.

65. D. Strutton, L.E. Pelton, and J.F. Tanner, "Shall We Gather in the Garden: The Effect of Ingratiatory Behaviors on Buyer Trust in Salespeople," *Industrial Marketing Management* 25 (1996): 151–62; J. O'Neil, "An Investigation of the Sources of Influence of Corporate Public Relations Practitioners," *Public Relations Review* 29 (2003): 159–69; C.A. Higgins, T.A. Judge, and G.R. Ferris, "Influence Tactics and Work Outcomes: A Meta-Analysis," *Journal of Organizational Behavior* 24 (2003): 90–106.

66. J. Foster, "Here Are Best Answers to Job Interview Questions," *The Herald (Rock Hill, S.C.)*, April 4, 2010; "Common Interview Questions and How to Answer Them," *Advice & Tips* (Sydney: Seek, September 19, 2013), https://www.seek.com.au/career-advice/common-interview-questions-and-how-to-answer-them (accessed July 3, 2017); J. Haden, "27 Most Common Job Interview Questions and Answers," *Inc.*, June 20, 2016; "Ten Tough Interview Questions and Ten Great Answers," *Job Search Advice* (Seattle: CollegeGrad, 2017), https://collegegrad.com/jobsearch/mastering-the-interview/ten-tough-interview-questions-and-ten-great-answers (accessed July 3, 2017); M. Cheary, "Common Interview Questions and Answers," *Interview Techniques* (London: Reed, 2017) (accessed July 3, 2017).

67. C.M. Falbe and G. Yukl, "Consequences for Managers of Using Single Influence Tactics and Combinations of Tactics," *Academy of Management Journal* 35 (1992): 638–52.

68. G. Yukl and J. Tracey, "Consequences of Influence Tactics Used with Subordinates, Peers, and the Boss," *Journal of Applied Psychology* 77, no. 4 (1992): 525–35; B. Oc and M.R. Bashshur, "Followership, Leadership and Social Influence," *Leadership Quarterly* 24, no. 6 (2013): 919–34; M.B. Wadsworth and A.L. Blanchard, "Influence Tactics in Virtual Teams," *Computers in Human Behavior* 44 (2015): 386–93.

69. P.P. Fu et al., "The Impact of Societal Cultural Values and Individual Social Beliefs on the Perceived Effectiveness of Managerial Influence Strategies: A Meso Approach," *Journal of International Business Studies* 35, no. 4 (2004): 284–305; A.N. Smith et al., "Gendered Influence: A Gender Role Perspective on the Use and Effectiveness of Influence Tactics," *Journal of Management* 39, no. 5 (2013): 1156–83; C.C. Lewis and J. Ryan, "Age and Influence Tactics: A Life-Stage Development Theory Perspective," *The International Journal of Human Resource Management* 25, no. 15 (2014): 2146–58.

70. This definition is founded on a cluster of definitions with similar core elements, including self-interest, damage to individuals and the organization, and perceived motivation of the political actor. See H. Mintzberg, *Power In and Around Organizations* (Englewood Cliffs, NJ: Prentice Hall, 1983); K. Michele Kacmar and G.R. Ferris, "Politics at Work: Sharpening the Focus of Political Behavior in Organizations," *Business Horizons* 36, no. 4 (1993): 70–74; C.-H. Chang, C.C. Rosen, and P.E. Levy, "The Relationship between Perceptions of Organizational Politics and Employee Attitudes, Strain, and Behavior: A Meta-Analytic Examination," *Academy of Management Journal* 52 (2009): 779–801; A. Bedi and A. Schat, "Perceptions of Organizational Politics: A Meta-Analysis of Its Attitudinal, Health, and Behavioural Consequences," *Canadian Psychology* 54 (2013): 246–59.

71. This famous quotation is attributed to both Nicolo Machiavelli and Sun-tzu. None of Machiavelli's five main books (translated) has any statement close to this quotation. Sun-tzu's book *Art of War* (translated) does not have this quotation either, but he makes a similar statement about spies: "Hence it is that with none in the whole army are more intimate relations to be maintained than with spies." See Sun-tzu, *The Art of War*, trans. L. Giles (Mineola, NY: Dover, 2002), 98.

72. Surveys of employees consistently identify organizational politics as self-serving behaviour that is dysfunctional for employee wellbeing and performance. See, for example, "Sloppy Worker Wake-Up Call: Sweating the Small Stuff Matters," news release (Menlo Park, CA: Accountemps, January 10, 2017); "Indian Millennials Lack Critical Skills: HBR Ascend Survey," *Hindustan Times*, July 18, 2017; Z. Mejia, "These Are the Top 10 Workplace Struggles Employees Face in 2018," *CNBC*, September 19, 2018; "New DDI Research: 57 Percent of Employees Quit Because of Their Boss," news release (Pittsburgh: Development Dimensions International, December 9, 2019).

73. D.L. Madison et al., "Organizational Politics: An Exploration of Managers' Perceptions," *Human Relations* 33, no. 2 (1980): 79–100; P. Kumar and R. Ghadially, "Organizational Politics and Its Effects on Members of Organizations," *Human Relations* 42, no. 4 (1989): 305–14; D. Buchanan and R. Badham, *Power, Politics, and Organizational Change: Winning the Turf Game* (Thousand Oaks, CA: Sage, 2008), 11; E.M. Landells and S.L. Albrecht, "Positive Politics, Negative Politics, and Engagement: Psychological Safety, Meaningfulness, and Availability as 'Black Box' Explanatory Mechanisms," in *Research in Occupational Stress and Well-Being*, ed. C.C. Rosen and P.L. Perrewé, vol. 15 (Bingley, UK: Emerald Publishing Limited, 2017), 33–49; E.M. Landells and S.L. Albrecht, "The Positives and Negatives of Organizational Politics: A Qualitative Study," *Journal of Business and Psychology* 32 (2017): 41–58.

74. E. Vigoda, "Stress-Related Aftermaths to Workplace Politics," *Journal of Organizational Behavior* 23, no. 5 (August 2002), 571–91. C.H. Chang, C.C. Rosen, and P.E. Levy, "The Relationship between Perceptions of Organizational Politics and Employee Attitudes, Strain, and Behavior: A Meta-Analytic Examination," *Academy of Management Journal* 52, no. 4 (2009): 779–801; A. Bedi and A. Schat, "Perceptions of Organizational Politics: A Meta-Analysis of Its Attitudinal, Health, and Behavioural Consequences," *Canadian Psychology* 54 (2013): 246–59.

75. Indian Millennials Lack Critical Skills: HBR Ascend Survey," *Hindustan Times*, July 18, 2017; "Your Best Employees Are Leaving. But Is It Personal or Practical?" news release (Atlanta: Randstad USA, August 28, 2018); J. Howington, "2018 Annual Survey Finds Workers Are More Productive at Home," *FlexJobs Job Search Tips and Blog* (blog), September 9, 2018, https://www.flexjobs.com/blog/post/2018-annual-survey-finds-workers-more-productive-at-home/; Z. Mejia, "These Are the Top 10 Workplace Struggles Employees Face in 2018," *CNBC*, September 19, 2018; P. Petrone, "Stress at Work Report: Who Is Feeling It the Most and How to Combat It," LinkedIn, *The Learning Blog* (blog), accessed February 25, 2020, https://learning.linkedin.com/blog/advancing-your-career/stress-at-work-report-who-is-feeling-it-the-most-and-how-to-com.

76. L.W. Porter, R.W. Allen, and H.L. Angle, "The Politics of Upward Influence in Organizations," *Research in Organizational Behavior* 3 (1981): 120–22; R.J. House, "Power and Personality in Complex Organizations," *Research in Organizational Behavior* 10 (1988): 305–57.

77. E. O'Boyle et al., "A Meta-Analysis of the Dark Triad and Work Behavior: A Social Exchange Perspective," *Journal of Applied Psychology* 97, no. 3 (2012): 557–79; A. Harrison, J. Summers, and B. Mennecke, "The Effects of the Dark Triad on Unethical Behavior," *Journal of Business Ethics* 153, no. 1 (2018): 53–77; M. Moshagen, B.E. Hilbig, and I. Zettler, "The Dark Core of Personality," *Psychological Review* 125, no. 5 (2018): 656–88; S.M. Spain, "The Dark Side of Personality," in *Leadership, Work, and the Dark Side of Personality*, ed. S.M. Spain (Cambridge, MA: Academic Press, 2019), 41–93.

78. C. Hardy, *Strategies for Retrenchment and Turnaround: The Politics of Survival* (Berlin: Walter de Gruyter, 1990), Chap. 14; G.R. Ferris et al., "Perceptions of Organizational Politics: Prediction, Stress-Related Implications, and Outcomes," *Human Relations* 49 (1996): 233–63; M.C. Andrews and K.M. Kacmar, "Discriminating among Organizational Politics, Justice, and Support," *Journal of Organizational Behavior* 22 (2001): 347–66.

10 Conflict and Negotiation in the Workplace

UpperCut Images/Getty Images

Learning Objectives

After you read this chapter, you should be able to:

LO10-1 Define conflict and debate its positive and negative consequences in the workplace.

LO10-2 Distinguish task conflict from relationship conflict and describe three strategies to minimize relationship conflict during task conflict episodes.

LO10-3 Diagram the conflict process model and describe six structural sources of conflict in organizations.

LO10-4 Outline the five conflict-handling styles and discuss the circumstances in which each would be most appropriate.

LO10-5 Apply the six structural approaches to conflict management and describe the three types of third-party dispute resolution.

LO10-6 Discuss activities in the negotiation preparation, process, and setting that improve negotiation effectiveness.

conflict the process in which one party perceives that its interests are being opposed or negatively affected by another party

The social distancing requirements of the COVID-19 pandemic may have temporarily halted the decade-long movement of employees from cubicles and private offices into open-plan and nonterritorial workspaces. These communal arrangements are now considered high-risk environments for spreading disease. But even before COVID-19, concern was growing that open-plan offices were fueling workplace conflict, most of which occurs as subtle irritation and resentment among coworkers.

Shared work space arrangements create higher interdependence among employees regarding the noise, visual movement, territorial privacy, and information privacy of that space. "Our open office has absolutely crippled my productivity," concludes a marketing professional in Idaho after three years in an open-office arrangement. "I can't hear myself think, I'm starting to feel bitter toward my coworkers, and my anxiety has shot through the roof."

Conflict may be even more intense in nonterritorial offices (where no one has an assigned desk) because they create ongoing competition over prized locations, such as desks in quieter areas, close to windows, and near strong Wi-Fi. "Each morning in my office is like a grown-up game of musical chairs, with six or so people competing for the last remaining hot desk," complains a British accountant. "Lost productivity spent hunting for somewhere to sit is the least of our concerns. Barely concealed resentment comes to the fore on regular occasions."[1]

The hostilities that employees experience in open-plan and nonterritorial workspaces illustrate that workplace conflict occurs in many ways. Yet, as we will learn in this chapter, some forms of conflict are also valuable to organizations. The challenge is to enable beneficial conflict and suppress dysfunctional conflict. We begin this chapter by defining conflict and discussing the age-old question: Is conflict good or bad? Next, we look at the conflict process and examine in detail the main factors that cause or amplify conflict. The five styles of handling conflict are then described, including its contingencies as well as gender and cross-cultural differences. This is followed by discussion of the most important structural approaches to conflict resolution. Next, we look at the role of managers and others in third-party conflict resolution. The final section of this chapter reviews key factors to consider when negotiating conflict resolution.

LO10-1 Define conflict and debate its positive and negative consequences in the workplace.

THE MEANING AND CONSEQUENCES OF CONFLICT

Conflict is a fact of life in organizations. Companies are continuously adapting to their external environment, yet there is no clear road map on what changes are best. Every day, employees disagree on which work objectives should receive priority, which norms they should abide by, and how even minor job tasks should be performed. These conflict episodes occur because of clashing work goals, divergent personal values and experiences, and a variety of other reasons that we discuss in this chapter.

Conflict is a process in which one party perceives that its interests are being opposed or negatively affected by another party.[2] It occurs when one party obstructs another's goals in some way, or when one party perceives that the other person or group is likely to do so. Conflict is ultimately based on perceptions; it exists whenever one party *believes* that another might obstruct its efforts, regardless of whether the other party actually has those intentions.

This definition—and the focus of this chapter—is on conflict with others, such as between people on the same team or department, between work units or business divisions, or between the organization and external stakeholders. However, conflict also

Conflict is ultimately based on perceptions; it exists whenever one party *believes* that another might obstruct its efforts, regardless of whether the other party actually intends to do so.
Goodboy Picture Company/Getty Images

occurs within each of us (called *intrapersonal conflict*), such as when our behavior conflicts with our beliefs and values (see Chapter 4 on cognitive dissonance).

Is Conflict Good or Bad?

One of the oldest debates in organizational behavior is whether conflict is good or bad—or, more recently, what forms of conflict are good or bad.[3] The dominant view over most of this time has been that conflict is dysfunctional.[4] This perspective argues that organizations work best through harmonious relations, whereas even moderately low levels of conflict tatter the fabric of workplace relations and sap energy from productive activities.

The "conflict-is-bad" perspective is now considered too simplistic, yet workplace conflict can indeed have negative consequences under some circumstances (see Exhibit 10.1).[5] Conflict potentially threatens personal needs and self-concept, which reduces job satisfaction and increases stress and turnover. It undermines job performance by consuming otherwise productive time, distracting employees from their work, and sapping their personal energy.[6]

Conflict also potentially undermines information sharing because employees are less motivated to ask for, pay attention to, and transmit information with discordant coworkers. Disagreements can also fuel organizational politics and thereby waste resources, such as when employees try to undermine the credibility of their opponents. Conflict among team members may hurt team cohesion and performance. Even when conflict occurs between work units or regions (such as when competing for budget funding), the interdepartmental conflict may lead to conflict and power struggles among employees *within* each group.[7]

Benefits of Conflict In the 1920s, when most organizational scholars viewed conflict as inherently dysfunctional, a few experts argued that conflict can have positive outcomes.[8] But it wasn't until the 1970s that conflict management experts began to embrace this idea that some level of conflict can be beneficial.[9] They formed an "optimal conflict" perspective, which states that organizations are most effective when employees experience a moderate level of conflict. Organizations are less effective when the intensity of conflict is very low or very high.

What are the benefits of conflict? First, it potentially improves decision making by energizing people to debate issues and evaluate alternatives more thoroughly. When employees disagree constructively, they probe and test one another's way of thinking to better understand the underlying issues that need to be addressed. They evaluate the logic of the opposing positions and reexamine each party's basic assumptions about the problem and its possible solution. Conflict also motivates creative thinking to discover novel solutions to the disagreement.[11]

> **"Conflict is the gadfly of thought. It stirs us to observation and memory. It instigates to invention. It shocks us out of sheeplike passivity, and sets us at noting and contriving.[10]"**
>
> —John Dewey, educational philosopher/psychologist

A second potential benefit is that moderate levels of conflict maintain vigilance with the external environment. Through disagreement, employees engage in active thinking, and this often involves ongoing questioning about how the organization can be more closely aligned with its customers, suppliers, and other stakeholders.[12] A third benefit occurs when team members experience conflict with external sources, such as competition with or threats from other teams or organizations. People tend to be more motivated to work together when faced with an external threat, which strengthens cohesion within the team (see Chapter 7). However, as we mentioned a few paragraphs ago, interdepartmental conflict sometimes undermines relations within the department.

Exhibit 10.1 Consequences of Workplace Conflict

Negative Consequences	Positive Consequences
• Lower performance • Higher stress, dissatisfaction, and turnover • Less information sharing and coordination • Increased organizational politics • Wasted resources • Weakened team cohesion (when conflict exists among team members)	• Better decision making —Tests logic of arguments —Questions assumptions —Generates creative thinking • More responsive to changing environment • Stronger team cohesion (when conflict exists between the team and outside opponents)

LO10-2 Distinguish task conflict from relationship conflict and describe three strategies to minimize relationship conflict during task conflict episodes.

THE EMERGING VIEW: TASK AND RELATIONSHIP CONFLICT

The "optimal conflict" perspective remains popular and may be true in some respects; too much of any conflict is probably dysfunctional.[13] However, the school of thought most widely accepted today is that there are two dominant types of conflict: task conflict and relationship conflict. These represent two distinct ways that people approach and interact with one another during disagreements.[14]

Task Conflict

Task conflict (also called *constructive conflict*) occurs when people focus their discussion around the issue (i.e., the "task") while showing respect for people involved in that disagreement. This type of conflict keeps the spotlight on the qualities of the ideas presented. With task conflict, participants examine behavior, ideas, and recommendations in terms of their factual accuracy, logic, and reasonable inferences. The discussion avoids any attention to the competence or power of the people involved. Although there is likely an upper limit to the intensity of any disagreement, research indicates that task conflict tends to produce the beneficial outcomes described earlier, particularly better decision making.[15]

We often hear about workplace conflicts caused by "personality clashes." Yet this label typically indicates that someone has oversimplified these interpersonal tiffs in terms of the opponent's personal characteristics rather than the task-related events that manifested the disagreement. Suppose an employee describes a disagreement with a coworker in terms of the latter's reckless personality. The coworker's behaviors or suggestions may be irritatingly risky. Yet, task-oriented conflict is possible by focusing on what the allegedly reckless employee does (the logic, ethics, and consequences of those actions) and on the logic and factual foundation of that person's suggestions, not on alleged personal attributes. The point here is that almost all workplace conflicts can be framed as task conflicts, even when some participants try to pin the problem on flaws on the other party's personal characteristics.

Relationship Conflict

In contrast to task conflict, **relationship conflict** occurs when the discussion focuses on characteristics of participants in the dispute. This type of conflict is evident when one party attacks another party's behavior or ideas by questioning the competence of those opponents. Rather than identifying logical and factual concerns with someone's suggestion (task conflict), relationship conflict attempts to dismiss the idea by arguing that it was proposed or supported by people who lack the ability, motivation, wisdom, thoughtfulness, and other virtuous characteristics to think of useful suggestions.

Relationship conflict also occurs more indirectly when people rely on status or expertise to defend their position ("My recommendation is better because I have the most experience!"). Arguing for an idea by claiming one's own superior talents implies the inferiority of those who present opposing arguments or recommendations. Relationship conflict even occurs when someone is abrasive or assertive to the extent that the behavior demeans others in the conversation.[16] For example, a manager who bangs a fist on the desk while presenting an argument is demonstrating that he or she has more power and the followers need harsh signals to get their attention.

Relationship conflict is dysfunctional because it threatens the other party's self-esteem (see Chapter 3). It usually triggers defense mechanisms and a competitive orientation between the opponents. It also reduces mutual trust by emphasizing interpersonal differences, thereby weakening any bond that might otherwise exist between the parties.[17] Relationship conflict escalates more easily than task conflict because the adversaries become less motivated to communicate and share information, making it more difficult for them to discover common ground and ultimately resolve the conflict. Instead, they rely increasingly on distorted perceptions and stereotypes, which tend to reinforce their perceptions of threat.

> Task conflict keeps the spotlight on the qualities of the ideas presented and avoids any attention to the competence or power of the participants.

task conflict a type of conflict in which people focus their discussion around the issue (i.e., the "task") in which different viewpoints occur while showing respect for people involved in that disagreement

relationship conflict a type of conflict in which people focus their discussion on qualities of the people in the dispute, rather than on the qualities of the ideas presented regarding a task-related issue

psychological safety a shared belief that it is safe to engage in interpersonal risk-taking; specifically, that presenting unusual ideas, constructively disagreeing with the majority, and experimenting with new work behaviors will not result in coworkers posing a threat to their self-concept, status, or career

Minimizing Relationship Conflict during Task Conflict

The logical recommendation from our discussion so far is to encourage task conflict and minimize relationship conflict. This sounds good in theory, but separating these two types of conflict isn't easy in practice. Research indicates that people experience some degree of relationship conflict whenever they engage in constructive debate.[18] No matter how diplomatically others question our ideas and actions, they potentially threaten our self-esteem and our public image, which usually triggers our drive to defend. The stronger the level of debate and the more the issue is tied to our self-view, the more likely that task conflict will evolve into (or mix with) relationship conflict. Fortunately, three conditions potentially minimize the level of relationship conflict during task conflict episodes.[19]

- *Emotional intelligence.* Relationship conflict is less likely to occur, or is less likely to escalate, when team members have high levels of emotional intelligence, as well as the related attributes of emotional stability and trait self-control.[20] Employees with higher emotional intelligence are better able to understand and regulate their own emotions during debate, which reduces the risk of escalating perceptions of interpersonal hostility. They are also more likely to view a coworker's emotional reaction as valuable information about that person's needs and expectations, rather than as a personal attack.
- *Team development.* Team development plays a critical role in suppressing relationship conflict during task conflict.[21] One reason is that as teams develop, their members become better at understanding and anticipating one another, which reduces the risk that a coworker's words or actions will be misinterpreted as a conflict trigger. A second reason is that team development produces higher team cohesion, in which employees feel a strong social identity with the group. Members of cohesive teams are motivated to minimize relationship conflict because these episodes threaten the team's stability and the member's future with that group.
- *Norms supporting psychological safety.* Task conflict is less likely to mutate into chronic relationship conflict when the team or broader organization adopts norms that support psychological safety.[22] **Psychological safety** refers to a shared belief that it is safe to engage in interpersonal risk-taking (see Chapter 7). In other words, employees are confident that presenting unusual ideas, constructively disagreeing with the majority, or experimenting with new work behaviors will not cause coworkers to threaten their self-concept, status, or career. Psychological safety flourishes when team and organizational norms encourage employees to respect and value one another, demonstrate interest in one another, be open-minded about and tolerant with coworkers' opinions, and show positive intentions toward one another. Showing positive intentions involves displaying positive emotions and nonthreatening behavior when discussing different points of view.

People experience some degree of relationship conflict whenever they engage in constructive debate, but relationship conflict can be minimized through emotional intelligence, team cohesion, and psychological safety norms.
DragonImages/Getty Images

LO10-3 Diagram the conflict process model and describe six structural sources of conflict in organizations.

CONFLICT PROCESS MODEL

Now that we have outlined the history and current perspectives of conflict and its outcomes, let's look at the model of the conflict process, shown in Exhibit 10.2.[23] This model begins with the sources of conflict, which we will describe in the next section. The sources of conflict lead one or both parties to perceive that conflict exists. They become aware that one party's statements and actions interfere with or otherwise threaten their own goals or beliefs. These perceptions produce and interact with emotions experienced about the conflict.

Conflict perceptions usually produce negative emotions, including stress, anxiety, fear, frustration, and/or anger.[24] However, some people experience positive emotions through cognitive reappraisal of the conflict, such as by perceiving the situation as a positive challenge, an opportunity to learn about other viewpoints, and a relief that nagging concerns about a possible conflict are out in the open and can now be addressed.

Manifest conflict represents each party's decisions and behaviors toward the other. These *conflict episodes* may range from subtle nonverbal communication to warlike aggression. Manifest conflict incidents are influenced by how the other party perceives and reacts emotionally to them.[25] Conflict is also behaviorally revealed by the style each side prefers using to resolve the conflict. Some people tend to avoid the conflict whereas others try to defeat those with opposing views. We discuss different conflict handling styles later in this chapter.

Exhibit 10.2 Model of the Conflict Process

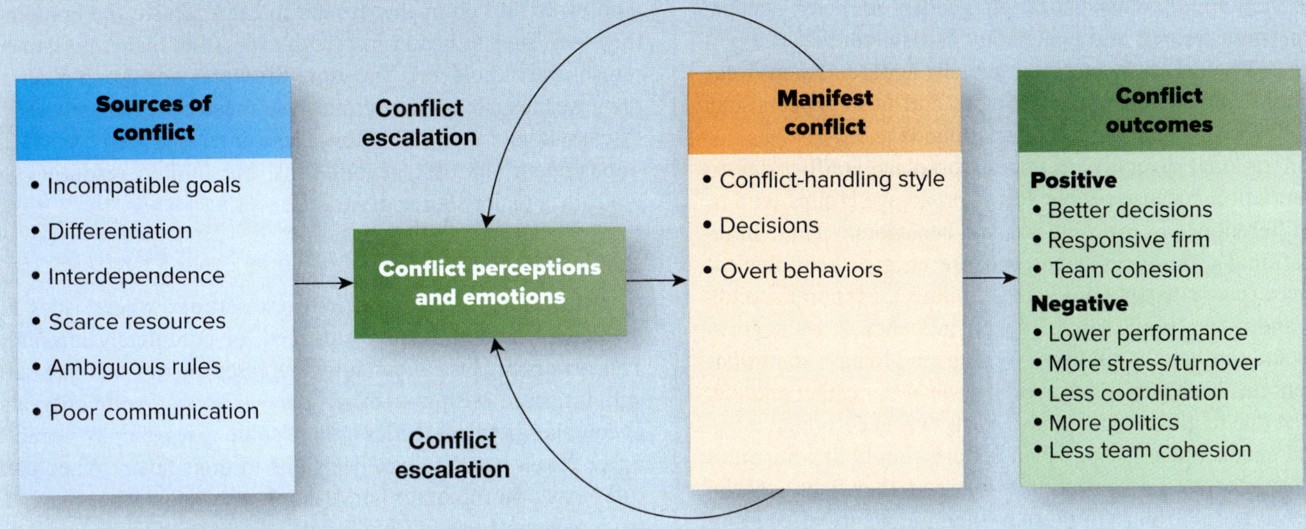

Exhibit 10.2 shows arrows looping back from manifest conflict to conflict perceptions and emotions. These arrows illustrate that the conflict process is really a series of episodes that potentially cycle into conflict escalation.[26] It doesn't take much to start this conflict cycle—just an inappropriate comment, a misunderstanding, or an action that lacks diplomacy. These behaviors cause the other party to perceive that conflict exists. Even if the first party did not intend to demonstrate conflict, the second party's response may create that perception.

STRUCTURAL SOURCES OF CONFLICT IN ORGANIZATIONS

The conflict model starts with the sources of conflict, so we need to understand these sources to effectively diagnose conflict episodes and subsequently resolve the disagreement or occasionally to generate conflict where it is lacking. The six main conditions that cause conflict in organizational settings are incompatible goals, differentiation, interdependence, scarce resources, ambiguous rules, and communication problems.

Incompatible Goals

Organizations divide work among departments and teams, who divide it further among individuals. Each division of work has associated goals, so employees and departments have different—and often conflicting—work objectives. Goal incompatibility occurs when the goals of one person or department seem to interfere with another person's or department's goals.[27] For example, the production department strives for cost-efficiency by scheduling long production runs whereas the sales team emphasizes customer service by delivering the client's product as quickly as possible. If the company runs out of a particular product, the production team would prefer to have clients wait until the next production run. This infuriates sales representatives who would rather change production quickly to satisfy consumer demand.

Differentiation

Another source of conflict is differentiation—differences among people and work units regarding their beliefs, values, experiences, and preferences. Differentiation is distinct from goal incompatibility; two people or departments may agree on a common goal (serving customers better) but have different beliefs about how to best achieve that goal (such as by introducing

Generational diversity produces workplace conflict due to differentiation because people across broad age groups tend to have different needs, expectations, and behaviors.
Michal Kowalski/Shutterstock

new technology versus employee customer service training). Employees form different beliefs, expectations, and worldviews due to their childhood socialization, gender, ethnicity, occupation, personal values, and personality.[28] Also, conflict is a perception, so before differences are actually apparent, employees form conflict beliefs from stereotypes and false expectations about coworkers from different backgrounds.

Generational diversity produces workplace conflict due to differentiation because people across broad age groups tend to have different needs, expectations, and behaviors.[29] These intergenerational differences occur because unique technological advances (e.g., smartphones versus Sputnik), economic conditions, and other "social forces" deeply influence us while growing up and throughout our lives. We also tend to have somewhat different needs and priorities at each stage of our career and life. Conflict due to differentiation also exists during corporate mergers and acquisitions.[30] Even when people from both companies want the integrated organization to succeed, they fight over the "right way" to do things because of their unique experiences in the separate companies.

Interdependence

All workplace conflict is caused to some extent by task interdependence. Conflict isn't possible between two people or work units that have no mutual involvement or shared resources (i.e., they are independent entities) because they would not have occasion to interfere with one another. Task interdependence exists when employees must share resources or coordinate work activities to perform their jobs (see Chapter 7). Conflict is inherently about relationships because people and work units are affected by others only when they have some degree of interdependence.

The probability and intensity of conflict increase with the level of interdependence.[31] Conflict is usually lowest when working with others in a pooled interdependence relationship, such as when sharing a common resource. The potential for conflict is higher in sequential interdependence work relationships, such as an assembly line. The highest risk and intensity of conflict tends to occur in reciprocal interdependence situations because employees in these situations quickly and significantly affect each other.

Scarce Resources

Resource scarcity generates conflict because each person or department requiring the same resource necessarily interferes with others who also need that resource to fulfill their goals.[32] Budget deliberations within organizations produce conflict because there isn't enough cash flow or debt facility to satisfy the funding aspirations of each work unit. Most labor strikes occur because there aren't enough financial and other resources for employees and company owners to each receive the outcomes they seek, such as higher pay (employees) and higher investment returns (stockholders). The more resources one group receives, the fewer resources other groups will receive. Fortunately, as we discuss later in this chapter, these interests aren't perfectly opposing in complex negotiations, but limited resources are typically a major source of friction.

Ambiguous Rules

Conflict is more common in work settings where rules are ambiguous, inconsistently enforced, or completely missing.[33] This occurs because uncertainty increases the risk that one party will interfere with the other party's goals. Ambiguity also encourages political tactics and, in some cases, employees enter a free-for-all battle to win decisions in their favor. When clear rules exist, on the other hand, employees know what to expect from one another and usually agree to abide by those rules.

Communication Problems

Conflict often becomes dysfunctional when employees lack the ability or motivation to state their disagreement in a diplomatic, nonconfrontational manner. It is difficult to craft a message that communicates dissent with neither too little nor too much assertiveness.[34] Influenced by their own strong feelings about an issue, employees tend to use emotion-laden language and aggressive nonverbal behavior when transmitting their concerns. The stronger the emotive language and other signals, the stronger the perception by receivers that the conflict not only exists, but is a high risk threat. Receivers often reciprocate with a similar response, which further escalates the conflict. Furthermore, aggressive and emotive communication typically fuels relationship conflict and makes it more difficult for the discussants to maintain a task conflict focus.

Poorly crafted communication is a source of conflict, but a lack of communication often amplifies that conflict. Occasionally, lack of communication exists because employees don't have the opportunity to discuss their differences. More often, the quarrel makes the relationship so uncomfortable that the parties actively avoid each other. Unfortunately, less communication can further escalate the conflict because each side increasingly relies on distorted images and stereotypes of the other party. Perceptions are further distorted because people in conflict situations tend to engage in more differentiation with those who are unlike themselves (see Chapter 3). This differentiation creates a more positive and reassuring self-concept and a more negative image of the opponent.[35]

> **Reciprocal interdependence tends to create the highest conflict because employees in these situations quickly and significantly affect each other.**

win–win orientation the belief that conflicting parties will find a mutually beneficial solution to their disagreement

win–lose orientation the belief that conflicting parties are drawing from a fixed pie, so the more one party receives, the less the other party will receive

Flashpoints of Conflict in the Workplace[36]

57% of 2,010 American knowledge workers in large firms say that the most common source of conflict with other departments or teams is conflicting goals (priorities) (highest source, lack of communication is second highest).

56% of 180,466 Canadian government employees say they are not at all stressed by coworker issues (17% are moderately or highly stressed).

13% of 5,136 UK employees say they have had shouting or very heated arguments at work within the past year.

44% of 2,211 UK employees who experienced a serious conflict with a coworker or manager within the past year say the conflict has been resolved (36% say it has not been resolved).

20% of 1,027 American employees believe that most people in their workplace are annoying.

14% of 1,027 American employees estimate that they experience coworker conflict weekly or more often.

donskarpo/Shutterstock

LO10-4 Outline the five conflict-handling styles and discuss the circumstances in which each would be most appropriate.

INTERPERSONAL CONFLICT-HANDLING STYLES

The six sources of conflict described in the previous section lead to conflict perceptions and emotions which, in turn, motivate people to respond in some way to the conflict. More than 70 years ago, organizational behavior pioneer Mary Parker Follett observed that people use a variety of interpersonal conflict-handling styles to address conflict situations. Follett's original list was expanded and refined over the years into the five-category model shown in Exhibit 10.3. This model recognizes that how people respond behaviorally to a conflict situation depends on the relative importance they place on maximizing outcomes for themselves and for the other party.[37]

- *Problem solving.* Problem solving tries to find a solution that is beneficial for both parties. This is known as the **win–win orientation** because people using this style believe the resources at stake are expandable rather than fixed if the parties work together to find a creative solution. Information sharing is an important feature of this style because both parties collaborate to identify common ground and potential solutions that satisfy everyone involved.
- *Forcing.* Forcing tries to win the conflict at the other's expense. People who use this style typically have a **win–lose orientation**—they believe the parties are drawing from a fixed pie, so the more one party receives, the less the other party will receive. Consequently, this style relies on "hard" influence tactics (see Chapter 9) to get one's own way. However, forcing is not necessarily aggressiveness or bullying. It also includes moderate degrees of assertiveness, such as when you speak up and show conviction for your idea or request.[38]
- *Avoiding.* Avoiding tries to smooth over or evade conflict situations altogether. A common avoidance strategy is to steer clear of the coworkers associated with the conflict. Another action is to minimize discussion of the sensitive topic when interacting with the other person. Although it is situated in the "low–low" sector of the model, avoidance does not necessarily mean that people always have a low concern for both one's own and the other party's interests. Instead, they might have low-low concern in the short run due to circumstances (i.e., avoidance is best conflict-handling option for now) but have high concern about one or both party's interests in the long run.[39]
- *Yielding.* Yielding involves giving in completely to the other side's wishes, or at least cooperating with little or no attention to your own interests. This style involves making unilateral concessions and unconditional promises, as well as offering help with no expectation that the other party needs to reciprocate in the future.
- *Compromising.* Compromising involves actively seeking a middle ground between the interests of the two parties. This involves calculating losses from concessions with equally valued gains, or at least trying to achieve similar levels of how much value each party sacrifices to reach agreement.

Mc Graw Hill connect

SELF-ASSESSMENT 10.1: What Is Your Preferred Conflict-Handling Style?

Choosing the Best Conflict-Handling Style

Chances are that you gravitate toward one or two conflict-handling styles that match your personality, personal

Exhibit 10.3 Interpersonal Conflict-Handling Styles

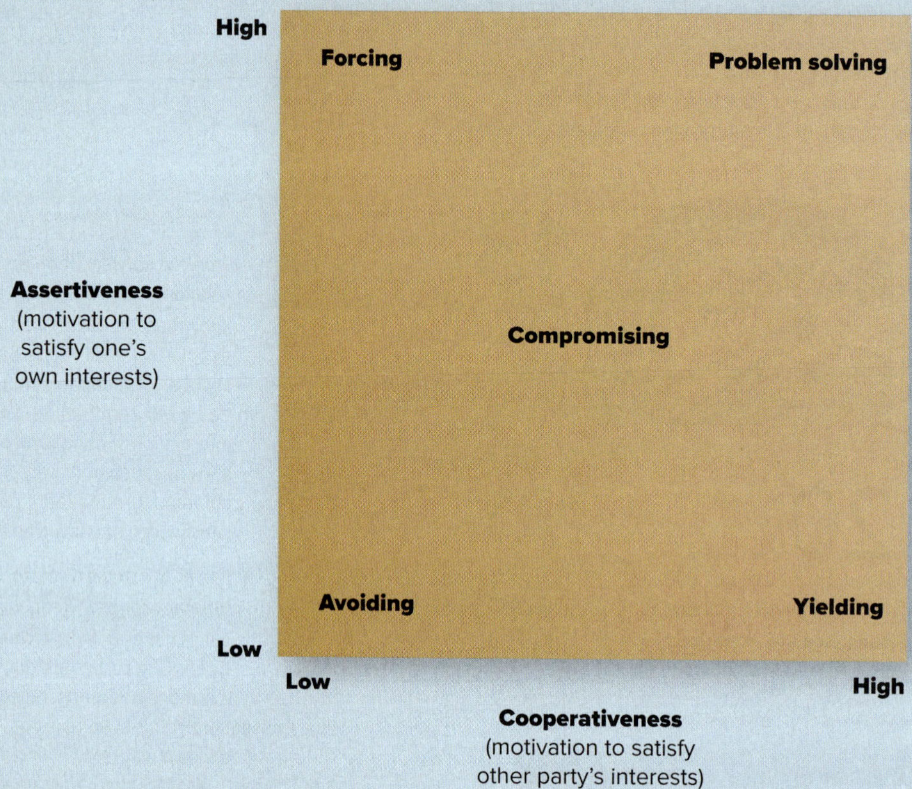

Source: C.K.W. de Dreu, A. Evers, B. Beersma, E.S. Kluwer, and A. Nauta, "A Theory-Based Measure of Conflict Management Strategies in the Workplace," *Journal of Organizational Behavior* 22 (2001): 645–68. Reprinted with permission of John Wiley & Sons, Inc.

and cultural values, and past experience.[40] You might typically use avoiding or yielding because disagreement makes you feel uncomfortable and is contrary to your self-view as someone who likes to get along with everyone. Or perhaps you prefer the forcing and compromising strategies because they reflect your strong need for achievement and to control the situation. However, the best style depends on the situation, so you need to understand and develop the capacity to use each style in the appropriate circumstances.[41]

Exhibit 10.4 summarizes the main contingencies and problems associated with using each conflict-handling style. Problem solving is the preferred conflict-handling style whenever possible. Why? Because this approach offers the best chance for the conflicting parties to reach a solution that is closest to their needs and goals. Through dialogue and clever thinking, the parties discover a win-win solution. In addition, the problem-solving style tends to improve long-term relationships, reduce stress, and minimize emotional defensiveness and other indications of relationship conflict.[42]

The problem-solving style is not the best conflict-handling style in all situations, however. If the conflict is simple and perfectly opposing (each party wants more of a single fixed pie), then this approach will waste time and increase frustration. It also takes more time and requires a fairly high degree of trust because there is a risk that the other party will take advantage of the information you have openly shared. The problem-solving style can be stressful and difficult when people experience strong feelings of conflict, likely because these negative emotions undermine trust in the other party.[43]

The forcing style is usually inappropriate because a high level of assertiveness tends to generate relationship conflict more quickly or intensely than occurs with other conflict-handling styles. Even so, a moderate degree of assertiveness may be appropriate where the dispute requires a quick solution or your ideas have a significantly and objectively stronger logical or moral foundation. This conflict-handling style may also be preferred when the other party would take advantage of a more cooperative conflict-handling style.

Avoiding is often ineffective as a conflict handling style because it produces uncertainty and frustration rather than resolution of the conflict.[45] However, avoiding may be the best short-term strategy when the conflict has become emotionally charged, conflict resolution would cost more than its benefits, or the parties prefer superficial harmony over resolving the conflict.

Exhibit 10.4 Conflict-Handling Style Contingencies and Problems

Conflict-Handling Style	Preferred Style When . . .	Problems with This Style
Problem solving	• Interests are not perfectly opposing (i.e., not pure win–lose) • Parties have trust, openness, and time to share information • Issues are complex	• Involves sharing information that the other party might use to their advantage
Forcing	• Dispute requires a quick solution • Your position objectively has a much stronger logical or moral foundation • Other party would take advantage of more cooperative strategies	• Highest risk of relationship conflict • May damage long-term relations, reducing future problem solving success
Avoiding	• Conflict has become too emotionally charged • Parties want to maintain a harmonious relationship • Cost of trying to resolve the conflict outweighs the benefits	• Doesn't usually resolve the conflict • May increase uncertainty and frustration
Yielding	• Issue is much less important to you than to the other party • The value and logic of your position isn't as clear • Parties want to maintain a harmonious relationship • Other party has substantially more power	• Increases other party's expectations in future conflict episodes
Compromising	• Single issue conflict with opposing interests • Parties lack time or trust for problem solving • Parties want to maintain a harmonious relationship • Parties have equal power	• Suboptimal solution where mutual gains are possible

> The more arguments you win, the fewer friends you will have.[44]
>
> —Unknown source, popular adage since late 1800s

The yielding style may be appropriate when the other party has substantially more power, the issue is not as important to you as to the other party, and you aren't confident that your position has superior logical or ethical justification.[46] On the other hand, yielding may give the other side unrealistically high expectations and motivate them to seek more from you in the future. In the long run, this style may produce more conflict, not less.

The compromising style may be best where the conflict is simple and perfectly opposing (each party wants more of a single fixed pie). Even if the conflict is sufficiently complex for potential mutual gains, compromising may be necessary when the parties lack time, trust, and openness to apply the problem-solving style. The compromising style is also popular where the parties prioritize harmony in their relationship over personal gains in the dispute.[47] Compromise also tends to occur where both parties have approximately equal power, which prevents one party from gaining advantage over the other. However, many conflicts have the potential for mutual gains, whereas the compromise style settles for a suboptimal solution. Research also suggests that employees are less happy with a compromise agreement under some conditions.

Cultural and Gender Differences in Conflict-Handling Styles

The preferred conflict handling style varies from one culture to another.[49] For example, people from high collectivist cultures—where people are expected to support and show allegiance to the group—are motivated to maintain harmonious relations and, consequently, are more likely than those from less collectivist cultures to manage disagreements through avoidance or problem solving. However, collectivism motivates harmony *within* the group, not necessarily with people outside the group.[50] Generally, cultural values and norms represent an important contingency when choosing the preferred conflict-handling approach in that culture.

Steering Clear of Workplace Conflict[48]

37% of 616 American managers surveyed say they are uncomfortable giving direct performance feedback/criticism to their employees to which they might respond badly.

36% of 500 American employees surveyed say the 2020 U.S. presidential election topic has led them to avoid talking to or working with a coworker because of his or her political views.

10% of 1,027 employed workers say they most often dealt with coworker conflict by avoiding that coworker completely.

35% of 701 UK employees who experienced serious conflict over the past year say the most common negative behavior resulting from that conflict was the refusal to work together or cooperate with each other.

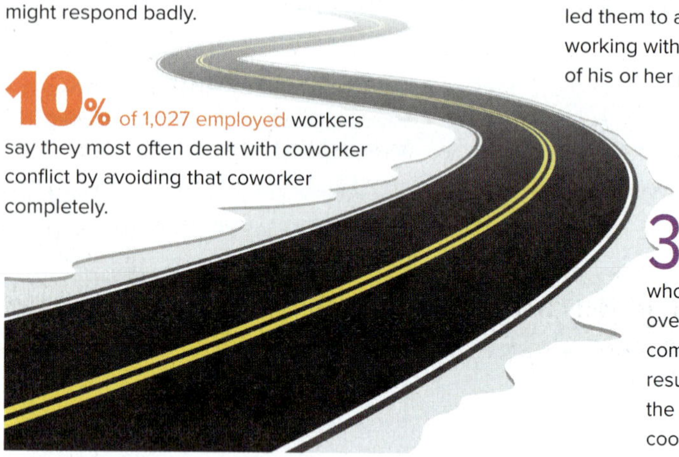

Alhovik/Shutterstock

Men and women also rely on different conflict-handling styles to some degree.[51] The clearest difference is that men are more likely than women to use the forcing style, whether as managers or nonmanagement employees. Also, women (whether as managers or employees) are more likely than male counterparts to use the avoiding style. Women are also slightly more likely than men to use problem solving, compromising, and yielding. One explanation for these differences is that, compared to men, women pay more attention to the relationship between the parties, so their preferred style tries to protect the relationship.

LO10-5 Apply the six structural approaches to conflict management and describe the three types of third-party dispute resolution.

STRUCTURAL APPROACHES TO CONFLICT MANAGEMENT

Conflict-handling styles describe how we approach the other party in a conflict situation. But conflict management also involves altering the underlying structural causes of potential conflict. The main structural approaches parallel the sources of conflict discussed earlier. Six structural approaches to minimize dysfunctional conflict are: emphasize superordinate goals, reduce differentiation, improve communication and understanding, reduce task interdependence, increase resources, and clarify rules and procedures.

Emphasize Superordinate Goals

One of the oldest recommendations for resolving conflict is to increase the parties' commitment to superordinate goals and decrease the importance of the conflicting subordinate goals.[52] **Superordinate goals** are goals that the conflicting employees or departments value and whose attainment requires the joint resources and effort of those parties.[53] These goals are called superordinate because they are higher-order aspirations such as the organization's strategic objectives rather than work unit operational goals or individual key performance objectives. Research indicates that the most effective executive teams frame their decisions as superordinate goals that rise above each executive's departmental or divisional goals. Similarly, effective leaders reduce dysfunctional organizational conflict through an inspirational vision that unifies employees and makes them less preoccupied with their subordinate goal differences.[54]

Suppose that marketing staff want a new product released quickly, whereas engineers want more time to test and add new features. Leaders can potentially reduce this interdepartmental conflict by reminding both groups of the company's mission to serve customers or by pointing out that competitors currently threaten sales of the company's existing products. By increasing commitment to companywide goals (customer focus, competitiveness), engineering and marketing employees pay less attention to their competing departmental-level goals, which reduces their perceived conflict with each other.[55]

Reduce Differentiation

Earlier in this chapter we explained that one of the main sources of workplace conflict is differentiation—differences among people regarding their training, values, beliefs, and experiences. Therefore, reducing differentiation is a logical approach to reducing dysfunctional conflict. As employees develop and recognize more similarities than differences with coworkers in other departments, they increase their trust in them and are more willing to coordinate activities and resolve their disputes through constructive discussion.[56]

Organizations can reduce differentiation among individuals or work units in several ways.[57] One strategy is for employees to have meaningful interaction with people in other groups, such as through participation in multidisciplinary projects.[58] A second strategy is to rotate staff to different departments or regions throughout their career. A third strategy is for leaders to build and maintain a strong organizational culture. Employees have shared values and assumptions and a stronger sense of community in a company with a strong culture (see Chapter 13). Each of these strategies creates common experiences or underlying beliefs that increase employee identification with the organization rather than just with a narrow business function, career specialization, or geographic region.

Improve Communication and Mutual Understanding

A third way to reduce dysfunctional conflict is to give the conflicting parties more opportunities to communicate and understand each other.[59] These activities don't necessarily reduce differentiation (employees still have divergent beliefs and experiences), but the interaction and discussion may create better awareness of and respect for one another's situation and point of view. The most basic application of this strategy is to change physical or reporting arrangements so employees across departments have more occasions to interact with one another. Employees also develop better mutual understanding with people in other departments through lunch-and-learn or poster session gatherings, in which one group summarizes its current projects to coworkers in other groups.

superordinate goals
goals that the conflicting parties value and whose attainment requires the joint resources and effort of those parties

Some companies improve mutual understanding through a variation of the Johari window model (see Chapter 3). In seminars with a trained facilitator, individuals disclose to coworkers information about themselves and their self-perceptions as well as feedback to others about how they are perceived.[61] Where conflicts have escalated, some embattled groups have participated in a deeper version of this process, called *intergroup mirroring*.[62] Led by an external consultant, the conflicting groups separately document their perceptions of (1) how the group perceives itself, (2) how it perceives the other group, and (3) how the group believes it is perceived by the other group. The "mirroring" stage follows, whereby each group discusses its three sets of perceptions with the other group. The two sides use this shared information to review their relationship problems and establish joint goals and action plans to improve their relationship.

Although communication and mutual understanding can reduce dysfunctional conflict, there are two important warnings. First, these interventions should be applied only for groups or individuals with moderate or low differentiation. If the parties have overwhelming differences, they tend to focus on information during the interaction that reinforces that view.[63] Consequently, dialogue could escalate rather than reduce relationship conflict. The second warning is that people in some cultures are less comfortable with the practice of resolving differences through direct and open dialogue.[64] This approach threatens harmony and risks loss of face, whereas people in collectivist and high power distance cultures, for example, prefer avoidance, yielding, and compromising to minimize the risk of any manifest conflict.

OB THEORY TO PRACTICE

Improving Mutual Understanding through Lunch Roulettes[60]

WeWork, the shared workspace company, expanded into Israel and within two years employed more than 100 people in its Tel Aviv technology group. Due to this rapid growth, informal subgroups and cliques were springing up, and newcomers had difficulty integrating. Aware of this trend, senior team members tried to think of ways to minimize dysfunctional conflict in the group by increasing mutual understanding.

The solution was lunch roulettes. Tel Aviv technology group employees participate (on average, about half of them do) by signing up through an app. The app organizes participants randomly—like a roulette wheel—into lunch groups of three people. To encourage conversation, attendees use the app to briefly state their hobbies and a "talk to me about" topic. The app organizes participants a couple of hours before the event and creates a private texting thread for each luncheon trio to coordinate where to eat and what to order.

"Lunch is a great time to talk and get to know one another," says WeWork software engineer Benny Sitbon, who helped create the event and the app. "Although our team is already medium-sized and in hypergrowth, the lunch roulette helps keeping that 'small team' feeling. Not only does this affect our team's happiness, it also improves our collaboration and approachability, and therefore, our efficiency."

vladans/Getty Images

Reduce Interdependence

Conflict occurs where people are dependent on one another, so another way to reduce dysfunctional conflict is to minimize the level of interdependence among the parties. Three ways to reduce interdependence among employees and work units are to create buffers, use integrators, and combine jobs.

- *Create buffers.* A buffer is any mechanism that loosens the coupling between two or more people or work units. This decoupling reduces the potential for conflict because the buffer reduces the effect of one party on the other. Building up inventory between people on an assembly line is a buffer, for example, because each employee is less dependent in the short term on the previous person along that line.[65]
- *Use integrators.* Integrators are employees who coordinate the activities of multiple work units toward the completion of a shared task or project.[66] Brand managers, for instance, are responsible for coordinating the efforts of the

research, production, advertising, and marketing departments regarding a specific product line. Integrators typically reduce the amount of direct interaction required among these diverse work units. Integrators rarely have direct authority over the departments they integrate, so they must rely on referent power and persuasion to manage conflict and accomplish the work.

- *Combine jobs.* Combining jobs is both a form of job enrichment and a way to reduce task interdependence. Consider a toaster assembly system where one person inserts the heating element, another adds the sides, and so on. By combining these tasks so that each person assembles an entire toaster, the employees now have a pooled rather than sequential form of task interdependence and the likelihood of dysfunctional conflict is reduced.

Managers as Third-Party Conflict Handlers[72]

54% of 1,027 employees surveyed who recently experienced conflict with a coworker took the dispute to their supervisor or human resources staff.

15% is the average percentage of management time that 2,200 U.S. chief financial officers say is "wasted resolving staff personality conflicts."

32% of 701 UK employees who've experienced serious conflict over the past year agree that their line manager helped to resolve the conflict (41% disagree).

32% of 701 UK employees who've experienced serious conflict over the past year agree that their line manager's involvement made the situation worse (45% disagree).

ATIC12/Getty Images

Increase Resources

Resource scarcity is a source of conflict, so increasing the amount of resources available would have the opposite effect.[67] This might not be a feasible strategy for minimizing dysfunctional conflict due to the costs involved. However, these costs need to be compared against the costs of dysfunctional conflict created by the resource scarcity.

Clarify Rules and Procedures

Conflicts that arise from ambiguous rules can be minimized by establishing clear rules and procedures. If two departments are fighting over the use of a new laboratory, a schedule might be established which allocates the lab exclusively to each team at certain times of the day or week.

THIRD-PARTY CONFLICT RESOLUTION

Most of this chapter has focused on people directly involved in a conflict, yet many disputes among employees and departments are resolved with the assistance of a manager, coworker, or other person outside the dispute. **Third-party conflict resolution** is any attempt by a relatively neutral person to help the parties resolve their differences.[68] There are three main third-party dispute resolution activities: arbitration, inquisition, and mediation. These interventions can be classified by their level of control over the process and control over the decision (see Exhibit 10.5).[69]

- *Arbitration.* Arbitrators have high control over the final decision, but low control over the process. Executives engage in this strategy by following previously agreed rules of due process, listening to arguments from the disputing employees, and making a binding decision. Arbitration is applied as the final stage of grievances by unionized employees in many countries, but it is also applied to nonunion conflicts in organizations with formal conflict resolution processes.
- *Inquisition.* Inquisitors control all discussion about the conflict. Like arbitration, the inquisition process has high decision control because it involves choosing the form of conflict resolution. However, it also has high process control because inquisitors choose which information to examine and how to examine it, and they generally decide how the conflict resolution process will be handled.[70]
- *Mediation.* Mediators have high control over the intervention process. In fact, their main purpose is to manage the process and context of interaction between the disputing parties. However, the conflicting parties make the final decision about how to resolve their differences. Thus, mediators have little or no control over the conflict resolution decision.[71]

Exhibit 10.5 Types of Third-Party Intervention

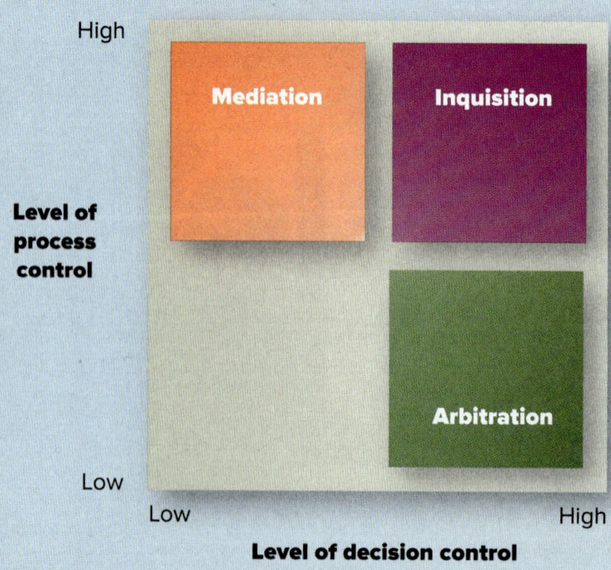

Choosing the Best Third-Party Intervention Strategy

Team leaders, executives, and coworkers regularly intervene in workplace disputes. Sometimes they mediate; at other times they serve as arbitrators. Occasionally, they begin with one approach then switch to another. Research suggests that managers usually adopt an inquisitional approach whereby they dominate the intervention process as well as make a binding decision.[73] They prefer the inquisition approach because it gives them control over the conflict process and outcome and tends to resolve disputes efficiently. This approach is also consistent with the traditional decision-oriented nature of managerial jobs.

Unfortunately, inquisition is usually the least effective third-party conflict resolution method in organizational settings.[74] One problem is that leaders who take an inquisitional role tend to collect limited information about the problem, so their imposed decision may produce an ineffective solution to the conflict. Another issue is that employees often view inquisitional procedures and outcomes as unfair because they have little control over this approach. In particular, the inquisitional approach potentially violates several practices required to support procedural justice (see Chapter 5).

Which third-party intervention is most appropriate in organizations? The answer partly depends on the situation, such as the type of dispute, the relationship between the manager and employees, and cultural values such as power distance.[75] Also, any third-party approach has more favorable results when it applies the procedural and interactional justice rules described in Chapter 5.[76] Generally, for everyday disagreements between two employees, the mediation approach is usually best because this gives workers more responsibility for resolving their own disputes. The third-party representative merely establishes an appropriate context for conflict resolution. Although not as efficient as other strategies, mediation potentially offers the highest level of employee satisfaction with the conflict process and outcomes.[77] When employees cannot resolve their differences through mediation, arbitration seems to work best because the predetermined rules of evidence and other processes create a higher sense of procedural justice.[78] Arbitration is also preferred where the organization's goals should take priority over individual goals.

LO10-6 Discuss activities in the negotiation preparation, process, and setting that improve negotiation effectiveness.

RESOLVING CONFLICT THROUGH NEGOTIATION

Think back through yesterday's events. Maybe you had to reach consensus with other students about what tasks to complete for a team project. Chances are that you shared transportation with someone, so you had to agree on the timing of the ride. Then perhaps there was the question of who made dinner. Each of these daily events created potential conflict and, most likely, they were resolved through negotiation.

third-party conflict resolution any attempt by a relatively neutral person to help conflicting parties resolve their differences

negotiation the process in which interdependent parties with divergent beliefs or goals attempt to reach agreement on issues that mutually affect them

Negotiation occurs when interdependent parties with divergent beliefs or goals attempt to reach agreement on issues that mutually affect them. In other words, people negotiate when they need to work together (mutual dependence), need to reach a consensus on decisions that affect them, and initially don't have identical preferences regarding those decisions.[79] This definition highlights the fact that negotiation skills are vital in organizations and everyday life because they help us achieve our goals, reduce conflict, and build collaborative relationships. In this section, we identify many of the strategies and conditions that effective negotiators consider in organizations and other settings.

Distributive versus Integrative Approaches to Negotiation

Earlier in this chapter, we noted that some conflict-handling styles adopt a win-lose orientation—the view that one party necessarily loses when the other party gains. In negotiations, this is called the *distributive* approach because the negotiator believes those involved in the conflict must distribute portions from a fixed pie. The opposing view is a win-win orientation, known as the *integrative* or *mutual gains* approach to negotiations. This approach exists when negotiators believe the resources at stake are expandable rather than fixed if the parties work creatively together to find a solution.

Distributive negotiation is most common when the parties have only one item to resolve, such as product price or starting salary. Integrative negotiation is more common when multiple issues are open for discussion. Negotiating multiple issues provides greater opportunity for mutual gains (integrative negotiation) because each issue or element in the negotiation has different value to each party. Consider the example of a buyer who wants to pay a low price for a large batch of manufactured items from a seller, doesn't need the entire order at the same time, but does need the payment schedule spread over time due to limited cash flow. The seller would like the buyer to pay a high price, but also values steady production to minimize overtime and layoffs. Through negotiation, the parties learn that spreading out the delivery schedule benefits both of them, and that the buyer would agree to a higher price if payments could be spread out with the delivery schedule.

Negotiators usually begin with a cautiously integrative approach to negotiations, but they switch to a distributive approach when they realize that their interests are perfectly opposing. Another factor is the individual's personality and past

Negotiating multiple issues provides greater opportunity for mutual gains (integrative negotiation) because each issue or element in the negotiation has different value to each party.
hjalmeida/123RF

experience. Some people have a natural tendency to be competitive and think more distributively whereas others more frequently believe that conflicts can result in mutual gains.

Preparing to Negotiate

Preparation is essential for successful negotiations.[80] You can't resolve disagreements unless you know what you want, why you want it, and what power you have to get it. You also need to anticipate the other party for each of these factors.

Develop Goals and Understand Needs Successful negotiators develop *goals* about what they want to achieve from the exchange. Equally important, they reflect on what *needs* they are trying to fulfill from those goals. The distinction between goals and needs is important because specific needs can be satisfied by different goals. For example, an employee might negotiate for a promotion (a goal), but what the employee really wants is more status and interesting work (underlying needs). Effective negotiators try to understand their own needs and avoid becoming locked into fixed goals. Focusing on needs enables negotiators to actively consider different proposals and opportunities, some of which could fulfill their needs better than their original negotiation goals. Preparation also includes anticipating the other party's goals and their underlying needs, based on available information before negotiation sessions begin.

Negotiators engage in a form of goal setting that identifies the three key positions shown in the bargaining zone model (see Exhibit 10.6).[81] The *initial offer point*—each party's opening offer to the other side—requires careful consideration

Exhibit 10.6 Bargaining Zone Model of Negotiations

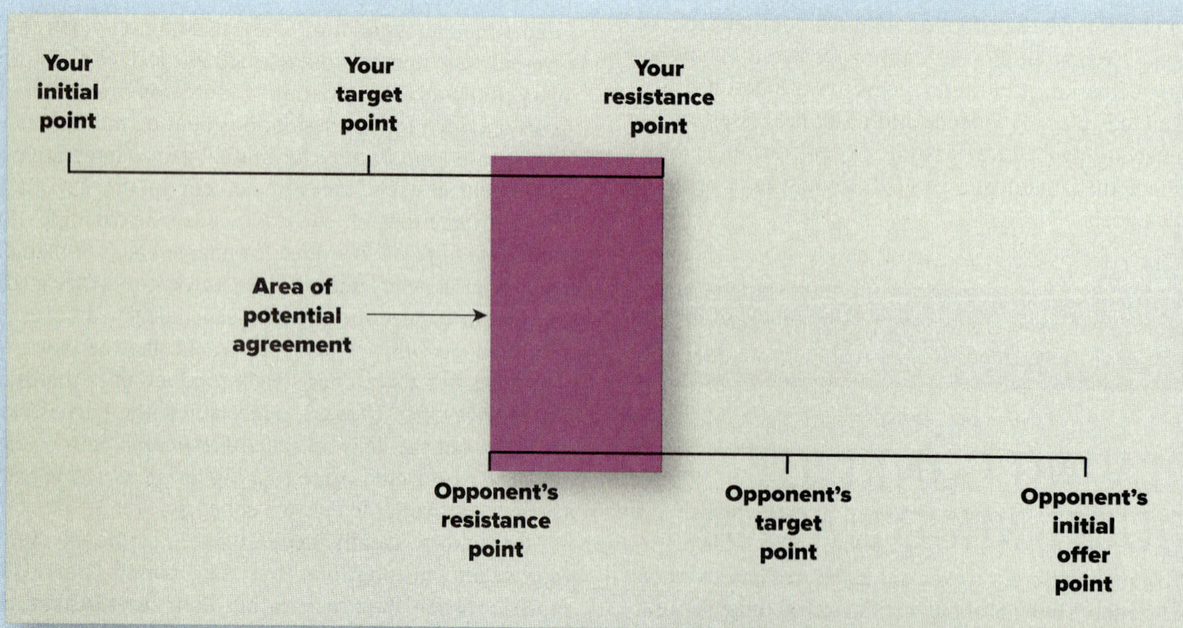

because it can influence the negotiation outcome. If the initial offer is set higher than the other party expected, it can anchor the negotiation at a higher point along the range by reframing the other party's perception of what is considered a "high" or "low" settlement (see Chapter 6).[82] In other words, a high initial offer point can potentially keep the outcome closer to your target point; it may even cause the other side to lower its resistance point. The challenge is to avoid an initial offer that is set so high that the other party breaks off negotiations or damages trust that cannot be rebuilt.

The *target point* is your realistic goal or expectation for a final agreement. This position must consider alternative strategies to achieve those objectives as well as test underlying assumptions about the situation.[83] Negotiators who set high, specific target points usually obtain better outcomes than those with low or vague target points. In this respect, a target point needs to possess the same characteristics as effective goal setting (see Chapter 5). Unfortunately, perceptual distortions cause inexperienced negotiators to form overly optimistic expectations, which can only be averted through careful reflection of the facts.[84]

The best alternative to a negotiated settlement (BATNA) estimates your power in the negotiation because it represents the estimated cost to you of walking away from the relationship.
Ryan McVay/Getty Images

best alternative to a negotiated settlement (BATNA) the best outcome you might achieve through some other course of action if you abandon the current negotiation

Know Your BATNA and Power

The *resistance point* in the bargaining zone model is the point beyond which you will make no further concessions and, instead, walk away from the negotiations. How do you determine the resistance point? The answer requires thoughtful comparison of how your goals and needs might be achieved through some other means. This comparison is called the **best alternative to a negotiated agreement (BATNA)**.[85] BATNA estimates your power in the negotiation because it represents the estimated cost to you of walking away from the relationship. If people outside the current negotiation are willing to negotiate with you and provide a reasonable agreement, then you have a high BATNA because it would cost you very little to walk away from the current negotiation.

Having more than one BATNA to a negotiation increases your power. A common problem, however, is that people tend to overestimate their BATNA.[86] They wrongly believe there are plenty of other ways to achieve their objective rather than through this specific negotiation. Wise advice here is to actively investigate multiple alternatives, not just assume they exist.

Your power in the negotiation depends on the sources and contingencies of power discussed in Chapter 9. For example, you have more power to negotiate a better starting salary and job conditions if you have valued skills and experience that few other people possess (high expertise with low substitutability), the employer knows that you possess these talents (high visibility), and the company will experience costs or lost opportunities fairly quickly if this position is not filled soon (high centrality). Not surprisingly, BATNA tends to be higher for those with more power, because they would be in demand in the marketplace.

The Negotiation Process

The negotiation process is a complex human interaction that draws on many topics in this book, including perceptions, attitudes, motivation, decision making, and communication. The most important specific negotiation practices are to gather information, manage concessions, manage time, and build the relationship.

Gather Information

Information is the cornerstone of effective negotiations.[87] It helps you to discover the other party's needs hidden behind their stated offers and negotiation goals. Some types of information reveal the other party's resistance point. Information can also potentially transform distributive negotiations into integrative negotiations by discovering multiple dimensions that weren't previously considered. For example, a simple negotiation over salary may reveal that the employee would prefer more performance-based pay and less fixed salary. Thus, mutual gains may be possible because there is now more than one variable to negotiate (amount and type of salary). Information is even more important in integrative negotiations because the parties require knowledge of each other's needs to discover solutions that maximize benefits for both sides.

Skilled negotiators spend most of the negotiation time listening closely to the other party and asking for details.[89] In

OB THEORY TO PRACTICE

Applying Mirroring to Gather Information in Negotiations[88]

Effective negotiators gather information about the opponent's underlying needs and expectations. They do this by listening more than talking, but also by encouraging the other party to reveal more information. "It's not just listening, but it's understanding how to get them to talk more," says former FBI hostage negotiator, Chris Voss.

One effective strategy used by the FBI is *mirroring*—repeating back as a question the last few words of what the other person said. If the opponent says "I need to receive your shipment within the next month," you would mirror by asking "Within the next month?" This usually motivates the other person to explain further. "By repeating back what people say, you trigger this mirroring instinct and your counterpart will inevitably elaborate on what was just said and sustain the process of connecting," Voss explains.

contrast, inexperienced negotiators mainly talk to the other side about their arguments and justifications. Skilled negotiators draw out more details by presenting open-ended questions, followed by probe questions ("Oh, why is that?"). Nonverbal communication is also observed as an associated source of information during this dialogue.

Skilled negotiators also test how well they understand the other side's facts and position by summarizing the information presented and by asking for clarification on specific points. They also communicate their inner thoughts and feelings, which encourages the other party to provide further information that will help dissolve concerns ("What you just said makes me hopeful, but I'm still concerned about the time frame expected.")

Manage Concessions A concession is one party's revision of a negotiating position so it comes closer to the other party's current position. Successful negotiators actually make fewer concessions and each concession is smaller than those of average negotiators, particularly in distributive negotiations where both parties know the bargaining zone.[90] Even so, the process of making concessions is important to all parties.

Concessions are a form of communication because they signal to the other party the relative importance of each issue being negotiated. They also symbolize each party's motivation to bargain in good faith. In fact, an important feature of negotiations is that each party reciprocates when the other side makes a concession.[91] Concessions need to be clearly labeled as such and should be accompanied by an expectation that the other party will reciprocate. They should also be offered in installments because people experience more positive emotions from a few smaller concessions than from one large concession.[92] Generally, the best strategy is to be moderately tough and give just enough concessions to communicate sincerity and motivation to resolve the conflict.

Manage Time Negotiators make more concessions as the deadline gets closer.[93] This can be a liability if you are under time pressure, or it can be an advantage if the other party alone is under time pressure. Negotiators with more power in the relationship sometimes apply time pressure through an "exploding offer" whereby they give the opponent a very short time to accept their offer.[94] These time-limited offers are frequently found in consumer sales ("on sale today only!") and in some job offers. They produce time pressure, which can motivate the other party to accept the offer and forfeit the opportunity to explore their BATNA. Another time factor is that the more time people have invested in the negotiation, the more committed they become to ensuring an agreement is reached. This commitment increases the tendency to make unwarranted concessions so that the negotiations do not fail.

Build the Relationship Building and maintaining trust is important in all negotiations.[95] In purely distributive negotiation situations, trust keeps the parties focused on the issue rather than personalities, motivates them to return to the bargaining table when negotiations stall, and encourages the parties to engage in future negotiations. Trust is also critical in integrative negotiations because it motivates the parties to share information and actively search for mutual gains.

Effective negotiators build trust by discovering common backgrounds and interests with the other party, such as places they have lived and favorite sports teams. In addition, trust tends to be higher when team members closely match the backgrounds of the other party. First impressions are also important. People form beliefs and emotions in a fraction of a second, so negotiators need to be sensitive to their nonverbal

Negotiators with more power in the relationship sometimes apply time pressure through an "exploding offer," whereby they give the opponent a very short time in which to accept their offer.
gstockstudio/123RF

> People form beliefs and emotions in a fraction of a second, so negotiators need to be sensitive to their nonverbal cues, appearance, and initial statements.

cues, appearance, and initial statements. Another way to build trust is by keeping promises in the negotiation and identifying shared goals and values with the other party. Trustworthiness also increases by developing a shared understanding of the negotiation process, including its norms and expectations about speed and timing.[96]

Finally, relationship building demands emotional intelligence.[97] This includes managing the emotions each person displays to the other party, particularly avoiding an image of superiority, aggressiveness, or insensitivity. Emotional intelligence also involves managing the other party's emotions. Well-placed flattery, humor, and other methods keep everyone in a good mood and diffuse dysfunctional tension.[98]

The Negotiation Setting

The effectiveness of negotiating depends to some extent on the environment in which the negotiations occur. Location is an important situational characteristic. It is easier to negotiate on your own turf because you are familiar with the negotiating environment and are able to maintain comfortable routines.[99] Also, there is no need to cope with travel-related stress or depend on others for resources during the negotiation. Due to these strategic advantages of home turf, many negotiators agree to neutral territory.

The physical distance between the parties and formality of the setting can influence how they perceive each other and the disputed issues. Seating arrangements have a similar effect. People who sit face-to-face are more likely to develop a win-lose orientation toward the conflict situation.

Most negotiators have audiences—anyone with a vested interest in the negotiation outcomes, such as executives, other team members, or the general public. Negotiators tend to act differently when their audience observes the negotiation or has detailed information about the process, compared to situations in which the audience sees only the end results.[100] When the audience has direct surveillance over the proceedings, negotiators tend to be more competitive, less willing to make concessions, and more likely to engage in assertive tactics against the other party. This "hard-line" behavior shows the audience that the negotiator is working for their interests. With their audience watching, negotiators also have more interest in saving face.

Study Checklist

Connect® is available for *M Organizational Behavior*. Additional resources include:

✓ Exercises:

- **Case Analysis:** Apply concepts within the context of a real-world situation.
- **Click and Drag:** Helps make the connection between theory and application through matching, ranking, or grouping activities.
- **Video Case:** See management in action through interactive videos.
- **Self-Assessment:** Designed to promote student self-awareness and reflection, these research-based surveys contain detailed feedback for students.
- **Application-Based Activities:** These highly interactive, application- and analysis-based exercises allow students to take on specific roles to complete management-related tasks within a real-world context.

✓ **SmartBook 2.0**™—Smartbook 2.0 is an adaptive learning solution that provides personalized learning to individual student needs, continually adapts to pinpoint knowledge gaps and focuses learning on concepts requiring additional study. It fosters more productive learning, takes the guesswork out of what to study, and helps students better prepare for class.

©Natthawat Jamnapa/123RF

Notes

1. P. Tomlin, " Hot Desk, Cold Shoulder," The Guardian, November 7, 2005; L. Green, "How Open Offices Are Killing Us," PsyPost, August 20, 2016; R. L. Morrison and K. A. Macky, "The Demands and Resources Arising from Shared Office Spaces," *Applied Ergonomics* 60 (April 2017): 103–15.
2. J.A. Wall and R.R. Callister, "Conflict and Its Management," *Journal of Management* 21 (1995): 515–58; M.A. Rahim, *Managing Conflict in Organizations*, 4th ed. (New Brunswick, NJ: Transaction, 2011), 15–17; D. Tjosvold, A.S.H. Wong, and N.Y.F. Chen, "Constructively Managing Conflicts in Organizations," *Annual Review of Organizational Psychology and Organizational Behavior* 1, no. 1 (2014): 545–68.

3. J.A. Litterer, "Conflict in Organization: A Re-Examination," *Academy of Management Journal* 9, no. 3 (September 1966): 178–86; M.A. Rahim, *Managing Conflict in Organizations,* 4th ed. (New Brunswick, NJ: Transaction, 2011), Chap. 1.

4. For example, see L. Urwick, *The Elements of Administration*, 2nd ed. (London: Pitman, 1947); H.L. Sheppard and S. Chase, "The Social and Historical Philosophy of Elton Mayo [with Comment]," *The Antioch Review* 10, no. 3 (1950): 396–406; C. Argyris, "The Individual and Organization: Some Problems of Mutual Adjustment," *Administrative Science Quarterly* 2, no. 1 (1957): 1–24; K.E. Boulding, "Organization and Conflict," *Conflict Resolution* 1, no. 2 (1957): 122–34; R.R. Blake, H.A. Shepard, and J.S. Mouton, *Managing Intergroup Conflict in Industry* (Houston: Gulf, 1964).

5. C.K.W. De Dreu and L.R. Weingart, "A Contingency Theory of Task Conflict and Performance in Groups and Organizational Teams," in *International Handbook of Organizational Teamwork and Cooperative Working*, ed. M.A. West, D. Tjosvold, and K.G. Smith (Chichester, UK: Wiley, 2003), 151–66; S. Rispens, "Benefits and Detrimental Effects of Conflict," in *Handbook of Conflict Management Research*, ed. O.B. Ayoko, N.M. Ashkanasy, and K.A. Jehn (Cheltenham, UK: Edward Elgar, 2014), 19–32; D. De Clercq and I. Belausteguigoitia, "Overcoming the Dark Side of Task Conflict: Buffering Roles of Transformational Leadership, Tenacity, and Passion for Work," *European Management Journal* 35, no. 1 (February 2017): 78–90, https://doi.org/10.1016/j.emj.2016.06.008.

6. F.R.C. de Wit, L.L. Greer, and K.A. Jehn, "The Paradox of Intragroup Conflict: A Meta-Analysis," *Journal of Applied Psychology* 97, no. 2 (2012): 360–90; L.L. Meier et al., "Relationship and Task Conflict at Work: Interactive Short-Term Effects on Angry Mood and Somatic Complaints," *Journal of Occupational Health Psychology* 18, no. 2 (2013): 144–56; N.L. Jimmieson, M.K. Tucker, and J.L. Campbell, "Task Conflict Leads to Relationship Conflict When Employees Are Low in Trait Self-Control: Implications for Employee Strain," *Personality and Individual Differences* 113 (July 2017): 209–18, https://doi.org/10.1016/j.paid.2017.03.035.

7. J. Meng, J. Fulk, and Y.C. Yuan, "The Roles and Interplay of Intragroup Conflict and Team Emotion Management on Information Seeking Behaviors in Team Contexts," *Communication Research* 42, no. 5 (July 2015): 675–700, https://doi.org/10.1177/0093650213476294; M.-H. Tsai and C. Bendersky, "The Pursuit of Information Sharing: Expressing Task Conflicts as Debates vs. Disagreements Increases Perceived Receptivity to Dissenting Opinions in Groups," *Organization Science* 27, no. 1 (December 2015): 141–56, https://doi.org/10.1287/orsc.2015.1025.

8. M.P. Follett, "Constructive Conflict," in *Dynamic Administration: The Collected Papers of Mary Parker Follett*, ed. H.C. Metcalf and L. Urwick (Bath, UK: Management Publications Trust, 1941), 30–49.

9. Although the 1970s marked a point when the benefits of conflict became widely acknowledged, a few earlier writers had also expressed this view. See H. Assael, "Constructive Role of Interorganizational Conflict," *Administrative Science Quarterly* 14, no. 4 (1969): 573–82; L.A. Coser, *The Functions of Social Conflict* (New York: Free Press, 1956); J.A. Litterer, "Conflict in Organization: A Re-Examination," *Academy of Management Journal* 9 (1966): 178–86.

10. J. Dewey, *Human Nature and Conduct: An Introduction to Social Psychology* (New York: Holt, 1922), 300.

11. P.J. Carnevale, "Creativity in the Outcomes of Conflict," in *The Handbook of Conflict Resolution: Theory and Practice*, ed. M. Deutsch, P.T. Coleman, and E.C. Marcus (San Francisco: Jossey-Bass, 2006), 414–35; T.A. O'Neill, N.J. Allen, and S.E. Hastings, "Examining the 'Pros' and 'Cons' of Team Conflict: A Team-Level Meta-Analysis of Task, Relationship, and Process Conflict," *Human Performance* 26, no. 3 (July 2013): 236–60, https://doi.org/10.1080/08959285.2013.795573; X.-Y. Xie, W.-L. Wang, and K. Luan, "It Is Not What We Have, but How We Use It: Reexploring the Relationship between Task Conflict and Team Innovation from the Resource-Based View," *Group Processes & Intergroup Relations* 17, no. 2 (March 2014): 240–51, https://doi.org/10.1177/1368430213502559; P. Petrou, A.B. Bakker, and K. Bezemer, "Creativity under Task Conflict: The Role of Proactively Increasing Job Resources," *Journal of Occupational and Organizational Psychology* (2018), https://doi.org/10.1111/joop.12250.

12. K.M. Eisenhardt, J.L. Kahwajy, and L.J. Bourgeois III, "Conflict and Strategic Choice: How Top Management Teams Disagree," *California Management Review* 39 (1997): 42–62; T. Greitemeyer et al., "Information Sampling and Group Decision Making: The Effects of an Advocacy Decision Procedure and Task Experience," *Journal of Experimental Psychology: Applied* 12, no. 1 (2006): 31–42; U. Klocke, "How to Improve Decision Making in Small Groups: Effects of Dissent and Training Interventions," *Small Group Research* 38, no. 3 (2007): 437–68.

13. C.K.W. De Dreu, "When Too Little or Too Much Hurts: Evidence for a Curvilinear Relationship Between Task Conflict and Innovation in Teams," *Journal of Management* 32, no. 1 (2006): 83–107; J.L. Farh, C. Lee, and C.I.C. Farh, "Task Conflict and Team Creativity: A Question of How Much and When," *Journal of Applied Psychology* 95, no. 6 (2010): 1173–80; G. Todorova, J.B. Bear, and L.R. Weingart, "Can Conflict Be Energizing? A Study of Task Conflict, Positive Emotions, and Job Satisfaction," *Journal of Applied Psychology* 99, no. 3 (2014): 451–67; L.R. Weingart et al., "The Directness and Oppositional Intensity of Conflict Expression," *Academy of Management Review* 40, no. 2 (2015): 235–62, https://doi.org/10.5465/amr.2013.0124.

14. This book adopts the long-held perspective (Fisher & Ury, Tjosvold, etc.) that task and relationship conflict refer to how the conflict is framed (the focus of attention). This "framing" perspective contrasts with some studies that define task, relationship, and two other types (process and status conflict) in terms of what the conflict is inherently about—that is, the conflict content or topic. This latter view is problematic because content- or topic-based typologies often expand into a long list of categories that undermines their usefulness for theory and practice. Furthermore, the content-based view inappropriately assumes that task conflict and relationship conflict cannot co-exist or be perceived in the same conflict episode. The "framing" perspective, which this book adopts, recognizes that almost all workplace conflicts can be viewed as task as well as relationship conflict. For example, "personality clashes" invariably manifest themselves in work-related tasks—how a task should it be performed, how employees should behave, etc. The framing perspective distinguishes whether the parties focus on factual/logical details of the stated positions (task conflict) or on the characteristics (personality, abilities) of people who support those positions (relationship conflict). It is a point of view and approach, not a typology of the event itself. Ultimately, it is how conflicts are framed—not whether the alleged topic is the task, process, status, or relationship—that affects the key outcomes in conflict episodes. For literature on the meaning of conflict types, see R.A. Baron, "Positive Effects of Conflict: A Cognitive Perspective," *Employee Responsibilities and Rights Journal* 4, no. 1 (March 1991): 25–36; A.C. Amason, "Distinguishing the Effects of Functional and Dysfunctional Conflict on Strategic Decision Making: Resolving a Paradox for Top Management Teams," *Academy of Management Journal* 39, no. 1 (February 1996): 123–48; R. Fisher and W. Ury, *Getting to Yes: Negotiating an Agreement without Giving In* (New York: Random House, 2012); K.A. Jehn, "Types of Conflict: The History and Future of Conflict Definitions and Typologies," in *Handbook of Conflict Management Research*, ed. O.B. Ayoko, N.M. Ashkanasy, and K.A. Jehn (Cheltenham, UK: Edward Elgar, 2014), 3–18; D. Tjosvold, A.S.H. Wong, and N.Y.F. Chen, "Constructively Managing Conflicts in Organizations," *Annual Review of Organizational Psychology and Organizational Behavior* 1 (2014): 545–68; T.A. O'Neill et al., "The Structure and Function of Team Conflict State Profiles," *Journal of Management* 44, no. 2

(February 2018): 811–36. One review recognizes this distinction between conflict type and how conflict is viewed (focus) or how it is expressed. See L.R. Weingart et al., "The Directness and Oppositional Intensity of Conflict Expression," *Academy of Management Review* 40, no. 2 (2015): 235–62.

15. F.R.C. de Wit, L.L. Greer, and K.A. Jehn, "The Paradox of Intragroup Conflict: A Meta-Analysis," *Journal of Applied Psychology* 97, no. 2 (2012): 360–90. Earlier meta-analyses reported either nonsignificant or somewhat negative correlations between task conflict and team outcomes. However, the recent meta-analysis and other writers point to several methodological problems with conflict research that explain the mixed findings. For a review, see M.L. Loughry and A.C. Amason, "Why Won't Task Conflict Cooperate? Deciphering Stubborn Results," *International Journal of Conflict Management* 25, no. 4 (2014): 333–58.

16. J.M. Leon-Perez et al., "The Relationship between Interpersonal Conflict and Workplace Bullying," *Journal of Managerial Psychology* 30, no. 3 (April 2015): 250–63, https://doi.org/10.1108/JMP-01-2013-0034; K.A. Graham et al., "Too Many Cooks in the Kitchen: The Effects of Dominance Incompatibility on Relationship Conflict and Subsequent Abusive Supervision," *The Leadership Quarterly*, December 2018, https://doi.org/10.1016/j.leaqua.2018.12.003.

17. R.S. Lau and A.T. Cobb, "Understanding the Connections between Relationship Conflict and Performance: The Intervening Roles of Trust and Exchange," *Journal of Organizational Behavior* 31, no. 6 (2010): 898–917.

18. C.K.W. De Dreu and L.R. Weingart, "Task versus Relationship Conflict, Team Performance, and Team Member Satisfaction: A Meta-Analysis," *Journal of Applied Psychology* 88 (2003): 587–604; A.C. Mooney, P.J. Holahan, and A.C. Amason, "Don't Take It Personally: Exploring Cognitive Conflict as a Mediator of Affective Conflict," *Journal of Management Studies* 44, no. 5 (2007): 733–58; K. Choi and B. Cho, "Competing Hypotheses Analyses of the Associations between Group Task Conflict and Group Relationship Conflict," *Journal of Organizational Behavior* 32, no. 8 (2011): 1106–26.

19. J.X. Yang and K.W. Mossholder, "Decoupling Task and Relationship Conflict: The Role of Intergroup Emotional Processing," *Journal of Organizational Behavior* 25 (2004): 589–605; B.H. Bradley et al., "Ready to Rumble: How Team Personality Composition and Task Conflict Interact to Improve Performance," *Journal of Applied Psychology* 98, no. 2 (2013): 385–92; B.H. Bradley et al., "Reaping the Benefits of Task Conflict in Teams: The Critical Role of Team Psychological Safety Climate," *Journal of Applied Psychology* 97, no. 1 (2012): 151–58.

20. P.L. Curseu, S. Boros, and L.A.G. Oerlemans, "Task and Relationship Conflict in Short-Term and Long-Term Groups: The Critical Role of Emotion Regulation," *International Journal of Conflict Management* 23, no. 1 (2012): 97–107; A. Schlaerth, N. Ensari, and J. Christian, "A Meta-Analytical Review of the Relationship between Emotional Intelligence and Leaders' Constructive Conflict Management," *Group Processes & Intergroup Relations* 16, no. 1 (2013): 126–36; N.L. Jimmieson, M.K. Tucker, and J.L. Campbell, "Task Conflict Leads to Relationship Conflict When Employees Are Low in Trait Self-Control: Implications for Employee Strain," *Personality and Individual Differences* 113 (July 2017): 209–18, https://doi.org/10.1016/j.paid.2017.03.035; H.R. Flores, X. Jiang, and C.C. Manz, "Intra-Team Conflict: The Moderating Effect of Emotional Self-Leadership," *International Journal of Conflict Management* 29, no. 3 (2018): 424–44, https://doi.org/10.1108/IJCMA-07-2017-0065.

21. F.R.C. de Wit, L.L. Greer, and K.A. Jehn, "The Paradox of Intragroup Conflict: A Meta-Analysis," *Journal of Applied Psychology* 97, no. 2 (March 2012): 360–90; S.E. Humphrey et al., "Team Conflict Dynamics: Implications of a Dyadic View of Conflict for Team Performance," *Organizational Behavior and Human Decision Processes* 142 (September 2017): 58–70, https://doi.org/10.1016/j.obhdp.2017.08.002; T.A. O'Neill and M.J.W. McLarnon, "Optimizing Team Conflict Dynamics for High Performance Teamwork," *Human Resource Management Review* 28, no. 4 (December 2018): 378–94, https://doi.org/10.1016/j.hrmr.2017.06.002.

22. A.C. Edmondson and Z. Lei, "Psychological Safety: The History, Renaissance, and Future of an Interpersonal Construct," *Annual Review of Organizational Psychology and Organizational Behavior* 1, no. 1 (2014): 23–43, https://doi.org/10.1146/annurev-orgpsych-031413-091305; D. Tjosvold, A.S.H. Wong, and N.Y.F. Chen, "Constructively Managing Conflicts in Organizations," *Annual Review of Organizational Psychology and Organizational Behavior* 1, no. 1 (2014): 545–68; A. Newman, R. Donohue, and N. Eva, "Psychological Safety: A Systematic Review of the Literature," *Human Resource Management Review* 27, no. 3 (September 2017): 521–35, https://doi.org/10.1016/j.hrmr.2017.01.001.

23. L. Pondy, "Organizational Conflict: Concepts and Models," *Administrative Science Quarterly* 2 (1967): 296–320; K.W. Thomas, "Conflict and Negotiation Processes in Organizations," in *Handbook of Industrial and Organizational Psychology*, ed. M.D. Dunnette and L.M. Hough (Palo Alto, CA: Consulting Psychologists Press, 1992), 651–718.

24. E. Halperin, "Emotion, Emotion Regulation, and Conflict Resolution," *Emotion Review* 6, no. 1 (January 1, 2014): 68–76, https://doi.org/10.1177/1754073913491844; G. Todorova, J.B. Bear, and L.R. Weingart, "Can Conflict Be Energizing? A Study of Task Conflict, Positive Emotions, and Job Satisfaction," *Journal of Applied Psychology* 99, no. 3 (2014): 451–67, https://doi.org/10.1037/a0035134; S. Čehajić-Clancy et al., "Social-Psychological Interventions for Intergroup Reconciliation: An Emotion Regulation Perspective," *Psychological Inquiry* 27, no. 2 (2016): 73–88, https://doi.org/10.1080/1047840X.2016.1153945; M. Caldara et al., "A Study of the Triggers of Conflict and Emotional Reactions," *Games* 8, no. 2 (2017): 21, https://doi.org/10.3390/g8020021; G.A. van Kleef and S. Côté, "Emotional Dynamics in Conflict and Negotiation: Individual, Dyadic, and Group Processes," *Annual Review of Organizational Psychology and Organizational Behavior* 5, no. 1 (2018): 437–64, https://doi.org/10.1146/annurev-orgpsych-032117-104714.

25. E. Halperin, "Emotion, Emotion Regulation, and Conflict Resolution," *Emotion Review* 6, no. 1 (2014): 68–76, https://doi.org/10.1177/1754073913491844; D. Motro, T. Kugler, and T. Connolly, "Back to the Basics: How Feelings of Anger Affect Cooperation," *International Journal of Conflict Management* 27, no. 4 (2016): 523–46, https://doi.org/10.1108/IJCMA-10-2015-0068; J. Folger, M.S. Poole, and R.K. Stutman, *Working through Conflict: Strategies for Relationships, Groups, and Organizations*, 7th ed. (Oxon, UK: Routledge, 2016), Chap. 2.

26. G.E. Martin and T.J. Bergman, "The Dynamics of Behavioral Response to Conflict in the Workplace," *Journal of Occupational & Organizational Psychology* 69 (1996): 377–87; K.A. Kennedy and E. Pronin, "When Disagreement Gets Ugly: Perceptions of Bias and the Escalation of Conflict," *Personality and Social Psychology Bulletin* 34, no. 6 (2008): 833–48, https://doi.org/10.1177/0146167208315158; L.F. Smyth, "Escalation and Mindfulness," *Negotiation Journal* 28, no. 1 (2012): 45–72, https://doi.org/10.1111/j.1571-9979.2011.00325.x.

27. R.E. Walton and J.M. Dutton, "The Management of Conflict: A Model and Review," *Administrative Science Quarterly* 14 (1969): 73–84; S.M. Schmidt and T.A. Kochan, "Conflict: Toward Conceptual Clarity," *Administrative Science Quarterly* 17, no. 3 (1972): 359–70.

28. For example, see K.A. Jehn, C. Chadwick, and S.M.B. Thatcher, "To Agree or Not to Agree: The Effects of Value Congruence, Individual Demographic Dissimilarity, and Conflict on Workgroup Outcomes," *International Journal of Conflict Management* 8, no. 4 (1997): 287–305; A.N. Garman, D.C. Leach, and N. Spector,

"Worldviews in Collision: Conflict and Collaboration across Professional Lines," *Journal of Organizational Behavior* 27, no. 7 (2006): 829–49, https://doi.org/10.1002/job.394; L.L. Greer et al., "Why and When Hierarchy Impacts Team Effectiveness: A Meta-Analytic Integration," *Journal of Applied Psychology* 103, no. 6 (2018): 591–613, https://doi.org/10.1037/apl0000291; X. "Paul" Zhang et al., "One World, Two Realities: Perception Differences between Software Developers and Testers," *Journal of Computer Information Systems* 58, no. 4 (2018): 385–94, https://doi.org/10.1080/08874417.2017.1289355.

29. D.R. Hillman, "Understanding Multigenerational Work-Value Conflict Resolution," *Journal of Workplace Behavioral Health* 29, no. 3 (2014): 240–57; S. Lyons and L. Kuron, "Generational Differences in the Workplace: A Review of the Evidence and Directions for Future Research," *Journal of Organizational Behavior* 35, no. S1 (2014): S139–57; M.J. Urick et al., "Understanding and Managing Intergenerational Conflict: An Examination of Influences and Strategies," *Work, Aging and Retirement* 3, no. 2 (2017): 166–85, https://doi.org/10.1093/workar/waw009.

30. R.M. Sarala, "The Impact of Cultural Differences and Acculturation Factors on Post-Acquisition Conflict," *Scandinavian Journal of Management* 26, no. 1 (2010): 38–56; J. Joseph, "Managing Change after the Merger: The Value of Pre-Merger Ingroup Identities," *Journal of Organizational Change Management* 27, no. 3 (2014): 430–48, https://doi.org/10.1108/JOCM-10-2013-0184; H.E. Yildiz, "'Us vs. Them' or 'Us over Them'? On the Roles of Similarity and Status in M&As," *International Business Review* 25, no. 1, Part A (2016): 51-65, https://doi.org/10.1016/j.ibusrev.2015.05.002. Differentiation conflict in mergers is similar to differentiation conflict between people and work units across national cultures. See, for example: J. Brett, "Intercultural Challenges in Managing Workplace Conflict–A Call for Research," *Cross Cultural & Strategic Management* 25, no. 1 (February 2018): 32–52, https://doi.org/10.1108/CCSM-11-2016-0190.

31. P.C. Earley and G.B. Northcraft, "Goal Setting, Resource Interdependence, and Conflict Management," in *Managing Conflict: An Interdisciplinary Approach*, ed. M.A. Rahim (New York: Praeger, 1989), 161–70; K. Jehn, "A Multimethod Examination of the Benefits and Detriments of Intragroup Conflict," *Administrative Science Quarterly* 40 (1995): 245–82; P.T. Coleman et al., "Navigating Conflict and Power at Work: The Effects of Power and Interdependence Asymmetries on Conflict in Organizations," *Journal of Applied Social Psychology* 43, no. 10 (2013): 1963–83.

32. J.G. March and H.A. Simon, *Organizations* (New York: John Wiley & Sons, 1958), 126.

33. Some scholars have noted that ambiguous rules may be the rule violator's opportunistic interpretation of rules that others believe are clear. For a discussion of the conditions under which conflict results from ambiguous or inconsistently enforced rules, see A.W. Martin et al., "Against the Rules: Synthesizing Types and Processes of Bureaucratic Rule-Breaking," *Academy of Management Review* 38, no. 4 (2013): 550–74, https://doi.org/10.5465/amr.2011.0223.

34. L.R. Weingart et al., "The Directness and Oppositional Intensity of Conflict Expression," *Academy of Management Review* 40, no. 2 (2015): 235–62, https://doi.org/10.5465/amr.2013.0124; D. Ames, A. Lee, and A. Wazlawek, "Interpersonal Assertiveness: Inside the Balancing Act," *Social and Personality Psychology Compass* 11, no. 6 (2017): e12317, https://doi.org/10.1111/spc3.12317; C. Samba, D. Van Knippenberg, and C.C. Miller, "The Impact of Strategic Dissent on Organizational Outcomes: A Meta-Analytic Integration," *Strategic Management Journal* 39, no. 2 (2018): 379–402, https://doi.org/10.1002/smj.2710.

35. M. Hewstone, M. Rubin, and H. Willis, "Intergroup Bias," *Annual Review of Psychology* 53 (2002): 575–604; T. Yamagishi and N. Mifune, "Social Exchange and Solidarity: In-Group Love or Out-Group Hate?" *Evolution and Human Behavior* **30**, no. 4 (2009): 229–37; N. Halevy, O. Weisel, and G. Bornstein, "'In-Group Love' and 'Out-Group Hate' in Repeated Interaction between Groups," *Journal of Behavioral Decision Making* 25, no. 2 (2012): 188–95; O. Weisel and R. Böhm, "'Ingroup Love' and 'Outgroup Hate' in Intergroup Conflict between Natural Groups," *Journal of Experimental Social Psychology* 60 (September 2015): 110–20, https://doi.org/10.1016/j.jesp.2015.04.008.

36. "The State of Work," 2018-2019 U.S. Edition (Lehi, UT: Workfront, August 29, 2018); D. Wheatley and J. Gifford, "UK Working Lives: The CIPD Job Quality Index" (London: Chartered Institute of Personnel and Development (CIPD), July 2019); "Co-Worker Conflicts," *Nulab* (blog), October 1, 2019, https://nulab.com/blog/collaboration/co-worker-conflicts/; "2019 Public Service Employee Survey Results for the Public Service" (Ottawa: Government of Canada, Treasury Board of Canada Secretariat, January 15, 2020); R. Suff, "Managing Conflict in the Modern Workplace" (London: Chartered Institute of Personnel and Development, January 2020).

37. M.P. Follett, "Constructive Conflict," in *Dynamic Administration: The Collected Papers of Mary Parker Follett,* ed. H.C. Metcalf and L. Urwick (Bath, UK: Management Publications Trust, 1941), 30–49; R.R. Blake, H.A. Shepard, and J.S. Mouton, *Managing Intergroup Conflict in Industry* (Houston: Gulf Publishing, 1964); T. Ruble and K. Thomas, "Support for a Two-Dimensional Model of Conflict Behavior," *Organizational Behavior and Human Performance* 16 (1976): 143–55; C.K.W. De Dreu et al., "A Theory-Based Measure of Conflict Management Strategies in the Workplace," *Journal of Organizational Behavior* 22 (2001): 645–68; D. Tjosvold, A.S.H. Wong, and N.Y.F. Chen, "Constructively Managing Conflicts in Organizations," *Annual Review of Organizational Psychology and Organizational Behavior* 1, no. 1 (2014): 545–68; K.E. Johnson and J.A. Hall, "Validity of Self-Reported Conflict Handling Preferences and the Role of Self-Enhancement," *International Journal of Conflict Management* 29, no. 4 (2018): 543–63, https://doi.org/10.1108/IJCMA-03-2018-0039.

38. D. Ames, A. Lee, and A. Wazlawek, "Interpersonal Assertiveness: Inside the Balancing Act," *Social and Personality Psychology Compass* 11, no. 6 (2017): e12317, https://doi.org/10.1111/spc3.12317.

39. Q. Wang, E.L. Fink, and D.A. Cai, "The Effect of Conflict Goals on Avoidance Strategies: What Does Not Communicating Communicate?" *Human Communication Research* 38, no. 2 (2012): 222–52.

40. Several studies have identified personal characteristics that predict a person's preferred conflict style. For example, see P.J. Moberg, "Linking Conflict Strategy to the Five-Factor Model: Theoretical and Empirical Foundations," *International Journal of Conflict Management* 12, no. 1 (2001): 47–68; J.E. Barbuto Jr., K.A. Phipps, and Y. Xu, "Testing Relationships between Personality, Conflict Styles and Effectiveness," *International Journal of Conflict Management* 21, no. 4 (2010): 434–47; M. Gunkel, C. Schlaegel, and V. Taras, "Cultural Values, Emotional Intelligence, and Conflict Handling Styles: A Global Study," *Journal of World Business* 51, no. 4 (2016): 568–85, https://doi.org/10.1016/j.jwb.2016.02.001; L. Parmer, "Relationships between Philosophical Values and Conflict Management Styles," *International Journal of Conflict Management* 29, no. 2 (2017): 236–52, https://doi.org/10.1108/IJCMA-11-2016-0091.

41. D.W. Johnson et al., "Effects of Cooperative, Competitive, and Individualistic Goal Structures on Achievement: A Meta-Analysis," *Psychological Bulletin* 89 (1981): 47–62; G.A. Callanan, C.D. Benzing, and D.F. Perri, "Choice of Conflict-Handling Strategy: A Matter of Context," *Journal of Psychology* 140, no. 3 (2006): 269–88; T.J. Hargrave and A.H. Van de Ven, "Integrating Dialectical and Paradox Perspectives on Managing Contradictions in Organizations," *Organization Studies* 38, no. 3-4 (April 2017): 319–39, https://doi.org/10.1177/0170840616640843.

42. X.M. Song, J. Xile, and B. Dyer, "Antecedents and Consequences of Marketing Managers' Conflict-Handling Behaviors," *Journal of Marketing* 64 (2000): 50–66; L.A. DeChurch, K.L. Hamilton, and C. Haas, "Effects of Conflict Management Strategies on Perceptions of Intragroup Conflict," *Group Dynamics* 11, no. 1

(2007): 66–78; D.G. Oore, M.P. Leiter, and D.E. LeBlanc, "Individual and Organizational Factors Promoting Successful Responses to Workplace Conflict," *Canadian Psychology* 56, no. 3 (2015): 301–10.

43. G.A. Chung-Yan and C. Moeller, "The Psychosocial Costs of Conflict Management Styles," *International Journal of Conflict Management* 21, no. 4 (2010): 382–99.

44. Several variations of this quotation have appeared over the past century. The field of marketing has an even older version of this quotation—Win an argument and lose a sale (or customer). Marketing textbooks and trade publications cited it in the 1890s. The "friends" version of this quotation has occasionally been attributed to Edward Wood, 1st Earl of Halifax, but we could not verify this. In any event, the earliest marketing/sales version appeared before Lord Halifax was an adult. Dale Carnegie definitely popularized the idea behind the notion that winning arguments loses friends. The entire first chapter of Part 3 in his best-selling book *How to Win Friends and Influence People* (1936) is devoted to this topic: "You Can't Win an Argument." The version of the quotation cited here is published in E. Knowles, *Little Oxford Dictionary of Proverbs* (Oxford, UK: Oxford University Press, 2009), 21.

45. J.B. Bear, L.R. Weingart, and G. Todorova, "Gender and the Emotional Experience of Relationship Conflict: The Differential Effectiveness of Avoidant Conflict Management," *Negotiation and Conflict Management Research* 7, no. 4 (2014): 213–31; A. Chunyan Peng and D. Tjosvold, "Social Face Concerns and Conflict Avoidance of Chinese Employees with Their Western or Chinese Managers," *Human Relations* 64, no. 8 (2011): 1031–50, https://doi.org/10.1177/0018726711400927; I. Yang, "Perceived Conflict Avoidance by Managers and Its Consequences on Subordinates' Attitudes," *Business Ethics: A European Review* 24, no. 3 (2015): 282–96, https://doi.org/10.1111/beer.12083; Z.-X. Zhang and X. Wei, "Superficial Harmony and Conflict Avoidance Resulting from Negative Anticipation in the Workplace," *Management and Organization Review* 13, no. 4 (2017): 795–820, https://doi.org/10.1017/mor.2017.48.

46. A. Ergeneli, S.M. Camgoz, and P.B. Karapinar, "The Relationship between Self-Efficacy and Conflict-Handling Styles in Terms of Relative Authority Positions of the Two Parties," *Social Behavior & Personality: An International Journal* 38, no. 1 (2010): 13–28.

47. K. Leung et al., "Harmony and Conflict: A Cross-Cultural Investigation in China and Australia," *Journal of Cross-Cultural Psychology* 42, no. 5 (2011): 795–816, https://doi.org/10.1177/0022022110363474; W.-F. Lin et al., "We Can Make It Better: 'We' Moderates the Relationship between a Compromising Style in Interpersonal Conflict and Well-Being," *Journal of Happiness Studies* 17, no. 1 (2016): 41–57, https://doi.org/10.1007/s10902-014-9582-8.

48. "New Interact Report: Many Leaders Shrink from Straight Talk with Employees" (Charlotte, NC: Interact, February 2016); "Co-Worker Conflicts," *Nulab* (blog), October 1, 2019, https://nulab.com/blog/collaboration/co-worker-conflicts/; R. Suff, "Managing Conflict in the Modern Workplace" (London: Chartered Institute of Personnel and Development [CIPD], January 2020); "Gartner Survey Shows 47% of Employees Report Being Distracted at Work by the U.S. Presidential Election," news release (Arlington, VA: Gartner, February 18, 2020).

49. C.H. Tinsley, "How Negotiators Get to Yes: Predicting the Constellation of Strategies Used across Cultures to Negotiate Conflict," *Journal of Applied Psychology* 86, no. 4 (2001): 583–93; M. Gunkel, C. Schlaegel, and V. Taras, "Cultural Values, Emotional Intelligence, and Conflict Handling Styles: A Global Study," *Journal of World Business* 51, no. 4 (2016): 568–85, https://doi.org/10.1016/j.jwb.2016.02.001.

50. F.P. Brew and D.R. Cairns, "Styles of Managing Interpersonal Workplace Conflict in Relation to Status and Face Concern: A Study with Anglos and Chinese," *International Journal of Conflict Management* 15, no. 1 (2004): 27–57; A. C-Y. Peng and D. Tjosvold, "Social Face Concerns and Conflict Avoidance of Chinese Employees with Their Western or Chinese Managers," *Human Relations* 64, no. 8 (2011): 1031–50, https://doi.org/10.1177/0018726711400927; X. Li, V. Worm, and P. Xie, "Towards an Integrative Framework of Conflict-Handling Behaviour: Integrating Western and Chinese Perspectives," *Asia Pacific Business Review* 24, no. 1 (2018): 22–36, https://doi.org/10.1080/13602381.2017.1357322; J. Brett, "Intercultural Challenges in Managing Workplace Conflict—A Call for Research," *Cross Cultural & Strategic Management* 25, no. 1 (2018): 32–52, https://doi.org/10.1108/CCSM-11-2016-0190.

51. J.L. Holt and C.J. DeVore, "Culture, Gender, Organizational Role, and Styles of Conflict Resolution: A Meta-Analysis," *International Journal of Intercultural Relations* 29, no. 2 (2005): 165–96; M. Davis, S. Capobianco, and L. Kraus, "Gender Differences in Responding to Conflict in the Workplace: Evidence from a Large Sample of Working Adults," *Sex Roles* 63, no. 7 (2010): 500–14; B.M. Gayle, R.W. Preiss, and M. Allen, "Where Are We Now? A Meta-Analytic Review of Sex Difference Expectations for Conflict Management Strategy Selection," in *Managing Interpersonal Conflict: Advances through Meta-Analysis,* ed. N.A. Burrell, et al. (New York: Routledge, 2014), 226–47.

52. K. Lewin, *Resolving Social Conflicts* (New York: Harper, 1948).

53. M. Sherif, "Superordinate Goals in the Reduction of Intergroup Conflict," *American Journal of Sociology* 63, no. 4 (1958): 349–56; J.D. Hunger and L.W. Stern, "An Assessment of the Functionality of the Superordinate Goal in Reducing Conflict," *Academy of Management Journal* 19, no. 4 (1976): 591–605.

54. K.M. Eisenhardt, J.L. Kahwajy, and L.J. Bourgeois III, "How Management Teams Can Have a Good Fight," *Harvard Business Review* (July/August 1997): 77–85; O. Doucet, J. Poitras, and D. Chenevert, "The Impacts of Leadership on Workplace Conflicts," *International Journal of Conflict Management* 20 (2009): 340–54; J. DiBenigno, "Anchored Personalization in Managing Goal Conflict between Professional Groups: The Case of U.S. Army Mental Health Care," *Administrative Science Quarterly* 63 (2018): 526–69.

55. R.S. Lau and A.T. Cobb, "Understanding the Connections between Relationship Conflict and Performance: The Intervening Roles of Trust and Exchange," *Journal of Organizational Behavior* 31 (2010): 898–917; D.E. Rast, M.A. Hogg, and D. van Knippenberg, "Intergroup Leadership across Distinct Subgroups and Identities," *Personality and Social Psychology Bulletin* 44 (2018): 1090–103.

56. M.-G. Seo and N.S. Hill, "Understanding the Human Side of Merger and Acquisition: An Integrative Framework," *The Journal of Applied Behavioral Science* 41 (2005): 422–43; H.E. Yildiz, "'Us vs. Them' or 'Us over Them'? On the Roles of Similarity and Status in M&As," *International Business Review* 25, Part A (2016): 51–65; F. Du and K. Xu, "The Path to Independence: Board Cohesion, Cognitive Conflict, and Information Sharing," *Journal of Management Accounting Research* 30 (2018): 31–54.

57. J. Sanchez-Burks, C.-Y. Cheng, and F. Lee, "Taking Advantage of Differences: Increasing Team Innovation through Identity Integration," in *Diversity and Groups*, vol. 11, *Research on Managing Groups and Teams* 11 (Bingley, UK: Emerald Group Publishing Limited, 2008), 55–73; A.M. Carton and B.A. Tewfik, "Perspective—A New Look at Conflict Management in Work Groups," *Organization Science* 27 (2016): 1125–41; H. Rubinstein, "The Importance of Multiple Perspectives," in *Applying Behavioural Science to the Private Sector: Decoding What People Say and What They Do*, ed. H. Rubinstein (Cham, Switzerland: Palgrave Pivot, 2018), 89–106; T. Wei and J. Clegg, "Effect of Organizational Identity Change on Integration Approaches in Acquisitions: Role of Organizational Dominance," *British Journal of Management* 29 (2018): 337–55.

58. J. DiBenigno, "Anchored Personalization in Managing Goal Conflict between Professional Groups: The Case of U.S. Army Mental Health Care," *Administrative Science Quarterly* 63, no. 3 (2018): 526–69.

59. J.F. Dovidio et al., "Reducing Intergroup Bias through Intergroup Contact: Twenty Years of Progress and Future Directions," *Group Processes & Intergroup Relations* 20 (2017): 606–20; R. Böhm, H. Rusch, and J. Baron, "The Psychology of Intergroup Conflict: A Review of Theories and Measures," *Journal of Economic Behavior & Organization*, 178 (October 2020): 947–62.

60. Based on information in B. Sitbon, "Meet, Eat, Scale, Repeat," *WeWork Technology* (blog), May 29, 2018, https://engineering.wework.com/meet-eat-scale-repeat-b33042383180.

61. J. Luft, *Of Human Interaction* (Palo Alto, CA: National Press, 1969); E.H. Schein, "Reactions, Reflections, Rejoinders, and a Challenge," *The Journal of Applied Behavioral Science* 45, no. 1 (2009): 141–58; L. Shamoa-Nir, "The Window Becomes a Mirror: The Use of the Johari Window Model to Evaluate Stereotypes in Intergroup Dialogue in Israel," *Israel Affairs* 23, no. 4 (2017): 727–46.

62. R.R. Blake and J.S. Mouton, "Reactions to Intergroup Competition under Win-Lose Conditions," *Management Science* 7 (1961): 420–35; R.R. Blake and J.S. Mouton, *Solving Costly Organizational Conflicts*, 1st ed. (San Francisco: Jossey-Bass Publishers, 1984), Chap. 6; M.L. Marks, "Merger Management HR's Way," *HRMagazine* 36, no. 5 (May 1991): 60; G. Gemmill and M. Elmes, "Mirror, Mask, and Shadow: Psychodynamic Aspects of Intergroup Relations," *Journal of Management Inquiry* 2 (1993): 43–51.

63. A.-K. Newheiser and J.F. Dovidio, "Individual Differences and Intergroup Bias: Divergent Dynamics Associated with Prejudice and Stereotyping," *Personality and Individual Differences* 53, no. 1 (2012): 70–74; L. Cosmides and J. Tooby, "Evolutionary Psychology: New Perspectives on Cognition and Motivation," *Annual Review of Psychology* 64 (2013): 201–29.

64. M.A. Von Glinow, D.L. Shapiro, and J.M. Brett, "Can We Talk, and Should We? Managing Emotional Conflict in Multicultural Teams," *Academy of Management Review* 29, no. 4 (2004): 578–92; X. Li, V. Worm, and P. Xie, "Towards an Integrative Framework of Conflict-Handling Behaviour: Integrating Western and Chinese Perspectives," *Asia Pacific Business Review* 24, no. 1 (2018): 22–36.

65. J.R. Galbraith, *Organization Design* (Reading, MA: Addison-Wesley, 1977), 132.

66. P.R. Lawrence and J.W. Lorsch, "New Management Job: The Integrator," *Harvard Business Review*, December 1967, 142–51; J.R. Galbraith, *Organization Design* (Reading, MA: Addison-Wesley, 1977), 152–58; R. Cappetta and P. Cillo, "Managing Integrators Where Integration Matters: Insights from Symbolic Industries," *The International Journal of Human Resource Management* 19 (2008): 2235–51.

67. J.G. March and H.A. Simon, *Organizations* (New York: John Wiley & Sons, 1958), 126.

68. A.R. Elangovan, "The Manager as the Third Party: Deciding How to Intervene in Employee Disputes," in *Negotiation: Readings, Exercises, and Cases*, ed. R.J. Lewicki, J.A. Litterer, and D. Saunders, 5th ed (New York: McGraw-Hill, 2007), 473–84; D.E. Conlon et al., "Third Party Interventions across Cultures: No 'One Best Choice,'" in *Research in Personnel and Human Resources Management* (Greenwich, CT: JAI, 2007), 309–49. A broader variation of third-party conflict resolution is peacemaking. See X. Zhang et al., "Peacemaking at the Workplace: A Systematic Review," *Negotiation and Conflict Management Research* 11 (2018): 204–24.

69. J.W. Thibaut and L. Walker, *Procedural Justice: A Psychological Analysis* (Hillsdale, N.J.: L. Erlbaum Associates, 1975); B.H. Sheppard, "Managers as Inquisitors: Lessons from the Law," in *Bargaining inside Organizations*, ed. M.H. Bazerman and R.J. Lewicki (Beverly Hills, CA: Sage, 1983).

70. D.J. Bussel, "A Third Way: Examiners as Inquisitors," *American Bankruptcy Law Journal* 90 (2016): 59–127.

71. J.A. Wall and T.C. Dunne, "Mediation Research: A Current Review," *Negotiation Journal* 28 (2012): 217–44; K. Bollen and M. Euwema, "Workplace Mediation: An Underdeveloped Research Area," *Negotiation Journal* 29 (2013): 329–53. Some researchers suggest that there are several forms of mediation, not all of which have high process and low decision control. See D.L. Shapiro and E.N. Sherf, "The Role of Conflict in Managing Justice," in *The Oxford Handbook of Justice in the Workplace*, ed. R. Cropanzano and M.L. Ambrose (New York: Oxford University Press, 2015), 443–60.

72. "Clash of the Coworkers," news release (Menlo Park, CA: Accountemps, March 9, 2017); "Co-Worker Conflicts," *Nulab* (blog), October 1, 2019, https://nulab.com/blog/collaboration/co-worker-conflicts/; R. Suff, "Managing Conflict in the Modern Workplace" (London: Chartered Institute of Personnel and Development [CIPD], January 2020).

73. B.H. Sheppard, "Managers as Inquisitors: Lessons from the Law," in *Bargaining inside Organizations*, ed. M.H. Bazerman and R.J. Lewicki (Beverly Hills, CA: Sage, 1983). Even in cultures that support managerial mediation, managers slip easily into inquisition and arbitration approaches where conflict has escalated. See M.K. Kozan, C. Ergin, and K. Varoglu, "Bases of Power and Conflict Intervention Strategy: A Study on Turkish Managers," *International Journal of Conflict Management* 25 (2014): 38–60.

74. R. Karambayya and J.M. Brett, "Managers Handling Disputes: Third Party Roles and Perceptions of Fairness," *Academy of Management Journal* 32 (1989): 687–704; B.M. Goldman et al., "The Role of Third Parties/Mediation in Managing Conflict in Organizations," in *The Psychology of Conflict and Conflict Management in Organizations*, ed. C.K.W. De Dreu and M.J. Gelfand (New York: Lawrence Erlbaum Associates, 2008): 291–319.

75. A.R. Elangovan, "Managerial Intervention in Organizational Disputes: Testing a Prescriptive Model of Strategy Selection," *International Journal of Conflict Management* 4 (1998): 301–35; P.S. Nugent, "Managing Conflict: Third-Party Interventions for Managers," *Academy of Management Executive* 16, no. 1 (2002): 139–54.

76. K. Bollen, H. Ittner, and M.C. Euwema, "Mediating Hierarchical Labor Conflicts: Procedural Justice Makes a Difference—For Subordinates," *Group Decision and Negotiation* 21, no. 5 (2012): 621–36; R. Nesbit, T. Nabatchi, and L.B. Bingham, "Employees, Supervisors, and Workplace Mediation: Experiences of Justice and Settlement," *Review of Public Personnel Administration* 32, no. 3 (2012): 260–87.

77. J.P. Meyer, J.M. Gemmell, and P.G. Irving, "Evaluating the Management of Interpersonal Conflict in Organizations: A Factor-Analytic Study of Outcome Criteria," *Canadian Journal of Administrative Sciences* 14 (1997): 1–13; L.B. Bingham, "Employment Dispute Resolution: The Case for Mediation," *Conflict Resolution Quarterly* 22, no. 1/2 (2004): 145–74; M. Hyde et al., "Workplace Conflict Resolution and the Health of Employees in the Swedish and Finnish Units of an Industrial Company," *Social Science & Medicine* 63, no. 8 (2006): 2218–27.

78. W.H. Ross and D.E. Conlon, "Hybrid Forms of Third-Party Dispute Resolution: Theoretical Implications of Combining Mediation and Arbitration," *Academy of Management Review* 25, no. 2 (2000): 416–27; W.H. Ross, C. Brantmeier, and T. Ciriacks, "The Impact of Hybrid Dispute-Resolution Procedures on Constituent Fairness Judgments," *Journal of Applied Social Psychology* 32, no. 6 (2002): 1151–88.

79. L.L. Thompson, J. Wang, and B.C. Gunia, "Negotiation," *Annual Review of Psychology* 61 (2010): 491–515; B. O'Neill, "International Negotiation: Some Conceptual Developments," *Annual Review of Political Science* 21 (2018): 515–33.

80. Several models of negotiations have been developed. Preparation (also called planning) is a key part of these models in organizational settings. See, for example, D. Jang, H.A. Elfenbein, and W.P. Bottom, "More than a Phase: Form and Features of a General Theory of Negotiation," *Academy of Management Annals* 12, no. 1 (2018): 318–56.

81. R. Stagner and H. Rosen, *Psychology of Union-Management Relations* (Belmont, CA: Wadsworth, 1965), 95–96, 108–10; R.E. Walton and R.B. McKersie, *A Behavioral Theory of Labor Negotiations: An Analysis of a Social Interaction System* (New York: McGraw-Hill, 1965), 41–46; L. Thompson, *The Mind and Heart of the Negotiator* (Upper Saddle River, NJ: Prentice Hall, 1998), Chap. 2.

82. A. Tversky and D. Kahneman, "Judgment under Uncertainty: Heuristics and Biases," *Science* 185, no. 4157 (1974): 1124–31; J.D. Jasper and S.D. Christman, "A Neuropsychological Dimension for Anchoring Effects," *Journal of Behavioral Decision Making* 18 (2005): 343–69.

83. S. Doctoroff, "Reengineering Negotiations," *Sloan Management Review* 39 (1998): 63–71; D.C. Zetik and A.F. Stuhlmacher, "Goal Setting and Negotiation Performance: A Meta-Analysis," *Group Processes & Intergroup Relations* 5 (2002): 35–52.

84. A. Caputo, "A Literature Review of Cognitive Biases in Negotiation Processes," *International Journal of Conflict Management* 24 (2013): 374–98; A.B.V. Zant and L.J. Kray, "Negotiation and Conflict Resolution: A Behavioral Decision Research Perspective," in *The Wiley Blackwell Handbook of Judgment and Decision Making*, ed. G. Keren and G. Wu (Chichester, UK: John Wiley & Sons, Ltd, 2015), 828–48; M. Schaerer, D.D. Loschelder, and R.I. Swaab, "Bargaining Zone Distortion in Negotiations: The Elusive Power of Multiple Alternatives," *Organizational Behavior and Human Decision Processes* 137 (2016): 156–71.

85. L.L. Thompson, J. Wang, and B.C. Gunia, "Negotiation," *Annual Review of Psychology* 61 (2010): 491–515. Some negotiation experts warn that BATNA is often misunderstood and that "no deal option" may be a better way of viewing such situations. See J.K. Sebenius, "BATNAs in Negotiation: Common Errors and Three Kinds of 'No,'" *Negotiation Journal* 33 (2017): 89–99.

86. R.L. Pinkley et al., "The Power of Phantom Alternatives in Negotiation: How What Could Be Haunts What Is," *Organizational Behavior and Human Decision Processes* 151 (2019): 34–48.

87. L.L. Thompson, "Information Exchange in Negotiation," *Journal of Experimental Social Psychology* 27 (1991): 161–79; R. Fells, *Effective Negotiation: From Research to Results*, 2nd ed. (Melbourne: Cambridge University Press, 2012), Chap. 6.

88. C. Voss and T. Raz, *Never Split the Difference: Negotiating as If Your Life Depended on It* (Random House, 2016), Chap.2; C. Clifford, "Ex FBI Negotiator Chris Voss: How to Get What You Want," *CNBC*, October 16, 2017.

89. N. Rackham and J. Carlisle, "The Effective Negotiator—Part I: The Behaviour of Successful Negotiators," *Journal of European Industrial Training* 2, no. 6 (1978): 6–11; J.M. Brett, "Managing Organizational Conflict," *Professional Psychology: Research and Practice* 15 (1984): 664–78; R. Fells et al., "Unraveling Business Negotiations Using Practitioner Data," *Negotiation and Conflict Management Research* 8, no. 2 (2015): 119–36.

90. A.R. Herrman and M. Allen, "Hardline versus Softline Bargaining Strategies: A Meta-Analytic Review," in *Managing Interpersonal Conflict: Advances through Meta-Analysis*, ed. N.A. Burrell, et al. (New York: Routledge, 2014), 213–25; J. Hüffmeier et al., "Being Tough or Being Nice? A Meta-Analysis on the Impact of Hard- and Softline Strategies in Distributive Negotiations," *Journal of Management* 40, no. 3 (2014): 866–92.

91. C. Thuderoz, "Why Do We Respond to a Concession with Another Concession? Reciprocity and Compromise," *Negotiation Journal* 33, no. 1 (2017): 71–83.

92. D. Malhotra, "The Fine Art of Making Concessions," *Negotiation* (2006): 3–5.

93. A.F. Stuhlmacher, T.L. Gillespie, and M.V. Champagne, "The Impact of Time Pressure in Negotiation: A Meta-Analysis," *International Journal of Conflict Management* 9 (1998): 97–116; C.K.W. De Dreu, "Time Pressure and Closing of the Mind in Negotiation," *Organizational Behavior and Human Decision Processes* 91 (2003): 280–95; P.J. Carnevale, "Strategic Time in Negotiation," *Current Opinion in Psychology*, 26 (2019): 106–12.

94. As with other forms of time pressure, the exploding offer effects on negotiation outcomes are complex. Those who apply these offers can be worse off in the negotiation under some circumstances. See N. Lau et al., "Exploding Offers Can Blow up in More Than One Way," *Decision Analysis* 11, no. 3 (2014): 171–88; W. Güth and M.G. Kocher, "More Than Thirty Years of Ultimatum Bargaining Experiments: Motives, Variations, and a Survey of the Recent Literature," *Journal of Economic Behavior & Organization* 108 (2014): 396–409.

95. M. Olekalns and P.L. Smith, "Moments in Time: Metacognition, Trust, and Outcomes in Dyadic Negotiations," *Personality and Social Psychology Bulletin* 31, no. 12 (2005): 1696–707.

96. D.W. Choi, "Shared Metacognition in Integrative Negotiation," *International Journal of Conflict Management* 21, no. 3 (2010): 309–33.

97. J.M. Brett et al., "Sticks and Stones: Language, Face, and Online Dispute Resolution," *Academy of Management Journal* 50 (2007): 85–99; D. Druckman and M. Olekalns, "Emotions in Negotiation," *Group Decision and Negotiation* 17 (2008): 1–11; M.J. Boland and W.H. Ross, "Emotional Intelligence and Dispute Mediation in Escalating and De-Escalating Situations," *Journal of Applied Social Psychology* 40 (2010): 3059–105.

98. P.J. Carnevale and A.M. Isen, "The Influence of Positive Affect and Visual Access on the Discovery of Integrative Solutions in Bilateral Negotiation," *Organizational Behavior and Human Decision Processes* 37 (1986): 1–13; L. Thompson, *The Mind and Heart of the Negotiator* (Upper Saddle River, NJ: Prentice-Hall, 1998), Chap. 2.

99. J.W. Salacuse and J.Z. Rubin, "Your Place or Mine? Site Location and Negotiation," *Negotiation Journal* 6 (1990): 5–10; G. Brown and M. Baer, "Location in Negotiation: Is There a Home Field Advantage?" *Organizational Behavior and Human Decision Processes* 114, no. 2 (2011): 190–200.

100. R. Lewicki, B. Barry, and D. Saunders, *Negotiation*, 8th ed. (New York: McGraw-Hill Education, 2020), Chap. 11.

11 Leadership in Organizational Settings

Drazen Zigic/Getty Images

Learning Objectives

After you read this chapter, you should be able to:

LO11-1 Define leadership and shared leadership.

LO11-2 Describe the four elements of transformational leadership and explain why they are important for organizational change.

LO11-3 Compare managerial leadership with transformational leadership and describe the features of task-oriented, people-oriented, and servant leadership.

LO11-4 Discuss the elements of path–goal leadership theory and leadership substitutes theory.

LO11-5 Describe the two components of the implicit leadership perspective.

LO11-6 Identify eight personal attributes associated with effective leaders and describe authentic leadership.

LO11-7 Discuss cultural and gender similarities and differences in leadership.

leadership influencing, motivating, and enabling others to contribute toward the effectiveness and success of the organizations of which they are members

shared leadership the view that leadership is a role, not a position assigned to one person; consequently, people within the team and organization lead each other

Airbus SE employs more than 130,000 people from 130 nationalities. The European aerospace company has thousands of managers and executives, yet has adopted the view that every employee should assume a leadership role no matter what position they hold. In fact, the company's recently launched Airbus Leadership University in Toulouse, France, ultimately serves all employees because "Airbus firmly believes that everyone is a leader!"[1]

Executives at Airbus recognize that leadership is a role, not a formal position assigned to specific people. As such, employees at all levels in the aerospace organization informally serve as leaders in various situations. Leadership is one of the most researched and discussed topics in the field of organizational behavior.[2] Google returns a whopping 1.4 billion web pages where *leadership* is mentioned. Google Scholar lists 337,000 journal articles and books with *leader* or *leadership* in the title. Every year over the past five years, Amazon has added an average of 2,500 English language books with *leadership* in the title.

The topic of leadership receives so much attention because we are captivated by the ability to influence and motivate others collectively beyond normal expectations. This chapter explores leadership from four perspectives: transformational, managerial, implicit, and personal attributes.[3] Although some of these perspectives are currently more popular than others, each helps us to more fully understand the complex subject of leadership. The final section of this chapter looks at cross-cultural and gender issues in organizational leadership. But first, we learn about the meaning of leadership as well as shared leadership.

LO11-1 Define leadership and shared leadership.

WHAT IS LEADERSHIP?

Several years ago, dozens of leadership experts from around the world reached a consensus that **leadership** is about influencing, motivating, and enabling others to contribute toward the effectiveness and success of the organizations of which they are members.[5] This definition has two key components. First, leaders motivate others through persuasion and other influence tactics. They use their communication skills, rewards, and other resources to energize everyone toward the achievement of challenging objectives. Second, leaders are enablers. They allocate resources, alter work relationships, minimize external disruptions, and establish other work environment changes that make it easier for employees to achieve organizational objectives.

Shared Leadership

Shared leadership is the view that leadership is a set of roles that everyone performs. It is not a position assigned to one person.[6] Companies are far more effective when everyone performs leadership responsibilities in various ways and at various times. The formal leader cannot—and should not—try to perform all leadership tasks. Instead, employees lead one another as the occasion arises. Shared leadership exists when an employee persuades coworkers to try out a new work activity or introduce new technology. It exists when employees help one another through social support or organizational citizenship behaviors. Shared leadership also exists when employees keep one another focused on the task and deadlines.

The Leadership Report Card[4]

79% of 181,662 Canadian federal government employees are satisfied with the quality of supervision they receive.

74% of 615,395 U.S federal government employees say their immediate supervisor is doing a good job (increasing annually from 69% approval five years earlier).

71% of 2,772 employees in North America, Europe, India, and Australia grade their boss's competence as an "A" or "B".

49% of 2,800 American employees say their manager is a good leader.

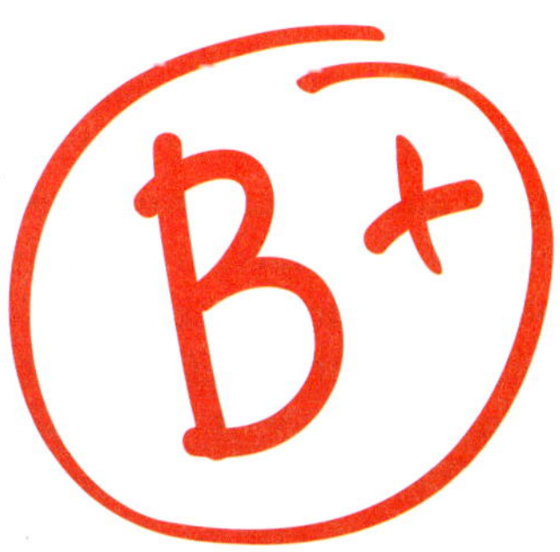

65% of 2,000 American and U.K full-time employees are confident their job performance would be as good or better WITHOUT their boss's input (only 11% believe they perform better with their boss's input).

18% of current managers have the high talent to effectively manage others (based on Gallup's analysis of 2.5 million manager-led teams).

vasilyrosca/123RF

transformational leadership a leadership perspective that explains how leaders change teams or organizations by creating, communicating, and modeling a vision for the organization or work unit and inspiring employees to strive for that vision

Shared leadership typically supplements formal leadership; that is, employees lead along with the formal manager, rather than as a replacement for that manager. However, W. L. Gore & Associates, Morning Star Company, Valve Corporation, and a few other unique companies rely almost completely on shared leadership because they don't have any formal managers on the organizational chart. In fact, when Gore employees are asked, "Are you a leader?" in annual surveys, more than 50 percent of them answer yes.[7]

Shared leadership flourishes in organizations where the formal leaders are willing to delegate power and encourage employees to take the initiative and risks without fear of failure (i.e., a learning orientation culture). Shared leadership also calls for a collaborative rather than internally competitive culture because employees succeed in shared leadership roles only when their coworkers support them in these roles. Furthermore, shared leadership lacks formal authority, so it operates best when employees learn to influence others through their enthusiasm, logical analysis, and involvement of coworkers in their idea or vision.

Shared leadership is the view that leadership is a set of roles, not a position; everyone should perform leadership responsibilities in various ways and at various times.
Inti St Clair/Blend Images LLC

LO11-2 Describe the four elements of transformational leadership and explain why they are important for organizational change.

TRANSFORMATIONAL LEADERSHIP PERSPECTIVE

Most leadership concepts and practices can be organized into four perspectives: transformational, managerial, implicit, and personal attributes. By far the most popular leadership perspective today—and arguably the most important in the domain of leadership—is transformational leadership. **Transformational leadership** views leaders as change agents. They move the organization or work unit in a new direction that will provide better opportunities and alignment with the external environment.

> **We've abandoned the Great Man model of leadership that long characterized Fiat and have created a culture where everyone is expected to lead.[8]**
>
> —Sergio Marchionne, former CEO of Fiat Chrysler Automobiles and Ferrari

There are several models of transformational leadership, but four elements are common throughout most of them and represent the core concepts of this leadership perspective (see Exhibit 11.1).[9] Transformational leaders create, communicate, and model a shared vision for the team or organization. They encourage experimentation so employees discover a better path to the future. Through these and other activities, transformational leaders also build commitment in followers to strive for that vision.

Develop and Communicate a Strategic Vision

The heart of transformational leadership is a strategic *vision*.[10] A vision is a positive image or model of the future that energizes and unifies employees.[11] Sometimes this vision is created by the leader; at other times, it is formed by employees or other stakeholders and then adopted and championed by the formal leader. An effective strategic vision has several identifiable features.[12] It describes an aspirational future with a higher purpose. This purpose is associated with personal values that directly or indirectly fulfill the needs of multiple stakeholders. A values-based vision is particularly meaningful and appealing to employees, which motivates them to strive for that ideal.

> The world is made up of those who make things happen, those who watch things happen, and those who ask what happened.[13]
>
> —Norman Augustine, aerospace business leader

Exhibit 11.1 Elements of Transformational Leadership

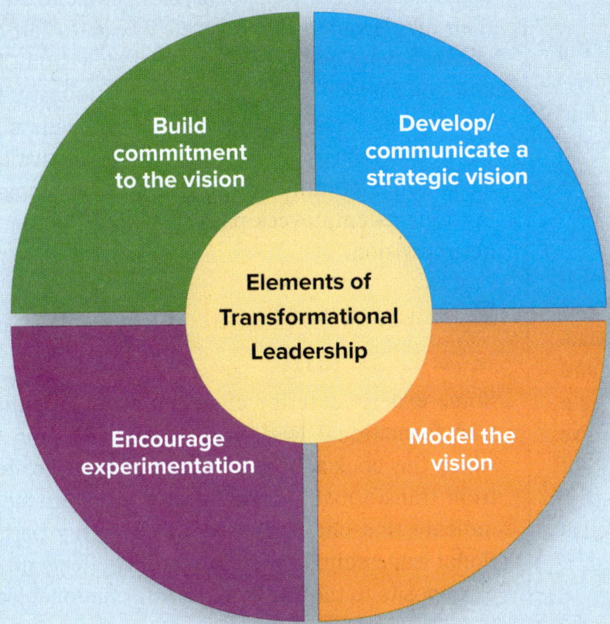

A strategic vision also engages employees because it is a distant goal that is both challenging and abstract. A vision of the future is challenging because it requires substantial change, such as new work practices and belief systems. It is necessarily abstract for two reasons. One reason is that the vision hasn't yet been experienced (at least, not in this company or industry), so it isn't possible to detail exactly what the vision looks like. The other reason is that an abstract description enables the vision to remain stable over time, yet is sufficiently flexible to accommodate operational adjustments in a shifting external environment. As such, a vision describes a broad noble cause related to fulfilling the needs of one or more stakeholder groups.

Another feature of an effective vision is that it is unifying. It is a superordinate objective that bonds employees together and aligns their personal values with the organization's values. In fact, a successful vision is a shared vision because employees collectively define themselves by this aspirational image of the future as part of their identification with the organization.

Not Quite Leading with Vision[14]

88% of 1,201 U.S. managers say it is important for companies to lay out a clear vision for the future.

79% of 5,113 adults in the U.S., UK, France, and Germany would consider a company's mission/purpose (vision) before applying for a job there.

21% of 31,000 employees globally say their manager is NOT effective at articulating the company's vision.

52% of 2,000 UK employees surveyed can't recall their organization's vision.

22% of 2.2 million employees surveyed worldwide strongly agree that their company's leaders have a clear direction for their organization.

Barbara Penoyar/Getty Images

Communicate the Vision The effectiveness of a strategic vision depends on how well leaders communicate it to followers and other stakeholders.[15] Transformational leaders generate meaning and motivation in followers by relying on symbols, metaphors, stories, and other vehicles that transcend plain language.[16] Metaphors and related communication tools "frame" the vision, meaning that they guide or construct the listener's mental model of the situation. Borrowing images from other experiences creates a richer understanding of the abstract vision that generates emotions and motivates people to pursue the vision.

Transformational leaders also convey the vision using verbal and nonverbal communication practices that show humility, sincerity, and a level of passion that reflects their personal belief in the vision and their optimism that employees can succeed. They strengthen team orientation and employee self-efficacy by referring to the team's strengths and potential. By focusing on shared experiences and

learning orientation a set of collective beliefs and norms that encourage people to question past practices, learn new ideas, experiment putting ideas into practice, and view mistakes as part of the learning process

the central role of employees in achieving the vision, transformational leaders suppress leader–follower differences, deflect attention from themselves, and avoid any image of superiority over the team.[17]

Model the Vision

Transformational leaders not only talk about a vision; they enact it. They "walk the talk" by stepping outside the executive suite and doing things that symbolize the vision.[18] Leaders model the vision through significant events such as visiting customers, moving their offices closer to (or further from) employees, and holding ceremonies to symbolize significant change. However, they also enact the vision by ensuring that routine daily activities—meeting agendas, dress codes, executive schedules—are consistent with the vision and its underlying values.

Modeling legitimizes the vision and demonstrates what it looks like in practice. Modeling the vision also builds employee trust in the leader. The greater the consistency between the leader's words and actions, the more employees will believe in and be willing to follow the leader. As Ceridian CEO David Ossip explains: "When employees are able to see their leadership live by the values that guide them, it helps to establish a sense of organizational trust and credibility."[19] Surveys report that "leading by example" is the most important attribute of effective leaders and is one of the most important characteristics of a company's culture.[20]

Encourage Experimentation

Transformational leadership is about change, and central to any change is discovering new behaviors and practices that are better aligned with the desired vision.[22] In other words, transformational leaders support a **learning orientation** (see Chapter 6). They encourage employees to continuously question the way things are currently done, to actively experiment with new ideas and practices that are potentially more consistent with the vision's future, and to view reasonable mistakes as a natural part of the learning process.[23]

Build Commitment toward the Vision

Transforming a vision into reality requires employee commitment, and transformational leaders build this commitment in several ways.[24] Their words, symbols, and stories create a contagious enthusiasm that energizes people to adopt the vision as their own. Leaders demonstrate a "can-do" attitude by enacting and behaving consistently with their vision. This persistence and consistency reflect an image of honesty, trust, and integrity. By encouraging experimentation, leaders involve employees in the change process so it is a collective activity. Leaders also build commitment through rewards, recognition, and celebrations as employees pass milestones along the road to the desired vision.

Transformational Leadership and Charisma

Some experts describe charisma as an essential ingredient of transformational leadership.[25] However, the emerging view, which this book adopts, is that charismatic leadership is distinct from transformational leadership. Several studies and reviews indicate that charisma is not necessarily part of transformational leadership; in fact, some of its effects on employees may be opposite to the effects of transformational leadership.[26]

> Great leaders walk the talk. They lead by example. There isn't anything they ask people to do they're not willing to do themselves.[21]
>
> —Mike Perlis, vice-chairman of Forbes Media

Charisma refers to a set of self-presentation characteristics and nonverbal communication behaviors (i.e. signaling) that generate interpersonal attraction and referent power over others as well as follower deference to the charismatic person (see Chapter 9).[27] In contrast, transformational leadership is a set of behaviors that engage followers toward a better future. Charismatic leadership motivates followers directly through the leader's referent power, whereas transformational leadership motivates followers through behaviors that persuade and earn trust. For instance, communicating an inspiring vision is a transformational leadership behavior that motivates followers to strive for that vision. This motivational effect exists separate from the leader's charismatic appeal.

Mc Graw Hill connect

SELF-ASSESSMENT 11.1: What Are Your Transformational Leadership Tendencies?

Transformational leaders are not necessarily charismatic, and charismatic leaders are not necessarily transformational.
Yuganov Konstantin/Shutterstock

Being charismatic is not inherently good or bad, but several research studies have concluded that charismatic leadership can produce negative consequences.[28] One concern is that charismatic leadership tends to produce dependency because, by definition, followers want to be associated with people who have charisma. Transformational leadership has the opposite effect; it builds follower empowerment, which tends to reduce dependence on the leader. Another concern is that leaders who are charismatic may become intoxicated by this power, which leads to a greater focus on self-interest than on the common good.[29] The main point here is that transformational leaders are not necessarily charismatic, and charismatic leaders are not necessarily transformational.

Evaluating the Transformational Leadership Perspective

Transformational leaders do make a difference.[30] Subordinates are more satisfied and have higher affective organizational commitment under transformational leaders. They also perform their jobs better, engage in more organizational citizenship behaviors, and make better or more creative decisions. Although transformational leadership is valuable, the theory has a few imperfections.[31] One problem is that some models engage in circular logic. They define and measure transformational leadership by its effects on employees (e.g., inspire employees), then (not surprisingly) report that this leadership is effective because it inspires employees. Instead, transformational leadership needs to be defined purely as a set of behaviors that people use to lead others through the change process.

A second concern is that some transformational leadership theories combine leader behaviors with the personal characteristics of leaders. For instance, transformational leaders are described as visionary, imaginative, sensitive, and thoughtful, yet these personal characteristics are really predictors of transformational leadership behaviors.[32] A third concern is that transformational leadership is usually described as a universal concept, that is, it should be applied in all situations. Only a few studies have investigated whether this transformational leadership is more valuable in some situations than others.[33] Preliminary evidence suggests that the transformational leadership perspective is relevant across cultures. However, there may be specific elements of transformational leadership, such as the way visions are communicated and modeled, that are more appropriate in North America than in other cultures.

managerial leadership a leadership perspective stating that effective leaders help employees improve their performance and well-being toward current objectives and practices

LO11-3 Compare managerial leadership with transformational leadership and describe the features of task-oriented, people-oriented, and servant leadership.

MANAGERIAL LEADERSHIP PERSPECTIVE

Leaders don't spend all (or even most) of their time transforming the organization or work unit. They also engage in **managerial leadership**—daily activities that support and guide the performance and well-being of individual employees and the work unit toward current objectives and practices. Leadership experts recognize that leading (transformational leadership) differs from managing (managerial leadership).[34] Although the distinction between these two perspectives remains somewhat fuzzy, each cluster has a reasonably clear set of activities and strong research foundation.

> **Managers are people who do things right and leaders are people who do the right thing.[35]**
>
> —Warren Bennis, leadership scholar (based on earlier writing by Peter Drucker)

One distinction between these two perspectives is that managerial leadership assumes the organization's or department's objectives are stable and aligned with the external environment.[36] In contrast, transformational leadership assumes the organization is misaligned with its environment and therefore needs to change its direction. An often-cited saying is that managers "do things right," which means that managerial leadership focuses on making employees and work units more effective at established objectives and practices. In contrast, leaders "do the right thing," which means that transformational leadership focuses on changing the workplace so its objectives are aligned more closely with the external environment.

A second distinction is that managerial leadership is more micro-focused and concrete because it relates to the specific performance and well-being objectives of individual employees and the immediate work unit. Transformational leadership is more macro-focused and abstract. It is directed toward an imprecise strategic vision for an entire organization, department, or team.

Managerial leadership requires transformational leadership to set the right direction (vision); transformational leadership requires managerial leadership to translate the abstract vision into specific operational behaviors and practices.
Rawpixel.com/Shutterstock

Interdependence of Managerial and Transformational Leadership

Although transformational and managerial leadership are discussed as two leadership perspectives, they are more appropriately viewed as *interdependent* perspectives.[37] In other words, transformational leadership and managerial leadership depend on each other. Transformational leadership identifies, communicates, and builds commitment to a better future for the organization or work unit. But these transformational leadership behaviors are not enough for organizational success. That success also requires managerial leadership to translate the abstract vision into specific operational behaviors and practices, and to continuously improve employee performance and well-being in the pursuit of that future ideal. Managerial leadership also depends on transformational leadership to set the right direction (vision). Otherwise, managers might produce operational excellence toward goals that are misaligned with the organization's long-term survival.

Senior executives typically engage in more transformational leadership than do middle managers, supervisors, and others further down the hierarchy. This greater emphasis on transformational leadership at higher levels likely occurs because senior leaders are more responsible for the organization's alignment with its environment and because they have more discretion to enable macro-level change. However, managerial and transformational leadership are not embodied in different people or positions in the organization. Every manager needs to apply both transformational and managerial leadership behaviors to varying degrees. Through shared leadership, even frontline employees apply managerial leadership (e.g., helping coworkers through a difficult project) and transformational leadership (e.g., championing more customer-friendly norms in the work unit).

Task-Oriented and People-Oriented Leadership

Managerial leadership research began in the 1940s when several universities launched intensive investigations to answer the question "What behaviors make leaders effective?" They studied first-line supervisors by asking subordinates to rate their bosses on many behaviors. These independent research teams essentially identified the same two clusters of leadership behavior from literally thousands of items (Exhibit 11.2).[38]

One cluster, called *task-oriented leadership*, includes behaviors that define and structure work roles. This leadership style includes assigning employees to specific tasks, setting goals and deadlines, clarifying work duties and procedures, defining work procedures, and planning work activities. The other cluster represents *people-oriented leadership*. This leadership style includes listening to employees for their opinions and ideas, creating a

Exhibit 11.2 Task- and People-Oriented Leadership Styles

Leaders are task-oriented when they . . .	Leaders are people-oriented when they . . .
• Assign work and clarify responsibilities. • Set goals and deadlines. • Evaluate and provide feedback on work quality. • Establish well-defined best work procedures. • Plan future work activities.	• Show interest in others as people. • Listen to employees. • Make the workplace more pleasant. • Show appreciation to employees for their performance contribution. • Are considerate of employee needs.

pleasant physical work setting, showing interest in staff, complimenting and recognizing employees for their effort, and showing consideration of employee needs.

These early managerial leadership studies tried to find out whether effective managers are more task-oriented or more people-oriented. This proved to be a difficult question to answer because each style has its advantages and disadvantages. In fact, evidence suggests that effective leaders rely on both styles, but in different circumstances.[39] When leaders apply the people-oriented style, their employees tend to have more positive attitudes as well as lower absenteeism, grievances, stress, and turnover. When leaders use task-oriented behaviors, their employees tend to have higher job performance. Not surprisingly, employees generally prefer people-oriented bosses, and they form negative attitudes toward bosses who are mostly task-oriented. However, task-oriented leadership also is appreciated to some degree. For example, college students value task-oriented instructors because those instructors provide clear expectations and well-prepared lectures that abide by the course objectives.[40]

Mc Graw Hill connect

SELF-ASSESSMENT 11.2: What Is Your Preferred Managerial Leadership Style?

Servant Leadership

Servant leadership is an extension or variation of people-oriented leadership because it defines leadership as serving others. In particular, servant leaders selflessly assist others in their need fulfillment, personal development, and growth.[41] Servant leaders ask, "How can I help you?" rather than expecting employees to serve them. They are typically described as selfless, egalitarian, humble, nurturing, empathetic, and ethical coaches. The main objective of servant leadership is to help followers and other stakeholders fulfill their needs and potential, particularly "to become healthier, wiser, freer, more autonomous, more likely themselves to become servants."[42] This description captures three key features of servant leadership:[43]

- *Natural desire or "calling" to serve others.* Servant leaders have a deep commitment to help others in their personal growth for that purpose alone. This commitment is not merely an instrument to achieve company objectives. It is a selfless desire to support others that goes beyond the leader's role obligation.
- *Humble, egalitarian, accepting relationship with followers.* Servant leaders do not view leadership as a position of power. Rather, they serve without drawing attention to themselves, without evoking superior status, and without being judgmental about others or defensive of criticisms received.
- *Ethical decisions and behavior.* Servant leaders display sensitivity to and enactment of moral values. They are not swayed by deviant social pressures or expectations. Servant leaders maintain moral integrity by relying on personal values to anchor their decisions and behavior. In this respect, servant leadership relies heavily on authentic leadership, which we discuss later in this chapter.

> Servant leaders selflessly assist others in their need fulfillment, personal development, and growth.

Servant leadership was introduced several decades ago and has since had a steady following, particularly among practitioners and religious leaders. Scholarly interest in this topic has bloomed recently, but the concept still faces a number of conceptual hurdles.[44] Although servant leadership writers generally agree on the three features we described here, many have included other characteristics that might confound the concept with its predictors and outcomes. Still, the notion that leaders should be servants has considerable currency and for many centuries has been embedded in the principles of major religions. One study also found that companies have higher performance (return on assets) when their chief executive officer exhibits servant leadership behaviors.[45]

servant leadership the view that leaders serve followers, rather than vice versa; leaders help employees fulfill their needs and are coaches, stewards, and facilitators of employee development

path–goal leadership theory a leadership theory stating that effective leaders choose the most appropriate leadership style(s), depending on the employee and situation, to influence employee expectations about desired results and their positive outcomes

LO11-4 Discuss the elements of path–goal leadership theory and leadership substitutes theory.

PATH–GOAL AND LEADERSHIP SUBSTITUTES THEORIES

Path–Goal Leadership Theory

The earliest managerial leadership studies not only identified the task-oriented and people-oriented leadership styles; they also concluded that the best leadership style depends on the situation.[46] This "it depends" view is consistent with the contingency anchor of organizational behavior discussed in Chapter 1. The dominant theory that applies this contingency approach to managerial leadership is **path–goal leadership theory**. The theory states that effective leaders choose one or more leadership styles to influence employee expectations (their preferred path) regarding achievement of desired results (their work-related goals), as well as their perceived satisfaction with those results (outcome valences). Leaders clarify the link between employee behaviors and outcomes, influence the valence of those outcomes, provide a work environment to facilitate goal accomplishment, and so forth.[47] Notice from this description that path–goal theory builds on the expectancy theory of motivation (Chapter 5) and its underlying formula of rational decision-making (Chapter 6).[48]

Path–Goal Leadership Styles Exhibit 11.3 presents the path–goal leadership theory model. It highlights four leadership styles and several contingency factors leading to three indicators of leader effectiveness. The four leadership styles are:[49]

- *Directive.* Directive leadership is the same as task-oriented leadership, described earlier. This leadership style consists of behaviors that provide a psychological structure for subordinates. It includes clarifying performance goals, the means to reach those goals, and the standards against which performance will be judged. Directive leadership also includes judicious use of rewards and disciplinary actions.
- *Supportive.* Supportive leadership is the same as people-oriented leadership, described earlier. This style consists of behaviors that provide psychological support for subordinates. The leader is friendly and approachable; makes the work more pleasant; treats employees with respect; and shows concern for the status, needs, and well-being of employees.
- *Participative.* Participative leadership consists of behaviors that encourage and facilitate employee involvement in decisions beyond their normal work activities. The leader consults with staff members, asks for their suggestions, and carefully reflects on employee views before making a decision. Participative leadership relates to involving employees in decisions (see Chapter 6).
- *Achievement-oriented.* This leadership style consists of behaviors that encourage employees to reach their peak performance. The leader sets challenging goals, expects employees to perform at their highest level, continuously seeks improvement in employee performance, and shows a high degree of confidence that employees will assume responsibility and accomplish challenging goals. Achievement-oriented leadership applies goal-setting theory as well as positive expectations in self-fulfilling prophecy.

Path–Goal Theory Contingencies As a contingency theory, path–goal theory states that each of the four leadership styles will be more effective in some situations than in others. The theory also contends that managers are able to apply the most appropriate leadership style (or styles) for each situation. Depending on the circumstances, this skill may involve using two or more leadership styles at the same time. The model specifies two sets of situational variables: (1) employee characteristics and (2) characteristics of the employee's work environment. Several employee and workplace contingencies have been studied, but the following four have received the most attention:[50]

- *Skill and experience.* A combination of directive and supportive leadership is best for employees who are (or perceive themselves to be) inexperienced and unskilled.[52] Directive leadership involves providing information about how to accomplish the task, whereas supportive leadership offers support to cope with the uncertainties of unfamiliar work situations. Directive leadership is detrimental when employees are skilled and experienced because it introduces too much supervisory control.
- *Locus of control.* People with an internal locus of control believe they have control over their work environment (see Chapter 3). Consequently, these employees prefer participative and achievement-oriented leadership styles and may become frustrated with a directive style. In contrast, people with an external locus of control believe their performance is due more to luck and fate, so they tend to be more satisfied with directive and supportive leadership.

Exhibit 11.3 Path–Goal Leadership Theory

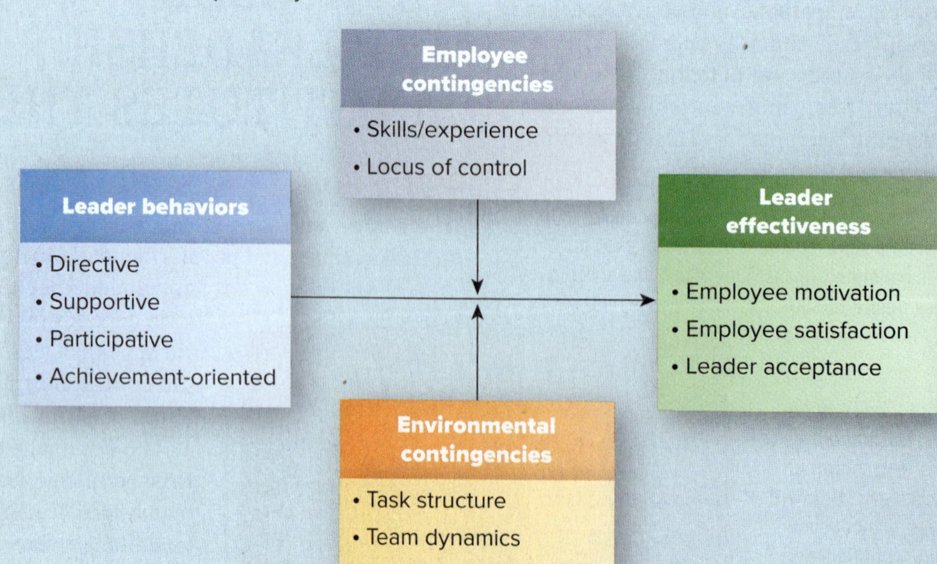

OB THEORY TO PRACTICE

Great Bosses Apply Path–Goal Leadership Theory[51]

When asked to describe their favorite boss, employees refer to leadership styles and situations that fit path–goal theory. For example, a junior employee at a pharmaceutical company in London, United Kingdom, praises his boss's supportive style. "She has this magical ability to lead with empathy, compassion and transparency." An experienced community education services worker in Minnesota appreciates participative leadership. "Is he perfect? No. But he listens to others' opinions and always considers them."

A financial services professional in Illinois says his manager is someone "you would walk on coals for" because of his balance of achievement and supportive leadership. "He pushed you but always had your best interest at heart and wanted you to succeed." And a school teacher in Michigan is happy that his current boss doesn't apply too much directive leadership, but instead "trusts that I am a veteran professional and does not micromanage."

FatCamera/E+/Getty Images

- *Task structure.* Leaders should adopt the directive style when the task is nonroutine because this style minimizes the role ambiguity that tends to occur in complex work situations (particularly for inexperienced employees).[53] The directive style is ineffective when employees have routine and simple tasks because the manager's guidance serves no purpose and may be viewed as unnecessarily micromanaging. Employees in highly routine and simple jobs may require supportive leadership to help them cope with the tedious nature of the work and lack of control over the pace of work. Participative leadership is preferred for employees performing nonroutine tasks because the lack of rules and procedures gives them more discretion to achieve challenging goals. The participative style is ineffective for employees in routine tasks because they lack discretion over their work.
- *Team dynamics.* Cohesive teams with performance-oriented norms act as a substitute for most leader interventions. High team cohesion substitutes for supportive leadership, whereas performance-oriented team norms substitute for directive and possibly achievement-oriented leadership. Thus, when team cohesion is low, leaders should use a supportive style. Leaders should apply a directive style to counteract team norms that oppose the performance objectives assigned to the team. For example, the team leader may need to exert authority if team members have developed a norm to "take it easy" rather than get a project completed on time.

leadership substitutes theory a theory identifying conditions that either limit a leader's ability to influence subordinates or make a particular leadership style unnecessary

Evaluating Path–Goal Theory Path-goal theory has received more research support than other managerial leadership models. In fact, one study reported that path-goal theory predicts effective leadership better than does transformational leadership.[54] This stronger effect likely exists because managers typically spend more of their time engaging in managerial rather than transformational leadership.[55]

Support for the path-goal model is far from ideal, however. Not all contingencies have research support and a few haven't been investigated at all.[56] Another concern is that path-goal theory assumes effective leaders can change managerial styles to fit the situation. In reality, it takes considerable effort to do so because leaders typically prefer one style that is most consistent with their personality and values. Some experts even suggest that leadership styles are hardwired.[57] In spite of these limitations, path-goal theory remains a relatively robust theory of managerial leadership.

Leadership Substitutes Theory

Path-goal leadership theory recommends applying different leadership styles to match the situation, whereas **leadership substitutes theory** suggests that the situation either limits the leader's ability to influence subordinates or renders a particular leadership style unnecessary.[58] The literature identifies several conditions that possibly substitute for task-oriented or people-oriented leadership (see Exhibit 11.4).

Exhibit 11.4 Possible Leadership Substitutes

Managerial Leadership Style	Possible Substitutes for That Style
Task-oriented	• Performance-based rewards • Employee is skilled and experienced • Guidance from coworkers • Team norms reinforce task objectives • Work is intrinsically motivating • Employee applies self-leadership
People-oriented	• Supportive coworkers • Employee is skilled and experienced • Work is intrinsically satisfying • Employee uses effective stress coping

Based on ideas in S. Kerr and J.M. Jermier, "Substitutes for Leadership: Their Meaning and Measurement," *Organizational Behavior and Human Performance* 22 (December 1978): 375–403; P.M. Podsakoff and S.B. MacKenzie, "Kerr and Jermier's Substitutes for Leadership Model: Background, Empirical Assessment, and Suggestions for Future Research," *Leadership Quarterly* 8 (1997): 117–32.

implicit leadership theory a theory stating that people evaluate a leader's effectiveness in terms of how well that person fits preconceived beliefs about the features and behaviors of effective leaders (leadership prototypes) and that people tend to inflate the influence of leaders on organizational events

Consistent with path-goal theory, task-oriented leadership is likely less valuable for employees as they gain skill and experience in the job.[59] This leadership style also may be unnecessary when performance-based rewards motivate employees to achieve organizational goals, when the work is intrinsically motivating, and when the employee has good self-motivation skills (called self-leadership, including engaging in self-set goals, self-reinforcement, and positive self-talk).

Under some conditions, teams likely substitute for task-oriented leadership.[60] Team norms that support organizational goals motivate team members to encourage (or pressure) coworkers to perform their tasks and possibly even to develop achievement-oriented performance expectations.[61] Coworkers also engage in organizational citizenship behaviors by instructing less-experienced employees, thereby requiring less task-oriented leadership from the formal manager.

People-oriented leadership may be less valuable when other forms of social support are available (such as supportive team members), when the work itself is enjoyable, and when the employee applies effective coping strategies to minimize stress. Skilled and experienced employees also have higher self-efficacy, which results in less stressful work and therefore less need for people-oriented leadership interaction from the boss.

The leadership substitutes model has intuitive appeal, but the evidence has been mixed. Some studies show that a few substitutes do replace the need for task- or people-oriented leadership, but others do not. The difficulties of statistically testing for leadership substitutes may account for some problems. However, a few writers contend that the weak support for substitutes indicates that formal leadership plays a critical role regardless of the situation.[62] Overall, we can conclude that leadership substitutes might reduce the need for managerial leadership behaviors, but they do not completely replace managers in these situations.

Task-oriented leadership may be unnecessary when performance-based rewards motivate employees to achieve organizational goals, when the work is intrinsically motivating, and when the employee has good self-motivation skills.
Maridav/Shutterstock

LO11-5 Describe the two components of the implicit leadership perspective.

IMPLICIT LEADERSHIP PERSPECTIVE

Research on transformational and managerial leadership has found that leaders do "make a difference"; that is, leaders significantly influence the performance of their departments and organizations. However, a third leadership perspective, called **implicit leadership theory**, explains that followers' perceptions also play a role in a leader's effectiveness. The implicit leadership perspective has two components: leader prototypes and the romance of leadership.[63]

Prototypes of Effective Leaders

One aspect of implicit leadership theory states that everyone has *leadership prototypes*—preconceived beliefs about the features

Leadership prototypes are preconceived beliefs about the features and behaviors of effective leaders, which shape the follower's expectations and acceptance of someone as a leader.
Syda Productions/Shutterstock

and behaviors of effective leaders.[64] These prototypes, which develop through socialization within the family and society, shape the follower's expectations and acceptance of others as leaders, and this in turn affects their willingness to remain as a follower. Leadership prototypes not only support a person's role as leader; they also influence follower perceptions of the leader's effectiveness. In other words, a leader is often perceived as more effective when he or she looks like and acts consistently with the prototype of a leader.[65]

This prototype comparison process occurs because people want to trust their leader before they are willing to serve as followers. However, the leader's actual effectiveness usually isn't known for several months or possibly years, so comparing the leader against a prototype is a quick (although faulty) way of estimating the leader's future success.

The Romance of Leadership

Along with relying on implicit prototypes of effective leaders, followers tend to inflate the perceived influence of leaders on the organization's success. This "romance of leadership" effect occurs for two reasons.[66] First, leadership is a useful way for us to simplify life events. It is easier to explain organizational successes and failures in terms of the leader's ability than by analyzing a complex array of other forces.

The second reason why people inflate their perception of the leader's influence over the environment is that people in the United States and many other cultures want to believe that life events are generated more from people than from uncontrollable natural forces.[67] This illusion of control is satisfied by believing that events result from the rational actions of leaders. In other words, employees feel better believing that leaders make a difference, so they actively look for evidence that this is so.

Fundamental attribution error (see Chapter 3) also explains why followers believe that leaders make a difference. Leaders are often given credit for the company's success because employees do not readily see the external forces that also influence these events. Leaders reinforce this belief by taking credit for organizational successes.[68]

The implicit leadership perspective highlights the fact that leadership is influenced by followers' perceptions, not only the actual behaviors and formal roles of people calling themselves leaders. Potential leaders must be sensitive to this fact and be aware of follower expectations. Individuals who do not naturally fit leadership prototypes need to provide more direct evidence of their effectiveness as leaders.

LO11-6 Identify eight personal attributes associated with effective leaders and describe authentic leadership.

PERSONAL ATTRIBUTES PERSPECTIVE OF LEADERSHIP

Since the beginning of recorded civilization, people have been interested in the personal characteristics that distinguish great leaders from the rest of us.[69] One groundbreaking review in the late 1940s concluded that no valid list of leadership traits could be distilled from previous research. A decade later, the review revised its conclusions to suggest that a few attributes are associated with effective leaders.[70] Even so, the initial review caused many scholars to give up their search for the personal characteristics of effective leaders.

Eight Important Leadership Attributes

Leadership experts have since returned to the notion that effective leaders possess specific personal attributes. Many leadership studies conducted long ago were apparently plagued by methodological problems, lack of theoretical foundation, and inconsistent definitions of leadership. Recent studies have mostly corrected these problems, with the result that several attributes are now consistently identified with effective leadership or leader emergence. Eight important attributes of effective leaders (not in any particular order) are personality, self-concept, leadership motivation, drive, integrity, knowledge of the business, cognitive and practical intelligence, and emotional intelligence (see Exhibit 11.5):[71]

Personality Most of the Big Five personality dimensions (see Chapter 2) are associated with effective leadership.[72] However, the strongest

McGraw Hill connect

SELF-ASSESSMENT 11.3: Do Leaders Make a Difference?

> Successful leaders have a complex, internally consistent, and clear self-concept as both a transformational and managerial leader.

Exhibit 11.5 Personal Attributes of Effective Leaders

Leadership attribute	Description
Personality	Effective leaders have higher levels of extraversion (outgoing, talkative, sociable, and assertive) and conscientiousness (careful, dependable, and self-disciplined).
Self-concept	Effective leaders have strong self-beliefs and a positive self-evaluation about their own leadership skills and ability to achieve objectives.
Leadership motivation	Effective leaders have a need for socialized power (not personalized power) to accomplish team or organizational goals.
Drive	Effective leaders have an inner motivation to pursue goals.
Integrity	Effective leaders have strong moral principles, which are demonstrated through truthfulness and consistency of words with deeds.
Knowledge of the business	Effective leaders have deep knowledge about the company's environment, enabling them to make more intuitive decisions.
Cognitive and practical intelligence	Effective leaders have above-average cognitive ability to process information (cognitive intelligence) and ability to solve real-world problems by adapting to, shaping, or selecting appropriate environments (practical intelligence).
Emotional intelligence	Effective leaders have the ability to recognize and regulate their own emotions and the emotions of others.

predictors are high levels of extraversion (outgoing, talkative, sociable, and assertive) and conscientiousness (careful, dependable, and self-disciplined). With high extraversion, effective leaders are comfortable having an influential role in social settings. With higher conscientiousness, effective leaders set higher goals for themselves (and others), are organized, and have a strong sense of duty to fulfill work obligations.

Self-Concept Successful leaders have a complex, internally consistent, and clear self-concept as both a transformational and managerial leader (see Chapter 3). This "leader identity" also includes a positive self-evaluation, which consists of high self-esteem, high self-efficacy, and an internal locus of control.[73] Many people in leadership positions default to daily managerial leadership and define themselves as managers. Effective leaders, on the other hand, view themselves as both transformational and managerial, and are confident with both of these self-views.[74]

Leadership Motivation Effective leaders are motivated to lead others. They have a strong need for *socialized power*, meaning that they want power to lead others in accomplishing organizational objectives and similar good deeds. This contrasts with a need for *personalized power*, which is the desire to have power for personal gain or for the thrill one might experience from wielding power over others (see Chapter 5).[75] Leadership motivation is also necessary because, even in organizations where managers support one another, they are in contests for positions further up the hierarchy. Effective leaders thrive rather than wither in the face of this competition.[76]

Drive Related to their high conscientiousness, extraversion, and positive self-evaluation, successful leaders have a moderately high need for achievement (see Chapter 5). This drive represents the inner motivation that leaders possess to pursue their goals and encourage others to move forward with theirs. Drive inspires inquisitiveness, an action orientation, and measured boldness to take the organization or team into uncharted waters.

Integrity Integrity involves having strong moral principles, which supports the tendency to be truthful and to be consistent in words and deeds. Leaders have a high moral capacity to judge dilemmas using sound values and to act accordingly. Notice that integrity is ultimately based on the leader's values, which

Employee Perceptions of Management Integrity[78]

64% of 6,119 employees in eight of the largest European countries agree that their line manager sets a good example of ethical business behavior (ranging from 72% in Ireland to 56% in France).

80% of 5,103 adults surveyed identify "honest" as one of the most common traits of great managers (2nd highest trait after "work ethic").

63% of 181,333 Canadian federal government employees somewhat or strongly agree that senior managers in their department/agency leads by example in ethical behavior (15% disagree).

56% of 615,395 U.S. federal government employees say their organization's senior leaders maintain high standards of honesty and integrity.

49% of 9,859 employees in the U.S. and seven other major countries (1,233 employees in each country) say they have a great deal of trust in their boss (ranging from 65% in Mexico to 22% in Japan).

Aquir/Shutterstock

provide an anchor for consistency. Several large-scale studies have reported that integrity and honesty are the most important characteristics of effective leaders.[77]

Knowledge of the Business Effective leaders understand the business environment in which they operate, including subtle indications of emerging trends. Knowledge of the business also includes a solid grasp of how their organization works effectively.

Cognitive and Practical Intelligence Leaders have above-average cognitive ability to process enormous amounts of information. Leaders aren't necessarily geniuses; rather, they have a superior ability to analyze a variety of complex alternatives and opportunities. Furthermore, leaders have practical intelligence. This means that they can think through the relevance and application of ideas in real-world settings. Practical intelligence is particularly evident where problems are poorly defined, information is missing, and more than one solution may be plausible.[79]

Emotional Intelligence Effective leaders have a high level of emotional intelligence. They are able to recognize and regulate emotions in themselves and in other people (see Chapter 4).[80] For example, effective leaders can tell when their conversations are having the intended emotional effect on employees. Also they can recognize and change their own emotional state to suit the situation, such as feeling optimistic and determined in spite of recent business setbacks.

Authentic Leadership

authentic leadership
the view that effective leaders need to be aware of, feel comfortable with, and act consistently with their values, personality, and self-concept

A few paragraphs ago, we said that successful leaders have a complex, internally consistent, and clear self-concept as a leader, and that they have a strong positive self-evaluation. These characteristics lay the foundation for **authentic leadership**, which refers to how well leaders are aware of, feel comfortable with, and act consistently with their values, personality, and self-concept.[82] Authenticity is mainly about knowing yourself and being yourself (see Exhibit 11.6). Leaders learn more about their personality, values, thoughts, and habits by reflecting on various situations and personal experiences. They also improve this self-awareness by receiving feedback from trusted people inside and outside the organization. Both self-reflection and receptivity to feedback require high levels of emotional intelligence.

As people learn more about themselves, they gain a greater understanding of their inner purpose, which, in turn, generates a long-term passion for achieving something worthwhile for the organization or society. Some leadership experts suggest that this inner purpose emerges from a life story, typically initiated by a transformative event or experience earlier in life.[83]

Authentic leadership is more than self-awareness; it also involves behaving in ways that are consistent with that self-concept rather than pretending to be someone else. It is difficult enough

OB THEORY TO PRACTICE

ITV CEO Carolyn McCall Identifies Important Leadership Attributes[81]

As one of the United Kingdom's most admired business executives, Carolyn McCall has had plenty of opportunity to observe the personal characteristics of great leaders. The CEO of ITV (the UK's largest commercial television company) and former CEO of easyJet and Guardian Media Group identifies drive as an important leadership attribute because the job is filled with hurdles and distractions. "You have to keep your energy and be resilient, and remember the long-term vision," she advises.

Integrity is another essential attribute of successful leaders. "A reputation takes years to build and you can lose it in two seconds," warns McCall, who recently received the British honor of Damehood (the female equivalent of knighthood). "I would rather tell people the truth, even if it's really hard, than avoid the problem."

A third leadership attribute that McCall emphasizes is understanding and managing emotions. "Emotional intelligence is important for leadership," she says. "For me, it's about being able to relate to other people and to show you want to nurture that relationship."

A fourth ingredient in successful leaders is self-concept, particularly the authentic leadership attributes of knowing yourself and being yourself in leadership roles. "You need to be comfortable with yourself to be confident," she says, warning that "if you change yourself to adapt to that, it's even harder." However, McCall distinguishes pretending to be someone else from adapting your leadership style to the situation. "Of course in different situations you have to have different behaviors. You sometimes have to be a lot more assertive in meetings, but that's a change of tone, not character."

Anthony Harvey/Getty Images

Exhibit 11.6 Authentic Leadership

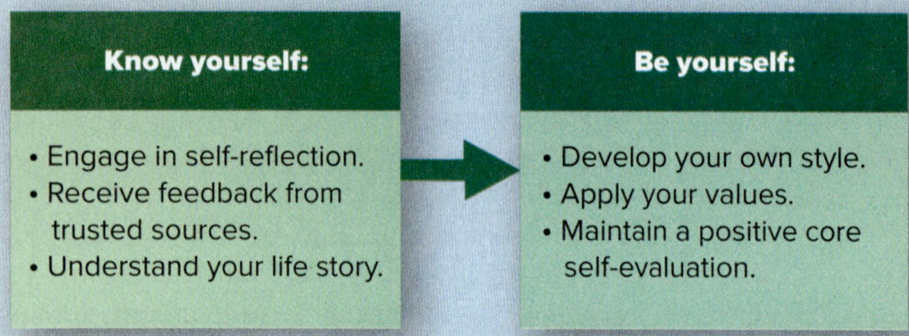

to lead others as your natural self; to lead others while pretending to be someone else is nearly impossible. To be themselves, great leaders regulate their decisions and behavior in several ways. First, they develop their own style and, where appropriate, move into positions where that style is most effective. Although effective leaders adapt their behavior to the situation to some extent, they invariably understand and rely on decision methods and interpersonal styles that feel most comfortable to them.

Second, effective leaders continually think about and consistently apply their stable hierarchy of personal values to those decisions and behaviors. Leaders face many pressures and temptations, such as achieving short-term stock price targets at the cost of long-term profitability. Experts note that authentic leaders demonstrate self-discipline by remaining anchored to their values. Third, leaders maintain consistency around their self-concept by having a strong, positive core self-evaluation. They have high self-esteem and self-efficacy as well as an internal locus of control (Chapter 3).

Authentic leadership begins by knowing yourself better through self-reflection and receptivity to feedback from trusted sources.
michaeljung/Shutterstock

Personal Attributes Perspective Limitations and Practical Implications

Personality, experience, self-concept, and other individual characteristics potentially contribute to a leader's effectiveness. Still, the personal attributes perspective has a few limitations.[84] First, it assumes that all effective leaders have the same personal characteristics that are equally important in all situations. This is probably a false assumption; leadership is far too complex to have a universal list of traits that apply to every condition. Some attributes might not be important all the time. Second, alternative combinations of attributes may be equally successful; two people with different sets of personal characteristics might be equally good leaders. Third, the personal attributes perspective views leadership as something within a person, yet experts emphasize that leadership is relational. People are effective leaders because of their favorable relationships with followers, not just because they possess specific personal characteristics.[85]

Also remember from our discussion earlier in this chapter that, in the short term, followers tend to define others as effective or ineffective leaders based on their personal characteristics rather than whether the leader actually makes a difference to the organization's success. People who exhibit self-confidence, extraversion, and other traits are called leaders because they fit the widely held prototype of an effective leader. Alternatively, if someone is successful, observers might assign several nonobservable personal characteristics to him or her, such as intelligence, confidence, and drive. In short, the link between personal characteristics and effective leadership is muddied by several perceptual distortions.

One important final point: The personal attributes perspective of leadership does not necessarily imply that leadership is a talent acquired at birth. On the contrary, attributes indicate only leadership *potential*, not leadership performance. People with these characteristics become effective leaders only after they have developed and mastered the necessary leadership behaviors through experience. However, even those with fewer leadership attributes may become very effective leaders by more fully developing their potential.

LO11-7 Discuss cultural and gender similarities and differences in leadership.

CROSS-CULTURAL AND GENDER ISSUES IN LEADERSHIP

Culture shapes the leader's values and norms, which influence his or her decisions and actions. Cultural values also shape the expectations that followers have of their leaders. An executive who acts inconsistently with cultural expectations is more likely to be perceived as an ineffective leader. Furthermore, leaders who deviate from those values may experience various forms of influence to get them to conform to the leadership norms and expectations of the society. Thus, differences in leadership practices across cultures are partly explained by implicit leadership theory, which was described earlier in this chapter.

Gender is another factor to consider in how leaders act and how followers perceive leaders. Studies in work settings have generally found that male and female leaders do not differ in their levels of task-oriented or people-oriented leadership. The main explanation is that real-world jobs require similar behavior from male and female job incumbents.[86] However, women do adopt a participative leadership style more readily than their male counterparts. One possible reason is that, compared to boys, girls are often raised to be more egalitarian and less status-oriented, which is consistent with being participative. There is also some evidence that, compared to men, women have somewhat better interpersonal skills, and this translates into their relatively greater use of the participative leadership style. A third explanation is that employees are motivated by their own gender stereotypes to expect female leaders to be more participative. Thus, female leaders comply with follower expectations to some extent.

Several studies report that women are rated higher than men on the emerging leadership qualities of coaching, teamwork, and empowering employees.[87] Yet research also suggests that women are evaluated negatively when they try to apply the full range of leadership styles, particularly more directive and autocratic approaches. Thus, ironically, women may be well suited to contemporary leadership roles, yet they often continue to face implicit leadership challenges due to followers' gender stereotypes and prototypes of leaders.[88] Overall, both male and female leaders must be sensitive to the fact that followers have expectations about how leaders should act.

Study Checklist

Connect® is available for *M Organizational Behavior*. Additional resources include:

✓ Exercises:

- **Case Analysis:** Apply concepts within the context of a real-world situation.
- **Click and Drag:** Helps make the connection between theory and application through matching, ranking, or grouping activities.
- **Video Case:** See management in action through interactive videos.
- **Self-Assessment:** Designed to promote student self-awareness and reflection, these research-based surveys contain detailed feedback for students.
- **Application-Based Activities:** These highly interactive, application- and analysis-based exercises allow students to take on specific roles to complete management-related tasks within a real-world context.

✓ **SmartBook 2.0™**—Smartbook 2.0 is an adaptive learning solution that provides personalized learning to individual student needs, continually adapts to pinpoint knowledge gaps and focuses learning on concepts requiring additional study. It fosters more productive learning, takes the guesswork out of what to study, and helps students better prepare for class.

Notes

1. "Leadership University," Airbus Industrie, Careers—Working for Airbus, accessed June 9, 2019, https://www.airbus.com/careers/working-for-airbus/leadership-university.html.
2. These statistics were collected in June 2019 using the advanced search features of Google, Google Scholar, and Amazon.
3. Many of these perspectives are summarized in R.N. Kanungo, "Leadership in Organizations: Looking Ahead to the 21st Century," *Canadian Psychology* 39 (1998): 71–82; G.A. Yukl, *Leadership in Organizations*, 8th ed. (Upper Saddle River, NJ: Pearson Education, 2013).
4. *State of the American Manager: Analytics and Advice for Leaders* (Washington, DC: Gallup, March 2015); "Survey Reveals Cities Where Workers Are Most (and Least) Happy with Bosses," news release (Menlo Park, CA: Robert Half, October 11, 2018); "Employees Worldwide Like Their Managers, yet Seven Out of 10 Claim They Can Do Their Boss's Job Better," news release (Lowell, MA: The Workforce Institute at Kronos, September 9, 2019); Office of Personnel Management, "2019 Federal Employee Viewpoint Survey" (Washington, DC: U.S. Government, October 2019); "2019 Public Service Employee Survey Results for the Public Service" (Ottawa: Government of Canada, Treasury Board of Canada Secretariat, January 15, 2020); "The Boss Barometer Report: US 2019," Kimble Applications, accessed March 21, 2020, https://www.kimbleapps.com/resources/boss-barometer-survey-us/; "The Boss Barometer Report: UK 2019," Kimble Applications, accessed March 21, 2020, https://www.kimbleapps.com/resources/boss-barometer-survey-uk/.
5. R. House, M. Javidan, and P. Dorfman, "Project GLOBE: An Introduction," *Applied Psychology: An International Review* 50 (2001): 489–505; R. House et al., "Understanding Cultures and Implicit Leadership Theories across the Globe: An Introduction to Project GLOBE," *Journal of World Business* 37 (2002): 3–10.
6. J.A. Raelin, "We the Leaders: In Order to Form a Leaderful Organization," *Journal of Leadership & Organizational Studies* 12, no. 2 (2005): 18–30; C.L. Pearce, J.A. Conger, and E.A. Locke, "Shared Leadership Theory," *Leadership Quarterly* 19, no. 5 (2008): 622–28; E. Engel Small and J.R. Rentsch, "Shared Leadership in Teams: A Matter of Distribution," *Journal of Personnel Psychology* 9, no. 4 (2010): 203–11.

7. D. Anfuso, "Core Values Shape W. L. Gore's Innovative Culture," *Workforce* 78, no. 3 (1999): 48–53.

8. S. Marchionne, "Fiat's Extreme Makeover," *Harvard Business Review* (2008): 45–48.

9. Most or all of these elements are included in W. Bennis and B. Nanus, *Leaders: The Strategies for Taking Charge* (New York: Harper & Row, 1985); N.M. Tichy and M.A. Devanna, *The Transformational Leader* (New York: Wiley, 1986); B.M. Bass and R.E. Riggio, *Transformational Leadership*, 2nd ed. (Mahwah, NJ: Erlbaum, 2006); J.M. Kouzes and B.Z. Posner, *The Leadership Challenge*, 5th ed. (San Francisco: Jossey-Bass, 2012).

10. Strategic collective vision has been identified as a key factor in leadership since Chester Barnard's seminal book in organizational behavior. See C. Barnard, *The Functions of the Executive* (Cambridge, MA: Harvard University Press, 1938), 86–89.

11. W. Bennis and B. Nanus, *Leaders: The Strategies for Taking Charge* (New York: Harper & Row, 1985), 27–33, 89; R.E. Quinn, *Building the Bridge as You Walk on It: A Guide for Leading Change* (San Francisco: Jossey-Bass, 2004), Chap. 11; R. Gill, *Theory and Practice of Leadership* (London: Sage, 2011), Chap. 4; D. O'Connell, K. Hickerson, and A. Pillutla, "Organizational Visioning: An Integrative Review," *Group & Organization Management* 36, no. 1 (2011): 103–25.

12. J.M. Strange and M.D. Mumford, "The Origins of Vision: Effects of Reflection, Models, and Analysis," *Leadership Quarterly* 16 (2005): 121–48; S. Kantabutra, "Toward a Behavioral Theory of Vision in Organizational Settings," *Leadership & Organization Development Journal* 30 (2009): 319–37; S.A. Kirkpatrick, "Lead through Vision and Values," in *Handbook of Principles of Organizational Behavior*, ed. E.A. Locke (Chichester, UK: Wiley, 2010), 367–87; R. Ashkenas and B. Manville, "You Don't Have to Be CEO to Be a Visionary Leader," *Harvard Business Review (Online)*, April 4, 2019.

13. N. Augustine, *Augustine's Laws*, 3rd ed. (New York: Viking, 1986), 32.

14. "Global Workforce Study" (London: Willis Towers Watson, September 29, 2016); Gallup Inc., *State of the American Workplace* (Washington, DC: Gallup, February 23, 2017; "Half of Employees Can't Recite Their Organisation's Vision or Values," *Small Business* (London), February 26, 2018; "2019 Edelman-LinkedIn B2B Thought Leadership Impact Study" (New York: Edelman, December 6, 2018); "Mission & Culture Survey 2019" (Mill Valley, CA: Glassdoor, July 9, 2019).

15. J.A. Conger and R.N. Kanungo, *Charismatic Leadership in Organizations* (Thousand Oaks, CA: Sage, 1998), 173–83; M. Venus, D. Stam, and D. van Knippenberg, "Leader Emotion as a Catalyst of Effective Leader Communication of Visions, Value-Laden Messages, and Goals," *Organizational Behavior and Human Decision Processes* 122, no. 1 (2013): 53–68; J. Mayfield, M. Mayfield, and W.C. Sharbrough, "Strategic Vision and Values in Top Leaders' Communications: Motivating Language at a Higher Level," *International Journal of Business Communication* 52, no. 1 (2015): 97–121.

16. D.A. Waldman, P.A. Balthazard, and S.J. Peterson, "Leadership and Neuroscience: Can We Revolutionize the Way That Inspirational Leaders Are Identified and Developed?" *Academy of Management Perspectives* 25, no. 1 (2011): 60–74; S. Denning, *The Leader's Guide to Storytelling: Mastering the Art and Discipline of Business Narrative*, rev. ed. (San Francisco: Jossey-Bass, 2011); J.C. Sarros et al., "Leaders and Their Use of Motivating Language," *Leadership & Organization Development Journal* 35, no. 3 (2014): 226–40; A.M. Carton, C. Murphy, and J.R. Clark, "A (Blurry) Vision of the Future: How Leader Rhetoric about Ultimate Goals Influences Performance," *Academy of Management Journal* 57, no. 6 (2014): 1544–70.

17. J.E. Baur et al., "More Than One Way to Articulate a Vision: A Configurations Approach to Leader Charismatic Rhetoric and Influence," *Leadership Quarterly* 27, no. 1 (2016): 156–71.

18. D.E. Berlew, "Leadership and Organizational Excitement," *California Management Review* 17, no. 2 (1974): 21–30; W. Bennis and B. Nanus, *Leaders: The Strategies for Taking Charge* (New York: Harper & Row, 1985), 43–55; T. Simons, "Behavioral Integrity: The Perceived Alignment between Managers' Words and Deeds as a Research Focus," *Organization Science* 13, no. 1 (2002): 18–35.

19. D. Ossip, "Create a Culture of Engagement for Successful Customer Outcomes," *The CEO Forum* 2015, 30–31.

20. The surveys on leading by example are reported in J.C. Maxwell, "People Do What People See," *BusinessWeek*, November 19, 2007, 32; Kronos, "Who's the Boss of Workplace Culture?" news release (Chelmsford, MA: Kronos, March 9, 2016). In the earlier survey, "leading by example" was the most important attribute of effective leaders. In the recent survey, HR professionals and managers rated "leading by example" as the top attribute of a company's culture, whereas employees ranked it below pay, coworker respect, and work–life balance. One recent study found that leading by doing has a positive correlation with employee productivity and service quality. See L. Eldor, "Leading by Doing: Does Leading by Example Impact Productivity and Service Quality?" *Academy of Management Journal*, March 26, 2020, amj.2018.0706.

21. S. Kolesnikov-Jessop, "You're the Conductor: Listen to the Music You Can Create with the Group," *The New York Times*, April 11, 2016.

22. B.M. Bass and R.E. Riggio, *Transformational Leadership*, 2nd ed. (Mahwah, NJ: Erlbaum, 2006), 7; J.M. Kouzes and B.Z. Posner, *The Leadership Challenge*, 5th ed. (San Francisco: Jossey-Bass, 2012), Chaps. 6 and 7.

23. W.E. Baker and J.M. Sinkula, "The Synergistic Effect of Market Orientation and Learning Orientation on Organizational Performance," *Academy of Marketing Science Journal* 27, no. 4 (1999): 411–27; Z. Emden, A. Yaprak, and S. T. Cavusgil, "Learning from Experience in International Alliances: Antecedents and Firm Performance Implications," *Journal of Business Research* 58, no. 7 (2005): 883–92.

24. J.M. Kouzes and B.Z. Posner, *The Leadership Challenge*, 6th ed. (San Francisco: Jossey-Bass, 2017).

25. R.J. House, "A 1976 Theory of Charismatic Leadership," in *Leadership: The Cutting Edge*, ed. J.G. Hunt and L.L. Larson (Carbondale: Southern Illinois University Press, 1977), 189–207; J.A. Conger, "Charismatic Leadership," in *The Sage Handbook of Leadership*, ed. A. Bryman et al. (London: Sage, 2011), 86–102.

26. J.E. Barbuto Jr., "Taking the Charisma out of Transformational Leadership," *Journal of Social Behavior & Personality* 12 (1997): 689–97; Y.A. Nur, "Charisma and Managerial Leadership: The Gift That Never Was," *Business Horizons* 41 (1998): 19–26; M.D. Mumford and J.R. Van Doorn, "The Leadership of Pragmatism: Reconsidering Franklin in the Age of Charisma," *Leadership Quarterly* 12, no. 3 (2001): 279–309; A. Fanelli, "Bringing Out Charisma: CEO Charisma and External Stakeholders," *Academy of Management Review* 31, no. 4 (2006): 1049–61; M.J. Platow et al., "A Special Gift We Bestow on You for Being Representative of Us: Considering Leader Charisma from a Self-Categorization Perspective," *British Journal of Social Psychology* 45, no. 2 (2006): 303–20.

27. W.H. Friedland, "For a Sociological Concept of Charisma," *Social Forces* 43 (1964): 18–26; K. Miyahara, "Charisma: From Weber to Contemporary Sociology," *Sociological Inquiry* 53 (1983): 368–88; J. Antonakis et al., "Charisma: An Ill-Defined and Ill-Measured Gift," *Annual Review of Organizational Psychology and Organizational Behavior* 3 (2016): 293–319; K.O. Tskhay, R. Zhu, and N.O. Rule, "Perceptions of Charisma from Thin Slices of Behavior Predict Leadership Prototypicality Judgments," *Leadership Quarterly*, 28 (2017): 555–62.

28. B. Shamir et al., "Correlates of Charismatic Leader Behavior in Military Units: Subordinates' Attitudes, Unit Characteristics, and Superiors' Appraisals of Leader Performance," *Academy of Management Journal* 41, no. 4 (1998): 387–409; R.E. de Vries, R.A. Roe, and T.C.B. Taillieu, "On Charisma and Need for Leadership," *European Journal of Work and Organizational Psychology* 8 (1999): 109–33; R. Khurana, *Searching for a Corporate Savior: The Irrational Quest for Charismatic CEOs* (Princeton, NJ: Princeton University Press, 2002); R.E. de Vries, R.D. Pathak, and A.R. Paquin, "The Paradox of Power Sharing: Participative Charismatic Leaders Have Subordinates with More Instead of Less Need for Leadership," *European Journal of Work and Organizational Psychology* 20, no. 6 (2010): 779–804. The effect of charismatic leadership on follower dependence also was noted earlier by U.S. government leader John Gardner. See J.W. Gardner, *On Leadership* (New York: Free Press, 1990), 34–36.

29. J. Lipman-Blumen, "A Pox on Charisma: Why Connective Leadership and Character Count," in *The Drucker Difference: What the World's Greatest Management Thinker Means to Today's Business Leaders*, ed. C.L. Pearce, J.A. Maciariello, and H. Yamawaki (New York: McGraw-Hill, 2010), 149–74.

30. A. Mackey, "The Effect of CEOs on Firm Performance," *Strategic Management Journal* 29, no. 12 (2008): 1357–67. However, one study reported that transformational leadership is less effective than authoritarian (command-control with punishment) leadership in resource scarcity environments. See X. Huang et al., "When Authoritarian Leaders Outperform Transformational Leaders: Firm Performance in a Harsh Economic Environment," *Academy of Management Discoveries* 1, no. 2 (2015): 180–200.

31. A. Bryman, "Leadership in Organizations," in *Handbook of Organization Studies*, ed. S.R. Clegg, C. Hardy, and W.R. Nord (Thousand Oaks, CA: Sage, 1996), 276–92; D. van Knippenberg and S.B. Sitkin, "A Critical Assessment of Charismatic-Transformational Leadership Research: Back to the Drawing Board?" *Academy of Management Annals* 7, no. 1 (2013): 1–60.

32. G. Yukl and J.W. Michel, "A Critical Assessment of Research on Effective Leadership Behavior," in *Advances in Authentic and Ethical Leadership*, ed. L.L. Neider and C.A. Schriesheim (Charlotte, NC: Information Age, 2014), 209–30.

33. B.S. Pawar and K.K. Eastman, "The Nature and Implications of Contextual Influences on Transformational Leadership: A Conceptual Examination," *Academy of Management Review* 22 (1997): 80–109; C.P. Egri and S. Herman, "Leadership in the North American Environmental Sector: Values, Leadership Styles, and Contexts of Environmental Leaders and Their Organizations," *Academy of Management Journal* 43, no. 4 (2000): 571–604.

34. A. Zaleznik, "Managers and Leaders: Are They Different?" *Harvard Business Review* 55, no. 3 (1977): 67–78; J.P. Kotter, *A Force for Change: How Leadership Differs from Management* (New York: Free Press, 1990); E.A. Locke, *The Essence of Leadership* (New York: Lexington Books, 1991); G. Yukl and R. Lepsinger, "Why Integrating the Leading and Managing Roles Is Essential for Organizational Effectiveness," *Organizational Dynamics* 34, no. 4 (2005): 361–75; D.V. Simonet and R.P. Tett, "Five Perspectives on the Leadership–Management Relationship: A Competency-Based Evaluation and Integration," *Journal of Leadership & Organizational Studies* 20, no. 2 (2013): 199–213.

35. W. Bennis and B. Nanus, *Leaders: The Strategies for Taking Charge* (New York: Harper & Row, 1985), 21. Peter Drucker also is widely cited as the source of this quotation. The closest passage we could find, however, is in the first two pages of *The Effective Executive* (1966) where Drucker states that effective executives "get the right things done." On the next page, he states that manual workers only need efficiency, "that is, the ability to do things right rather than the ability to get the right things done." See P.F. Drucker, *The Effective Executive* (New York: Harper Business, 1966), 1–2.

36. R.J. House and R.N. Aditya, "The Social Scientific Study of Leadership: Quo Vadis?" *Journal of Management* 23, no. 3 (1997): 409–73.

37. G. Yukl and R. Lepsinger, "Why Integrating the Leading and Managing Roles Is Essential for Organizational Effectiveness," *Organizational Dynamics* 34, no. 4 (2005): 361–75. One recent critique of leadership theories suggests that scholars need to further clarify the distinction, if any exists, between leading and managing. See S.T. Hannah et al., "Debunking the False Dichotomy of Leadership Idealism and Pragmatism: Critical Evaluation and Support of Newer Genre Leadership Theories," *Journal of Organizational Behavior* 35, no. 5 (2014): 598–621.

38. E.A. Fleishman, "The Description of Supervisory Behavior," *Journal of Applied Psychology* 37, no. 1 (1953): 1–6. For discussion on methodological problems with the development of these people-versus-task-oriented leadership constructs, see C.A. Schriesheim, R.J. House, and S. Kerr, "Leader Initiating Structure: A Reconciliation of Discrepant Research Results and Some Empirical Tests," *Organizational Behavior and Human Performance* 15, no. 2 (1976): 297–321; L. Tracy, "Consideration and Initiating Structure: Are They Basic Dimensions of Leader Behavior?" *Social Behavior and Personality* 15, no. 1 (1987): 21–33.

39. A.K. Korman, "Consideration, Initiating Structure, and Organizational Criteria–A Review," *Personnel Psychology* 19 (1966): 349–62; E.A. Fleishman, "Twenty Years of Consideration and Structure," in *Current Developments in the Study of Leadership*, ed. E.A. Fleishman and J.C. Hunt (Carbondale: Southern Illinois University Press, 1973), 1–40; T.A. Judge, R.F. Piccolo, and R. Ilies, "The Forgotten Ones? The Validity of Consideration and Initiating Structure in Leadership Research," *Journal of Applied Psychology* 89, no. 1 (2004): 36–51; D.S. DeRue et al., "Trait and Behavioral Theories of Leadership: An Integration and Meta-Analytic Test of Their Relative Validity," *Personnel Psychology* 64, no. 1 (2011): 7–52; G.A. Yukl, *Leadership in Organizations*, 8th ed. (Upper Saddle River, NJ: Pearson Education, 2013), 62–75.

40. V.V. Baba, "Serendipity in Leadership: Initiating Structure and Consideration in the Classroom," *Human Relations* 42 (1989): 509–25.

41. S.J. Peterson, B.M. Galvin, and D. Lange, "CEO Servant Leadership: Exploring Executive Characteristics and Firm Performance," *Personnel Psychology* 65, no. 3 (2012): 565–96.

42. R.K. Greenleaf, *Servant Leadership: A Journey into the Nature of Legitimate Power & Greatness* (Mahwah, NJ: Paulist Press, 1977; repr., 2002), 27.

43. S. Sendjaya, J.C. Sarros, and J.C. Santora, "Defining and Measuring Servant Leadership Behaviour in Organizations," *Journal of Management Studies* 45 (2008): 402–24; R.C. Liden et al., "Servant Leadership: Development of a Multidimensional Measure and Multi-Level Assessment," *Leadership Quarterly* 19 (2008): 161–77; D. van Dierendonck, "Servant Leadership: A Review and Synthesis," *Journal of Management* 37 (2011): 1228–61; R. VanMeter et al., "In Search of Clarity on Servant Leadership: Domain Specification and Reconceptualization," *AMS Review* 6 (2016): 59–78.

44. R. VanMeter et al., "In Search of Clarity on Servant Leadership: Domain Specification and Reconceptualization," *AMS Review* 6 (2016): 59–78.

45. S.J. Peterson, B.M. Galvin, and D. Lange, "CEO Servant Leadership: Exploring Executive Characteristics and Firm Performance," *Personnel Psychology* 65, no. 3 (2012): 565–96.

46. S. Kerr et al., "Towards a Contingency Theory of Leadership Based Upon the Consideration and Initiating Structure Literature," *Organizational Behavior and Human Performance* 12 (1974): 62–82; L.L. Larson, J.G. Hunt, and R.N. Osborn, "The Great Hi-Hi Leader Behavior Myth: A Lesson from Occam's Razor," *Academy of Management Journal* 19 (1976): 628–41.

47. R.J. House, "A Path Goal Theory of Leader Effectiveness," *Administrative Science Quarterly* 16, no. 3 (1971): 321–39; M.G. Evans, "Extensions of a Path-Goal Theory of Motivation," *Journal of Applied Psychology* 59 (1974): 172–78; R.J. House and T.R. Mitchell, "Path-Goal Theory of Leadership," *Journal of Contemporary Business* (1974): 81–97; M.G. Evans, "Path Goal Theory of Leadership," in *Leadership*, ed. L.L. Neider and C.A. Schriesheim (Greenwich, CT: Information Age, 2002), 115–38.
48. For a thorough study of how expectancy theory of motivation relates to leadership, see R.G. Isaac, W.J. Zerbe, and D.C. Pitt, "Leadership and Motivation: The Effective Application of Expectancy Theory," *Journal of Managerial Issues* 13 (2001): 212–26.
49. R.J. House, "Path-Goal Theory of Leadership: Lessons, Legacy, and a Reformulated Theory," *The Leadership Quarterly* 7, no. 3 (1996): 323–52.
50. J. Indvik, "Path-Goal Theory of Leadership: A Meta-Analysis," *Academy of Management Proceedings* (1986): 189–92; J.C. Wofford and L.Z. Liska, "Path-Goal Theories of Leadership: A Meta-Analysis," *Journal of Management* 19 (1993): 857–76.
51. These testimonials are reported in S. Sahadi, "We Asked CNN Business Readers What Makes a Great Boss. Here's What You Said," *CNN Business*, March 27, 2019.
52. J.D. Houghton and S.K. Yoho, "Toward a Contingency Model of Leadership and Psychological Empowerment: When Should Self-Leadership Be Encouraged?" *Journal of Leadership & Organizational Studies* 11, no. 4 (2005): 65–83.
53. R.T. Keller, "A Test of the Path-Goal Theory of Leadership with Need for Clarity as a Moderator in Research and Development Organizations," *Journal of Applied Psychology* 74 (1989): 208–12.
54. R.P. Vecchio, J.E. Justin, and C.L. Pearce, "The Utility of Transactional and Transformational Leadership for Predicting Performance and Satisfaction within a Path-Goal Theory Framework," *Journal of Occupational and Organizational Psychology* 81 (2008): 71–82.
55. B. Carroll and L. Levy, "Defaulting to Management: Leadership Defined by What It Is Not," *Organization* 15, no. 1 (2008): 75–96; I. Holmberg and M. Tyrstrup, "Well Then—What Now? An Everyday Approach to Managerial Leadership," *Leadership* 6, no. 4 (2010): 353–72.
56. C.A. Schriesheim and L.L. Neider, "Path-Goal Leadership Theory: The Long and Winding Road," *Leadership Quarterly* 7 (1996): 317–21.
57. N. Nicholson, *Executive Instinct* (New York: Crown, 2000); T.A. Judge, R.F. Piccolo, and R. Ilies, "The Forgotten Ones? The Validity of Consideration and Initiating Structure in Leadership Research," *Journal of Applied Psychology* 89, no. 1 (2004): 36–51; T.A. Judge, R.F. Piccolo, and T. Kosalka, "The Bright and Dark Sides of Leader Traits: A Review and Theoretical Extension of the Leader Trait Paradigm," *Leadership Quarterly* 20 (2009): 855–75. One pioneering managerial leadership expect specifically argued that managers cannot easily switch leadership styles. See FE. Fiedler, "Engineer the Job to Fit the Manager," *Harvard Business Review* 43, no. 5 (1965): 115–22.
58. S. Kerr and J.M. Jermier, "Substitutes for Leadership: Their Meaning and Measurement," *Organizational Behavior and Human Performance* 22 (December 1978): 375–403.
59. This observation also has been made by C.A. Schriesheim, "Substitutes-for-Leadership Theory: Development and Basic Concepts," *Leadership Quarterly* 8 (1997): 103–08.
60. D.F. Elloy and A. Randolph, "The Effect of Superleader Behavior on Autonomous Work Groups in a Government Operated Railway Service," *Public Personnel Management* 26 (1997): 257–72; C.C. Manz and H. Sims Jr., *The New SuperLeadership: Leading Others to Lead Themselves* (San Francisco: Berrett-Koehler, 2001).
61. M.L. Loughry, "Coworkers Are Watching: Performance Implications of Peer Monitoring," *Academy of Management Proceedings* (2002): O1–O6.
62. P.M. Podsakoff and S.B. MacKenzie, "Kerr and Jermier's Substitutes for Leadership Model: Background, Empirical Assessment, and Suggestions for Future Research," *Leadership Quarterly* 8 (1997): 117–32; S.D. Dionne et al., "Neutralizing Substitutes for Leadership Theory: Leadership Effects and Common-Source Bias," *Journal of Applied Psychology* 87, no. 3 (2002): 454–64; J.R. Villa et al., "Problems with Detecting Moderators in Leadership Research Using Moderated Multiple Regression," *Leadership Quarterly* 14, no. 1 (2003): 3–23; S.D. Dionne et al., "Substitutes for Leadership, or Not," *Leadership Quarterly* 16, no. 1 (2005): 169–93.
63. J.R. Meindl, "On Leadership: An Alternative to the Conventional Wisdom," *Research in Organizational Behavior* 12 (1990): 159–203; L.R. Offermann, J.K. Kennedy, and P.W. Wirtz, "Implicit Leadership Theories: Content, Structure, and Generalizability," *Leadership Quarterly* 5, no. 1 (1994): 43–58; R.J. Hall and R.G. Lord, "Multi-Level Information Processing Explanations of Followers' Leadership Perceptions," *Leadership Quarterly* 6 (1995): 265–87; O. Epitropaki and R. Martin, "Implicit Leadership Theories in Applied Settings: Factor Structure, Generalizability, and Stability over Time," *Journal of Applied Psychology* 89, no. 2 (2004): 293–310. For a broader discussion of the social construction of leadership, see G.T. Fairhurst and D. Grant, "The Social Construction of Leadership: A Sailing Guide," *Management Communication Quarterly* 24, no. 2 (2010): 171–210.
64. R.G. Lord et al., "Contextual Constraints on Prototype Generation and Their Multilevel Consequences for Leadership Perceptions," *Leadership Quarterly* 12, no. 3 (2001): 311–38; K.A. Scott and D.J. Brown, "Female First, Leader Second? Gender Bias in the Encoding of Leadership Behavior," *Organizational Behavior and Human Decision Processes* 101 (2006): 230–42; S.J. Shondrick, J.E. Dinh, and R.G. Lord, "Developments in Implicit Leadership Theory and Cognitive Science: Applications to Improving Measurement and Understanding Alternatives to Hierarchical Leadership," *Leadership Quarterly* 21, no. 6 (2010): 959–78.
65. S.F. Cronshaw and R.G. Lord, "Effects of Categorization, Attribution, and Encoding Processes on Leadership Perceptions," *Journal of Applied Psychology* 72 (1987): 97–106; J.L. Nye and D.R. Forsyth, "The Effects of Prototype-Based Biases on Leadership Appraisals: A Test of Leadership Categorization Theory," *Small Group Research* 22 (1991): 360–79.
66. R. Meindl, "On Leadership: An Alternative to the Conventional Wisdom," *Research in Organizational Behavior* 12 (1990): 163; B. Schyns, J.R. Meindl, and M.A. Croon, "The Romance of Leadership Scale: Cross-Cultural Testing and Refinement," *Leadership* 3, no. 1 (2007): 29–46; J. Felfe and L.E. Petersen, "Romance of Leadership and Management Decision Making," *European Journal of Work and Organizational Psychology* 16, no. 1 (2007): 1–24.
67. J. Pfeffer, "The Ambiguity of Leadership," *Academy of Management Review* 2 (1977): 102–12.
68. R. Weber et al., "The Illusion of Leadership: Misattribution of Cause in Coordination Games," *Organization Science* 12, no. 5 (2001): 582–98; N. Ensari and S.E. Murphy, "Cross-Cultural Variations in Leadership Perceptions and Attribution of Charisma to the Leader," *Organizational Behavior and Human Decision Processes* 92 (2003): 52–66; M.L.A. Hayward, V.P. Rindova, and T.G. Pollock, "Believing One's Own Press: The Causes and Consequences of CEO Celebrity," *Strategic Management Journal* 25, no. 7 (2004): 637-53.
69. The history of the personal attributes perspective of leadership, as well as current research on this topic, is nicely summarized in S. J. Zaccaro, C. Kemp, and P. Bader, "Leader Traits and Attributes," in *The Nature of Leadership*, ed. J. Antonakis, A. T. Cianciolo, and R. J. Sternberg (Thousand Oaks, CA: Sage, 2004), 101–24.
70. R. M. Stogdill, *Handbook of Leadership* (New York: Free Press, 1974), chap. 5.

71. This list is based on S.A. Kirkpatrick and E.A. Locke, "Leadership: Do Traits Matter?" *Academy of Management Executive* 5 (1991): 48–60; S.J. Zaccaro, C. Kemp, and P. Bader, "Leader Traits and Attributes," in *The Nature of Leadership*, ed. J. Antonakis, A.T. Cianciolo, and R.J. Sternberg (Thousand Oaks, CA: Sage, 2004), 101–24; G.A. Yukl, *Leadership in Organizations*, 8th ed. (Upper Saddle River, NJ: Pearson Education, 2013), Chap. 6.

72. T.A. Judge et al., "Personality and Leadership: A Qualitative and Quantitative Review," *Journal of Applied Psychology* 87, no. 4 (2002): 765–80; D.S. Derue et al., "Trait and Behavioral Theories of Leadership: An Integration and Meta-Analytic Test of Their Relative Validity," *Personnel Psychology* 64, no. 1 (2011): 7–52; A. Deinert et al., "Transformational Leadership Sub-Dimensions and Their Link to Leaders' Personality and Performance," *Leadership Quarterly* 26, no. 6 (2015): 1095–120; A.D. Parr, S.T. Lanza, and P. Bernthal, "Personality Profiles of Effective Leadership Performance in Assessment Centers," *Human Performance* 29, no. 2 (2016): 143–57.

73. D.V. Day, M.M. Harrison, and S.M. Halpin, *An Integrative Approach to Leader Development: Connecting Adult Development, Identity, and Expertise* (New York: Routledge, 2009); D.S. DeRue and S.J. Ashford, "Who Will Lead and Who Will Follow? A Social Process of Leadership Identity Construction in Organizations," *Academy of Management Review* 35, no. 4 (2010): 627–47; H. Ibarra et al., "Leadership and Identity: An Examination of Three Theories and New Research Directions," in *The Oxford Handbook of Leadership and Organizations*, ed. D.V. Day (New York: Oxford University Press, 2014), 285–301; L. Guillén, M. Mayo, and K. Korotov, "Is Leadership a Part of Me? A Leader Identity Approach to Understanding the Motivation to Lead," *Leadership Quarterly* 26, no. 5 (2015): 802–20.

74. B. Carroll and L. Levy, "Defaulting to Management: Leadership Defined by What It Is Not," *Organization* 15, no. 1 (2008): 75–96.

75. One study suggests that leaders sometimes retain their power by undermining followers' power. See C. Case and J. Maner, "Divide and Conquer: When and Why Leaders Undermine the Cohesive Fabric of Their Group," *Journal of Personality and Social Psychology* 107, no. 6 (2014): 1033–50.

76. J. B. Miner, "Twenty Years of Research on Role Motivation Theory of Managerial Effectiveness," *Personnel Psychology* 31 (1978): 739–60; C.J. Vinkenburg et al., "Arena: A Critical Conceptual Framework of Top Management Selection," *Group & Organization Management* 39, no. 1 (2014): 33–68; B.L. Connelly et al., "Tournament Theory: Thirty Years of Contests and Competitions," *Journal of Management* 40, no. 1 (2014): 16–47; Y. Baruch and Y. Vardi, "A Fresh Look at the Dark Side of Contemporary Careers: Toward a Realistic Discourse," *British Journal of Management* 27, no. 2 (2016): 355–72.

77. For surveys on the importance of leader integrity, see J.M. Kouzes and B.Z. Posner, *The Leadership Challenge*, 5th ed. (San Francisco: Jossey-Bass, 2012), Chap. 2; R. Half, "What Is the Most Important Leadership Attribute?" news release (Menlo Park, CA: PR Newswire, September 22, 2016); S. Giles, "The Most Important Leadership Competencies, According to Leaders around the World," *Harvard Business Review Digital Articles*, March 2016, 2–6.

78. "Could Trust Cost You a Generation of Talent? Global Generations 3.0: A Global Study on Trust in the Workplace" (London: EY, June 2016); G. Dondé, "Ethics at Work: 2018 Survey of Employees: Europe" (London: Institute of Business Ethics, July 2018); J. Dube, "8 Questions That Need to Be on Every Manager Evaluation Form," *The Predictive Index* (blog), September 11, 2018, https://www.predictiveindex.com/blog/8-questions-that-need-to-be-on-every-manager-evaluation-form/; Office of Personnel Management, "2019 Federal Employee Viewpoint Survey" (Washington, DC: U.S. Government, October 2019); "2019 Public Service Employee Survey Results for the Public Service" (Ottawa: Government of Canada, Treasury Board of Canada Secretariat, January 15, 2020).

79. J. Hedlund et al., "Identifying and Assessing Tacit Knowledge: Understanding the Practical Intelligence of Military Leaders," *Leadership Quarterly* 14, no. 2 (2003): 117–40; R.J. Sternberg, "A Systems Model of Leadership: WICS," *American Psychologist* 62, no. 1 (2007): 34–42.

80. J.M. George, "Emotions and Leadership: The Role of Emotional Intelligence," *Human Relations* 53 (2000): 1027–55; D. Goleman, R. Boyatzis, and A. McKee, *Primal Leaders* (Boston: Harvard Business School Press, 2002); R.G. Lord and R.J. Hall, "Identity, Deep Structure and the Development of Leadership Skill," *Leadership Quarterly* 16, no. 4 (2005): 591–615; C. Skinner and P. Spurgeon, "Valuing Empathy and Emotional Intelligence in Health Leadership: A Study of Empathy, Leadership Behaviour and Outcome Effectiveness," *Health Services Management Research* 18, no. 1 (2005): 1–12.

81. "Three Leadership Secrets from easyJet Boss Carolyn McCall," *O2 BusinessBlog, O2*, September 19, 2014, http://businessblog.o2.co.uk/three-leadership-secrets-easyjet-boss-carolyn-mccall/; C. Zillman, "easyJet CEO: 'I'm Not a Turnaround Expert,'" *Fortune*, June 15, 2015; L. Roderick, "easyJet CEO Carolyn McCall Explains How Marketers Can Soar," *Marketing Week*, March 9, 2016; K. Magee, "'Women Don't Need to Defeminise, They Need to Be Themselves,' easyJet CEO McCall Says," *Advertising Week*, April 19, 2016; D. Medland, "EasyJet CEO Dame Carolyn McCall on Transformative Leadership," *Insights (Chartered Management Institute)*, April 26, 2017; G. Spanier, "ITV's Carolyn McCall: 'We Have Got to Evolve Quickly,'" *Campaign*, February 18, 2019.

82. B. George, *Authentic Leadership* (San Francisco: Jossey-Bass, 2004); W.L. Gardner et al., "'Can You See the Real Me?' A Self-Based Model of Authentic Leader and Follower Development," *Leadership Quarterly* 16 (2005): 343–72; B. George, *True North* (San Francisco: Jossey-Bass, 2007), Chap. 4; M.E. Palanski and F.J. Yammarino, "Integrity and Leadership: Clearing the Conceptual Confusion," *European Management Journal* 25, no. 3 (2007): 171–84; F.O. Walumbwa et al., "Authentic Leadership: Development and Validation of a Theory-Based Measure," *Journal of Management* 34, no. 1 (2008): 89–126.

83. W.G. Bennis and R.J. Thomas, "Crucibles of Leadership," *Harvard Business Review* 80, no. 9 (2002): 39–45; R.J. Thomas, *Crucibles of Leadership: How to Learn from Experience to Become a Great Leader* (Boston: Harvard Business Press, 2008).

84. R. Jacobs, "Using Human Resource Functions to Enhance Emotional Intelligence," in *The Emotionally Intelligent Workplace*, ed. C. Cherniss and D. Goleman (San Francisco: Jossey-Bass, 2001), 161–63; J.A. Conger and D.A. Ready, "Rethinking Leadership Competencies," *Leader to Leader* (2004): 41–47.

85. R.G. Lord and D.J. Brown, *Leadership Processes and Self-Identity: A Follower-Centered Approach to Leadership* (Mahwah, NJ: Erlbaum, 2004); R. Bolden and J. Gosling, "Leadership Competencies: Time to Change the Tune?" *Leadership* 2, no. 2 (2006): 147–63.

86. G.N. Powell, "One More Time: Do Female and Male Managers Differ?" *Academy of Management Executive* 4 (1990): 68–75; M.L. van Engen and T.M. Willemsen, "Sex and Leadership Styles: A Meta-Analysis of Research Published in the 1990s," *Psychological Reports* 94, no. 1 (2004): 3–18.

87. A. H. Eagly, M. C. Johannesen-Schmidt, and M. L. van Engen, "Transformational, Transactional, and Laissez-Faire Leadership Styles: A Meta-Analysis Comparing Women and Men," *Psychological Bulletin* 129 (2003): 569–91; S. Paustian-Underdahl, L. Walker, and D. Woehr, "Gender and Perceptions of Leadership Effectiveness: A Meta-Analysis of Contextual Moderators," *Journal of Applied Psychology* 99, no. 6 (2014): 1129–45.

88. A.H. Eagly, S.J. Karau, and M.G. Makhijani, "Gender and the Effectiveness of Leaders: A Meta-Analysis," *Psychological Bulletin* 117 (1995): 125–45; M.E. Heilman et al., "Penalties for Success: Reactions to Women Who Succeed at Male Gender-Typed Tasks," *Journal of Applied Psychology* 89, no. 3 (2004): 416–27; A.H. Eagly, "Achieving Relational Authenticity in Leadership: Does Gender Matter?," *Leadership Quarterly* 16, no. 3 (2005): 459–74; A.J. Anderson et al., "The Effectiveness of Three Strategies to Reduce the Influence of Bias in Evaluations of Female Leaders," *Journal of Applied Social Psychology* 45, no. 9 (2015): 522–39.

PART 4

12 Designing Organizational Structures

pcruciatti/Shutterstock

Learning Objectives

After you read this chapter, you should be able to:

LO12-1 Describe three types of coordination in organizational structures.

LO12-2 Discuss the role and effects of span of control, centralization, and formalization and relate these elements to organic and mechanistic organizational structures.

LO12-3 Identify and evaluate five types of departmentalization.

LO12-4 Explain how the external environment, organizational size, technology, and strategy are relevant when designing an organizational structure.

organizational structure the division of labor as well as the patterns of coordination, communication, workflow, and formal power that direct organizational activities

Robert Bosch GmbH has been replacing its hierarchical organizational structure with a team-based structure. For example, the power tools division of the German engineering and technology company replaced a seven-layer hierarchy with cross-functional self-directed teams, each with less than one dozen employees. The home and gardens business unit alone has 54 teams. Most teams are responsible for designing or manufacturing specific products (hedging products, cleaning technology, etc.). However, some teams are assigned support roles, such as engineering services and brand management.

"In terms of achieving a flatter organization, for a lot of projects we now work in a "podular" structure," explains a Bosch executive. "So, not in a kind of pyramid organization, but by creating teams, or pods, with people from multiple departments with different expertise who can work together on projects much faster." The team-based structure enables the company to respond more quickly and effectively to changes and customized client requests. "As these teams are mostly independent of any hierarchical constraints, they can connect and act in a much more agile way and really focus on the results."[1]

Robert Bosch GmbH is relying on a new organizational structure to support creativity and agility at the German engineering and technology company. **Organizational structure** refers to the division of labor as well as the patterns of coordination, communication, workflow, and formal power that direct organizational activities. Structure formally dictates the allocation of financial, power, and information resources, as well as what activities receive the most attention. For example, Bosch's new structure reorganizes employees around cross-functional teams rather than specialized departments. It also decentralizes more authority and accountability to these self-directed teams.

The topic of organizational structure typically conjures up images of an organizational chart. Organizational structure includes these reporting relationships, but it also includes other features that relate to work standards and rules, team dynamics, power relationships, information flow, and job design. The organization's structure is an important instrument in an executive's toolkit for organizational change because it establishes new communication patterns and aligns employee behavior with the corporate vision. Indeed, one recent global survey of 7,000 business and human resources leaders in 130 countries reported that organizational design was their firm's most important trend or priority to improve human capital (leadership and corporate culture were second and third most important, respectively).[2]

This chapter begins by introducing the two fundamental processes in organizational structure: division of labor and coordination. This is followed by a detailed investigation of the four main elements of organizational structure: span of control, centralization, formalization, and departmentalization. The latter part of this chapter examines the contingencies of organizational design, including external environment, organizational size, technology, and strategy.

LO12-1 Describe three types of coordination in organizational structures.

DIVISION OF LABOR AND COORDINATION

All organizational structures include two fundamental requirements: the division of labor into distinct tasks and the coordination of that labor so employees are able to accomplish common goals.[3] Organizations are groups of people who work interdependently toward some purpose. To effectively accomplish this common purpose, most work is divided into manageable chunks, particularly when there are many different tasks required to complete the work. Organizations also introduce various coordinating mechanisms to ensure that everyone is working effectively toward the same objectives.

Division of Labor

Division of labor refers to the subdivision of work into separate jobs assigned to different people. Subdivided work leads to job specialization because each job now includes a narrow subset of the tasks necessary to complete the product or service. Bosch divides its employees into thousands of specific jobs to more effectively design, manufacture, and market new products. As companies get larger, this horizontal division of labor is usually accompanied by vertical division of labor. Some people are assigned the task of supervising employees, others are responsible for managing those supervisors, and so forth.

Why do companies divide the work into several jobs? As we described in Chapter 5, job specialization increases work efficiency.[4] Job incumbents can master their tasks more quickly when work cycles are shorter. Less time is wasted changing

All organizational structures include two fundamental requirements: the division of labor into distinct tasks and the coordination of that labor.
Vetta/Getty Images

from one task to another. Training costs are lower because employees require fewer physical and mental skills to accomplish the assigned work. Finally, job specialization makes it easier to match people with specific aptitudes or skills to the jobs for which they are best suited. It is almost impossible for one person working alone to competitively design, manufacture, and market to retailers a new Bosch precision digital inclinometer (a trade tool that electronically measures angles); instead, this work requires hundreds of people with diverse knowledge and skills.

Coordination of Work Activities

When people divide work among themselves, they require coordinating mechanisms to ensure that everyone acts in concert. In fact, the extent to which work can be effectively divided among several people and departments depends on how well the divided work can be coordinated. When an organization divides work beyond its capacity to coordinate that work, individual effort is wasted due to misalignment, duplication, and mistiming of tasks. Coordination also tends to become more expensive and difficult as the division of labor increases. Therefore, companies specialize jobs only to the point where it isn't too costly or challenging to coordinate the people in those jobs.[5]

Every organization—from the two-person tax accounting business to the largest corporate entity—uses one or more of the following coordinating mechanisms:[6] informal communication, formal hierarchy, and standardization (see Exhibit 12.1). These forms of coordination align the work of staff within the same department as well as across work units. Coordinating mechanisms are also critical when several organizations work together, such as in joint ventures and humanitarian aid programs.[7]

Coordination through Informal Communication All organizations rely on informal communication as a coordinating mechanism. This process includes sharing information on mutual tasks as well as forming common mental models so that employees synchronize work activities using the same cognitive road map.[8] Informal communication is vital in nonroutine and ambiguous situations because employees need to exchange a large volume of information through face-to-face communication and other media-rich channels. Bosch's new structure encourages more informal communication because much of the work among product development teams relates to novel ideas, which are nonroutine and ambiguous.

Coordination through informal communication is easiest in small firms, but digital technologies have further enabled this coordinating mechanism at Bosch and in other large organizations.[9] Companies employing thousands of people also support informal communication by keeping each production site small. Magna International follows this principle by keeping many of its plants—including its recently opened paint shop in Hoče,

Exhibit 12.1 Coordinating Mechanisms in Organizations

Form of Coordination	Description	Subtypes/Strategies
Informal communication	Sharing information on mutual tasks; forming common mental models to synchronize work activities.	• Direct communication • Liaison roles • Integrator roles • Temporary teams
Formal hierarchy	Assigning legitimate power to individuals, who then use this power to direct work processes and allocate resources.	• Direct supervision • Formal communication channels
Standardization	Creating routine patterns of behavior or output.	• Standardized skills • Standardized processes • Standardized output

Sources: Based on information in J. Galbraith, *Designing Complex Organizations* (Reading, MA: Addison-Wesley, 1973), 8–19; H. Mintzberg, *The Structuring of Organizations* (Englewood Cliffs, NJ: Prentice Hall, 1979), Chap. 1; D.A. Nadler and M.L. Tushman, *Competing by Design: The Power of Organizational Architecture* (New York: Oxford University Press, 1997), Chap. 6.

Large organizations encourage coordination through informal communication by organizing employees from several departments into temporary cross-disciplinary teams.
stockbroker/123RF

Slovenia–to a maximum size of around 200 employees. The global auto-parts manufacturer has found that employees have difficulty remembering each other's names in plants that are any larger, a situation that makes informal communication more difficult as a coordinating mechanism.[10]

Some large firms encourage informal communication through *liaison roles.* These employees transmit information between two work units that seldom communicate or coordinate directly with each other. Coordination through informal communication is also possible in larger firms through *integrator roles*. These people coordinate a work process by encouraging employees in each work unit to directly share information and coordinate work activities with each other. Brand managers for luxury perfumes have integrator roles because they ensure that fragrance developers, bottle designers, advertising creatives, production, and other groups work together to develop the product and brand's image.[11]

Large organizations also encourage coordination through informal communication by organizing employees from several departments into temporary teams. Known as *concurrent engineering*, this cross-disciplinary team-based coordination was pioneered by Toyota almost four decades ago and is now widespread throughout several industries. As design engineers work on product specifications, team members from production engineering, manufacturing, marketing, purchasing, and other departments provide immediate feedback as well as begin their contribution to the process. Without concurrent engineering teams, employees at each stage of product development face the cumbersome task of passing their work "over the wall" to the next department with limited or significantly delayed feedback.[12]

Coordination through Formal Hierarchy Informal communication is the most flexible form of coordination, but it can become chaotic as the number of employees increases. Consequently, as organizations grow, they rely increasingly on a second coordinating mechanism: formal hierarchy.[13] Hierarchy assigns legitimate power to individuals, who then use this power to direct work processes and allocate resources. In other words, work is coordinated through direct supervision–the chain of command. For instance, Walmart stores have managers and assistant managers who are responsible for ensuring that employees are properly trained, perform their respective tasks, and coordinate effectively with other staff.

A century ago, management scholars applauded formal hierarchy as the best coordinating mechanism for large organizations. They argued that organizations are most effective when managers exercise their authority and employees receive orders from only one supervisor. The chain of command–in which information flows across work units only through supervisors and managers–was viewed as the backbone of organizational strength.

Although still important, formal hierarchy is much less popular today. One problem, which Bosch is trying to minimize with its new structure, is that hierarchical organizations are not as agile for coordination in complex and novel situations. Formal communication through the chain of command is rarely as fast or accurate as informal direct communication among employees. Another concern with formal hierarchy is that managers are able to closely supervise only a limited number of employees. As the business grows, the number of supervisors and layers of management must increase, resulting in a costly bureaucracy. A third problem is that today's workforce demands more autonomy over work and more involvement in company decisions. Coordination through formal hierarchy tends to limit employee autonomy and involvement, which increases employee complaints of being "micromanaged."

Coordination through Micromanagement[14]

71% of 889 Koreans say that they have experienced a militaristic (authoritarian, patriarchic, oppressive management) culture at school and work.

23% of 2,800 American office workers say their current supervisor is a micromanager.

39% of 2,000 American employees say that being a micromanager is the worst quality in a boss (most frequent choice, followed by being "overly critical").

Steve Hamblin/Corbis

31% of 1,525 working Canadians say they have experienced an overbearing micromanager, someone who is constantly hovering and asking for status updates.

59% of 450 American office workers say they have worked for a micromanager.

span of control the number of people directly reporting to the next level above in the hierarchy

Coordination through Standardization Standardization, the third means of coordination, involves creating routine patterns of behavior or output. This coordinating mechanism takes three distinct forms:

- *Standardized processes.* Quality and consistency of a product or service often can be improved by standardizing work activities through job descriptions and procedures.[15] For example, flowcharts represent coordination through standardized processes. This coordinating mechanism works best when the task is routine (such as mass production) or simple (such as stocking shelves), but it is less effective in nonroutine and complex work such as product design or executive decision making.
- *Standardized outputs.* This form of standardization involves ensuring that individuals and work units have clearly defined goals and output measures (e.g., customer satisfaction, production efficiency). For instance, to coordinate the work of salespeople, companies assign sales targets rather than specific behaviors.
- *Standardized skills.* When work activities are too complex to standardize through processes or goals, companies often coordinate work effort by extensively training employees or hiring people who have learned precise role behaviors from educational programs. Hospitals, accounting firms, and other organizations that employ professionals rely on coordination through standardized skills. They carefully hire people for their education, training, and past experience so they can perform tasks without continuous supervision, precise job descriptions, or exacting work process guidelines. Training is also a form of standardization through skills. Many companies have in-house training programs where employees learn how to perform tasks consistent with company expectations.

Division of labor and coordination of work represent the two fundamental ingredients of all organizations. But how work is divided, which coordinating mechanisms are emphasized, who makes decisions, and other issues are related to the four elements of organizational structure that we discuss over the next two sections of this chapter.

LO12-2 Discuss the role and effects of span of control, centralization, and formalization and relate these elements to organic and mechanistic organizational structures.

ELEMENTS OF ORGANIZATIONAL STRUCTURE

Every organizational structure consists of four elements. This section introduces three of them: span of control, centralization, and formalization. The fourth element—departmentalization—is presented in the next section of this chapter.

Span of Control

Span of control (also called *span of management*) refers to the number of people directly reporting to the next level above in the hierarchy. A narrow span of control exists when very few people report directly to a manager, whereas a wide span exists when a manager has many direct reports.[16] A century ago, French engineer and management scholar Henri Fayol strongly recommended a relatively narrow span of control, typically no more than 20 employees per supervisor and 6 supervisors per manager. Fayol championed formal hierarchy as the primary coordinating mechanism, so he believed that supervisors should closely monitor and coach employees. His views were similar to those of Napoleon, who declared that senior military leaders should have no more than five officers directly reporting to them. These prescriptions were based on the belief that managers simply could not monitor and control any more subordinates closely enough.[17]

Today, we know better. The best-performing manufacturing plants currently have an average of 38 production employees per supervisor (see Exhibit 12.2).[18] What's the secret here? Did Fayol, Napoleon, and others miscalculate the optimal span of control? The answer is that those sympathetic to hierarchical control believed employees should perform the physical tasks, whereas supervisors and other management personnel should make the decisions and monitor employees to make sure they performed their tasks. In contrast, the best-performing manufacturing operations today rely on self-directed teams, so direct supervision (formal hierarchy) is supplemented with other coordinating mechanisms. Self-directed teams coordinate mainly through informal communication and various forms of standardization (i.e., training and processes), so formal hierarchy plays more of a supporting role.

Managers often can accommodate a wider span of control because staff members are self-managing and coordinate mainly through standardized skills. For instance, nurse managers often have between 25 and 50 direct reports because nurses are professionally trained and have specific protocols to guide most of their work activity.[20]

A second factor influencing the best span of control is whether employees perform routine tasks. A wider span of control is possible when employees perform routine jobs because they require less direction or advice from supervisors. A narrow span of control is necessary when employees perform novel or complex tasks because these employees tend to require more supervisory decisions and coaching. This principle is illustrated in a survey of property and casualty insurers. The average span of control in commercial-policy processing departments is around 15 employees per supervisor, whereas the span of control is 6.1 in claims service and 5.5 in commercial underwriting. Staff members in the latter two departments perform more technical work, so they have more novel and complex tasks, which requires more supervisor involvement. Commercial-policy processing, on the other hand, is like production work. Tasks are routine and have few exceptions, so managers have less coordinating to do with each employee.[21]

A third influence on span of control is the degree of interdependence among employees within the department or team.[22] Generally, a narrow span of control is necessary for highly

Exhibit 12.2 Recommended, Actual, Estimated, and Enforced Spans of Control[19]

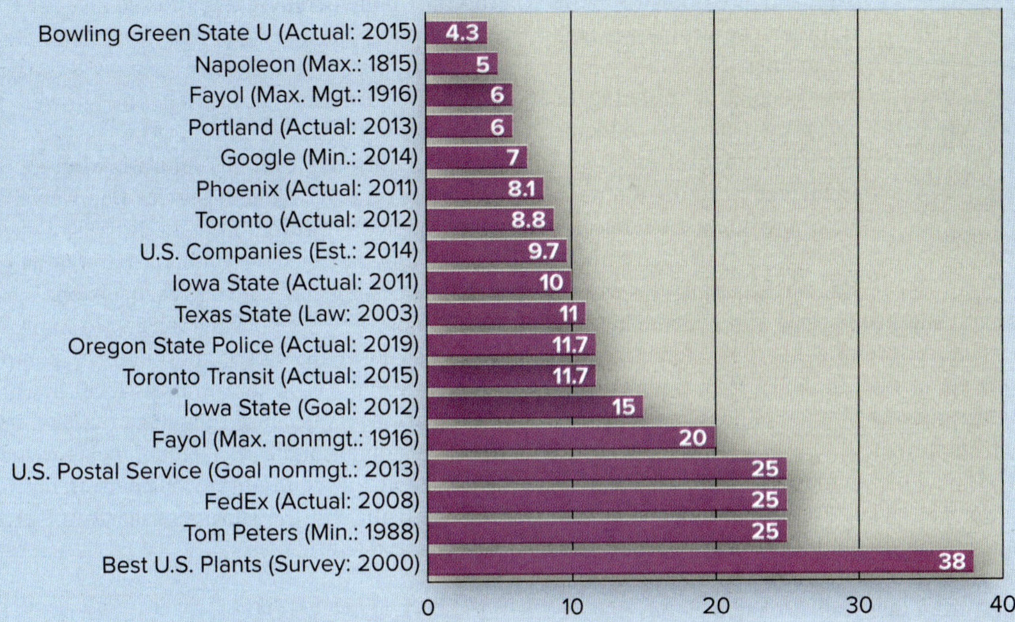

Note: Data represent the average number of direct reports per manager. "Max." is the maximum spans of control recommended by Napoleon Bonaparte and Henri Fayol. "Min." is the minimum span of control applied to teams by Google and recommended by Tom Peters. "Est." is the estimated average span of control across all major U.S. companies, according to consulting firm Deloitte. "Goal" refers to the span of control targets that the U.S. Postal Service and State of Iowa are trying to achieve. (USPS currently exceeds its goal.) The State of Texas number is the span of control mandated by law. The Best U.S. Plants number is the average span of control in American manufacturing facilities identified by *Industry Week* magazine as the most effective. "Actual" refers to the spans of control reported in the cities of Phoenix, Portland, and Toronto; the public service of the U.S. state of Iowa; Bowling Green State University; the Toronto Transit Commission; the Oregon State Police; and FedEx Corporation in the years indicated. The City of Toronto number excludes firefighters and parks, which have unusually high spans of control. When these units are included, Toronto's span of control is 16.29.

interdependent jobs because employees tend to experience more conflict with each other, which requires more of a manager's time to resolve. Also, employees are less clear on their personal work performance in highly interdependent tasks, so supervisors spend more time providing coaching and feedback.

Tall versus Flat Structures Span of control is interconnected with organizational size (number of employees) and the number of layers in the organizational hierarchy. Consider two companies with the same number of employees. If Company A has a wider span of control (more direct reports per manager) than Company B, then Company A necessarily has fewer layers of management (i.e., a flatter structure). The reason for this relationship is that a company with a wider span of control has more employees per supervisor, more supervisors for each middle manager, and so forth. This larger number of direct reports is possible only by removing layers of management.

As companies grow and employ more people, they usually build taller structures to enable some degree of direct supervision as a coordinating mechanism.
Rosemary Calvert/Getty Images

The interconnection of span of control, organizational size (number of employees), and number of management layers has important implications. As organizations grow and employ more people, they must widen the span of control, build a taller hierarchy, or both. Most companies end up building taller structures because they rely on direct supervision to some extent as a coordinating mechanism and there are limits to how many people each manager can coordinate.

Unfortunately, building a taller hierarchy (more layers of management) creates problems. One concern is that executives in tall structures tend to receive lower-quality and less timely information. People tend to filter, distort, and simplify information before it is passed to higher levels in the hierarchy because they are motivated to frame the information in a positive light or to summarize it more efficiently. In contrast, information receives less manipulation in flat hierarchies, and is often received much more quickly than in tall hierarchies.

centralization the degree to which formal decision authority is held by a small group of people, typically those at the top of the organizational hierarchy

formalization the degree to which organizations standardize behavior through rules, procedures, formal training, and related mechanisms

A second problem is that taller structures have higher overhead costs. With more managers per employee, tall hierarchies necessarily have more people administering the company, thereby reducing the percentage of staff who are actually making the product or providing the service. A third issue with tall hierarchies is that employees usually feel less empowered and engaged in their work. Hierarchies are power structures, so more levels of hierarchy tend to draw power away from people at the bottom of that hierarchy. Indeed, the size of the hierarchy itself tends to focus power around managers rather than employees.[24]

These problems with tall hierarchies have prompted companies to reduce management layers. For example, Thomson Reuters recently slashed its hierarchy to a maximum of six layers. The media conglomerate previously had up to 12 layers between the top executive and front-line staff. Conagra Foods also restructured into a flatter organization. CEO Sean Connolly says the packaged food company now has "fewer layers, broader spans of control and the workforce, we believe, is right-sized for speed, empowerment, agility, all the things we need to do."[25]

Although flattening the hierarchy has advantages, this necessarily widens the span of control, which can have negative consequences.[26] With a wider span of control, managers have less time to effectively coach employees, resolve conflicts, and make operational decisions within the work unit. Fewer layers also reduce the company's ability to develop managerial skills because there are fewer positions and steps to develop management talent. Promotions are also riskier because they involve a larger jump in responsibility in flatter, compared to taller, hierarchies. Finally, managers translate corporate strategy into coherent daily operations, but there is less time to perform this vital task when supervising more employees.

Centralization and Decentralization

Centralization means that formal decision-making authority is held by a small group of people, typically those at the top of the organizational hierarchy. Most organizations begin with centralized structures because the founder makes most of the decisions and tries to direct the business toward his or her vision. As organizations grow, however, they diversify and their environments become more complex. Senior executives aren't able to process all the decisions that significantly influence the business. Consequently, larger organizations typically *decentralize*; that is, they disperse decision authority and power throughout the organization.

The optimal level of centralization or decentralization depends on several contingencies that we will examine later in this chapter. However, different degrees of decentralization can occur simultaneously in different parts of an organization. For instance, 7-Eleven centralizes decisions about information technology and supplier purchasing to improve buying power, increase cost-efficiencies, and minimize complexity across the organization. Yet it decentralizes local inventory decisions to store managers because they have the best information about their customers and can respond quickly to local market needs. "We could never predict a busload of football players on a Friday night, but the store manager can," explains a 7-Eleven executive.[27]

Formalization

Formalization is the degree to which organizations standardize behavior through rules, procedures, formal training, and related mechanisms.[28] In other words, companies become more formalized as they increasingly rely on various forms of standardization to coordinate work. Fulfillment by Amazon is well-known—and sometimes infamously identified—for its very high formalization. The warehouse operations for Amazon's third-party sellers relies on standardization of work processes as a coordinating mechanism. Computer algorithms determine how many products employees should pick, move, pack, and store per hour. Even bathroom breaks are apparently timed. As soon as one product is picked, the employee's scanner displays the next item with a countdown of the time allowed to find and scan that item.[29]

Older companies tend to be more formalized because work activities become routinized, making them easier to document into standardized practices. Large organizations tend to have more formalization because coordinating a large number of people only through direct supervision and informal communication is difficult and costly. External influences, such as government safety legislation and strict accounting rules, also encourage formalization.

> Any new idea condemned to struggle upward through multiple levels of rigidly hierarchical, risk-averse management is an idea that won't see daylight . . . until it's too late.[23]
>
> —Sergio Marchionne, former CEO of Fiat Chrysler Automobiles and Ferrari

mechanistic structure an organizational structure with a narrow span of control and a high degree of formalization and centralization

organic structure an organizational structure with a wide span of control, little formalization, and decentralized decision making

Large organizations tend to have more formalization because coordinating a large number of people only through direct supervision and informal communication is difficult and costly.
sefa ozel/Getty Images

Formalization may increase efficiency and compliance, but it also can create problems.[30] Rules and procedures reduce organizational flexibility, so employees follow prescribed behaviors even when the situation clearly calls for a customized response. High levels of formalization tend to undermine creativity. Some work rules become so convoluted that organizational efficiency would decline if they were actually followed as prescribed. Formalization is also a source of job dissatisfaction and work stress.

Finally, rules and procedures have been known to take on a life of their own in some organizations. They become the focus of attention rather than the organization's ultimate objectives of producing a product, providing a service, and satisfying stakeholder needs.

Mechanistic versus Organic Structures

We discussed span of control, centralization, and formalization together because they cluster around two broader organizational forms: mechanistic and organic structures (see Exhibit 12.3).[31] A **mechanistic structure** is characterized by a narrow span of control and a high degree of formalization and centralization. Mechanistic structures have many rules and procedures, limited decision making at lower levels, tall hierarchies of people in specialized roles, and vertical rather than horizontal communication flows. Tasks are rigidly defined and are altered only when sanctioned by higher authorities. Although now changing, Bosch has traditionally had a mechanistic structure, which was apparent by the German firm's centralized decision making, clearly defined job descriptions, and work activities heavily guided by established rules and procedures.

Companies with an **organic structure** have the opposite characteristics. They operate with a wide span of control, decentralized decision making, and little formalization. Tasks are fluid, adjusting to new situations and organizational needs. In extremely organic organizations, decision making is decentralized down to teams and individuals, and employees have enough autonomy to adapt their job duties to fit the situation.

As a general rule, mechanistic structures operate better in stable environments because they rely on efficiency and routine behaviors. Organic structures work better in rapidly changing (i.e., dynamic) environments because they are more flexible and responsive to the changes. Organic structures are also more compatible with human capital development (see Chapter 1) because they emphasize information sharing and an empowered workforce rather than hierarchy and status. However, the effectiveness of organic structures depends on how well employees have developed their roles and expertise.[32] Without these conditions, employees are unable to coordinate effectively with each other, resulting in errors and gross inefficiencies.

Exhibit 12.3 Contrasting Mechanistic and Organic Organizational Structures

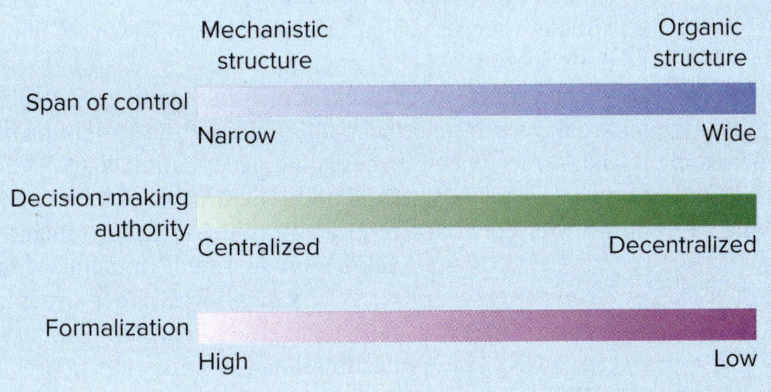

connect

SELF-ASSESSMENT 12.1: Which Organizational Structure Do You Prefer?

functional structure an organizational structure in which employees are organized around specific knowledge or other resources

LO12-3 Identify and evaluate five types of departmentalization.

FORMS OF DEPARTMENTALIZATION

Span of control, centralization, and formalization are important elements of organizational structure, but most people think about organizational charts when the discussion of organizational structure arises. The organizational chart represents the fourth element in the structuring of organizations, called *departmentalization*. Departmentalization specifies how employees and their activities are grouped together. It is a fundamental strategy for coordinating organizational activities because it influences organizational behavior in the following ways:[33]

- Departmentalization establishes the chain of command—the system of common supervision among positions and units within the organization. It frames the membership of formal work teams and typically determines which positions and units must share resources. Thus, departmentalization establishes interdependencies among employees and subunits.
- Departmentalization focuses people around common mental models or ways of thinking, such as serving clients, developing products, or supporting a particular skill set. This focus is typically anchored around the common budgets and measures of performance assigned to employees within each departmental unit.
- Departmentalization encourages specific people and work units to coordinate through informal communication. With common supervision and resources, members within each configuration typically work near each other, so they can use frequent and informal interaction to get the work done.

There are almost as many organizational charts as there are businesses, but the five most common pure types of departmentalization are simple, functional, divisional, team-based, and matrix.

Simple Structure

Most companies begin with a *simple structure*.[34] They employ only a few people and typically offer only one distinct product or service. There is minimal hierarchy—usually just employees reporting to the owners. Employees perform broadly defined roles because there are insufficient economies of scale to assign them to specialized jobs. The simple structure is highly flexible and minimizes the walls that form between employees in other structures. However, the simple structure usually depends considerably on the owner's direct supervision to coordinate work activities, so it is very difficult to operate as the company grows and becomes more complex.

Functional Structure

As organizations grow, they typically shift from a simple structure to a functional structure. Even after they adopt more complex organizational structures that we discuss later, they will have a functional structure at some level of the hierarchy. A **functional structure** organizes employees around specific knowledge or other resources (see Exhibit 12.4). Employees with marketing expertise are grouped into a marketing unit, those with production skills are located in manufacturing, engineers are found in product development, and so on. Organizations with functional structures are typically centralized to coordinate their activities effectively.

Evaluating the Functional Structure The functional structure creates specialized pools of talent that typically serve everyone in the organization. Pooling talent into one group improves economies of scale compared to dispersing functional specialists over different parts of the organization. The functional structure also increases employee identity with the specialization or profession. Direct supervision is easier in a functional structure because managers oversee people with common issues and expertise.[35]

The functional structure also has limitations.[36] Grouping employees around their skills tends to focus attention on those skills and related professional needs rather than on the company's products, services, or client needs. Unless people are transferred from one function to the next, they might not develop a broader understanding of the business. Compared with other structures, the functional structure usually produces more dysfunctional conflict and poorer coordination in serving clients or developing products. These problems occur because employees need to work with coworkers in other departments to complete organizational tasks, yet they have different subgoals and mental models about how to perform the work effectively. Together, these problems require substantial formal controls and coordination when people are organized around functions.

Exhibit 12.4 A Functional Organizational Structure

Compared with other organizational structures, the functional structure usually produces more dysfunctional conflict and poorer coordination in serving clients or developing products.
tkemot/Shutterstock

divisional structure an organizational structure in which employees are organized around geographic areas, outputs (products or services), or clients

Divisional Structure

The **divisional structure** (sometimes called the *multidivisional* structure) groups employees around geographic areas, outputs (products or services), or clients. Exhibit 12.5 illustrates these three variations of divisional structure.[37] The *geographic divisional structure* organizes employees around distinct regions of the country or world. Exhibit 12.5(a) illustrates the geographic divisional structure adopted by global dairy foods company Saputo. The *product/service divisional structure* organizes employees around distinct outputs. Exhibit 12.5(b) illustrates the four product divisions at Medtronic, the American medical devices company. The *client divisional structure* organizes employees around specific customer groups. Exhibit 12.5(c) illustrates the client-focused divisional structure at Thomson-Reuters, the digital information services company.[38]

Exhibit 12.5 Three Types of Divisional Structure

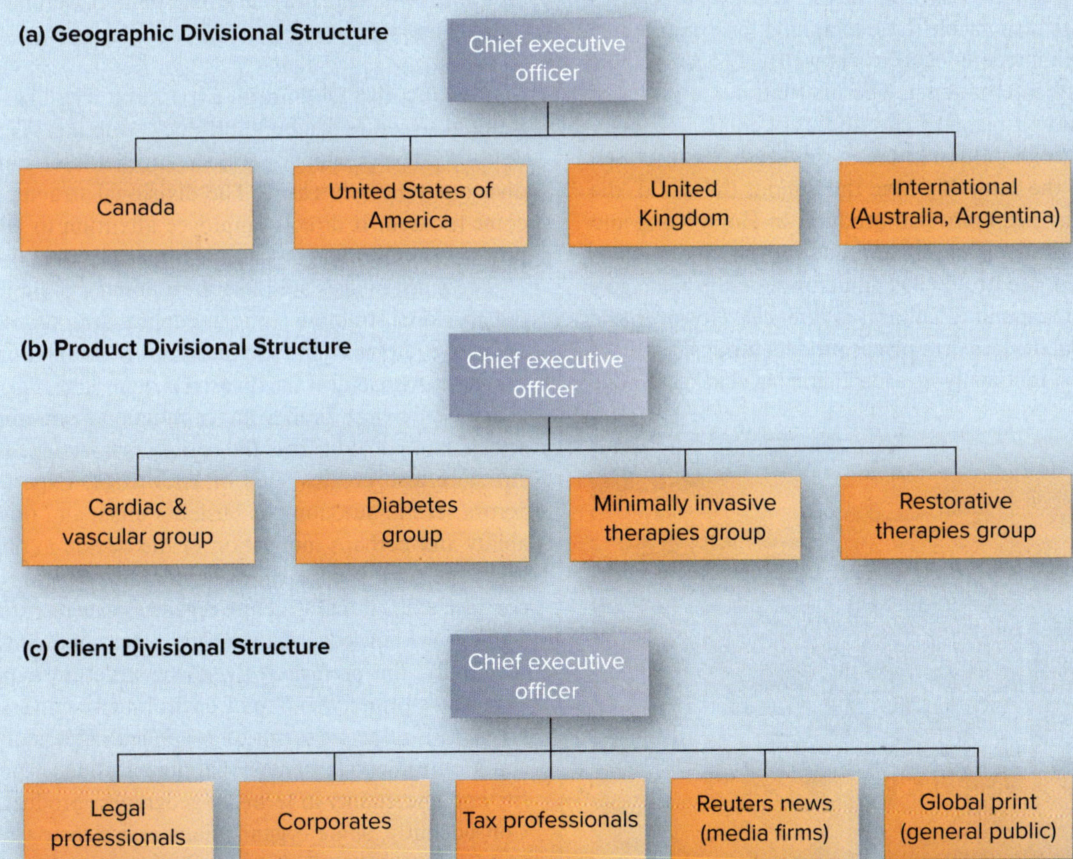

Note: Diagram (a) shows the geographic divisions at Saputo; diagram (b) depicts the four product divisions of Medtronic; diagram (c) shows the five client divisions of Thomson Reuters. None of these firms has a pure divisional structure. At all three companies the top executive team also includes the heads of functional units. Medtronic executives reporting to the CEO are responsible for products (shown), geographic areas, or functional responsibilities.

The divisional structure is outcome-focused; it directs employee attention to customers and products, rather than to their own specialized knowledge.

Which form of divisional structure should large organizations adopt? The answer depends mainly on the primary source of environmental diversity or uncertainty.[39] Suppose an organization has one type of product sold to people across the country. If customers have different needs across regions, or if state governments impose different regulations on the product, then a geographic structure would be best so the company can be more vigilant about this diversity. In contrast, if the company sells several types of products across the country and customer preferences and government regulations are similar everywhere, then a product structure would likely work best.

Saputo, the dairy foods company, is organized mainly around geographic regions, likely because regulations and sales channels vary more by country than by product. Top-level executives at McDonald's are responsible for several functions (marketing, finance, information technology, etc.) as well as two geographic divisions: US and International. The international division of the fast food chain is organized into dozens of countries.[40]

McDonald's geographic structure makes sense because even though it makes the same Big Mac throughout the world, the fast-food company has more fish products in Hong Kong and more vegetarian products in India, in line with traditional diets in those countries. Medtronic has numerous country managers to anticipate and respond to cultural differences. However, the American medical devices firm places product groups (cardiac/vascular, diabetes, minimally invasive therapies, and restorative

Whether an organization should adopt a geographic, product, or client-focused structure depends mainly on the primary source of environmental diversity or uncertainty.
David Pearson/Shutterstock

therapies) at the top of its organizational structure, likely because marketing and manufacturing activities vary much more across product divisions than across regions.

Many companies are moving away from structures that organize people around geographic clusters.[41] One reason is that clients can purchase products online and communicate with businesses from almost anywhere in the world, so local representation is becoming less important. Reduced geographic variation is another reason for the shift away from geographic structures; freer trade has reduced government intervention, and consumer preferences for many products and services are becoming more similar (converging) around the world. The third reason is that large companies increasingly have global business customers who demand one global point of purchase, not one in every country or region.

Evaluating the Divisional Structure The divisional organizational structure is a building-block structure. As the company develops new products, services, or clients, it can sprout new divisions relatively easily. The divisional structure is also outcome-focused. It directs employee attention to customers and products, rather than to their own specialized knowledge.[42]

These advantages are offset by a number of limitations. First, the divisional structure tends to duplicate resources, such as production equipment and engineering or information technology expertise. Also, unless the division is quite large, resources are not used as efficiently as they are in functional structures where resources are pooled across the entire organization. The divisional structure also creates silos of knowledge. Expertise is spread across several autonomous business units, and this reduces the ability and perhaps motivation of the people in one division to share their knowledge with counterparts in other divisions. In contrast, a functional structure organizes experts together, thereby supporting knowledge sharing within areas of expertise.

Finally, the preferred divisional structure depends on the company's primary source of environmental diversity or uncertainty. This principle seems to be applied easily enough at Saputo and Medtronic, but many global organizations experience diversity and uncertainty in terms of geography, product, *and* clients. Consequently, some organizations revise their structures back and forth or create complex structures that attempt to give all three dimensions equal status. This muddling generates further complications because organizational structure decisions shift power and status among executives. If the company switches from a geographic to a product structure, people who lead the

team-based structure an organizational structure built around self-directed teams that complete an entire piece of work

matrix structure an organizational structure that overlays two structures (such as a geographic divisional and a product divisional structure) in order to leverage the benefits of both

geographic fiefdoms suddenly get demoted under the product chiefs. In short, leaders of global organizations struggle to find the best divisional structure, often resulting in the departure of some executives and frustration among those who remain.

Team-Based Structure

A **team-based structure** is built around self-directed teams that complete an entire piece of work, such as manufacturing a product or developing an electronic game. This type of structure is usually organic. There is a wide span of control because teams operate with minimal supervision. There is no formal leader in its most extreme variation, just someone selected by other team members to help coordinate the work and liaise with top management.

Team structures are highly decentralized because almost all day-to-day decisions are made by team members rather than someone further up the organizational hierarchy. Many team-based structures also have low formalization because teams are given relatively few rules about how to organize their work. Instead, executives assign quality and quantity output targets, and often productivity improvement goals, to each team. Teams are then encouraged to use available resources and their own initiative to achieve those objectives.

Team-based structures are usually found within the manufacturing or service operations of larger divisional structures. Several GE aircraft engine plants are organized as team-based structures, but these plants operate within GE's larger divisional structure. A small number of firms apply the team-based structure from top to bottom, including Morning Star Company, W. L. Gore & Associates, and Valve Corporation, where almost all employees work in teams.

Evaluating the Team-Based Structure The team-based structure has gained popularity because it is more flexible and responsive in turbulent environments.[43] It tends to reduce costs because teams have less reliance on formal hierarchy (direct supervision). A cross-functional team structure improves communication and cooperation across traditional boundaries. With greater autonomy, this structure also allows quicker and more informed decision making.[44] For this reason, some hospitals have shifted from functional departments to cross-functional teams. Teams composed of nurses, radiologists, anesthetists, a pharmacology representative, possibly social workers, a rehabilitation therapist, and other specialists communicate and coordinate more efficiently, thereby reducing delays and errors.[45]

Some hospitals have shifted from functional departments to cross-functional teams to improve communication and cooperation across traditional specialist boundaries.
PeopleImages/Getty Images

The team-based structure also has several limitations. It can be costly to maintain due to the need for ongoing interpersonal skills training. Teamwork potentially takes more time to coordinate than formal hierarchy during the early stages of team development. Employees may experience more stress due to increased ambiguity in their roles. Team leaders also experience more stress due to increased conflict, loss of functional power, and unclear career progression ladders. In addition, team structures suffer from duplication of resources and potential competition (and lack of resource sharing) across teams.[46]

Matrix Structure

Randon S.A., one of Brazil's largest private companies, manufactures truck bodies (transport truck trailers), car and truck parts (brake pads, wheel ends, etc.) railcars, and earth-moving vehicles. Although these businesses operated independently, Randon executives felt that they needed to be more responsive to headquarters initiatives on product innovation, cost efficiency, and aftermarket business opportunities (field force). Therefore, the company now has a matrix organizational structure that combines the four main business divisions with four functional groups that champion these initiatives. "One of the main gains of the organizational change is to accelerate the growth of operations through the development of new technologies, product innovation and cost management," says Randon CEO Daniel Randon.[47]

Randon and many other organizations have adopted a **matrix structure**, which overlays two structures (in this case, product divisions with a functional structure) to leverage the benefits of both.[48] Exhibit 12.6 shows a product-functional matrix structure, similar to what Randon has recently introduced. The dots represent the individuals (functional leaders within each product division) who have two bosses. For example, the head of purchasing in the brake parts division (a company called Fras-le) reports to Randon's head of procurement at headquarters as well as to the head of Fras-le.

A common mistake is to assume that everyone in this type of matrix organizational structure reports to two bosses. In reality, this particular type of matrix structure has only managers at one

Exhibit 12.6 Matrix Organizational Structure Similar to Randon S.A.

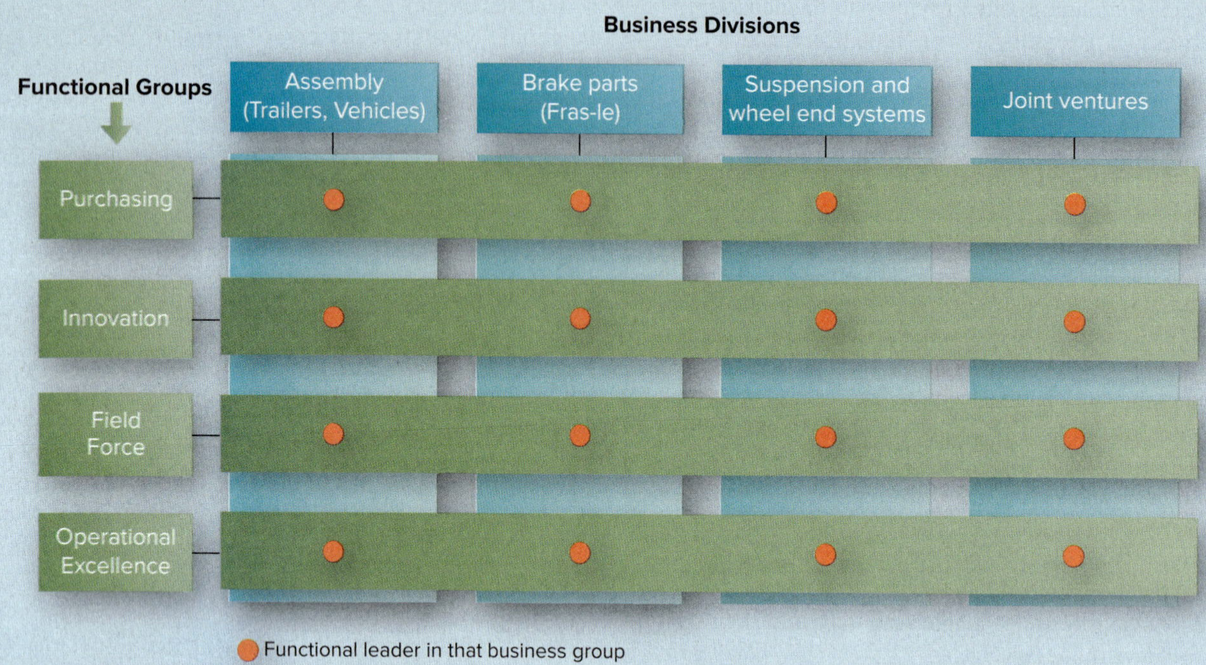

Note: This diagram, which is created for illustrative purposes only, is a representation of part of Randon's most recent structure. The complete top-level structure also has nonmatrixed functional executives reporting to the CEO or COO. This diagram also assumes a pure matrix structure, in which both product and functional chiefs have equal power. However, it is possible that one of these leader groups will have more authority over the people represented by the dots.

level in the organization reporting to two bosses. The executive responsible for product innovation at Fras-le (Randon's brake parts business) reports to both the head of Fras-le and to the headquarters leader responsible for innovation. All employees below the innovation leader at Fras-le report to only one manager in the Fras-le operations.

Hennes & Mauritz AB has a matrix organizational structure similar to Randon. Specifically, the Swedish fashion retailer intersects its store brands (H&M, H&M Home, & Other Stories, Monki, Cos, etc.) with almost a dozen functional groups (logistics, production, accounting, human resources, etc.). A related form of matrix organization, particularly among global companies, is the product-geographic structure. One such example is the matrix structure at Shiseido, which has five product groups intersected with six regions. The Japanese cosmetics and personal care firm adopted the product-geographic structure because it needed to assign equal power and attention to regional groups as to its product groups.[49]

Global organizations tend to have complex designs that combine different types of structures, so a "pure" matrix design is relatively uncommon. A pure matrix gives equal power to leaders of both groups (products and regions, for example), whereas in reality companies often give more power to one set of groups while the other set of groups has mostly "dotted line" or advisory authority.

A considerably different form of matrix structure, which can be applied to small or large companies, overlays a functional structure with projects.[50] BioWare adopted this project-functional matrix structure soon after the electronic games company was born two decades ago. Most BioWare employees have

> **One matrix structure overlays functions with projects; employees have a permanent functional unit but are continuously assigned to temporary project teams.**

two managers. One manager leads the specific project to which employees are assigned, such as *Star Wars*, *Mass Effect*, and *Dragon Age*; the other manager is head of the employee's functional specialization, such as art, programming, audio, quality assurance, and design.[51] Employees are assigned permanently to a functional unit but are continuously assigned to temporary project teams. When the project nears completion, the functional boss reassigns employees in his or her functional specialization to another project.

Evaluating the Matrix Structure The project-functional matrix structure usually makes very good use of resources and expertise, making it ideal for project-based organizations with fluctuating workloads. When properly managed, it improves communication efficiency, project flexibility, and innovation, compared to purely functional or divisional designs. It focuses employees on serving clients or creating products, yet keeps people organized around their specialization. The result is that knowledge sharing improves and people are more efficiently assigned to work where they are most needed.

Matrix structures for large organizations are also a logical choice when two different dimensions are equally important (such as regions and products at Shiseido). Structures determine executive power and what should receive priority; the matrix structure works best when the business environment is complex and two different dimensions deserve equal attention and integration. Executives who have worked in a global matrix also say they have more freedom, likely because their two bosses are more advisory and less oriented toward command-and-control leadership.[52]

In spite of these advantages, the matrix structure has several well-known problems.[53] One concern is that it increases conflict among managers who equally share power. Employees working at the matrix level have two bosses and, consequently, two sets of priorities that aren't always aligned with each other. Project leaders might squabble with functional leaders regarding the assignment of specific employees to projects as well as regarding the employee's technical competence. However, successful companies manage this conflict by developing and promoting leaders who can work effectively in matrix structures. "Of course there's potential for friction," says an executive at IBM India. "In fact, one of the prerequisites to attaining a leadership position at IBM is the ability to function in a matrix structure."[54]

Ambiguous accountability is another challenge with matrix structures. In a functional or divisional structure, one manager is responsible for everything, even the most unexpected issues. But in a matrix structure, the unusual problems don't get resolved because neither manager takes ownership of them.[56] Due to this ambiguous accountability, matrix structures have been blamed for corporate ethical misconduct, such as embezzlement at Hana Financial Group in Korea and massive bribery at Siemens AG in Germany. The combination of dysfunctional conflict and ambiguous accountability in matrix structures also explains why some employees experience more stress and why some managers are less satisfied with their work arrangements.

LO12-4 Explain how the external environment, organizational size, technology, and strategy are relevant when designing an organizational structure.

CONTINGENCIES OF ORGANIZATIONAL DESIGN

Most organizational behavior theories and concepts have contingencies: Ideas that work well in one situation might not work as well in another situation. This contingency approach is certainly relevant when choosing the most appropriate organizational structure.[57] In this section, we introduce four contingencies of organizational design: external environment, size, technology, and strategy.

External Environment

The best structure for an organization depends on its external environment. The external environment includes anything outside the organization, including most stakeholders (e.g., clients, suppliers, government), resources (e.g., raw materials, human resources, information, finances), and competitors. Four characteristics of external environments influence the type of organizational structure best suited to a particular situation: dynamism, complexity, diversity, and hostility.[58]

Dynamic versus Stable Environments Dynamic environments have a high rate of change, leading to unfamiliar situations and a lack of identifiable patterns. Organic structures operate well in dynamic environments. Employees are experienced and coordinate well in teams, which enables the

> The more accountable I can make you, the easier it is for you to show you're a great performer. The more I use a matrix, the easier I make it to blame someone else.[55]
>
> —Mark Hurd, former Oracle and Hewlett-Packard executive

Mechanistic structures are better suited to stable environments, which have regular cycles of activity, as well as predictable changes in supply for raw materials and demand for finished products.
Monty Rakusen/Getty Images

organization to adapt more quickly to changes.[59] For instance, the U.S. Army learned from difficult confrontations against guerrilla insurgents that the battlefield has become too dynamic and complex for its rigid mechanistic structure. It has since evolved into a more organic structure consisting of teams with increased autonomy to accomplish their missions. "We became what we called 'a team of teams': a large command that captured at scale the traits of agility normally limited to small teams," explains General Stanley McChrystal, who led America's Joint Special Operations Command and NATO forces in the war in Afghanistan.[60]

In contrast, stable environments are characterized by regular cycles of activity, as well as predictable changes in supply for raw materials and demand for finished products. Events are more predictable, enabling the firm to apply rules and procedures. Mechanistic structures are more efficient when the environment is predictable, so they tend to be more profitable than organic structures under these conditions.

Complex versus Simple Environments Complex environments have many elements, whereas simple environments have few things to monitor. As an example, a major university library operates in a more complex environment than a small-town public library. The university library's clients require several types of services—book borrowing, online full-text databases, research centers, course reserve collections, and so forth. A small-town public library has fewer of these demands placed on it. The more complex the environment, the more decentralized the organization should become. Decentralization is a logical choice for complex environments because decisions are pushed down to people and subunits who possess the information needed to make informed choices.

Diverse versus Integrated Environments Organizations located in diverse environments have a greater variety of products or services, clients, and regions. In contrast, an integrated environment has only one type of client and product and serves only one geographic area. The more diversified the environment, the more the firm needs to use a divisional structure aligned with that diversity. If it sells a single product around the world, a geographic divisional structure would align best with the firm's geographic diversity, for example. Diverse environments also call for decentralization. By pushing decision making further down the hierarchy, the company can adapt better and more quickly to diverse clients, government requirements, and other circumstances related to that diversity.

Hostile versus Munificent Environments Firms located in hostile environments face resource scarcity and more competition in the marketplace. These conditions are typically dynamic as well because they reduce the predictability of access to resources and demand for outputs. Organic structures tend to be best in hostile environments. However, when the environment is extremely unfavorable—such as during the COVID-19 pandemic or when there is a severe shortage of raw production materials—organizations tend to temporarily centralize so that decisions can be made more quickly and executives feel more comfortable being in control.[61] Ironically, centralization may result in lower-quality decisions during organizational crises because top management has less information, particularly when the environment is complex.

Organizational Size

The organizational structures of large firms differ from those of smaller ones, for good reason.[63] As the number of employees increases, job specialization increases due to a greater division of labor. The greater division of labor requires more elaborate coordinating mechanisms. Thus, larger firms make greater use of standardization (particularly work processes and outcomes) to coordinate work activities. These coordinating mechanisms create an administrative hierarchy and greater formalization. Historically, growing organizations reduced their reliance on informal communication as a coordinating mechanism. However, emerging digital technologies have enabled large firms to coordinate work more through informal communication than was previously possible.[64]

Larger organizations also tend to be more decentralized than are smaller organizations. Executives have neither sufficient time nor expertise to process all the decisions that significantly influence the business as it grows. Therefore, decision-making authority is pushed down to lower levels, where employees are able to make decisions on issues within their narrower range of responsibility.

Technology

Technology is another factor to consider when designing the best organizational structure for the situation.[65] *Technology*

OB THEORY TO PRACTICE

The Risk of Centralizing Authority during Pandemics[62]

Luis Alvarez/Getty Images

Organizational leaders often make the mistake of temporarily centralizing authority during pandemics, such as during the COVID-19 crisis. Unfortunately, centralization when the external environment becomes hostile can produce worse decisions because headquarters executives have less information than managers on the front lines.

"The temptation in a time of crisis is for leaders to put themselves at the center of all activity," warns Manley Hopkinson, a leadership consultant and McKinsey advisor who served as an officer in the British Royal Navy during the first Gulf War. "It is vital that a leader resist centralizing control."

Hugo Bague, who was a senior Rio Tinto executive during the Ebola crisis, agrees. "Local teams are often the best positioned to judge the situation on the ground—and their decisions should not be second-guessed." During the Ebola crisis, for instance, Rio Tinto executives in Guinea, West Africa, were asked to recommend whether the expatriates should leave, a decision that would have undermined the mining firm's credibility in that country. They determined that the expats should stay, but their families should be sent home.

Although Rio Tinto's Guinea executives made the decision, senior executives at headquarters monitored the decision process. "We said clearly, whether you stay in Guinea or not is your call," says Bague. "But we want to have a discussion with you to ensure that you've looked at it at every angle."

refers to the mechanisms or processes an organization relies on to make its products or services. In other words, technology isn't just the equipment used to make something; it also includes how the production process is physically arranged and how the production work is divided among employees.

The two main technological contingencies are task variability and task analyzability, both of which we described as job characteristics in Chapter 5. *Task variability* refers to how predictable the job duties are from one day to the next. In jobs with high variability, employees perform several types of tasks, but they don't know which of those tasks are required from one day to the next. Low variability occurs when the work is highly routine and predictable. *Task analyzability* refers to how much the job can be performed using known procedures and rules. In jobs with high task analyzability, employees have well-defined guidelines to direct them through the work process. In jobs with low task analyzability, employees tackle unique situations with few (if any) guidelines to help them determine the best course of action.

An organic structure should be introduced where employees perform tasks with high variability and low analyzability, such as in a research setting. The reason is that employees face unique situations with little opportunity for repetition. In contrast, a mechanistic organizational structure is preferred where production work has low task variability and high task analyzability, such as an assembly line. Assembly work is routine, is highly predictable, and has well-established procedures—an ideal situation for a mechanistic structure to operate efficiently.

McGraw Hill connect

SELF-ASSESSMENT 12.2: Does Your Job Require an Organic or Mechanistic Structure?

> A mechanistic organizational structure is preferred where production work has low task variability and high task analyzability, such as an assembly line.

organizational strategy the way the organization positions itself in its environment in relation to its stakeholders, given the organization's resources, capabilities, and mission

Organizational Strategy

Organizational strategy refers to the way the organization positions itself in its environment in relation to its stakeholders, given the organization's resources, capabilities, and mission.[66] In other words, strategy represents the decisions and actions applied to achieve the organization's goals. Although size, technology, and environment influence the optimal organizational structure, these contingencies do not necessarily determine structure. Instead, corporate leaders formulate and implement strategies that shape both the characteristics of these contingencies as well as the organization's resulting structure.

This concept is summed up with the simple phrase "structure follows strategy."[67] Organizational leaders decide how large to grow and which technologies to use. They take steps to define and manipulate their environments, rather than let the organization's fate be entirely determined by external influences (see the open systems view in Chapter 1). Furthermore, organizational structures don't evolve as a natural response to environmental conditions; they are the outcomes of conscious human decisions. Thus, organizational strategy influences both the contingencies of structure and the structure itself.

If a company's strategy is to compete through innovation, a more organic structure would be preferred because it is easier for employees to share knowledge and be creative. If a company chooses a low-cost strategy, a mechanistic structure is preferred because it maximizes production and service efficiency.[68] Overall, it is now apparent that organizational structure is influenced by size, technology, and environment, but the organization's strategy may reshape these elements and loosen their connection to organizational structure.

OB THEORY TO PRACTICE

Choosing the Best Organizational Structure

Contingency Variable	Recommendation
Dynamic versus stable environment	Organic structures are better in dynamic environments; mechanistic structures are usually more effective for stable environments.
Complex versus simple environment	Organizations should be more decentralized as environments become more complex.
Diverse versus integrated environment	A divisional structure aligned with the highest form of diversity tends to work well in diverse environments.
Hostile versus munificent environment	Organic structures are more suitable for hostile environments; mechanistic structures are usually more effective in munificent environments.
Organizational size	As companies grow, they should make greater use of standardization for coordination and should become more decentralized.
Technology: task variability and task analyzability	Organic structures are better where tasks have high variability and low analyzability; mechanistic structures are better where production involves low variability and high analyzability tasks.
Organizational strategy	Organic structures are better when the company's strategy is to compete through innovation, a more mechanistic structure is preferred when the organization chooses a low-cost strategy.

Study Checklist

Connect® is available for *M Organizational Behavior.* Additional resources include:

✓ Exercises:

- **Case Analysis:** Apply concepts within the context of a real-world situation.
- **Click and Drag:** Helps make the connection between theory and application through matching, ranking, or grouping activities.
- **Video Case:** See management in action through interactive videos.
- **Self-Assessment:** Designed to promote student self-awareness and reflection, these research-based surveys contain detailed feedback for students.
- **Application-Based Activities:** These highly interactive, application- and analysis-based exercises allow students to take on specific roles to complete management-related tasks within a real-world context.

✓ **SmartBook 2.0**™—Smartbook 2.0 is an adaptive learning solution that provides personalized learning to individual student needs, continually adapts to pinpoint knowledge gaps and focuses learning on concepts requiring additional study. It fosters more productive learning, takes the guesswork out of what to study, and helps students better prepare for class.

Notes

1. P. Tate, "Pioneering an Industrial Revolution at Bosch," *Manufacturing Leadership Journal*, June 2, 2018; T. Jakob and M.-O. Griesshaber, "How Big Companies Can Survive in the Digital Age: New Models for Culture, Leadership, and Collaboration" (Presentation, Singapore, September 28, 2018); P. Wainewright, "How Bosch Broke Free from Silos to Reorganize as Agile Teams," *Diginomica*, February 7, 2019.
2. S. Ranson, R. Hinings, and R. Greenwood, "The Structuring of Organizational Structure," *Administrative Science Quarterly* 25 (1980): 1–14; J.E. Johanson, "Intraorganizational Influence," *Management Communication Quarterly* 13 (2000): 393–435; K. Walsh, "Interpreting the Impact of Culture on Structure," *Journal of Applied Behavioral Science* 40, no. 3 (2004): 302–22. The recent survey is reported in J. Bersin et al., "The New Organization: Different by Design," in *Global Human Capital Trends 2016* (Westlake, TX: Deloitte University Press, 2016), 1–14.
3. H. Mintzberg, *The Structuring of Organizations* (Englewood Cliffs, NJ: Prentice Hall, 1979), 2–3.
4. E.E. Lawler III, *Motivation in Work Organizations* (Monterey, CA: Brooks/Cole, 1973); M.A. Campion, "Ability Requirement Implications of Job Design: An Interdisciplinary Perspective," *Personnel Psychology* 42 (1989): 1–24.
5. G.S. Becker and K.M. Murphy, "The Division of Labor, Coordination Costs, and Knowledge," *Quarterly Journal of Economics* 107, no. 4 (1992): 1137–60; L. Borghans and B. Weel, "The Division of Labour, Worker Organisation, and Technological Change," *The Economic Journal* 116, no. 509 (2006): F45–F72.
6. H. Mintzberg, *The Structuring of Organizations* (Englewood Cliffs, NJ: Prentice Hall, 1979), Chap. 1; D.A. Nadler and M.L. Tushman, *Competing by Design: The Power of Organizational Architecture* (New York: Oxford University Press, 1997), Chap. 6; J.R. Galbraith, *Designing Organizations: An Executive Guide to Strategy, Structure, and Process* (San Francisco: Jossey-Bass, 2002), Chap. 4.
7. J. Stephenson Jr., "Making Humanitarian Relief Networks More Effective: Operational Coordination, Trust and Sense Making," *Disasters* 29, no. 4 (2005): 337.
8. A. Willem, M. Buelens, and H. Scarbrough, "The Role of Inter-Unit Coordination Mechanisms in Knowledge Sharing: A Case Study of a British MNC," *Journal of Information Science* 32, no. 6 (2006): 539–61; R.R. Gulati, "Silo Busting," *Harvard Business Review* 85, no. 5 (2007): 98–108.
9. L. Borghans and B. Weel, "The Division of Labour, Worker Organisation, and Technological Change," *The Economic Journal* 116, no. 509 (2006): F45–F72.
10. T. Van Alphen, "Magna in Overdrive," *Toronto Star*, July 24, 2006; "Production at Magna Paint Shop Finally under Way," news release (Hoče, Slovenia: Magna Steyr, March 19, 2019).
11. J.R. Galbraith, *Designing Organizations: An Executive Guide to Strategy, Structure, and Process* (San Francisco, CA: Jossey-Bass, 2002), 66–72; D. Aaker, *Spanning Silos: The New CMO Imperative* (Cambridge, MA: Harvard Business Press, 2008), 95–96; A. Pike, *Brands and Branding Geographies* (Cheltenham, UK: Edward Elgar, 2011), 133.
12. S.M. Sapuan, M.R. Osman, and Y. Nukman, "State of the Art of the Concurrent Engineering Technique in the Automotive Industry," *Journal of Engineering Design* 17, no. 2 (2006): 143–57; D.M. Anderson, *Design for Manufacturing: How to Use Concurrent Engineering to Rapidly Develop Low-Cost, High-Quality Products for Lean Management* (Boca Raton, FL: CRC Press/Taylor & Francis, 2014), Chap. 2.
13. A.H. Van De Ven, A.L. Delbecq, and R.J. Koenig Jr., "Determinants of Coordination Modes within Organizations," *American Sociological Review* 41, no. 2 (1976): 322–38.
14. "Survey: More Than Half of Employees Have Worked for a Micromanager," news release (Menlo Park, CA: Accountemps, July 1, 2014); "The Beast in the Corner Office: A Living Nightmare for Many Canadians," news release (Toronto: Monster Canada, October 28, 2015); T.K. Ock, "Top-Down Corporate Culture Continues to Take Its Toll," *Korea Herald*, July 19, 2016; "Study: The Worst Traits in a Boss," *Comparably* (blog), March 28, 2018, https://www.comparably.com/blog/study-the-worst-traits-in-a-boss/; "Survey Reveals Cities where Workers Are Most (And Least) Happy with Bosses," news release (Menlo Park, CA: Robert Half, October 11, 2018).
15. Y.M. Hsieh and A.T. Hsieh, "Enhancement of Service Quality with Job Standardisation," *Service Industries Journal* 21 (2001): 147–66.
16. B. Davison, "Management Span of Control: How Wide Is Too Wide?" *Journal of Business Strategy* 24, no. 4 (2003): 22–29; N.A. Theobald and S. Nicholson-Crotty, "The Many Faces of Span of Control: Organizational Structure across Multiple Goals," *Administration Society* 36, no. 6 (2005): 648–60; R.M. Meyer, "Span of Management: Concept Analysis," *Journal of Advanced Nursing* 63, no. 1 (2008): 104–12.
17. D.D. Van Fleet and A.G. Bedeian, "A History of the Span of Management," *Academy of Management Review* 2 (1977): 356–72; H. Fayol, *General and Industrial Management*, trans. C. Storrs (London: Pitman, 1949); D.A. Wren, A.G. Bedeian, and J.D. Breeze, "The Foundations of Henri Fayol's Administrative Theory," *Management Decision* 40, no. 9 (2002): 906–18.
18. D. Drickhamer, "Lessons from the Leading Edge," *IndustryWeek*, February 21, 2000, 23–26.
19. D. Thompson, "More on the Span of Control Issue," *Statesman Journal Blog* (Oregon), May 16, 2011; Iowa State Legislative Services Agency, *Span of Control*, Fiscal Note, Iowa State (Des Moines: Iowa Legislature, March 10, 2011); Western Management Consultants, *Service Efficiency Study Program Management Span of Control Review Report to the City Manager* (Toronto: City of Toronto, October 31, 2012); U.S. Postal Service, *Supervisor Workhours and Span of Control: Management Advisory* (Washington, DC: U.S. Postal Service, April 4, 2013); N. Fish and S. Novick, *FY 2013-14 Budget Subcommittee #1 Final Report* (Portland, OR: City of Portland, April 8, 2013); E. Schmidt and J. Rosenberg, *How Google Works* (New York: Grand Central, 2014), 42–44; S. Stoll, *Accenture Update: Progress Report through August 31, 2015* (Bowling Green, OH: Bowling Green State University, September 18, 2015); WMC Consultants, *Toronto Transit Commission Organizational Review Report* (Toronto: Toronto Transit Commission, July 2015); *The New Organization: Different by Design*, Global Human Capital Trends 2016 (New York: Deloitte University Press, 2016).
20. For examples of nurse manager span of control, see: D. Jones et al., "Nurse Manager Scope and Span of Control: An Objective Business and Measurement Model" (AONE 45th Annual Conference, Denver, 2013); R.O. Sherman, "Span of Control in Nurse Leader Roles," *Emerging Nurse Leader* (blog), June 27, 2013, https://www.emergingrnleader.com/span-of-control-in-nurse-leader-roles/; J.M. Kendall, "Nurse Manager Span of Control and the Impact on Employee Engagement," DNP Projects (University of Kentucky, 2018), https://uknowledge.uky.edu/dnp_etds/185.

21. J. Greenwald, "Ward Compares the Best with the Rest," *Business Insurance*, August 26, 2002, 16. One recent article also emphasized that claims managers require a narrow span of control. See M.T. Murdock, "Getting Claim Costs under Control: Improve Your Loss Ratio Using These Proven Fundamentals," *Claims Journal*, March 1, 2016.

22. J.H. Gittell, "Supervisory Span, Relational Coordination and Flight Departure Performance: A Reassessment of Postbureaucracy Theory," *Organization Science* 12, no. 4 (2001): 468–83.

23. S. Marchionne, "Navigating the New Automotive Epoch," *Vital Speeches of the Day* (2010): 134–37.

24. T.D. Wall, J.L. Cordery, and C.W. Clegg, "Empowerment, Performance, and Operational Uncertainty: A Theoretical Integration," *Applied Psychology: An International Review* 51 (2002): 146–69.

25. Conagra Foods, "Conagra Brands Investor Day," news release (Chicago: CQ FD Disclosure, October 18, 2016); J. Tashea, "With Significant Changes, Thomson Reuters Wants to Be Closer to Its Customers," *ABA Journal*, May 15, 2019.

26. Q.N. Huy, "In Praise of Middle Managers,"*Harvard Business Review* 79 (2001): 72–79; C.R. Littler, R. Wiesner, and R. Dunford, "The Dynamics of Delayering: Changing Management Structures in Three Countries," *Journal of Management Studies* 40, no. 2 (2003): 225–56; H.J. Leavitt, *Top Down: Why Hierarchies Are Here to Stay and How to Manage Them More Effectively* (Cambridge: Harvard Business School Press, 2005); L. McCann, J. Morris, and J. Hassard, "Normalized Intensity: The New Labour Process of Middle Management," *Journal of Management Studies* 45, no. 2 (2008): 343–71; "Why Middle Managers May Be the Most Important People in Your Company," *Knowledge @ Wharton*, May 25, 2011.

27. The variations of decentralization within a company are discussed in G. Masada, "To Centralize or Decentralize?" *Optimize*, May 2005, 58–61. The 7-Eleven example is described in J.G. Kelley, "Slurpees and Sausages: 7-Eleven Holds School," *Richmond* (VA) *Times-Dispatch*, March 12, 2004, C1; S. Marling, "The 24-Hour Supply Chain," *InformationWeek*, January 26, 2004, 43.

28. H. Mintzberg, *The Structuring of Organizations* (Englewood Cliffs, NJ: Prentice Hall, 1979), Chap. 5.

29. J. Bloodworth, "I Worked in an Amazon Warehouse," *The Guardian*, September 17, 2018; M. Burin, "When You Click 'Buy Now', This Is What Happens inside Amazon Australia's Warehouse," *ABC News (Australia)*, February 27, 2019; M. Zahn and S. Paget, "'Colony of Hell': 911 Calls From Inside Amazon Warehouses," *The Daily Beast*, March 11, 2019.

30. W. Dessein and T. Santos, "Adaptive Organizations," *Journal of Political Economy* 114, no. 5 (2006): 956–95; A.A.M. Nasurdin et al., "Organizational Structure and Organizational Climate as Potential Predictors of Job Stress: Evidence from Malaysia," *International Journal of Commerce and Management* 16, no. 2 (2006): 116–29; C.J. Chen and J.W. Huang, "How Organizational Climate and Structure Affect Knowledge Management–The Social Interaction Perspective," *International Journal of Information Management* 27, no. 2 (2007): 104–18.

31. T. Burns and G. Stalker, *The Management of Innovation* (London: Tavistock, 1961).

32. W.D. Sine, H. Mitsuhashi, and D.A. Kirsch, "Revisiting Burns and Stalker: Formal Structure and New Venture Performance in Emerging Economic Sectors," *Academy of Management Journal* 49, no. 1 (2006): 121–32.

33. H. Mintzberg, *The Structuring of Organizations* (Englewood Cliffs, NJ: Prentice Hall, 1979), 106.

34. H. Mintzberg, *The Structuring of Organizations* (Englewood Cliffs, NJ: Prentice Hall, 1979), Chap. 17; R.M. Burton, B. Obel, and G. DeSanctis, *Organizational Design: A Step-by-Step Approach*, 2nd ed. (Cambridge, UK: Cambridge University Press, 2011), 61–63.

35. J.R. Galbraith, *Designing Organizations: An Executive Guide to Strategy, Structure, and Process* (San Francisco: Jossey-Bass, 2002), 23–25; R.M. Burton, B. Obel, and G. DeSanctis, *Organizational Design: A Step-by-Step Approach*, 2nd ed. (Cambridge, UK: Cambridge University Press, 2011), 63–65.

36. E.E. Lawler III, *Rewarding Excellence: Pay Strategies for the New Economy* (San Francisco: Jossey-Bass, 2000), 31–34.

37. The evolutionary development of the divisional structure is described in J.R. Galbraith, "The Evolution of Enterprise Organization Designs," *Journal of Organization Design* 1, no. 2 (2012): 1–13.

38. These structures were identified from corporate websites and annual reports. The organizations typically rely on a mixture of structures (typically functional units along with the divisional units shown here), so the charts shown have been adapted and simplified for learning purposes.

39. M. Goold and A. Campbell, "Do You Have a Well-Designed Organization?" *Harvard Business Review* 80 (2002): 117–24. Others have added factors such as economies of scale and what resources need to be controlled the most. See G. Kesler and A. Kates, *Leading Organization Design: How to Make Organization Design Decisions to Drive the Results You Want* (San Francisco: Jossey-Bass, 2011), Chap. 3.

40. "5 Things to Know About Ian Borden," news release (Chicago: McDonald's Corporation, December 10, 2019).

41. J.R. Galbraith, "Structuring Global Organizations," in *Tomorrow's Organization*, ed. S.A. Mohrman et al. (San Francisco: Jossey-Bass, 1998), 103–29; C. Homburg, J.P. Workman Jr., and O. Jensen, "Fundamental Changes in Marketing Organization: The Movement toward a Customer-Focused Organizational Structure," *Academy of Marketing Science Journal* 28 (2000): 459–78; T.H. Davenport, J.G. Harris, and A.K. Kohli, "How Do They Know Their Customers So Well?" *Sloan Management Review* 42 (2001): 63–73; J.R. Galbraith, "Organizing to Deliver Solutions," *Organizational Dynamics* 31 (2002): 194–207.

42. R.M. Burton, B. Obel, and G. DeSanctis, *Organizational Design: A Step-by-Step Approach,* 2nd ed. (Cambridge, UK: Cambridge University Press, 2011), 65–68.

43. J.R. Galbraith, E.E. Lawler III, and Associates, *Organizing for the Future: The New Logic for Managing Complex Organizations* (San Francisco: Jossey-Bass, 1993); R. Bettis and M. Hitt, "The New Competitive Landscape," *Strategic Management Journal* 16 (1995): 7–19.

44. P.C. Ensign, "Interdependence, Coordination, and Structure in Complex Organizations: Implications for Organization Design," *Mid-Atlantic Journal of Business* 34 (1998): 5–22.

45. M.M. Fanning, "A Circular Organization Chart Promotes a Hospital-Wide Focus on Teams," *Hospital & Health Services Administration* 42 (1997): 243–54; B. Cougot et al., "Impact at Two Years of an Intervention on Empowerment among Medical Care Teams: Study Protocol of a Randomised Controlled Trial in a Large French University Hospital," *BMC Health Services Research* 19, no. 1 (2019): 1–13; N. Wellman et al., "Beyond the Pyramid: Alternative Formal Hierarchical Structures and Team Performance," *Academy of Management Journal*, July 9, 2019.

46. R. Cross, "Looking before You Leap: Assessing the Jump to Teams in Knowledge-Based Work," *Business Horizons* 43, no. 5 (2000): 29–36; M. Fenton-O'Creevy, "Employee Involvement and the Middle Manager: Saboteur or Scapegoat?" *Human Resource Management Journal* 11 (2001): 24–40; C. Douglas and W.L. Gardner, "Transition to Self-Directed Work Teams: Implications of Transition Time and Self-Monitoring for Managers' Use of Influence Tactics," *Journal of Organizational Behavior* 25 (2004): 47–65; G. Garda, K. Lindstrom, and M. Dallnera, "Towards a Learning Organization: The Introduction of a Client-Centered Team-Based Organization in Administrative Surveying Work," *Applied Ergonomics* 34 (2003): 97–105.

47. "Randon Companies Announce Change in Organizational Structure," news release (Caxias do Sul, Brazil: Randon S.A., February 3, 2020).

48. S.M. Davis and P.R. Lawrence, *Matrix* (Reading, MA: Addison-Wesley, 1977); J.R. Galbraith, *Designing Matrix Organizations That Actually Work* (San Francisco: Jossey-Bass, 2009); G. Kesler and A. Kates, *Leading Organization Design: How to Make Organization Design Decisions to Drive the Results You Want* (San Francisco: Jossey-Bass, 2011), Chap. 7.

49. "Corporate Governance Report 2018" (Stockholm: H&M Hennes & Mauritz AB, April 15, 2019); "Annual Report 2018 Digest" (Tokyo: Shiseido Company, Limited, October 11, 2019).

50. R.C. Ford and W.A. Randolph, "Cross-Functional Structures: A Review and Integration of Matrix Organization and Project Management," *Journal of Management* 18 (1992): 267–94.

51. R. Muzyka and G. Zeschuk, "Managing Multiple Projects," *Game Developer*, March 2003, 34–42.

52. J.X.J. Qiu and L. Donaldson, "Stopford and Wells Were Right! MNC Matrix Structures *Do* Fit a 'High-High' Strategy," *Management International Review (MIR)* 52, no. 5 (2012): 671–89; D. Ganguly and M. Mitra, "Survive the Matrix," *Economic Times* (Mumbai, India), March 29, 2013.

53. G. Calabrese, "Communication and Co-operation in Product Development: A Case Study of a European Car Producer," *R&D Management* 27 (1997): 239–52; T. Sy and L.S. D'Annunzio, "Challenges and Strategies of Matrix Organizations: Top-Level and Mid-Level Managers' Perspectives," *Human Resource Planning* 28, no. 1 (2005): 39–48; J. Wolf and W.G. Egelhoff, "An Empirical Evaluation of Conflict in MNC Matrix Structure Firms," *International Business Review* 22, no. 3 (2013): 591–601.

54. D. Ganguly, "Matrix Evolutions," *Economic Times* (Mumbai, India), February 18, 2012.

55. D. Ciampa and M. Watkins, "Rx for New CEOs," *Chief Executive*, January 2008.

56. D.A. Nadler and M.L. Tushman, *Competing by Design: The Power of Organizational Architecture* (New York: Oxford University Press, 1997), Chap. 6; M. Goold and A. Campbell, "Structured Networks: Towards the Well-Designed Matrix," *Long Range Planning* 36, no. 5 (2003): 427–39.

57. L. Donaldson, *The Contingency Theory of Organizations* (Thousand Oaks, CA: Sage, 2001); J. Birkinshaw, R. Nobel, and J. Ridderstråle, "Knowledge as a Contingency Variable: Do the Characteristics of Knowledge Predict Organizational Structure?" *Organization Science* 13, no. 3 (2002): 274–89.

58. P.R. Lawrence and J.W. Lorsch, *Organization and Environment* (Homewood, IL: Irwin, 1967); H. Mintzberg, *The Structuring of Organizations* (Englewood Cliffs, NJ: Prentice Hall, 1979), Chap. 15.

59. T. Burns and G. Stalker, *The Management of Innovation* (London: Tavistock, 1961); P.R. Lawrence and J.W. Lorsch, *Organization and Environment* (Homewood, IL: Irwin, 1967).

60. G.S. McChrystal et al., *Team of Teams: New Rules of Engagement for a Complex World* (New York: Penguin, 2015); R. Feloni, "Retired 4-Star Gen. Stanley McChrystal Explains How the Realisation the US Was Losing the Iraq War in 2004 Led to the Transformation of Special Operations," *Business Insider*, January 4, 2019.

61. H. Mintzberg, *The Structuring of Organizations* (Englewood Cliffs, NJ: Prentice Hall, 1979), 282.

62. Based on information in G. Tolub, "Applying Past Leadership Lessons to the Coronavirus Pandemic," McKinsey & Company, March 2020.

63. D.S. Pugh and C.R. Hinings, *Organizational Structure: Extensions and Replications* (Farnborough, UK: Lexington Books, 1976); H. Mintzberg, *The Structuring of Organizations* (Englewood Cliffs, NJ: Prentice Hall, 1979), Chap. 13.

64. J.R. Galbraith, *Designing Matrix Organizations That Actually Work* (San Francisco: Jossey-Bass, 2009), 52–55; G. Hertel, S. Geister, and U. Konradt, "Managing Virtual Teams: A Review of Current Empirical Research," *Human Resource Management Review* 15 (2005): 69–95.

65. C. Perrow, "A Framework for the Comparative Analysis of Organizations," *American Sociological Review* 32 (1967): 194–208; D. Gerwin, "The Comparative Analysis of Structure and Technology: A Critical Appraisal," *Academy of Management Review* 4, no. 1 (1979): 41–51; C.C. Miller et al., "Understanding Technology-Structure Relationships: Theory Development and Meta-Analytic Theory Testing," *Academy of Management Journal* 34, no. 2 (1991): 370–99.

66. R.H. Kilmann, *Beyond the Quick Fix* (San Francisco: Jossey-Bass, 1984), 38.

67. A.D. Chandler, *Strategy and Structure* (Cambridge, MA: MIT Press, 1962).

68. D. Miller, "Configurations of Strategy and Structure," *Strategic Management Journal* 7 (1986): 233–49.

13 Organizational Culture

Learning Objectives

After you read this chapter, you should be able to:

LO13-1 Describe the elements of organizational culture and discuss the importance of organizational subcultures.

LO13-2 Describe four categories of artifacts through which corporate culture is deciphered.

LO13-3 Discuss the importance of organizational culture and the conditions under which organizational culture strength improves organizational performance.

LO13-4 Compare and contrast four strategies for merging organizational cultures.

LO13-5 Discuss five strategies for changing and strengthening an organization's culture, including the application of attraction–selection–attrition theory.

LO13-6 Describe the organizational socialization process and identify strategies to improve that process.

organizational culture
the values and assumptions shared within an organization

The phrase "organizational culture" was rarely uttered before 1982.[1] Today, the concept is on the minds of most executives and is almost daily the subject of popular-press articles. Whenever a company is in deep trouble or very successful, its organizational culture is usually implicated as a key part of the explanation. The following recent newspaper headlines illustrate this point.[2]

- "Crisis Reveals 'Sick' Culture Inside Boeing." This *New York Times* investigative feature provides evidence from internal emails that Boeing's safety-focused engineering culture has long been replaced with a culture that values revenue and cost-efficiency, even if it involves deceiving government regulators. The article suggests that Boeing's current culture is responsible for Boeing's latest product, the safety-plagued 737 Max, which has had two deadly crashes.
- "Tesla Needs Its Battery Maker. A Culture Clash Threatens Their Relationship ." This article in *The Wall Street Journal* describes the frequent corporate culture collisions between the risk-oriented impatience of electric-car pioneer Tesla and its battery manufacturing partner, Panasonic—well known for its conservative and slow consensus-driven decision-making culture.
- "Have Australia's Scandal-Hit Banks Changed Their Culture?" An Australian Royal Commission exposed dysfunctional corporate cultures that led to unethical and illegal practices among that country's leading banks. This article in London's *Financial Times* questions whether the Royal Commission's findings will change the dysfunctional cultures of these organizations.

Organizational culture consists of the values and assumptions shared within an organization.[3] It defines what is important and unimportant in the company and, consequently, directs everyone in the organization toward the "right way" of doing things. You might think of organizational culture as the company's DNA–invisible to the naked eye, yet a powerful template that shapes what happens in the workplace.

This chapter begins by identifying the elements of organizational culture and then describing how culture is deciphered through artifacts. Next, we examine the relationship between organizational culture and organizational effectiveness, including the effects of cultural strength, fit, and adaptability. Our attention then turns to the challenges of and solutions to merging organizational cultures. The latter part of this chapter examines ways to change and strengthen organizational culture and looks more closely at the related topic of organizational socialization.

LO13-1 Describe the elements of organizational culture and discuss the importance of organizational subcultures.

ELEMENTS OF ORGANIZATIONAL CULTURE

Organizational culture consists of shared values and assumptions. Exhibit 13.1 illustrates how these shared values and assumptions relate to each other and are associated with artifacts, which are discussed in the next section of this chapter. *Values* are stable, evaluative beliefs that guide our preferences for outcomes or courses of action in a variety of situations (see Chapters 1 and 2).[4] They are conscious perceptions about what is good or bad, right or wrong. In the context of organizational culture, values are discussed as *shared values*, which are values that people within the organization or work unit have in common and place near the top of their hierarchy of values.[5]

Organizational culture also consists of *shared assumptions*–a deeper element that some experts believe is the essence of corporate culture. Shared assumptions are nonconscious, taken-for-granted perceptions or ideal prototypes of behavior that are considered the correct way to think and act toward problems and opportunities. Shared assumptions are so deeply ingrained that you probably wouldn't discover them by surveying employees. Only by observing employees, analyzing their decisions, and debriefing them on their actions would these assumptions rise to the surface.

Espoused versus Enacted Values

Most corporate websites have "Careers" web pages for job candidates, and many of these sites proudly list the company's core values. Do these values really represent the organization's culture? Some do, but these pages more likely describe *espoused values*–the values that corporate leaders hope will eventually become the organization's culture, or at least the values they want others to believe guide the organization's decisions

> **The thing I have learned at IBM is that culture is everything.**[6]
>
> —Louis V. Gerstner Jr., former CEO of IBM and RJR Nabisco

Exhibit 13.1 Organizational Culture Assumptions, Values, and Artifacts

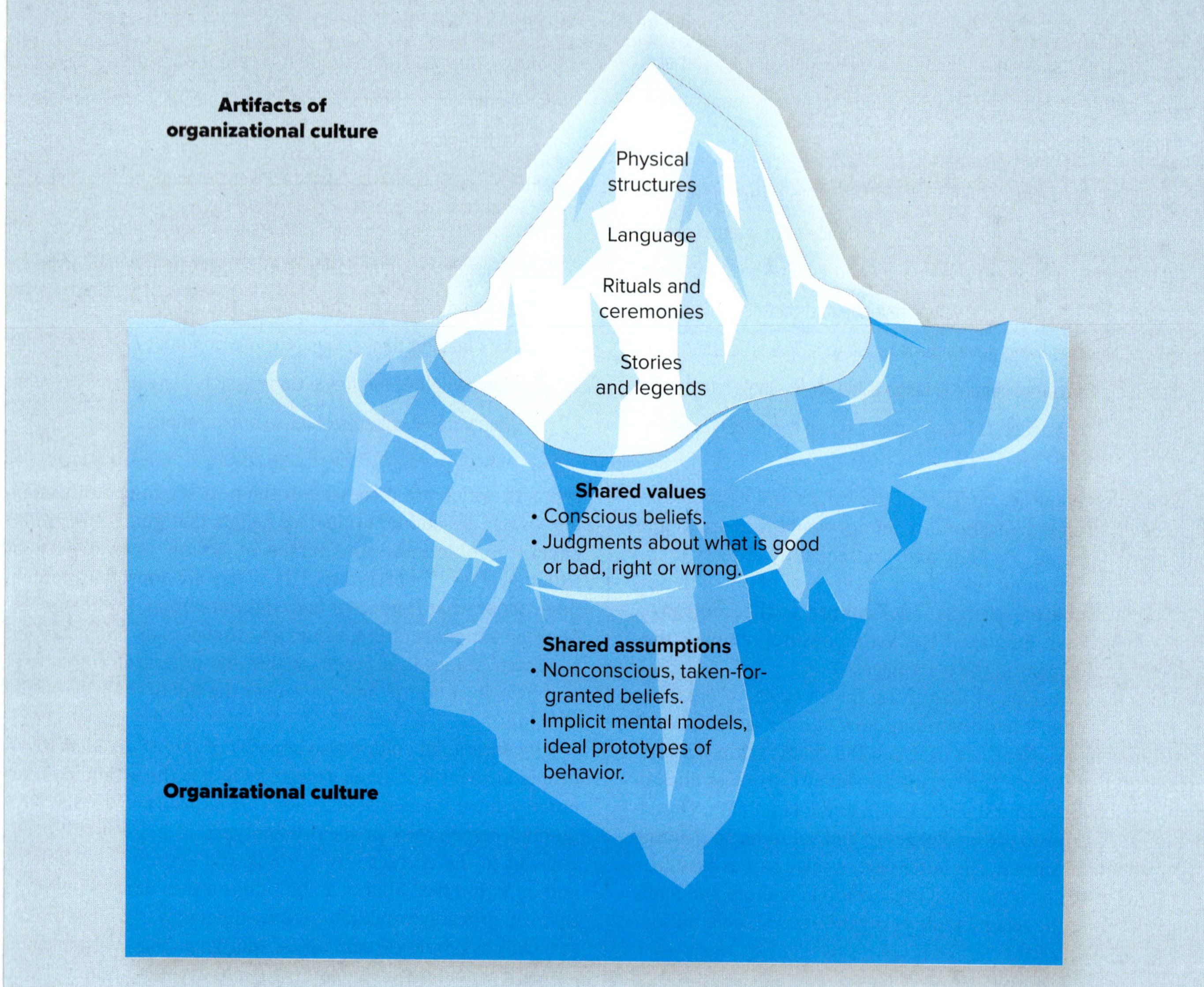

and actions.[7] Espoused values are usually socially desirable, so they present a positive public image. Even if top management acts consistently with the espoused values, lower-level employees might not do so. Employees bring diverse personal values to the organization, some of which might conflict with the organization's espoused values. Some companies even describe espoused values that are completely different from their actual culture.[8]

An organization's culture is defined by its *enacted values*, not its espoused values. Values are *enacted* when they actually guide and influence decisions and behavior. They are values put into practice. Enacted values are apparent when watching executives and other employees in action, such as where they focus their attention and resources, how they behave toward stakeholders, what decisions they make, and the outcomes of those decisions and behavior.

Content of Organizational Culture

Organizations differ in their cultural content, that is, the relative ordering of shared values.[10] Compare Pinterest and Netflix, for example. Pinterest, the image-focused social media site, has a decidedly collaborative culture that avoids contested debate and other risks of offending coworkers. "We aspire to create a culture where people feel respected and valued," says a Pinterest spokesperson. In contrast, Netflix's culture seems to prioritize individual performance and undertones of internal competitiveness. The online streaming media provider reminds employees that its managers "hire, develop, and cut smartly" and that

How Important Is Organizational Culture?[9]

93% of employee reviews on Glassdoor discuss some element of the company's culture.

86% of more than 7,000 business leaders across 130 countries identify organizational culture as one of the most important business issues (3rd most important, after organization design and leadership).

80% of 1,204 employees across 50 countries say their company's success and growth over the next five years depends on changing the organization's culture.

56% of 5,113 working adults in the U.S., UK, France, and Germany say that company culture is more important than salary when it comes to being satisfied at work.

50% of 548 human resources practitioners agree that leaders uphold the stated values of their organization.

30% of 25,000 employees surveyed worldwide rate their organization's culture as "poor" (29% rate it as "very good").

ozgur_oral/Shutterstock

"adequate performance gets a generous severance package." Employees say that getting fired is never far from anyone's mind, which seems to fuel organizational politics and undermine collaboration.[11]

How many corporate cultures are there? Several models and measures classify organizational culture into a handful of easy-to-remember categories. One of these, shown in Exhibit 13.2, identifies seven corporate cultures. Another popular model identifies four organizational cultures organized in a two-by-two table representing internal versus external focus and flexibility versus control. Other models organize cultures around a circle with 8 or 12 categories. These circumplex models suggest that some cultures are opposite to others, such as an avoidance culture versus a self-actualization culture, or a power culture versus a collegial culture.[12]

Organizational culture models and surveys are popular with corporate leaders faced with the messy business of diagnosing their company's culture and identifying what kind of culture they want to develop. Unfortunately, the models oversimplify the diversity of cultural values in organizations. There are dozens of individual values, and many more combinations of values, so the number of organizational cultures that these models describe likely falls considerably short of the full set.

The diversity of corporate cultures is evident in a study of espoused values at the top 500 American companies.[13] The study distilled these values down to nine categories. Integrity appeared most often, followed by teamwork, innovation, respect, quality, safety, community, communication, and hard work. But each of these categories includes a large number of specific values. The "respect" category, for instance, includes the specific values of diversity, inclusion, development, empowerment, and dignity. As you can see, there are dozens of espoused values, so there would be an equally long list of enacted values.

Another concern is that organizational culture models and measures typically ignore the shared assumptions aspect of culture. This oversight likely occurs because measuring shared assumptions is even more difficult than measuring shared values. A third concern is that many organizational culture models and measures incorrectly assume that organizations

Exhibit 13.2 Organizational Culture Profile Dimensions and Characteristics

Organizational Culture Dimension	Characteristics of the Dimension
Innovation	Experimenting, opportunity seeking, risk taking, few rules, low cautiousness
Stability	Predictability, security, rule-oriented
Respect for people	Fairness, tolerance
Outcome orientation	Action-oriented, high expectations, results-oriented
Attention to detail	Precise, analytic
Team orientation	Collaboration, people-oriented
Aggressiveness	Competitive, low emphasis on social responsibility

Sources: Based on information in C.A. O'Reilly III, J. Chatman, and D.F. Caldwell, "People and Organizational Culture: A Profile Comparison Approach to Assessing Person–Organization Fit," *Academy of Management Journal* 34, no. 3 (1991): 487–518.

artifacts the observable symbols and signs of an organization's culture

have a fairly clear, unified culture that is easily decipherable.[14] In reality, an organization's culture is typically blurry and fragmented. Every employee has a somewhat distinct hierarchy of values, so an organization's culture necessarily has noticeable variability. Also, organizations consist of clusters of employees across the organization, and these groups prioritize different values than the company's culture. Thus, many of the popular organizational culture models and measures oversimplify the variety of organizational cultures and falsely presume that organizations can easily be identified within these categories.

Mc Graw Hill connect

SELF-ASSESSMENT 13.1: Which Corporate Culture Do You Prefer?

Organizational Subcultures

When discussing organizational culture, we are really referring to the *dominant culture*, that is, the values and assumptions shared most consistently and widely by the organization's members. The dominant culture is usually supported by senior management, but it sometimes persists even when the executive team desires another culture.

Organizations are also composed of *subcultures* located throughout their various divisions, geographic regions, and occupational groups.[15] Some subcultures enhance the dominant culture by espousing parallel assumptions and values. Others differ from but do not conflict with the dominant culture. Still others are called *countercultures* because they embrace values or assumptions that directly oppose the organization's dominant culture. It is also possible that some organizations (including some universities, according to one study) consist of subcultures with no decipherable dominant culture at all.[16]

Some subcultures enhance the dominant culture, whereas others are called *countercultures* because their values or assumptions oppose the organization's dominant culture.
mediaphotos/Getty Images

Subcultures, particularly countercultures, may cause conflict and dissension among employees, but they also serve two important functions.[17] First, they maintain the organization's standards of performance and ethical behavior. Employees who hold countercultural values are an important source of surveillance and critical review of the dominant order. They encourage constructive conflict and more creative thinking about how the organization should interact with its environment. Subcultures potentially support ethical conduct by preventing employees from blindly following one set of values. Subculture members continually question the "obvious" decisions and actions of the majority, thereby making everyone more mindful of the consequences of their actions.

Subcultures serve a second valuable function: they are spawning grounds for emerging values that keep the firm aligned with the evolving needs and expectations of customers, suppliers, communities, and other stakeholders. Companies eventually need to replace their existing dominant values with ones that are more appropriate for the changing environment. Those emerging cultural values and assumptions usually exist in subcultures long before they are ideal for the organization. If subcultures are suppressed, the organization may take longer to discover, develop, and adopt the emerging desired culture.

LO13-2 Describe four categories of artifacts through which corporate culture is deciphered.

DECIPHERING ORGANIZATIONAL CULTURE THROUGH ARTIFACTS

Shared values and assumptions are not easily measured through surveys and might not be accurately reflected in the organization's values statements. Instead, as Exhibit 13.1 illustrated earlier, an organization's culture needs to be deciphered through a detailed investigation of artifacts. **Artifacts** are the observable symbols and signs of an organization's culture, such as the way visitors are greeted, the organization's physical layout, and how employees are rewarded.[18] A few experts suggest that artifacts are the essence of organizational culture, whereas most others (including the authors of this book) view artifacts as symbols or indicators of culture. In other words, culture is cognitive (values and assumptions inside people's heads), whereas artifacts are observable manifestations of that culture. Either way, artifacts are important because they represent and reinforce an organization's culture.

Artifacts provide valuable evidence about a company's culture.[19] An organization's ambiguous (fragmented) culture is best understood by observing workplace behavior, listening to everyday conversations among staff and with customers, studying written documents and emails, viewing physical structures and settings, and interviewing staff about corporate stories. In other words, to truly understand an organization's culture, we need to sample information from a variety of organizational artifacts. In this section, we review four broad categories of artifacts: organizational stories and legends, organizational language, rituals and ceremonies, and physical structures and symbols.

Organizational Stories and Legends

Stories and legends about the company's founders and past events permeate strong organizational cultures. Some tales recount heroic deeds, whereas others ridicule incidents that deviated from the firm's core values. Organizational stories and legends add human realism to corporate expectations, individual performance standards, and the criteria for getting fired. They also produce emotions, which tend to improve listeners' memory of the lesson within the story.[20] Stories have the greatest effect on communicating corporate culture when they describe real people, are assumed to be true, are known by employees throughout the organization, and convey clear messages about the way things should (or should not) be done.[21]

Organizational Language

The language of the workplace speaks volumes about the company's culture. How employees talk to each other, describe customers, express anger, and greet stakeholders are all verbal symbols of shared values and assumptions. An organization's culture particularly stands out when employees habitually use customized phrases and labels, even when that language isn't complimentary. Not long ago at Goldman Sachs, employees infamously spoke about "elephant trades," which apparently were large investment transactions with huge profit potential. The investment firm's salespeople were allegedly rewarded for going "elephant hunting" (seeking out these large trades from clients). Some staff also referred to "muppets," a label for unsophisticated clients. Under new leadership, Goldman Sachs is apparently changing its culture, but the derogatory language it generated is still used in the investment industry.[23]

OB THEORY TO PRACTICE

Galvanize Puts the Moose on the Table[22]

yvdavyd/Getty Images

Galvanize employees often utter the phrase "put the moose on the table," which means talking openly about a known problem or issue that everyone has avoided (i.e., the elephant in the room). "It's a symbolic invitation to have the awkward—but necessary—conversation," says Laurie Schultz, CEO of the Canadian security software company. "We say it all the time. It's a huge, huge, huge part of our culture."

As a reminder, Galvanize has stuffed toy moose and moose drawings throughout its offices. Schultz adds: "One thing I've learned is the power of symbols, values, and language when reinforcing a risk-taking culture."

> **What we say—and how we say it—can deeply affect a company's culture.[24]**
>
> —Tom Kelley and David Kelley, partner (Tom) and founder (David) of IDEO

rituals the programmed routines of daily organizational life that dramatize the organization's culture

ceremonies planned displays of organizational culture, conducted specifically for the benefit of an audience

Rituals and Ceremonies

Rituals are the programmed routines of daily organizational life that dramatize an organization's culture.[25] They include how visitors are greeted, how often senior executives visit subordinates, how people communicate with one another, how much time employees take for lunch, and so forth. Cultural rituals are repetitive, predictable events that have symbolic meaning of underlying cultural values and assumptions. For instance, BMW's fast-paced culture is quite literally apparent in the way employees walk around the German automaker's offices. "When you move through the corridors and hallways of other companies' buildings, people kind of crawl, they walk slowly," observes a BMW executive. "But BMW people tend to move faster."[26] **Ceremonies** are more formal artifacts than rituals. Ceremonies are planned activities conducted specifically for the benefit of an audience. This would include publicly rewarding (or punishing) employees or celebrating the launch of a new product or newly won contract.

> We shape our buildings; thereafter, they shape us.[29]
>
> —Winston Churchill, former Prime Minister of the United Kingdom

Physical Structures and Symbols

The size, shape, location, and age of buildings both reflect and influence an organization's culture. Buildings might support a company's emphasis on teamwork, environmental friendliness, hierarchy, or any other set of values.[27] Even if the building doesn't make much of a statement, there is a treasure-trove of physical artifacts inside. Desks, chairs, office space, and wall hangings (or lack of them) are just a few of the items that might convey cultural meaning.[28] Each physical artifact alone might not say much, but put enough of them together and an image emerges of how they symbolize the organization's culture.

For example, one prominent workspace design and manufacturing company recently identified the workspace features typically found at companies with different organizational cultures. Exhibit 13.3 summarizes the physical space design of collaborative and creative cultures compared to cultures that emphasize efficiency (control) and

Exhibit 13.3 Workspace Design and Organizational Culture

Collaborative and Creative Cultures	Controlling and Competitive Cultures

• More team space • Informal space • Low/medium enclosure • Flexible environment • Organic layout	• More individual space • More formal than informal space • High/medium enclosure • More fixed environment • More structured, symmetrical layout

Photos: (Left) PeopleImages/Getty Images; (Right) Westend61 Premium/Shutterstock

Sources: Based on information in *How to Create a Successful Organizational Culture: Build It—Literally* (Holland, MI: Haworth Inc., June 2015).

competition. Collaborative and creative cultures value more teamwork and flexibility, so space design is informal and enables spontaneous group discussion. Controlling and competitive cultures tend to have more structural office arrangements and provide more space for individual work than teamwork.[30]

LO13-3 Discuss the importance of organizational culture and the conditions under which organizational culture strength improves organizational performance.

IS ORGANIZATIONAL CULTURE IMPORTANT?

Does a strong organizational culture improve organizational effectiveness? Tony Guzzi thinks so. "I am a firm believer that my job is to define the culture we want, model the culture we want, and nourish the culture we want," says the CEO of EMCOR Group, a *Fortune* 500 company that provides construction, industrial and energy infrastructure, and facilities services. "In the end, the biggest thing you [as CEO] can try to shape is the culture in the organization."[31]

> **Culture is one of the most precious things a company has, so you must work harder on it than anything else.[32]**
>
> —Herb Kelleher, cofounder and former CEO of Southwest Airlines

Tony Guzzi and many other leaders believe that an organization's success partly depends on its culture. Several popular-press management books similarly assert that the most successful companies have strong cultures.[33] Does OB research support this view that companies are more effective when they have a strong culture? Yes, potentially, but the evidence indicates that the relationship depends on a few conditions.[34]

The Meaning and Potential Benefits of a Strong Culture

Before discussing the contingencies of an effective organizational culture, let's examine the meaning of a "strong" organizational culture and its potential benefits. Culture strength refers to how widely and deeply employees understand and embrace the organization's dominant values and assumptions. In a strong organizational culture, the company's core values are "shared" by most employees across all subunits. Values are "shared" when employees hold a similar understanding of them and internalize them as part of their personal set of values.

In a strong culture, the company's values and assumptions are also institutionalized through well-established artifacts, which further entrench the culture. In addition, strong cultures tend to be long-lasting; some can be traced back to personal attributes and behaviors of the company's founder. In contrast, companies have weak cultures when the dominant values are held mainly by a few people at the top of the organization, employees lack awareness or agreement on the meaning of those values, the values and assumptions are unstable over time or highly varied across the organization, and the culture is difficult to interpret from artifacts.

Under specific conditions, companies are more effective when they have strong cultures because of the three important functions listed in Exhibit 13.4 and described as follows:

- *Control system.* Organizational culture is a deeply embedded form of social control that influences employee decisions and behavior.[35] Culture is an automatic pilot, nonconsciously directing employees so their behavior is consistent with organizational expectations. For this reason, organizational culture is often described as a compass that points everyone in the same direction.
- *Social glue.* Organizational culture is the social glue that bonds people together and makes them feel part of the organizational experience.[36] Employees are motivated to internalize the organization's dominant culture because it fulfills their need for social identity. This social glue attracts new staff and retains top performers. It also becomes the common thread that holds employees together in global organizations.
- *Sense making.* Organizational culture helps employees to make sense of what goes on and why things happen in the company.[37] Corporate culture also makes it easier to understand what is expected of them. For instance, research has found that sales employees in companies with stronger organizational cultures have clearer role perceptions and less role-related stress.[38]

> **We cannot provide [employees] with a playbook that covers every eventuality, but we can explicitly share a set of values to help them make the best possible choices.[39]**
>
> —Angela Brown, CEO of Moneris

Exhibit 13.4 Potential Benefits and Contingencies of Culture Strength

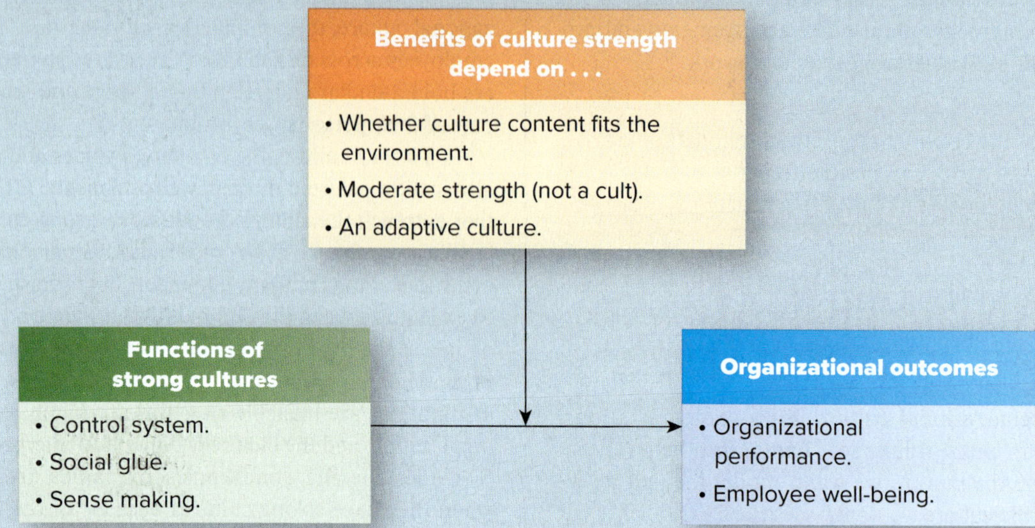

Contingencies of Organizational Culture and Effectiveness

Studies have found only a moderately positive relationship between culture strength and organizational effectiveness. The reason for this weak link is that strong cultures improve organizational effectiveness only under specific conditions (see Exhibit 13.4). The three main contingencies are (1) whether the culture content is aligned with its external environment; (2) whether the culture is moderately strong, not cult-like; and (3) whether the culture incorporates an adaptive culture.

Culture Content Is Aligned with the External Environment The benefits of a strong culture depend on whether its content—the culture's dominant values and assumptions—is aligned with the external environment. If the culture is congruent with the environment, then employees are more motivated and have clearer role perceptions to practice behaviors that improve the organization's interaction with its environment. But when the culture is misaligned with the environment, a strong culture encourages decisions and behaviors that can undermine the organization's connection with its stakeholders.

Consider Microsoft, which has had a strong culture for many years. Until recently, the technology giant's dominant values were noticeably dysfunctional, meaning that they undermined rather than enhanced the organization's capacity to innovate, adapt, and collaborate internally and externally. "Innovation was being replaced by bureaucracy. Teamwork was being replaced by internal politics. We were falling behind," recalls current CEO Satya Nadella. Indeed, some observers predicted that if Microsoft's existing culture continued, the company would be "fading toward irrelevance." Nadella successfully transformed Microsoft's culture by instilling a new set of dominant values around a growth mindset of innovation, information sharing (collaboration), and customer focus—values that are much more aligned with what the technology firm needs to thrive.[40]

Culture Strength Is Not the Level of a Cult A second contingency is the degree of culture strength. Various experts suggest that companies with very strong cultures—known as corporate "cults"—may be less effective than companies with moderately strong cultures.[41] One reason corporate cults may undermine organizational effectiveness is that they lock people into mental models, which can blind them to new opportunities and unique problems. The effect of these very strong cultures is that people overlook or incorrectly define subtle misalignments between the organization's activities and the changing environment.

Corporate cults tend to undermine organizational effectiveness by locking people into mental models, which can blind them from seeing new opportunities and unique problems.
mediaphotos/Getty Images

adaptive culture an organizational culture in which employees are receptive to change, including the ongoing alignment of the organization to its environment and continuous improvement of internal processes

learning orientation a set of collective beliefs and norms that encourage people to question past practices, learn new ideas, experiment putting ideas into practice, and view mistakes as part of the learning process

The other reason why very strong cultures may be dysfunctional is that they suppress dissenting subcultures. The challenge for organizational leaders is to maintain not only a strong culture but one that allows subcultural diversity. Subcultures encourage task-oriented conflict, which improves creative thinking and offers some level of ethical vigilance over the dominant culture. In the long run, a subculture's nascent values could become important dominant values as the environment changes. Corporate cults suppress subcultures, thereby undermining these benefits.

Culture Is an Adaptive Culture A third condition influencing the effect of cultural strength on organizational effectiveness is whether the culture content includes an **adaptive culture**.[42] An adaptive culture embraces change, creativity, open-mindedness, growth, and learning. It is one in which employees recognize that the organization's survival and success depends on their ability to discover emerging changes in the external environment and to adapt their own behavior to those changes. Thus, employees in adaptive cultures adopt an open systems view and take responsibility for the organization's performance and alignment with the external environment.

> You have to create a culture that not only accepts change but seeks out how to change.[43]
>
> —Dan Akerson, former GM CEO

In an adaptive culture, receptivity to change extends to internal processes and roles. Employees believe that satisfying stakeholder needs requires continuous improvement of internal work processes. They also recognize the importance of remaining flexible in their own work roles. The phrase "That's not my job" is found in nonadaptive cultures. Finally, an adaptive culture has a strong **learning orientation** because being receptive to change necessarily means that the company also supports action-oriented discovery. With a learning orientation, employees welcome new learning opportunities, actively experiment with new ideas and practices, view reasonable mistakes as a natural part of the learning process, and continuously question past practices (see Chapter 6).[44]

Organizational Culture and Business Ethics

An organization's culture influences the ethical conduct of its employees. This makes sense because good behavior is driven by ethical values, and ethical values become embedded in an organization's dominant culture. The opposite is equally true. There are numerous instances where an organization's culture has been the apparent cause of unethical conduct. For instance, Uber suffered from an organizational culture that resulted in allegations of sexual harassment, bullying, privacy violations, anti-competitive activities, and theft of proprietary technology. It also created an infamously competitive, political, and conflict-ridden workplace. "The culture and approach that got Uber where it is today is not what will get us to the next level," said Dara Khosrowshahi diplomatically, soon after he replaced Uber's founder as CEO. "Our values define who we are and how we work, but I had heard from many employees that some of them simply didn't represent the kind of company we want to be."[45]

Some leaders also try to improve ethical conduct by changing and strengthening the organization's culture around more socially desirable values. This strategy occurred at Barclays Bank PLC, which was found guilty of rigging interest rates a decade ago. After the British bank's most senior executives were forced out due to the scandal, the new CEO focused on establishing a clear set of ethical values (respect, integrity, service, excellence, stewardship). He then advised all 140,000 Barclays employees that these values should guide their behavior so Barclays could become a more ethical organization.

"There might be some who don't feel they can fully buy in to an approach which so squarely links performance to the upholding of our values," warned Barclays' CEO. "My message to those people is simple: Barclays is not the place for you. The rules have changed. You won't feel comfortable at Barclays and, to be frank, we won't feel comfortable with you as colleagues."[46] The point here is that organizational culture and ethics go hand-in-hand. To create a more ethical company, leaders need to instill enacted values that steer employees toward morally correct behavior.

LO13-4 Compare and contrast four strategies for merging organizational cultures.

MERGING ORGANIZATIONAL CULTURES

Mergers and acquisitions often fail financially when the merging organizations have incompatible cultures.[47] Unless the acquired firm is left to operate independently, companies with clashing

bicultural audit a process of diagnosing cultural relations between companies and determining the extent to which cultural clashes will likely occur

Corporate Culture Risks in Mergers and Acquisitions[49]

53% of 803 executives who were recently involved in M&A activity say they ensured the cultures of the two companies were aligned by interviewing employees from both companies about their needs and concerns.

20% of 1,000 corporate and private equity executives say M&A deals underperform because the parties did not achieve cultural alignment.

30% of 1,438 M&A professionals in 54 countries say that M&A transactions failed to ever meet financial targets due to culture issues.

23% of 400 American C-level executives say their M&A performance on corporate culture due diligence is strong.

48% of 230 top-level executives of Australian companies identify cultural fit as one of the top three factors in the success of M&A deals (90% of M&A specialist executives identify cultural fit as a top factor).

(Photo left): Volodymyr Krasyuk/Shutterstock; (Photo right): Mike Flippo/Shutterstock

cultures tend to undermine employee performance and customer service. Consequently, several studies estimate that only between 30 and 50 percent of corporate acquisitions add value.[48]

Bicultural Audit

Organizational leaders can minimize cultural collisions in corporate mergers and fulfill their duty of due diligence by conducting a bicultural audit.[50] A **bicultural audit** diagnoses cultural relations between the companies and determines the extent to which cultural clashes will likely occur. The process begins by identifying cultural differences between the merging companies. This might occur by surveying employees or through an extended series of meetings where executives and staff of both firms discuss how they think through important decisions in their business. From the survey data or meetings, the parties determine which differences between the two firms will result in conflict and which cultural values provide common ground on which to build a cultural foundation in the merged organization. The final stage involves identifying strategies and preparing action plans to bridge the two organizations' cultures.

Strategies for Merging Different Organizational Cultures

In some cases, the bicultural audit results in a decision to end merger talks because the two cultures are too different to merge effectively. However, even with substantially different cultures, two companies may form a workable union if they apply the appropriate merger strategy. The four main strategies for merging different corporate cultures are assimilation, deculturation, integration, and separation (see Exhibit 13.5).[51]

Exhibit 13.5 Strategies for Merging Different Organizational Cultures

Merger Strategy	Description	Works Best When . . .
Assimilation	Acquired company embraces acquiring firm's culture.	Acquired firm has a weak culture and acquiring firm's culture is strong and successful.
Deculturation	Acquiring firm imposes its culture on unwilling acquired firm.	Rarely works—may be necessary only when acquired firm's culture is dysfunctional but its employees aren't yet aware of the problems.
Integration	Merging companies combine the two or more cultures into a new composite culture.	Existing cultures at both firms are relatively weak or have overlapping values and can be improved.
Separation	Merging companies remain distinct entities with minimal exchange of culture or organizational practices.	Firms operate successfully in different businesses requiring different cultures.

Sources: Based on ideas in A.R. Malekzadeh and A. Nahavandi, "Making Mergers Work by Managing Cultures," *Journal of Business Strategy* 11 (May/June 1990): 55–57; K.W. Smith, "A Brand-New Culture for the Merged Firm," *Mergers and Acquisitions* 35 (June 2000): 45–50.

Assimilation Assimilation occurs when employees at the acquired company willingly embrace the cultural values of the acquiring organization. Typically, this strategy works best when the acquired company has a weak culture or is dysfunctional, whereas the acquiring company's culture is strong and aligned with the external environment. The cultural assimilation strategy seldom produces cultural clashes because the acquiring firm's culture is highly respected and the acquired firm's culture is fairly easily altered.

Deculturation Assimilation is rare. Employees usually resist organizational change, particularly when they are asked to abide by significantly different corporate values. Under these conditions, some acquiring companies apply a *deculturation* strategy by imposing their culture and business practices on the acquired organization. The acquiring firm strips away reward systems and other artifacts that support the old culture. People who cannot adopt the acquiring company's culture often lose their jobs. Deculturation may be necessary when the acquired firm's culture doesn't work, even when employees in the acquired company aren't convinced of this. However, this strategy is difficult to apply effectively because the acquired firm's employees resist the cultural intrusions from the buying firm, thereby delaying or undermining the merger process.

Integration A third strategy is to combine the cultures of the two firms into one new composite culture that preserves the best features of the previous cultures. Integration is slow and potentially risky because there are many forces preserving the existing cultures. Still, this strategy should be considered when the companies have relatively weak cultures or when their cultures include several overlapping values. Integration works best when the cultures of both merging companies could be improved, which motivates employees to adopt the best cultural elements of the separate entities. Incorporating the best cultural elements of the original companies symbolizes that employees from both firms have meaningful values for the combined organization. "Find one thing in the organization that was good and use it as a cornerstone for a new culture," advises a respected executive who has led several mergers and acquisitions. "People don't want to work for an organization for years and then be told it's rubbish."[52]

Separation A separation strategy occurs when the merging companies agree to remain distinct entities with minimal exchange of culture or organizational practices. This strategy is most appropriate when the two merging companies are in unrelated industries because the most appropriate cultural values tend to differ by industry. Separation is also the preferred approach for the corporate cultures of diversified conglomerates. The cultural separation strategy is rare, however. Executives in acquiring firms usually have difficulty keeping their hands off the acquired firm. According to one estimate, only 15 percent of mergers leave the acquired company as a stand-alone unit.[53]

Integration works best when the cultures of both merging companies could be improved, which motivates employees to adopt the best cultural elements of the separate entities.
dotshock/Shutterstock

LO13-5 Discuss five strategies for changing and strengthening an organization's culture, including the application of attraction–selection–attrition theory.

CHANGING AND STRENGTHENING ORGANIZATIONAL CULTURE

Is it possible to change an organization's culture? Yes, but doing so isn't easy, the change rarely occurs quickly, and often the culture ends up changing (or replacing) corporate leaders. A few experts argue that an organization's culture "cannot be managed," so attempting to change the company's values and assumptions is a waste of time.[54] This may be an extreme view, but organizational culture experts generally agree that changing an organization's culture is a monumental challenge. At the same time, the external environment changes over time, so organizations eventually need to shift their culture to maintain alignment with the emerging environment.

This section looks at five strategies that have had some success at altering and strengthening corporate cultures. These strategies, illustrated in Exhibit 13.6, are not exhaustive, but each seems to work well in most circumstances.

Model Desired Culture through the Actions of Founders and Leaders

Whether deliberately or haphazardly, the company's founder usually forms an organization's culture.[56] The founder's

> **If you don't spend time to create a culture in your organization, one will create itself. And the one that creates itself is probably not going to be good.**[55]
>
> —Bill Emerson, Vice Chair of Rock Holdings Inc. (parent company of Quicken Loans)

Exhibit 13.6 Strategies for Changing and Strengthening Organizational Culture

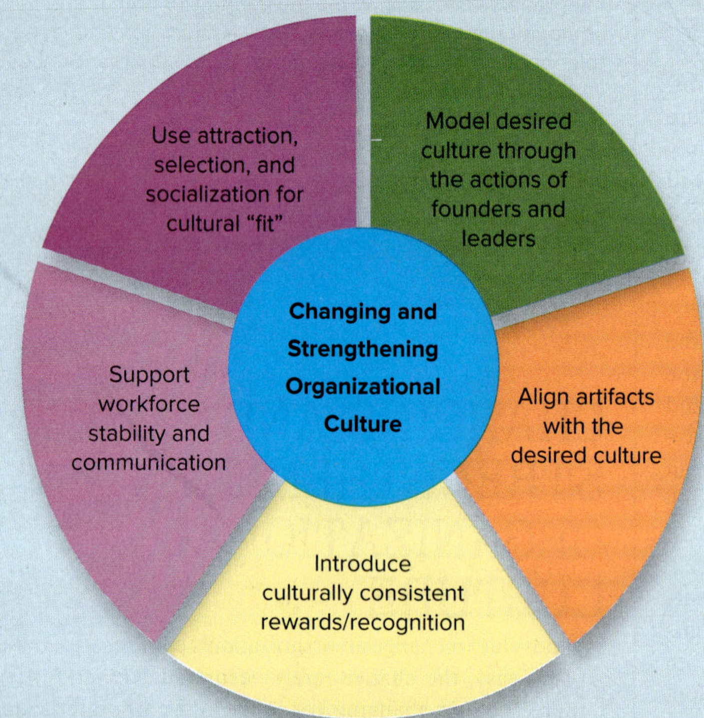

personality, values, habits, and critical events all play a role in establishing the firm's core values and assumptions. The founder is often an inspiring visionary who provides a compelling role model for others to follow. In later years, organizational culture is reinforced through stories and legends about the founder that symbolize the core values.

Although founders usually establish an organization's culture, subsequent leaders need to actively guide, reinforce, and sometimes alter that culture.[57] The process of leading cultural change is associated with both transformational leadership and authentic leadership (see Chapter 11). In each of those models, leaders base their words and actions on personal values, and those values potentially become a reflection of the organization's values. For instance, one study found that the preferred conflict-handling style of leaders influences the work unit's or organization's cultural expectations on how employees address conflict situations. Another study reported that work units or companies with strong servant leadership were more likely to have a culture that valued providing service to others.[58]

Align Artifacts with the Desired Culture

Artifacts represent more than just the visible indicators of a company's culture. They are also mechanisms that keep the culture in place or shift the culture to a new set of values and assumptions.[59] As we discuss in the next chapter on organizational change, systems and structures are important instruments to support the desired state of affairs. These systems and structures are artifacts, such as the workplace layout, reporting structure, office rituals, type of information distributed, and language that is reinforced or discouraged. Corporate cultures also can be strengthened through the artifacts of stories and behaviors. According to Max De Pree, former CEO of furniture manufacturer Herman Miller Inc., every organization needs "tribal storytellers" to keep the organization's history and culture alive.[60] Leaders play a role by creating memorable events that symbolize the cultural values they want to develop or maintain.

Introduce Culturally Consistent Rewards and Recognition

Reward systems and informal recognition practices are artifacts, but they deserve separate discussion because of their powerful effect on strengthening or reshaping an organization's culture.[61] Uber created a new reward system to help replace its "toxic" culture with one that is more compatible with societal expectations. The transportation network

Artifacts don't just symbolize a company's culture; they also keep the culture in place or shift the culture to a new set of values and assumptions.
mixetto/Getty Images

company previously had an internally competitive (rank-and-yank) merit system and allegedly biased performance review process tied to its original list of dysfunctional values. Uber's new reward system asks employees to document specific performance goals as well as one "citizenship goal" (e.g., helping coworkers, volunteering outside the company). This reward system encourages cooperation, community involvement, and individual development without competing against coworkers. "We're shifting the culture very significantly through this process," says the Uber human resources executive who championed the new reward system.[62]

Support Workforce Stability and Communication

An organization's culture is embedded in the minds of its employees. Organizational stories are rarely written down; rituals and ceremonies do not usually exist in procedure manuals; organizational metaphors are not found in corporate directories. Thus, a strong culture depends on a stable workforce. Workforce stability is important because it takes time for employees to fully understand the organization's culture and how to enact it in their daily work lives. The organization's culture can literally disintegrate during periods of high turnover and precipitous downsizing because the corporate memory is lost with the departing employees. A strong organizational culture also depends on a workplace in which employees regularly interact with one another. Through ongoing communication, everyone in the organization develops shared language, stories, and other artifacts.

Use Attraction, Selection, and Socialization for Cultural Fit

A valuable way to strengthen and possibly change an organization's culture is to recruit and select job applicants whose values are compatible with the culture. This process is explained by **attraction–selection–attrition (ASA) theory**.[63] ASA theory states that organizations have a natural tendency to attract, select, and retain people with values and personality characteristics that are consistent with the organization's character, resulting in a more homogeneous organization and a stronger culture.

- *Attraction.* Job applicants engage in self-selection by avoiding prospective employers whose values seem incompatible with their own values.[65] They look for subtle artifacts during interviews and through public information that communicate the company's culture. Some organizations encourage this self-selection by actively describing their cultures.

attraction–selection–attrition (ASA) theory a theory that states that organizations have a natural tendency to attract, select, and retain people with values and personality characteristics that are consistent with the organization's character, resulting in a more homogeneous organization and a stronger culture

Corporate Culture Fit during the Hiring Process[64]

46% of 1,509 American job seekers say that the organization's culture is very important in applying to a company.

77% of 5,113 working adults in the United States, United Kingdom, France, and Germany say they would consider a company's culture before applying there.

90% of 1,500 American and Canadian hiring managers say a candidate's fit with the company's culture is equal to or more important than their skills and experience.

37% of 1,500 American and Canadian employees say they would decline an offer for the perfect job if the corporate culture wasn't a good fit.

13% of 1,064 hiring employers in the U.S. and Canada say that the most challenging attributes to find in job candidates is corporate culture fit.

alxpin/Getty Images

organizational socialization the process by which individuals learn the values, expected behaviors, and social knowledge necessary to assume their roles in the organization

- *Selection.* Hiring managers increasingly assess how well a job candidate "fits in" with the company's culture when deciding whether to hire that person.[66] IKEA is a values-driven organization, so it determines how well applicants' personal values are compatible with the global retailer's corporate values as well as how well those applicants are aware of IKEA's values. The idea is that this cultural alignment is good for both the company and the employee. "Be clear of your personal values and connect those with your company values," advises an IKEA human resource manager. "We know that tomorrow's candidates are not necessarily looking for the perfect job; they're looking for the perfect cultural fit."[67]

People seek workplaces that are reasonably congruent with their personal values and are motivated to leave workplaces that are a poor fit.

- *Attrition.* People seek workplaces that are reasonably congruent with their personal values and are motivated to leave workplaces that are a poor fit. This occurs because person–organization values congruence supports their social identity and minimizes internal role conflict. Even if employees aren't forced out, many quit when values incongruence is sufficiently high.[68] Several companies (Zappos, G Adventures, etc.) will even pay newcomers to quit within the first few weeks of employment if the new employees think their personal values conflict with the company's culture.

LO13-6 Describe the organizational socialization process and identify strategies to improve that process.

ORGANIZATIONAL SOCIALIZATION

Organizational socialization is the process by which individuals learn the values, expected behaviors, and social knowledge necessary to assume their roles in the organization.[69] It is a valuable set of practices to help companies change and strengthen their organizational culture. Equally important, it helps newcomers adjust to coworkers, work procedures, and other conditions in organizational life. Research indicates that when evidence-based organizational socialization practices are applied, new hires tend to perform better, have higher job satisfaction, and remain longer with the organization.[70]

Some writers claim that organizational socialization can change employee values to become more aligned with the company's culture. However, personal values are fairly stable beyond early adulthood and therefore are not so easily altered by short-term training and related socialization events. Instead, effective organizational socialization offers newcomers a clearer understanding about the company's values which, in turn, gives them guidelines to more accurately engage in values-consistent behaviors on the job.[71] Better awareness of the company's culture also motivates new hires to reject the job offer or more quickly leave if their personal values are incompatible with the organization's values and assumptions.

Learning and Adjustment Process

Organizational socialization is a process of both learning and adjustment. It is a learning process because newcomers try to make sense of the company's physical workplace, social dynamics, and strategic and cultural environment. They learn about the organization's performance expectations, power dynamics, corporate culture, company history, and jargon. They also need to form successful and satisfying relationships with other people from whom they can learn the ropes.[72] In other words, effective socialization supports newcomers' *organizational comprehension*. It accelerates development of an accurate cognitive map of the physical, social, strategic, and cultural dynamics of the organization. Ideally, this learning should be distributed over time to minimize information overload.

Organizational socialization is also an adjustment process because individuals need to adapt to their new work environment. They develop new work roles that reconfigure their social identity, adopt new team norms, and practice new behaviors.[73] The adjustment process is fairly rapid for many people, usually occurring within a few months. However, newcomers with diverse work experience seem to adjust better than those with limited previous experience, possibly because they have a larger toolkit of knowledge and skills to make the adjustment possible.[74]

Stages of Organizational Socialization

Organizational socialization is a continuous process, beginning before you submit a job application and continuing throughout your career within the company. However, it is most intense during movement across organizational boundaries, such as when you first join a company or get transferred to an international assignment. Each of these transitions is a process that can be divided into three stages. Our focus here is on the socialization of new employees, so the three stages are called preemployment socialization, encounter, and role management (see

Exhibit 13.7 Stages of Organizational Socialization

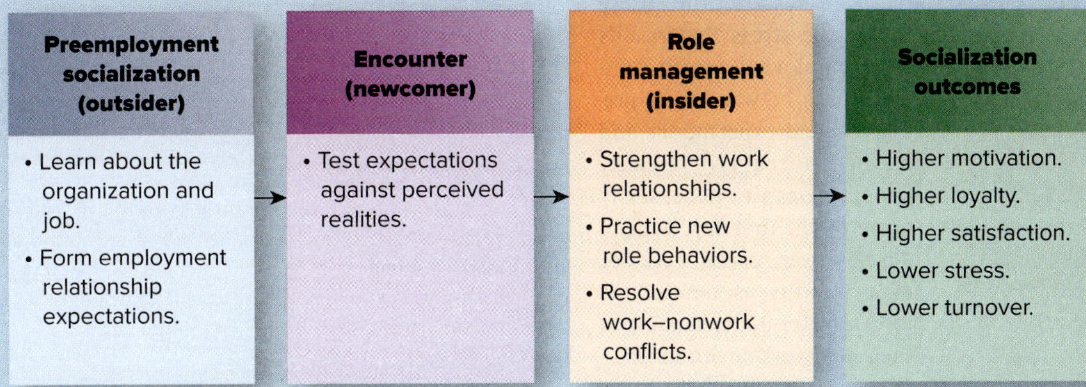

Exhibit 13.7). These stages parallel the individual's transition from outsider to newcomer and then to insider.[75]

Stage 1: Preemployment Socialization Think back to the months and weeks before you began working in a new job (or attending a new school). You actively searched for information about the company, formed expectations about working there, and felt some anticipation about fitting into that setting. The preemployment socialization stage encompasses all the learning and adjustment that occurs before the first day of work. In fact, a large part of the socialization adjustment process occurs during this stage.[76]

The main problem with preemployment socialization is that outsiders rely on indirect information about what it is like to work in the organization. This information is often distorted by inherent conflicts that arise during the mating dance between employer and applicant.[77]

The main problem with preemployment socialization is that outsiders rely on indirect information about what it is like to work in the organization.
Rawpixel.com/Shutterstock

- The employer's motivation to attract many high-quality job applicants conflicts with the applicant's need to receive complete and accurate information for choosing the best job offer. Many firms describe only positive aspects of the job and company, causing applicants to accept job offers based on misleading expectations about working at that organization.
- The job applicant's motivation to receive job offers conflicts with the employer's need to receive complete and accurate information for choosing the best job applicants. Applicants engage in impression management when seeking employment, motivating them to hide negative information, act out of character, and occasionally embellish information about their past accomplishments. Due to this distorted information, the employer chooses applicants that are less qualified or have a poorer cultural fit with the organization.
- Employers are motivated to attract many high-quality job applicants, which conflicts with their need to receive complete and accurate information for choosing the best job applicants. Employers are sometimes reluctant to ask some types of questions to applicants or use potentially valuable selection methods because those information-gathering activities might scare off the best job candidates. Without the additional information about applicants, the employer forms inaccurate expectations about job candidates and hires people who might not be sufficiently qualified or compatible with the organization's culture.
- Job applicants are motivated to receive job offers, which conflicts with their need to receive complete and accurate information for choosing the best job offer. Applicants avoid asking important questions about the company because they want to convey a favorable image to their prospective employer. For instance, applicants usually don't like to ask about starting salaries and promotion opportunities because it makes them seem greedy or aggressive. Yet, unless the employer provides this information, applicants might fill in the missing details with false assumptions that produce inaccurate job expectations.

Stage 2: Encounter The first day on the job typically marks the beginning of the encounter stage of organizational socialization. This is the stage in which newcomers test how well their

reality shock the stress that results when employees perceive discrepancies between their preemployment expectations and on-the-job reality

realistic job preview (RJP) a method of improving organizational socialization in which job applicants are given a balance of positive and negative information about the job and work context

preemployment expectations fit reality. Many companies fail that test, resulting in **reality shock**—the stress that results when employees perceive discrepancies between their preemployment expectations and on-the-job reality.[78] Reality shock doesn't necessarily occur on the first day; it might develop over several weeks or even months as newcomers form a better understanding of their new work environment.

Reality shock is common in many organizations.[79] Newcomers sometimes face *unmet expectations* whereby the employer doesn't deliver on its promises, such as failing to provide challenging projects or the resources to get the work done. However, new hires also experience reality shock due to *unrealistic expectations*, which are distorted work expectations formed from the information exchange conflicts described earlier. Whatever the cause, reality shock impedes the learning and adjustment process because the newcomer's energy is directed toward managing the resulting stress.[80]

Stage 3: Role Management Role management, the third stage of organizational socialization, really begins during preemployment socialization, but it is most active as employees make the transition from newcomers to insiders. They strengthen relationships with coworkers and supervisors, practice new role behaviors, and adopt attitudes and values consistent with their new positions and the organization. Role management also involves resolving the conflicts between work and nonwork activities, including resolving discrepancies between their personal values and those emphasized by the organizational culture.

Improving the Socialization Process

Companies have a tendency to exaggerate positive features of the job and neglect to mention the undesirable elements. Their motivation is to attract as many job applicants as possible, which they assume will improve the selection choices. Unfortunately, this flypaper approach often ends badly. Those hired soon discover that the actual workplace is not as favorable as the employer's marketing hype (i.e., unmet expectations), resulting in reality shock. In contrast, a **realistic job preview (RJP)** offers a balance of positive and negative information about the job and work context.[81] This balanced description of the company and work helps job applicants decide for themselves whether their skills, needs, and values are compatible with the job and organization.

OB THEORY TO PRACTICE

Selected Organizational Socialization Practices[84]

Newcomer swag. Before or during their first day of work, new hires receive a welcome kit (often called a "swag") symbolizing that the individual really has been hired and is valued. New hires at Element Three, a marketing firm in Indianapolis, receive a water bottle, t-shirt, keychain, pencils, and other items branded with the company's logo or elephant mascot. TE Connectivity's swag includes a company backpack. Slack's kit includes a pair of socks with Slack's quasi-tartan design.

Connecting newcomers—quickly! Newcomers start bonding with coworkers and develop organizational comprehension more quickly when they are given access to the company's digital collaborative platform and associated apps soon after accepting the job offer. This might include access to all communication channels and apps or to a few of them designed for newcomers and employees who bring them on board. Slack, the collaborative platform, has a special onboarding app (ChiefOnboarding) that assigns newcomer tasks, provides access to resources, and directs newcomers to specific coworkers for information.

First day readiness and welcome. The first day on the job needs to be well planned and a positive experience. Twitter tackles newcomer readiness planning with its 75-step "Yes to Desk" process from the moment applicants say "yes" to the job offer through to the first day on the job at their desk. Twitter's system keeps new hires informed about what to expect, and the company has the resources ready for newcomers to join the team and begin their orientation on or before the first day of work.

Team training tasks for remote newcomers. UK-based company OutreachPete helps new hires to successfully bond together even though it has an almost entirely remote workforce located around the world. "All new workers are put into a separate [Slack] channel together and given instructional materials and initial training tasks to complete," explains the founder of the SEO link-building company. "You'd be amazed at how it creates an immediate sense of teamwork despite these individuals being spread across the globe."

Newcomers sometimes face *unmet expectations* whereby the employer doesn't deliver on its promises, such as failing to provide challenging projects or the resources to get the work done.

RJPs scare away some applicants, but they also tend to reduce turnover and increase job performance.[82] This occurs because RJPs help applicants develop more accurate preemployment expectations, which, in turn, minimize reality shock. RJPs represent a type of vaccination by preparing employees for the more challenging and troublesome aspects of the work context. There is also some evidence that RJPs increase affective organizational commitment. One explanation is that companies providing candid information are easier to trust. Another explanation is that RJPs show respect and concern for the employee's expectations and welfare.[83]

Socialization Agents If you ask new employees what provided the greatest assistance adjusting to their jobs, they will probably credit helpful coworkers, bosses, or maybe even friends who work elsewhere in the organization. The fact is, socialization agents play a central role in the socialization process.[85] Supervisors tend to provide technical information, performance feedback, and information about job duties. They also improve the socialization process by giving newcomers reasonably challenging first assignments, buffering them from excessive demands, helping them form social ties with coworkers, and generating positive emotions around their new work experience.[86]

Coworkers are important socialization agents because they are easily accessible, can answer questions when problems arise, and serve as role models for appropriate behavior. New employees tend to receive this information and support when coworkers welcome them into the work team. Coworkers also aid the socialization process by being flexible and tolerant in their interactions with new hires.

Organizational socialization is most successful when companies help newcomers strengthen their social bonds with other employees. This can occur casually through immediate involvement with a welcoming team of veteran employees. It also occurs through various social interaction events, particularly where current staff members help newcomers get acquainted with people elsewhere in the organization. For newcomers who work remotely, the best advice is to have them meet coworkers face-to-face within a few months after joining the company. However, distant workers can also build a sense of community through regular video interactions and access to the internal digital communication platform as soon as they accept the job offer.

Study Checklist

Connect® is available for *M Organizational Behavior.* Additional resources include:

✓ Exercises:

- **Case Analysis:** Apply concepts within the context of a real-world situation.
- **Click and Drag:** Helps make the connection between theory and application through matching, ranking, or grouping activities.
- **Video Case:** See management in action through interactive videos.
- **Self-Assessment:** Designed to promote student self-awareness and reflection, these research-based surveys contain detailed feedback for students.
- **Application-Based Activities:** These highly interactive, application- and analysis-based exercises allow students to take on specific roles to complete management-related tasks within a real-world context.

✓ **SmartBook 2.0**™—Smartbook 2.0 is an adaptive learning solution that provides personalized learning to individual student needs, continually adapts to pinpoint knowledge gaps and focuses learning on concepts requiring additional study. It fosters more productive learning, takes the guesswork out of what to study, and helps students better prepare for class.

Notes

1. The terms *organizational culture* and *corporate culture* were popularized in 1982 in T.E. Deal and A.A. Kennedy, *Corporate Cultures* (Reading, MA: Addison-Wesley, 1982); T.J. Peters and R.H. Waternam, *In Search of Excellence: Lessons from America's Best-Run Companies* (New York: Warner, 1982). However, this phrase did appear more than a decade earlier in N. Margulies, "Organizational Culture and Psychological Growth," *The Journal of Applied Behavioral Science* 5, no. 4 (1969): 491–508; S. Silverzweig and R.F. Allen, "Changing the Corporate Culture," *Sloan Management Review* 17, no. 3 (1976): 33–34. The notion that organizations have dominant values can be traced back to P. Selznick, *Leadership in Administration: A Sociological Interpretation* (Evanston, IL: Row, Peterson and Company, 1957), 19–22.
2. T. Higgins and T. Mochizuki, "Tesla Needs Its Battery Maker. A Culture Clash Threatens Their Relationship," *The Wall Street Journal*, October 8, 2019; D. Gelles, "Crisis Reveals 'Sick' Culture Inside Boeing," *The New York Times*, January 11, 2020, A1; J. Smyth, "Have Australia's Scandal-Hit Banks Changed Their Culture?" *Financial Times*, February 11, 2020.
3. A. Williams, P. Dobson, and M. Walters, *Changing Culture: New Organizational Approaches* (London: Institute of Personnel Management, 1989); E.H. Schein, "What Is Culture?" in *Reframing Organizational Culture*, ed. P.J. Frost et al. (Newbury Park, CA: Sage, 1991), 243–53.

4. B.M. Meglino and E.C. Ravlin, "Individual Values in Organizations: Concepts, Controversies, and Research," *Journal of Management* 24, no. 3 (1998): 351–89; B.R. Agle and C.B. Caldwell, "Understanding Research on Values in Business," *Business and Society* 38, no. 3 (1999): 326–87; S. Hitlin and J.A. Pilavin, "Values: Reviving a Dormant Concept," *Annual Review of Sociology* 30 (2004): 359–93.
5. N.M. Ashkanasy, "The Case for Culture," in *Debating Organization*, ed. R. Westwood and S. Clegg (Malden, MA: Blackwell, 2003), 300–10.
6. J. Dewey, *Human Nature and Conduct: An Introduction to Social Psychology* (New York: Holt, 1922), 300.
7. B. Kabanoff and J. Daly, "Espoused Values in Organisations," *Australian Journal of Management* 27, Special issue (2002): 89–104; H. Bourne and M. Jenkins, "Organizational Values: A Dynamic Perspective," *Organization Studies* 34, no. 4 (2013): 495–514.
8. At least one study suggests that espoused values have a positive influence on organizational performance by motivating employees (emotional contagion), signaling desired behaviors, and enhancing public reputation. However, in many firms studied, these espoused values may also have been enacted values. See K. Jonsen et al., "Evaluating Espoused Values: Does Articulating Values Pay Off?" *European Management Journal* 33, no. 5 (2015): 332–40.
9. J. Bersin et al., "The New Organization: Different by Design," in *Global Human Capital Trends 2016* (Westlake, TX: Deloitte University Press, 2016), 1–14; "Where Organizational Culture Is Headed," *Strategy&* (blog), 2018, https://www.strategyand.pwc.com/gx/en/insights/2018/global-culture-survey.html; "The TINYpulse 2019 Employee Engagement Report: The End of Employee Loyalty" (Seattle: TINYpulse, February 2019); D. Sull, C. Sull, and A. Chamberlain, "Measuring Culture in Leading Companies," *MIT Sloan Management Review*, June 24, 2019; "Mission & Culture Survey 2019" (Mill Valley, CA: Glassdoor, July 9, 2019); "New Survey Reveals Toxic Cultures and Negative Behaviors Are Prevalent in the Workplace," News Release (Washington DC: EVERFI, November 20, 2019).
10. C. Ostroff, A.J. Kinicki, and R.S. Muhammad, "Organizational Culture and Climate," in *Handbook of Psychology*, 2nd ed., ed. I.B. Weiner (New York: Wiley, 2012), 643–76.
11. R. Hastings and P. McCord, *Netflix Culture: Freedom and Responsibility* (Los Gatos, CA: Netflix, August 2009); R. Hastings, *Culture at Netflix* (Los Gatos, CA: Netflix, 21 June 2017), https://jobs.netflix.com/culture (accessed July 11, 2017); S. Ramachandran and J. Flint, "At Netflix, Radical Transparency and Blunt Firings Unsettle the Ranks," *The Wall Street Journal*, October 25, 2018; B. Murphy Jr., "You Don't Just Get Fired at Netflix," *Inc*, October 27, 2018; S. Rodriguez, "Pinterest: Overly 'Nice' Culture Has Hurt Growth, Ex-Employees Say," *CNBC News*, April 10, 2019. Netflix updated its famous original organizational culture statement, but the underlying values are similar. This culture is also evident from many recent posts on Glassdoor by current and former employees.
12. C.A. O'Reilly III, J. Chatman, and D.F. Caldwell, "People and Organizational Culture: A Profile Comparison Approach to Assessing Person-Organization Fit," *Academy of Management Journal* 34 (1991): 487–516; J.J. van Muijen, "Organizational Culture," in *A Handbook of Work and Organizational Psychology: Organizational Psychology*, ed. P.J.D. Drenth, H. Thierry, and C.J. de Wolff (East Sussex, UK: Psychology Press, 1998), 113–32; P.A. Balthazard, R.A. Cooke, and R.E. Potter, "Dysfunctional Culture, Dysfunctional Organization: Capturing the Behavioral Norms That Form Organizational Culture and Drive Performance," *Journal of Managerial Psychology* 21, no. 8 (2006): 709–32; C. Helfrich et al., "Assessing an Organizational Culture Instrument Based on the Competing Values Framework: Exploratory and Confirmatory Factor Analyses," *Implementation Science* 2, no. 1 (2007): 13. For reviews of organizational culture survey instruments, see T. Scott et al., "The Quantitative Measurement of Organizational Culture in Health Care: A Review of the Available Instruments," *Health Services Research* 38, no. 3 (2003): 923–45; D.E. Leidner and T. Kayworth, "A Review of Culture in Information Systems Research: Toward a Theory of Information Technology Culture Conflict," *MIS Quarterly* 30, no. 2 (2006): 357–99; S. Scott-Findlay and C.A. Estabrooks, "Mapping the Organizational Culture Research in Nursing: A Literature Review," *Journal of Advanced Nursing* 56, no. 5 (2006): 498–513.
13. L. Guiso, P. Sapienza, and L. Zingales, "The Value of Corporate Culture," *Journal of Financial Economics* 117, no. 1 (2015): 60–76.
14. J. Martin, P.J. Frost, and O.A. O'Neill, "Organizational Culture: Beyond Struggles for Intellectual Dominance," in *Handbook of Organization Studies*, ed. S. Clegg et al. (London: Sage, 2006), 725–53; N.E. Fenton and S. Inglis, "A Critical Perspective on Organizational Values," *Nonprofit Management and Leadership* 17, no. 3 (2007): 335–47; K. Haukelid, "Theories of (Safety) Culture Revisited—An Anthropological Approach," *Safety Science* 46, no. 3 (2008): 413–26.
15. G. Hofstede, "Identifying Organizational Subcultures: An Empirical Approach," *Journal of Management Studies* 35, no. 1 (1990): 1–12; J. Martin and C. Siehl, "Organizational Culture and Counterculture: An Uneasy Symbiosis," *Organizational Dynamics* (1983): 52–64; E. Ogbonna and L.C. Harris, "Organisational Culture in the Age of the Internet: An Exploratory Study," *New Technology, Work and Employment* 21, no. 2 (2006): 162–75.
16. H. Silver, "Does a University Have a Culture?" *Studies in Higher Education* 28, no. 2 (2003): 157–69.
17. A. Sinclair, "Approaches to Organizational Culture and Ethics," *Journal of Business Ethics* 12 (1993); T.E. Deal and A.A. Kennedy, *The New Corporate Cultures* (Cambridge, MA: Perseus Books, 1999), Chap. 10; A. Boisnier and J. Chatman, "The Role of Subcultures in Agile Organizations," in *Leading and Managing People in Dynamic Organizations*, ed. R. Petersen and E. Mannix (Mahwah, NJ: Erlbaum, 2003), 87–112; C. Morrill, M.N. Zald, and H. Rao, "Covert Political Conflict in Organizations: Challenges from Below," *Annual Review of Sociology* 29, no. 1 (2003): 391–415.
18. J.S. Ott, *The Organizational Culture Perspective* (Pacific Grove, CA: Brooks/Cole, 1989), Chap. 2; J.S. Pederson and J.S. Sorensen, *Organizational Cultures in Theory and Practice* (Aldershot, UK: Gower, 1989), 27–29; M.O. Jones, *Studying Organizational Symbolism: What, How, Why?* (Thousand Oaks, CA: Sage, 1996).
19. A. Furnham and B. Gunter, "Corporate Culture: Definition, Diagnosis, and Change," *International Review of Industrial and Organizational Psychology* 8 (1993): 233–61; E.H. Schein, "Organizational Culture," *American Psychologist* (1990): 109–19; E.H. Schein, *The Corporate Culture Survival Guide* (San Francisco: Jossey-Bass, 1999), Chap. 4.
20. T.E. Deal and A.A. Kennedy, *Corporate Cultures* (Reading, MA: Addison-Wesley, 1982), chap. 5; C.J. Boudens, "The Story of Work: A Narrative Analysis of Workplace Emotion," *Organization Studies* 26, no. 9 (2005): 1285–306; S. Denning, *The Leader's Guide to Storytelling* (San Francisco: Jossey-Bass, 2005).
21. J.C. Meyer, "Tell Me a Story: Eliciting Organizational Values from Narratives," *Communication Quarterly* 43 (1995): 210–24; W. Swap et al., "Using Mentoring and Storytelling to Transfer Knowledge in the Workplace," *Journal of Management Information Systems* 18 (2001): 95–114; A.L. Wilkins, "Organizational Stories as Symbols Which Control the Organization," in *Organizational Symbolism*, ed. L.R. Pondy et al. (Greenwich, CT: JAI Press, 1984), 81–92; R. Zemke, "Storytelling: Back to a Basic," *Training* 27, no. 3 (1990): 44–50.
22. F. Stone, "The Conversation: ACL Services Boss Laurie Schultz Knows Fraud When She Sees It," *BC Business*, February 7, 2017; "5 Questions on Culture with Laurie Schultz, CEO, Galvanize," *Business in Vancouver*, January 2020, pp. 30-31.

23. G. Smith, *Why I Left Goldman Sachs: A Wall Street Story* (New York: Grand Central Publishing, 2012); B. Tuttle, "16 Amazing Facts about the Muppets That'll Make You Laugh, Cry & Sing Along," *Money*, September 22, 2015; L. Burton, "David Solomon Getting Goldman Sachs on Track to a Softer Culture," *Telegraph*, November 9, 2019. The word "muppet" is frequently mentioned in the investment industry to describe naive or gullible clients. See, for example, V. Guida, "Wells Fargo CEO Steps Down amid Rebukes from Regulators, Congress," *Politico*, March 28, 2019.
24. T. Kelley and D. Kelley, *Creative Confidence: Unleashing the Creative Potential within Us All* (New York: Random House, 2013), 198.
25. A.C.T. Smith and B. Stewart, "Organizational Rituals: Features, Functions and Mechanisms," *International Journal of Management Reviews* 13 (2011): 113–33.
26. "The Ultimate Chairman," *Business Times Singapore*, September 3, 2005.
27. G. Turner and J. Myerson, *New Workspace New Culture: Office Design as a Catalyst for Change* (Aldershot, UK: Gower, 1998); J.C. McElroy and P.C. Morrow, "Employee Reactions to Office Redesign: A Naturally Occurring Quasi-Field Experiment in a Multi-Generational Setting," *Human Relations* 63 (2010): 609–36; T.J. Kallio, K.-M. Kallio, and A.J. Blomberg, "Physical Space, Culture and Organisational Creativity–A Longitudinal Study," *Facilities* 33 (2015): 389–411; S. Zerella, K. von Treuer, and S.L. Albrecht, "The Influence of Office Layout Features on Employee Perception of Organizational Culture," *Journal of Environmental Psychology* 54 (2017): 1–10.
28. K.D. Elsbach and B.A. Bechky, "It's More Than a Desk: Working Smarter through Leveraged Office Design," *California Management Review* 49, no. 2 (2007): 80–101.
29. Churchill apparently made this statement on October 28, 1943, in the British House of Commons, when London, damaged by bombings in World War II, was about to be rebuilt.
30. *How to Create a Successful Organizational Culture: Build It–Literally* (Holland, MI: Haworth Inc., June 2015).
31. G. Forsythe, K. Kuhla, and D. Rice, "The CEO's Role in Shaping an Organization's Culture," *Chief Executive*, February 6, 2018.
32. T.E. Deal and A.A. Kennedy, *The New Corporate Cultures* (Reading, MA: Perseus Books, 1999), 22.
33. J.C. Collins and J.I. Porras, *Built to Last: Successful Habits of Visionary Companies* (London, UK: Century, 1994); T.E. Deal and A.A. Kennedy, *The New Corporate Cultures* (Cambridge, MA: Perseus Books, 1999); R. Barrett, *The Values-Driven Organization*, 2nd ed. (New York: Routledge, 2017); J.M. Kouzes and B.Z. Posner, *The Leadership Challenge*, Sixth ed. (Hoboken, NJ: John Wiley & Sons, 2017), Chap. 3.
34. C. Siehl and J. Martin, "Organizational Culture: A Key to Financial Performance?," in *Organizational Climate and Culture*, ed. B. Schneider (San Francisco: Jossey-Bass, 1990), 241–81; G.G. Gordon and N. Di-Tomaso, "Predicting Corporate Performance from Organizational Culture," *Journal of Management Studies* 29 (1992): 783–98; J.P. Kotter and J.L. Heskett, *Corporate Culture and Performance* (New York: Free Press, 1992); C.P.M. Wilderom, U. Glunk, and R. Maslowski, "Organizational Culture as a Predictor of Organizational Performance," in *Handbook of Organizational Culture and Climate*, ed. N.M. Ashkanasy, C.P.M. Wilderom, and M.F. Peterson (Thousand Oaks, CA: Sage, 2000), 193–210; A. Carmeli and A. Tishler, "The Relationships between Intangible Organizational Elements and Organizational Performance," *Strategic Management Journal* 25 (2004): 1257–78; S. Teerikangas and P. Very, "The Culture–Performance Relationship in M&A: From Yes/No to How," *British Journal of Management* 17, no. S1 (2006): S31–S48.
35. Y. Wiener, "Forms of Value Systems: A Focus on Organizational Effectiveness and Cultural Change and Maintenance," *Academy of Management Review* 13, no. 4 (1988): 534–45; J.A. Chatman and S.E. Cha, "Leading by Leveraging Culture," *California Management Review* 45 (2003): 20–34; M. Alvesson, *Understanding Organizational Culture*, 2nd ed. (London: Sage, 2013).
36. B. Ashforth and F. Mael, "Social Identity Theory and the Organization," *Academy of Management Review* 14 (1989): 20–39; M. Alvesson, *Understanding Organizational Culture*, 2nd ed. (London: Sage, 2013).
37. M.R. Louis, "Surprise and Sensemaking: What Newcomers Experience in Entering Unfamiliar Organizational Settings," *Administrative Science Quarterly* 25 (1980): 226–51; S.G. Harris, "Organizational Culture and Individual Sensemaking: A Schema-Based Perspective," *Organization Science* 5 (1994): 309–21.
38. J.W. Barnes et al., "The Role of Culture Strength in Shaping Sales Force Outcomes," *Journal of Personal Selling & Sales Management* 26, no. 3 (2006): 255–70.
39. A.A. Brown, "How to Create a Values Framework and Make It Work," *Financial Post*, August 9, 2018.
40. H. McCracken, "Satya Nadella Rewrites Microsoft's Code," *Fast Company*, September 18, 2017; H. Ibarra, A. Rattan, and A. Johnston, "Microsoft: Instilling a Growth Mindset," *London Business School Review* 29, no. 3 (October 2018): 50–53.
41. C.A. O'Reilly III and J.A. Chatman, "Culture as Social Control: Corporations, Cults, and Commitment," *Research in Organizational Behavior* 18 (1996): 157–200; B. Spector and H. Lane, "Exploring the Distinctions between a High Performance Culture and a Cult," *Strategy & Leadership* 35 (2007): 18–24. Organizational cults are closely associated with high organizational identification, which has several known dysfunctional outcomes for companies and individuals. See S. Conroy et al., "Where There Is Light, There Is Dark: A Review of the Detrimental Outcomes of High Organizational Identification," *Journal of Organizational Behavior* 38 (2017): 184–203.
42. J.P. Kotter and J.L. Heskett, *Corporate Culture and Performance* (New York: Free Press, 1992), Chap. 4; B.M. Bass and R.E. Riggio, *Transformational Leadership*, 2nd ed. (New York: Routledge, 2006), Chap. 7; D.P. Costanza et al., "The Effect of Adaptive Organizational Culture on Long-Term Survival," *Journal of Business and Psychology* (2015): 1–21.
43. T. Krisher and D.A. Durbin, "General Motors CEO Akerson Leads Comeback from Bankruptcy by Ruffling Company's Bureaucracy," *Associated Press Newswires*, December 17, 2011.
44. W.E. Baker and J.M. Sinkula, "The Synergistic Effect of Market Orientation and Learning Orientation on Organizational Performance," *Academy of Marketing Science Journal* 27, no. 4 (1999): 411–27; O. Pesämaa et al., "How a Learning Orientation Affects Drivers of Innovativeness and Performance in Service Delivery," *Journal of Engineering and Technology Management* 30 (2013): 169–87; J.C. Real, J.L. Roldán, and A. Leal, "From Entrepreneurial Orientation and Learning Orientation to Business Performance: Analysing the Mediating Role of Organizational Learning and the Moderating Effects of Organizational Size," *British Journal of Management* 25 (2014): 186–208.
45. G. Bensinger and J.S. Lublin, "Uber Fires More Than 20 People in Harassment Investigation," *The Wall Street Journal*, June 7, 2017; S. Levin, "Uber's Scandals, Blunders and PR Disasters: The Full List," *Guardian*, June 18, 2017; B. Edelman, "Uber Can't Be Fixed–It's Time for Regulators to Shut It Down," *Harvard Business Review*, June 21, 2017); D. Khosrowshahi, "Uber's New Cultural Norms," Linkedin Blog (blog), November 7, 2017, https://www.linkedin.com/pulse/ubers-new-cultural-norms-dara-khosrowshahi; S. Nicholls, "The Uber Story," transcript, Four Corners (Sydney: ABC Australia, March 13, 2019).

46. "Antony Jenkins to Staff: Adopt New Values or Leave Barclays," *The Telegraph (London)*, 17 January 2013. Also, original email to Barclays employees distributed in January 2013.

47. M.L. Marks, "Adding Cultural Fit to Your Diligence Checklist," *Mergers & Acquisitions* 34, no. 3 (1999): 14–20; E.H. Schein, *The Corporate Culture Survival Guide* (San Francisco: Jossey-Bass, 1999), Chap. 8; S. Teerikangas and P. Very, "The Culture-Performance Relationship in M&A: From Yes/No to How," *British Journal of Management* 17, no. S1 (2006): S31–S48; G.K. Stahl and A. Voigt, "Do Cultural Differences Matter in Mergers and Acquisitions? A Tentative Model and Examination," *Organization Science* 19, no. 1 (2008): 160–76.

48. J.P. Daly et al., "The Effects of Initial Differences in Firms' Espoused Values on Their Postmerger Performance," *Journal of Applied Behavioral Science* 40, no. 3 (2004): 323–43; C. Cook and D. Spitzer, *World Class Transactions* (London: KPMG, 2001); J. Krug, *Mergers and Acquisitions: Turmoil in Top Management Teams* (Williston, VT: Business Expert Press, 2009).

49. "Integration Report 2015: Putting the Pieces Together" (New York: Deloitte M&A Institute, March 2015); "Defining What Is Vital for Deal Success: Value Curve Study Validates Holistic Approach to M&A" (Chicago: GrantThornton LLP, May 2018); "Australia's Evolving Deals Landscape: Corporate Australia's Attitudes and Perspectives on Deal Activity" (Sydney: KPMG Australia, August 2018); "Mercer Survey Reveals Culture Issues Derail M&A Transactions at an Alarming Rate," news release (New York: Mercer, September 24, 2018); "The State of the Deal: M&A Trends 2019" (New York: Deloitte, December 2018).

50. C.A. Schorg, C.A. Raiborn, and M.F. Massoud, "Using a 'Cultural Audit' to Pick M&A Winners," *Journal of Corporate Accounting & Finance* (2004): 47–55; W. Locke, "Higher Education Mergers: Integrating Organisational Cultures and Developing Appropriate Management Styles," *Higher Education Quarterly* 61, no. 1 (2007): 83–102.

51. A.R. Malekazedeh and A. Nahavandi, "Making Mergers Work by Managing Cultures," *Journal of Business Strategy* (1990): 55–57; K.W. Smith, "A Brand-New Culture for the Merged Firm," *Mergers and Acquisitions* 35 (2000): 45–50.

52. A. Hyland, "Howzat? Wesfarmers and Boral Chairman Bob Every on Career and Overcoming Adversity," *Australian Financial Review*, July 6, 2015.

53. Hewitt Associates, "Mergers and Acquisitions May Be Driven by Business Strategy—but Often Stumble over People and Culture Issues" (Lincolnshire, IL: PR Newswire, 1998).

54. J. Martin, "Can Organizational Culture Be Managed?" in *Organizational Culture*, ed. P.J. Frost et al. (Beverly Hills, CA: Sage, 1985), 95–98.

55. B. O'Connor, "CEO Credits Quicken Loans' Culture for Firm's Success," *Detroit News*, May 1, 2013, C2.

56. E.H. Schein, "The Role of the Founder in Creating Organizational Culture," *Organizational Dynamics* 12, no. 1 (1983): 13–28; A.S. Tsui et al., "Unpacking the Relationship between CEO Leadership Behavior and Organizational Culture," *Leadership Quarterly* 17 (2006): 113–37; Y. Berson, S. Oreg, and T. Dvir, "CEO Values, Organizational Culture and Firm Outcomes," *Journal of Organizational Behavior* 29, no. 5 (2008): 615–33; B. Schneider, M.G. Ehrhart, and W.H. Macey, "Organizational Climate and Culture," *Annual Review of Psychology* 64, no. 1 (2013): 361–88.

57. Y. Berson, S. Oreg, and T. Dvir, "CEO Values, Organizational Culture and Firm Outcomes," *Journal of Organizational Behavior* 29, no. 5 (2008): 615–33; A.S. Klein, J. Wallis, and R.A. Cooke, "The Impact of Leadership Styles on Organizational Culture and Firm Effectiveness: An Empirical Study," *Journal of Management & Organization* 19 (2013): 241–54; D.V. Day, M.A. Griffin, and K.R. Louw, "The Climate and Culture of Leadership in Organizations," in *The Oxford Handbook of Organizational Climate and Culture*, ed. B. Schneider and K.M. Barbera (New York: Oxford University Press, 2014), 101–17.

58. M.J. Gelfand et al., "Conflict Cultures in Organizations: How Leaders Shape Conflict Cultures and Their Organizational-Level Consequences," *Journal of Applied Psychology* 97, no. 6 (2012): 1131–47; R.C. Liden et al., "Servant Leadership and Serving Culture: Influence on Individual and Unit Performance," *Academy of Management Journal* 57, no. 5 (2014): 1434–52.

59. J.C. McElroy and P.C. Morrow, "Employee Reactions to Office Redesign: A Naturally Occurring Quasi-Field Experiment in a Multi-Generational Setting," *Human Relations* 63 (2010): 609–36; S.J. Hogan and L.V. Coote, "Organizational Culture, Innovation, and Performance: A Test of Schein's Model," *Journal of Business Research* 67 (2014): 1609–21; S. Zerella, K. von Treuer, and S.L. Albrecht, "The Influence of Office Layout Features on Employee Perception of Organizational Culture," *Journal of Environmental Psychology* 54 (2017): 1–10.

60. M. De Pree, *Leadership Is an Art* (East Lansing: Michigan State University Press, 1987).

61. J. Kerr and J.W. Slocum Jr., "Managing Corporate Culture through Reward Systems," *Academy of Management Executive* 1 (1987): 99–107; J.M. Higgins et al., "Using Cultural Artifacts to Change and Perpetuate Strategy," *Journal of Change Management* 6, no. 4 (2006): 397–415; H. Hofstetter and I. Harpaz, "Declared versus Actual Organizational Culture as Indicated by an Organization's Performance Appraisal," *International Journal of Human Resource Management* (2011): 1–22.

62. A. Griswold, "Uber Is Designed so That for One Employee to Get Ahead, Another Must Fail," *Quartz*, February 27, 2017; M.R. Dickey, "Inside Uber's New Approach to Employee Performance Reviews," *TechCrunch*, August 1, 2017.

63. B. Schneider, "The People Make the Place," *Personnel Psychology* 40, no. 3 (1987): 437–53; B. Schneider et al., "Personality and Organizations: A Test of the Homogeneity of Personality Hypothesis," *Journal of Applied Psychology* 83, no. 3 (1998): 462–70; T.R. Giberson, C.J. Resick, and M.W. Dickson, "Embedding Leader Characteristics: An Examination of Homogeneity of Personality and Values in Organizations," *Journal of Applied Psychology* 90, no. 5 (2005): 1002–10.

64. Kelly Services, "Career Resilience: Key Insights from Kelly into the Global Talent Market" (Troy, MI: Kelly Services, June 2016); "2018 Job Seeker Nation Study" (San Mateo, CA: Jobvite, April 26, 2018); "More Than One-Third of Workers Would Pass on Perfect Job if Corporate Culture Was Not a Fit, Survey Finds," news release (Menlo Park, CA: Robert Half, November 27, 2018); "Mission & Culture Survey 2019" (Mill Valley, CA: Glassdoor, July 9, 2019).

65. T.A. Judge and D.M. Cable, "Applicant Personality, Organizational Culture, and Organization Attraction," *Personnel Psychology* 50, no. 2 (1997): 359–94; D.S. Chapman et al., "Applicant Attraction to Organizations and Job Choice: A Meta-Analytic Review of the Correlates of Recruiting Outcomes," *Journal of Applied Psychology* 90, no. 5 (2005): 928–44; A.L. Kristof-Brown, R.D. Zimmerman, and E.C. Johnson, "Consequences of Individuals' Fit at Work: A Meta-Analysis of Person–Job, Person–Organization, Person–Group, and Person–Supervisor Fit," *Personnel Psychology* 58, no. 2 (2005): 281–342; C. Hu, H.C. Su, and C.I.B. Chen, "The Effect of Person-Organization Fit Feedback via Recruitment Web Sites on Applicant Attraction," *Computers in Human Behavior* 23, no. 5 (2007): 2509–23.

66. A. Kristof-Brown, "Perceived Applicant Fit: Distinguishing between Recruiters' Perceptions of Person–Job and Person–Organization Fit," *Personnel Psychology* 53, no. 3 (2000): 643–71; A.E.M. Van Vianen, "Person–Organization Fit: The Match between Newcomers' and Recruiters' Preferences for Organizational Cultures," *Personnel Psychology* 53 (2000): 113–49.
67. E. Keating, "'Leadership Is Not Genetics': How Ikea Australia's National Talent Manager D'neale Prosser Puts Authentic Leadership into Practice," *SmartCompany*, March 8, 2018; "'We Believe That Your Values Are More Important than Your CV,'" *Human Resources Director Australia*, April 11, 2018.
68. D.M. Cable and J.R. Edwards, "Complementary and Supplementary Fit: A Theoretical and Empirical Integration," *Journal of Applied Psychology* 89, no. 5 (2004): 822–34.
69. J. Van Maanen, "Breaking In: Socialization to Work," in *Handbook of Work, Organization, and Society*, ed. R. Dubin (Chicago: Rand McNally, 1976).
70. D.G. Allen, "Do Organizational Socialization Tactics Influence Newcomer Embeddedness and Turnover?" *Journal of Management* 32, no. 2 (2006): 237–56; A.M. Saks, K.L. Uggerslev, and N.E. Fassina, "Socialization Tactics and Newcomer Adjustment: A Meta-Analytic Review and Test of a Model," *Journal of Vocational Behavior* 70, no. 3 (2007): 413–46.
71. S.L. McShane, G. O'Neill, and T. Travaglione, "Managing Employee Values in Values-Driven Organizations: Contradiction, Façade, and Illusions" (paper presented at the 21st Annual ANZAM Conference, Sydney, Australia, December 2007); S.L. McShane, G. O'Neill, and T. Travaglione, "Rethinking the Values-Driven Organization Process: From Values Engineering to Behavioral Domain Training" (paper presented at the Academy of Management 2008 Annual Meeting, Anaheim, CA, 2008).
72. G. T. Chao et al., "Organizational Socialization: Its Content and Consequences," *Journal of Applied Psychology* 79 (1994): 450–63; H. D. Cooper-Thomas and N. Anderson, "Organizational Socialization: A Field Study into Socialization Success and Rate," *International Journal of Selection and Assessment* 13, no. 2 (2005): 116–28.
73. N. Nicholson, "A Theory of Work Role Transitions," *Administrative Science Quarterly* 29 (1984): 172–91; A. Elfering et al., "First Years in Job: A Three-Wave Analysis of Work Experiences," *Journal of Vocational Behavior* 70, no. 1 (2007): 97–115; B.E. Ashforth, D.M. Sluss, and A.M. Saks, "Socialization Tactics, Proactive Behavior, and Newcomer Learning: Integrating Socialization Models," *Journal of Vocational Behavior* 70, no. 3 (2007): 447–62; T.N. Bauer, "Newcomer Adjustment during Organizational Socialization: A Meta-Analytic Review of Antecedents, Outcomes, and Methods," *Journal of Applied Psychology* 92, no. 3 (2007): 707–21.
74. J.M. Beyer and D.R. Hannah, "Building on the Past: Enacting Established Personal Identities in a New Work Setting," *Organization Science* 13 (2002): 636–52; H.D.C. Thomas and N. Anderson, "Newcomer Adjustment: The Relationship between Organizational Socialization Tactics, Information Acquisition and Attitudes," *Journal of Occupational and Organizational Psychology* 75 (2002): 423–37.
75. L.W. Porter, E.E. Lawler III, and J.R. Hackman, *Behavior in Organizations* (New York: McGraw-Hill, 1975), 163–67; J. Van Maanen, "Breaking In: Socialization to Work," in *Handbook of Work, Organization, and Society,* ed. R. Dubin (Chicago: Rand McNally, 1976), 67–130; D.C. Feldman, "The Multiple Socialization of Organization Members," *Academy of Management Review* 6 (1981): 309–18.
76. B.E. Ashforth and A.M. Saks, "Socialization Tactics: Longitudinal Effects on Newcomer Adjustment," *Academy of Management Journal* 39 (1996): 149–78; J.D. Kammeyer-Mueller and C.R. Wanberg, "Unwrapping the Organizational Entry Process: Disentangling Multiple Antecedents and Their Pathways to Adjustment," *Journal of Applied Psychology* 88, no. 5 (2003): 779–94.
77. L.W. Porter, E.E. Lawler III, and J.R. Hackman, *Behavior in Organizations* (New York: McGraw-Hill, 1975), Chap. 5.
78. M.R. Louis, "Surprise and Sensemaking: What Newcomers Experience in Entering Unfamiliar Organizational Settings," *Administrative Science Quarterly* 25 (1980): 226–51.
79. S.L. Robinson and D.M. Rousseau, "Violating the Psychological Contract: Not the Exception but the Norm," *Journal of Organizational Behavior* 15 (1994): 245–59.
80. D.L. Nelson, "Organizational Socialization: A Stress Perspective," *Journal of Occupational Behavior* 8 (1987): 311–24; A. Elfering et al., "First Years in Job: A Three-Wave Analysis of Work Experiences," *Journal of Vocational Behavior* 70 (2007): 97–115; C.-M. Alcover et al., "Understanding the Changing Nature of Psychological Contracts in 21st Century Organizations: A Multiple-Foci Exchange Relationships Approach and Proposed Framework," *Organizational Psychology Review* 7, no. 1 (2017): 4–35.
81. J.P. Wanous, *Organizational Entry* (Reading, MA: Addison-Wesley, 1992); J.A. Breaugh and M. Starke, "Research on Employee Recruitment: So Many Studies, So Many Remaining Questions," *Journal of Management* 26, no. 3 (2000): 405–34.
82. J.M. Phillips, "Effects of Realistic Job Previews on Multiple Organizational Outcomes: A Meta-Analysis," *Academy of Management Journal* 41 (1998): 673–90.
83. Y. Ganzach et al., "Social Exchange and Organizational Commitment: Decision-Making Training for Job Choice as an Alternative to the Realistic Job Preview," *Personnel Psychology* 55 (2002): 613–37.
84. W. Harris, "5 Ways Company Swag Boosts Company Culture," *Element Three* (blog), June 13, 2018, https://elementthree.com/blog/5-ways-company-swag-boosts-company-culture/; KemptonBeth, "Improve Your Employee Onboarding: Lessons from Twitter and Pinterest," *Hireology* (blog), July 10, 2019, https://hireology.com/blog/improve-your-employee-onboarding-lessons-from-twitter-and-pinterest/; N. Davies, "5 Secrets of Onboarding 100% Remote Workers Revealed by Hiring Experts and Leaders," *Forbes*, November 6, 2019; "ChiefOnboarding," Slack App Directory, accessed May 31, 2020, https://slack.com/apps/A4BDDF8SU-chiefonboarding.
85. C. Ostroff and S.W.J. Koslowski, "Organizational Socialization as a Learning Process: The Role of Information Acquisition," *Personnel Psychology* 45 (1992): 849–74; H.D. Cooper-Thomas and N. Anderson, "Organizational Socialization: A Field Study into Socialization Success and Rate," *International Journal of Selection and Assessment* 13, no. 2 (2005): 116–28; S. Nifadkar and T. Bauer, "Breach of Belongingness: Newcomer Relationship Conflict, Information, and Task-Related Outcomes during Organizational Socialization," *Journal of Applied Psychology* 101, no. 1 (2016): 1–13.
86. S. Nifadkar, A.S. Tsui, and B.E. Ashforth, "The Way You Make Me Feel and Behave: Supervisor-Triggered Newcomer Affect and Approach-Avoidance Behavior," *Academy of Management Journal* 55, no. 5 (2012): 1146–68.

14 Organizational Change

Learning Objectives

After you read this chapter, you should be able to:

LO14-1 Describe the elements of Lewin's force field analysis model.

LO14-2 Discuss the reasons why people resist organizational change and how change agents should view this resistance.

LO14-3 Outline six strategies for minimizing resistance to change and debate ways to effectively create an urgency to change.

LO14-4 Discuss how leadership, coalitions, social networks, and pilot projects assist organizational change.

LO14-5 Describe and compare action research and appreciative inquiry as formal approaches to organizational change.

LO14-6 Discuss two cross-cultural and three ethical issues in organizational change.

Over the past half-dozen years, Tanya Domier has transformed Advantage Solutions into a more proactive, performance-driven organization with a stronger global footprint. The change process at the California-based provider of technology-enabled sales and marketing business solutions included redefining jobs, retraining staff, and hiring people with skills more closely aligned with the new business model. Domier also communicated the change vision in terms of five pillars to success: people, culture, creating raving fans of clients and customers, operational efficiency, and growth.

The changes at Advantage Solutions have been highly successful. Under Domier's leadership, the company has expanded into several countries, almost doubled its workforce, and has become North America's leading marketing services firm for more than 3,500 clients and brands. Its marketing division is the top-ranked promotion agency network and experiential/event marketing agency in the United States.

This transformation did not occur easily. In the early days, it triggered strong resistance from some long-serving managers and employees. "There were many people who did not believe in our strategy," acknowledges Domier, an award-winning executive and a board member at Nordstrom, Yum! Brands, and other organizations. "There were many people who undermined the strategy."

Employee resistance to change at Advantage Solutions has since subsided, but Domier says she learned valuable lessons about leading change. "Anybody can captain a ship on calm seas, but if you really want [to be] a leader, you have to learn to weather a storm," she advises.[1]

The transformation of Advantage Solutions illustrates a few of the challenges in organizational change. Although Domier's strategy for organizational renewal now seems clear-cut, most organizational change is messy, requiring considerable leadership effort and vigilance. As we will describe throughout this chapter, the challenge of change is not just in deciding which way to go; the challenge is in the execution of this strategy. When leaders discover the need for change and identify some ideas about the preferred route to a better future, the change process involves navigating around the numerous obstacles and gaining organization-wide support for that change.

This chapter unfolds as follows. We begin by introducing Lewin's model of change and its component parts. This discussion includes sources of resistance to change, ways to minimize this resistance, and ways to stabilize desired behaviors. Next, the chapter examines two approaches to organizational change—action research and appreciative inquiry. The final section of this chapter considers both cross-cultural and ethical issues in organizational change.

LO14-1 Describe the elements of Lewin's force field analysis model.

LEWIN'S FORCE FIELD ANALYSIS MODEL

Change is the norm, not the exception, in successful organizations. One of the fundamental messages throughout this book is that organizations operate as open systems. As such, they

Ready for Organizational Change?[2]

50% of Google teams in an organizational change initiative (reorganization) say they understood why the changes were made.

49% of 1,512 American employees surveyed believe that management is honest about their reasons and objectives for organizational changes.

82% of 1,487 American employees and managers involved in a corporate transformation agree that their CEO communicates a compelling change story to the organization.

28% of 1,512 American employees surveyed say they doubt that current organizational changes will achieve their objectives or have the desired effects.

41% of 935 business leaders surveyed believe their organization DOES NOT have a good track record when it comes to managing change.

sarahdesign/Shutterstock

force field analysis Kurt Lewin's model of systemwide change that helps change agents diagnose the forces that drive and restrain proposed organizational change

unfreezing the first part of the change process, in which the change agent produces disequilibrium between the driving and restraining forces

refreezing the latter part of the change process, in which systems and structures are introduced that reinforce and maintain the desired behaviors

need to continually evolve with ongoing changes in their external environment, such as consumer needs, global competition, technology, community expectations, government (de)regulation, and environmental standards. Successful organizations monitor their environments and take appropriate steps to maintain a compatible fit with new external conditions. Rather than resist change, employees in successful companies embrace change as an integral part of organizational life.

It is easy to see environmental forces pushing companies to change the way they operate. What is more difficult to see is the complex interplay of these forces on individuals, teams, and work units. Social psychologist Kurt Lewin developed a model to describe this process using the metaphor of a force field (see Exhibit 14.1).[4] Although it was developed a half century ago, contemporary reviews of this subject affirm that Lewin's **force field analysis** model remains one of the most widely respected ways of viewing the change process.[5]

One side of the force field model represents the *driving forces* that push organizations toward a new state of affairs. These might include new competitors or technologies, evolving client expectations, or a host of other environmental changes. Corporate leaders also produce driving forces even when external forces for change aren't apparent. For instance, even when companies are successful, their leaders urge employees to strive for higher standards or better practices. David Ogilvy, one of the world's most successful advertising executives, stated this view decades ago when describing the culture of his agency: "We have a habit of divine discontent with our performance. It is an antidote to smugness."[6]

The other side of Lewin's model represents the *restraining forces* that maintain the status quo. These restraining forces are commonly called "resistance to change" because they appear to block the change process. Stability occurs when the driving and restraining forces are roughly in equilibrium—that is, they are of approximately equal strength in opposite directions.

> I've always believed that when the rate of change inside an institution becomes slower than the rate of change outside, the end is in sight.[3]
>
> —Jack Welch, former General Electric CEO

Exhibit 14.1 Lewin's Force Field Analysis Model

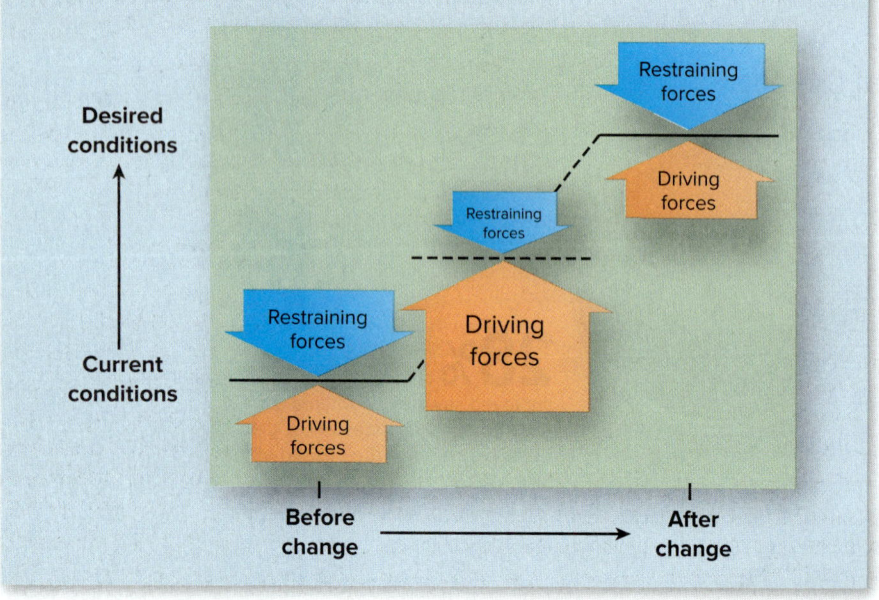

Lewin's force field model emphasizes that effective change occurs by **unfreezing** the current situation, moving to a desired condition, and then **refreezing** the system so it remains in the desired state. Unfreezing involves producing disequilibrium between the driving and restraining forces. As we will describe later, this may occur by increasing the driving forces, reducing the restraining forces, or doing a combination of both. Refreezing occurs when the organization's systems and structures are aligned with the desired behaviors. They must support and reinforce the new role patterns and prevent the organization from slipping back into the old way of doing things. In the next two sections of this chapter, we use Lewin's model to understand why change is blocked and how the process can evolve more smoothly.

LO14-2 Discuss the reasons why people resist organizational change and how change agents should view this resistance.

UNDERSTANDING RESISTANCE TO CHANGE

Mention organizational change to anyone who has attempted to lead these initiatives and the phrase "resistance to change" will inevitably enter the conversation. Resistance to change takes many forms, ranging from overt work stoppages to subtle attempts to continue the old ways.[7] A study of bank employees reported that covert resistance is much more common than overt resistance. Some employees in that study avoided the desired changes by moving into different jobs. Others continued to perform tasks the old way as long as management didn't notice. Even when employees complied with the planned changes, they showed resistance by performing the new task while letting customers know that they disapproved of these changes forced on them![8]

Resistance to change takes many forms, ranging from overt work stoppages to subtle attempts to continue the old ways.
(left): Jacob Wackerhausen/Getty Images; (right): Mark Dierker/McGraw-Hill

> **People don't resist change. They resist being changed.[11]**
>
> —unnamed organizational change consultant, cited by MIT scholar Peter Senge

Most change agents are understandably frustrated by passive or active resistance to their planned change. However, resistance is a common and natural human response. Even when people support change, they typically assume that it is others—not themselves—who need to do the changing. Resistance is a form of conflict, but change agents sometimes interpret that disagreement as relationship conflict (see Chapter 10). They describe the people who resist as unreasonable, dysfunctional, and irrational reactionaries to a desirable initiative. By perceiving the situation as relationship conflict, change agents attack the competence of those who resist the change, which further escalates the conflict and generates even stronger resistance to the change initiative.

A more productive approach is to view resistance to change as task conflict. From this perspective, resistance is a signal either that the change agent has not sufficiently prepared employees for change or that the change initiative should be altered or improved.[9] Employees might not feel a sufficiently strong urgency to change, or they might believe the change strategy is ill-conceived. Even if they recognize the need for change and agree with the strategy, employees might resist because they lack confidence to change or believe the change will make them worse off than the current situation. Resistance takes many forms, and change agents need to decipher those different types of resistance to understand their underlying causes.[10]

Resistance is also a form of voice, so giving employees an opportunity to discuss their concerns potentially improves procedural justice (see Chapter 5) as well as decision making about the change (see Chapter 6). By redirecting initial forms of resistance into constructive conversations, change agents can generate a feeling of fairness among employees. Furthermore, resistance is motivated behavior; it potentially engages people to think about the change strategy and process. Change agents can harness that motivational force to ultimately strengthen commitment to the change initiative.

Why Employees Resist Change

Change management experts have developed a long list of reasons why people resist change.[12] Some people inherently oppose change because of their personality and values.[13] Aside from these dispositional factors, employees typically oppose organizational change because they lack sufficient motivation, ability, role clarity, or situational support to change their attitudes, decisions, and behavior.[14] In other words, an employee's readiness for change depends on all four elements of the MARS model. These MARS elements are the foundations of the six most commonly cited reasons for why people resist change: (1) negative

connect

SELF-ASSESSMENT 14.1: Are You Ready for Change?

valence of change, (2) fear of the unknown, (3) not-invented-here syndrome, (4) breaking routines, (5) incongruent team dynamics, and (6) incongruent organizational systems and structures.

Negative Valence of Change Employees usually resist change when they believe the post-change situation will have more negative than positive outcomes.[15] In other words, they apply (although imperfectly) the rational choice decision-making model (Chapter 6) to estimate whether the change will make them better or worse off (i.e., positive or negative valence). This cost-benefit analysis mainly considers how the change will affect them personally. However, resistance also increases when employees believe the change will do more harm than good to the team, organization, or society.[16]

Fear of the Unknown Organizational change usually has a degree of uncertainty, and employees tend to assume the worst when they are unsure whether the change will have good or bad outcomes. Uncertainty also is associated with lack of personal control, which is another source of negative emotions.[17] Consequently, the uncertainty inherent in most organizational change is less desirable than the relative certainty of the status quo. This "status quo bias" adds more negative valence to the cost-benefit calculation we described above.

Not-Invented-Here Syndrome Employees sometimes oppose or even discreetly undermine organizational change initiatives that are introduced by people outside their group. This "not-invented-here" syndrome is most apparent among employees who are usually responsible for the knowledge or initiative.[18] For example, information technology staff are more likely to resist implementing new technology championed by marketing or finance employees. If the IT staff support the change, they are implicitly acknowledging another group's superiority within IT's own area of expertise. To protect their self-worth, some employees deliberately inflate problems with changes they did not initiate, just to "prove" that those ideas were not superior to their own. As one consultant warned: "Unless they're scared enough to listen, they'll never forgive you for being right and for knowing something they don't."[19]

> When you are leading for growth, you know you are going to disrupt comfortable routines and ask for new behavior, new priorities, new skills. Even when we want to change, and do change, we tend to relax and the rubber band snaps us back into our comfort zones.[20]
>
> —Ray Davis, former CEO and chair of Umpqua Bank

Employees usually resist change when they believe the post-change situation will have more negative than positive outcomes.
Krakenimages.com/Shutterstock

Breaking Routines People are creatures of habit. They typically resist initiatives that require them to break those automated routines and to learn new role patterns. And unless the new patterns of behavior are strongly supported and reinforced, employees tend to revert to their past routines and habits.

Incongruent Team Dynamics Teams develop and enforce conformity to a set of norms that guide behavior (see Chapter 7). However, conformity to existing team norms may discourage employees from accepting organizational change. For instance, organizational initiatives to improve customer service may be thwarted by team norms that discourage the extra effort expected to serve customers at this higher standard.

Incongruent Organizational Systems Rewards, information systems, patterns of authority, career paths, selection criteria, and other systems and structures are both friends and foes of organizational change. When properly aligned, they reinforce desired behaviors. When misaligned, they pull people back into

Facing the Challenge of Resistance to Change[21]

57%
of 1,000 American employees say that change makes them less happy or has no effect on their happiness.

46%
of 1,000 nonmanagement employees are willing to challenge the status quo (compared with 89% of chief executives).

34%
of more than 2,000 employees in the U.S. and UK say they feel anxiety over new or changing work processes.

44%
of 1,778 change management professionals surveyed globally say their organization is at or past the point of "change saturation."

25%
of 10,000 employees surveyed say they don't like to leave their comfort zone when change is occurring (16% of top level executives say this).

Brand X Pictures/Getty Images

their old attitudes and behavior. Even enthusiastic employees lose momentum after failing to overcome the structural confines of the past.

LO14-3 Outline six strategies for minimizing resistance to change and debate ways to effectively create an urgency to change.

UNFREEZING, CHANGING, AND REFREEZING

According to Lewin's force field analysis model, effective change occurs by unfreezing the current situation, moving to a desired condition, and then refreezing the system so it remains in this desired state. Unfreezing occurs when the driving forces are stronger than the restraining forces. This happens by making the driving forces stronger, weakening or removing the restraining forces, or doing both.

The first option is to increase the driving forces, which motivates employees to change through fear or threats (real or contrived). This strategy rarely works, however, because the action of increasing the driving forces alone is usually met with an equal and opposing increase in the restraining forces. A useful metaphor is pushing against the coils of a mattress. The harder corporate leaders push for change, the stronger the restraining forces push back. This antagonism threatens the change effort by producing tension and conflict within the organization.

The second option is to weaken or remove the restraining forces. The problem with this change strategy is that it provides no motivation for change. To some extent, weakening the restraining forces is like clearing a pathway for change. An unobstructed road makes it easier to travel to the destination but does not motivate anyone to go there. The preferred option, therefore, is to both increase the driving forces and reduce or remove the restraining forces. Increasing the driving forces creates an urgency for change, while reducing the restraining forces lessens motivation to oppose the change and removes obstacles such as lack of ability and situational constraints.

Creating an Urgency for Change

Organizational change is more likely to succeed when employees develop a sufficiently strong urgency for change.[22] In rare situations, such as the COVID-19 pandemic, the forces for change are widely known and worrisome to most employees. As such, they are motivated (or compliant) to dive into new practices, such as working from home, learning new digital communication technology, altering work schedules, wearing protective clothing, and engaging in unusual forms of interaction with coworkers and clients that minimize transmission of disease.

Unfreezing occurs by making the driving forces stronger, weakening or removing the restraining forces, or doing both.
Lightspring/Shutterstock

Most of the time, leaders buffer employees from the external environment to such an extent that the prevailing driving forces are hardly felt by anyone below the top executive level. The result is that employees don't understand why they need to change and leaders are surprised when their change initiatives do not have much effect. Consequently, the change process needs to begin by making the external forces for change known to employees and explaining their seriousness for the organization's future. These are the main driving forces in Lewin's model. They push people out of their comfort zone, energizing them to face the risks that change creates.

Some companies fuel the urgency for change by putting executives and employees in direct contact with customers. Dissatisfied customers and other stakeholders represent a compelling driving force for change because the organization's survival typically depends on having customers who are satisfied with the product or service. Personal interaction with customers also provides a human element that further energizes employees to change current behavior patterns.[23]

OB THEORY TO PRACTICE

Instilling an Urgency for Change at Slack[24]

Until recently, Slack didn't have any serious competitors. This worried Stewart Butterfield, the entrepreneur who cofounded the collaborative communication platform. "We don't have any effective competitors," he observed a year before Microsoft Teams and Facebook for Work were launched. "It's handy in one way, but it's also very motivating to have a real competitor."

To generate an urgency for change and minimize complacency, Butterfield persuasively warned Slack employees of the limited time they had remaining to build an unbeatable product. "It's up to me to instill the message that we have a year, maybe 18 months, before we really have to lock horns with anyone," said Butterfield.

Creating an Urgency for Change without External Forces Exposing employees to external forces can strengthen the urgency for change, but leaders often need to begin the change process before problems come knocking at the company's door. The challenge is greatest when companies are successful in their markets. Studies have found that when the organization is performing well, decision makers become less vigilant about external threats and are more resistant to change. "The biggest risk is that complacency can also come with that success," warns Richard Goyder, who recently stepped down as CEO of Wesfarmers, Australia's largest conglomerate. "That complacency may result in risk-aversion, or it may simply show up as a lack of urgency, as people take the foot off the accelerator and just assume that success will come as it always has."[25]

Creating an urgency for change when the organization is the market leader requires a lot of persuasive influence that helps employees visualize future competitive threats and environmental shifts. Experts warn, however, that employees may see this strategy as manipulative, which produces cynicism about change and undermines trust in the change agent.[26] Fortunately, the urgency for change doesn't need to originate from problems or threats to the company; this motivation also can develop through the leader's vision of a more appealing future. A future vision of a better organization makes the current situation less appealing. When the vision connects to employees' values and needs, it can be a motivating force for change even when external problems are insignificant.

Reducing the Restraining Forces

Earlier, we used the mattress metaphor to explain that increasing the driving forces alone will not bring about change because employees often push back harder to offset the opposing forces. To minimize this push-back, change agents need to address each of the sources of resistance. Six of the main strategies for minimizing resistance to change are outlined in Exhibit 14.2. Communication, learning, employee involvement, and stress management should be the first priorities for leading change.[27] However, negotiation and coercion may be required where some people will clearly lose something from the change and in cases where the speed of change is critical.

Communication Communication is the highest priority and first strategy required for any organizational change. Communication improves the change process in at least two ways.[28] First, communication generates the urgency for change that

Mc Graw Hill connect

SELF-ASSESSMENT 14.2: Are You Tolerant of Change?

> **The most practical piece of advice I can offer others is to recognize the critical importance of open communication in times of change.[29]**
>
> —Chris Catliff, CEO of Blueshore Financial

Exhibit 14.2 Strategies for Minimizing Resistance to Change

Strategy	Example	When Applied	Problems
Communication	Customer complaint letters are shown to employees.	When employees don't feel an urgency for change, don't know how the change will affect them, or resist change due to a fear of the unknown.	Time-consuming and potentially costly.
Learning	Employees learn how to work in teams as company adopts a team-based structure.	When employees need to break old routines and adopt new role patterns.	Time-consuming, potentially costly, and some employees might not be able to learn the new skills.
Employee involvement	Company forms a task force to recommend new customer service practices.	When the change effort needs more employee commitment, some employees need to protect their self-worth, and/or employee ideas would improve decisions about the change strategy.	Very time-consuming. Might lead to conflict and poor decisions if employees' interests are incompatible with organizational needs.
Stress management	Employees attend sessions to discuss their worries about the change.	When communication, training, and involvement do not sufficiently ease employee worries.	Time-consuming and potentially expensive. Some methods may not reduce stress for all employees.
Negotiation	Employees agree to replace strict job categories with multiskilled job clusters in return for increased job security.	When employees will clearly lose something of value from the change and would not otherwise support the new conditions. Also necessary when the company must change quickly.	May be expensive, particularly if other employees want to negotiate their support. Also tends to produce compliance but not commitment to the change.
Coercion	Company president tells managers to "get on board" the change or leave.	When other strategies are ineffective and the company needs to change quickly.	Can lead to subtler forms of resistance, as well as long-term antagonism with the change agent.

Sources: Adapted from P.R. Lawrence, "How to Deal with Resistance to Change," *Harvard Business Review* (May/June 1954): 49–57; J.P. Kotter and L.A. Schlesinger, "Choosing Strategies for Change," *Harvard Business Review* 57 (1979): 106–14.

we described a few paragraphs ago. Leaders motivate employees to support the change by candidly telling them about the external threats and opportunities that make change so important. The second way that communication minimizes resistance to change is by illuminating the future and thereby reducing fear of the unknown. The more leaders communicate details about the vision as well as milestones already achieved, the more easily employees can understand their own roles in that future.

Learning Learning is an important process in most organizational change initiatives because employees need new knowledge and skills to fit the organization's evolving requirements. Learning not only helps employees perform better following the change; it also increases their readiness for change by strengthening their belief about working successfully in the new situation (called *change self-efficacy*). And when employees develop stronger change self-efficacy, they develop a stronger acceptance of and commitment to the change.[30]

Employee Involvement Employee involvement is almost essential in the change process, although only a low level of involvement may be possible when the change must occur quickly or employee interests significantly conflict with the organization's needs. The potential benefits of employee involvement, which were discussed in Chapter 6, are relevant to organizational change. Rather than being disinterested agents of someone else's decisions, involved employees tend to feel more personal responsibility for successful implementation of the change.[31] This sense of ownership also minimizes the not-invented-here syndrome and fear of the unknown. Furthermore, the work environment is so complex that determining the best direction of the change effort requires ideas and knowledge of many people.

Stress Management Organizational change is a stressful experience for many people because it threatens self-esteem and creates uncertainty about the future.[32] Communication, learning, and employee involvement can reduce some of the stressors.[33] However, research indicates that stress management practices are also needed to help employees cope with changes.[34] In particular, stress management minimizes resistance by removing some of the negative valence and fear of the unknown about the change process. Stress also saps energy, so minimizing stress potentially increases employee motivation to support the change process.

Negotiation As long as people resist change, organizational change strategies will require a variety of influence tactics.

Applying assertive influence (coercion) is the least desirable way to bring about organizational transformation, but it is sometimes necessary when speed is essential and other tactics are ineffective.
Elnur/Shutterstock

Negotiation is a form of influence that involves the promise of benefits or resources in exchange for the target person's compliance with the influencer's request. This strategy potentially gains support from those who would otherwise lose out from the change. However, this support usually goes no further than compliance with the change effort. Negotiation rarely produces commitment to change, so it might not be effective in the long term.

Coercion If all else fails, leaders rely on coercion as part of the change process. Coercion includes a range of assertive influence behaviors (see Chapter 9), such as persistently reminding people of their obligations, frequently monitoring behavior to ensure compliance, confronting people who do not change, and using threats of punishment (including dismissal) to force adherence to the expected changes.

Applying assertive influence on those who will not support the change is the least desirable way to bring about organizational transformation. However, these forms of coercion are sometimes necessary when speed is essential and other tactics are ineffective. In particular, it may be necessary to remove executives who are unwilling or unable to change their existing mental models of the ideal organization. This is also a radical form of "unlearning" the organization's past routines that have become dysfunctional.[35] Even so, coercion is a risky strategy because survivors (employees who do not leave) may have less trust in corporate leaders and engage in more political tactics to protect their own job security.

Refreezing the Desired Conditions

Unfreezing and changing behavior won't produce lasting change. People are creatures of habit, so they easily slip back into familiar patterns. Therefore, leaders need to refreeze the new behaviors by realigning organizational systems and team dynamics with the desired changes. The desired patterns of behavior can be "nailed down" by changing the physical structure and situational conditions. Organizational rewards are also powerful systems that refreeze behaviors.[36] If the change process is supposed to encourage efficiency, then rewards should be realigned to motivate and reinforce efficient behavior.

Information systems play a complementary role in the change process, particularly as conduits for feedback.[37] Feedback mechanisms help employees learn how well they are moving toward the desired objectives, and they provide a permanent architecture to support the new behavior patterns in the long term. The adage "What gets measured, gets done" applies here. Employees concentrate on the new priorities when they receive a continuous flow of feedback about how well they are achieving those goals.

LO14-4 Discuss how leadership, coalitions, social networks, and pilot projects assist organizational change.

LEADERSHIP, COALITIONS, AND PILOT PROJECTS

Kurt Lewin's force field analysis model is a useful template to explain the dynamics of organizational change. But it overlooks four other ingredients in effective change processes: leadership, coalitions and social networks, and pilot projects.

Transformational Leadership and Change

Effective change requires one or more change champions who apply the elements of transformational leadership that were discussed in Chapter 11. Leaders develop a vision of the organization's desired future state, communicate that vision in ways that are meaningful to others, make decisions and act in ways that are consistent with that vision, and encourage employees to experiment with ways to align work activities more closely with the vision.[38]

A key element of leading change is a strategic vision.[39] A leader's vision provides a sense of direction and establishes the critical success factors against which the real changes are evaluated. Furthermore, a vision provides an emotional foundation for the change because it links the individual's values and self-concept to the desired change.[40] A strategic vision also minimizes employee fear of the unknown and provides a better understanding of what behaviors employees must learn for the desired future.

Coalitions, Social Networks, and Change

One of the great truths of organizational change is that change agents cannot lead the initiative alone. They need the assistance of several people with a similar degree of commitment to the transformation.[41] Indeed, some research suggests that this

A leader's vision provides a sense of direction and establishes the critical success factors against which the real changes are evaluated.
Rawpixel.com/Shutterstock

group—often called a *guiding coalition*—may be the most important factor in the success of public-sector organizational renewal programs.[42]

Membership in the guiding coalition extends beyond the executive team. Ideally, it includes a diagonal swath of employees representing different functions and most levels of the organization. The guiding coalition is sometimes formed from a special task force that initially investigates the opportunities for change. Members of the guiding coalition also should be influencers who are highly respected by peers in their area of the organization.

Social Networks and Viral Change The change process can be strengthened through social networks, which are structures of people connected to each other through one or more forms of interdependence (see Chapter 9). They have an important role in communication and influence, both of which are key ingredients for organizational change. To some extent, coalition members support the change process by feeding into these networks. But social networks contribute to organizational change whether or not the change agent has a formal coalition.

Social networks are not easily controlled, yet some change agents have tapped into them to build a groundswell of support for a change initiative. *Viral change* is a variation of word-of-mouth and viral marketing, whereby information is seeded to a few people and then spread to others through friendship connections.[43] Within organizations, social networks represent the channels through which news and opinions about change initiatives are transmitted. Participants in that network have relatively high trust, so their opinions are more persuasive than information from formal channels. Social networks also provide opportunities for behavior observation—employees observe one another's behavior and eventually adopt that behavior themselves. As key people in the network change their actions, they are copied by others in the network.[44]

Viral change is a variation of word-of-mouth and viral marketing, whereby information is seeded to a few people and then spread to others through friendship connections.

action research a problem-focused change process that combines action orientation (changing attitudes and behavior) and research orientation (testing theory through data collection and analysis)

Pilot Projects and Diffusion of Change

Many companies rely on a pilot project, which involves introducing change to one work unit or section of the organization. This cautious approach tests the effectiveness of and employee support for the transformation. Furthermore, a pilot project is more flexible and less risky than a companywide initiative.[45] It is also easier to select organizational groups with high readiness for change, thus increasing the likelihood that the transformation will be successful.

How does change get diffused from the pilot project to other parts of the organization? The answer is guided by the MARS model of individual behavior and performance (see Chapter 1). First, employees are more likely to adopt the practices of a pilot project when they are motivated to do so.[46] This occurs when they see that the pilot project is successful and people in the pilot project receive recognition and rewards for changing their previous work practices. Diffusion also occurs more successfully when managers support and reinforce the desired behaviors. More generally, change agents need to minimize the sources of resistance to change that we discussed earlier in this chapter.

Second, employees must have the ability—the required skills and knowledge—to adopt the practices introduced in the pilot project. According to innovation diffusion studies, people adopt ideas more readily when they have an opportunity to interact with and learn from those who have already applied the new practices.[47]

Third, pilot projects get diffused when employees have clear role perceptions—that is, when they understand how the practices in a pilot project apply to them even though they are in a completely different functional area. The challenge here is for change agents to provide guidance that is not too narrowly defined around the pilot project environment because it might not seem relevant to other areas of the organization. At the same time, the pilot project intervention should not be described too broadly or abstractly to other employees because this makes the information and role model too vague. Finally, employees require supportive situational factors, including the resources and time necessary to adopt the practices demonstrated in the pilot project.

OB THEORY TO PRACTICE

Strategies for Diffusing Change from a Pilot Project

Motivation

- Widely communicate and celebrate the pilot project's success.
- Reward and recognize pilot project employees as well as those who work at transferring that change to other parts of the organization.
- Ensure that managers support and reinforce the desired behaviors related to the pilot project's success.
- Identify and address potential sources of resistance to change.

Ability

- Give employees the opportunity to interact with and learn from pilot project team members.
- Reassign or temporarily transfer some pilot project employees to other work units, where they can coach and serve as role models.
- Give employees technical training to implement practices identified in the pilot project.

Role Perceptions

- Communicate and teach employees how the pilot project practices are relevant for their own functional areas.
- Ensure that the pilot project is described in a way that is neither too specific nor too general.

Situational Factors

- Give staff sufficient time and resources to learn and implement the pilot project practices in their work units.

LO14-5 Describe and compare action research and appreciative inquiry as formal approaches to organizational change.

TWO APPROACHES TO ORGANIZATIONAL CHANGE

So far, this chapter has examined the dynamics of change that occur every day in organizations. However, organizational change agents and consultants also apply various structured approaches to organizational change. This section introduces two of the leading approaches: action research and appreciative inquiry.

Action Research Approach

Along with introducing the force field model, Kurt Lewin recommended an **action research** approach to the change process. The philosophy of action research is that meaningful change is a combination of action orientation (changing attitudes and behavior) and research orientation (testing theory).[48] The change process needs to be action-oriented because the ultimate goal is to improve workplace behaviors and practices. An action orientation involves diagnosing current problems and applying interventions that resolve those problems. At the same time, the change process is a research study because change agents apply a conceptual framework (such as team dynamics or organizational culture) to a real situation. As with any good research, the

The philosophy of action research is that meaningful change is a combination of action orientation (changing attitudes and behavior) and research orientation (testing theory).
Monty Rakusen/Getty Images

change process involves collecting data to diagnose problems more effectively and to systematically evaluate how well the theory works in practice.[49]

Within this dual framework of action and research, the action research approach adopts an open systems view. It recognizes that organizations have many interdependent parts, so change agents need to anticipate both the intended and the unintended consequences of their interventions. Action research is also a highly participative process because open-systems change requires both the knowledge and the commitment of members within that system. Indeed, employees are essentially co-researchers as well as participants in the intervention. Overall, action research is a data-based, problem-oriented process that diagnoses the need for change, introduces the intervention, and then evaluates and stabilizes the desired changes. The main phases of action research are illustrated in Exhibit 14.3:[50]

1. *Form client–consultant relationship.* Action research usually assumes that the change agent originates outside the system (such as a consultant), so the process begins by forming the client–consultant relationship. Consultants need to determine the client's readiness for change, including whether people are motivated to participate in the process, are open to meaningful change, and possess the abilities to complete the process.
2. *Diagnose the need for change.* Action research is a problem-oriented activity that carefully diagnoses the problem to determine the appropriate direction for the change effort. Organizational diagnosis relies on systematic analysis of the situation. It involves gathering and analyzing data about an ongoing system, including interviews and surveys of employees and other stakeholders. Organizational diagnosis also involves employees so they understand, support, and improve the appropriate change method, the schedule for the actions involved, and the expected standards of successful change.
3. *Introduce intervention.* This stage in the action research model applies one or more actions to correct the problem. It may include any of the prescriptions mentioned in this book, such as building more effective teams, managing conflict, building a better organizational structure, or changing the corporate culture. An important issue is how quickly the changes should occur.[51] Some experts recommend *incremental change*, in which the organization fine-tunes the system and takes small steps toward a desired state. Others claim that *rapid change* is often required, in which the system is overhauled decisively and quickly.
4. *Evaluate and stabilize change.* Action research recommends evaluating the effectiveness of the intervention against the standards established in the diagnostic stage. Unfortunately, even when these standards are clearly stated, the effectiveness of an intervention might not be apparent for several years or might be difficult to separate from other factors. If the activity has the desired effect, the change agent and participants need to stabilize the new conditions. This refers to the refreezing process that was described earlier in this chapter. Rewards, information systems, team norms, and other conditions are redesigned so they support the new values and behaviors.

The action research approach has dominated organizational change thinking since it was introduced in the 1940s. However, some experts are concerned that the problem-oriented nature of action research—in which something is wrong that must be fixed—focuses on the negative dynamics of the group or system rather than its positive opportunities and potential. This concern with action research has led to the development of a more positive approach to organizational change, called *appreciative inquiry*.[52]

Exhibit 14.3 The Action Research Process

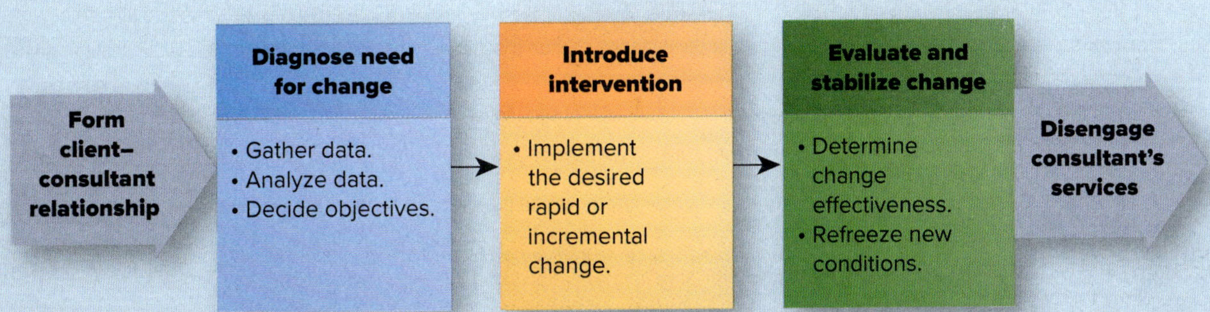

appreciative inquiry an organizational change strategy that directs the group's attention away from its own problems and focuses participants on the group's potential and positive elements

positive organizational behavior a perspective of organizational behavior that focuses on building positive qualities and traits within individuals or institutions as opposed to focusing on what is wrong with them

Appreciative Inquiry Approach

Appreciative inquiry tries to break out of the problem-solving mindset of traditional change management practices by reframing relationships around the positive and the possible. It searches for organizational (or team) strengths and capabilities and then applies that knowledge for further success and well-being. Appreciative inquiry is therefore deeply grounded in the emerging philosophy of **positive organizational behavior**, which suggests that focusing on the positive qualities and traits within individuals or institutions rather than on what is wrong with them will improve organizational success and personal well-being. In other words, this approach emphasizes building on strengths rather than trying to directly correct problems.[53]

Appreciative inquiry improves open dialogue by redirecting the group's attention away from its own concerns. This is especially useful when participants are aware of their problems or already suffer from negativity in their relationships. The positive orientation of appreciative inquiry enables groups to overcome these negative tensions and build a more hopeful perspective of their future by focusing on what is possible.[54] This positive approach to change also suggests that change agents should adapt an optimistic view of possibilities, such as seeing a glass half full rather than half empty. Therefore, appreciative inquiry actively frames reality in a way that provides constructive value for future development.

Appreciative inquiry's positive focus is illustrated by the intervention conducted a few years ago at Heidelberg USA. The American arm of the world's largest printing press manufacturer (Heidelberger Druckmaschinen AG) had experienced morale-busting product setbacks as well as downsizing due to an economic recession. To rebuild employee morale and engagement, Heidelberg held a two-day appreciative inquiry summit involving one-third of its staff. Organized into diverse groups from across the organization, participants envisioned what Heidelberg would ideally look like in the future. From these sessions emerged a new vision and greater autonomy for employees to serve customers. "Appreciative inquiry can energize an organization even in tough times because it begins the conversation with possibilities instead of problems," says a senior executive at Heidelberg USA.[55]

Appreciative inquiry tries to break out of the problem-solving mentality of traditional change management practices by reframing relationships around the positive and the possible.
Colin Anderson/Blend Images LLC

Appreciative Inquiry Principles Appreciative inquiry embraces the five principles summarized in Exhibit 14.4. One of

Exhibit 14.4 Five Principles of Appreciative Inquiry

Appreciative Inquiry Principle	Description
Positive principle	Focusing on positive events and potential produces more positive, effective, and enduring change.
Constructionist principle	How we perceive and understand the change process depends on the questions we ask and language we use throughout that process.
Simultaneity principle	Inquiry and change are simultaneous, not sequential.
Poetic principle	Organizations are open books, so we have choices in how they may be perceived, framed, and described.
Anticipatory principle	People are motivated and guided by the vision they see and believe in for the future.

Sources: Based on D.L. Cooperrider and D.K. Whitney, *Appreciative Inquiry: A Positive Revolution in Change* (San Francisco: Berrett-Koehler, 2005), Chap. 7; D.K. Whitney and A. Trosten-Bloom, *The Power of Appreciative Inquiry: A Practical Guide to Positive Change,* 2nd ed. (San Francisco: Berrett-Koehler, 2010), Chap. 3.

these is the positive principle, which we have just described. A second principle, called the *constructionist principle*, recognizes that the questions we ask and the language we use construct different realities. How questions are stated determines the information we receive, which in turn affects which change intervention we choose. A third principle, called the *simultaneity principle*, states that inquiry and change are simultaneous, not sequential. We begin the change process the moment we ask questions because the questions themselves influence those who hear and answer those questions. Consequently, change agents need to be mindful of effects that the inquiry has on the direction of the change process.

A fourth appreciative inquiry principle, called the *poetic principle*, states that organizations are open books, so we have choices in how they may be perceived, framed, and described. The poetic principle encourages change agents to actively frame reality in a way that provides constructive value for future development. The fifth principle, called the *anticipatory principle*, recognizes that people are motivated and guided by an abstract vision of the future that is aligned with their personal values. We noted the importance of visions earlier in this chapter (change agents) and in our discussion of transformational leadership (Chapter 11).

The Four-D Model of Appreciative Inquiry Appreciative inquiry follows the "Four-D" process shown in Exhibit 14.5. The model's name refers to its four stages, which begins with *discovery*–identifying the positive elements of the observed events or organization.[56] This might involve documenting positive customer experiences elsewhere in the organization. Or it might include interviewing members of another organization to discover its fundamental strengths. As participants discuss their findings, they shift into the *dreaming* stage by envisioning what might be possible in an ideal organization. By pointing out a hypothetical ideal organization or situation, participants feel safer revealing their hopes and aspirations than they would if they were discussing their own organization or predicament.

As participants make their private thoughts public to the group, the process shifts into the third stage, called *designing*. In the designing stage, participants listen with selfless receptivity to each other's views and assumptions and eventually form a collective image for thinking within the team. In effect, they create a common mental model of "what should be." As this model takes shape, group members shift the focus back to their own situation. In the final stage of appreciative inquiry, called *delivering* (also known as *destiny*), participants establish specific objectives and direction for their own organization on the basis of their model of "what will be."

Appreciative inquiry was introduced more than three decades ago, but it gained popularity only within the past dozen years. The City of Cleveland recently held the Cleveland Rising Summit, an appreciative inquiry event in which 600 participants developed numerous ideas to improve the region and clarify aspirations for the next decade. Several dozen health professionals at a hospital in Vancouver, Canada, were involved in appreciative inquiry sessions to discover how to improve medical practice for dementia patients. Appreciative inquiry has also been successfully applied across a range of other organizations, including Heidelberg USA, British Broadcasting Corporation, the State of Massachusetts, and Hunter Douglas.

Appreciative inquiry has much to offer, but it is not always the best strategy for change and, indeed, has not always been successful. This approach depends on participants' ability to let go of the problem-oriented approach, including the "blame game" of determining who may have been responsible for past failures. It also requires leaders who are willing to accept appreciative inquiry's less structured process. Another concern is that research has not yet examined the contingencies of this approach.[57] In other words, we don't yet know under what conditions appreciative inquiry is a useful approach to organizational change and under what conditions it is less effective. Overall, appreciative inquiry can be an effective approach to organizational change, but we are still discovering its potential and limitations.

Exhibit 14.5 The Four-D Model of Appreciative Inquiry

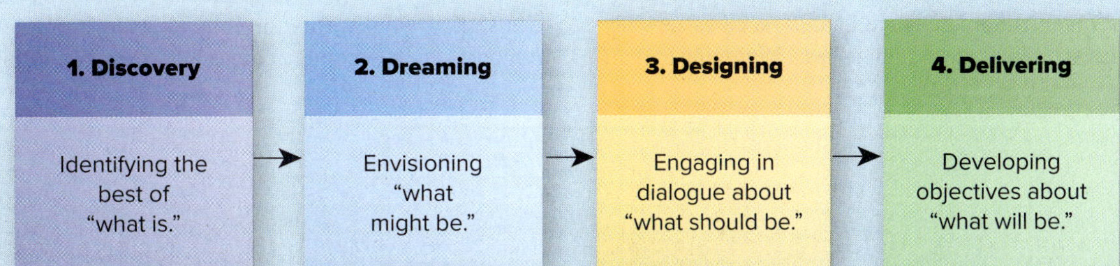

Sources: Based on F.J. Barrett and D.L. Cooperrider, "Generative Metaphor Intervention: A New Approach for Working with Systems Divided by Conflict and Caught in Defensive Perception," *Journal of Applied Behavioral Science* 26 (1990): 229; D. Whitney and C. Schau, "Appreciative Inquiry: An Innovative Process for Organization Change," *Employment Relations Today* 25 (Spring 1998): 11–21; D.L. Cooperrider and D.K. Whitney, *Appreciative Inquiry: A Positive Revolution in Change* (San Francisco: Berrett-Koehler, 2005), Chap. 3.

OB THEORY TO PRACTICE

Appreciative Inquiry Guides the Future at Lewis County General Hospital[58]

Lewis County General Hospital has adopted appreciative inquiry principles and practices for its long-term strategy development process. "I wanted to focus on what we can do, not on what we can't," says Gerald R. Cayer, CEO of the county-owned medical centre in upstate New York.

Instead of focusing on problems, Lewis County General Hospital began with "Discovery and Aspirations" discussion sessions, which reviewed the best practices of rural hospitals around the country. This was followed by the "designing" phase of strategy development. The hospital's appreciative inquiry process involved numerous stakeholders, including hospital administration, employees, labor unions, service providers, the hospital foundation, and community members.

"The point is to bring forward great minds, encourage dialogue, and to think about what can make the most sense for the community and for the hospital," Cayer explains.

Monkey Business Images/Shutterstock

LO14-6 Discuss two cross-cultural and three ethical issues in organizational change.

CROSS-CULTURAL AND ETHICAL ISSUES IN ORGANIZATIONAL CHANGE

Throughout this chapter, we have emphasized that change is inevitable and often continuous because organizations need to remain aligned with the dynamic external environment. Yet, we also need to be aware of cross-cultural and ethical issues with any change process. Many organizational change practices are built around Western cultural assumptions and values, which may differ from and sometimes conflict with assumptions and values in other cultures.[59] One possible cross-cultural limitation is that Western organizational change models, such as Lewin's force field analysis, often assume change has a beginning and an ending in a logical linear sequence (i.e., a straight line from point A to point B). Yet in some cultures change is viewed more as a cyclical phenomenon, such as the earth's revolution around the sun or a pendulum swinging back and forth. Other cultures have an interconnected view of change whereby one change leads to another (often unplanned) change, which leads to another change, and so on, until the change objective is ultimately achieved in a more circuitous way.

Some interventions assume that effective organizational change is necessarily punctuated by tension and overt conflict. Indeed, these events often encourage open conflict. But this direct confrontation view is incompatible with cultures that emphasize harmony (see Chapter 10). These cross-cultural differences suggest that a more contingency-oriented perspective is required for organizational change to work effectively in this era of globalization.

Organizational change practices also need to consider ethical issues.[60] One ethical concern is the risk of violating individual privacy rights. The action research model is built on the idea of collecting information from organizational members, yet this asks employees to provide personal information and reveal emotions they would not normally divulge.[61] A second ethical concern is that some change activities potentially increase

> Some interventions assume that effective organizational change is necessarily punctuated by tension and overt conflict, whereas this practice is incompatible with cultures that emphasize harmony.

management's power by inducing compliance and conformity in organizational members. For instance, action research is a systemwide activity that requires employee participation rather than allowing individuals to get involved voluntarily. A third concern is that some organizational change interventions undermine the individual's self-esteem. The unfreezing process requires that participants disconfirm their existing beliefs, sometimes including their own competence at certain tasks or interpersonal relations.

Organizational change is usually more difficult than it initially seems. Yet the dilemma is that most organizations operate in hyperfast environments that demand continuous and rapid adaptation. Organizations survive and gain competitive advantage by mastering the complex dynamics of moving people through the continuous process of change as quickly as the external environment is changing.

Andrew Carnegie
Bettmann/Getty Images

ORGANIZATIONAL BEHAVIOR: THE JOURNEY CONTINUES

More than a century ago, industrialist Andrew Carnegie said: "Take away my people, but leave my factories, and soon grass will grow on the factory floors. Take away my factories, but leave my people, and soon we will have a new and better factory."[62] Carnegie's statement reflects the message woven throughout this textbook: Organizations are not buildings or machinery or financial assets; rather, they are the people in them. Organizations are human entities–full of life, sometimes fragile, and always exciting.

Study Checklist

Connect® is available for *M Organizational Behavior.* Additional resources include:

✓ Exercises:
- **Case Analysis:** Apply concepts within the context of a real-world situation.
- **Click and Drag:** Helps make the connection between theory and application through matching, ranking, or grouping activities.
- **Video Case:** See management in action through interactive videos.
- **Self-Assessment:** Designed to promote student self-awareness and reflection, these research-based surveys contain detailed feedback for students.
- **Application-Based Activities:** These highly interactive, application- and analysis-based exercises allow students to take on specific roles to complete management-related tasks within a real-world context.

✓ **SmartBook 2.0**™—Smartbook 2.0 is an adaptive learning solution that provides personalized learning to individual student needs, continually adapts to pinpoint knowledge gaps and focuses learning on concepts requiring additional study. It fosters more productive learning, takes the guesswork out of what to study, and helps students better prepare for class.

©Natthawat Jamnapa/123RF

Notes

1. "Our Annual Inventory of Influence," *Orange County Business Journal* 39, no. 9 (2016): 1-2, 4-15; J.L. Jones, "Head of a Small Class: Tanya Domier, a Rare Female CEO in Orange County, Talks Diversity, Corporate Gender Gap," *Orange County Register* (CA), March 20, 2016; "25 Years of OC 50 2018," *Orange County Business Journal* 41, no. 19 (May 7, 2018): 5-6, 8, 10, 12-22; https://advantagemarketingpartners.com/about/ (accessed June 11, 2020).
2. D. Maor, A. Reich, and L. Yocarini, "The People Power of Transformations" (New York: McKinsey & Company, February 2017); American Psychological Association, "2017 Work and Well-Being Survey" (Washington, DC: Center for Organizational Excellence, May 30, 2017); L.-M. Pu and L. Schramm, "Changing the Change Rules at Google," *Re:Work* (blog), July 12, 2018, https://rework.withgoogle.com/blog/changing-the-change-rules-at-google/; D. DeRosa, "People Are Not the Problem: Eight Tips for Managing Change Successfully," *Business 2 Community* (blog), September 4, 2019, https://www.business2community.com/human-resources/people-are-not-the-problem-eight-tips-for-managing-change-successfully-02236206.

3. J. Welch, *Jack: Straight from the Heart* (New York: Warner Business Books, 2001), 432.

4. K. Lewin, *Field Theory in Social Science* (New York: Harper & Row, 1951).

5. D. Coghlan and T. Brannick, "Kurt Lewin: The 'Practical Theorist' for the 21st Century," *Irish Journal of Management* 24, no. 2 (2003): 31–37; B. Burnes, "Kurt Lewin and the Planned Approach to Change: A Re-appraisal," *Journal of Management Studies* 41, no. 6 (2004): 977–1002.

6. M. Young, *Ogilvy on Advertising in the Digital Age* (London: Goodman Books, 2017), 267. For details about the likely origins of "divine discontent," see the annotation/reference near the end of the "Identifying Problems and Opportunities" section in Chapter 6 (Decision Making and Creativity) of this book.

7. Some experts suggest that employee "resistance to change" is a misnomer because the resistance isn't to change; it is resistance to the perceived negative outcomes of the change. See E.B. Dent and S.G. Goldberg, "Challenging 'Resistance to Change,'" *Journal of Applied Behavioral Science* 35 (1999): 25–41.

8. S. Chreim, "Postscript to Change: Survivors' Retrospective Views of Organizational Changes," *Personnel Review* 35, no. 3 (2006): 315–35.

9. E.B. Dent and S.G. Goldberg, "Challenging 'Resistance to Change,'" *Journal of Applied Behavioral Science* 35 (1999): 25–41; D.B. Fedor, S. Caldwell, and D.M. Herold, "The Effects of Organizational Changes on Employee Commitment: A Multilevel Investigation," *Personnel Psychology* 59, no. 1 (2006): 1–29.

10. B.J. Tepper et al., "Subordinates' Resistance and Managers' Evaluations of Subordinates' Performance," *Journal of Management* 32, no. 2 (2006): 185–209; J.D. Ford, L.W. Ford, and A. D'Amelio, "Resistance to Change: The Rest of the Story," *Academy of Management Review* 33, no. 2 (2008): 362–77.

11. This quotation is incorrectly attributed to MIT scholar Peter Senge. Senge cites this memorable quotation in his highly regarded book *The Fifth Discipline*, but he states that it originated from an unnamed "seasoned organizational change consultant." See: P.M. Senge, *The Fifth Discipline: The Art and Practice of the Learning Organization* (New York: Doubleday Currency, 1990), 155.

12. D.A. Nadler, "The Effective Management of Organizational Change," in *Handbook of Organizational Behavior*, ed. J.W. Lorsch (Englewood Cliffs, NJ: Prentice Hall, 1987), 358–69; R. Maurer, *Beyond the Wall of Resistance: Unconventional Strategies to Build Support for Change* (Austin, TX: Bard Books, 1996); P. Strebel, "Why Do Employees Resist Change?" *Harvard Business Review* (1996): 86–92; D.A. Nadler, *Champions of Change* (San Francisco: Jossey-Bass, 1998).

13. S. Oreg et al., "Dispositional Resistance to Change: Measurement Equivalence and the Link to Personal Values across 17 Nations," *Journal of Applied Psychology* 93, no. 4 (2008): 935–44.

14. R.R. Sharma, *Change Management: Concepts and Applications* (New Delhi: Tata McGraw-Hill, 2007), Chap. 4; I. Cinite, L.E. Duxbury, and C. Higgins, "Measurement of Perceived Organizational Readiness for Change in the Public Sector," *British Journal of Management* 20, no. 2 (2009): 265–77; A.A. Armenakis and S.G. Harris, "Reflections: Our Journey in Organizational Change Research and Practice," *Journal of Change Management* 9, no. 2 (2009): 127–42; S. Jaros, "Commitment to Organizational Change: A Critical Review," *Journal of Change Management* 10, no. 1 (2010): 79–108.

15. D.T. Holt et al., "Readiness for Organizational Change: The Systematic Development of a Scale," *Journal of Applied Behavioral Science* 43, no. 2 (2007): 232–55; G. Bohner and N. Dickel, "Attitudes and Attitude Change," *Annual Review of Psychology* 62, no. 1 (2011): 391–417; A.M. García-Cabrera and F. García-Barba Hernández, "Differentiating the Three Components of Resistance to Change: The Moderating Effect of Organization-Based Self-Esteem on the Employee Involvement-Resistance Relation," *Human Resource Development Quarterly* 25, no. 4 (2014): 441–69.

16. R. de la Sablonnière et al., "Profound Organizational Change, Psychological Distress and Burnout Symptoms: The Mediator Role of Collective Relative Deprivation," *Group Processes & Intergroup Relations* 15, no. 6 (2012): 776–90.

17. S. Oreg, M. Vakola, and A. Armenakis, "Change Recipients' Reactions to Organizational Change: A 60-Year Review of Quantitative Studies," *Journal of Applied Behavioral Science* 47, no. 4 (2011): 461–524.

18. D. Grosse Kathoefer and J. Leker, "Knowledge Transfer in Academia: An Exploratory Study on the Not-Invented-Here Syndrome," *Journal of Technology Transfer* 37, no. 5 (2012): 658–75; A.L.A. Burcharth, M.P. Knudsen, and H.A. Søndergaard, "Neither Invented nor Shared Here: The Impact and Management of Attitudes for the Adoption of Open Innovation Practices," *Technovation* 34, no. 3 (2014): 149–61.

19. V. Newman, "The Psychology of Managing for Innovation," *KM Review* 9, no. 6 (2007): 10–15.

20. R. Davis, *Leading for Growth: How Umpqua Bank Got Cool and Created a Culture of Greatness* (San Francisco: Jossey-Bass, 2007), 40.

21. "Addison Group Survey Finds Nearly Half of Staff Level Employees Don't Feel Confident Their Industry," news release (Chicago: Addison Group, June 5, 2017); D. Meinert, "How to Avoid Common Mistakes in Change Management," *HR Magazine*, February 2018; B. Sanzenbacher, "Why 42% of Workers Are Fed Up and Ready to Bolt," *Wrike Blog* (blog), February 15, 2018, https://www.wrike.com/blog/why-42-of-workers-are-fed-up-and-ready-to-bolt/; "How Operational Inefficiencies Result In Employee Burnout (UK Survey)," *Wrike Blog* (blog), February 22, 2018, https://www.wrike.com/blog/how-operational-inefficiencies-result-in-employee-burnout-uk-survey/; M. Murphy, "Resistance to Change in Organizations Comes from These 5 Factors (New Data)," *Leadership IQ* (blog), October 15, 2019, https://www.leadershipiq.com/blogs/leadershipiq/resistance-to-change-in-organizations-comes-from-these-5-factors-new-data; L. de Boer, "Study: Resistance to Change at Work Holds Back Automation," *Signavio* (blog), March 4, 2020, https://www.signavio.com/post/change-at-work/.

22. J.P. Kotter, *A Sense of Urgency* (Boston: Harvard Business School Press, 2008); S.H. Appelbaum et al., "Back to the Future: Revisiting Kotter's 1996 Change Model," *Journal of Management Development* 31, no. 8 (2012): 764–82.

23. L.D. Goodstein and H.R. Butz, "Customer Value: The Linchpin of Organizational Change," *Organizational Dynamics* 27 (1998): 21–35.

24. A. Weckler, "You Don't Have Mail: How Slack Reinvented Chat," *Irish Independent*, January 26, 2017, 6.

25. D. Miller, *The Icarus Paradox: How Exceptional Companies Bring about Their Own Downfall* (New York: HarperBusiness, 1990); S. Finkelstein, *Why Smart Executives Fail* (New York: Viking, 2003); A.C. Amason and A.C. Mooney, "The Icarus Paradox Revisited: How Strong Performance Sows the Seeds of Dysfunction in Future Strategic Decision-Making," *Strategic Organization* 6, no. 4 (2008): 407–34. Richard Goyder's quotation is from "Sustaining High Performance (Richard Goyder: Wesfarmers)," *CEO Forum*, September 2006.

26. T.F. Cawsey and G. Deszca, *Toolkit for Organizational Change* (Los Angeles: Sage, 2007), 104.

27. J.P. Kotter and L.A. Schlesinger, "Choosing Strategies for Change," *Harvard Business Review* (1979): 106–14.

28. J.P. Kotter and D.S. Cohen, *The Heart of Change* (Boston: Harvard Business School Press, 2002), 83–98; J. Allen et al., "Uncertainty during Organizational Change: Managing Perceptions through Communication," *Journal of Change Management* 7, no. 2 (2007): 187–210; A.E. Rafferty, N.L. Jimmieson, and A.A. Armenakis, "Change Readiness: A Multilevel Review," *Journal of Management* 39, no. 1 (2013): 110–35; M. van den Heuvel et al., "Adapting to Change: The Value of Change Information and Meaning-Making," *Journal of Vocational Behavior* 83, no. 1 (2013): 11–21.

29. Jostle, "Culture Hero Series: Chris Catliff, Blueshore Financial," *The Jostle Blog*, October 30, 2013, http://blog.jostle.me/blog/culture-hero-series-chris-catliff-north-shore-credit-union.

30. D. M. Herold and S. D. Caldwell, "Beyond Change Management: A Multilevel Investigation of Contextual and Personal Influences on Employees' Commitment to Change," *Journal of Applied Psychology* 92, no. 4 (2007): 942–51; D. T. Holt and J. M. Vardaman, "Toward a Comprehensive Understanding of Readiness for Change: The Case for an Expanded Conceptualization," *Journal of Change Management* 13, no. 1 (2013): 9–18.

31. K.T. Dirks, L.L. Cummings, and J.L. Pierce, "Psychological Ownership in Organizations: Conditions under Which Individuals Promote and Resist Change," *Research in Organizational Change and Development* 9 (1996): 1–23; E.A. Lofquist, "Doomed to Fail: A Case Study of Change Implementation Collapse in the Norwegian Civil Aviation Industry," *Journal of Change Management* 11, no. 2 (2011): 223–43; L.K. Lewis and T.L. Russ, "Soliciting and Using Input during Organizational Change Initiatives: What Are Practitioners Doing," *Management Communication Quarterly* 26, no. 2 (2012): 267–94.

32. S.G. Bamberger et al., "Impact of Organisational Change on Mental Health: A Systematic Review," *Occupational and Environmental Medicine* 69, no. 8 (2012): 592–98.

33. N.T. Tan, "Maximising Human Resource Potential in the Midst of Organisational Change," *Singapore Management Review* 27, no. 2 (2005): 25–35; A.E. Rafferty and S.L.D. Restubog, "The Impact of Change Process and Context on Change Reactions and Turnover during a Merger," *Journal of Management* 36, no. 5 (2010): 1309–38.

34. M. McHugh, "The Stress Factor: Another Item for the Change Management Agenda?" *Journal of Organizational Change Management* 10 (1997): 345–62; D. Buchanan, T. Claydon, and M. Doyle, "Organisation Development and Change: The Legacy of the Nineties," *Human Resource Management Journal* 9 (1999): 20–37.

35. J.P. Hausknecht and J.A. Holwerda, "When Does Employee Turnover Matter? Dynamic Member Configurations, Productive Capacity, and Collective Performance," *Organization Science* 24, no. 1 (2013): 210–25.

36. E.E. Lawler III, "Pay Can Be a Change Agent," *Compensation & Benefits Management* 16 (2000): 23–26; D.S. Cohen and J.P. Kotter, *The Heart of Change Field Guide* (Boston: Harvard Business School Press, 2005), 161–77; M.A. Roberto and L.C. Levesque, "The Art of Making Change Initiatives Stick," *MIT Sloan Management Review* 46, no. 4 (2005): 53–60.

37. L.D. Goodstein and H.R. Butz, "Customer Value: The Linchpin of Organizational Change," *Organizational Dynamics* 27 (1998): 21–35; R.H. Miles, "Leading Corporate Transformation: Are You up to the Task?" in *The Leader's Change Handbook,* ed. J.A. Conger, G.M. Spreitzer, and E.E. Lawler III (San Francisco: Jossey-Bass, 1999), 221–67.

38. R.E. Quinn, *Building the Bridge as You Walk on It: A Guide for Leading Change* (San Francisco: Jossey-Bass, 2004), Chap. 11; S. Oreg and Y. Berson, "Leaders' Impact on Organizational Change: Bridging Theoretical and Methodological Chasms," *Academy of Management Annals* 13 (2019): 272–307.

39. M.S. Cole, S.G. Harris, and J.B. Bernerth, "Exploring the Implications of Vision, Appropriateness, and Execution of Organizational Change," *Leadership & Organization Development Journal* 27, no. 5 (2006): 352–67; S. Kirkpatrick, "Leading through Vision and Values," in *Handbook of Principles of Organizational Behavior: Indispensable Knowledge for Evidence-Based Management*, ed. E. Locke (Hoboken: Wiley, 2010), 367–87; V. Lundy and P.P. Morin, "Project Leadership Influences Resistance to Change: The Case of the Canadian Public Service," *Project Management Journal* 44, no. 4 (2013): 45–64.

40. J.P. Kotter and D.S. Cohen, *The Heart of Change* (Boston: Harvard Business School Press, 2002), 61–82; D.S. Cohen and J.P. Kotter, *The Heart of Change Field Guide* (Boston: Harvard Business School Press, 2005).

41. J.P. Kotter, "Leading Change: Why Transformation Efforts Fail," *Harvard Business Review* (1995): 59–67.

42. J.B. Cunningham and S.K. James, "Implementing Change in Public Sector Organizations," *Management Decision* 47, no. 2 (2009): 330.

43. A. De Bruyn and G.L. Lilien, "A Multi-Stage Model of Word-of-Mouth Influence through Viral Marketing," *International Journal of Research in Marketing* 25, no. 3 (2008): 151–63; J.Y.C. Ho and M. Dempsey, "Viral Marketing: Motivations to Forward Online Content," *Journal of Business Research* 63, no. 9/10 (2010): 1000–06; M. Williams and F. Buttle, "The Eight Pillars of WOM Management: Lessons from a Multiple Case Study," *Australasian Marketing Journal* 19, no. 2 (2011): 85–92.

44. L. Herrero, *Homo Imitans* (Beaconsfield Bucks, UK: meetingminds, 2011).

45. M. Beer, R.A. Eisenstat, and B. Spector, *The Critical Path to Corporate Renewal* (Boston: Harvard Business School Press, 1990).

46. M. Beer, R.A. Eisenstat, and B. Spector, *The Critical Path to Corporate Renewal* (Boston: Harvard Business School Press, 1990), Chap. 5; R.E. Walton, "Successful Strategies for Diffusing Work Innovations," *Journal of Contemporary Business* (1977): 1–22; R.E. Walton, *Innovating to Compete: Lessons for Diffusing and Managing Change in the Workplace* (San Francisco: Jossey-Bass, 1987).

47. E.M. Rogers, *Diffusion of Innovations*, 4th ed. (New York: Free Press, 1995).

48. P. Reason and H. Bradbury, *Handbook of Action Research* (London: Sage, 2001); D. Coghlan and T. Brannick, "Kurt Lewin: The 'Practical Theorist' for the 21st Century," *Irish Journal of Management* 24, no. 2 (2003): 31–37; C. Huxham and S. Vangen, "Researching Organizational Practice through Action Research: Case Studies and Design Choices," *Organizational Research Methods* 6 (2003): 383–403.

49. V.J. Marsick and M.A. Gephart, "Action Research: Building the Capacity for Learning and Change," *Human Resource Planning* 26 (2003): 14–18.

50. L. Dickens and K. Watkins, "Action Research: Rethinking Lewin," *Management Learning* 30 (1999): 127–40; J. Heron and P. Reason, "The Practice of Co-operative Inquiry: Research 'with' Rather Than 'on' People," in *Handbook of Action Research*, ed. P. Reason and H. Bradbury (Thousand Oaks, CA: Sage, 2001), 179–88.

51. D.A. Nadler, "Organizational Frame Bending: Types of Change in the Complex Organization," in *Corporate Transformation: Revitalizing Organizations for a Competitive World*, ed. R.H. Kilmann, T.J. Covin, and Associates (San Francisco: Jossey-Bass, 1988), 66–83; K.E. Weick and R.E. Quinn, "Organizational Change and Development," *Annual Review of Psychology* 50 (1999): 361–86.

52. T.M. Egan and C.M. Lancaster, "Comparing Appreciative Inquiry to Action Research: OD Practitioner Perspectives," *Organization Development Journal* 23, no. 2 (2005): 29–49.

53. N. Turner, J. Barling, and A. Zacharatos, "Positive Psychology at Work," in *Handbook of Positive Psychology*, ed. C.R. Snyder and S. Lopez (Oxford, UK: Oxford University Press, 2002), 715–30; K. Cameron, J.E. Dutton, and R.E. Quinn, eds., *Positive Organizational Scholarship: Foundation of a New Discipline* (San Francisco: Berrett-Koehler, 2003); S.L. Gable and J. Haidt, "What (and Why) Is Positive Psychology?" *Review of General Psychology* 9, (2005): 103–10; M.E.P. Seligman et al., "Positive Psychology Progress: Empirical Validation of Interventions," *American Psychologist* 60 (2005): 410–21. On the origins of appreciative inquiry, see G.R. Bushe, "Foundations of Appreciative Inquiry: History, Criticism and Potential," *AI Practitioner* 14 (February 2012): 8–20.

54. D.K. Whitney and D.L. Cooperrider, "The Appreciative Inquiry Summit: Overview and Applications," *Employment Relations Today* 25 (1998): 17–28; J.M. Watkins and B.J. Mohr, *Appreciative Inquiry: Change at the Speed of Imagination* (San Francisco: Jossey-Bass, 2001).

55. D. Meinert, "Positive Momentum," *HR Magazine* 58, no. 6 (2013): 68–74.

56. F.J. Barrett and D.L. Cooperrider, "Generative Metaphor Intervention: A New Approach for Working with Systems Divided by Conflict and Caught in Defensive Perception," *Journal of Applied Behavioral Science* 26 (1990): 219–39; D.K. Whitney and D.L. Cooperrider, "The Appreciative Inquiry Summit: Overview and Applications," *Employment Relations Today* 25 (1998): 17–28; J.M. Watkins and B.J. Mohr, *Appreciative Inquiry: Change at the Speed of Imagination* (San Francisco: Jossey-Bass, 2001), 15–21.

57. G.R. Bushe, "Five Theories of Change Embedded in Appreciative Inquiry" (paper presented at the 18th Annual World Congress of Organization Development, Dublin, Ireland, July 14–18, 1998); T.F. Yaeger, P.F. Sorensen, and U. Bengtsson, "Assessment of the State of Appreciative Inquiry: Past, Present, and Future," *Research in Organizational Change and Development* 15 (2004): 297–319; G.R. Bushe and A.F. Kassam, "When Is Appreciative Inquiry Transformational? A Meta-Case Analysis," *Journal of Applied Behavioral Science* 41 (2005): 161–81.

58. Based on information in J. Abbass, "Lewis County Hospital Takes a Positive Approach to Planning," *Watertown Daily Times (NY)*, February 25, 2019.

59. T.C. Head and P.F. Sorenson, "Cultural Values and Organizational Development: A Seven-Country Study," *Leadership and Organization Development Journal* 14 (1993): 3–7; R.J. Marshak, "Lewin Meets Confucius: A Review of the OD Model of Change," *Journal of Applied Behavioral Science* 29 (1993): 395–415; C.M. Lau, "A Culture-Based Perspective of Organization Development Implementation," *Research in Organizational Change and Development* 9 (1996): 49–79; C.M. Lau and H.Y. Ngo, "Organization Development and Firm Performance: A Comparison of Multinational and Local Firms," *Journal of International Business Studies* 32, no. 1 (2001): 95–114.

60. M. McKendall, "The Tyranny of Change: Organizational Development Revisited," *Journal of Business Ethics* 12 (1993): 93–104; C.M.D. Deaner, "A Model of Organization Development Ethics," *Public Administration Quarterly* 17 (1994): 435–46.

61. G.A. Walter, "Organization Development and Individual Rights," *Journal of Applied Behavioral Science* 20 (1984): 423–39.

62. The source of this often-cited quotation was not found. It does not appear, even in other variations, in the books that Andrew Carnegie wrote (such as *Gospel of Wealth*, 1900; *Empire of Business*, 1902; and *Autobiography*, 1920). However, Carnegie may have stated these words (or similar ones) elsewhere. He gave many speeches and wrote numerous articles, parts of which have been reported by other authors.

Organization Index

Name Index

A

B

C

D

E

F

G

H

L

M

N

O

P

Q

R

S

T

U

V

W

X

Y

Z

Glossary/Subject Index

C

D

F

G

H

I

Information overload *A condition in which the volume of information received exceeds the person's capacity to process it*, 198–199

Inoculation effect *A persuasive communication strategy of warning listeners that others will try to influence them in the future and that they should be wary of the opponent's arguments*, 222–223

Interactional justice *The perception that appropriate rules have been applied in the way the people involved are treated throughout the decision process*, 117, 119–120

Intrinsic motivation *Motivation that occurs when people are fulfilling their needs for competence and autonomy by engaging in the activity itself, rather than from an externally controlled outcome of that activity*, 108

Intuition *The ability to know when a problem or opportunity exists and to select the best course of action without conscious reasoning*

J

Job characteristics model *A job design model that relates the motivational properties of jobs to specific personal and organizational consequences of those properties*, 122, 123

Job enlargement *The practice of adding more tasks to an existing job*, 124

Job enrichment *The practice of giving employees more responsibility for scheduling, coordinating, and planning their own work*, 124–125

Job satisfaction *A person's evaluation of his or her job and work context*, 86

Job specialization *The result of a division of labor, in which work is subdivided into separate jobs assigned to different people*, 121

Johari window *A model of mutual understanding that encourages disclosure and feedback to increase our own open area and reduce the blind, hidden, and unknown areas*, 67

K

L

Leadership *Influencing, motivating, and enabling others to contribute toward the effectiveness and success of the organizations of which they are members*

M

Power distance *A cross-cultural value describing the degree to which people in a culture accept unequal distribution of power in a society*, 44

Primacy effect *A perceptual error in which we quickly form an opinion of people based on the first information we receive about them*, 66

Procedural justice *The perception that appropriate procedural rules have been applied throughout the decision process*, 117, 119–120

Process losses *Resources (including time and energy) expended toward team development and maintenance rather than the task*, 161

Production blocking *A time constraint in team decision making due to the procedural requirement that only one person may speak at a time*, 176

Prospect theory effect *A natural tendency to feel more dissatisfaction from losing a particular amount than satisfaction from gaining an equal amount*, 145

Psychological safety *A shared belief that it is safe to engage in interpersonal risk-taking; specifically, that presenting unusual ideas, constructively disagreeing with the majority, and experimenting with new work behaviors will not result in coworkers posing a threat to their self-concept, status, or career*, 177

Psychopathy *A personality trait of people who ruthlessly dominate and manipulate others without empathy or any feelings of remorse or anxiety, use superficial charm, yet are social predators who engage in antisocial, impulsive, and often fraudulent thrill-seeking behavior*, 35

R

Rational choice decision making *The process of using pure logic and all available information about all alternatives to choose the alternative with the highest value*, 135–137

Realistic job preview (RJP) *A method of improving organizational socialization in which job applicants are given a balance of positive and negative information about the job and work context*, 312

Reality shock *The stress that results when employees perceive discrepancies between their preemployment expectations and on-the-job reality*, 312

Recency effect *A perceptual error in which the most recent information dominates our perception of others*, 66

Referent power *The capacity to influence others on the basis of an identification with and respect for the power holder*, 214–215

Refreezing *The latter part of the change process, in which systems and structures are introduced that reinforce and maintain the desired behaviors*, 320, 326

Relationship conflict *A type of conflict in which people focus their discussion on qualities of the people in the dispute, rather than on the qualities of the ideas presented regarding a task-related issue*, 235

Remote teams *Teams whose members operate across space, time, and organizational boundaries and are linked through information technologies to achieve organizational tasks*, 174–175

Representativeness heuristic *A natural tendency to evaluate probabilities of events or objects by the degree to which they resemble (are representative of) other events or objects rather than on objective probability information*, 141

Rituals *The programmed routines of daily organizational life that dramatize the organization's culture*, 302

Role *A set of behaviors that people are expected to perform because they hold specific formal or informal positions in a team and organization*, 170

Role perceptions *The degree to which a person understands the job duties assigned to or expected of him or her*, 18–19

S

Satisficing *Selecting an alternative that is satisfactory or "good enough," rather than the alternative with the highest value (maximization)*, 141–142

Social presence *The extent to which a communication channel creates psychological closeness to others, awareness of their humanness, and appreciation of the interpersonal relationship*, 195

Span of control *The number of people directly reporting to the next level above in the hierarchy*, 280–282

Stakeholders *Individuals, groups, and other entities that affect, or are affected by, the organization's objectives and actions*, 8–9

Stereotype threat *An individual's concern about confirming a negative stereotype about his or her group*, 62

Stereotyping *The process of assigning traits to people based on their membership in a social category*, 61–63

Strengths-based coaching *An approach to coaching and feedback that focuses on building and leveraging the employee's strengths rather than trying to correct his or her weaknesses*, 115–116

Stress *An adaptive response to a situation that is perceived as challenging or threatening to the person's well-being*, 90–91

Stressors *Any environmental conditions that place a physical or emotional demand on the person*, 92–93

Structural hole *An area between two or more dense social network areas that lacks network ties*, 364

Superordinate goals *Goals that the conflicting parties value and whose attainment requires the joint resources and effort of those parties*, 242

Surface-level diversity *The observable demographic or physiological differences in people, such as their race, ethnicity, gender, age, and physical disabilities*, 12, 13

Synchronicity *The extent to which the channel requires or allows both sender and receiver to be actively involved in the conversation at the same time (synchronous) or at different times (asynchronous)*, 195

T

Task analyzability *The degree to which job duties allow the application of established procedures and rules to guide decisions and behavior (high analyzability); employee creativity and judgment are necessary to perform jobs with low task analyzability*, 124, 291

Task conflict *A type of conflict in which people focus their discussion around the issue (i.e., the "task") in which different viewpoints occur while showing respect for people involved in that disagreement*, 235

Task identity *The degree to which a job requires completion of a whole or an identifiable piece of work*, 123

Task interdependence *The extent to which team members must share materials, information, or expertise in order to perform their jobs*, 165

Task performance *The individual's voluntary goal-directed behaviors that contribute to organizational objectives*, 20, 21

Task significance *The degree to which a job has a substantial impact on the organization and/or larger society*, 123

Task variability *The degree to which job duties are nonroutine and unpredictable; employees perform diverse tasks from one day to the next because they are faced with unfamiliar and unexpected issues*, 124, 291

Team-based structure *An organizational structure built around self-directed teams that complete an entire piece of work*, 287

U

V

W

Win-lose orientation *The belief that conflicting parties are drawing from a fixed pie, so the more one party receives, the less the other party will receive*, 239

Win-win orientation *The belief that conflicting parties will find a mutually beneficial solution to their disagreement*, 239

Work-life integration *The degree that people are effectively engaged in their various work and nonwork roles and have a low degree of role conflict across those life domains*, 13-15

Y

Z